Dale MORGAN
ON EARLY MORMONISM

DALE LOWELL MORGAN
1914 - 1971

My viewpoint about Mormon history is that of the sociologist, the psychologist, the political, economic, and social historian. I do not expect that the average Mormon will accept in its entirety the evaluation of Mormon history that I shall make, but I do expect that he will acknowledge my integrity within what he regards as the limitations of my understanding, or point of view. On such a basis we can get along very equably, and we may find that my interpretation of Mormon history will not, after all, do such violence to Mormon ideas of that history.

Morgan to S.A. Burgess, April 26, 1943

Dale MORGAN ON EARLY MORMONISM

CORRESPONDENCE & A NEW HISTORY

John Phillip Walker,
Editor

with a Biographical
Introduction by
John Phillip Walker

and a Preface by
William Mulder

Signature Books

Salt Lake City, Utah

Printed in the United States
of America

ISBN 0-941214-36-2
LC 86-60251

design by Diane Valantine

frontispiece photo courtesy
Utah State Historical Society

TABLE OF CONTENTS

EDITOR'S ACKNOWLEDGEMENTS

In bringing the present volume to press some obligations are so large as to require a personal expression of appreciation.

I am indebted to three institutions which house Dale L. Morgan papers. The University of Utah Marriott Library, Special Collections division, was under the direction of Everett L. Cooley when Della Dye first drew my attention to the "marvelous" letters of Dale to Madeline McQuown. Gregory Thompson, who succeeded Dr. Cooley, and Nancy Young have continued the policy of making these materials more widely available.

The Utah State Historical Society Library responded to my every request. I am particularly grateful to Gary Topping, Martha Stewart, and Jean Anne McMurrin for their help.

Employees of the Bancroft Library at the University of California at Berkeley generously allowed access to the materials from their splendid collection even though it meant for them several trips between Berkeley and Richmond, California, where their Morgan papers are stored.

Dale's brother and literary executor, Jim Morgan, graciously allowed access and granted publication rights to all of the materials that were requested.

Both Trudy McMurrin and Sterling M. McMurrin steered the project towards George D. Smith, president of Signature Books, where his staff labored to make the published book one of which Dale would have approved. Thanks particularly to Gary James Bergera, Ronald Priddis, Diane Valantine, Ian G. Barber, Mary Brockert, and Susan Staker for their careful preparation of the documents.

I also wish to thank several individuals who assisted with comments and suggestions. I acknowledge the gracious help of LaMar Petersen, H. Michael Marquardt, Wesley P. Walters, Everett L. Cooley, C. G. Walker, and Beverly Walker.

I owe much to Kent L. Walgren. It was he who asked me once, when I was going on about Dale's letters, "Did you realize that part of his unfinished manuscript is in the Madeline McQuown Collection?" Kent's question set this undertaking in motion. Since then he has urged the project along and improved it by his thoughtful readings and suggestions.

Without the continuous support of Renae P. Walker none of my efforts would have been possible.

John Phillip Walker
January 1986

PREFACE

William Mulder

The publication of a selection of Dale L. Morgan's correspondence and chapters from his unfinished history of Mormonism is a happy event. Dale has put every researcher and writer on both the Mormons and the Far West since him in his debt because of his wide-ranging industry and his fabled generosity. The industry and generosity went together, with Dale modestly disclaiming that whatever grist he was grinding for others also fed his own mill. "Any problem existing for anybody, in Mormon research," he wrote to fledgling Mormon historian Juanita Brooks in April 1942, "was a problem also for me. . . . In answering their limited needs, I answer larger needs of my own. . . . All these individual things are parts of an infinitely complex organism that I am trying to see whole."

I am myself a beneficiary of Dale's generosity with his materials and the example of his method in trying to see whole. On a tip from Dale to the publisher Alfred A. Knopf that A. Russell Mortensen and I were putting together a collection of observers' accounts about the Mormons, Mr. Knopf, passing through Salt Lake City in the early 1950s with his wife Blanche, called us from the airport. He kindly invited us to lunch and, after chit-chat that curiously never mentioned our project, put the prospectus for our book in his pocket as he left and said we would hear from him soon. Within days we did, in words now historic to our ears: "I am inclined," he wrote, "to take a flyer on your book." Several years and many vicissitudes later *Among the Mormons* appeared (in 1958), with, as one of its inclusions, an essay by Dale on the contemporary scene. The essay in fact forms his unsurpassed introduction to *Utah: A Guide to the State* (1941) that opens with that memorable line, "The Mormon habitat has always been a vortex of legend and lie." Other notable inclusions in *Among the Mormons* came from the newspapers Dale had ransacked for Mormon items at the Library of Congress and the New York Public Library and in every state on the way west during a cross-country trek in his old Hudson in 1947-48, an epic copying spree on an equally old typewriter, a labor of Hercules that provided scholars with a major resource, an indispensable "tool book" long before the Xerox revolution.

It was hard to be one up on Dale in terms of historical finds, and it gave Russ Mortensen and me no end of pleasure to discover that the letters of Utah governor Alfred Cumming's wife Elizabeth, which on a tip from Ray R. Canning I had tracked down in the Manuscripts Division of Duke University Library, were new to Dale. "Could I get a print of your Cumming microfilm?" he asked Russ. "That is a mighty fetchin' lady, and I want to know her better." The request came as a footnote in a letter of 7 April 1958, in which he endorsed *Among the Mormons* with a warm comment that "the whole thing was brought off with a sense of style" but with a warning that he had been asked to review it for John Caughey's *Pacific Historical Review*. "So," wrote Dale, "I will have to check up on what you have deleted, as well as what you have put into it. Let us hope the book will stand up under this investigation!"

Dale was a professional and would not allow friendship to compromise criticism. His review did, in fact, find some shortcomings in our anthology: he found the early section, "Genesis," "a bit overloaded with excerpts by Mormons themselves—perhaps," he charitably observed, "because articulate outsiders were not always conveniently at hand during the successive crises in New York, Ohio, Missouri, and Illinois." And he also found that we had "often leaned upon reminiscences rather than the exactly contemporary record" we would doubtless have preferred. At the same time he found that the selections gave "the general reader a living sense of earliest Mormon history." In the section entitled "Chronicles and Judges," dealing with the first decades after the Mormons arrived in the Salt Lake Valley, Dale found the gravest weakness our selection of an address by Juanita Brooks recounting the Mountain Meadows Massacre. "Her remarks are indeed moving," he wrote, "but within the framework of this book, the editors might better have printed one of the accounts written by the investigators of 1858-1860—or even portions of John D. Lee's 'Confession.'"

In his correspondence Dale was the "patron saint" many historians found him to be. And he was the explorer. Dale's letters are explorations, the intellectual equivalent of the travels of his mountain men, filled with his forays into libraries and the field, alive with information and agendas, acute observations, creative speculations, and restless searchings as he maps the historical and literary landscape of the Mormons and the West. What he writes of Jedediah Smith and the opening of the West may be metaphorically applied to Dale's opening of Mormon and western historiography. Dale prefaces his *Jedediah*: "He entered the West when it was still largely an unknown land; when he left the mountains, the whole country had been printed on the living maps of his trappers' minds. Scarcely a stream, a valley, a pass or a mountain range but had been named and become known for good or ill. A new kind of American, the mountain man, had come into existence during those eight years, and Jedediah Smith and his associates had had the shaping of him." Substitute Dale Morgan for Jedediah Smith in this description, scholars for mountain men, and Mormon and western historiography for the actual topography and we have a suggestive figure, by no means far-fetched, of the magnitude of Dale's achievement.

Archivists David Atkinson and Gary Topping, who prepared a description of the scope and content of the Dale Lowell Morgan Collection at the Utah State Historical Society, remark on Dale's "tenacious devotion to accuracy in even the minutest detail as well as his curiously limited conception of the nature of the historical process. History, to Dale Morgan," they write, "meant primarily geographical movement. Larger social forces and the role of personality did not entirely escape him, but he was always at his best when meticulously reconstructing the route followed by a mountain man or emigrant party. On occasion Morgan let his passion for minutiae trap him into applying emphasis to relatively minor points." And they cite the time Dale wrote to Marguerite Sinclair at the Utah Historical Society, suggesting she do "history a service and ask Charles Kelly to write a piece for this year's *Quarterly* demonstrating that Escalante actually crossed at Padre Creek, not at the Crossing of the Fathers." Dale may have suffered the faults of his virtues, but "meticulous reconstruction" and "passion for minutiae" have proved to be salutary correctives in Mormon and western history, so often the preserve of the well-meaning but undisciplined amateur.

Dale's insistence on factual accuracy and verbal precision served his larger naturalistic aim of seeing the whole, the total environment–physical, social, cultural, intellectual–of a time and a place. His environmental method, his dogged pursuit of "the background of the background of the background," got him into trouble with literary critic and western historian Bernard DeVoto, whose review of Fawn M. Brodie's biography of Joseph Smith, *No Man Knows My History* (in the New York *Herald Tribune*, 16 December 1945), provoked Dale to write DeVoto a sharply critical letter. DeVoto, in fact, called it a "blast," and his angry reply of 28 December 1945 fills eight pages in Wallace Stegner's edition of *The Letters of Bernard DeVoto* (Doubleday, 1975). Stegner's commentary only whets the appetite: "The irritation evident in DeVoto's reply," he writes, "though some of it had been simmering for a good while, reflected partly the heat of argument and partly the profound differences in personality and historical method between the two." DeVoto did not think Dale understood metaphor (Stegner suggests Dale may have been "somewhat baffled by DeVoto's difficult and allusive style") and objected to Dale's listing "mistakes" in DeVoto's review that "weren't mistakes. I could not," insisted DeVoto, "imagine anyone's understanding them as mistakes. I had never experienced the kind of mind that could think of them as mistakes. There was no way my mind and yours could meet over them." DeVoto confessed to "flow[ing] naturally into psychiatric judgments," to being "warped and writhen and tied in a double lover's knot in that direction." He called himself a "spoiled psychiatrist" and hazarded the guess that Morgan was a "spoiled sociologist." "At least it appears to me," he wrote, "that when you have found an environmental explanation of something, you are content, you feel that you have settled matters, and depart about some new and proper business, whistling in the carefree consciousness of a job well done."

DeVoto told Morgan that "there are a very great many things in [Joseph] Smith and in Mormonism [about] which I cannot accept your explanation as explaining. . . . It seems to me," he wrote, "that your vast factual knowledge of Mormonism, your enormous store of data, rests on and is implemented by conceptions that have only a verbal meaning. . . . You deal with pure verbalisms as if they were realities as solid as bricks. What seems to me to weigh a pound seems to you to strike C-sharp and there is no way of bringing us to discuss things in the same terms." DeVoto warned Morgan to look to his own preconceptions and to be a little more careful of his own statements of fact.

> But most particularly this, when you think of Smith as a "product and exemplar of his times," take care that you sufficiently realize that those times did not, anywhere outside his church, center on him. In short, if you are going to deal with him on the basis of what seems to you a historical theory but is, if I diagnose it aright, a sociological theory which accepts only a static psychology—then make sure, make a damned sight surer than it appears to me you now do, that you avoid the cardinal fallacy of practically everyone who writes about Mormonism. . . . That fallacy consists in overstating the importance and the typicalness of Mormonism in the United States of its time. It was not typical of American life at that time and it was, even in sum total, of exceedingly minute importance in or to American life. It is at best a minor thing in America as a whole, and at best an aberration of the principal energies involved in it. Something of the state of mind of the true believer seems to linger on in everyone who writes about Mormonism.

DeVoto's parting sally was that he would "not acknowledge" that Dale's ideas about American life at large in the first half of the nineteenth century were any more authoritative than his or rested on any more intimate or more detailed knowledge.

Stegner assures us that "squabbling was not their characteristic relationship. Both before and after this altercation, DeVoto drew on Morgan's encyclopedic knowledge of the West and the fur trade, and valued him both for his learning and for his generosity with it. We all did." DeVoto once confided to Garrett Mattingly, another eminent historian, "I can't ever be a historian for I hate detail and can't spare the time for original research. I'm a journalist, my boy, . . . a mere literary gent who can be a nice press agent for history." Both DeVoto and Morgan, however, took Francis Parkman as a master of narrative history to heart, and Parkman knew, as Van Wyck Brooks writes of him, that "no good writer has ever liked drudgery, nor has any good writer ever permitted anyone else to do his drudgery for him." Dale Morgan was a good writer and did his own drudgery.

A comparison with Parkman may illuminate Dale's own career. Both were heroic historians, heroic in a double sense: they were heroic in overcoming crippling handicaps—Parkman's nearly total loss of sight and Dale's complete loss of hearing; and they were heroic in their grand designs—Parkman's the prolonged conflict involving England, France, and Spain for the mastery of the New World in the context of events in the Old; Dale's the exploration and settlement of the West and the rise and movement of the Mormons in the context of national events. Both turned their handicaps to advantage, Parkman's near blindness intensifying his pictorial imagination, Dale's deafness freeing him from distractions and compensated by his artist's eye for shape and color. They were both strenuous men in a way Teddy Roosevelt would have admired, dedicated and driven like Jesuits as they buried themselves for months in libraries and archives or followed a trail for the exhilaration of standing on the sites where history was made. And both were pioneers: Parkman, taking his cue from Irving, made the writing of American history significant at a time when reputations, like Prescott's and Motley's, rested in an established interest in European history; Dale made the local and regional history of the trans-Mississippi West significant, tracing the tributaries that fed the mainstream of national history: the Humboldt, the Great Salt Lake, Jedediah Smith, William H. Ashley, Catholic fathers, Mormon settlers, Forty-Niners, and Overlanders—all parts that would eventually make the whole greater than the sum of these parts—names without the ring perhaps of Bunker Hill and Bull Run, the Alamo and Little Big Horn, but magnified and luminous in Dale's artful narratives and vivid descriptions.

Dale, so often the hack in order to earn a living (Dale was poor where Parkman was affluent), never wrote like one. He had style and a sense of humor. Afflicted as he was, unable to hear the tones of his own voice, much less another's, he spoke in a high-pitched monotone, words pouring out in answer to questions and fragments put to him on scraps of paper. I remember using up a pad of note cards in conversation with him once on a park bench in Washington, D.C., when he sat by the hour like a patient academic Bernard Baruch sharing his wisdom. Dale once described Washington, by the way, as "a historian's paradise" and the National Archives as "enough to make one weep with joy." Dale was quick in repartee, the wit, often satirical, flashing in conversation as it did in his letters. In one letter to Russ Mortensen, dated 19 July 1951 and preserved at the Utah State Historical Society, he responded with a question and a quip to the news that the society might be moving to the Kearns Mansion. "How fireproof is the place?" he wanted to know. "And how sure could the Society be that its collection would be safe? A burned-up governor is easily replaced, but not so a library."

The photograph of Dale that accompanies Everett Cooley's admiring and affectionate memorial tribute in the *Utah Historical Quarterly* (Winter 1971) looks at once severe and serene, even benign, the face of a man who has taken his own measure in success as well as adversity and knows his worth. Had Alvin Gittins painted Dale's portrait, as I wish he had, he would have caught the unflinching look in Dale's eyes, the granitic purpose in repose in the square angles of his face, the hint of an enigmatic smile at the corners of the mouth, the strength of the stubby fingers closed around one of his books. In the photograph the hands do, in fact, rest with deliberate weight on an up-ended copy, spine forward, of *The West of William H. Ashley*. The iconography is fitting and completes the image of Dale Lowell Morgan as patron saint of Mormon and western historians. "Dale Morgan," writes Dr. Cooley, "was a man of many ideas and more projects for himself and others to do than could be undertaken in a half dozen lifetimes. . . . Dale compressed more projects into his too short life than many of us would do were we given a dozen lives."

Thomas Jefferson wanted only three of his achievements memorialized on his tombstone: his authorship of the Virginia Statute of Religious Freedom, his drafting of the Declaration of Independence, and his founding of the University of Virginia. Dale Morgan would be glad to be remembered, I think, for the three major contributions John Phillip Walker identifies in the following biographical essay: his tireless collecting of original source materials, his grandly conceived and superbly written histories, and his seminal correspondence. For today his epitaph might read, in the manner of the elegies on headstones in the graveyards of colonial New England:

Though dead, he lives
In works heroic,
Memorials of
A spirit stoic.

BIOGRAPHICAL INTRODUCTION

John Phillip Walker

Dale Lowell Morgan (1914-1971) stands in the front rank of historians of the American West. To this day, his books, *Jedediah Smith and the Opening of the West, The West of William H. Ashley, The Humboldt: Highroad of the West*, and *The Great Salt Lake* remain classics in their field. They earned Dale the reputation of a painstaking and skilled historian of the American Frontier. Yet the fur laden trappers and trail blazers, which provided the grist for his seminal studies, were not Dale's first historical interest. The figure who first caught, and then held his curiosity throughout the better part of his life, was Joseph Smith, the nineteenth-century founder of the Church of Jesus Christ of Latter-day Saints, who, not unlike his explorer contemporaries, charted a new path to heaven for his followers.

Sadly, however, the story of Dale Morgan and Mormon history is not a happy one, but one of a brilliant scholar and his unfinished masterpiece—a mere fragment of the work he had envisioned. Nor was this the only tragedy in Dale's short life. His father, James Lowell, died when Dale was only five, leaving his mother, Emily Holmes, a family of four small children to raise. When Dale was thirteen he contracted meningitis, which left him permanently deaf and cost him a year of school. Through the help of skilled tutors and his mother, he learned to cope with his handicap. But oral communication proved difficult, and normal speech was soon substituted by passing notes.

Perhaps to compensate, Dale immersed himself in the printed word. Only rarely did he discuss the difficulties his deafness caused for him as a historian. "While history is still alive and walking around, it presents some problems, as you can realize," he wrote. "This is the one area where my inability to hear is a genuine handicap, because I cannot easily enable people to talk informally or even off the record, for my private information. The act of writing becomes an inhibition, if you see what I mean." Later he would struggle with eye problems, fearing that he would not be able to either read a manuscript or hear it read to him. But even this prospect did not cloud his literary future. Witness to his stamina and courage, Dale decided that, if both blind and deaf, he would simply abandon history and dictate novels to support himself financially.

Born in Salt Lake City on 18 December 1914, Dale graduated from the University of Utah in 1937 with a bachelor's degree in commercial art. Jobs were scarce under the best of circumstances, and Dale's handicap made job-hunting even more difficult. He was denied a series of openings with advertising agencies because of his difficulties. Finally in 1938, at the age of twenty-three, he was hired by the Historical Records Survey of the Works Progress Administration (WPA) to develop a bibliography of Utah from 1847 to statehood—thus launching his career as a professional historian. He began as a clerk for the project but was soon editor and finally supervisor for the Utah Writers' Project.

Dale's first published works as a historian stemmed from his job at the Utah Writers' Project. His first monograph was a book-length essay on "The State of Deseret," appearing in the *Utah Historical Quarterly* in 1941. This study was preceded by several historical sketches of Utah counties in the *Inventory of the County Archives of Utah*, published between 1939 and 1941. Also in 1941, Dale published a small work, *A History of Ogden* (Utah), and edited and wrote sections of *Utah: A Guide to the State*, since recognized as one of the best guides in the WPA series. The following year he published his final WPA project, *Provo, Pioneer Mormon City*.

Dale continued to write about Mormon subjects throughout his career. Most notably, he reviewed virtually every major book on the Mormons, Utah, and the West for the *Saturday Review of Literature* from 1945 to 1957. He wrote a chapter on Mormon novels, entitled "Mormon Storytellers," for Ray B. West's 1946 *Rocky Mountain Reader*. Three years later West invited Dale to contribute the chapter on Salt Lake City for his book *Rocky Mountain Cities*. In 1959 Dale published in the *Utah Historical Quarterly* "The Changing Face of Salt Lake City," which traced the capital's physical alterations over the years.

Dale's most important published work on Mormonism was his 1947 *The Great Salt Lake*. Published in a Bobbs-Merrill series on American lakes, *The Great Salt Lake* contains Dale's rich version of Mormon history along the shores of Utah's largest body of water. His carefully written chapters about the Mormon trek to Utah and the establishment of "the foundations of the Kingdom of God" in Deseret display a panoramic knowledge of Mormon development.

These published works, however, represent only a small part of what Dale contributed to Mormon historiography. He also labored to make basic research materials and bibliographies available to other scholars interested in the Mormon movement. He encountered firsthand the dearth of reference materials for Mormon historians while working for the WPA during the late 1930s. "The resources of the wide world of scholarship were essentially unavailable to the Utah student of 1940," he wrote. Again and again, he found it basically:

> impossible to write definitively on any topic relating to Utah and the Mormons. . . . If one knew that relevant titles existed, or once had existed, in the outside world, blind search after them was the only real expedient. As for tapping distant repositories by microfilm, if you did succeed in locating an item and could have it filmed, . . . there was [not] a viewer within a thousand miles of Salt Lake City other than that in the LDS Genealogical Society; and photostating entire books (or pamphlets, even) very quickly ran into real money.

While working for the Utah Writers' Project, Dale began to remedy the lack of source materials by compiling primary reference "tool books" for Mormon historians. The documents he subsequently collected often appeared in the published works of other writers. His generosity is evident, for example, in the following 1941 letter to Juanita Brooks, who, at the time, was researching her book on the Mountain Meadows massacre.

> I am sending you herewith something that will be far more interesting to you than anything I could write as a letter. . . . About 11 this morning I wandered around the [LDS church] Historian's Office to see if by any chance they had the History of the Santa Clara Mission, [Jacob] Hamblin says he handed in; there was nothing in the History of [the] St. George Stake; . . . I then asked Alvin Smith if he knew of such a history in manuscript. He couldn't recall anything of the sort and was doubtful that they would have it if it wasn't in the *Journal History* or *Stake History*. I then asked if they had any of Hamblin's Journals. He looked up the index and found that they were supposed to have a mutilated journal by Hamblin. Most obligingly, he looked through a couple of steel cupboards and gave it to me.
>
> Naturally I was highly delighted. I sat down at a typewriter there in the office, I borrowed some paper . . . and without so much as five minutes' intermission, hammered the typewriter for six hours. . . . I got up with the complete copy of the journal that I send you. Please take every care of this, because there is no carbon copy.

In 1942 Dale left Salt Lake City for Washington, D.C., to work for the federal government. He took with him the idea of developing a comprehensive bibliography of the churches of Mormonism, and he soon discovered that the nation's capital was rich in research materials about Mormonism. In his spare hours, he copied in minute detail the card catalogs of the libraries he visited, including the Library of Congress and the New York City Public Library. Five years later, in 1947, he embarked on a nationwide trip to the major libraries and sites of Mormon history, adding to his bibliography at each stop. He published his finished bibliography on the "lesser Mormon churches" in three issues of the *Western Humanities*

Review between 1949 and 1953. But his comprehensive bibliography of the Mormon church from 1830 to 1849 was not published in his lifetime. He did, however, send a preliminary copy to the Utah State Historical Society, which was typed in quadruplicate so that the listing could be accessed by author, title, chronological date, or imprint date. He was also the moving force behind the first National Union Catalogue of works about Mormonism, which others expanded from its 700 entries to the much larger *A Mormon Bibliography* eventually published under the direction of Chad Flake in 1978.

While in Washington, D.C., Dale also began reading and making transcriptions from the newspaper collections in the Library of Congress. By the end of the summer of 1947, he could claim that he had read virtually every newspaper in the Library of Congress published before 1849 in Ohio, Vermont, Illinois, Missouri, and Iowa. During his year-long research pilgrimage across the United States in 1947-48, he read and typed entries from newspapers in every area where the Mormon church had been located. Copying methods are so much better today that it is easy to forget that Dale's transcriptions from the seventy-five volumes of the *Niles Weekly Register*, for example, had to be pounded out by hand on a standard typewriter. These priceless transcriptions were kept in a file titled "The Mormons and the Far West." In 1949 Dale sold carbon copies of the set to the Henry B. Huntington Library, Yale University, and the Utah State Historical Society. This rich newspaper collection, sadly ignored by most researchers today, provides access to many of the earliest accounts of events in Mormon history.

In August 1947, Dale wrote to Fawn Brodie, author of the controversial biography of Joseph Smith, *No Man Knows My History*, about his newspaper transcriptions:

> All this has been arduous in the extreme, but it had to be done some day by somebody. . . . Maybe future researchers, instead of going over the same ground again, can take up where I have left off and scan other areas of the newspaper press—and thus, by a collective effort over a long period of time, history may come to have the benefit of the vast amount of materials scattered in newspapers which, from the sheer labor involved, has remained unmined down to the present time. I think that newspapers represent probably the greatest source of untouched material yet awaiting researchers in Mormon history, so this particular job is my contribution to research in general, apart from the necessities of my particular work-in-progress.

Dale also transcribed many sections from the LDS Journal History, a multi-volume daily history of Mormonism, to which he had access in the LDS Church Historian's Office between 1940 and 1942. Although access to this mammoth compilation is no longer as restricted as it once was, as late as 1971 Dale wrote that his collection of excerpts, which he kept in a set of binders, was "irreplaceable." He was convinced that ranking church leaders would never allow anyone to copy from the Journal History as he had in the early 1940s.

Dale called these newspaper transcriptions, bibliographies, and collections of unpublished source material his "tool books." "It is sad to think how anyone who works in the field of Mormonism must do everything for himself," he once lamented about this phase of his work. "The tools of the trade are simply nil. You must first fashion the tools, and only then can you set about your proper labors. Well, before I get through with the Saints [i.e., Mormons] this will be changed in some degree." By the end of a decade of such collecting and organizing, he was convinced that there was "hardly a phase of Trans-Mississippi history for that period that I could not rewrite." And though Dale always shared his research with others, his remarkable exertions were, as he indicates, primarily for one purpose: his own history of the Mormon church.

Soon after beginning work for the WPA, Dale decided to write a major history, in three volumes, of the rise and development of Mormonism. In 1942 he explained to Juanita Brooks, herself a promising Mormon historian:

> For the last several years I have been soaking up everything about the Mormons I could find. Nothing was without significance. Any problem existing for anybody, in Mormon research, was a problem also for me. Those people (and I encountered a diverse group) with whom I came in contact supply me with provocative viewpoints on this major interest of my life. In answering their limited needs, I answer larger ones of my own . . . all these individual things are parts of an infinitely complex organism that I am trying to see whole. I didn't begin this research with that end in view, but things have developed that I believe I am now capable of writing that definitive history of the Mormons and this state that has been so badly needed. I am not yet ready to write it; but I believe that I am fortunate enough to have the equipment, I have an emotional understanding of Mormonism, I also have an intellectual detachment essential to the critical appraisal of it. My work of the Historical Records Survey and the Writers Project during the last four years, has been, in effect, a fellowship in the history of this state; I have a pretty good educational background, and I have sunk enough time in research to have a pretty extensive command of resources. So you see what these things add up to.

His decision to leave the WPA and move to Washington, D.C., was dictated, in large measure, by his drive to continue his research. His evenings and weekends could be spent in the various book, manuscript, newspaper, and map collections of the Library of Congress and in the "staggering and largely unplumbed manuscript collections" of the National Archives.

In January 1945 Dale applied for a post-service fellowship from the Guggenheim Foundation. He believed he needed two years to complete his history of the Mormons: one year of field research and at least one year of writing. He received a $2,000 stipend in the spring of that year, with a possible $2,000 renewal for an extra year. He spent the rest of 1945, all of 1946, and most of 1947 finishing his exhaustive newspaper search in the Library of Congress.

In the fall of 1947, Dale quit his job, activated the Guggenheim grant, and set out in a 1943 Hudson for a crosscountry study of Mormonism. His first stop was New York City where he spent six weeks in the New York Public Library and the New York Historical Society, working principally in the newspaper files. While in New York he almost bankrupted himself microfilming early Mormon publications such as *The Return*, *The Elder's Journal*, *The Gospel Herald*, *The Prophet*, *The Messenger and Advocate*, and *The Evening and the Morning Star*.

During the rest of 1947 Dale made his way through the New England states where Mormonism was born. From New York he struck out for Vermont where he retraced the meanderings of Joseph Smith's family. First he went to Woodstock, then Windsor, where, nearly 136 years before, Solomon Mack, Joseph's maternal grandfather, had published a pamphlet entitled *Narrative of Solomon Mack*. Dale next went down to the old Smith farm at South Royalton in search of something more than manuscripts. "Biography," he had once written to a friend, "demands a certain feeling, a sense of the texture of life." That evening, as on so many others, he recorded his impressions.

> The air was winey and fresh, wholly delicious, the very smell of October in the hills. The rolling adjacent land seems still to be farmed after a fashion. I noticed that the soil was rocky still. I climbed over a barbed wire fence north of the place and climbed the higher of the hills looming above it until checked by a more formidable barbed wire fence I didn't think it worthwhile to climb, as I had altitude enough for the picture I wanted. I noticed that in this field above the old farm was a good deal of cutover land, with small stumps to give me an idea of some of the problems this land may have afforded when the original stand of timber was cleared off by the Smiths. Scenically the place was lovely even at this season, when the greys and russets and duns of November reign in the hills, for the hills still were carpeted by a brave fresh green of grass.

From Windsor he drove five miles to Tunbridge, where the Smiths had also lived for a time, and then on to Sharon, Norwich, Whitingham, and the old Brigham Young farm. From Vermont he went to Massachusetts, spending several days in the libraries of Boston.

All through the winter of 1947 Dale followed the paths that Mormonism had wandered from New York through Pennsylvania and Ohio. He spent Thanksgiving that year near Afton, New York, where Joseph Smith had married Emma Hale in 1827. Then he went to Colesville, site of an 1830 trial of Joseph, and on to Harmony to see where the couple had buried their first child. Late in November, he visited Palmyra, where the Book of Mormon was first published in 1830. Kirtland, Ohio, and the first Mormon temple followed; there Dale spent several days in the extensive newspaper collections of the Western Reserve Historical Society. He moved on from Cleveland to the Detroit Public Library where he worked in the Burton Historical Collection. Then on to Chicago where he discovered affidavits concerning Joseph's life, collected but not published by A. B. Deming in his expose *Naked Truths About Mormonism*, and also the stockbook of the church's ill-fated attempt at banking, the Kirtland Anti-banking Safety Society.

After a few days Dale moved on to Fort Leavenworth, Kansas, from where he made research forays to the many schismatic churches of Mormonism in the vicinity. He spent several days at the headquarters of the Reorganized Church of Jesus Christ of Latter Day Saints in Independence, Missouri, and received permission from RLDS church president Israel Smith to examine anything in their library, including photostats of their manuscript copy of the Book of Mormon. After spending a day with the manuscript, with the help of RLDS library research assistant S. A. Burgess, Dale concluded that the RLDS manuscript was the second, or printer's copy, of the Book of Mormon. Dale also examined the Hiram Page seerstone. Burgess "gave a demonstration of how it was used, holding it up to his eyes and peering through it. But Burgess said he could not make it work." Neither could Dale. He also examined such curiosities as the Reformed Egyptian "caractors" reportedly transcribed from the Book of Mormon and was allowed to read the Book of John Whitmer, an early official history of Mormonism, and also the original printer's copy of the Book of Commandments, an early compilation of Mormon scripture.

He finished his visits to the other churches in the Independence area by the end of January and then visited other sites in Missouri—Columbia, St. Louis, and St. Joseph. From there he visited Nauvoo, Illinois. Finally he turned west, tracing the Mormon Battalion route to California. There he worked in the Huntington Library, the Stanford University Library, and the Bancroft Library at Berkeley.

He reached his mother's home in Salt Lake City in March 1948, prepared to spend the next year to eighteen months writing the first volume of his history of the Mormons. But he arrived to find a letter from the Guggenheim Foundation notifying him that the second year fellowship, which he needed to support his writing, had been denied. He was out of funds and out of a job, having resigned his federal government position in order to work full-time on his Mormon history. Now, he felt, he would have to start again, not "from scratch, but some distance back of scratch."

Still reeling from this disappointment, Dale soon received yet another setback. He had written to LDS church president George Albert Smith requesting cooperation from the Church Historian's Office in Utah similar to that he had been granted by the RLDS church in Independence. He received a letter dated 14 April 1948 from Joseph Anderson, secretary to the Utah church's governing First Presidency:

> An experience running over several years has persuaded us of the unwisdom of giving access to our manuscript records to people writing books, because that same experience has shown that people writing such books are rarely qualified to appraise accurately what they read, and too frequently, whether conscious or unconsciously, they misrepresent what they find. Such manuscripts will therefore not be available for general inspection or use.

The Historian's Office, Anderson concluded, was not a research library "but a private library, maintained and operated for the benefit of the Church." The Utah church would allow Dale access to some printed materials in its library but not to manuscripts, which included first and rare editions of books. This was the first time a library or a church had refused Dale access to Mormon materials, and early the following year the first counselor to President Smith, J. Reuben Clark, Jr., further urged the Guggenheim Foundation not to renew its funding of Dale's research. Still, Dale followed up on the offer to let him look at the non-rare, non-first edition books in the church's collections, hoping to add titles to his bibliography. He was surprised to find only 190 out of the 700 titles already on his list in the Church Historian's Office, a smaller number than he had found in the New York Public Library, the Harvard Library, or the Coe Collection at Yale University.

By mid-1948 finding work had become Dale's most pressing priority. He wrote to John Selby, his editor at Rinehart and Company, in July and requested an advance on the first volume of the Mormon history, promising the first draft of the book by April 1949. This resulted in a signed contract and an advance of $750 within the next few weeks. But even as he wrote Dale was accepting projects that stole time away from his Mormon history—so as to raise "the water table of my financial well," as he put it. On 6 September 1949 he wrote to his friend Dean Brimhall:

> In the last month my decision has definitely crystallized to return to Washington [D.C.], permanently insofar as I am able to establish myself. The year and a half I have spent in Utah has graphically demonstrated to me that it is wholly unrealistic of me to try to maintain myself here. Both economically and culturally it is impossible–if not impossible, unwise and impracticable. Apart from the cultural handi-

> caps under which one must work here, the basic tools of research [are] not even at hand, [and] the economic disability [is] serious. What it amounts to is that I should either have to give up the writing of the histories for which I have prepared myself through so many years, or be content to live forever at a worse than substandard subsistence level.

Dale left Utah that winter. As he later wrote, "For better or worse, I am an expatriate now." He had no job waiting in Washington, D.C., so in addition to working on his Mormon history he was also accepting whatever work came his way, mainly writing book review articles for the *Saturday Review of Literature* and cataloging manuscript collections for the Eberstadt Company, a rare book dealer in New York City. By March 1950 he wrote to Fawn Brodie that he had completed about 125 pages of his Mormon history, plus a 19-page appendix on Joseph Smith's 1826 "glass looking" trial in Bainbridge, New York. He sent this portion of the manuscript to the Utah State Historical Society to be typed.

Unfortunately, a January 1952 letter from Dale's publisher, Stanley Rinehart, stopped work on the Mormon history altogether. Dale had been working on the project for at least seventeen years, four years under contract with them, Rinehart wrote, and they had received only three chapters. Not only was the project two and a half years past the projected completion date, Rinehart continued acidly, but the "volume of correspondence [about the book] far outweighs this amount of manuscript." Consequently, Rinehart advised, they were no longer committed to publication of Dale's Mormon history.

Stunned by the tone of the letter, Dale left his apartment that morning and went to the Library of Congress where he remained through the day. In the evening he wrote to his friend D. L. Chambers, president of Bobbs-Merrill Publishing Company. Chambers, who had been "extraordinarily kind and courteous through all our relations," had previously expressed interest in Dale's Mormon book. Dale asked Chambers for an immediate advance of $750 in order to purchase his old obligation from Farrar and Rinehart. The advance would be for a biography of Jedediah Smith. In effect, the Mormon history was traded for the biography. Later that month Dale confessed to long-time confidant Madeline McQuown, "I have many times regretted that I committed myself on this book when as it proved the circumstances of my life were such that I was not able to make good on the commitment; and as I have not been willing to throw a text together to satisfy a merely legal obligation, I have been in a cruel situation."

For the rest of Dale's life he would refer periodically to the Mormon history he would one day finish. He never did. In all he wrote some seven chapter and two appendices. But when one realizes that Dale's chapters were all written before 1952, his remarkable insight into Joseph Smith and the beginnings of Mormonism becomes apparent.

Dale's contribution to history is not limited to his unfinished manuscript; all of his writings embody his sense of history. He once wrote that his point of view as a historian was primarily "that of the taxonomist—to describe *what* has happened rather than to criticize the happening." In 1948 Dale was considering an invitation to speak to the Salt Lake City Lion's Club. "I may finally agree to give out with something," he explained to Fawn Brodie.

> If so, it will be a discussion of "New Ways of Thinking about Mormon History," and will present the case for the primarily sociological viewpoint on Mormon history, getting away from the old right-and-wrongness of things and emphasizing the how of things, also dwelling upon the organic wholeness of the Mormon story, in which nothing that happens anywhere is the history of the major church, social and political; Mormon colonization considered in its larger aspects, and not merely as an exclusive possession of B[righam]. Young's followers.

He realized that such an approach would not be popular among some of the faithful. "I don't think this [his Mormon history] will make me any more popular in my native state," he wrote, "for it comes to conclusions which not only parallel Fawn Brodie's in many places, but documents them even more precisely. Luckily the Destroying Angels are now dead and gone, and I can cope with the Annoying Angels." But then, he would add to close friends, Joseph Smith himself would have probably had a difficult time in the contemporary church. "I am afraid that a reincarnation of Joseph would get called upon the carpet about the third week after his baptism," he quipped, "and very likely he wouldn't last out his first six months in the Church."

Dale was as concerned with the style as with the substance of his histories. "While it is being written with what literary grace I can summon to the task," he explained, "my main objective is to have a reader say not 'What a brilliant writer this fellow Morgan is' but 'So that's the truth of the matter.'" He wrote at length to Juanita Brooks in 1945, counseling her about what revisions he would recommend in the language of her own book.

> But don't let the prose stand as pedestrian merely because you wrote it that way in a hurry to get your ideas down. The point is, strike a balance between a prose which is a medium for the conveyance of ideas (a valuable kind of prose, by the way), and a prose which has an intrinsic interest of its own, for its fresh and attractive way of saying things. Every writer has to face this individual problem of saying what he wants to say in the simplest possible way, and of availing himself of the rich resources of the English language in such a way as to extend the popular comprehension and appreciation of that language. Simplicity, carried to an extreme, steadily flattens vocabulary into a barren-

> ness of narrow compass; language over-ornate becomes polysyllabic exhibitionism. No writer can tell another how he is to solve this problem. It is a matter of temperament, equipment, and taste. But it does help to be aware of the nature of the problem confronting one.

The seven chapters Dale more or less completed of his Mormon history reveal both the artist and the scholar in full command of his material.

Dale's correspondence must be included with his "tool books" and his unfinished history as significant contributions to Mormon historiography. "No one ever asked advice or direction from him without receiving it," wrote his colleague and friend Juanita Brooks. "He has consistently encouraged writers and furnished both factual materials and expert criticism. The whole field of historical research has been greatly enriched and stimulated by this man."

Dale was at his best writing long, lively letters, full of anecdotes, observations, and speculations mixed with a rich smattering of his latest finds in the recipient's field of interest. These letters constitute an intellectual history of Mormonism during the period and display the many controversies and problems which Dale encountered in researching Mormon history. His own frustration in finding materials made him a sympathetic friend and generous colleague to other researchers working on Mormon topics. For years he supplied a steady stream of material for Madeline McQuown's still unpublished biography of Brigham Young. When Juanita Brooks once asked why he would spend precious hours on someone else's work, he responded, "You need not be puzzled at the interest I take in what you are doing. . . . It's the kind of thing I'd do in your place, and I get a personal pleasure out of what you're doing, so in a sense when I can lay hold of something you can use and can make it available to you, it has the value and interest of a personal experience."

He was also a prodder and promotor. In February 1944, he wrote to Madeline McQuown about Brooks:

> I want to tell you about Juanita Brooks and a new book of which I am what you might call the spiritual father. Some weeks back I got to thinking about Juanita, her valiant and rather extraordinary life, her remarkable knowledge of the history and folkways of the Southern Mormon Frontier, and so on. Accordingly I wrote her that she was commanded to write a book, in some degree autobiographical, but with a large basis of social history, a kind of passionately personal book about that life she knows so well. I outlined in general what the book would be, and told her that her whole life had literally been a preparation to write it. Well, the idea struck fire in her mind, and she now sends me thirty or forty pages she has dashed off. . . . The material is absolutely wonderful! She tells some of the most marvelous stories you ever heard; but more than that, the tone of all she

> writes is warm, human, witty and wise, and as I have just written her, it is full of sunlight.

The material to which Dale was referring grew into Brooks's *Quicksand and Cactus*. Unfortunately, the book was not published until some thirty-eight years after this letter was written, a decade after Dale's death. He also maintained an active collaboration on each of Brooks's major works, including *The Mountain Meadows Massacre*, *John D. Lee*, and *The Diary of Hosea Stout*.

As a silent partner, Dale could be a helpful, if sometimes nitpicking, critic. Fawn Brodie sent him drafts of her work-in-progress, *No Man Knows My History*, which he returned with detailed comments and suggestions. He recommended that she expand her section on Nauvoo, Illinois, to give the book more coherence and also suggested she "make a final evaluation of [Joseph] Smith's character" and his magnetic hold on his followers. "He gave them," Dale wrote, "something they never got from anyone else; he left an indelible impression upon their minds, and they gave him a love they had never given anyone else." He also cautioned her to evaluate carefully every area in the book that might lead to criticism—thus anticipating the intensive examination which followed its publication in 1945. "You occupy a somewhat singular position in this historiography of the Mormons," he wrote to her,

> in pioneering a certain viewpoint on Joseph and the Church. You are fortunate in one respect, in that anyone who uses the same material must come to much the same conclusions as yours, and you will have the distinction of having got there first. But the cost of this pioneering is that there are bound to be errors of commission and omission in what you say, and you are now much more a target than anyone who comes after you will be—particularly as those to follow will have the benefit of the discussions you have set on foot, and may be able to avoid some of the pitfalls you are bound to have fallen into. So you'll just have to take the good with the bad!

Dale and Fawn Brodie shared research materials, a similar naturalistic outlook toward Mormon history, and a protective sympathy for each other's works throughout their careers. Their mutual admiration once led to a rare heated exchange between Dale and the pugnacious author of *Harper's* magazine's "Easy Chair" column, Bernard DeVoto.

In December 1945, Utah-born literary critic DeVoto reviewed Brodie's *No Man Knows My History* in the *New York Herald Tribune* and referred to his own theory that Joseph Smith was a paranoid. "Stirred from [his] lethargy," Dale fired off a seven-page, single-spaced, closely-argued letter accusing DeVoto of misrepresenting Brodie's book and letting his preconceptions about Joseph Smith influence his judgment. DeVoto's reply, as quoted by William

Mulder in the Preface, was filled with personal invective. DeVoto then wrote to Brodie:

> In common with God knows how many others I have frequently wished that I didn't write books. Today I could almost bring myself to wish that you didn't, for this morning I took a half a day off to write Dale Morgan about yours, and the afternoon's mail has now impelled me to take the other half day off and write you about it, and the last day I could afford to take off was back around the turn of the century.

DeVoto's response inspired another seven-page riposte from Dale, this time less provocative and signed cordially. Still Dale concluded, "I think it would be close to impossible to write a book-length study of Joseph Smith which would seriously maintain the paranoid thesis and show forth his life as exemplifying it."

Dale's view that the founder of Mormonism did not act out of paranoid delusions appears most fully developed in the seven surviving chapters of his Mormon history which he once outlined in a letter to Madeline McQuown:

> How [did] Joseph Smith happen to start a church[?] I definitely subscribe to the one-thing-led-to-another theory. He had been a peepstone seer, but was forced beyond that by the bad reaction of his old moneydigging associates to his tale of the golden plates, and also by the religious note upon which his plea to Martin Harris for help was predicated. In writing an attenuation of the Bible, his ideas were further pent up in religious channels, and the revelation that was wrung from him by the dilemma of the loss of the first part of the B[ook] of M[ormon] manuscript took him over the borderline. . . . The first intimation that there was going to be a church occurs in [the] B[ook of]. C[ommandments]. [Chapter] IV, the revelation of March, 1829, and the idea recurs thereafter, but you will see that in most of the revelations down to April 6, 1830, the true faith is equated with the acceptance of Joseph, his gift, and his book.

More often than not, Dale's letters reveal wit and a sense of humor. "I have an interesting new theory on Joseph the Prophet I would like your opinion on," he wrote to Mormon researcher Stanley Ivins in 1955.

> I have entertained this theory for a long while, but what has led me to formulate it in so many words is a little research job a friend did for me in Archives. He looked up the Joseph Smith family in Ontario, N.Y., in 1820, Farmington township, and located them all right. The age groups all checked except that the children were shy two males. One of these would have been Joseph Smith, the other I forget at the moment, but I have a theory about him too. In short, my

> theory is that there never was any such person as Joseph Smith, Junior; he was simply an optical illusion, perhaps discovered originally in a peepstone. Although this is a radical new theory, consider how well it fits the facts. It explains how such an improbable person never existed anyhow, and most triumphantly of all, it accounts for the fact that all of Joseph's reputed plural wives never bore him any children. You might object that this would not explain Joseph Smith III, etc., but I ask you, and this is unanswerable, Emma was human, wasn't she? As for the other little man who wasn't there in the census, no doubt this was William. I never quite believed in William either.

Perhaps if the theory caught on, he closed, they could start a new Mormon church—"Perhaps we could call it the Reformed or Swearing-off Mormon Church."

Dale's correspondence also documents his involvement with the Utah State Historical Society. During one period, he sent detailed letters from his Washington, D.C., apartment suggesting publishing schedules for a year at a time—what articles would be in which issues, who would write them, what they would contain, and where the material could be found. He even recommended that writers be required to follow the University of Chicago's *Manual of Style*.

Following Washington, D.C., Dale returned briefly to Salt Lake City. In 1954, he joined the staff of the Bancroft Library at the University of California, Berkeley, as an editor and author. By the 1960s, Dale, the professional historian who had forged his way without conventional institutional degrees and support, began at last to receive the recognition he rightly deserved. In 1960 he was made a Fellow of the Utah State Historical Society. The California Historical Society next presented him with their Henry R. Wagner Memorial Award in 1961 and its Fellowship Award in 1962. He received the University of Utah Alumni Association's Distinguished Alumni Award in 1964 and the Award of Merit from the American Association for State and Local History in 1965. Finally in 1970, twenty years after the renewal of his first grant had been denied, he received a second Guggenheim Foundation fellowship, this time to write a single-volume history of the fur trade in North America which he hoped to tackle the following year.

He was scarcely able to begin, however. He died of cancer in Maryland on 30 March 1971 at the age of fifty-six, leaving behind a clutch of major unfinished works. His papers, spanning some thirty-five years of research and study, filled a hundred crates and were deposited with his employer, the Bancroft Library. A priceless legacy of one of the West's "most productive and influential historians during the 1950s and 1960s," to borrow a phrase from Everett Cooley, director of Special Collections at the University of Utah Library, the contents have unfortunately remained unprocessed and are unavailable to most researchers.

Prior to Dale's death, Fawn Brodie wrote to a friend on hearing of his serious illness, "He has some great books inside him, and I simply can't bear to think of their not being written. No one but he can do what ought to be done on Mormon history." Following his untimely passing, Juanita Brooks could only echo, "I have long since ceased trying to figure out the WHY's of the Universe. I can only accept these tragedies with what grace I can muster. The cause of Utah history suffers greatly from his loss." "It's a great loss," added western novelist Wallace Stegner; "he was so fine a scholar that almost one's first thought is of the unwritten book—and not only the Mormon one but the fur trade one. And that's heartless, really, because he was also so fine and decent and generous and long-suffering a man that one should think first of the person we've lost, and not the books."

THE LETTERS

Dale Morgan cultivated a voluminous correspondence during his brief life. Confined to a world of silence, his articulate letters became his major means of communicating with those around him. They were, for him, an essential part of his personality and are thus filled with the stuff of human relationships: wit, gossip, advice, criticism, elation, dejection, humor, consolation, encouragement, and, above all, warmth. One cannot read them without experiencing a renewed sense of humanity. Few men or women are as exposed and vulnerable in their personal correspondence as is Morgan. But, as Morgan himself would probably have been quick to add, few men and women have been as accessible.

The following fifty letters chosen for inclusion were written over a period of nearly thirty years, from 1942 to 1970. They were selected from approximately three hundred available letters dealing more or less with Mormon themes. The total number of Morgan letters is difficult to determine, but it may be safely assumed that they number in the thousands. Because Morgan's papers, housed at the Bancroft Library in Berkeley, California, have not been processed, the majority of letters included here are more easily located in the various archives housing the papers of Morgan's correspondents: the Utah State Historical Society for the letters to Juanita Brooks, Stanley Ivins, Marguerite Sinclair, and Elizabeth Lauchnor; and the University of Utah Marriott Library, Special Collections division, for the letters to Fawn Brodie, Joseph Anderson, S. A. Burgess, Francis W. Kirkham, John Selby, Wesley P. Walters, Bernard DeVoto, and Madeline McQuown.

The task of determining which letters to reprint verbatim was difficult. Generally, the following three criteria were used in efforts to simplify the problem: letters which provide autobiographical details, letters which offer insights into Morgan's approach to Mormon historiography and methodology, and letters which contain information regarding his unfinished history, "The Mormons."

In editing the letters for publication, the bulk of which are typewritten copies, obvious errors, including Morgan's rare misspellings and grammatical mistakes, have been corrected. Morgan tended not to underline magazine and book titles, and was sometimes inconsistent regarding capitalization, especially with words such as "church," "president," "apostle," "mother," "ms," and "mss." In these instances, no attempt at standardization has been made. The parentheses and ellipses are Morgan's, but the brackets have been added to supply necessary clarification where needed without distracting the reader by referring him or her to a footnote. Where more information may be required by the reader, footnotes are supplied following the letter to which they refer. What follows then is, as far as it is possible to convey from original to printed page, what Dale Morgan felt, believed, and wrote.

1. To JUANITA BROOKS[1]

Salt Lake City, Utah
12 April 1942

Dear Juanita,

This is my sixth letter this afternoon, after which my correspondence will be fairly well caught up; as yours is latest in point of time, it becomes last answered.

It is refreshing to have your letters. I often gallop at so frantic a pace that the world gets to spinning pretty furiously, and your good common sense and urbane view of the world is a tonic, even when this tonic is far from refreshing to you personally. (It is curious, the effect we can have on people independent of the effect we are having on ourselves.)

It was nice having you down here, but there certainly was little enough leisure to enjoy life with you. I wanted to break a few trails for you, so to speak, which you could tread with some assurance when opportunity offered; I probably was not overwhelmingly successful in that, except that you will know where to lay hands on things when you want them, I think. The only other places you really need to know about are the Tribune-Telegram library, on the third floor of the T-T building, the U[niversity] of U[tah] library (for some of its theses only) on the U campus, and the [LDS[2]] Genealogical Society library, about which I know nothing much myself yet, but will in due course, as one of my research workers is a genealogist in good standing, to say the least.

I am rather amused, in a way, by a sort of misconception of me that you evidence in talking about my "unselfishness." It is far from being as simple as that, though I can see how you look at it. You see, Juanita, in a purely practical sense, I get as much out of everything I do as anybody who partially or wholly shares in this action. For the last several years I have been soaking up everything about the Mormons I could find. Nothing was without significance. Any problem existing for anybody, in Mormon research, was a problem also for me. These people (and I have encountered an exceedingly diverse group—a folklorist in Los Angeles, a novelist in Terra Haute, a highway employee interested in Nevada trails in Carson City, Wallace Stegner[3] in Cambridge, Bernard DeVoto[4] in the same place, etc., etc.) with whom I come in contact supply me with provocative viewpoints on this major interest of my life. In answering their limited needs, I answer larger needs of my own. For example, your interest is primarily in southwestern Utah, the Indian missions, [the] Dixie [region of southern Utah], etc. I can almost exactly parallel your interest and enthusiasm (except for a geographical and local knowledge I can't possess); what is important to you is important to me; and the ways these things are important to you are also the ways they are important to me; but also, all these individual things are parts of an infinitely complex organism that I am trying to see whole. I didn't begin this research with that end in view, but things have so developed that I believe I am now capable of writing that definitive history of the Mormons and this state that has been so badly needed. I am not yet ready to write it; I have a very great deal of research still to do; but I believe that I am fortunate enough to have the equipment. I have an emotional understanding of Mormonism, and also an intellectual detachment essential to the critical appraisal of it; my work for the Historical Records Survey and the Writers' Project, during the past four years, has been, in effect, a fellowship in the history of this state; I have a pretty good educational background, and I have sunk enough time in research to have a pretty extensive command of resources. So you see what these things add up to.

In a letter about Christmas-time, you speculated a little about me; I couldn't take the time then to remark on myself. However, there isn't much to say. I was born into a thoroughly orthodox Mormon family (except that the orthodoxies of each succeeding generation are not, of course, the same orthodoxies) and was, to my fourteenth birthday, probably a more dutiful Mormon than the average—president of my quorum of deacons, etc., etc. My father died soon after my fifth birthday, and my mother has taught school (second at first, then first grade) ever since to support her children, which included a sister and two brothers younger than I, all three of whom now are married. I lost my hearing through meningitis in the summer of 1929, and was out of school a year convalescing. The loss of my hearing pretty well broke up the world I had lived in, in one way and another; it confirmed a tendency to introspection and living in a personal world; it broke me out of most social contacts and faced me with various difficult problems of adjustment, not least among which was a grave doubt as to my competency to survive in the kind of depression world we had during my high school years. I studied commercial art in high school, seeing that as the best possibility for myself, but my senior year English teacher, after some investigation, found that I was eligible to be helped by the state Vocational Rehabilitation Department; I was given a probational year at the University, and then three more years. My tuition fees were paid by this department, and my mother scraped up enough money for books, carfare, etc., although I rarely had a nickel to rub one against another. I did a good deal of writing at the U and, in my junior year especially, recovered a measure of self respect and confidence in myself. After graduation I had a difficult time for a period, as I did not find employment at once and there were other complications in my living which I won't discuss except to say that they ended with putting me together as a person. I spent much of the time that year studying advertising at home, but then an opening [was] offered with the H[istorical] R[ecords] S[urvey] in Ogden. I worked there nine months, then moved back to Salt Lake. I went to San Francisco, or rather stopped off there after a trip into the Northwest with some of my family, in the summer of 1939, and tried to stir up something in advertising, as I wanted to get into something more demanding than what I had been doing, and wanted to get out of Utah for awhile. However, that was a bad season, so I went back to Utah to work for the HRS until things should open up in the fall. Then my mother had a heart attack, so I decided to stay on till the end of the year, then in December Farrar & Rinehart offered me a contract on the Humboldt book which I had proposed to them, and I decided to stick around doing research until the next July. But in February Darel McConkey[5] came from Washington to help get the Guide finished, and as he had heard about me from Maurice Howe[6] and Nels Anderson,[7] he tried to draft my services. HRS squawked, and it was arranged that I should work mornings for Writers, and afternoons for HRS. That was accordingly quite a busy spring for me, and Darel thought pretty highly of me and leaned on me quite heavily; as he had come out with instructions to try to find a supervisor adequate to the job, he finally asked me if I would be interested in taking it over. There were various complications, but it finally worked out that way. I accordingly took over the project in July, 1940, and have run it since, at the same time spending all my spare hours doing research for the Mormon books that have gradually evolved in my mind. That research is now mostly finished here, and I am going to make a determined effort, perhaps before the end of summer, to get to Washington, to finish up my research in the National Archives and Library of Congress. History has been perhaps the largest value in my life in the last couple of years, but it is not a paying kind of history, and I shall have to find jobs to support it, so to speak.

I graduated from the U with an art major, expecting to make a living in commercial art and advertising, but use this talent solely for recreation. When I lived alone in an Ogden apartment, I sometimes pinned up stuff on the walls, not that it was good, but for the educational effect of looking it over; however, since I came back to live somewhat crowded with my family, the stuff has stayed packed down [in] the basement; anyway, I gave to various friends the best things I had done. I haven't done any finished clay pieces; my first will be cast soon, but it's just a journeyman's find-out-how piece, if you know what I mean. I like to sketch nudes in pastel, and now and then drop in on the life classes at the Art Center for this purpose; sometimes they come out well, and sometimes they're lousy. But I'm strictly nothing but an amateur, grade B, as an artist. I have played chess since the summer of 1936, and have been a factor in most of the tournaments played since—I won the city championship in 1938, 1940, and 1941, lost out by half a point in 1936 and 1939, was four points down in 1937, and how this year's event will come out remains to be seen (it is reported round by round in the sports pages of the [Deseret] News each Saturday, and the Tribune each Sunday, so you can follow this yourself, if interested). In the state championship, I won in 1940 and 1941, missed out by half a point in 1937 and 1938, and was about four points down in 1939.

I expect to marry ultimately, but won't predict when. If things had broken a little better several years ago, I would probably have been married now, although my family would be amazed to know this; I don't talk about it but may write about it sometime in a novel I want to write. As to religion, I had a period of adjustment through my teens which more or less precipitated itself during my final college years and the year thereafter. I could no longer believe the things I had formerly believed, but made the transition without bitterness, as some persons I know have not been so fortunate in accomplishing. I do not see the necessity of a God in the scheme of things, and on the plane of ethics think that things are in a hell of a state if we order our behavior purely in hope of reward or fear of punishment in a hereafter; if I have a religion, it is a belief in what I call "the decencies of human relations." I live life as I see it from day to day and hour to hour, and in my way I think I am a better Mormon than those who go to church on Sunday and pay their tithing. I don't ask that others believe or think as I do, but also ask that they try not to enforce their beliefs and thinking upon me. In other words, I'll let them live as they want to, and mind my own business; and I expect that they shall let me live as I want to, and mind their own business. This is an ideal of tolerance which probably does not work out uniformly, and is not the kind of religion that can be effectively preached; it is a purely personal religion. At the same time, I have no quarrel with those who find that formal religion, in orthodox patterns, fills a definite need in their lives; nor am I critical of the Mormon Church on these grounds. Historically, I think there are certain imbecilities in the social development of the Mormon Church; its history is riddled with inconsistencies, and the church membership and its ideals today would be utterly unacceptable to the fanatic founders of the religion; the whole scheme of values has changed, as Mormonism has evolved from a millennial church to an ordinary, or more ordinary, type of church. These are matters for historical evaluation, and in the course of time I mean to evaluate them—what the church was and what it has become, and why it was inevitable that it should so become. But in the field of pure religion, the Mormon Church offers as much as any other church—perhaps more, aside from some of the absurdities consequent upon an authoritarian-type church—and if one desires to worship God, he can do it with as much grace and dignity within the sanctions of Mormonism as anywhere. I might remark that I respect you for your own type of religious thinking. It is a primary criticism I hold of the

Church that it tends, fundamentally, to stifle independent thinking by straitjacketing it with the demands of faith. For the independence of mind to which you hold I admire you, and I hope that it will always characterize your thinking, about the church, about life, and about yourself, regardless of environmental demands.

This letter has gone into a larger quantity of detail than is usual with my letters. Possibly it will explain to you a few things about me, though you will find in it not one fact of any but personal history!

Dale

[1] Juanita Brooks, an LDS historian from southern Utah, corresponded regularly with Morgan throughout the 1940s and 1950s. She accepted his generous help during the writing of several of her books, including *The Mountain Meadows Massacre* (1950) and *John Doyle Lee: Zealot-Pioneer Builder-Scapegoat* (1962). Brooks/Morgan correspondence is housed in both the Utah State Historical Society and the University of Utah Marriott Library, Special Collections division.

[2] LDS is a common acronym referring to the Utah-based Church of Jesus Christ of Latter-day Saints; also Mormon.

[3] Wallace Stegner, a graduate of the University of Utah, was a western novelist, historian, and conservationist. He authored several books about Utah and the Mormons. Morgan's reference in this letter probably refers to one of Stegner's two works-in-progress, *Mormon Country* (1942) and *The Big Rock Candy Mountain* (1943).

[4] Bernard DeVoto, a noted western historian and literary critic, was born in Ogden, Utah. He was, at the time of this letter, curator of the Mark Twain papers, teaching at Harvard University, and was completing work on his *Year of Decision*. His life is chronicled in Wallace Stegner's *The Uneasy Chair*.

[5] Darel McConkey was the director of the Utah Writers' Project which produced *Utah: A Guide to the State*, edited by Morgan.

[6] A close friend of Morgan, Maurice Howe later helped convince him to move to Washington, D.C.

[7] Nels Anderson, another of Morgan's friends who prompted his move east, was a convert to the Mormon church. After graduating from Brigham Young University and the University of Chicago, he published in 1942 a major contribution to the sociology of Mormonism, *Desert Saints*.

2. To JUANITA BROOKS

Salt Lake City, Utah
21 May 1942

Dear Juanita,

Here is the rest of the [Thomas D.] Brown journal, completed today. Copying it has been a most laborious job, but I wish all my time were spent as profitably. Apart from the new light this journal sheds on the Indian mission, it provides interesting material on [John D.] Lee[1] that I have not seen before; and also it echoes in the Utah outlands things that were going on at headquarters, especially the consecration agitation, as no other journal I have seen does. I was disappointed, however, that Brown didn't either confirm or deny that tale you have heard about how [Jacob] Hamblin happened to leave Harmony for Santa Clara. The dictatorial character of Lee, as brought out in the journal, might supply a little indirect substantiation, though.

Before I forget, I'll ask you to make corrections on the carbon material sent you earlier. In the entry for June 24, 1854, last line, read "these two days" for "these day days." In the entry for June 30, first line, insert "and" after "ago." In the poem on July 24, 3rd verse, first line, read "he would build up" for "he would built up." I notice, too, that there is no 10th verse. I think that is my error, and will investigate, possibly before I mail this to you.

After the beginning I didn't number the pages—I think I told you the reason—they could be numbered later, after the job was done, when no question could arise about how much of the journal had been copied for profane eyes.

When you have returned the part of the journal you have, so that I can review it as a whole, I will offer some comment on passages of the journal, etc. But aside from that, don't you think it's a pretty fine ms. [i.e., manuscript], taken altogether?

Incidently, I might make some remarks now which are applicable to earlier material I have lent you also. Anything I have given you or obtained for you, you may make free use of in any writing you do; but I should prefer that no acknowledgments be made direct to me for such material. For example, in the case of this Brown material, as also in the case of the Hamblin material, use the journals as boldly as you want, but don't intimate that you obtained it, through my courtesy, from the [LDS Church] Historian's Office, or anything like that. If people wonder how you have got your hands on certain things, let them wonder.

I say this because in some respects I haven't always been quite ethical in drawing upon the Historian's Office for stuff. I don't always say, "I want a copy of such and such. May I obtain it?" There is an automatic tendency to say no, on the part of [A. William] Lund[, a long-time employee of the Historian's Office], at least, irrespective of one's motives in these matters. I shall of course make only the most ethical use of the material I have gathered to date, and may gather hereafter; I shall use it only within the canons of the highest historical objectivity. I have therefore felt justified, and my conscience has never bothered me. Material that might be used by enemies of the church, or critics of the church, to attack the church I have never placed at the disposal of other persons for this reason. Although Charles Kelly[2] has been more than kind in all our relations, and has done me many favors, I should not permit him to see the [Jacob] Hamblin[3] journal for this ethical reason. I might, on request, offer criticisms of his thinking or writing, based on what I know, but I should regard the sources as inviolate. In one respect our own relationship has been unusually pleasant because I have been able to hold every confidence in you, and anything that crossed your special field of research I have passed on to you. But as I say, neither in personal intercourse nor in professional acknowledgments should I like you to identify any specific material as having been derived from me. And, as one other point in this respect, which you will recall I brought up last fall, I should like you to ask my permission before you let anyone, no matter how much trust you might have in such a person, use this material I have given you. It is a part of my feeling of responsibility, which I am sure you understand. There are absolutely no restrictions upon your own work, and the personal uses you find for this stuff, but I feel better to know that it will not go beyond you without my knowledge and permission. I am not talking specifically about any person or set of circumstances, you understand; I am just outlining a personal problem in morals.

I am sorry your Hamblin book did not achieve the fellowship, but there has of course been more than a probability of that ever since the war broke out. In the light of a war crisis, any book of primarily regional interest would suffer in the eye of the contest readers. However, I would not pay any attention to this setback; I would just go right ahead and work on your book as time, opportunity, and money will permit. For the moment, if I were you, I would not bother my head about a publisher. You might or might not be able to strike terms with one just now, with all this unpredictable dislocation of our society, contingent on the war effort and the increase in taxes, rationing, priorities, etc., making the future so unpredictable—if you were unlucky, that might be discouraging to you. Look at it like this, Juanita: You aren't interested in this book for the money there might be in it, not even for the reputation you might gain out of it. It is a labor of love with you, for the most part. Working on the book, directing all your creative energies toward its fulfillment, will be a rich experience for you. I know you and your writing well enough to know that the end product will be an immeasurably rich book, and one certain of publication. You may not have the same confidence, but you could take my word for it, this time. Anyway, by the time you are ready to publish, I may be in a position to give you a lift with a publisher; or Bernard DeVoto has expressed a willingness to do what he can for any book I feel really worth while, and if I have no influence in the book world, he has, at least.

I suggest that you try to orient your life as well as you can to let you do the job you want to do. Your case is not dissimilar to mine. I have been holding down a job which at some points has a coinciding field of interest with my primary absorption, Utah history, but this job has been in large part a means to an end; it has been financing my leisure hours. This will also be true to some extent of whatever job I pass on to during this year. Whatever the job means to me, it will mean most the freedom to use my leisure hours in this way.

You yourself have a family to take care of, and other responsibilities. But perhaps you can make some arrangements. You say in your letter that you might make more money by taking a regular part-time job at the college. Had it occured to you that you might take some of the bright edge from your leisure hours during the school months, through handling a family job and a school job, but thereby set aside enough money so that in summer you could go where you wanted to do such research as you felt to be necessary? There are ways to sacrifice some things in life to acquire others; I am better aware of this than are most people. I am not going to philosophize to you, but you might think this over.

I don't know just when I'll be able to get away, but as I told you, I am going to try to manage it as soon after August 1 as I can. It is not a matter of money, so much, as of opportunity. I need certain resources in my writing that are not to be had here in the local libraries. I need background materials on American life to give me a perspective for the books I want to write. For instance, you can't find books here on morals in the United States between 1700 and 1850 (except some of the secondary summaries of such books); you can't find books which give an idea of the state of medical thinking in the country for the above period, etc. Neither is there the monograph material on the early socialistic and communistic experimentalism of the early 19th century. Except that Bernard DeVoto lent me his copy of Nordhoff's "Communistic Societies of the United States," I should never yet, for instance, have had a look at this book. I want to look into the government archives at Washington, also. I have a vast quantity of Mormon material, now—as I told you a while ago, I have very nearly obtained all I want from the Church library, several millions of words; and now I begin to suffer from the malnutrition of the local libraries. Apart from all this, I want to become external to Utah for a while and look the place over from a distance. And also, I confess, I am becoming a little fed up on WPA and all its red tape, especially now that we on this project are losing all individual identity, and are being merged into a sort of anonymous "War Service" program. (Technically there has been no Utah Writers' Project for the last week or so; we are now merely a "phase" of the War Service Division, like all the other white collar projects.) And the constriction of our activities somewhat gets on my nerves. If I have to spend all my time on defense stuff, I'd like it to be big, rather than piddling, defense stuff. Well, I won't go on in this vein except to say that you will be able to draw upon me as freely, wherever I go, as you have in the past. There isn't a whole lot of material now in this town that would be fresh to you. The research from here on will be like chasing gophers out of their holes—when you can find the gophers.

I wondered, when I received your last letter, what you expected to find in the Temple archives. It didn't occur to me that you meant the St. George Temple, rather than the Salt Lake Temple—although there were sealings in Brigham's house, as well as in the Endowment House before there was a St. George temple, I would have been willing to bet money that Jacob [Hamblin] never brought an Indian wife to Salt Lake to be married to her. I am doubtful whether any vital statistics record in the church would record an Indian marriage. But of course I don't know for sure.

The article you mention for the [Utah Historical] Quarterly sounds interesting. By all means go ahead. And as another thought, any time some interesting phase of the *social* history of the state occurs to you, give serious thought to writing it up. "History" to most Utah writers means what is found in the [multi-volume] Journal History [of the LDS church] or Brigham [Young]'s letters. We are badly in need of some informed historical comment on home life, agricultural practices, irrigation developments, recreation, etc., etc. That is one service [LDS novelist] Maurine Whipple did state history; and it is a crying shame that the job had to be left for a novelist to do in the form of fiction. The Quarterly really needs to be broadened this way. The forthcoming issue, with its material on pioneer midwives, is a step in the right direction.

I've spent a good part of the afternoon, when I should have been attending to office affairs, on this letter; so you will excuse me if I write no more now. Thanks ever so much for the information on the journal-gathering. I'll ask some more questions later. It has definitely been arranged that I shall write an article on the subject for the Autumn number of the Rocky Mountain Review. They offered to serialize it in two numbers, if I needed that much space.

Dale

[1] John Doyle Lee (1812-77) was a participant in the Mormon/Indian massacre of an Arkansas emigrant company near Cedar City, Utah, in 1857. The bloody massacre at Mountain Meadows and the tragic life of John D. Lee were both subjects of books by Juanita Brooks.

[2] Charles Kelly (1889-1971) corresponded regularly with Morgan about early pioneer routes and western outlaws, two of Kelly's favorite research topics. He and Morgan subsequently collaborated on a revision of his *Old Greenwood: The Story of Caleb Greenwood*. Kelly's letters with Morgan and J. Roderic Korns are maintained at the Utah State Historical Society.

[3] Jacob Hamblin (1819-86) was an early Utah settler and LDS missionary to the Paiute Indians on the Utah frontier. Juanita Brooks was trying to establish if Hamblin had been a participant in the Mountain Meadows massacre.

3. To S. A. BURGESS[1]

Salt Lake City, Utah
1 July 1942

Dear Mr. Burgess:

Owing to the pressure of our war work, your kind letter of June 5, critical of the Utah Writers' Project's *Utah: A Guide to the State* has had to wait some time for answer. I may say that your letter is interesting and stimulating throughout, but many points you make seem irrelevant or even misconceived, and I am sure you will not object if I answer you generally as well as with specific reference to matters criticized in the *Utah Guide*.

[Here follow six paragraphs responding to Burgess's criticisms of the American Series project in general that are unrelated to the *Utah Guide* and Mormon history and have therefore been deleted.]

Propaganda is a term used very loosely. In popular thinking it has the significance of facts or pseudo-facts designed to convert people to some given viewpoint usually conceived as being disparate from abstract truth. In point of fact, any written or spoken utterance, any human communication designed to effect some purpose or end is "propaganda." You characterize the *Utah Guide* as being indirect propaganda for the Utah Mormon church; had it occurred to you that the American Guide as a whole might be called indirect propaganda for the American way of life? Certain bases of thinking underlay the production of the American Guide series; we took it for granted that America was worth examining, worth interpreting—in a word, worth writing about. This naturalistic viewpoint applied as well to a segment of America, the Utah Mormon church, as to America as a whole. The L.D.S. church is central to Utah's way of life; it is an existing fact, conditioning the lives of all who dwell in Utah, whether Mormon or non-Mormon. We were concerned first of all with this cultural fact. By picturing a condition of culture, we did a service to all who are interested in the development and nature of America and its people. I could argue to you, though I will not, that the Utah Guide would constitute a perfect achievement, as a picture of Mormon Utah, if it uncritically accepted everything the Utah Mormons believe about themselves and their history, and drew a graphic picture of these beliefs. All who examined the Utah Guide should then be able to draw their own conclusions about the validity or nature of Mormon beliefs about any given subject. This was not, however, our purpose. We desired to draw a picture of Mormon beliefs from an objective point of view, reserving to ourselves the privilege of exhibiting or not exhibiting a skepticism about those beliefs. I believe that we fully accomplished, in the Utah Guide, all that we aimed to do.

Let me discuss a little further this question of propaganda. Essentially your letter criticizes the Utah Writers' Project because it accepted for facts, or presented for facts, certain beliefs about its history entertained by the L.D.S. church. But at the same time the Massachusetts Writers' Program is criticized because it exhibited a skepticism of a prevailing view in that state about the Sacco-Vanzetti case. The Massachusetts Guide is objected by the governor of Massachusetts, and therefore the Writers' Program is censurable; the Utah Guide is *not* objected to by the President of the L.D.S. church, and therefore the Writers' Program is censurable. You will perceive the incompatibility of these criticisms. The Massachusetts Writers' Program, in my opinion, interpreted controversial facts as it saw them, just as did the Utah Writers' Program, and this honesty of intention is a reflection of the essential integrity of the whole American Guide series. I may say that I am proud to have been associated with the Writers' Program, and proud of the integrity of its work.

I should like to take the liberty of pointing out the fact that your narrow viewpoint on the Utah Guide, revolving about your central interest in the beliefs of the Reorganized Church, prevents your seeing the Utah Guide for what it is. One would judge from your letter that the whole Utah Guide is subservient to the large purposes of "Utah Mormon propaganda." Now I should like you to reexamine this book. You will please observe that all the material published in Part I except "Contemporary Scene," "History," and "Mormon Church," is concerned only incidently with the L.D.S. church, and when concerned is as often critical as not. The percent of Mormon material in Part IV is even more negligible. Parts II and III, concerned with the towns and the by-ways, naturally have more to do with the Mormons as a people, but in view of the fact that the Mormons settled Utah, I am sure you will admit that these sections could not have been written without attention for the Mormon people, and I think that any reasoned consideration of these pages will confirm the honesty and the objectivity of our observation and our judgment of the Utah scene.

You do not object to the essays, "Contemporary Scene" and "Mormon Church"—because, I believe, you see these essays for what they are, an exposition of the mental climate of the people of Utah. They could hardly have been written in any other form and serve their essential purpose. Your criticisms of the *Utah Guide* and your characterization of the book as propaganda rest almost entirely upon exceptions taken to certain statements made in the essay on "History," and the statements to which exceptions are made cannot be considered as susceptible of easy disposition in the light of facts at present available to history.

Having said so much by way of preface, I will now take up your specific criticisms.

1. The question of whether Brigham Young held the Church together: You have attacked our statement on p. 52 on the basis of the probable membership of the Church prior to the death of Joseph Smith as compared to the number Brigham Young demonstrably drew to Utah. Obviously here the question is how reliable the pre-Young statistics are, and one's judgment of the matter depends upon the seriousness with which one regards the statistics you quote. Every man must be his own judge in this matter, but I for one place no reliance whatever in the figures which, on the average, would place the total membership of the Church on June 27, 1844, as approaching 200,000. You will observe that in almost every case, when the estimates you quote were made, some question of church prestige was involved. It is my experience that any group contending its own importance always tends to give itself the benefit of a great many doubts. Although I should not give this as a finally considered opinion, pending further study of the matter, I very greatly doubt if there were as many as 40,000 members of the Church on June 27, 1844, in the United States, and the figure is probably lower than this. Estimates I would regard as reliable give the number of Mormons scattered between Nauvoo and Council Bluffs, at the end of 1846, as about 15,000 (including the Battalion), and in view of the fact that no other organized group in 1846 numbered, I should judge, over 300 members (I allot this many to Strang and to Wight), I don't think any objective critic can question that the group headed by the Twelve constituted the central church organization. If you will permit me to hazard this personal opinion, I might say that had the Utah Church not constituted a core of organized activity between 1844 and 1860, the Reorganized Church might never have been able to found an effective organization. This is a question much too involved for easy discussion here, but I think you will realize what I mean, even though you may not agree.

The census figure for 1850 may be taken as entirely reliable, I believe, but it by no means reflects the full influence of the Twelve Apostles among the church membership, as from the date of the census it covered only the emigrations of 1847-1849. The first movement from the midwestern frontier to Utah was not completed until 1852, and if census figures were available for this year, they would give a possibly truer picture of the extent to which Brigham Young held the allegiance of the Mormon people, although by 1852 European emigration was becoming much stronger and is a disturbing influence in any conclusions that may be reached.

2. The question of Sidney Rigdon's sermon of July 4, 1838: Your objections do not seem to be altogether well taken, for even though, as you say, the only extant report of this "salt sermon" may be that in Hunt's *Missouri War*, I am not aware that any Mormon writers

have ever seriously denied that Rigdon gave voice to the sentiments quoted on p. 54 of the Guide. I have seen many contemporary references to this speech, and whether or not he was correctly reported in what he said, the impression of his speech that got abroad may be boiled down to what was quoted in the Guide, and the historical effect remains the same. However, it is my understanding that the speech in question was printed in *The Far West*, a weekly newspaper which was published, I believe, at Liberty, and that it was further printed in pamphlet form and distributed about the countryside. Ebenezer Robinson, in vol. 1 of *The Return*, makes a statement to this effect. I have been greatly desirous of getting a transcript of the entire speech, and if one is to be obtained, I should much appreciate your aid in this matter; in the original draft of the History essay Rigdon's words were quoted without source, and the "according to Bancroft," which is stylistically most disruptive, was inserted to please a consultant who remarked that he had never seen Rigdon's speech printed in any Mormon source (which in itself I regard as significant, by the way).

3. The question of whether Brigham Young led the church out of Missouri: Your objection here seems to me more well founded than others you voice. The assertion in the Utah Guide followed the account of M. R. Werner, whose biography of Brigham Young remains the most important biography about him. Werner distinctly was not a Mormon, and had no propagandic purpose to serve, but on the other hand there is a tendency for biographers to overemphasize the influence of their subjects in their times, and Werner may have fallen into this error. I will say frankly that I have not given enough attention to the sources to be able to comment authoritatively on this matter, although for some months past I have wanted to inquire into the extent of Young's leadership in the exodus from Nauvoo. I thank you for crystallizing in my mind the necessity for reexamining this phase of Mormon history.

4. The question of stealing by Mormons during the Nauvoo period: You inquire how much stealing was by Mormons, and phrase your remarks to indicate that if there was any stealing it probably commenced after Brigham Young's accession to power. As a matter of fact, Mormon literature both before and after the death of Joseph Smith abundantly attests the fact that some stealing was going on in and around Nauvoo. Rebukes were periodically administered to the people for not ridding themselves of the blacklegs who dwelt among them. I have a number of references which I will elaborate upon when I am enabled to examine the Nauvoo period of Mormon history, and these sufficiently confirm the existence of some thievery and robbery, by Mormons as well as by non-Mormons. However, I will say that in my belief (and this was expressed in brief in the Guide), because of the situation of the Mormon group in an antagonistic society, any and all crime in the Hancock County area was automatically attributed to the Mormons. The columns of the *Warsaw Signal* and *Quincy Whig* abundantly attest this. They were cer-

tainly members of the criminal elements among the Mormon people, but by and large I think they were not guilty of charges so frequently laid at their door. This is what might be called the abstract truth of the matter. But in Illinois abstract truth did not count for much; what counted was what people believed, and a great many people believed that the Mormons were guilty of charges alleged by their enemies.

5. "Rumors of adultery and polygamy": You cite this as though it were an objection, but in actual fact you are in evident agreement with me that there *were* rumors of this kind, regardless of their truth. You will please remember that our point of view in the essay was what people *believed*, the levels of belief in contemporaneous society contributing to the difficulties of the Mormons. I don't think you will contest the idea that even before June 27, 1844, there was a widely voiced suspicion that the Mormons were guilty of unorthodox marriage practices.

6. The migration to the Rocky Mountains: You are not very clear in discussing this, and I experience some difficulty in knowing exactly what to say to you. However, it is my understanding from reading controversial works involving the Reorganized Church that you have combatted the idea that Joseph Smith ever intended leading the Mormons out of the Mississippi Valley to the West, and that you tend to regard proofs advanced by the L.D.S. church as being revisions of original history to serve the propagandic purposes of this church. This is a matter to which I have given especial attention, and in the work on the Mormons that I have conceived, I believe I shall be able to demolish once and for all any argument that Joseph Smith did not entertain this purpose. Two years ago I commenced to write a monograph on the subject, but after I had written forty-odd pages, I began to see that my materials had a significance too wide for monograph treatment, involving a whole reorientation of Nauvoo history from 1843 on, and I therefore shelved the subject until I could undertake a large treatment of Mormon history. My materials have been drawn in some part, though by no means wholly, from the L.D.S. archives here, but I do not think historians of the Reorganized Church will seriously question my findings when I am enabled to publish them. I cannot speak so authoritatively about the authenticity of the Rocky Mountains prophecy, but I am by no means disposed to doubt it, in view of what I have learned about Smith's purposes in the winter of 1844. I cannot undertake to discuss the whole subject at length here, so for the present I must content myself with assuring you that the statements in the Utah Guide about the proposal to migrate to the Rocky Mountains have a firm factual foundation, and I will publish the proofs in due course.

7. The question whether Brigham Young talked with the voice of Joseph: The Guide mentions this only as a folk tale ("it is said"). I consider it quite probable that this was a later rationalization by the supporters of Brigham Young; I have not seen any journal entry of that day which mentions the impression spoken of. However, I am

not disposed to doubt the possibility that some of Brigham Young's auditors thought they heard Joseph's voice in Brigham's. To my mind, what they really heard was a man's voice speaking confidently and with power, a purposeful voice such as they had known Joseph's to be, and after so much indecision and weakness in the voices of other leaders who had spoken to them since Joseph's death, they were ripe for the authentic sound of leadership. Since my own personal views are at least agnostic in character, you will understand that I am not much disposed to believe that Joseph actually spoke through Brigham. However, there is no question that at an early date the belief was disseminated among the Mormon people that this thing actually had happened, and this was the reason the belief merited inclusion in the essay on history. I am sure you will grant me the commonplace fact in social psychology that it is not things themselves but what people believe about things and how they react to things that shape the development of society.

8. Your critical remarks about Brigham Young are well taken, on the whole. It is quite true that no proper critical study has yet been made of him. During his lifetime and for a while thereafter there was a tendency by his enemies to squeeze down and belittle his stature; only in recent years has a proper recognition of his abilities and accomplishments begun to emerge, but this recognition has fallen into the opposite error of praising him for qualities he did not possess and generally overestimating him. Within the frame of his environment Young was a brilliantly able personality, and an adequate evaluation of this must now be made; at the same time he had the defects of his qualities; in many respects he was narrow, intolerant, autocratic, and provincial. All this must enter into an appraisal of him. But recognizing all this, I see no reason for altering anything that was said about him within the restricted compass of the History essay. I should like to offer one correction about your own remarks. You say that the Mormons in Utah today "would place Mr. Young as the greatest of all L.D.S. and Joseph much inferior." This is an entirely erroneous impression, as I can assure you from my own certain knowledge. The reinterpretation of Young as a great man, a greater man in his way than Smith, must be attributed to non-Mormon writers. Mormons themselves are not disposed to go as far as non-Mormons in this reappraisal. Joseph Smith has approached the stage of semi-deification, and many orthodox Mormons will not even permit discussion of Joseph Smith as a man with human failings, whereas Brigham Young may be so criticized.

9. The question of polygamy: This is, of course, a very old source of contention between the Reorganized and L.D.S. Churches, and I am sure that nothing is to be gained by resuming the argument here. I am not aware that any non-Mormon historian of repute has accepted the view of the matter put forth by the Reorganized Church, and while you may attribute this simply to effective propaganda by the Utah church and to the tendency of people to believe the worst about other people, you will at least grant me that the

view of polygamy set forth by the Utah Guide has ample justification in published history. Although I recognize that there are problems about the institution and development of polygamy among the Mormons, and I propose to devote further attention to these problems before publishing the work on the Mormons I contemplate, for the present I am content to let the Utah Guide represent the viewpoint of history on the subject of polygamy among the Mormons. I am very well acquainted with the social background out of which Mormonism arose, the influence of the "burnt over district," the influence of the numerous small communistic and socialistic societies, the influence of prevailing religious beliefs, etc. We are entirely in agreement here. But I conceive these influences to have worked on Joseph Smith equally with Brigham Young, and do not see that their existence alters in any way the general argument of polygamy as having been instituted by Smith.

In connection with the argument that moral standards were higher in polygamy than out, I had general reference to the whole fact of polygamy and the whole fact of monogamy in the United States. I have read through hundreds of diaries, and have had access to scores of official minute books and other documents concerned with the practical working of polygamy as a social system, and there can be no question about the almost fanatic morality and the entire integrity of polygamy among the Mormons. There were abuses, naturally; I have no doubt that there were polygamists who had their eye less on heavenly glories than on earthly pleasures; but the Guide said this in so many words. Conditions of morality among the Mormon people are adequately set forth in print, and although the picture drawn by Mormon elders of the iniquity of the nation's large cities may be regarded as exaggerated, the kernel of truth cannot be ignored. I have no doubt that monogamy in specific localities, particularly in rural districts, existed on as high or higher a plane morally speaking than polygamy among the Mormons. But there was a tight moral rein exerted generally on the Mormons as a people that was not exerted on monogamic society at large, and from this large viewpoint I regard the statements in the Utah Guide as true to the facts of history. Polygamy can be endlessly debated; it has been too much debated in the past, and history has been astigmatic in consequence of it. The point was made in the Utah Guide because it seemed about time someone made it in a popular book about the Mormons.

10. Finally I should like to correct your impression that an effort was made in the Utah Guide to discredit Joseph Smith. The portrait drawn of him was an honest picture of him as a man, although within the limitations afforded by the book it was impossible to devote more than a few paragraphs to him. If you will re-read the essay on History, I believe you will grant the integrity of our intention and the objectivity of our interpretation.

This letter has drawn out to intolerable length. No doubt you will not regard it as a reply satisfactory in all respects, since you have been answered in general terms, and not with a documentation, chapter and verse, from history; however, I am sure that you will recognize, at the same time, that all questions you have brought up have long been violently controversial questions, and whole books have been printed to argue one viewpoint or another; it is hardly possible for me to undertake anything so ambitious within the compass of a letter of this sort. But I am grateful for your critical viewpoint; I find that any divergent expression of views stimulates one to a greater awareness of any subject, and since I personally entertain a large project in Mormon history, your own viewpoint as expressed in this letter has a high personal value which I wish to acknowledge. Opportunities will offer later, I hope, to discuss with you the minutiae of certain controversial phases of the history of the Mormons.

Sincerely yours,

Dale L. Morgan
Assistant State Supervisor
War Service Program[2]

[1] S. A. Burgess was a research assistant and staff member in the Historian's Office of the Reorganized Church of Jesus Christ of Latter Day Saints (RLDS), headquartered in Independence, Missouri.

[2] Though written by Morgan, this letter also carries the signature of Gail Martin, Morgan's supervisor at the War Service Program.

4. To S. A. BURGESS

Arlington, Virginia
26 April 1943

Dear Mr. Burgess,

I have no doubt that you will be surprised, even confounded, that it should have taken me this long to reply to the kind letter you wrote me last August. A thousand times since then I have thought about writing, but a combination of pressing circumstances has always intervened, and for various reasons I have been unable to write you until today. I hope that this long delay will not make my letter any the less acceptable.

Your letter reached me when my affairs were in a particularly tangled condition. I had resigned my job, effective the first week of October, and was moving heaven and earth to get things straightened out for the Writers' Project so I could turn things over to my successor and come East with some peace of mind. At the same time, I was working every possible minute to finish my research in the Mormon archives in Salt Lake, and to put the manuscript of my book, THE HUMBOLDT: HIGHROAD OF THE WEST, in shape to mail it to its publisher. Under such circumstances, I had to put off a number of things I should have liked to do.

I had hoped that I might be able to come East through Independence, and stop off en route to see you and make your personal acquaintance, but I had to come by train and direct through Omaha and Chicago, so that pleasure was denied me. Then, after reaching Washington I had to locate a place to live, a job, etc., not to speak of making final revisions of my book so it could go to the printer. There have been plenty of other troubles, but even so I should have written earlier had I not mislaid your letter of last August, which somehow disappeared among my papers. It was not until yesterday, when I ransacked the place, that I turned up the missing letter, and now I do myself the honor to address you again.

Now that I am free of my book on the Humboldt River, which will be published in a few weeks, I have freed myself for the more important books I wish to write about the Mormons. The big book on this subject, one I hope will have real claims to definitiveness, I shall commence to write about a year from now. At the moment I am preparing to write a preliminary book dealing with American society between 1800 and 1861, which will constitute a background study of American social life and the forces operating on that life—a very relevant approach to any broad study of the Mormons, as I am sure you will acknowledge. This work is tentatively called *This Was America*, and I have contracted to deliver it to my publishers a year from this coming July. While I am engaged on writing this book, I expect to complete my research for THE MORMONS.

I have studied rather exhaustively the Mormon archives in Salt Lake City, and have copies of all or most documents of major interest or importance in those archives, I think, so that I have ample materials to write the history of the Utah church (of course, that material must be supplemented by other material from government archives, newspapers, books, etc.). However, I feel that I must conduct a search, as exhaustive in its way, for materials bearing on the other subdivisions of Mormonism than the Utah church, before I shall be in a position to evaluate properly the Mormon experience as a whole. You may be able to give me signal aid in calling to my attention materials relating to the Reorganized Church which you feel to be important to a study of Mormon history.

I don't know whether any comprehensive bibliography of "Josephite" literature has ever been published, or compiled. If one has, I should appreciate your telling me where I can find it. If not, I wonder whether you would undertake to give me a list of works that you feel to be basic to a study of Mormonism from the viewpoint of the Reorganized Church? While, of course, I shall arrive at my own conclusions about Mormon history, as a whole and in part, I should like first to think that I have fully comprehended the view that each segment of the Mormon church entertains concerning itself.

I should appreciate it, also, if you could give me a general description of the holdings of the Emma Hale Memorial Library—published works, including important and rare periodicals and newspapers; and manuscript works (particularly this latter). I should also like to know whether it would be possible to arrange to view any of the holdings of this library at a distance—for instance, by interlibrary loan through the Library of Congress—or whether these materials can be consulted only by coming to Independence in person.

Having discussed these points, let me turn to some matters you brought up in your letter of August last. First, as to myself and my background:

I was born of orthodox Mormon parents, and was baptized into the Utah church. As I grew up, however, and as my education progressed, my views inclined to agnosticism, or perhaps even to passive atheism. By "passive," I mean that I feel no compulsions to convert other people to what I think; my point of view is that other men are free to believe what they will about themselves, about life, and about religion, so long as they permit me the same freedom in my own living. Religion for me has nothing to do with the concept of God, but is a personal code only; on the other hand, I have nothing to say against, and even sympathize with, those who find that religion gives a higher meaning to life.

From this outline of my views, it will be understood that my approach to Mormon history is what we might call naturalistic, i.e., disbelieving in the concept of God, I do not accept ideas about Mormon history that are fundamental to the Mormon viewpoint on that history—the immediate intervention of God in Mormon affairs. While for my part I think that my examination of Mormon history will be "objective" and "unbiased," I realize that from the Mormon point of view this examination will exhibit bias in a basic characteristic—the disinclination to accept the idea that the evidence in Mormon history confirms the intervention of God in this history. However, as a practical historian, one must take the standpoint that causes and effect proceed directly out of human behavior, that men's difficulties are occasioned by human inadequacy, not by any special favor or disfavor granted to individuals by "God." So my viewpoint about Mormon history is that of the sociologist, the psychologist, the political, economic, and social historian. I do not expect that the average Mormon will accept in its entirety the evaluation of Mormon history that I shall make, but I do expect that he will acknowledge my integrity within what he regards as the limitations of my understanding, or point of view. On such a basis we can get along very equably, and we may find that my interpretation of Mormon history will not, after all, do such violence to Mormon ideas of that history.

I do not think that my early associations with the Mormon church have any effect on my thinking about Mormon history except to make me understand how the Mormon mind functions—what the Mormon way of life is—to know that the generality of Mormons are good and solid people, and that for the most part they always have been; and to know, finally, how and wherein non-Mormons have misconceived Mormons and their religion. At the same time, the development of my personal views has given me an intellectual detachment concerning the Mormons and Mormon history. It is in this that I consider myself especially fortunate, and more than usually well-fitted to examine Mormon history: I have an emotional understanding of the Mormon way of life, and an intellectual detachment concerning that life that enables me to examine it with what I feel to be a scientific attitude.

Polygamy has been injected into our correspondence, especially my point of view toward it, and yours. My paternal grandmother is a daughter of Orson Pratt, but otherwise all my ancestors are of monogamous origin. I have no prejudice about polygamy one way or the other; and my viewpoint about it does not, as you ventured to suggest, proceed out of any imbibition of the Utah point of view, but from certain basic conceptions of human behavior. I do not see things in black and white; rather, I am sensitive to the shades of gray. I am not one of those who think that you can prove anything at all about the integrity of Joseph Smith's character by proving that he did or did not conceive and promulgate polygamy; this ties in too closely with the old ideas, still implicit in Mormon exegesis, that Joseph Smith must be accounted either the blackest villain or the purest-hearted saint who ever lived, depending on whether Mormonism was or was not an "imposture." I don't think he was either. I think he was a man subjected to a singular environmental pressure, and that his behavior must be interpreted as the effect of this pressure upon distinctive psycho-physiological components of his character. It seems to me a fundamental weakness of most Mormon thinking, in any broad sense, that it tends to exhibit this *either-or* attitude, which really reflects a viewpoint of theoretical ethics, not of personal and social psychology.

As to polygamy conceived as an institution, apart from questions about its origin in Mormon history, I would not argue that it was as desirable as monogamy. At the same time I would point out (I have in the past and will do so hereafter in my writings) that it was not the hell-on-earth that popular prejudice has conceived it. It was a way of living together—in some ways, a more difficult way of living together—and whether that way was successful boiled down in the end to human beings and how they were able to get along together: a never-ending problem for the human race, and not in marriage only.

It will be seen that by reason of my point of view (as to God) many points of argument between the Utah church and other branches of the Mormon organism strike me as virtual irrelevancies in connection with Mormon history. (I have reference especially to controversies over the true succession published around the turn of the century by Roberts and others.) There is a lot of hair splitting over unnecessary points—unnecessary, that is, to one not emotionally involved, and much of this kind of controversy will be quite beside the point as far as my own study of Mormon history goes. However, I will not develop this point further at the moment, though I may venture to take up some angles of it with you at a later date, as my book progresses, especially some questions as to Joseph Smith and polygamy.

For the present, however, my primary concern is with the gathering of facts, and in particular, facts from the sources. It is my experience that if you gather enough facts, and organize them properly, they provide their own conclusions. I wrote a long monograph last year on the [phonetic] Deseret Alphabet, which I imagine will be published in due course by the Utah Historical Quarterly, and the pattern of fact here was sufficient almost to say everything that needed to be said about the Alphabet; this is a useful case in point. Right now I am anxious to gather all the material I can about the Reorganized Church, and about such Mormon sects as the Reorganized Church may possess. I am not fully acquainted with what you possess, and therefore am not sure as to developing means of access—particularly while we have a world war on our hands—so that any sort of catalogue you could give me would be most serviceable in my work.

I venture also to ask you again for the name of the person in Independence who owns a collection of material relevant to Lyman Wight. Wight's Texas venture requires careful study, in my opinion, and I have already gathered a variety of material about it without, however, getting my hands on source documents that would illustrate Wight's own point of view. I am particularly desirous of obtaining information about his movements from the fall of 1844 to the end of 1849—how he traveled south, problems of establishing his colony, etc. While I have many odds and ends enabling me to get a rough idea as to all this, I cannot feel that I have as yet got at the heart of Wight and his enterprise. If I could possibly borrow, or obtain photostatic or typewritten copies of source documents bearing on him, his colony, and his point of view, I should be very pleased, and any help you can provide in this respect I shall appreciate very much.

This letter is one written in general terms, very general terms indeed, but I am sure you will understand what I am saying. And I hope that I may turn to you again as from time to time I am faced with problems where your help will be fruitful for me.

Sincerely,

Dale L. Morgan

5. To FAWN BRODIE[1]

Arlington, Virginia
10 September 1943

Dear Fawn,

I would say I was highly amused by the tale of your misadventures, [but I do not want] to put too great a strain on your sense of humor. With the McKay angle brought up the way it was, I am not in the least surprised at the outcome of your relations with the Church Historian's Office. For the fact is, anybody who becomes an Apostle becomes a prospective President of the Church, and I think regards himself, and conducts himself, accordingly. I think [LDS apostle] David O. [McKay[2]] really was thinking that it would be a hell of a note to be uncle to a naturalistic biographer of the Prophet; it would be a reflection on him. If he couldn't keep the members of his own family converted, what future was there for him as President of the Church? Etc., etc.

Reminds me of a session I had with [A. William] Lund in the spring of 1940, which gave me a curious insight into the churchly mind. As a consultant he had been asked to read the MS [i.e., manuscript] of the monograph I wrote for the Utah Historical Quarterly on the State of Deseret. If you have read that monograph (published in 1940) you will agree that there are things in it which one would imagine would fall strangely on the ears of orthodoxy. To my everlasting astonishment, however, Lund passed by all those things (and fortunately asked me no embarrassing questions about how certain extracts from the Journal History had turned up in this essay without the excerpts being approved by him when originally copied) and argued about the most inconsequential things you could imagine. Anyway, in one section I had a trivial remark on the subject of how the assumption of authority by the Twelve in 1844 had been a turn for democracy in the church (as against the divine right and patrilineal succession ideas) because, said I, any man presumably could become a member of the Quorum of the Twelve and so could aspire one day to be president of the Church. Lund shook his head gravely over this. It wasn't true, he said. If a man aspired in his heart to be president of the Church, he wouldn't be selected as an apostle in the first place! (Idea, God chose His servants from among the meek and humble of heart.) I gaped at Lund for a minute, wondering if he could possibly be serious, wondering if he had no better an insight into the nature of man than this. But he was eminently serious, so I made a minor change in that sentence to obviate his criticism. Lund was always an instructive character for me; I never ceased to marvel at the way his mind worked.

I am interested to know that I haven't yet been read out of the Church. I have astonished everybody except myself in this respect, and maybe it's just my naivete that has preserved me from that astonishment. However, the really acid test will come when I write a serious monograph on the Danites, something I hope to do this fall. Maybe I'll publish it in the Pacific Historical Review or the California Folklore Quarterly. An objective study of that subject has long been needed, and I don't require much more material to be able to write it. If they still love me after *that* is published, I guess we'll stay happily wedded the rest of our natural lives.

It is something that you were permitted to see the Wasp and the Nauvoo Neighbor. I understand that sometimes now even orthodox church members are not permitted to examine those files. I never asked to see them myself, as I thought it more important to occupy myself with manuscript material while I could. I never saw a copy of either paper, in fact, until I examined the partial file in the New York Public Library a month ago.

What you tell me about the Reorganized Church being so poor surprises me but by no means astonishes me. If you saw some of the letters Burgess had written me, you would understand. They look as though they had been typewritten by a half-blind stenographer. I thought they had a more imposing establishment than you describe, however. I certainly hope an opportunity will offer for me to spend some time there before Burgess dies. I have heard of the William Smith pamphlet you mention, but have never inquired after it. It, or some excerpts from it, was published in the anti-Mormon press in Illinois after Smith's death, if the thing I have in mind is the same as that to which you refer.

The Book of Mormon you bought was a reasonable, though not sensational bargain. It ordinarily sells at about $25 or $30 a copy, I think. The really rare edition of the Book of Mormon is that of Kirtland—1837, I think—which is the second. Professor [M. Wilford] Poulson of B[righam]. Y[oung]. U[niversity]. a couple of years ago showed me this, one he had just bought. He has a collection of the various editions of the Book of Mormon. I think one of these days I'll drop him a line prodding him further about that [James] Strang monograph he has worked at for some years.

I'm glad you met Juanita Brooks. I had a letter from her a couple of weeks ago, mentioning her trip to Salt Lake, but she didn't say she'd met you. I'm rather fond of her. She looks like the meekest kind of member of the [LDS women's] Relief Society, but she has a keen mind, extraordinary energy, and great independence of outlook. In fact, she is the only professing Mormon for whom I have any respect as a historian, and Juanita has her fears about just how orthodox she really is. Between us, we have been working on the M[outain] M[eadows] M[assacre] for a couple of years. We have exchanged quite fully our information on that. Ultimately Juanita will write a special piece on the subject, and still more ultimately I'll write a full treatment of it in the larger frame of Mormon reference. Charles Kelly has also been engaged on this subject, for ten years and more; he considers that the book will be his master-work, and he is patient enough to wait years for little odds and ends of his picture to be filled in. He has shown me his MS, but didn't offer to let me read it, and I certainly did not ask. (You know, Hoffman Birney's Grim Journey, a novelized version of the Donner affair, was stolen from a MS that Kelly had entrusted to Birney for the purpose of finding a publisher! I'll tell you what I know of the story sometime. Anyhow, that understandably has made Kelly a little cautious, and under such circumstances I would never ask to see what he was doing.) So two independent investigations of the MMM have been going on, that by Kelly and that by Juanita and me.

When you are feeling better, I suggest that you and your husband come over to my place some evening for supper (note that I don't say *dinner*, as I don't get home until about 7, usually). We could arrange the date if you would call my office. Rosemary Reich, the secretary of our branch, is very good about accepting telephone calls for me. The number is REpublic 7500, Extension 6855. I know that your baby presents a problem, but if you could bring him along too, he would be no less welcome. My place can be reached either via the Rosslyn streetcar (No. 10), or via bus. By streetcar, you catch #10 anywhere along Penn. or M Street in Georgetown, and cross the Key Bridge to the loop on the other side of the river which is the end of the line. Walk straight south, up Moore Boulevard, for two of the short blocks, then (with service stations on both corners) go west along this street two short blocks. Key Boulevard begins there, the natural continuation of this street. It curves slightly, then climbs a hill about a block long, and then levels off. Half a block beyond there it levels off; on the south side of the street is a group of three apartment buildings, and my apartment is in the westernmost of these.

To reach my place by bus, take any of several busses which have "via Wilson Boulevard" on (they leave from 11th and E in town, but come out through Georgetown, and have a stop in Georgetown just west of Wisconsin). This bus crosses the bridge and goes straight up Moore Boulevard to Wilson, which is the street just above this one. It climbs the hill west, and the second stop after turning into Wilson Boulevard is in Colonial Village, almost in front of the Wilson theater. A street goes south, between an apartment building on the west and a schoolhouse on the east, and one block down it runs into Key Boulevard, just half a block west of the apartment buildings in which I am located.

Most of my books on the West are here with me now, though the great majority of my Mormon books are in Utah. However, you might find useful those that I do have here. They include my copy of [William A.] Linn [*The Story of the Mormons, from the Date of Their Origin to the Year 1901*, 1902], a copy of [I. Woodbridge] Riley [*The Founder of Mormonism; A Psychological Study of Joseph Smith, Jr.*, 1902] which I found in New York last month, the 7 volumes of the Joseph Smith history of the Church edited by [B. H.] Roberts, a file of the Millennial Star running from July 1844 to December 1855, the last volume of the Times and Seasons, vol. 4 of the Journal of Discourses, and a few others like Figures of the Past, Ferris's Utah and the Mormons, etc.

with best wishes,

Dale

[1] Fawn McKay Brodie (1915-81), author of the 1945 biography of Mormon prophet Joseph Smith, *No Man Knows My History*, was the daughter of LDS leader Thomas E. McKay and the niece of future church president David O. McKay. Following the publication of her Joseph Smith biography, she was excommunicated from the LDS church for apostasy in 1946.

[2] David O. McKay (1873-1970), named an apostle of the LDS church in 1906, would later be appointed church president on 8 April 1951.

6. To JUANITA BROOKS

Arlington, Virginia
9 December 1943

Dear Juanita,

We have lately come to exhibit a remarkable, if not a fatal, capacity for writing each other at identical times. I believe four of our last five letters have crossed in the mails, and let no one tell you that isn't eccentric, as we have both written at irregular intervals. You probably received my last within a day or so of the time you mailed your note of the 30th with the extraordinary [Mary Elizabeth Rollins] Lightner[1] material.

I am indeed sorry to hear that you have been ill again. It really must have been something, if it paled an appendectomy. You are cryptic, not to tell me about it. I am glad to hear, though, that you are on the way to recovery. Please take proper care of yourself, for our sake if not for yours.

I have been wondering through the day whether we have a malaria case out at my place. You know, my small niece, Anne, picked up some malaria in Trinidad in 1941, which did not break out until she got back home in January 1942. She was doctored for a while and apparently rid of it, but a few months later there was a recurrence of the chills and fever. She was doctored again, and this time we hoped it was gone for good, as over a year has passed with no further signs of the disease. However, last night about 7 she had a chill, followed by a fever which shot up to 105, and if there is another chill in 24 or 48 hours, the likelihood is that the malaria is back again. I hope it will turn out to be something else—there is a good deal of mild flu around here at present, and this kind of flu would be easier for her to take than malaria. Anyhow, I'm anxious to get home from the office today to see how she is getting along. I am damned glad she and Ruth are at my place instead of at a hotel, if she is going to be ill in any way.

Within a few days, when I've finished proofreading it, I will ship you some mss. [i.e., manuscripts] that will interest you even if they don't have anything to do with Jacob the Hamblin. I guarantee! Beyond that, I will say nothing, so as to screw up your anticipation a little.

The Lightner material, you may be sure, is highly interesting to me. I am as greatly interested in any phase of Mormon history as any specialist in that phase; I consider myself, indeed, a potential specialist, at least, anywhere I happen to be in Mormon history. So you can be sure I will always be grateful to have copies of things like this.

Mrs. Lightner's claim to have been sealed to Joseph brings up that old puzzler. Personally, Juanita, I am fully convinced that Joseph took all these wives the Utah Mormons have credited to him. But in view of [Joseph's first wife] Emma's children, how are we to explain the barrenness of all these other wives? It is inconceivable that all could have been barren in relation to him; some of them bore children to other men. And I can't exactly couple Joseph with contraceptives; neither does it seem likely to me that he practiced what John Humphrey Noyes's Oneida colony called "male continence"—that is, a deliberately arrested intercourse in which the male remained quiescent, short of orgasm in either man or woman. Noyes's community was able to exercise considerable control over childbirth through this mechanism. But even if he knew about this (and I haven't checked dates; I am merely feeling my way along in my thinking as I write this), Joseph to me seems too much an egocentric type to concern himself greatly about the physical consequences that might attend intercourse with any woman he desired.

Well, it is a great puzzle, and I have turned it over in the back of my mind for several years, without however investigating the circumstances too closely, being sufficiently occupied with other things. Fawn [Brodie] was told by LeRoi Snow of the [LDS] Historian's Office that, according to a tradition in the Snow family, Eliza

[R. Snow, another of Joseph Smith's plural wives,] had a miscarriage when pushed down a flight of stairs by Emma [Smith]. But he had only the tradition for this. And such tradition must be regarded with due suspicion.

While we're on the subject of plural marriage, things certainly have been popping in Utah lately. I don't know how much truth there is in the rumor, but I hear that [LDS apostle Richard R.] Lyman had had three wives for years, but recently took a new one 30 years old, which became so widely known that he was thrown overboard [i.e., excommunicated].[2] This is too bad; I respected Lyman more than many of the other apostles. If I had to pick out anybody for the heave-ho, I think it would be [LDS apostle and official Church Historian] Joseph Fielding Smith![3] There is a good deal of the bigot in him, and I don't go much for bigots, in churches or out.

Yesterday at the Library of Congress I had a look at a new book by Paul Bailey called Sam Brannan and California Mormons. It gave me a more discouraged feeling about Mormon scholarship than I've had for a long time. For hell's sake, Juanita, what is the matter with these young Mormon scholars? Are they all imbeciles, or just what is wrong? I made only an incidental investigation into Brannan's life for my own book, but even so I learned enough to know that Bailey bowdlerized some original sources, misquoted others, badly misinterpreted others, didn't even trouble himself about others, and emerged with a pseudo-documented rehash that was a disgrace even to the pages of the Improvement Era [official organ of the LDS church], where the piece seems to have been originally serialized. Books like this are assuming a regular pattern; there are a quantity of them being turned out, also, in the U of Chicago's Divinity School, as masters' theses. They have the forewords by [LDS apostle John A.] Widtsoe, who doesn't know what he's talking about but unfortunately thinks he does; they have the professional form; they deal in more or less unused materials. But third-rate merchandise is what is being produced. It would be in the interests of the Mormon Church to train a consultant who would bring to bear upon such manuscripts the most rigorous critical standards. The literature that would result would be less extensive in dimensions, and less eulogistic in purpose, and the church would not always appear as a shimmeringly holy thing; but it would be literature having a chance of enduring, and it would establish a confidence in the integrity and honesty of the church such as will never result from a thousand tons of this Bailey bilge.

Are you still with me?!

I haven't heard any reports on the progress of the U[tah]. H[istorical]. Q[uarterly]., but hope Marguerite [Sinclair] pulls herself together and gets it out soon now. I guess they need a little more system in the Historical Society, so as to get out the annual volume by October, at least. I'm curious to see what finally was done to or with your fine piece.

Time has been marching while I have worked on this, and the office is about to shut up shop for the day. So, as an interim letter only, I'll ship this along and hope it will suffice to amuse you through five minutes of any day. Remember, Juanita, take good care of yourself. We have a right to expect this of you.

Dale

[1] Mary Elizabeth Rollins Lightner was a plural wife of Joseph Smith. The reference here is probably to her autobiography, later published as *The Life and Testimony of Mary Lightner*.

[2] Richard R. Lyman (1870-1963) was appointed a member of the LDS church's Quorum of the Twelve Apostles in 1918. On 12 November 1943, he was dropped from the quorum and excommunicated from the church for "violation of the Christian Law of Chastity," or adultery.

[3] Joseph Fielding Smith (1876-1972) was appointed an LDS apostle in 1910. He also acted as official Church Historian. He served as church president from 1970 through 1972.

7. To FAWN BRODIE

Arlington, Virginia
27 April 1944

Dear Fawn,

Figuratively speaking, I think one of these days one of these missionaries will catch you with your slip off, and he will slap a garment on you so fast it will knock your eye out. And after that, posterity will cease to have to worry about you; you'll be a righteous woman of good works the rest of your days, and on your tombstone will be engraved something by Edgar A. Guest. I tell you this to comfort you and let you know in advance of the time that all will yet turn out well.

I know very well the harassed feeling you experience. When I moved to Ogden in 1938 to take the job with the Historical Records Survey, I rented an upstairs apartment from a family on Jackson Avenue. A week or so later I found a note under my door advising me that special services were held by the Church for the hard of hearing and the deafened in such and such a ward every Sunday at such and such a time. What I felt then is how you feel now. I shall go to hell, I know, but I'm enjoying myself now, and I wouldn't be surprised if I enjoy myself somewhat in hell too. After all, just think of all the living headaches who are figuring on putting up in heaven. . . . Why don't you suggest to [Edgar A.] Brossard [a local church official] that you give a reading from one of your chapters at Sacrament Meeting some Sunday night? He could advertise it in the papers as a special preview of the prize-winning biography, etc.

I have [Fitz Hugh] Ludlow's book here now, in case you ever want to see it. I agree that the characterization of [Orrin Porter] Rockwell[1] is striking. In fact, [Charles] Kelly & [Hoffman] Birney quoted from it on the dust jacket of their *Holy Murder[, the Story of Porter Rockwell]*. I think you must have reference to [Wilhelm] Wyl's book [*Mormon Portraits*], in the case of Rockwell's brag. That is the only thing I can recall, and it is the only instance of the kind that Kelly & Birney cite.

Wyl says, on p. 255, that in an interview with Brigadier General Patrick Edward Connor on June 23 (1886 apparently), Connor told him that Rockwell used to tell him "many of the horrible deeds he had committed for the church. Among other things he told me once that HE HAD SHOT BOGGS. *'I shot through the window,'* said he, *'and thought I had killed him*, but I had only wounded him; *I was damned sorry that I had not killed the son of a b——!'* "

Wyl, in printing the Fanny Brewer affidavit on pp. 249-50, dates it Boston, Sept. 13, 1842, and follows it with one by G. B. Frost, same place, Sept. 19, 1842. Presumably the affidavits were printed in the Boston Recorder subsequent to the latter date. If it is merely the text rather than the citation you want, you are welcome to borrow my Wyl. In the long run, of course, you will want to cite the original source. That is my own policy, never citing a secondary source if I can authenticate the original source.

I'm not sure what your Improvement Era citation is (on Ludlow), but maybe it is the Rockwell sketch they serialized some time back. I have never got around to scanning that, although I glanced at one of the issues when it appeared. Kelly told me that George Albert Smith had remarked to [J. Cecil] Alter[2] that this piece was about as bad in its way as Holy Murder was in the other. (Or words to that effect; I forget the precise wording now.)

Incidently, you greatly underestimate the E. R. Snow diary. It has no earth-shaking entries, but it has a number of important stray facts tying in with a dozen phases of early Utah history. I am very glad to have the parts dealing with the first years in Utah. Biographically, it's not much good, but historically, it is more than respectable. Did you read F. Y. Fox's two-part piece on the Consecration Movement of the [18]50s? There's some sound scholarship in that. I've devoted a lot of attention to the Consecration movement of the 50s myself, and there are very few angles that Fox missed. He also did, some years ago, an excellent thesis for Northwestern on The Mormon Land System. If the Historian's Office were staffed with men of his caliber, I think Mormon history as written by Mormon historians would take a great stride foward. I've never met the fellow, and know nothing about him, but by his works I am willing to judge him.

I just got around today to looking at Reva Stanley's [biography of LDS apostle Parley P. Pratt] Archer of Paradise. A most curious work, a mixture of the amateur and the professional, the skeptic and the zealot, and with an effort at casual interpretation positively astonishing in places, as when the American point of view toward the Mormons a hundred years or so ago is summed up as being the same thing as the popular idea of the "Reds" at the time the book was written. (That reads as a very curious rebuke to today's ultra-conservative church leaders.)

I'm glad you enjoyed Juanita's jam and preserves. If you get around before it has vanished, I'll give you some more of the plum jam, as I have found another suitable bottle around here. I should feel myself to betray Juanita in her generosity if I did not spread out to the uttermost her beneficence. So I'll look for you to drop in again sometime soon.

The Sinclair Lewis piece is very amusing. It is not criticism, it's "you're another!" It is in full fellowship with the satiric passages he writes in his books; this time he got off on the subject of B[ernard]. DeV[oto]. instead of the clergy or Babbitt. Yet the interesting thing is that in this case, as usual, he got just enough truth into his picture to give it a certain cockeyed recognition. Incidently, have you read [Wallace] Stegner's Big Rock Candy Mountain? I read it in December and have since recommended it to everyone I know. It is to my mind the best novel anyone has ever written about the West; it is inconceivably better than anything he has ever written before (perhaps because, unquestionably, it is his own story, basically). It is the only book I have ever seen which dealt naturally with the Utah scene, especially the modern Utah scene; and I think no one who has ever lived in the West can read it without a thousand recognitions. I would give a great deal to have written this novel myself. I was glad to see Lewis give Stegner a boost, though he was really panning DeVoto rather than praising Stegner, and I can't agree with Lewis that Stegner's On A Darkling Plain has any particular significance.

I've thought it all over, and have finally come to the conclusion that Joseph Smith is a damned lie, and no such person ever existed. This proposition is so plain, on the basis of the numerous facts available, that I'm surprised nobody ever realized it before. I mention it to you in case the information might come in handy.

Dale

[1] Orrin Porter Rockwell was a bodyguard to Joseph Smith. His feats of courage and terrorism were legendary among Mormons. Following the attempted assassination of Missouri governor Lilburn W. Boggs, an anti-Mormon, in May 1842, Rockwell was widely thought to be the assailant.

[2] J. Cecil Alter was editor of the *Utah Historical Quarterly*.

8. To MADELINE MCQUOWN[1]

Arlington, Virginia
1 June 1944

Madeline darling,

Your letter of Sunday came yesterday—very appropriately, I thought, since I had reckoned that your new dress most probably would reach you yesterday, though I *hoped* it would come on Memorial Day. I await your verdict on it with much interest, because I rather fancy myself as a selecter of wardrobes for you, and, as I told you once, would greatly enjoy clothing you entirely in things of my own selection from the skin out. I think my taste in general tends toward simplicity of cut and color, but with color that is bright and fresh. Not that this is an invariable criterion, but as a generality it is good, I think.

The hospital has certainly been giving you the works; you are going through an ordeal of the first grade. But I am happy about it, because it is something upon which you embarked of your own will—that is, you went to the hospital in search of health, not being hauled there helplessly with no voice of your own in the matter. I hope that all these examinations will get to the root of your trouble and give you an opportunity to begin leading a half-decent life as soon as you leave the hospital. I shall be daily expecting further word on how things are going with you. And maybe by the time the week is out I will have a bulletin about your dress.

I've been pretty much on the run since I wrote you Friday night. When I got home Saturday night, on the step in front of my apartment was the steel file [cabinet] Mother had shipped me—it had been too heavy for the express people to carry upstairs (350 lbs.). So I had to dig up tools to tear the crate open, then carry up the individual drawers, and finally take the empty filing cabinet up, reassembling them in my apartment. This occupied the greater part of the evening. Maurice Howe spent Sunday with me, coming about 12:30 and staying till about 11:30. He is looking much better than I had anticipated, and enjoyed himself a great deal without seeming to get too tired. In fact, I was probably more exhausted than he at the end of the day, since of course I made him take it easy while I cooked dinner and otherwise made myself useful around the apartment.

When I got home on Monday night I found myself in possession of a complete set (lacking only the first index volume) of the

32-volume Early Western Travels series. This is something I have had an ambition to own for years, without much expectation of ever having the $200-plus that is the asking price for this series in these days. Rosenstock in Denver shipped me this set on the understanding that I might take as much time as I wanted to pay for it. The cost shocks me a little—$170. But I think I could sell them overnight for more than that, and the books almost completely fill in the foundation of my historical library. There are not more than a dozen basic source narratives that I still lack dealing with Western history as I approach it, and I am now in a position to sit tight and work with what I have. Incidently, Rosenstock has told me all sorts of interesting things about really big-time collecting (he is one of the country's best known Americana sellers) with leave to use the information in a magazine article. I had intended writing one for Publishers' Weekly about his adventures with the Ferris journal, but I think I will see if I can't slant this yarn so as to hit one of the big-circulation magazines. I have a number of interesting ideas about it. Incidently, when I speak of big-time collecting, I mean this matter of paying from $3,000 to $10,000 for a single book.

Anyhow, I spent most of the evening Monday cutting the leaves of the books. (Though 40 years old now, two-thirds of them were uncut. I abominate uncut books.)

Tuesday night, I fulfilled a promise I had made the Federal Chess Club some weeks before, to come around and with others of the top players play three games at once against the membership, at odds of the knight. Last night, Wednesday, I was occupied till midnight baking a new batch of bread. And tonight, after seeing Maurice off on his train at 5:30, I must do some things at National Archives. Tomorrow night I'm going to try to get some writing done. Thus my week goes!

I have spoken now and then of my "basic" library, gradually assembled over the last five years. I'll give you a more concrete idea of what I have. I own all the Bancrofts, all the Pacific Railroad Exploration Reports, all of the Hulbert Overland to the Pacific volumes (8 of them), the 12-volume Southwest Historical Series published by Clark, 7 of the 8 Princeton University Trans-Mississippi Series, the 6 most important of the 8-volume Original Journals of Lewis & Clark, and now the Early Western Travels. I have Mrs. Victor's River of the West, Osborne Russell, James Bridger, Sabin's Kit Carson Days (and four or five other Carson items, including his Own Story), Ghent & Hafen's Broken Hand, Catlin's North American Indians, Hodge's Handbook of American Indians, Bryant, Thronton, Nidever . . . and so on and so on, plus the Mormon stuff. It is simpler to list the important stuff that I lack than that I still need. The only real deficiencies in my functional collection are Zenas Leonard's Narrative, Larpenteur's Forty Years a Fur Trader, Ross's Fur Hunters, Rose's Four Years in the Rockies (these latter two customarily sell for around $40 and I have no expectation of owning them), John Ball's Autobiography, Allen's Ten Years in Oregon, and one or two others. A couple of others it would be convenient to have but I already have the privilege of using them, Darel [McConkey] owning Gass's Journal (of the L & C expedition), and Maurice owning James's Three Years Among the Indians and Mexicans, Luttig's Journal of a Fur Trading Expedition, James Clyman, and Chittenden's Am. Fur Trade. You see, we can write a lot of history out of this group of books.

The file that Mother shipped here contains practically everything of importance of my MS materials except the stuff that you had. I had asked Mother to enclose that if there was room, but quite evidently there was not, and I shall have to have her make a supplementary shipment. I have had some trouble discussing this point with her because I don't know precisely what it was that you did return, and Mother is not clear in her mind as to what she did with the stuff you brought back. You didn't tell me whether you ever received those photographs I mailed you from the train, going east, but I assume that you had them. To judge from the files I now have here, and my recollection of what I left with you, you had all my Journal History notes up to 1845, plus the folders for 1849 and 1850, and also the journal of Priddy Meeks. Whether you had other MS stuff I don't know. Some of the books you had have already been sent on to me, notably the Journal of Discourses. One book I lent you, Mrs. Waite's *Mormon Prophet and His Harem*, Mother was not able to find when she shipped me some of my books two months or so ago, but I asked her to search again before I queried you. I am going to have her send me the rest of the Mormon books I require to write about Mormon history, so that I will have all the stuff here. If any of the stuff you had should not turn up at my place, there would be some presumption that it might have got mixed up with your own stuff when you stored your books and notes and the like. I bring up the point now, because if we get these things all straightened out at this time and know where we stand, when I come West for you I can, if necessary, stop off in Ogden and dig out any stuff of yours that you are likely to be in need of after you get here, or any stuff of mine that might have got mixed up therein. At all events, I will discuss this with you when Mother has made her search and sent off her final shipment to me.

Dale

[1]Madeline Reeder McQuown and Morgan had a complex thirty-five relationship, during which time a rich and lively correspondence was generated. Although she destroyed some of his letters before her death, her papers at the University of Utah's Marriott Library, Special Collections division, contain many letters both to and from Morgan (though occasionally some portions have been excised). Her papers also include the first four chapters and first appendix to Morgan's unfinished Mormon history, her unpublished biography of Brigham Young, and a novelized account of her relationship with Morgan.

9. To MADELINE MCQUOWN

Arlington, Virginia
10 July 1944

[The preceding pages are missing.]

Here it is Monday morning, and since I began this letter I have picked up what I hope will turn brown into a tan, but which might just as easily turn into a peeling party. The last few Sundays I have taken off my shirt and moved out to the "sun beach" at the side of the apartment. Yesterday I thought I could take two hours in the sun, but the fact is not yet demonstrated. I am more red than brown to this point. Sunday is the only time I can get into the sun, really, so soaking up the sunshine presents some difficulties.

Saturday morning I had to stop in at the post office to pick up two of my books [Maurice] Howe had mailed back to me, and on passing my laundry I was shocked to see that the populace was warned to pick up its laundry by July 8, on account [of the proprietor having been] "DRAFTED." At that moment I had approximately 7 cents in my pocket—I had intended picking up the laundry today, which was payday. But stern measures obviously were demanded. So at the office I extracted $5 from a person of temporary wealth, and got out to Rosslyn just in time to meet the Chinese fellow walking down the street from his place. He turned around and went back with me and so I am again in possession of my linens. All my sheets but two, and all my towels but two were at the laundry, so you can see the crisis that confronted me. It was just plain luck I happened to pass the laundry that morning, as customarily in going to and from the streetcar terminal I take another course which perhaps saves a hundred yards or two of walking. Today's check will go rapidly to hell, but it is some comfort to get all my obligations under the hatches, and after the end of this month I should not only be able to help you constructively (aside from the minimum sums I have been sending you) but to put together a bank balance of more satisfying proportions than I have had so far this year.

During these sunning periods I have put on my dark glasses and occupied myself in going through [Bernard] DeVoto's Year of Decision critically, by way of making it more factually water-tight and thus more useful; I finished the job yesterday. Since I have been working intermittently at this, it is interesting to have you discuss him as a historian in your letter. Although a memory is an important adjunct for anyone who works with history, I don't think it is by any means the prime prerequisite for a historian. I have reflected upon DeVoto as a historian, and I should say that his weaknesses are part and parcel of his strength. His characteristic errors are not the errors in which memory itself is much of a factor. Rather, they come through the tendency he has for sweeping generalizations and striking literary effect. These of course are the things that make his writing most challenging and alive; his mind sweeps broadly so that he puts large facts together in interesting new ways, flavored by allusion and language. But in putting his facts together in this way, frequently he subjects his details to a pressure of distortion. You have to take the bad with the good in his historical writing—and I for one will take it.

The allusion in [Wallace] Stegner's letter I did not take seriously. He was either flattering me more or less, or having himself a good-natured dig at my proclivity for pointing out errors of detail in other guys' writing. (For instance, when I wrote him some months back congratulating him on the fine job he did with his novel, I mentioned a very few details that were out of line—speaking of the "continental divide" at Brighton in Big Cottonwood Canyon, "Brigham City High" instead of "Box Elder High," and one or two others.) I don't know precisely what he has in mind, but the other day I stumbled over a piece he wrote on Boston which perhaps indicates his method of approach—if so, he might do an interesting job. I'll try to collar this issue of the Atlantic Monthly from the magazine editor's desk here, and send it along to you. Iffen I do, take note of the remarks on fish cookery in the end pages. In fact, tear 'em out and save 'em!

At this point interruption seized me in its iron grasp, and I resume next morning. Even 18 hours later I still love you! I'm sure you will be pleased with this tidbit of information.

I'd enjoy gossiping about some more of the people around here this morning, but with some jobs I have to do, I'd better not, for this time.

We are promised a really scorching day today, with very high humidity and temperatures up to 95 (it got to 91 yesterday). The humidity has turned up, all right, but so far the sky is overcast, and if it stays that way all day, nobody around here will be heard groaning. Darling, you ought to make your way here. You could get all the sunshine you are not getting in California. In fact, there are two stretches of lawn around the group of apartments which are a virtual sun beach. I don't know how it is on weekdays, not being around, but on Sundays there are always two or three people at a time soaking up the sun on one side or the other. The lawn is fresh and green and pleasant, the location, while not board-fenced, is not out in the middle of the street, and in other respects one may pick up a respectable tan there—if he is around when the sun is giving off the means of a tan.

Well, why *not* make your way here? Returning to our subject of yesterday, suppose you name a date when you will leave San Francisco, and I will lay out an itinerary, etc., for you. Put up or shut up, darling!

With your letter Monday came one from Juanita Brooks. A while back I learned that the original transcripts of the [John D.] Lee trials were in the Huntington Library. I wrote Juanita Brooks about it, and she wrote them. They had a copy of her little biography of her grandfather, Dudley Leavitt, and were cordial, being particularly interested in what she had said about having been interested in collecting diaries, and so on. Well, on the 10th she went to Los Angeles for the dual purpose of visiting with her brother's family and of looking things over at Huntington. In both respects, she had a very satisfying time. You know, a while back the Rockefeller foundation made a series of regional grants, about $50,000 each, for research projects in American history. The Huntington Library is the administrator of the Southwestern grant, and they are interested in a program of gathering Mormon diaries, among other things. They intimated as much to Juanita before she went there. I told her I was both in favor and against the idea—that is, one can only look with favor on a collecting program designed to preserve materials for history—but one cannot look with such favor on a program by which the State of Utah will be looted of its historical treasures for an out-of-state institution. Juanita told them she could not be enthusiastic about collecting originals for them, except when they were not being taken care of properly, or when the owners were poor and need to sell. The upshot is that they will be fully satisfied with photostating the journals; and accordingly Juanita is to be given $50 a month plus traveling expenses, postage, and other incidental expenses, for a new collecting program. The arrangement has to be okayed by the Board of Directors, but Dr. [Robert G.] Cleland told Juanita he presumed they would accept his recommendation. So this is to my mind a perfect arrangement, from which history can only be the gainer. Huntington does not, so Juanita reports, have a very extensive collection of Mormon manuscript material right now—she sends me notes on what they do have. But in future something should result from Juanita's efforts—and nobody is better equipped to find stuff. Besides, photostats are much more satisfactory than typed copies. So I am in a mood to say hooray!

Juanita has also ordered a microfilm of the Lee trial testimony—something like 900 pages for the two trials. Between us, Juanita and I will soon have everything available on the M[outain] M[eadows] M[assacre]. We have been putting all our findings into a mutual pool, and both of us have contributed material of high value.

I've been sitting here reading and rereading the two poems. I hope you will send me all the poems you write. They give me a special insight into you I obtain in no other way, and they are a way of enjoying you, deep down inside where you live most vitally. I've already said that I particularly like the one called "June 7." I like the original version of the poem, but it did occur to me in time that it possibly was subjective in some ways, and it might mean more to me and to you than to one who knew nothing of the Wasatch and the desert country. The poem now written strikes fire in a great many more recesses of the heart, perhaps; you have expanded the experience to a more universal level. All this apart from the almost shattering force of the title and all it implies for all that you say.

In the other poem, is the parenthesis around "in place" intended for a deletion of those words? I like the poem better without them.

Now, at this late stage of my letter, I actually take up your letter. With all my heart I hope you got away to the Sacramento Valley and that you had a thoroughly enjoyable little vacation from San Francisco. There must be another one in the Santa Cruz Mountains even if the one in the Sacramento Valley went as planned. I like to think of you enjoying yourself. I prefer to think of you enjoying yourself with me, but as next best, I like to think of you enjoying yourself anywhere at all.

I am most interested, too, in what you tell me about this woman endocrinologist, and I hope she really is right in thinking she knows what your endocrine upset has been. Good luck to us!

About the [Brigham] Young biography, I think you are wrong in imagining that the sample chapters must be the opening chapters. The chapters that you have written would, indeed, be much more to the point—because they are chapters from a significant period of his life, and the earlier years were not really his most significant years. I think you ought to have as many as five or six chapters altogether, to show a substantial bulk of writing already done, and to illustrate your method, but these need not necessarily be consecutive chapters. An outline of what you propose to do, and some indication of how your chapters fit into the whole, is all you will require.

You might send along those novels at your convenience, but make sure it is at your convenience, and forget about the Lauritzen book if it is in Utah.

[The remainder of this page has been torn away. The next page begins:]

The enclosed note from Stegner might interest you. He wrote me a week or so ago asking advice about a picture story on the Mormons for Look [magazine]—he is doing a larger story on the problems of minorities, racial and otherwise, and thought he would like to pull in the Mormons as an example of a problem which has been largely dissipated by the force of history. I interpreted his letter to mean that he was doing a primarily West Coast job, and therefore recommended San Bernardino rather than a Utah town; or if he felt the need of a Utah locale, maybe Beaver would be a good bet because of the background of Mormon-Gentile conflict there (it was headquarters for the southern Utah polygamy prosecutions, locale of the Lee trials, etc). From this second letter it would appear he has something larger in view, a national approach to a problem, and I should judge that the Look angle is only incidental and that he means to have a book out of it.

Dale

P.S. On second thought, I'm enclosing my key to Mother's place . . .

[The remainder of this page has been torn away.]

10. To JUANITA BROOKS

Arlington, Virginia
25 July 1944

Dear Juanita,

At the moment this is the only paper I have around, and this is a good moment for writing you a note, so let's let it go at that.

I much enjoy the deteriorating effect I have on your character. If it is any comfort to you, yours is not the only integrity I undermine. The other day one of my friends remarked that he was a little leary of something he'd been doing—"for Gossakes," he said, "remember—" By which he meant that a few ill- or well chosen words could do him great quantities of no good at all. I told him, of course, that I was a walking cemetery, and his grave should be held undisturbed like all the others I carry around in me. So the same thing can apply to yours. I'll discuss these [John D. Lee] journals with you presently; but for right now all I'll say is I'm damned glad they exist, and I only hope that others are to be found. I have an idea that no personal journal by him will ever be found for the period between December, 1850, and about July, 1851, because he kept the official journal of the Iron County Mission during that period, and I should imagine that satisfied his journal-keeping proclivities. I have all the excerpts from this record that were copied into the Journal History, incidently. Did Huntington give you any reason to think that they might be able to lay hands on others of his journals? I hope so, for heaven's sake. When you look in on them again, ask them to put my name on the subscription list for their publication of the journals. You needn't tell them I know about them—just tell them I have a standing order for every Mormon journal that is published by anyone. Incidently, I think they would be smart to hire you to edit the journals. With the possible exception of [Charles] Kelly, you know more about his life than anyone else, I'm willing to bet.

The mircrofilms of the Lee trials arived Thursday night, and the upshot was that willy-nilly I immediately squeezed out of this month's budget $5.50 for a "viewer." It is a very simple device, consisting of a lens set in an adjustable cylinder a couple of inches long, with a slide arrangement at the back through which the microfilm can be drawn—like looking into a very short telescope. It doesn't "lift" the microfilm very far, but it does lift it into readability, and at the cost of a certain amount of eye-strain, one could go through the entire microfilm with the use of this "viewer" alone. But I have been contemplating this device, and it seems to me that it should be possible to use it as a projector. That is, by shining a strong light back of the film, it should be possible to use the lens to project an enlarged version of the film on a screen or something. I have made some (as yet unsatisfactory) experiments with a flashlight, but I mean to mess around further and see what I can do with this lens. It will be far easier to use microfilms with this device if it can be made to enlarge them further. I'll report in due time. Meanwhile you can rest assured that we have already a means of using these microfilms, if something still better cannot be figured out.

One by-product of my getting this "Viewer" is that I am now going to go ahead and write the Danite[1] piece. Up till now I have been stymied by two things—I haven't had my files here, and I had no means of getting at two microfilms I possessed, bearing on the Missouri phase. But my files have been at hand since early last month, and on Sunday I used this Viewer to extract from the two microfilms the information I needed. So as rapidly as time will permit, I shall now write the piece. I'm going to see if the Pacific Historical Review will publish it.

As a dividend to you on the arrival of my files, I enclose an excerpt in regard to [Jacob] Hamblin and another in regard to Indian wives. The latter is interesting when read in conjunction with Hosea Stout's journal entry, because this lecture to the Green River Saints was delivered some months before Stout appeared on the scene, and it is evident from what Stout tells us that the good humor, if not even the ribaldry, of the men was far from subdued by Nebeker's lecture! I do not remember clearly, but isn't this journal entry one of the very earliest of all the entries evidencing a policy of taking Indian wives? This mission to the Shoshones antedates by some months the organization of the Southern Indian mission.

What you're suffering from right now, in the case of your book, is a characteristic case of "authoritis." I have experienced the disease myself from time to time and recognize all the symptoms. Personally, I am expecting from day to day to hear that you have been given the award you are after, though as I have observed to you, I always admit the capacity for people's going haywire, and there is always the chance that H[oughton]-M[iflin] will get smart on you. But when and if that happens, all you have to do is send your MS to me, because I have appointed myself your authorized agent in all contingencies except a straight award by H-M. I have a place on my bookshelf already reserved for *Quicksand and Cactus*, and it is only a question of time until the space is filled.

While I think about it, I want to ask you a question. What is Salt Lake City characteristically called by the Mormon outlanders? One of my friends once wrote a story in which a character, a farmer, called it "The Lake." I have wondered whether that name was peculiar to the section he was writing about, or whether it was generally used. The reason I ask is that I am going to write a piece on Salt Lake City for the Rocky Mountain Review, probably their autumn number. They are inaugurating a series called "Rocky Mountain Cities," and plan to publish an article on the major city in each of the Rocky Mountain states. Since I have various ideas about S[alt] L[ake] C[ity] I never could write into a W[orks] P[rogress] A[dministration] production a completely personal point of view; in other words, I was pleased to be asked to do the Salt Lake City piece. But I would like this item of imformation on Salt Lake City as viewed from the outside. My own point of view has been largely internal, of course.

In a day or so I shall send you something that will interest you—to wit, the rest of Gunnison's journal. Just when I thought I had finished with the Stansbury journals, I found a homeward-bound journal by Gunnison which I had taken to be only a field-book. I expect to finish copying it at National Archives today, and after a spell of proof-reading, I will send you a copy to supplement what I sent you before—the entries run to November 30, 1850, by which time he was on a river steamer heading up the Ohio. There is not so much information about the Mormons in this, but while homeward bound he was told by one fellow who had boarded with Lyman that Amasa Lyman had six wives, all of whom were "profane swearers," and a juicy item of gossip is thrown in for good measure.

You speak of going back to Huntington August 2. I hope that all arrangements have been cleared with respect to the Rockefeller grant, and also that they are paying your expenses there! Such details are always helpful. If by any chance you should have the time while there, I'd appreciate your having a closer look at the [Oliver] Cowdery docket book, particularly for 1837, to see whether it does contain anything of importance for Mormon history during that period of violent upset in Kirtland [Ohio]. Fawn [Brodie], by the way, is off to New England with her husband and her youngster for a two-week vacation. She always gets worried when she goes off somewhere with her husband, because, as she says, she has such a vested interest in her book that she couldn't stand not having it published. So, against the contingency that a truck might run them down, she dropped me a note before leaving vesting in me all rights and whatnot in her MS and notes "just in case." Fire also troubles her, but she is able to safeguard against that somewhat by keeping a carbon copy of her MS in her husband's desk in the Navy building. I know somewhat how she feels. I drew up a formal will a year ago to insure that my papers would not just be sold for waste paper in case I slipped in getting out of the bathtub some day. Fawn ordered a microfilm of the miscellaneous Cowdery letters, but they had not arrived up to the time she left, a week ago today.

I expect to go over to N.Y. to see my mother and sister between August 10 and 15, and will also spend some of that time at the N[ew] Y[ork] P[ublic] L[ibrary]. If anything occurs to you that you'd like looked into while I'm there, speak up and I'll attend to it.

Your tale of Dixie [i.e., southern Utah] puts me in mind of what Orson Huntsman once wrote, that he "believed Dixie was close to hell, for it was the hottest place I ever was in." Not that it will be any comfort to you, you can be glad you have only the heat and not the humidity. It is my experience that Utah's dry-kiln variety of heat is greatly to be preferred to the steam pressure-chamber they have in this section of the country. But this year to date has not been so bad as last year.

* * * One of the secretaries here, a young Negro wife, just walked down the aisle. She is in a state of extreme expectation, if you know what I mean. I don't know what she expects, but personally I am expecting the child to arrive almost any hour now.

This reminds me of a story I heard yesterday which in a way is a small cross-section of a world. Naomi Peres, one of my associates here, was telling me about the janitor and wife in the apartment building where she and her husband live. This couple, who are just "ordinary colored folks," acquired a baby about three months ago. Naomi just learned the details in the last couple of weeks, when the woman came up to do some ironing for her to enable her to get away on a vacation. The woman said that God had sent the child to her, which sounded rather odd until she explained. In the spring she was riding on the streetcar one day when she saw a young colored girl, about 18, on the seat ahead carrying a baby boy about 10 months old. The baby was rather dirty, and it was plain that the girl was very poor. The woman began to talk to the baby as women do, and then she began to talk to the girl who, it developed, had reached so desperate a point that she was almost in a mood to kill the child to get rid of it. She was not married, and the child's father was overseas. With this baby to take care of, she couldn't hold down a job, find a decent place to stay, or anything else; it was a millstone around her neck. The janitor's wife said, "Don't you dare harm this little baby! If you can't take care of him, give him to someone." "You take him, then," the girl said. The woman gasped, then said, "You can't do just like that. Come to my place and talk to my husband and me and see what you want to do." So the girl came with her and they talked it over, then she said to the girl, "You don't want to do anything in a hurry that you'll regret. So you think it all over for a week or two, and then if you still want me to have the baby, you come back with him." So the girl went off. And the woman told Naomi that she prayed to God every night that the girl would decide to give her the baby. Finally she did come back. The woman said, "But don't you want to investigate us or something?" The girl shook her head, and said she could see from their place and how they acted the kind of people they were. So she went off and left her child behind, and now this couple has a baby of its own. Naomi asked about a formal adoption, since they might grow to love the baby and then the mother might come and demand him back; the woman said they would manage that when they could get $25 to pay a lawyer to fix up the papers. And now the woman says she prays that sometime they can get $180 to pay for an operation on her so she can bear a little sister for the boy. She is 38 years old, so let us hope she is able to raise that money before very long.

It appears that at first the woman's husband, and all the in-laws, were very much set against the idea. But she brought her husband around to at least a neutral point of view at the time the girl brought the baby back, and now, Naomi says, the fellow is even crazier about this baby, now 13 months old, than his wife is. An enormous, sober-looking fellow over six-feet tall, he goes everywhere, the baby's hand in his toddling along by his side! All the relatives have now fallen in love with the child in the same way.

There is something deeply pathetic, and also something rather heartwarming, about this story. It is the kind of story that must be duplicated many times over in the submerged part of the population.

And this story puts me in mind of an observation Darel McConkey made to my mother last summer. "There's nothing cuter than a colored baby," he said, "—except mine!"

Dale

[1] The Danites were a secret fraternity of vigilante Mormons organized in 1838 in Far West, Missouri. Reportedly, their purpose was to "waste away the Gentiles [i.e., non-Mormons] by robbing and plundering them." The "Danite piece" Morgan refers to has never been published, and may be among his uncatalogued papers at the Bancroft Library, Berkeley, California.

11. To FAWN BRODIE

Arlington, Virginia
28 August 1944

Dear Fawn,

For a week I've done practically nothing in my spare time but read in your manuscript [*No Man Knows My History*]. It has been thoroughly engrossing. I picked up your MS after you left last Monday, and only put it down at 2 a.m. because I was supposed to show up at the office [the] next day and have to be my own alarm clock. Since then I have read it on the streetcar going to and from work, at lunch, after hours, etc., etc. To a considerable extent I have marked up the manuscript, but I think it would also be well to summarize for you some of my reactions.

In the first place, I think the book is downright fascinating. It is fascinating to me, a specialist, and I think it will be to the general reader. The research is wide and deep without being ostentatious; the prose is clean and on the whole admirably muscular; it is frequently full of stimulating ideas, and at all times it moves rapidly. These add up to notable virtues indeed.

When I first saw your MS, my reaction was that you had a history of Joseph's life, not a biography. In the job of rewriting, you have dealt effectively with that criticism. The same chapters have now become a biography. Joseph dominates them in a way he did not before; and they illuminate his life—a personality emerges from the history. I feel that right up to the end of the Missouri chapters, you are clearly master of your material. You write with insight and understanding, not to say with much practical shrewdness and deftness. The only really grave defect in the first 25 chapters is the handling of the Nauvoo material. I am frank to say that I think more work is required of you here.

I have written on the manuscript itself some of my reactions and suggestions with respect to this part of the book, but I'll restate my ideas in general terms. I, at least, got the impression from the Nauvoo chapters that you were no longer in command of your material, as you clearly were in the earlier parts of the book. You have done precision jobs on some aspects of the Nauvoo history, very fine segments, considered in isolation. But they stand in isolation; they don't build together into a larger coherence. On thinking it over, I believe that the greatest part of your trouble is that (a) you have not made the necessary final analysis of [Joseph] Smith's character which will at once explain and be explained by the events you narrate; (b) the manner in which you have chopped up the [John C.] Bennett material seriously disorganizes the narrative; and (c) the amount of space you give to polygamy sets up strains of disproportion—that is, while all this material should be retained, as it is of greatest importance and significance, it was not of such critical significance to the outward course of his life as other actions and events of the period, and when you have subtracted the inner life (polygamy), you do not have a sufficient skeleton to support the body of your narrative. I very much think that you must expand your discussion of the situation in Illinois and Nauvoo, the pattern of outward event and motivation. Also I think this discussion will have more weight when you have done what I regard as still more essential, written a chapter of analysis of Smith's character.

It may be that you have proposed such an examination of him for one of the last chapters, which I have not seen yet. But if so, I recommend that you incorporate the body of such material into the earlier time scheme. Because an understanding of Smith's character in all its final complexity is essential to the reader's understanding of the final events of his life; a post mortem simply won't do.

This chapter I speak of is essential for your sake as well as the reader's. I don't get the impression that you have been willing to make a final evaluation of Smith's character, and in consequence there is a certain tentativeness or unwillingness to what you have to say about him through the Nauvoo era. You put forward the facts, but I get the impression that you don't throw your weight behind them. And, moreover, this gives an illusory aspect of simplicity to the final years of Joseph's life. I am firmly of the opinion that he was not in the least a simple personality at the time of his death. I agree with you that he was perfectly sane, and you have hit exactly upon my own point of view, that his career in major degree is best interpreted as an astonishing reflection of the Jacksonian upsurge of the common man; he was perfectly the expression of the *zeitgeist*. But at the same time he was definitely not a simple personality. This rich complexity remains to be built into his portrait for the Nauvoo era. And one element you must also get into this is the extraordinary magnetism he had for his followers. You have not yet exactly explained this. He gave them something they never got from anyone else; he left an indelible impress upon their minds, and they gave him a love they never have given anyone else. The martyrdom was a factor in this, of course, because it sanctified all they felt about him. But Joseph owes his semi-deification today quite as much to the quality in him which gave his people a renewed and enriched sense of their own life and of the meaning of life. This quality, living on, has tended to cancel out of history and legend certain elements of the profoundly human, even the earthiness that also made them enjoy him while he lived—and which also, perhaps, served in its time to heighten his meaning for them (he lived more intensely than they, and they found a vicarious satisfaction in this aliveness, which empathically enlivened their own existences).

I have also a general criticism of your book, to which I think you would do well to give careful attention before publishing it. It is one of the strengths as well as one of the weaknesses of your book that you have not hesitated to come to bold judgments on the basis of assumptions. Sometimes these come off astonishingly, and are bound to be fruitful in further thinking about Joseph and the Mormons. But also, sometimes, they leave you out on limbs. A few such cases I have pointed out, in the course of marking up the MS. But I seriously advise you to go carefully over your entire book and make a final evaluation of all such judgments before you publish it.

The point is, by their very boldness, these generalizations expose you to attack as you are exposed in no other way. Mormons who don't like your book, and there are bound to be many, are going to go over it with a fine-tooth comb looking for ways to discredit you. And if you have been rash and have left yourself wide open in some ways, they are going to jump all over you. The psychology is simple—if they can prove or seem to prove that your mind goes haywire on certain matters, even if these are matters unrelated to the large issues of your book, then they can cast doubt on your mental processes in arriving at judgments in other areas of the book, areas where they cannot question the facts themselves. Many Mormons are likely to be discomfited by what you have to say concerning the origins of the Book of Mormon and of polygamy, so you had better take measures to protect yourself from counterassaults while you still have time. Let me give you an example. After [Vardis] Fisher's [1939] novel [*The Children of God*] came out—and this was merely a novel, mind you—an astonishing number of Mormons took comfort in pointing out Fisher's error in stating that the company brought to America by Lehi was a part of the lost tribes.[1] The fact that this was an utterly irrelevant element of Fisher's larger story made no difference at all. ("Oh, it's full of errors. Why, Fisher is so uninformed about Mormon history that he even thinks the Nephites and Lamanites descended from the Lost Tribes.") In other words, the error was a starting point for rationalization.

As history, rather than as fiction, your book is likely to be subjected to an examination far more intensive. And nowhere will you be more vulnerable, in the light of such fault-finding, than in the area of generalizations. Because your generalizations about Smith's character and related matters are of key importance to your book. Without a minute study of the book in relation to its sources, a job I have not been able to attempt, I cannot say where your generalizations are abundantly supported in fact and where they represent, to a degree, your own intuitions. But you should have some inner knowledge on this point, and on reviewing your MS, you should know where it would be wise of you to make a final check on your sources and see whether your statements are too flat and positive in the light of the facts that are available to you. Many of your judgments you can set forward tentatively, after the fashion I have indicated in some places. But it is highly important that you should not talk like God on insubstantial foundations.

The Mormons themselves are not likely to challenge you on the point, but I would suggest that you carefully re-evaluate what you have to say about [Sidney] Rigdon, especially from the time of the break-up at Kirtland. Your judgment is that he was finally crushed as a personality in Missouri and was never significant thereafter. But this, I think, goes too far. I have begun to think that much requires to be explained about Rigdon during the Nauvoo period. What, for example, are we to make of that entry in the first week of January, 1841, that he had been ordained a "prophet, seer, and revelator to the Church"? This is damned near inexplicable, Joseph being what he was. Rigdon, you know, after Joseph's death brought forth a revelation of January 7, 1841, which he claimed as a basis of legitimacy in the church he established. I have not examined this revelation in the Messenger and Advocate (at [the] L[ibrary of]. C[ongress].) yet, but I find it coincidental, to say the least, that this claimed revelation should be dated only a few days after the entry in the official History of the Church to which I refer above. I mean to look into this matter presently—and maybe you would do well to look into it youself before too readily or too cavalierly disposing of Rigdon in your book. I gain the impression that you arrive at other flat judgments about Rigdon which one day you may regret as overstatements, hence I would advise reviewing all you have to say about him while the opportunity is still fluid.

I suggest too that somewhere, in discussing Brigham Young, you stick in a few words about the profound impression Joseph made on Brigham. About all you have to say now is that Brigham recognized that there was something in Joseph that made him the better man. Joseph made an imperishable impression upon Brigham, and Brigham is said to have died with Joseph's name on his lips—you would do well to make the reader understand why.

As a matter of personal taste, I would suggest that you write out all abbreviations of months and names; it looks more graceful in print. I think your footnoting system, or method of citation, can be worked out more satisfactorily and in condensed fashion, but I will reserve specific recommendations here until I have learned what you plan in the way of a bibliography.

You will observe that, however regrettably, I have recommended expansion rather than cutting in my general approach to the book. But I have also indicated, in ma[r]king up the MS, a kind of interior cutting which you might well utilize in going over your manuscript prior to typing the draft for Knopf. This, in a far greater degree, was the sort of job I did on the Humboldt [book], when I found I had to cut 40,000 words from it without impairing its substance. I sweat blood on that job, and there was no word published in my book which had not been individually weighed in my mind for its necessity; but when I got through I felt much better about the prose; it had become incomparably leaner and more muscular—all the fatty tissue that had vaguely bothered me before was missing. So if you feel the need to cut, I would suggest going over your MS in ways I have indicated, to see whether you can say the same thing as effectively (or more effectively) in fewer words.

You will appreciate that all my annotations are suggestive only. Another person may contribute ideas of value, but when it comes right down to it, the author must fashion his book according to his own conception of interior necessity.

Dale

[1] Vardis Fisher was an Idaho-born writer of thirty-six books, most of which were historical novels.

12. To MADELINE MCQUOWN

Arlington, Virginia
8 December 1944

Dear Madeline,

It won't be news to you that I have had damned little news from you for too long a time. Your last letter was dated the 25th, and 13 days later the only assurance I have about you is a package I obtained from the P.O. this morning, which is dated the 28th. I shall place this package "on file" till further instructions are received from you. But I can tell you, I should much rather have had a nice, warm (if not fat) letter from you than whatever this "fragile" package may prove to contain. I want to know that you are feeling better and not monkeying around with carbon monoxide any more,[1] and otherwise living a righteous life . . . and thinking of me once in a while.

It's a gloomy sort of day here today, dripping rain and mist all over the town. It has been fairly cold for a week past—25-32 minimums—but has gradually warmed up, only to cloud up and start drizzling. A hell of a note. I like my warmth and my sunshine both at the same time.

I was over to see Fawn [Brodie] last night. She has embarked upon having a new baby, and since the early stages always get her down, she won't be feeling up to snuff till after Christmas. The new arrival is scheduled for next June. I joked with her about whether she had books between babies or babies between books. She says babies come along faster than books—her first took her six years—but even so, the scheduling could be improved.

She has not yet received her manuscript back from [M. Wilford] Poulson at B[righam] Y[oung] U[university] or from [Milo M.] Quaife, but has reports from both. The Quaife one was amusing because it was what you would term a favorable book review rather than a specialist's report on a manuscript. In sending Fawn the report, [Alfred] Knopf also summed up his irate reply to Quaife. He said they didn't have to be told it was a serious job, well done, etc., etc.—they knew that already. What they wanted from him was consideration in detail as to the proportions of the parts, treatment, etc!

At BYU Poulson wrote Fawn a curious reaction. His approval was grudging and tentative, and yet he seemed to have no major quarrels with the book. His criticism was almost entirely criticism in detail, and bibliographical suggestion. His letters which Fawn showed me rather made me wonder about him. His being a BYU professor, even if of psychology, automatically bespeaks a certain orthodoxy in him, but I was interested to see him speak of "our group," and "we,"—placing himself squarely within the church—inasmuch as in my own conversations with him he had not committed himself personally one way or the other. This being so, it seems odd that he did not express himself from the larger philosophical point of view, taking issue with Fawn on certain of her conclusions. From an earnest Mormon, I expected such difference of opinion, and in fact recommended to Fawn when I read her MS that if Poulson did not give her such a reaction, she ought to get one from some person like Juanita Brooks, as I warned her my point of view was much the same as hers, and I would tend to be uncritical from certain bases of assumption just as she would, so that for a mature book, she ought to have the rounded thinking that would come from an independent Mormon's point of view.

Fawn is looking around for a subject for a new book. She doesn't known what she wants to do next, except that it must not be about the Mormons. I suggested the possibility of a study of the Grant administration after the Civil War, and its impact upon American life, political, social, and economic, with special reference to the kind of baronial finance that got its start then, and to the unfortunate handling of the South, which has left a scar upon American life to this day. I thought there were contemporary parallels which would give such a book impact and importance. Fawn was interested, but a little appalled at the formidable nature of the undertaking.

The Great Salt Lake book is still in stasis, pending word from Stanley Rinehart as to the contractual angle. Therefore the Guggenheim idea is still in stasis also, as I am sitting tight there until I see what bearing the Quaife proposal may have on my application.

At [the National] Archives I continue slowly plowing my way through Vol. 1 of the Utah Territorial Records. I've not quite reached the half-way mark in the first of the two volumes. There is an incredible amount of 1858-59 material—most of the first volume is composed of documents dating from those years, while the second volume covers the 14 years from 1860 to 1873. I enclose a carbon copy of the last document I copied, an extra specimen copy I made for your benefit. It is not in itself particularly important, but it offers some insight into the viewpoint of Brocchus and how his mind worked, and also locates him seven years after the big fuss. The printed document is really of more historical importance, but at Archives I am restricting myself to MS material. Printed stuff can be picked up later—and elsewhere, if necessary—at my leisure.

And here and now, while I happen to think about it, let me add a postscript to my recent discussion of your Ely story. I recommended, if you will recall, that the scene of the three men riding out on the desert be recast to present it from Joe's point of view. But I meant to discuss one of the angles involved, to which I devoted some thought at the time. In a word, the story would be more coherent and more compact, and you would get away from a tendency toward loose ends that the story displays, and for these reasons I am inclined to think you should follow my suggestions. But on the other side, there is to be said that the story is given greater depth, and a larger sense of dimension, through borrowing the Englishman's mind to experience the desert with. It may be argued whether the story is not made a little too craftsmanlike, too neatly tailored at the edges, and therefore a little too artificial or formular in acting upon my suggestion. I could see two sides to this. But still I felt that the scene as it stood pulled more out of the story than it put into it. I don't think this is a purely personal reaction. Maybe you could incorporate the substance of that scene, retaining the Englishman's viewpoint, and still attain a firmer texture if you looked into the man's mind more consistently in other parts of the story.

So much for Dr. Morgan, the well-known authority on the short story. This charge is rendered without service.

Damn it, why aren't you somewhere around, so I can buy a flower for you when the fancy takes me—or even grow one for you that we can enjoy together? Give me a good answer, if you can.

Dale

[1] It is unclear what Morgan was referring to here.

13. To JUANITA BROOKS

Arlington, Virginia
January 1945

Dear Juanita,

The new year could not begin right if I didn't take a few minutes off this evening to write you a little note. I have wanted to write it for five or six days now, but believe me, I have really been busy, at home and at the office. I was run ragged at the office today, and will be tomorrow, and probably the following day too—and into next week, for that matter.

However, we can find more interesting topics than that. For instance, the Christmas present you sent me. Juanita, you are an incredible woman! You not only send me a present as valued as any I have received in my life, but practically apologize because it has no dust jacket! I assure you, Juanita, my dear, that I would have considered it one of the finest presents of the year merely to be informed where I could obtain these volumes of the Journal of Discourses. Since Friday night I have poked my nose into them at virtually every free moment. These volumes will be immensely valuable to me for a long time to come, and I hardly know how to express fully my indebtedness to you and my appreciation. Perhaps one of these days I can send you something you will value similarly. In fact, I've been looking for something specific for some time now, and think there are prospects of laying my hands on it. When I do and when it comes along, you will understand that I hoped to please you to somewhat the degree you have delighted my own heart.

On top of all this, your collective Dixie salad came too! The apples and pomegranates did not do so well on the long trip, about half of each going the way of all flesh, but I have been on a constant Dixie diet ever since, just the same! I've lacked whipping cream, but I am not a person to let that faze me; I have thinned out some mayonnaise with milk, and that makes an entirely satisfactory salad dressing. The Dixie salad is one of my favorites already, I assure you; it is a wonderful addition to the American cuisine, and the originator deserves well of the republic. Who originated that salad in the first place, by the way? And when? It might date back to early days, but if so, I suspect it was not called a "salad." That is a word of fairly recent popularity in the American food vocabulary.

Do you remember once when I sent you some excerpts from Beattie's Heritage of the Valley, relating to the break-up of the San Bernardino colony after the M[ountain] M[eadows] M[assacre]? I now fortunately have a copy of that book. I've wanted a copy ever since I first saw it, since it is a definitive study of its kind—and there are precious few of those in Mormon history. Beattie was given access at the [LDS] Church Historian's office to the official mission journals kept by Richard Hopkins, and also the journals of [Amasa] Lyman and [Charles] Rich, hence the 13 chapters he devotes to the Mormons are authoritative. Months ago I asked the Denver bookseller, Fred Rosenstock, to try to find me a copy, and he finally tracked the author down and got one from him. The author is now 84 years old; he was therefore 78 when the book was published. Here is a case where age has served to ripen a man as a historian. Anyway, I mention to you that I own this book now, just in case you ever have need to refer to it.

We had an icing storm here last Wednesday, and it has been cold and dangerous out, until today, when a thaw with a dripping rain set in. The rain got rid of the ice and then let up, and it was fairly temperate, though gray and gloomy, when I came home tonight. But the weather forecast is for some cold and clear weather for a spell. It has been colder the last couple of weeks than since the notably cold first Janauary I was here—two years ago. But is has been still colder in the plains states, if that's ever any comfort to anyone. In Dixie, let us hope, things are ordered better.

A happy new year, Juanita, to you and yours, in St. George and all over this great world.

Dale

14. To JUANITA BROOKS

Arlington, Virginia
30 May 1945

Dear Juanita,

On this holiday-that's-not-a-holiday I'll make a beginning on a letter now, before lunch, and finish it later in the evening. Just by way of showing how things run, ever since I got back to D.C. I've been looking for a note from you, and have also [been] trying to get in touch with Darel [McConkey] so I could take him to a delayed birthday lunch (his birthday was May 10). Then all of a sudden your letter and MS came last night, while half an hour ago Darel suddenly phoned to say he could lunch with me today. So friendship is getting back on a functional basis again!

Your MS looks very good on a preliminary glance-over. I'll read it with care, put it aside for a week or 10 days to get perspective, then ship it back to you. And I want to commend you all over again for your contribution to the [Utah Historical] Quarterly. It is one of the most admirable pieces that has been published in the Quarterly; it presents a balanced over-all background picture, it minutely examines a particular area (both in subject and in geography) of Indian relations, and it draws upon a great amount of source material not hitherto published. Combined with a generally good writing job, that is a fine performance by any criteria.

Naturally I have devoted a good deal of thought to your situation since [LDS church president Heber J.] Grant's death. If I were to give you some advice, it would be to wait about six weeks or two months until George Albert Smith[1] has had a chance to get settled in his new job, and then go see *him*, the President of the Church direct, about your M[ountain] M[eadows] M[assacre] project. I believe he has possibly a more realistic view of Mormon history than most of the General Authorities, and the fact that he is at the very top would make his help count for something. Argue to him along the lines I earlier discussed in connection with [David O.] McKay. Moreover, I urge you to go about this as soon as Smith has had a chance to take hold and get out from under the first press of business. I don't know whether you have noticed the current apostolic seniority list, but after [George F.] Richards[,] Joseph Fielding Smith and David O. McKay stand in line, and if something should happen in succession to George Albert Smith and Richards, you would be confronted with about as reactionary a pair of historical minds as you could find in a month's search in the Church. So if you are going to try to write your MMM study within the bounds of Church sanction, you had better make the most of the situation now prevailing. You may not get anywhere with Smith, but at least he will receive you kindly, I think, especially if you point out all the angles involved. You should of course come armed with your letters of accreditation from Huntington, your letters from any local authorities, your letters from the Morris family, etc., etc. And while you are at it, you might boldly ask Smith's help in getting the notes Andrew Jenson took on the MMM as related in his Autobiography.

As I remarked to you, I am still in good standing around the Historian's Office. [A. William] Lund even said he liked my book on the Humboldt, which faintly surprised me. My time was too limited to do a great deal, but I did root around the H.O. a little. And for one thing, the Journal of the Southern Indian Mission is right there with all the other mission journals, on the other side of the shelf where the Journal Histories are. It was a little out of alphabetical order and was easily to be overlooked unless you looked carefully, but it was there, all right. If you ever get in there, just look for it for yourself, and you will find it without any difficulty.

Most of the time I spent in the H.O. was occupied in making extensive notes from the Nauvoo Wasp, of which the Church has the only complete file. I waded through 42 numbers, but didn't have time to go through the last 10, unfortunately. I hope I can finish that job some day, at which time I would also like to see 70 specific issues of the Neighbor between 1843 and 1845. The Chicago Historical Society and N.Y. Public Library have extensive files of the [Nauvoo] Neighbor, but there are 70 numbers known to exist only at the H.O.

My search for Millennial Stars was unluckily unavailing (I had particularly hoped to get the volume, 1863 or 1864, which contains the first half of the History of Brigham Young, but dammit, no luck!), but I did pick up a few other useful items. One was the Memoirs of John R. Young. I don't know whether you have looked into this; but it has a number of references to Hamblin over a period of years. I had meant to check up on Mrs. Shepard, to see if by any chance she had a copy of the Lee journals, but got tied up the last day and couldn't manage it. If you are in Salt Lake again, you might check on this yourself. If she does have a copy, it might be a good idea to buy one as an opening gambit for the subject of the Ginn narrative!

The blank space above indicates a not-so-blank interval spent with Darel [McConkey] at the Smorgasbord restaurant on K street. Even though we took a "bureaucratic luncheon," if you can figure out that cryptic term, the time went all too fast. He inquired after you very particularly and was delighted to know we had had a session in Salt Lake City. He has been burning the midnight oil on rush jobs for the past three weeks, and has another on his hands now, but next week is taking a vacation of sorts for the purpose of moving, at last, into the house in Alexandria he bought in December.

I'm looking for Maurice Howe to turn up in town next week, or at latest the week following, for the annual Social Security conferences. I hope you got a chance to see him at the U[niversity] of U[tah] before he left town.

Adverting again to Grant's death, I've been thinking about him since the news came along, and especially since reading the S[alt]. L[ake]. newspapers which my mother sent me. I'd like to have you tell me what the generality of the Church have thought about Grant, as you have heard them casually speak of him from time to time, both before and after his death. It seems to me that all the talk about his being "beloved" in the Church publications in recent years and in the obituaries is untrue in some degree. It strikes me that he has always been more respected than loved in the true sense of that word, that few people have ever felt particularly close to him or been warmed by his personality, and that few if any felt at his death the sense of personal loss that nearly everyone felt on the occasion of President Roosevelt's death. I'd like to have you check my viewpoint against that of the membership generally.

Did you succeed in getting the Maguire diaries? And if so, how do they strike you? Did you get to talk to Poulson at B. Y. U.? Your elliptical letter leaves me guessing at any number of interesting topics! I spent one evening with Fawn, the Monday night after I saw you, and she told me of talking briefly with him in Provo. She thought he had an amazing library. On V-E afternoon my mother and I drove down to Orem to visit my sister-in-law and nieces, and I tried to see Poulson then, but he has moved to a new home and had no phone, so I couldn't reach him by phone. I located his new home, but he was not there so I missed out on talking with him. Fawn has been in San Francisco and should be back this way soon. I understand her husband has been successful in getting a release from the Navy as soon as the S.F. conference is over, so they will be moving to New Haven almost at once after their return East. Another good neighbor blown away on the winds!

Tell me all about your plans for tackling the MMM theme, and what you have found out about the grant-in-aid. It has long struck me that there is nothing more true than that "he who has gits," and whereas you have tended to interpret my sundry "successes" in terms of my having the stuff, I have taken the more practical point of view that each thing I have embarked upon has very largely contributed to my getting the next thing I went after. We are having a demonstration of that in your life now. Your earlier jobs led to the Huntington work, that has led to the grant-in-aid, and other consequences yet to shape up will emerge in turn out of that. A lot hinges in this world on the simple matter of getting started. After that, you just have to keep your wits normally about you, and you are surprised with what results.

Have you heard from your boy in Germany since the big European bust-up came? I hope you will be seeing him soon.

Dale

[1] An LDS apostle since 1903, George Albert Smith had been appointed church president on 21 May 1945. He would die six years later.

15. To FAWN BRODIE

Arlington, Virginia
28 October 1945

Dear Fawn,

Up to the time the mailman arrived yesterday, I was on my way to getting a vigorous day's work done. But from 11 a.m. to midnight I accomplished absolutely nothing except a visit to the grocery store. I think that is a sufficient summation of your book [*No Man Knows My History*], that on the third reading in three years, and after all that has gone into it, I can be spellbound by it still, and read in it with absolute fascination. I am glad the book is in print at last, and congratulate you on the final fruition of all your work. It is a distinguished book in every way, in the research and the writing, and in its physical format. I am proud to have the book for my Mormon shelf, and I am warmed by your inscription.

I had anticipated that your book would be dedicated to Bernard [her husband]. I had thought that fewer dedications could be more completely appropriate, for he is the cause as well as the symbol of your personal liberation from the oppressions of Mormon orthodoxy. And yet to me as to a few other persons, the actual dedication is even more beautifully fitting. Your book is an act of freedom, of liberation, and the dedication to McKeen [Eccles Brimhall] is your obeisance, your act of devotion and consecration, to something much larger than yourself—to the human spirit itself, to the things men live for and die for. There were doubtless other and more personal things you meant to express by this dedication, but this is the significance it has for me. You could not well express all this or even any part of it in words, but that is how I feel about it, and I am sure how Darel [McConkey] and Dean [Brimhall] and Bernard will feel.

In browsing through the book as I did all day yesterday and for several hours this morning, I have been especially impressed by its literary quality. The prose is distinguished, Fawn, full of light and meaning, and heightening one's sense of the richness of language. Your patient work with the prose, improving it through each draft I have seen, has been richly rewarded. One has the constant sense of an experience of your mind as well as an experience of Joseph, and it is a rich and satisfying experience.

In another month, the letters will start coming in on this book—as for that matter they have already, evidenced by Israel Smith's. I think you will find this correspondence an invigorating experience, and you may find also that it will bring to light lost and unknown facts of the greatest interest. It is amazing what follows upon the publication of a book, or even a magazine article, at times. Charles Kelly, for instance, first got wind of the John D. Lee journals when a Lee descendant, passing his printing company, saw in the window some of his books, including Holy Murder, and came in to tell of the 1859 journal she had. Another woman who read his Post article on the Colorado River sent him the original journals of Clement Powell, Major Powell's nephew on the exploration of 1871. And in my own case there was the woman in Ogden who learned from my book that she owned the Bible C. T. Stanton of the Donner Party carried with him when he died in the snow in 1846. You will probably get your full share of scurrilous letters, but I think you have a sufficiently balanced point of view not to get upset by any such.

It strikes me as not altogether coincidental that the Reorganized Church has learned of the book prior to publication. I suspect Knopf's publicity department knows something about that. There is nothing like a good, rousing controversy to sell a few books, and a lawsuit is manna from heaven. Reminds me of when the Historical Records Survey published its history of Ogden, back in 1940. The Brown family got exceedingly exercised over some remarks on Captain James Brown, and there were mutterings about a libel suit. Some of the people in W[orks] P[rogress] A[dministration] were a little upset by the idea, but the state administrator, Greenwell, took a very philosophic view of the matter; a suit, he said, might sell 40,000 copies or so. Incidently, I think I will send in a subscription to the [RLDS] Saints' Herald. I have been going to do so for some time, to get the contemporary feel of that church, and it would seem that now is a very appropriate time to begin a subscription! I am making a copy of Israel's letter, and will let you know how it works out in the Herald.

A couple of minor things occurred to me in browsing through your book. Your preface leaves me with a feeling of incompletion, as though the concluding paragraph had been lopped off. After thinking it over, it occurs to me that you might have done well to invert or transpose your last two sentences. In other words, to make it read: "He was a mythmaker of prodigious talents. The moving power of Mormonism was a fable—one that few converts stopped to question, for its meaning seemed profound and its inspiration was contagious. And after a hundred years the myths he created are still an energizing force in the lives of a million followers." Put that way, it seems to me, there is a great finality about your statement, though of course finality is the very thing you might have wanted to avoid!

Other matters that strike my eye are mostly typographical errors or inadvertances. On p. 172 you speak of the geography Joseph had read "as a boy," and then give as a reference a work published in

1824, when Joseph would be 18 or 19. You do not say explicitly, of course, that this was the book he had read in "as a boy," but I think there is a certain looseness of statement here, by and large. On p. 307 and in your bibliography, the [John C.] Bennett affidavits should more properly be called a Broadside than a Pamphlet, as I realize since seeing the original. This would apply again on p. 318. On p. 330 you are actually right but literally or technically incorrect in giving Charles Kelly as sole author of Holy Murder. Hoffman Birney is coauthor, though I believe he contributed little more to it than the sales value of his name. On p. 365, although I haven't looked it up, I seem to recall that it was John Bennett, not Joseph [Smith], who carried on the correspondence with C. V. Dyer. On p. 437, in the sentence about George Harris, the double dash seems an impropriety in connection with the use of "either." On p. 440, Hall was a Mormon till 1847, but not "a Mormon in Nauvoo" during that time, since he accompanied the Camp of Israel across Iowa, and this is important in some of the things he has to say. For instance, as I recall, he says that while the Camp was going across Iowa Brigham formally notified [Henry] Jacobs that Zina could no longer be his wife—something to that effect. This becomes of interest in the light of your statement on p. 443 that Jacobs stood as witness to Zina's marriage to Brigham in January, 1846, before the evacuation from Nauvoo. On p. 458, Woodworth's name has inadvertently been spelled "Lucien."

In reflecting upon the Bibliography, with the text itself at head, I am not entirely satisfied with its completeness. Even on the grounds of delimitation you specify, there are works in your texts that should clearly be in your bibliography. For instance, "A Girl's Letters from Nauvoo," cited from the Overland Monthly. It seems to me also that the bibliography itself, as well as the introduction thereto, should include the Cowdery letters.

Finally, let me say that I like the index very much. You can find things with it, which is a virtue not shared by very many indices.

Of late I have been looking into Strangite sources, a compartment of Mormon history I have hitherto not stirred up very much. I wrote [Milo M.] Quaife about the Strang MSS. He is willing to let me see them, but doesn't want their texts published in any degree. I imagine he wants to keep up their monetary value for the benefit of his estate; their sales value would be higher unpublished than published, of course. Incidently, he tells me that Chicago U recently asked him to read a new book about Strang they were contemplating publishing, but he declined doing so for lack of time. The author seems to be from Wisconsin, so apparently this is not Poulson who is being heard from. I wanted to get a photostatic copy of the original letters Strang produced as from Joseph Smith. My idea was that if Joseph didn't write it, and I simply can't see Joseph writing anybody such a letter, then Strang must have done so, because he would hardly admit another person into a conspiracy so important to his pretensions. The investigations of the past have simply hinged about whether the signature was Joseph's or was forged, but it occurred to me it might be possible to prove by a handwriting expert that Strang had written the body of the letter, in the assumed hand of a clerk. Quaife was willing to have the letter photostated, he said, providing I would not publish it in facsimile. But yesterday he wrote me that he had looked at the document for the first time in years and noted what he had forgotten, that the body of it was not in script. It was hand printed, he said, hence would be of no service to me and he would spare me the expense of having it photostated. Well this is too bad, but I for one would say that Strang proved himself no fool in printing the letter!

I took Juanita to task about the [Eliza] Partridge diary, and she replied, "The Eliza Marie Partridge Smith Lyman book gave a few pages of summary, and began with daily entries on the trip across the plains. According to a grandson, she kept a daily record during her time as wife of Joseph, but there were things in it which she did not wish her family to see, so she burned it and made this abbreviated copy . . . I had little time there to sit down with it. The lady who had it was very reluctant to let it go; I had to telephone long distance to Mayfield to get consent of a brother before she would let me take it at all. Once that was secured, I got it off before she should change her mind. In fact, she wanted to see it wrapped and registered, lest I might appropriate it unto myself. It is now at the [B]Y[U] also, being copied, and will be returned to her from there."

A later letter, this last week, tells of her late visit to S.L. to see President [George Albert] Smith about prying the M[ountain] M[eadows] M[assacre] affidavits out of David O. [McKay]. She was a little early for her appointment, she said, "but he called me in immediately. I was struck with the change of the whole atmosphere of the office. When I went some time ago to talk to David O. McKay the attitude of the girl [secretary] was one of suspicion and her business seemed to be to keep people out. Now when the girl answered the telephone, she always said, 'The President is busy right now, but I am sure that he will be glad to see you,' or 'The President is a little behind in his appointments, but I am sure that it can be arranged.' A little lady from Idaho who looked funnier even than I did was greeted cordially and assured that the President would be glad to talk to her; a bright young solider from England, a deacon, he told one of the men, a new convert just before he entered the service and for three years a prisoner in Japan, was treated so well that it warmed my heart. At least the new president is a warm-hearted, Christian human being, and maybe that is worth as much as just being the Mouthpiece of God. And it makes up for the fact that he is neither handsome nor eloquent.

"He was kind to me. He would prefer not to have the MMM stirred up, naturally, but he listened to my reasons for feeling that it would be good to do it. He knew nothing of the affidavits I wanted, but told me to talk to Brother McKay, and shook hands with me twice saying 'I hope that whatever you do in this matter, you will be happy about it, permanently happy.'

"Well, Brother McKay wasn't in, but I had a long talk with the secretary who accepted the papers, Joseph Anderson. He was nice to me, but of course could do nothing. He advised me to wait over until Friday morning if I could to see Bro. McKay. I did, and waited an hour and a half. Bro. Anderson seemed to feel that I would get my chance, but finally came and told that he had given my message and explained what I wanted, and Bro. McKay referred me to Joseph Fielding. I said no, that Joseph Fielding did not know of the papers and I preferred to wait until I could talk to David O. So that's how it stands. I'll have to go back again."

Altogether, an interesting letter!

Last Monday the Saturday Review sent me Maurine Whipple's book, which is to be published November 8 (apparently Knopf transposed the dates of yours and hers), and I sent them my review Friday. I don't know whether Maurine will be pleased or infuriated with my review, which should indicate the kind of job it is.

Speaking of plans for books, have you ever looked into the possibilities of a biography of Horace Greeley? I don't know whether anybody has done an adequate job on him; if not, he would certainly merit investigation. His life was not melodramatic as Joseph's was, but he was an important figure in memorable times, and there is a certain pathos about how quickly the life went out of him after his bid for the Presidency failed, as though it had crushed his ego and all desire to live. I have run into Greeley at various times in my researches in Western and Mormon history, so if he should interest you, let me know.

I can think of two other men who ought to be written up, for the first time, but they may not appeal to you in sweep if not for stature. One is Major J. W. Powell, who revolutionized large areas of our social thinking with his work instituting the Geological Survey and the Bureau of American Ethnology, apart from his adventurous early years. The other is Philip St. George Cooke, whom you probably know principally as commander of the Mormon Battalion, but who led an extraordinarily varied career on the frontier and in the army. Still a fourth possible subject, here mentioned because your own point of view on her and her movement would be damned interesting, I think, is Susan B. Anthony of the women's suffrage movement. We have enough perspective on that movement to be able to evaluate it now. However, I am not certain someone hasn't written her up.

I have to go around to the Library of Congress to type copies of some items about Gunnison from the Milwaukee papers of 1853, so this must suffice us for this time. I'm always happy to hear from you, so spread youself in a letter whenever you feel expansive.

Dale

P.S. I've been pondering that court record [against Joseph Smith for "glass looking" in 1826] in your Appendix A. I certainly would like either to see that court record or a contemporary newspaper mention of that case. Has it occurred to you that if by some chance, somewhere along the line, a single word had inadvertantly been omitted, it would have altered a great many things? In other words, a "not" before "guilty" would make quite a difference, and Cowdery's statement would become good, honest fact. "Guilty" is the logical verdict on the basis of the evidence, but the question must be raised whether the evidence had any relevance in law. He may have done all these things as testified, but did they come within the purview of the law? I think probably the truth was as you have it, but as I say, I wish we had confirmatory evidence of some kind.

16. To JUANITA BROOKS

Arlington, Virginia
15 December 1945

Dear Juanita,

I received last night your extremely interesting letter of the 9th outlining your reaction to Fawn [Brodie]'s book [*No Man Knows My History*]. As I am pressed for time this weekend, I should have waited for a few days to comment, but it is necessary that I write you about another matter, so I will tackle both birds with one stone.

This other matter is that I received in today's mail a dishonest squawk from Maurine [Whipple][1] about my review of her book. I say dishonest not so much from some of the misstatements in her letter as from her obvious motives in writing it. She didn't mail the protest to me direct, but instead sent it in care of [Alfred] Knopf for him to send on to me, and I suppose it was intended as much for its effect on him as on me. Well, my naturally sweet disposition has soured with advancing age, so I sat down this afternoon and wrote a four-page documentation of what I merely said in general terms in the S[aturday] R[eview of] L[iterature]—and I am shipping off a carbon copy of the letter to Knopf at the same time I send the ribbon copy to her. I don't know what Knopf thought about her letter; he seems to have done nothing but to put Maurine's unsealed envelope and letter into one of his own envelopes and shipped the thing off to me.

Maurine began with some acid thanks for a "selling" review, selling because it would cause the book to be talked about and thus "all-important" as a consideration, then saying she was sorry I think she would have stooped to plagiarism, that she didn't include a bibliography because there simply wasn't room for the two-hundred-odd books and pamphlets she consulted, that the Utah Guide was credited four or five times (sic!) and was only one of many sources, and that she did not use Desert Saints "except to read it some years ago." She now raised the entirely irrelevant point about her use of pictures from the Utah Guide, etc., to which I did not refer in any way in my review, and saying that if I have any further quarrel, she would suggest I contact "Governor Herbert B. Maw, the Utah State Publicity Committee, and Mr. Randall Jones." She wound up by asking that I point out the paragraphs or sentences in her book which I thought needed quotation marks.

Well, I said frankly that I regarded her letter as disingenuous in some part and irrelevant in large degree, and then put on my demonstration of varying kinds of borrowing from the Utah Guide. I doubt that she will show you the letter, so just for your own information in case you want to hunt them up, you can find sundry correspondences on the following pages (the first number being from the Guide, the second from Maurine's book) 227 and 28; 226 and 7-8; 68 and 54; 70 and 54; 76 and 56; 7 and 63; 239 and 63; 8, 9 and 83; 457 to 463 and 88, 89; 473 and 89 (this is amazing; she quotes from the Cedar Breaks essay for her own remarks on Bryce!); 9 and 90; 455 and 91; 9 and 91; 3 and 137; 65 and 138; 66, 83 and 139; 5 and 140, 141; 9 and 142; 439 and 181.[2] Most flagrant among these are 455 and 91 and 439 and 181. Since I had to spend several of my good hours this afternoon writing this damned letter, I wasn't disposed to fool around with Nels' book, so I contented myself with an illustrative example, the passage on pp. 86-7 which she appropriated for p. 53 of her book. I wound up the letter feeling out of temper with her so I read her a lecture, saying she could write, with passion, brains, and skill, and there was no reason why she shouldn't do so independently, "without living on the fat of other people's minds."

The reason I have gone into all this is that at one point in the letter I incidently commented that I was amused to hear "that the phrase 'bucking like a wild steer' which I quoted in the review as being presumably a phrase of your own, was originally the conception (as applied to a country) of a writer in *Arizona Highways.*" Since you made that remark to me, I want to give you this forewarning in case Maurine comes around to knock suspiciously on your door.

I can't say that this business gives me any particular pleasure. But there is no doubt that Maurine has been overdue for a spanking, and I like to think that she and the people in her life may alike benefit from having one administered to her.

Let's get on to Fawn's book. Juanita, if every member of the church united your feeling for the Mormon way of life with your intellectual objectivity and reasonableness, no religion on earth would rival Mormonism, and the Kingdom of God would have a fair chance of early realization. I can count on the fingers of both hands if not on those of one the members of the church who could sit down and read a book like Fawn's and then discuss it without rancor, appreciating its merits without accepting its arguments. I have told you before that you are a rare and wonderful person, but for the record let me say so all over again right now.

In many things you say I am inclined to concur—and if you were to discuss them with Fawn, so would she, in the main. The point you make, for example, about the indifference with which the Mormon laiety will regard the book. I think Fawn began her book with the zealot's gleam in her eye, to present "the truth" and overwhelm any unhappy Mormon who might chance to read her disquisition. But acquired maturer ideas as she went along, and probably a year or more before the book was finished, she could see it in proper perspective. In these matters, Juanita, it all boils down finally to that old philosophical conundrum, "What is Truth?" There is no absolute or final definition of truth. It has emotional values for some people, intellectual values for others. Our confusions are consequent in some degree upon the fact that people try to square their emotional truths with the intellect, while their intellectual truths they try to invest with emotional meanings.

Let's discuss some concrete cases. You may hear someone—a returned missionary in the pulpit, say—pronounce a judgment like this: "I *know* that God lives. I *know* that Joseph was a prophet of God. I *know* that the gospel is true, and will be the salvation of mankind." You cannot challenge that knowledge; you can't bring any logic to bear against it. He knows what he knows, and there is nothing more that can be said. Except that his ideas may change if he is left to himself. When I was eight or ten or so and a regular Sunday-school goer, in our ward I saw a rather handsome boy four or five years older than I named Edwin Wells. He was then a deacon, I think. He looked to me somehow sanctified and set apart, beautiful and holy. Well, Juanita, as I contemplated him, revelation came upon me, and I *knew*, I *knew* that I was seeing there before me in the flesh a future President of the Church. It was a knowledge superior to reason; in short, it was of the very stuff of our returned missionary's knowledge above. Except that for some fifteen years or so I have felt a certain skepticism about the validity of that revelation.

Essentially this was an emotional experience, with its intellectual consequents merely trailing along behind. It is at the other extreme from my present predominantly intellectual point of view upon religious topics.

Consider again how our individual points of view upon Mormonism and all religion are rooted in our fundamental viewpoint on God. It is in part a consequence of your experience of life, your upbringing and certain things that have befallen you, that you have an unshakable conviction of the reality of God. That is basic in your whole attitude toward Mormonism. It gives an emotional color that subtly shapes all your thinking on every subject, and all your reactions to what we call the objective facts of your life. The result is that when you contemplate Mormon history, there is a vast area of the probable and the possible that you accept without much question.

At the other extreme we have my attitude (which I believe is substantially Fawn's). I feel absolutely no necessity to postulate the existence of God as explanation of anything whatever. To me God exists only as a force in human conduct consequent upon the hypothecation of such a being by man. I find infinitely more interesting than abstract philosophical ideas of deity the quirk in men's minds by which they have found it necessary to originate the concept of God. Essentially my views are atheist, but I call myself an agnostic because I regard professing atheists as being as much deluded as professing theists. The one says, "I *know* there isn't a God"; the other, "I *know* that there is." And I find the proof lacking in either case. Thus when I formulate my views, I say that I have no personal belief in God and see no necessity for the existence of such a being; I say further that I think this is the only life we'll ever have, and that we'd better make the most of it. But I feel no compulsion to enforce these views upon anyone who chooses to think otherwise and do not respond to the missionary endeavors of either theist or atheist. Nor do I find my life and my conception of life rendered in any way less beautiful or satisfying by my view that death is a final end to it; indeed, I rather pity those who must have an after life to recompense them for the spiritual poverty of this one.

I have been at pains to define my attitude because it is important in the matter of our approach to the problems of Mormon history. Mine becomes an essentially inductive method. I put together the facts that I can find, after assessing them according to what I think their worth may be, and thus slowly and painfully I build toward central conceptions. I do not think it misrepresents your own point of view too much to say that you start with central conceptions and (all the while testing your facts by those conceptions) work toward a factual structure that will articulate those conceptions and give them life and meaning according to our everyday standards of objective reality—"historical facts," in other words. I believe I have about as great a reasonableness of spirit as anyone who has made inquiries in Mormon history. But I am aware also of a fatal defect in my objectivity. It is an objectivity on one side only of a philosophical Great Divide. With my point of view on God, I am incapable of accepting the claims of Joseph Smith and the Mormons, be they however so convincing. If God does not exist, how can Joseph Smith's story have any possible validity? I will look everywhere for explanations except to the ONE explanation that is the position of the church. You in your turn will always be on the other side of that Great Divide. You may believe or disbelieve in the truth of Mormonism itself, but your acceptance or rejection of Mormonism does not in any way affect your final religious conviction, your acceptance of God. Indeed, you might remain a good church member when fundamentally you were in a state of apostasy, in the sense that you might conceive that Mormonism, perhaps "false" in detail or doctrine, was nevertheless "true" as an instrumentality of God, a way of life shot through with perverse and even absurd error, but good and satisfying because conducive to what we call a "Christian" manner of life. You understand, I am not trying to define your ideas for you; I do not for a moment maintain that these are necessarily your ideas. But I am explaining the different ways different minds may grapple with the concept of God and the influence of this concept on formal religion. It may serve to illustrate that whereas I am supremely uninterested as far as the question of the nature and actuality of God is concerned, I am supremely interested in what men's minds do with the concept of God, and how their behavior may be dictated by the prevalence of such concepts.

Well, then, in the light of all that I have been saying, let me take up your letter and some of the points you raise for discussion. I do not disagree particularly with your point of view on Joseph's boyhood as Fawn pictures it. I do not think, indeed, that Fawn regarded Joseph's boyhood as anything but normal in most ways. What came of the boyhood interests and activities may be regarded as important, however. I am reminded, incidentally, of Priddy Meeks' journal. You may recall Priddy's bafflement and awe at the boy he took into his family who had such a great way with peepstones and second sight. I always felt that Tom Sawyer would have understood William Titt very well, far better than Priddy was ever capable of understanding him. Because Priddy was blinded with his own religious conceptions and his own superstitions, for one thing; and also Tom Sawyer had a genius entirely comparable with William's. So also both Tom Sawyer and William Titt might have felt well at home with Joseph Smith as a boy. I do not recall having read any writer who intimated that Joseph displayed homo-sexual proclivities as a boy, and think you may have in mind Vardis Fisher's conception of auto-erotic (masturbatory) practices of which Joseph may have been guilty. I do not think Fisher's conception is in the least far-fetched; anyone who has ever read Havelock Ellis's great work could not regard a certain amount of this as other than normal. But I agree with you that Joseph's talk about youthful indiscretions hardly had reference to such ideas which may have persisted in Joseph's mind. It is inconsistent with his character as we know it that he should have exhibited a type of self-revelation of this kind. The idea may shock Victorian religious minds, that a future prophet should, even as a possibility, have been addicted at any time to auto-erotism. But no one who approaches Joseph as a human being can be in any way shocked or even surprised by such a postulate. "Why not?"

We come to an interesting point of departure, however, when we arrive at the question whether Joseph was indeed a conscious fraud and impostor. Fawn has clarified my thinking in this connection.

She and I approached Mormonism from two different angles. I began with the Utah era and worked backwards, while she began with the Book of Mormon and worked forward. I was half disposed to accept a median point of view where Mormon and non-Mormon may almost meet. The Mormon may consent to the idea that the plates were only apparently real, that Joseph gained access to them through a series of visions, as a concession from the original Mormon contention that the plates could be felt and hefted. And the non-Mormon may conceive of Joseph as a victim of delusions, a dreamy mystic, so to speak. But when you get at the hard core of the situation, the Book of Mormon as an objective fact, there isn't any middle ground; it becomes as simple a matter as the Mormon and anti-Mormons originally said it was. Either Joseph was all he claimed to be, or during the period at least of the writing of the Book of Mormon he was a "conscious fraud and impostor." I think what is called the "Isaiah problem" of the Book of Mormon admirably illustrates the issues. Either, as the Mormons claim, the Isaiah text is integral to the Book of Mormon as well as to the Bible, or one must conceive that Joseph had an open Bible before him while he was dictating the Book of Mormon behind his curtain. It is hard to conceive that he had memorized the thousands of words of [the] Isaiah text so that in his "delusions" he could have dictated this text automatically.

I have yet to make my own independent examination of the question of the origin of the Book of Mormon; that is a job I will do independently, and any verdict I offer meantime is only provisional. But for the present I find Fawn's theory the one most reasonable in the light of the available facts, and her theory is the more important in that for the first time the official church theory is challenged as to its historicity. The Mormon laiety won't know or care what Fawn has written, but the scholars of the church cannot ignore what she says. Hence in my point of view, hers is a constructive contribution to the question. If the Mormons can bring up new evidence to support their thesis, Fawn's book has imposed that responsibility upon them; it will serve to ventilate an important question. If they cannot, there may be good reason to think that Fawn has actually hit upon the "truth" of the matter. In either event, the legacy of her book is an aroused historical curiosity which can only be regarded as socially fruitful.

It seems to me that your idea is not well taken, that Joseph could not have been a conscious fraud and impostor because he inspired loyalties too deep in too many. This over-simplifies Fawn's idea; as I understand her, she does not maintain that he was forever a conscious fraud and impostor—he acquired, indeed, a compensating psychology; he made a psychological adjustment which had the practical effect of amounting to sincere conviction. Fundamentally it was Joseph's personal magnetism that bound people to him originally; and then after the church began to grow, it acquired an almost independent existence. It acquired a dignity from the lives of its converts; it became a social force energizing the lives of innumerable people swept up in its course. Mormonism is by no means the only illustration of this social phenomenon. It is exemplified in Ann Lee and the Shakers, in William Miller and the Seventh-day Adventists. It has been exemplified in politics time and again. And lately in Europe we have seen the spectacle of a gangster regime and a gangster mentality invested with social sanctity, and for which men were willing to die—or to conduct murder like an organized science. I do not mean to discount your point of view, but I am not willing that we should be limited by it in our appraisal of Joseph.

Your slant on polygamy is interesting but a little confusing, for you would seem to argue against what in logic the church should be glad to see, Fawn's fresh point of view on the question whether Joseph had children by plural wives. The church has always been hard put to explain why there were no children by those wives; except for the embarrassments involved, one could conceive that it might welcome Fawn's hypotheses. I do not agree with you that wives who had borne him chidlren would necessarily have testified to it. For if Fawn's facts be accepted, the women could not have *proved* anything; the Reorganized Church was in a position to ask how they could show Joseph as the father of their children instead of their legal husbands. Their own position would have been equivocal without any commensurate gain resulting. Altogether, a singular situation! And it seems obvious to me that the Church will not care for the thesis that plural marriage was originally (for Joseph, that is) something other than what it became. I am satisfied that Fawn is entirely correct in her conception that Joseph married a considerable number of other men's wives. The thesis makes sense out of a lot of isolated facts I have, apart from those she cites. As for instance, some remarks by Brigham Young before the Twelve [Apostles] in 1849, to the effect that "the Lord allowed Joseph privileges that are denied to us because He knew that Joseph's time on earth was short." (This was imbedded in the middle of a discourse on plural marriage and how the men should conduct themselves in their relations with their wives.)

Getting back to where my remarks started, I am reminded of something in a letter Fawn sent me this week. Some anonymous soul in Utah, she says, sent her a report of [LDS apostle] J. Reuben Clark's speech installing a new president [Howard S. McDonald] at BYU, with the following heavily underscored: "He wounds, maims and cripples a soul who raises doubts about or destroys faith in the ultimate truths. God will hold such a one strictly accountable, and who can measure the depths to which one shall fall who wilfully shatters in another the opportunity for celestial glory. These ultimate truths are royal truths to which all human wisdom and knowledge are subjects. These truths point the way to celestial glory."

So we may inquire again, what is truth? In this instance, Truth obviously is what J. Reuben Clark happens to believe.[3] He knows what "ultimate truths" are, even; he knows all about God and God's intentions. Or can it be that he merely has the social power to make people listen to his idea of Truth? If we were to pursue this matter far enough, I think we would find that Truth, in the end, is what makes J. Reuben Clark feel good, whether it is his conception of religion, politics, or economics. The only trouble is, we need a more generally applicable definition of truth. Too many different things make too many different people feel good in ways that are too contradictory for ready definition.

And consider, as a final illustration, what one of Fawn's pious uncles lately wrote her: "You will be required, sooner or later, to admit and correct EVERY ONE OF YOUR ERRORS. This is much easier accomplished while your soul and body are together. When you leave your earthly house, you have no place to hide your errors. They are apparent both to yourself and to those with whom you come in contact. Your shame will be so mortifying that it will place you in an environment of darkness where you will see no one else and 'think' no one else sees you. There you will wander until you become so tired with your condition and so weakened and exhausted that a feeling of repentence will begin to manifest itself. At that moment relief will come to you and some repentant soul a little farther along than yourself will help you. But it is a very slow process and entails much suffering. All this can be avoided by taking advantage of repentance in this life . . . "

He also, you see, knows the Truth. He has, indeed, an astonishing fund of information about it. One would do him an injustice to say that he has evolved a punishment for people who don't adopt his conception of the Truth, because plainly he *knows* about these unpleasant arrangements he describes. And thus he is my brother, for as brought out earlier in this letter, I too have had my experience of *knowing* with a transcendent knowledge beyond analysis or explanation.

If I don't watch out, I am likely to get sidetracked from the more or less high plane of seriousness on which this letter has been written; and since it is almost midnight anyhow, I will break off and get some sleep. But don't think I don't respect your point of view very highly, Juanita. I am, in fact, going to send your letter to Fawn so that she also may read it. Certainly it will interest her and it will serve, as with any serious point of view urbanely put, to broaden her viewpoint and mine, I am confident.

Dale

[1] Maurine Whipple was a Mormon novelist who published in 1941 the best-selling *The Giant Joshua*. Her 1945 book, *This is the Place: Utah*, is here criticized by Morgan.

[2] To separate the page numbers from the two books, Morgan used dashes. This tends to be confusing, however, and the word "and" has been inserted in their place.

[3] J. Reuben Clark (1871-1961), a forceful ranking LDS church leader whose views continue to influence Mormon policy, was openly suspicious of intellectualism and secular approaches to religious studies. See also Letter Number 41.

17. To BERNARD DEVOTO

Arlington, Virginia
20 December 1945

Dear DeVoto:

I read with great interest your review of Fawn Brodie's book [*No Man Knows My History*] in Sunday's *Herald-Tribune*. You had some excellent things to say, expressed with your customary precision and felicity of phrase. I think on the whole Fawn will be more than gratified by your critical appraisal.

But also—and this is the occasion of my letter—I am rather astonished at some things in your review. It isn't often that one can feel you have misrepresented a book in some important particular, or that you have failed to read it with attention, but that is the impression with which I am left by your review. I must conjecture that your preconceptions about Joseph Smith in this instance intervened upon your judgment, or at any rate upon your statement of the facts.

I refer, of course, to your paranoid theory. Four years or more ago I told you that in due course I would challenge some of your views about Joseph. I had in mind then doing essentially the job Fawn has done now; I had become convinced that he could be more completely interpreted as a product and exemplar of his times than through any other avenue of approach; and although I am not in complete agreement with Fawn's organization and interpretation of the facts of Joseph's life, her book as it stands sufficiently represents my views on Joseph's character and personality to serve us as the basis of a discussion.

You maintain that Fawn "pretty consistently avoids the crucial issue," which you explain to mean that she does not adequately deal with his "basic drive," but which I would take to mean more exactly that nowhere in her book does she make an effort to grapple directly with the paranoid thesis, an idea you have wrestled with so determinedly that any interpretation of Joseph which does not argue the merits of this thesis directly you must necessarily feel incomplete. Yet Fawn's entire book is essentially a refutation of the paranoid thesis, and it is at least arguable whether, in the light of her organization of the facts, it was required of her that she face what you call "the crucial issue."

I mean to discuss this at length, but first let me dispose of some lesser matters which exemplify the misrepresentation I speak of above. I do not think you can justify from her book your statements, "She endows it (the Book of Mormon) with an integrated, carefully wrought structure and subtle, eloquent and moving English style. . . . Actually, the gold Bible has neither form nor structure of any kind, its imagination is worse than commonplace, it is squalid, and the prose is lethal. The book Smith wrote is not a novel to any literary critic."

Really, this is a pronouncement of a curse upon the Book of Mormon, not a measured critical appraisal of it. I believe you are inclined to caricature Joseph and his literary production, perhaps in part out of unconscious defense of your matured theory about his personality, and in part as a vindication of the characterization of the Book of Mormon which had appeared in the original version of "The Centennial of Mormonism" [in *American Mercury*, January 1930], but which had been deleted from the definitive version, as I supposed, as the result of sober second thought. At all events, I do not see how you can justify your summation of Fawn's position and your verdict upon the Book of Mormon in the light of her passages on pp. 62-3, and 68-73.

Granted that the book is not a novel in the sense that *Anna Karenina* or *The Red Badge of Courage* or *Huckleberry Finn* is a novel. But the author's intention, equipment, and background must be taken into account. If the Book of Mormon is at all to be interpreted as a kind of frontier fiction, it must be regarded as a primitive, and interpreted in the light in which all primitives are interpreted. And this particular primitive was written by a young man with little schooling, with no depths of experience to draw upon, of no introspective bent, and with a literary background inevitably theological in coloration, thanks to the Bible and contemporary religious excitement. You may hold the end product in no great respect, but the history of the book is itself a denial that it altogether lacked in some kind of form and structure. One may say, indeed, that the historical importance of the Book of Mormon is that it supplied an intellectual content for religious emotions, giving them a justification and a rationalization, something the mind could chew upon and return to as a fixed point of reference. Observe that John A. Clark, who was not favorably impressed either by the Mormons or the book of Mormon, wrote in his *Gleanings by the Way* (1842), that there were "certainly striking marks of genius and literary skill displayed in the management of the main story." From the naturalistic point of view that is mine and Fawn's and yours it is not to be expected that the Book of Mormon should be regarded as the product of a matured intelligence with something to say (*vide* your remarks about young writers in our own time, in *Minority Report*). Nobody would contend that Joseph was an artist in the sense that Thoreau, say, was an artist. But neither can the Book of Mormon be cavalierly dismissed as a mere excrescence upon literature. And of course if you say that

Fawn endows the book with a "subtle, eloquent and moving English style," you are merely demolishing a straw man you have yourself set up. If this is not an absolute misstatement of Fawn's position, it is certainly a misstatement in the sense that it connotes for the reader what our more sophisticated vocabulary expresses in this terminology—a connotation quite foreign to the times and the content of the Book of Mormon. It also ignores what she has to say about the dullness of the book's style, a matter on which she expressed herself with such vigor that the devout are certainly going to feel affronted and abused.

Before getting back to the main concern of this letter, I should like to advert to a couple of misunderstandings embodied in your review. The first of these is entirely justifiable since you had only the evidence of the book to go upon. But Fawn is well aware that some part of the Book of Mormon was pirated in the local newspaper before publication. Indeed, this knowledge has been public property ever since Francis W. Kirkham published his book on source material relating to the Book of Mormon in 1937, reprinted and revised in 1942 as *A New Witness for Christ in America*. If I recall correctly, Hamlin Cannon stumbled over the same information and published it in the *Mississippi Valley Historical Review* a year or so ago without knowing it had already been published. The second point is that I believe you are mistaken in feeling that Brigham Young has been impossibly cut down from life size in the biography; at any rate, you are mistaken about any bias on Fawn's part. I say this out of a two-and-a-half year acquaintance with her and much discussion of her book with her. I am in agreement with you that the biography gives inadequate attention to those who ultimately held the church together, but Brigham cannot be separated out from the other apostles in this respect. Brigham Young was so long underestimated in his greatness that in reaction there is now a tendency to overestimate him, and particularly is this the case for the period before 1844. I expect to demonstrate all this in detail if I keep my health and strength, but the parallel is not dissimilar to that between Roosevelt and Truman. Truman has turned out to be much more of a man than anybody expected, though his greatness, if any, is not yet established. The point is, Roosevelt's death gave him the opportunity to grow. So also with Joseph and Brigham. The point cannot be pushed too far, because there is every difference in running a nation and running (or even holding together) a church. But the parallel exists nevertheless. This is my point of view on Joseph and Brigham, not Fawn's. But her treatment of Brigham, based on the facts as they presented themselves to her, is not individually, only collectively, out of proportion.

But let's get at the central subject-matter of my letter. It seems to me that in reviewing the book you evade or ignore a contribution it makes that is of cardinal significance. No theory about Joseph can have the least validity about him except insofar as it may be measured against the facts of his life. One may start with a theory and marshal facts to support it, but as you are well aware, the only historically valid method is to marshal the facts and see what they add up to. Only then is a theory, and particularly a theory dealing in the intangibles of psychology and psychiatric investigation, in the least apposite. The great importance of Fawn's book is the immensely competent and painstaking job of fact-finding she has done. Although something more can be done in this direction, she has performed a pioneer work of the highest significance. This has to be the point of departure for our thinking about Joseph, the facts of his life as she has assessed and organized them.

The initial weakness of the paranoid theory of his personality is that it has been postulated on insufficient evidence. Maybe there will always be insufficient evidence to permit a final pronouncement upon him, as indeed you say in your review, but your theory, however brilliantly conceived and argued, must be reconsidered from the ground up in the light of Fawn's fact-finding job.

The springboard for the whole paranoid theory has been that Joseph had visions or hallucinations. You expressed the opinion that there was no reason to doubt Joseph's own account of his visions—in part perhaps because of the solid social insistence upon the vision by the Mormons through a century . . . and in part perhaps because you wanted to make use of the fact for your own purposes. I regard it as a contribution by this biography that is of the highest importance that the authenticity of the First Vision (of the Father and the Son) has been called in question, that Mormon history has been challenged on one of its most fundamental assumptions. According to Fawn's exploration of the facts, it is possible that this conception was not evolved until 1838; in all the literature available to us, there is only one indicated possibility that anything had been said of the First Vision as early as 1835, even. If the First Vision is thrown overboard on grounds of insufficient proof—and on Fawn's showing this is what objective historians are likely to do unless and until the Mormons can document their history on this point—a keystone in the structure of the paranoid theory has been destroyed.

There remains, of course, the matter of the visions involving the Angel Moroni, and the actual coming-forth of the Book of Mormon. Yet this vision is infinitely less ambitious than the so-called First Vision, and of far less value or significance for psychological theory. The idea of Joseph as moody, tranced, or dedicated, in any religious sense, emerges as nothing but an idea without foundation in fact. There was no necessary motivation in the First Vision (always taking the point of view of our naturalism rather than that of Mormon faith). But there was abundant motivation in the vision involving the Angel Moroni. You find Fawn's account of Joseph's Palmyra years "superb," hence I take it that you find her account of Joseph's formative years entirely plausible. You have not committed yourself as to her theory and her fact-finding as to the motivation and immediate events leading to the writing of the Book of Mormon, but it would be interesting to know, for our present purposes, if you reject her ideas at any point. The visions of the Angel Moroni, by this interpretation, are not at all established. All that is established is that Joseph told people he had visions—and made them believe it.

Of course, this raises the question of the extent to which Joseph was a conscious fraud and impostor. But this question must be raised anyhow. No visions or hallucinations in themselves can explain the physical text of the Book of Mormon. I was at one time half inclined to the belief that Joseph's might have been a borderline personality, subject indeed to hallucinations, and that he may as he supposed have seen the Golden Plates with the eye of faith (call it delusion), dictating the book from something like a trance state. This idea has the advantage of leaving Joseph's sincerity unimpaired, and makes less troublesome the analysis of his subsequent career. But as I face the actual fact of the Book of Mormon and contemplate some of its physical characteristics—in other words, as I get out of the realm of beautiful thinking and wrestle with obstinate facts which have to be set one in front of another in some kind of order—I find this conception untenable. One hard fact alone seems to me to require us to come to grips with a decision that Joseph either was all he said he was, a prophet of the living God translating from plates of gold, or a conscious fraud and impostor. This is the matter contained in the Book of Mormon and constituting what is called the Isaiah problem. I cannot find it logical that Joseph committed these thousands of words from Isaiah to memory. I find it a good deal more reasonable to conjecture that he had an opened Bible with him on the other side of his curtain. And that idea seems to me to enforce a conception that conscious deception entered into the writing of the Book of Mormon, though I do not mean to say he did not make a psychological adjustment later; on the contrary, I believe that he did, and I believe a better job of demonstrating the mechanism of the adjustment can be done than Fawn has done, though her own demonstration is not to be undervalued.

So far we are not necessarily is disagreement, since you have yourself announced your conviction that Joseph was the author of the Book of Mormon. But suppose we go on from this point. Your review is not altogether consistent in some respects, in its viewpoint on the Book of Mormon and what it may tend to demonstrate about Joseph as a person, so we can more profitably go on to *Forays and Rebuttals* [DeVoto's 1936 compilation of essays].

In this book, p. 96, you make a generalized statement about what I might call the context, or perhaps the content, of Joseph's personality. In this summation there is a dangerous potential of fallacy because it telescopes a man's life without due regard for the time factor or for social consecutiveness. I should imagine that one could make a similar demonstration about many lives that we accept as normal. There is something of the incredible about every man's life, if you stop to add it up, if you pile the details, out of context, atop each other; and particularly is this the case with what I might call energized or energizing personalities. Not that Joseph's was in any sense an ordinary personality. But before I regarded it as too significant that a man told me he had "seen and conversed with God the Father, Jesus, various personages of the Old and New Testaments and various angels and archangels," I should want to know something about his social background. I might find all this, if not less strange, at least more explainable, if I were informed that itinerant preachers were wandering about the neighborhood announcing that the Millennium had alrady arrived and the Resurrection had taken place; if preachers were announcing themselves as a reincarnation or embodiment of God; if his neighbors were seeing celestial steamboats chugging across the sky, complete with crew and passengers. And, an *if* of hardly less importance, he was ignorant of the psychiatric investigation of dreams and invested them with supernormal significances. (I have myself had dreams which persisted as waking memories and then faded into a generalized memory in which, after a lapse of time, for all my critical apparatus and detachment, I have found it almost impossible to distinguish details actually remembered and dream details inextricably intermingled. I find this experience a useful one for probing a personality to whom dream images might come even more readily and more persuasively.) I might conclude that all this was symptomatic of a lunatic world. Or I might find in these facts something indicative of prevailing social excitations, social thought-patterns, and intercommunicable emotions. Set against such a background, a fellow who on the record is the possessor of a vivid and unorthodox imagination—such a fellow who claims to have conversed with God the Father and His Son—may be simply a fellow with a hunger to be noticed, an overdeveloped capacity for fantasy working on the social stuff of his life. You may simplify all this and say that the fellow is suffering from delusions. But for that matter, where is the man who doesn't suffer from delusions about himself—in his relations with women, for instance, or his professional life: anything involving his ego.

Much of what you say in the key paragraph I have cited is in some part untrue because it ignores the factor of immediate causation, the context of event. You may say that the heavens were always opening to give Joseph guidance, and let inferences be drawn from that. But also you may picture a man driven by circumstances to find an unassailable answer to some question of policy or action—and a man with the most unbounded confidence in himself, assertive and autocratic. You do not need the factor of delusion to explain him. Joseph may have used the apparatus of revelation in clear charlatanry. Or he may have adapted that apparatus (evolved originally to extricate himself from grave difficulties in connection with the Book of Mormon) to the formulation of ideas sincerely believed to have been "revealed" to him, but which was akin to that process which in our workaday world we call "getting an inspiration." Let me draw another illustration out of personal experience. When I was seven or eight years old, I was much struck with the appearance and air of an older boy I saw only on Sundays, a boy then a deacon in

Wells Ward in Salt Lake City. He looked to me somehow sanctified and set apart, beautiful and holy. Looking at him, I knew, I *knew*, that I was looking upon a future President of the Church. It was a knowledge I could not have argued, but it was Ultimate Truth, beyond reason or argument. It was, in fact, something like a consciously developed revelation. Well, maybe it was, though I have my doubts about it now and do not look for his early accession to the Presidency of the Church. But remembering that experience, and remembering further what it is like to get struck with a Big Idea, I can conceive that Joseph's revelations were honestly arrived at (some of them, at any rate), if not precisely after the fashion his followers may have believed. With no opening of the heavens in any way involved.

I think, at this point, we had better establish some working definitions as to what constitutes the paranoid personality. If the "paranoid reaction type" you describe on p. 97 of your book [*Forays and Rebuttals*] be given a sufficiently wide application, it will encompass almost anybody who ever had an "original" idea, who exhibited energy in pursuit of a purpose or an idea, or was concerned to accomplish things. On such a finding Joseph was a paranoid, you another, I also, and Babe Ruth, Gypsy Rose Lee, General Eisenhower, and Franklin D. Roosevelt for good measure. But we both have in mind something more clearly aberrant. You endeavor to get at this by matching some assumed correspondences against Henderson and Gillespie's text.

I will grant you persecution as a constant theme in Mormon history, and some of it is real. But of that which is not real, how much stems from abnormal psychology and how much of it was purposive propaganda? Joseph in his history has much to say about persecution while he was translating the Book of Mormon. The record will not bear him out on this. But did Joseph feel himself actually persecuted? This is certainly doubtful. A lot of Joseph's history is retrospective; it is an instrument in the furtherance of specifically evolved purposes. When he came to dictate his history, the kind of history he needed to have was the history of a prophet of the living God. It was a characteristic of biblical prophets that they had been persecuted; that was almost the hallmark of their prophetic authenticity. And, moreover, by 1838 Joseph had got into various and sundry scrapes with people and the law. It was easier to discount all these as "persecution" than to face the facts, particularly for a personality not given to introspective analysis. Persecution was, moreover, not only a name for his troubles but a name of force to his followers. Before we begin making something of Joseph's talk of persecution, I think we had better inquire pretty closely into how much of this was merely verbal and how much of it was integral in Joseph's view of himself and the world.

Henderson and Gillespie's next point, about the auditory and visual hallucinations, have already had sufficient comment in my appraisal of the implications of Fawn's fact-finding job. And in this respect it may be important that "hallucinations," if granted an initial existence or validity, have to be borne with to the end. It is not enough to say Joseph had hallucinations up to 1830, say, or to 1835. What of his mental state after that time? So far from being able to trace the stages of psychic disintegration, one finds something approaching more nearly to psychic integration. Joseph had less and less need of the apparatus of revelation as he grew in personal status and in power. His word sufficed where once he had had to invoke the Word of God. Revelation practically ceased in the last five years of his life. And among the exceptions we find such concessions to necessity as the revelation on plural marriage.

Let us turn to Webster for a moment. Hallucination is defined as "perception of objects with no reality, or experience of sensations with no external cause, usually arising from disorder of the nervous system." It should be borne in mind that practically all the evidence brought to bear to support the theory of hallucinations is adduced from the early years, when the volume of information about Joseph is least satisfactory, and when his own version of his career is least susceptible to being checked against observation and the facts of history. One should imagine that the operation of paranoia should exhibit wilder and wilder hallucinations. The exact contrary is the case. Joseph's life and his exegesis of doctrine for his church both illustrate the evolution of a career and a metaphysics in no way abnormal. As for the former, consider the profound influence of the Jacksonian epoch, with its insistence upon the unlimited capacities of the common man; and reflect, further, upon some of the political and social developments of the Thirties and Forties. I was struck five years ago with the extraordinary degree to which Joseph reflected the temper of his times. One can find his enlarging ambitions *outre* only if one completely ignores his background. And as for his doctrines, the spelling out of his metaphysics, in what way does he differ from any thinker, or any writer, who occupies himself with certain ideas? Our book review columns are full of summations of writers discussing books as capstones to their careers, fruitions of their philosophical systems, and so on.

It is a further difficulty about the paranoid thesis that Joseph cannot be shown to be shifting from one preoccupation to another; there is absolutely nothing that can be adduced to show the progression of paranoia or psychic disintegration. There are his social and political ambitions, his grandiose metaphysics, his sexual adventures. Yes, but the first of these is the reflection of mere being, the commonest exemplification of the American success story. If men didn't enlarge their ambitions as accomplishment and opportunity permitted, we would all still be living in trees. His metaphysics I have discussed, after a fashion. His sexuality is found to be simultaneous with all the other facets of his character and with his interests and ambitions. It was not a development of the Forties; it dates well back into the Thirties. And if we were privileged to catechize the girls of Palmyra and vicinity, if we knew all that went on in the barns and the bushes between 1815 and 1825, we might not be hasty in our conclusions as to when Joseph began to exhibit a vigorous sexuality. There is no way to check this against experience, against history, that is to say. But we have to apply to Joseph what common sense tells us about the generality of boys, youths, and young men, and always allow for possibility. The difference between Joseph and the average country boy sexually interested in girls might be that life took Joseph up and set him down in an environment not favorable to whore houses and casual mistresses, and an environment, moreover, profoundly colored by power on the one hand and theological rationalization on the other. And all these things we see going on at the same time—his hunger for power, his use of and sustenance of a church, his sexuality. You can find here no progression of paranoia, nothing more concrete than the evolution of a man's interests and activities.

All this discussion has been essentially negative, in that it contends against your own integrated theory and does not attempt to tie Joseph up in a neat little package which may be set against your own. Indeed, perhaps Joseph cannot be tied up in any such package, perhaps in no lesser package than a comprehensive account of his life such as Fawn has attempted. It must be remarked that nothing I say here is particularly inharmonious with her large-scale account of Joseph; and most of what I say is said against the background of fact-finding represented in her book. I think that Joseph's personality can be explained more perfectly than Fawn has explained it, and that some enigmas that are left by her treatment can be cleared up by a thoughtful operation of the facts. But I think also that she has done the large pioneer work, that with some exceptions within the boundaries she has set up the truth about Joseph's character can be worked out—insofar as any man can ever finally be known through the elliptical medium of a book.

Lengthily yours,

Dale L. Morgan

P.S. Let me add one comment I neglected to make at the proper point above. I am inclined to agree that Joseph's church would have exploded from internal strains had he lived much longer; too many forces too violent for adjustment in American mores were operating in it. The dynamism in Mormonism, at least, would have exploded out of it, and if Joseph had survived, it would have been as prophet to the wholly innocuous and wholly dedicated—if he were capable of accepting such a diminishment of prestige and function. But the internal strains were social in character. The Mormon church had grown too greatly in numbers and power for the pieces to be put back together again as they had been in Ohio and Missouri. There comes a time for any organism when it must survive as such or tear itself apart. Mormonism was approaching that stage in June, 1844. But

Joseph's state of mind was almost an irrelevance. He was destroyed, finally, by his arrogance, by his handling of the [Nauvoo] Expositor affair. But it was an arrogance inherent in his career, and it cannot be shown to be pathological in terms of modern psychology. I might add that Joseph's death may have been the salvation of the church in more ways than in settling upon it the seal of martyrdom. When all the angles are considered, the social shock of his death and the effect of this upon the psychological fabric of the church, may alone have made it possible for Brigham to evacuate Illinois on an organized basis. (And it is to be remarked that Brigham required a year to crystallize the possibility of evacuation; it is also to be remarked that it was his psychological astuteness in clinging to Nauvoo during that last year which, more than anything else, enabled Brigham to establish himself against his rivals—he held Nauvoo and Nauvoo was Joseph. Thereafter he could risk emigration out of Illinois, and he did so as rapidly as he could.)

18. To FAWN BRODIE

Arlington, Virginia
22 December 1945

Dear Fawn,

It would be nice, and I am sure it would prove something or other, if I felt industrious tonight, and like writing on books. But I don't, and so what? I feel more like loafing, even on a typewriter.

For no particular reason I have been reflecting on a note you wrote me while on vacation some 18 months or more ago. You were discussing some reading you had been doing, [Wallace] Stegner's Big Rock Candy Mountain, and Lilliam Smith's Strange Fruit. The latter, you said, for its very spareness made more of an impression on you than the former. I had not read Strange Fruit then, but I did read it last winter. I was not overly impressed with it. It was too craftsmanlike. All the points were too neatly made; it was put together like a woman's hairdress for some particular occasion, impressive at the moment but not the way people live on a 24-hour basis. I have wondered how the two novels stack up in your mind now. I was interested on a couple of occasions to have you mention Stegner's novel, yet you have never referred to Strange Fruit since that time, in conversation with me. I have not felt any urge to go back to the latter novel, but Stegner's book sticks in my mind; it stays with me, and I keep thinking about its own peculiar triangle, the relations between father, mother, and son, and the dislocated life the father led and what came of it in the end. I think Stegner said something about human beings, and about their relationships with one another and the world, and about the West. I think his book has about as good a chance of lasting as any novel that has yet come out of the West. And I wonder, too, if Stegner has it in him to write another book compounded from such bitterness and love, because of course this was plainly his own story in its essentials, and a man's explanation of his own being in the end is the most important story he is ever likely to be able to tell.

Well, the note on which this letter has opened is not particularly relevant to anything. Maybe I should show signs of intelligence and talk about things of more immediate interest.

I am glad that [Bernard] DeVoto wrote so warmly of your book [*No Man Knows My History*]. Indeed, I rejoice with you and for you for every success your book has. It is pleasant to see good things happen to one's friends. Not that you need to be told that, of course. I have remembered it as somehow characteristic of you how your eyes lighted and your face filled with pleasure last spring when I finally got around to telling you that the Guggenheim thing had materialized. You didn't have to say anything, though you did say the words; your expression bespoke your feelings before the words got there.

Anyhow, DeVoto's review led me to take up a labor I had promised five years or so ago—I think it was in 1941 when he and I were carrying on some correspondence with respect to his Year of Decision, then in preparation. I told him in due course I should challenge his views on a basis of social background. He remarked that he had lately pronounced Joseph [Smith] a paranoid in some lecture of importance in Boston, and that no member of the congregation had even hissed, then went on to insist that a man was an individual before he became a member of society, and argued for psychology on this basis for a paragraph or so. I would not accept the idea, but was not prepared to argue, not at that moment. Well, that was five years ago, and when he reviewed your book Sunday, he stirred me from my lethargy and I tackled the subject. Not, obviously, in a formal essay for publication; just an organization of ideas that occurred to me in the course of writing a letter. You might be interested in my angle of view, so I enclose a carbon of this letter, asking that you return it at your convenience. Some of the points you mention in your note of the 18th, which appropriately enough was written on my birthday, I took up with D-V myself.

It is interesting to reflect upon the three major reviews of the biography, by DeVoto, [Vardis] Fisher, and myself. Each of us started with a theory about Joseph, and our reviews were conditioned by the theory. My theory, as it happens, coincides with yours in large measure, and the majority of my criticisms had already been argued out with you before publication. I think some of DeVoto's ideas are not so much legitimate criticism as a re-formulation of his article on Joseph in the Dict[ionary of]. Am[erican]. Biog[raphy]., plus ideas as expanded in Forays and Rebuttals. Almost all the points he made against you in the review, he had previously made in his own publications, so you had to deal with habit-patterns in his thinking as well as with the operating critic. Nevertheless, he said some extraordinarily fine and deserved things about your book, and you are fully entitled to glow a little inside in contemplating them.

I think the most important specific criticisms I would bring to bear against the biography are criticisms I made earlier. I don't think the motivations involved in the founding of the church, as a development from the labor with the Book of Mormon, have been adequately explored; nor on the basis of his early life as you picture it is there quite adequate explanation of the religious content of the Book of Mormon, for one thing, and of the religion he founded, for another. On a more general basis, I think the book has a weakness in that it displays a tendency to over-simplification of event along the avenue of individual personality and character. Maybe that is only a criticism of you for writing a biography and not a complete history, but still I think it is legitimate. An especially notable example, to my mind, is the treatment of the final Missouri imbroglio in terms of [Sidney] Rigdon's disintegrating personality. I felt this all along, as you may recall, and I think these chapters, as much as anything, centered Fisher's and DeVoto's criticism on novelizing events, and inadequate handling of Rigdon. I suspect that if you had been writing Rigdon's biography instead of Joseph's, you might have come up with a more rounded view of Rigdon. This was what I was getting at in my own review, when I talked about chiaroscuro of character. (For space reasons I had tossed out a brief comment on over-simplification along the lines of my remarks above.)

I am spending Christmas Day with the McConkeys, and I obtained a copy of your book to present to them. When opportunity offers, I shall ask you to sign it for them. I have seen your book around town in the various bookstores, but never in any quantity and never for long until Thursday, when I noticed a stack of no less than 18 copies at Brentano's. I was in again yesterday, so had another look at the pile, which now consisted of 16. So people obviously are buying the book! It would be wonderful if it really started to sell—not after the fashion of a Forever Amber, but still selling.

Earlier in the week I had a Christmas card from Dick Scowcroft, who was leaving to spend the holidays in Utah. If he doesn't get shot, maybe you can set foot in the state in the course of time. Watch your daily newspaper. Incidentally, a letter from Juanita which came in the same mail with yours yesterday discusses Scowcroft's book, which she has just read. She enjoyed it very much and thinks he really can write; she thought Ester and Caroline were marvelously done. She goes on to say, "But somehow I couldn't make Burton ring true. He should not have been a moron, exactly, I thought, and yet he acted like one from first to last—a spineless nitwit who would lie around three months without doing one earthly thing, nothing but eat his three meals and lie and try vacantly to think or try to decide whether or not he should smoke a cigarette. Perhaps instead of criticizing him, I'd rather just say that I've never seen a boy like him. If these are at all typical Mormons, we're in a pretty low grade, aren't we—from Albert and the Johnson girl up and down. I know mothers who are just as dramatic on the question of smoking; I know the church under Presidents [Heber J.] Grant and J. Reuben Clark has made the use of tobacco one of the major sins. I hope for a more tolerant regime from here on for a while—except of course, for Joseph Fielding [Smith] and a few of the other good stand-patters."

Juanita fascinates me, anyhow. She is always half-expecting to get bounced by the church for her unorthodox thinking. Thus she teaches a Sunday school class such heretical doctrines as this: "It is not a matter of being just good, but good for something—negations never lead to positive righteousness. I would rather have a smoker and a drinker who is fundamentally and aggressively Christian than a man who boasts that he has never tasted either liquor or tobacco, and at the same time has never done anything worth while in his life. I get so tired of our 'Thou Shalt Not's.' I'd like us to put our emphasis on some good, positive 'Thou Shalt's.' " She told me once that while she was studying at Columbia she saw a good deal of a girl from her own country who had got an education and become a social worker, and had gone in thoroughly for smoking and drinking. This friend thought Juanita ought to take up both and then go back to Dixie College and be a rebel. That would require and show courage, and might do some good. But Juanita's philosophy was and still is, "When a cowboy wants to turn a herd of stampeding cattle, he doesn't run directly counter to them. If he did, he'd be run over. He rides with them, and turns them gradually. So if I don't like the stand of the church, I can do more about it by staying in."

One of these days I am going to put Juanita into a book. Maybe even the Great Salt Lake book, though not referred to specifically by name, merely an example of the hard core of integrity and common sense that can be found in the Mormon way of life and the Mormon society if you are willing to look around a little.

In an earlier letter you mentioned Hamlin Cannon. About the first of November I ran into him in Archives one day, and he wanted to know if your book "was worth buying." It would have done your heart good to see his eyes pop when I told him it was the best job of research ever done in Mormon history. He inquired as to its nature, then wanted to know if you had used his article in Miss[issippi]. Valley Hist[orical]. Rev[iew]. on the Palmyra [New York] newspapers and the Book of Mormon. I told him you had had all that long ago, and expressed my surprise that he hadn't known that [Francis] Kirkham had already published that information. This was the first he had heard about it! Cannon is a very odd fellow. I half respect him and half dislike him. He is somehow rigid both in mind and personlity, but he has a consuming interest in history, not too well-balanced yet informed by the scientific spirit. His personality apart, I think he is handicapped chiefly by a lack of a sort of over-all shrewdness. Or maybe you could call it a fundamental lack of imagination.

I hope the [RLDS Saints'] Heralds have arrived by now and that you know all about the "Brodie 'Atrocity'." This week's issue leaves you in peace, and it may indeed be some time before Israel [Smith] ventures to overthrow your weak but vicious effort to overthrow the Kingdom. I sent for the two earlier Hearlds containing his first two articles on "The Origin of Mormon Polygamy," and find that they contain nothing new, simply an exposition of a certain state of mind. He denies the Plural Marriage revelation, among other reasons, because no copy in Joseph's hand can be adduced, hence it would not be admissible in a court of law! I wonder if he would submit the Doctrine & Covenants generally to that criterion. It is futile to argue with the zealots, of course. Man can find infinite reason for not changing his mind about something he wants to believe. Double and triple meanings can be read into language, legalistic objections brought to bear—anything and everything so that one does not have to change his opinions about something. It was in the light of this viewpoint that I "reviewed" your book for the [LDS] Improvement Era a year or more ago in one of my notes to you.

It would be nice if Hayes could turn up his diary, but I suspect that what he heard about was your own manuscript. Any written memoir is a "diary" to the uninitiated. However, Hayes is a sufficiently experienced historian to be able to figure that out, too, and if he is going to make a search anyhow, more power to him.

I don't go in much for Christmas cards any more, but I do try to write to my friends at Christmas and let them know they are remembered. So let me express to you and Bernard and Dickie, who will doubtless be forgetting me with great rapidity, my affection and respect, and my best wishes both for a happy holiday season and for a fruitful new year.

Dale

19. To BERNARD DEVOTO

Arlington, Virginia
January 1946

Dear DeVoto:

I had on Monday your vigorous letter of December 28, and today, while I am still trying to get acclimated to the new year, I have a letter from Fawn Brodie enclosing a carbon copy of a letter to you which makes an extremely interesting contribution to this paranoid discussion I opened up. Thus we have three people sitting in our sanity commission and can quarrel amiably among ourselves (comforted by the knowledge that regardless of our findings, few people will ever find out about them and fewer still give a damn). You are, as you insist, a peaceable fellow: Fawn has an altogether pacific nature, or so she maintains in public; while for myself, I am a perfect paragon of sweet reasonableness. So "quarrel" is not the mot juste, but let it ride.

As an appropriate introduction to the discussion following, permit me an anecdote in which I figure as victim. A year or so ago I was conducting with [J.] Rod[eric] Korns[1] a long-distance argument on some question or other relating to Western history, and in the course of the argument we arrived at a point where certain evidences were in dispute. I would not allow them the status of "facts," and Rod with his usual combativeness assured me that that was precisely what they were, facts, brother, facts. So then he told me a story. Once upon a time he had gone duck-hunting with a friend, and in the dawn's early light a duck and a mudhen flew overhead. Both men blasted away with their shotguns, and the two birds fell into the water. "I'll retrieve them," Rod's friend said, and he clambered out of the boat and went sloshing away through the mud and muck, the while Rod glowed in contemplation of this high altruism. So a few minutes later the friend came back to the boat, the duck in one hand and the mudhen in the other, and he tossed the latter into Rod's lap. "Here's your mudhen, Rod," he said graciously.

Now, Rod said, he had been hunting ducks for a good many years, and was a pretty fair shot. Moreover, he'd gotten a clear crack at the duck. So, said he to me now, when *you* shoot at a fact, you bring down a duck, every time! But when I blast away, it's a mudhen. "Nuts to you," said J. Roderic Korns.

With this devastating story green in my memory, it would be something less than intelligent of me to suppose that I alone am capable of bringing down ducks, or that I never turn up without mudhens in my bag. I am at pains to make this point clear because I believe you read out of my last letter a greater harshness, perhaps a more superior air, than was either intended or, as I would like to think, written into the letter. I did not conceive of this letter as a "blast," but simply as a probing into what struck me as some curious judgments curiously arrived at; indeed, I hardly recognize my letter as it is reflected back to me in yours. This is not of any particular importance, except that I should like to make some things plain about my attitudes respecting history and myself. Anything I ever say, I like to have accepted as being within the proportions of my ignorance and according to my understanding of the facts, which on occasion may be quite inadequate. When I make judgments in print, I prefer to restrict myself to opinions I can nail down if necessary, but in my correspondence with my friends I permit myself some latitude and feel free to discuss not alone error but the possibility of error—not always clearly distinguished in my letters, I grant you. I have no illusions that all the bugs can ever be gotten out of any kind of history; history made absolutely "straight" is a snare and a delusion. The very terms on which history is written insure this in perpetuity. But it is nevertheless absorbing, as well as necessary, to work with the facts we have, and insofar as we can establish their status as facts, see what they add up to, straighten out such distortions as we become aware of and have tools to work on. (This is your own view, of course, amply stated in your letter to me.) For myself, I take an active personal interest in doing what I can toward straightening out books which capture my respect and my enthusiasm. It comes out as an idiosyncrasy, perhaps: I wrote Nels Anderson about everything that struck upon my attention when his book [*Desert Saints*] came out; I did as much with Wally Stegner's book, and yours, and Fawn's, notwithstanding I'd had two earlier cracks at Fawn's book. (And as a matter of fact, when I get up the ambition to separate out the new from the old, I am going to write Fawn another catalogue of things that have come to my attention since I wrote her at the end of October.) I am in hopes that all my friends will serve me equally with my own books, and I should have been happy to have you give way to your low instincts, as you put it, and write me about everything debatable you found in my book on the Humboldt. There are preposterous errors in that book, such incomprehensible misstatements as having the South Fork of the Humboldt run south, for instance. And only the other day I turned up five gross errors in connection with my discussion of the Stevens-Townsend-Murphy party of 1844 (and this party is important, because in conjunction with an Oregon group they took wagons over precisely the trail the Mormons followed in 1847, from Council Bluffs to the Greenwood Cutoff.) One can only derive such comfort as is possible from the fact that as author you yourself turn up more things that are wrong with your book than all your critics combined.

I've been at pains to make these various points since it would seem that we have to dispose of an earlier letter I wrote you before we can get at the position you have taken on my new one. I had remembered that letter as simply a page-by-page recital of detail you would do well to check up before you published a revised edition, so I spent half an hour rooting around in my papers, and after blowing the dust off, came up with a carbon copy of that letter which I have reexamined in the light of your comments. I think you must remember it somewhat inexactly, and I believe it exhibits rather less of verbal gymnastics than your present letter would lead us to believe. Although no literary production, it answers the purpose I had in view. I have checked up all the page references I gave, and find them in my copy of your book, for example. I don't follow you in the matter of verbalizing. I began that letter by personally objecting to the thesis that any year of the period could be conceived, finally and irrevocably, as the year of ultimate decision for the Civil War, and I hazarded the opinion that emphasis given this point had obscured for some of the critics and readers the large things your book had to say about American life and which were wholly independent of this thesis. But beyond this I concerned myself principally with factual details. Some of these details remain matter of opinion, and my remarks could serve the function only of a stated dissent from stated conclusions. On a couple of points I was clearly in error, for example my questioning of there being "two well known maps" (p. 41)—I can now name you a great many more than two. My second point was not too well put in the light of facts as complex as I have since ascertained them to be, in connection with the movement of [William H.] Ashley's men upon the mountains. And my provisional correction for p. 87 is perfectly irrelevant, since it is not the Josephites who hold the temple site. In some cases I suggested the desirability of more reserved phraseology, to militate against misunderstanding or ambiguity, and I took you to task for polishing off Colonel Kane too slickly. But this is about the sum and substance of that letter, and I think it does not necessarily present us with any difficulties in pursuing our present discussion. Incidently, if the time comes that you undertake a revised edition, give me a little advance notice and I will translate for such as you can make of it some marginalia that has accrued from using your book and cross-checking in sources during the last couple of years.

So much for preliminaries. We seem to have three principal topics requiring discussion, my underlying attitudes toward and basic conceptions of Mormon history; the Book of Mormon in its literary qualities, with some related questions; and the question of the paranoid thesis. Suppose I take the latter two first. Or on second thought, maybe I'd better tackle the questions in order since my qualities of judgment and perception affect in some degree the validity of my arguments, and it might serve a useful purpose to ascertain whether an intelligence in some degree consistent informs my reasoning.

First let me say that your portrait of me as being something like a "spoiled sociologist" is closer to reality than Fawn's presentation of me as a painter. I took an art major in college with a view to using it in advertising and commercial art, but I at no time ever took myself seriously as an artist and as a painter I am below classification, even. My principal interest always remained the social sciences, and it was in social psychology that I first found the tools that enabled my mind to grasp the Mormon phenomenon and see the history in perspective. So to that extent I am your sociologist, although my interest has never been for sociology as such. Not that there is anything original in my discovery or use of these tools. You have used certain of them yourself, and to fruitful effect, in literary researches and criticism. This insistence upon social causation at any rate has had the effect of persuading me to look first in the environment for an explanation of a social situation or of a person, even. I would not say of myself as you say of me, however, that I am willing to go whistling about my business once I have established certain matters of background. Indeed, if environment were all-important, we would have had twenty dozen Mormonisms, an infinity of them, even—or none. I try rather to evolve an integrated view of the individual as a biological organism and as a factor in society; perhaps, indeed, I insist upon the terms of this integration more than you do. I recall that you wrote me once, for example, that "every man is a study in the psychology of the individual before he is an item in sociology." I would not accept that dictum. Even if one were to maintain that life in the womb were to be taken into account, the social angle remains, the physiological relationship of the mother and the child. After parturition the biological organism and the individual in society are one and the same. Nothing can be subtracted from the whole without leaving a nullity. Every man is the product of total environment acting upon the biological organism, as I call it for lack of a better term, the "life" itself. It is hardly possible to conceive even an adult withdrawing wholly from society and remaining what we could define as a man. Take him out of society and what have you left? An Alexander Selkirk reduced almost to gibbering idiocy within a relatively brief period. Or a wild woman of the Santa Barbara Channel Islands. The pattern of behavior that we call sanity disintegrates very rapidly indeed when any man ceases to feel the impact upon his personality of society. And you could define that the other way around, if you wanted: we define a man's sanity in terms of his ability to maintain contact with "reality," with society and its norms. At the same time, of course, subtract the "life" and you will have left only a hundred pounds or more of an organic substance that very quickly requires to be cremated or buried. And I am not willing to grant the possibility of either a static psychology or a static environment. Stasis is impossible if for no other reason than that men inevitably grow old and die.

None of this is in any part either brilliant or profound, but it may serve to indicate that I have a dynamic view of the possibilities of any man in any given social situation, and no doctrinaire ideas: I am willing to look narrowly into the specific situation or the specific individual with a sense of discovery. And the "sociological" coloring of my thinking and of my techniques of historical approach may, in what I have said above, have been more clearly defined than has hitherto been the case.

You wonder what conceptions my factual investigations rest upon, what my controlling theory on Mormonism and its significance is. Well, for one thing let me say I have been at pains *not* to formulate theories of large views about the Mormons. I have been aided in this by the oddity of much of my research; I have worked backward instead of forward in time—an accident consequent upon the fact that I have had to use libraries and archives as I have found them, exhausting them in turn. No complete inversion of research and no complete lack of controlling ideas is possible, of course, for any intelligent person engaged upon gathering and evaluating facts. But in large part, I think, I have kept myself free from the formulation of theories before all possible facts had been collected. I have tested the theories of others as I have acquired reagents I could bring to bear upon them (as is evidenced by the fact that at the very moment you read this you are peremptorily dragged up out of the depths of your proper preoccupations to read these words). I was at one time inclined to be persuaded by your paranoid theory, as offering a naturalistic explanation of Joseph [Smith] which did not insult the intelligence as those of the past had done; I am now very much inclined to reject your theory for reasons quite different from Fawn's. But let me not anticipate myself on that subject. I was saying that I have carefully steered away from most theories; I decline to let academic historians, for example, require me to declare myself on the [Frederick Jackson] Turner hypothesis in relation to Mormonism. I've been making a collection of facts about places, people, and time, and of course something of a collection of ideas that people have held about the Mormons.

But still it is obvious that I have some controlling theory about the Mormons, regardless of how much we will grant to my judicial fact-gathering. And the theory has a societal base. In defining myself, I may make somewhat clearer what is in my mind when I talk of Joseph as both a product and exemplar of his times. (It seems to me that you hold too narrow a view here, as though only one type of person or one range of interests could qualify within this definition. I think a thousand men, or five thousand, all within the range of their individuality, could stand as "products and exemplars of their time"—you have the infinitely variable factor of individual personality and the factor more nearly approaching the common denominator, of energies and tendencies in society.) Anyway, I conceive of Mormonism as an extremely interesting type-specimen of the Jacksonian democratization of American society. By "Jacksonian" I have reference to the same forces in society that operated to bring forth [Andrew] Jackson and his associates and adherents, rather than the social causation originating in Jackson's own acts. The energies that produced Jackson, the sway and surge of ideas and emotions, produced Mormonism simultaneously. Mormonism can therefore properly and instructively be examined as another dimension of the Jacksonian upsurge, and our ultimately rounded idea of the full significance of the Jacksonian age may wait upon the opening of a number of such new channels of thinking, new ways of looking at the period. [Arthur M.] Schlesinger has lately published a book on the Age of Jackson, but observe that outside the economic and political field his purview is narrow—for instance, his discussion of religion is primarily a discussion of religion as an instrument influenced by and influencing political ideas and socio-economic change. This is not to criticize him for hewing to his thesis, merely to say that new awarenesses of the religious scene of that period are possible and desirable. You may remember what Walter Prescott Webb had to say in his The Great Plains, that none of his facts was new but that we should look at them in new ways. I think the idea is perfectly applicable to the Mormons. Indeed, if I did not, I should be infinitely discouraged by the extraordinary job Fawn has done for Mormonism's opening period. Within her restricted compass, she has had a tremendous lot of things to say. What I propose has to be done, of course, with a sense of history's proportions—with due attention to the number of people involved in proportion to the size of the population itself, the ways in which Mormonism has affected American life, what it has drawn from as well as given back to that life, and so on. I regard Mormonism as an infinitely more fruitful avenue of approach for some thinking about American life than Millerism, for example. Although Millerism was not without its typical elements, it may be studied much more nearly in a vacuum than may Mormonism—a theological vacuum. It was, in a sense, something imposed upon the daily lives of people, and it could congeal about its collapsed ideas leaving hardly a ripple in society. Mormonism, on the other hand, proceeded out of American life at more points, from millennialism to the evangelical communisms, with religious, political, social, and economic ideas indiscriminately sucked into the vortex to be digested or spewed out, with the central energies and structure of the church always different because of what it experienced or took to itself. I don't say, with you, that Mormonism was at best an aberration of the principal energies involved; I do say that it is an interesting vehicle for some of the social energies of its time, and that something can be learned about the nature of American society from a critical scrutiny of the Mormon phenomenon. That is all I will ever claim for any history of the Mormons. Unless, of course, after we are all dead and buried it turns out that Joseph was, after all, a prophet of the living God who established the consummating dispensation and was thus the most important thing to happen since Christ. But unless we are set to writing that history in another existence, I think we can dismiss this anxiety from our minds.

So much for the background of my thinking. Suppose now we take up the Book of Mormon, and the verbalisms you detected in my last letter. I should describe those elements of my letter as being elliptical statement instead, assuming in you a very considerable knowledge of what I was talking about which would enable you to follow me without my having to spell things out as I would in print or for the uninitiated. But if you want to call those passages plain, bad writing, I won't quarrel with you. You took particular exception to my view that the Book of Mormon could not be conceived as absolutely lacking in form and structure, that "the history of the book itself is a denial that it altogether lacked in some kind of form and structure." Let me for present convenience itemize the ideas thus elliptically disposed of: What would a book with "neither form nor structure of any kind" be? In the nature of things, could it be anything but a patternless collection of words taken at random from the dictionary? "Form" and "structure" may be abstract ideas, but for everyone they have connotations of *organization*, of pattern and design. Was it an inchoate book of the above type that was used in Mormon proselyting with such immense early effect? Would such a book have given the church any kind of foundation, any intellectual justification, any glamour of ideas? May it not be established in Mormon history that converts did get something out of the Book of Mormon? If not, how could two persons have derived the same thing from an utterly inchoate mass of words, and how could they have found an identity of feeling and an intellectual satisfaction in reading the book? Does not the history of the book show a compulsive force which may be traced concretely in the source literature? Does not the book in its history therefore deny any thesis that it was "absolutely lacking" in form and structure?

All this simplifies my ideas to the point of absurdity. Really, you don't mean what you say, that the Book of Mormon had no form or structure of any kind. You know that there was a story of sorts, that the narrative moved along after a fashion, that people read it then and now as a more or less convincing history, that people have found religious sentiments in it they have been able to adapt to their purposes, that it also incorporated a fund of comment on contemporary American life and ideas. What you really mean is that all this was done without "style."

After receiving your letter, I had intended to point up what I thought to be an odd limitation of viewpoint on your part, in that you would not conceive of the idea of "novel" as having any real meaning outside a 20th century definition of the word. This seemed to be a viewpoint arbitrarily arrived at and irrelevant, for all we need concern ourselves with is the creative energies involved, the mechanism of literary creation on however primitive a level, not with the end-product. We are all three agreed that Joseph wrote the book; from our viewpoint it is immaterial what type-name we give to it.

But Fawn has made it unnecessary to argue this point, for in the carbon copy she sends me of her letter to you, I think she has disposed of the subject satisfactorily to all of us through by-passing any argument about the 19th or 20th century novel. So I will wind up this section of the letter by saying simply that I have reread all the citations you give me with respect to the imagination, style, and structure of the book, and do not think that they materially affect my own position as set forth in my last letter, or support yours. I am not in any way concerned with this part of the discussion, however, and do not think argument is likely to be of any particular value; I would not have brought up the [issue as fully,] as a matter of fact, except that the evaluation of the Book of Mormon that was involved had some bearing on our common judgment as to the paranoid thesis. Except for my interest in this latter, I should not have opened this present discussion at all, for you and Fawn were quite capable, between you, of thrashing out any differences between what she seemed to be saying and what you seemed to think she had said. But since I did think a useful purpose was to be served in inquiring into your view of the paranoid thesis in the light of Fawn's job, I also took occasion to call attention to what I then and still conceive to be some distortions of language if not of viewpoint on your part.

So without further delay let's get into the paranoid question. Between our letters Fawn herself has had something to say on this subject, something of great interest, and I feel that it is much to be regretted that she didn't formulate these ideas within the framework of her book. If she had challenged the psychologists with a problem, maybe someone with the technical equipment would be spurred to see what he could find out. It is really a little obligatory on authors to phrase, at least, the questions for which there are no answers; being able to phrase a question sometimes is half the effort involved in getting an answer. I have remarked to Fawn in the past, and again said in my review, that there were more difficult problems involved about the selection and assessment of fact than her text always made clear, though I have recognized literary difficulties involved. Nevertheless, when the occasion arises for a revision of the book, I think Fawn would be well advised to incorporate a discussion of this kind among the appendices, at least. The point of view is certainly one that must operate in any evaluation of the objective "facts" and her interpretation thereof.

Fawn goes far to harmonize our differences in her letter to you. For all your insistence upon the paranoid color of [Joseph's] personality, you are not disposed to dispute the influence of social causation. And for all my emphasis upon social causation, I am not disposed to dispute a psychological abnormality. For regardless of what you may find in a normal man's background, you don't find him bringing forth revelations from God and founding churches with sweeping claims. In the area of personality, there is certainly a mystery to be grasped after, how Joseph's mind worked, what his values were, and all the rest of it. He quite possibly had the capacity for fantasy which other circumstances might have made him a writer as we customarily think of this term; there is indeed little question of this, though one may indict his talents for insufficiency. There is a cloudy and shifting borderline, as you say, between sanity and insanity, between perception of reality and employment of dream images. But if everyone is a little insane in some way or another, still I am not disposed to accept the thesis that Joseph ever was insane in the usual meaning we give this word.

A little earlier I remarked that Fawn and I had come to reject your paranoid thesis for different reasons. She has explained an area of investigation in which I had not worked, research into Joseph's youth. I knew the importance of such an investigation and refused to open a discussion of Joseph as a paranoid before someone had done such a job. But my own rejection of your thesis came at the other end, the Nauvoo end to which Fawn barely adverts in her letter. You had to say on pp. 97-8 of your "Centennial," "The finding that Joseph Smith comes somewhere within the wide limits of the paranoid reaction type does not attempt to appraise the degree of his insanity nor the regularity and duration of its attacks. That its rhythm was uneven, that for long periods he was free of it, that at other times his delusions did not affect his behavior apart from the dominant ideas—all this seems to me to show plainly in the record. But that some form of the paranoid constitution is the explanation of him seems necessitated by all the available facts."

This is persuasively put, but I do not think a demonstration can be made against the record to which you must appeal, the day-to-day story of his life. You cannot anywhere select out individual acts and say that he here reveals himself insane, not if you use those facts in context, and have reference to chronology. You cannot, I feel well assured, document the stated conclusions from a pattern of fact. I think it would be close to impossible to write a booklength study of Joseph which would seriously maintain the paranoid thesis and show forth his life as exemplifying it. I grant you that [Harry M.] Beardsley tried something of the sort, but you and I both know that his biography [*Joseph Smith and His Mormon Empire*] was shallow and a little silly, exhibiting the paradox of being skeptical without being critical. Beardsley at no time achieved other than a muddy view of Joseph, and the contradictions in which his book abounds are the logical consequence. As far as the paranoid thesis goes, he interlards psychiatric language into his book at intervals, and that is about all. My own rejection of your thesis, then, found its roots in my utter inability to demonstrate in a sustained pattern of fact, in Joseph's life lived from one day to the next, the validity of a paranoid conception. I have very grave doubts, indeed, that anyone can do so. I outlined some reasons for skepticism in my last letter, and I am also in accord with what Fawn says, that Joseph is best explained in evolutionary terms, that he was a different psychological phenomenon at 17 than at 38. That would apply as well in the case of the paranoid thesis, but I think the evolution for all practicable purposes can be traced within the limits of working sanity, as we conceive of sanity. Not "normality," no, but sanity.

The test I speak of can also, profitably I think, be applied to the earlier years and the revelations, which serve as much as anything to give comfort in the abstract to the paranoid thesis. Some time ago Fawn expressed to me a difficulty here: At just what point in the revelations can you say with assurance that Joseph was honestly deluded instead of an unabashed fraud? Which revelation first partakes of delusion, and how can you thereafter separate the conscious fraud from the delusion? (Perhaps recognizing this difficulty, you have yourself observed that he eked out his deluded revelations with conscious inventions.) This is an appeal to the record the paranoid thesis must face, since as you have yourself said often in print and have repeated in your letter to me, retrospective psychoanalysis of a dead man is at best speculative and uncontrolled, and justifiable only if no other proper tools exist for getting at the dead man's personality. It may be an injustice, but in the nature of things the paranoid thesis must be subjected to a more rigorous testing and must make a better showing under close examination than any other.

This entire letter may have served to clarify the background to my thinking on the paranoid question, perhaps exhibiting some evidence that I have a more solid philosophy in my appeal to social causation, and a more liberal attitude toward the x-factor of personality, than was immediately apparent. I emphasize the point only that I may not seem to evade your effective burlesque of my point of view, your neighborhood of Napoleons. I submit in your instance, however, that there is a difference between personality-substitution and the kind of thing I have had under discussion; the one is subject to being checked against experience, while the whole history of religion insists upon the personal relationship between man and God, with the frontiers of this relationship so tenuously defined as constantly to defy exact delineation. Any time you deal with the God-concept in society, what men think about God, you come a little unstuck from [what] we may choose to call either experience or reality, and I submit, again, that there is a vast field for the operation of "self-deception" within our definition of normality.

Well, I'm not sure where all this has brought us. I don't even guarantee that this letter reads intelligibly. It has been written subject to constant interruption by every imaginable circumstance over a period of some days since it was begun. But writing these letters has not been without some personal value to me; you have served me very well as an anvil on which to hammer into greater concreteness some of my ideas about Joseph's personality. If you've got nothing comparable out of the correspondence, you'll just have to derive whatever consolation anvils do derive from being anvils!

Cordially,

Dale L. Morgan

[1] During the 1940s, J. Roderic Korns participated with Morgan and Charles Kelly in a three-way correspondence regarding western trails. Following Korns's death, Morgan prepared his unfinished manuscript, "West from Fort Bridger," for publication in the 1951 *Utah Historical Quarterly*, volume 19, numbers 1 through 4.

20. To FAWN BRODIE

Arlington, Virginia
January 1946

Dear Fawn,

Here it is, the new year a week old, and I am just answering your letter. The trouble is that the [Bernard] DeVoto letter had first priority, and I couldn't get opportunity to complete it until this afternoon. My affairs have been complicated by the fact that Charlie Wood, who went to college with me and who comes from Ogden (you may well know him) has been named executive secretary to Gossett, the new Idaho senator. I wrote him airmail on Christmas Day inviting him to put up with me till he could find a house or apartment for his wife and three kids. He arrived Friday morning and things have been somewhat turned around ever since, as you can imagine.

DeVoto's reply to me surprised me a little, but only on first reading. The tone of my letter was on the tactless side, and since for some years he has been in a position where criticism of him represented an attack upon him, he was bound to have an emotional reaction. I imagine also that he had felt some little irritation that I didn't write him in unreserved praise of his '46 book [*Year of Decision*] when it came out—after all, he had sunk years into it and by now would yearn for a little more appreciation. Also my consistent interest in detail can be irritating to people who don't share my enthusiasm for it. Hence DeVoto's letter to me blew up into verbalisms whereas you own tactful letter brought a very ingratiating reply. Under the circumstances, I think his letter to me was tolerant as well as testy, and the only thing I regret is that he seems to have got me involved in some emotional reactions, saying to you and perhaps thinking to himself that I believe him "dishonest" in certain matters. Actually, I regard him as human instead, as you may gather from these remarks. So I was at some pains in my letter not to quarrel with him. I don't quarrel as a rule, anyhow, except with extremely disagreeable people, and only with them when I have to.

I return to you the letter he wrote (and also the rather touching letter from your aunt). I chose not to refer to this letter in any way that would indicate I had seen it, as you will observe. Much of my letter to him, a carbon of which I enclose, you will note to have been addressed to you over his shoulder, particularly with respect to your intervention in the paranoid discussion.

Madeline [McQuown] still hasn't received your book, but I have hopes she will lay hands on it this week. It must have arrived at the San Francisco hospital a day or so after she left there, and the forwarding service of the post office was so inefficient that finally they returned the book to me instead. Madeline meanwhile returned to Ogden just before Christmas, and I have sent the book off again. She is beginning to feel a little recovered from her trip, and better, apparently, in general, which is welcome news. The mountains just now are magnificent, she says, as I can well imagine, though temperatures seem to be quite mild and pleasant there at present.

Meanwhile Juanita [Brooks] writes me from St. George [Utah] that Maurine [Whipple] has evidently got an $1800 advance out of Simon & Schuster for a sequel to The Giant Joshua, and is settling down in S[alt]. L[ake]. on this $150 a month income to write the book. Whatever I have to say in criticism of Maurine as a person doesn't extend to her talents as a business woman. You and I are the merest amateurs, I assure you.

Speaking of Juanita, you somewhat misconstrued her letter to me and my reply, though this was natural enough. Juanita did not make a special point of writing this letter to me, nor did I reply in quite that vein. When she is moved to communicate on any subject, she sits down and writes me like that. I give her a kind of intellectual companionship, if you get what I mean. She is very reserved in St. George about her ideas and ambitions; in fact, nobody but her husband even knows she has been writing that book about Bunkerville. Her husband is not at all a literary person, or a person of literary interests, but I gather that he is a very fine, understanding fellow, wholly sympathetic to Juanita's interests and ambitions, and willing to take on his own shoulders certain of the family responsibilities and labor so that Juanita may, from time to time, have the freedom and the opportunity to get into things like books and history. Although I know him only as I find him reflected through Juanita, as our own intercourse has been limited to the few occasions he has written me from special circumstances, as when Juanita had an appendectomy a couple of years ago, I have a great deal of respect for him as a person, and could wish that more husbands were as kind, patient, and understanding with their wives when it comes to things not precisely held in common. Juanita doesn't "give out" at all with Maurine, and she has for her somewhat mixed feelings, not liking, precisely, but a certain amount of understanding and forebearance. Maurine is temporarily off her, but when she needs her for something, she'll be around again, Juanita remarks without any acidity at all.

Your own comments on Juanita's case interested me for the insight they afforded into your own personality as at present constituted. You seem to find it much more necessary to place things on a clearly rational level than I do. (For instance, without accepting the intervention of God in Juanita's experience, I am willing to admit of a dozen explanations of this, including pure chance, and feel no impulse to "explain" anything, merely being content with the fact that something happened and that it had an emotional impact upon Juanita.) I have an idea that you haven't come full circle yet in liberating yourself from the church. You have an intellectual but not yet an emotional objectivity about Mormonism. You are still in certain of a mood of rebellion and you sometimes give vent to a sharp intellectual scorn for the Mormon way of life which practically speaking is an intolerance for it. I suspect that you won't begin to have really generous feelings, a live-and-let-live philosophy, until you have finished disentangling yourself from the religion. Your intellectual detachment is only a way-station in your development—it aligns you with another culture, that of the world outside, but does not yet equip you to come to terms with the Mormons on the emotional plane. I am inclined to believe that this reflects a sense of emotional insecurity which may require several more years to overcome. You feel a need to maintain yourself in a status of rebellion, sharp, constant, and unequivocal, and on an unassailable intellectual plane, argument held within the limits of reason, and the quicksands of emotion fenced out. Your Achilles heel, of course, is your feeling about your father, and being conscious of that vulnerability you defend it at all times. After a while, I think you will no longer feel the need of fortification, no longer feel the imminent danger that if you relax you will be dragged by the heels back into the Mormon complex. When you reach that stage, you will feel more comfortable about Mormonism generally and your critical reactions, I think, will be softened with a wide acceptance of some of the human values.

And while we are psychologizing like this, let me hazard the opinion that your inability to settle upon a proper subject for a new book is an effect of this emotional complex. Otherwise I think you would be crammed with new ideas, bursting and running over with them, as authors tend to be. I don't think you fully recognize the extent to which your book was written out of an emotional compulsion, and the extent to which that compulsion persists. You are looking for something that will occupy and satisfy your emotions as Mormonism has done, and it is hardly likely that you will find such a topic or subject. Because writing Joseph's biography was your act of liberation and of exorcism. You might write on Mormonism again with the same pleasure and intensity—but this violates your idea of your growth as an artist, to be so limited in your subject-matter; you want to find something that will let you develop in new dimensions of your mind. This of course is a good and valid artistic impulse. I have brought up this subject, however, so you can wonder whether your decision about the desirability of doing any new subject suggested to you is not subconsciously affected by your feeling of emotional flatness. Maybe—and maybe not. I don't say decisively so, but I have been interested to wonder about the coloration of your thinking, and the formation of your essential attitudes.

The gossip about you is getting interesting! Now "adopted," and perhaps in due time, as you suggest, "bastard." Let's hope it doesn't reach the stage where they start to call you a bitch! Enough is too much!

A (somewhat delayed) happy new year to you!

Dale

21. To JUANITA BROOKS

Arlington, Virginia
23 May 1946

Dear Juanita,

While the spuds (or spud, rather; just one was left in the sack) are making up their minds to boil, let me get off a rebuke to you. Sister Brooks, I'll have you know that the time will never come when I will be too busy to read and enjoy any letter you may have the time and energy to write me, and don't you forget it. I may not be equal to replying in the moment, but this nevertheless holds true on the incoming end. It is always a delight to hear from you and to see your own characteristic (which is to say, vigorous, honest, and sensible) intelligence at work.

You had yourself quite a time in S[alt]. L[ake]., but the occurrence was by no means a waste. Even in the negative sense, you got something out of it. If nothing more than a consciousness of your own freedom.

. . . At this moment I hopped to the window to see if the plane in the sky was one of the Shooting Stars. It may well have been. They are much on everybody's mind here since a flight criss-crossed the town Sunday. They move less swiftly across the sky than my mind's eye had pictured, but just the same, they move so fast and with such a slim grace as to have an incredible beauty of their own. An ordinary plane looks like the sheerest earth-bound machine by contrast; the heart lifts to follow them. For all the world it is like seeing a half dozen flung stones across the sky, or a flock of starlings, with the curiously *flung* look they have always had for me. I wondered about their sound. Darel [McConkey] says it is a kind of shuddering roar, louder than ordinary planes. I imagine your kids would be delighted to see and hear them, airplanes bulking as they do in small boys', minds, these days.

. . . By this time the spud, with miscellaneous other things, is tucked under my belt. But I'll let things digest for a few moments while I gossip further with you.

The G[reat] S[alt] L[ake] book continues to be my No. 1 headache. And not the text only. I worked on it all day yesterday, till past midnight, without writing a word. I was assembling some base maps to send to the publisher so that he can start a cartographer on the maps. Fortunately the publisher sees eye to eye with me on the provision of adequate maps. They are most cooperative about it. But if I want maps that are accurate as to trails and routes, I must provide adequate base maps. You ought to see the collection I am sending as a starter—gasoline company maps, national forest maps, Geological Survey quadrangles, maps dating back to the Wheeler survey of the '80s, Bear River survey maps, and heaven knows what else. The job would be simple if quadrangles existed for the entire region. But map coverage has been of only the most spotty variety. Fortunately I hear that plans are on foot for the U[niversity] of U[tah] to cooperate with the G[eographical]. S[urvey]. in getting the rest of the state mapped. But that does me no good right now. The map I worked on yesterday is designed to show the country from Pilot Peak to Fort Bridger, and from Fort Fall to Utah Lake, with routes of the Bartleson company of 1841, Fremont of 1843 and 1845, Clyman, Bryant, Hastings, and the Donners, 1846, and the Mormons, 1847, plus some odds and ends. There will be at least three other maps in the book, one showing most of the West, one showing Great Salt Lake in some detail, and one showing the mythical lakes and rivers of the period before exploration. I have been thinking of one to illustrate my Mormon text, illustrating the spread of settlement, etc., but haven't made up my mind what I want. Maybe a kind of "Mormon empire" map to illustrate its geographic reach. Then also I am having to round up pictures from here, there, and everywhere (there will be 22 pages of pictures). All this, and I am not yet past the two-thirds mark! Sometimes I wonder why I ever took up authorship.

One thing that continues to astonish me is all this speculation about why Fawn [Brodie] wrote her book. It is so apparent to me that I've never even asked her, though she has made various remarks to confirm my understanding of her. It is strange that every motive is seized upon except for the obvious one. It makes me wonder if the generality of the Mormons don't know what it is to be scourged by a driving intellectual curiosity, to have the drive, the urge, and the will to *know* how something came about. You yourself understand this well enough, in your absorption with the M[ountain] M[eadows] M[assacre]. But how is it the people you talk to, even the ones with generous intentions, are such dead sticks? The origins of Fawn's book are akin to the origins of mine and of yours. There was more than met the eye in certain circumstances of history. How to account for it, and why had no one ever accounted for it? As a matter of fact, Fawn did not originally set out to write a biography of Joseph [Smith]. She got curious about the origin of the Book of Mormon, and what the scientific method could decide about that. This gave her, as she felt, a new way of looking at Joseph and the church, and her expanding interests ramified finally into a book. That was the basic drive. To it you must add the attraction exerted upon an artist by a vacuum in the literature, a craftsman's urge to do a job well—and also, in Fawn's case, the desire to interpret her own origins to herself. As she has remarked to me, the book has served her as the autobiographical novel serves many other writers; it has been a kind of catharsis for her.

The motivation is not greatly dissimilar in my own inquiries into Mormon history. It is a challenge to me to try to tread objectively between warring points of view, to get at the facts, uncover them for facts, and see what the facts have to say to a reasonable intelligence. If somebody else had already done this, my interest might have been deflected into something else. But as it is, I am neck-deep in the Mormons!

As a matter of fact, I have a parallel specialism, fur trade and exploration in the Far West. Here the challenge is not that the facts are so contradictory but that they are so sparse and so hard to come by. You have to piece out what you can from the merest skeleton of fact. About three-fourths of my library consists of "Western" source narratives, as distinguished from Mormon books. I think you would be surprised to run over my collection—the Lewis & Clark original journals, the Astorian books and journals, and dozens of others covering the era of the mountain men and the immigrants. When I get the Mormons off my chest, about five years from now, perhaps, I shall have some books to write on this general subject.

Getting back to Fawn's book, and leaving my autobiography to take care of itself, I find it interesting also, this need the people in Utah feel to interpret Fawn's book in terms of what her intention was, whether she was "sincere" or not. This seems to me an entire abdication of the critical function. Even if her intent had been malicious, that would not affect the solid fact of her book itself. Are the things she has written good history or not? Are they susceptible of being tested as fact or not? People leave these things aside and feel around for ideas about her to occupy their emotions. This is natural enough, perhaps. But one would look for more perceptive attitudes on the part of those who avowedly use their minds to think with, this fellow [Daryl] Chase,[1] for instance. The first rule for any book is to begin with the book, not the author. I think I apply this in my own critical reactions. I don't have an elevated idea of Maurine Whipple as a person, but I still feel that her Giant Joshua is the best romantic novel about the Mormons yet written; and I didn't qualify that with "romantic" until Scowcroft's book came along. Similarly I was not favorably impressed with Virginia Sorenson on the one occasion I met her, four years or so ago; I liked her husband much better. But the lady can write, there's no doubt about it; she can probably write still better than she has up to now. And if she can and does, more power to her, no matter what my personal reaction is to her.

[LDS writer] Claire Noall flitted through town last week, but I didn't see her. She expected to be back from N.Y. about the middle of this week, but I have not yet heard from her. In re[gard to] the diaries you speak of, I wonder if there isn't some mistake, when you say the ones she borrowed are missing. At least, the ones she had copied were those for 1846 and for 1849-50, and you include these among those you itemize to me.

Your anecdote of Marguerite [Sinclair[2]] is perfectly characteristic. Oh, well, if they [the *Utah Historical Quarterly*] expurgate the Tracy journal, I will promptly unexpurgate my copy by proofreading it against the original in the N[ew] Y[ork] P[ublic] L[ibrary], so I, at least, have nothing to lose. I waged the same battle once over the Priddy Meeks journal, and it was because of my announced intention to quote from the original instead of an emasculated version when, in due course, I used the material that [J. Cecil] Alter elaborately prefaced his editing with a statement of what he did to the journal. So I figure that if only in a negative way, I sometimes have a good influence on Utah historical publication!

I am interested to hear that you have several times reviewed Children of the Covenant. Summarize for me what you tell your audiences, Juanita. You talked about it when you first read it, but what you said to me is not necessarily what you would say in a formal public review of it.

I picked up a copy of Lillian McQuarrie's book off Brentano's library discard table a week or so ago but haven't had any time to look into it. This summer, sometime. Do you know her personally? What do you think of her?

Returning to another old theme, I asked my mother again about the James S. Brown papers. She has learned that they are in the possession of a daughter, Louette, who is a Mrs. Henry Tanner (a 5th or 6th wife, hence evidently getting on in years). I gather that she is found a somewhat different person by some of her own family, so if you follow up on her in S[alt]. L[ake]., you will no doubt want to play your cards close to your chest. I don't know what the address is, but it is doubtless in the city directory or phone book. I also asked Mother if Nora Shumway knew anything about the Charles Shumway journals, if he kept any. She says she will ask when she sees her next. As I understand you know her also, you might want to inquire yourself, though I imagine his journals, if any, will turn out to be in the [LDS] H[istorian's]. O[ffice].

And speaking of journals, there is a typewritten copy of an Oregon journal of 1854 in the Library of Congress which is something of a treasure. It has certain naturalistic comments such as I have seen in few if any other journals. Although it is several years since I looked at it, I remember, for example, one entry about like this: "Got up at daybreak and you know what was the first thing we done, as ussual." (I've sometimes thought that it would make an interesting chapter in social history to know just how people managed this part of their lives along the Overland Trail—how it accorded with their notions of modesty and convenience, and so on. But for the most part one has to fill in this part of the record of the trail from one's own imagination.)

Well, as you can see, it is easy to talk to you, once I get started. I had better break off, I guess. I'll just squeeze in a comment that Ray West's introduction to his anthology, which was published Monday, strikes me as having a lot of philosophical nonsense in it. He is talking with his eye on Big League Criticism, not the authors and materials, in discoursing on moral facts, etc. Not that there aren't some interesting observations made, but in my view his discourse is inadequate and in large part irrelevant. He should look to social history, not to esthetics, if he wants to know why we have some writers now and didn't have some a while back. I might add that I am annoyed with him over his reprinting my piece on Mormon novelists. I gave my permission if he made certain necessary corrections, but I'll be damned if he made the corrections, and there are some brand new errors and elisions to boot. Incidently, I think his excerpt from [Maurine Whipple's] The Giant Joshua, when stacked up alongside the excerpt from [Vardis Fisher's] Children of God, neatly demonstrates my point that the former is much superior as a novel.

Sister Brooks, thassall! Good night, sleep tight.

Dale

P.S. Juanita, I'm going to ask you to do something for me, if, as, and when you can. I would like very much to get a record of Brigham Young's wives and of the women sealed to him. Fawn told me she saw the card catalogue containing this information at the Genealogical Society while in Utah last year, but the time equation was such that she couldn't copy any of these cards, and just barely did get the dope on Joseph, in fact. I am well assured that Brigham had more wives than the family has ever acknowledged. For example, my Journal History notes record the death in 1846 of his wife, Mary Pierce, who has never been listed as a wife in any published record. This was not the same person as Margaret Pierce, who lived to a ripe old age. It may be that since Fawn's book was published the records are inaccessible. But if by hook or crook they can be got at, I would give a great deal to have the authentic information. If you know someone doing genealogical research, for instance, I would be glad to employ such a person to do this particular job of research. I would like to have such records for everyone who was an apostle in 1844 or became one by 1849, but I would settle for the information about Brigham Young if I couldn't do better.

Also, I ran into Nels [Anderson] on the streetcar earlier this week. For a month past he has been with National Housing and is, he says, busier than hell. He showed me the notes of the speech he was going to make about Harry Hopkins at the Hopkins memorial services Wednesday, a speech he has since made. He looks well and says his wife and son are fine.

[1] Daryl Chase, a graduate of the University of Chicago Divinity School, had written in 1944 *Joseph Smith the Prophet, as He Lives in the Hearts of His People*. In 1954, he became president of Utah State University in Logan, Utah.

[2] Marguerite Sinclair was a secretary at and later secretary/manager of the Utah State Historical Society between 1940 and 1949.

22. To FAWN BRODIE

Arlington, Virginia
June 1946

Dear Fawn,

The date being what it is, it is to be hoped that you are somebody's mother by now, and that you have come safe and sound and triumphant through the ordeal. I shall be anxiously waiting to hear that you have made out all right, for notwithstanding medical advances, childbearing is serious business and there is always that great big IF to worry about. I've been looking for some word from my sister, who has been daily if not hourly looking for her big moment for two weeks past, but up to Wednesday night the mad dash to the hospital had not commenced, and the lack of news is to be taken as probably meaning that things are still status quo. My mother is driving east with her sister and two friends, and who knows, they may yet arrive in New York for zero hour. They are due here Thursday night, and may stay on with me a day or two, depending on what the news is from Brooklyn. Things worked out very well at my mother's end, for my younger brother, who has been in Japan since October, arrived back home Thursday in time for Mother to see something of him before she shoved off Saturday morning. That is more split-second timing than I am able to manage. Unless [the] O[ffice of] P[rice] A[dministration] is killed dead, the probability is that I won't launch into the Guggenheim thing until March, what with my inability to get a car, and the G[reat S[alt] L[ake] book taking so much time that should have gone into Mormon research. So my timing is months off, a sad contrast to my mother's.

Incidentally, my mother writes me that she found out that [Albert E.] Bowen[1] wrote the onslaught on your book, though she didn't specify how she knew. Perhaps through one of her friends who is a friend of the Harold B. Lees.[2] As you remarked, the Bowen piece was more cogent than many of the critiques we have seen. I believe you will be interested, however, to read Juanita Brooks's reaction to this, written me some weeks ago before I had seen it myself. The letter is perfectly characteristic of Juanita herself, and typical of the kind she writes me every now and then, so for that reason also I think it will interest you.

Returning to Bowen, however: I think it is a comment on the Mormon provincial mind that Bowen did not have the intelligence to be urbane in his review. If [Robert Joseph] Dwyer stuck his neck out and asked to have his block knocked off, Bowen would have been smart to be ever so much the gentleman and do the job with a scalpel instead of a bludgeon. As it is, he and his church come out as a pair of plug-uglies—capable, of course, but still plug-uglies. Bowen is perfectly right in his contention that the naturalism of your book can be turned as tellingly on the Roman Catholics as upon the Mormons. This was a good point and he could have shown up Dwyer and at the same time made himself out a very forbearing Christian. But his mind is evidently not of that caliber. I don't know whether the churlish headline for the review is his idea or that of the [Deseret] News, but this is of the same kidney.

But as you guess, I am definitely annoyed at his use of the quotation from my S[aturday] R[eview of] L[iterature] review. For one thing, he quotes as much as, if not more so, out of context in using this review as you do in any accusation he levels against you. For another thing, his use of part of my review is based on nothing more substantial than a printer's boner! You may recall that when my review was published, I mentioned to you a word transposition in the next to the last paragraph. Well, let me now be explicit. The original text of my review read, " . . . may be subject to both a kinder and a *more far-rangingly objective* reinterpretation." The way it came out in print was, "a *far more rangingly objective* reinterpretation," and this, I submit, is something else again. However, this review proves me wrong in one thing. When Darrell Greenwell told me that my review of your book would probably exile me permanently, I asked him how any church member would ever find out I had reviewed it. I can only suppose that Bowen read the blurb Knopf used and looked up the entire review at the library!

The [Hugh] Nibley pamphlet [*No Ma'am That's Not History*] came just after your letter did. I think it is something of a slapstick performance, and the irony of it is, Nibley [a professor at LDS church-owned Brigham Young University] is much more intoxicated with his own language than you, the "glib English major," are. Nibley's law of parsimony is all right, but no church member has ever been willing to apply that law to the *record* of Joseph's life. It is applied only to the *belief* about Joseph's life, which is another proposition entirely. The interesting thing is that both Nibley and Bowen actually leave severely alone the factual structure of your book. Their quarrel is with words alone. Change, say, 20 phrases in your book and you have eliminated nine-tenths of their criticisms without in any way impairing the structure of the biography. Actually, you are being challenged on very few fundamental grounds. The court record, chiefly. I am surprised at how that has aroused everybody. You recall that it aroused Durham, also. Well, if that record is to be found in any town or county archives, you may be sure I will find it when I lay hands on a car. The thing that worries me is whether the Saints may not undertake such a hunt in advance of me. I can just imagine some zealous missionary confiscating the page from a record and shipping it to Salt Lake City so that the experts can look it over and put it away, satisfied it is a forgery!

If you knew as much about [German historian Eduard] Meyer as you tell me, you knew more than I did. All I knew about Meyer was that [George B.] Arbaugh used him [in his 1932 *Revelation in Mormonism*]. I wouldn't have thought that any foreign scholar ever made a critical investigation that was worth a damn about Mormonism, and even Meyer will have to convince me, no matter what his attainments may have been in other fields. But it will be a damnably annoying chore for me to find out what he had to say.[3] Someone could translate aloud to you, but for me such a translation would involve an actual written translation, a tough proposition to face. I suppose I will have to get someone to read it and summarize what it's all about, then in one fashion or another, I can get an abstract or translation of anything worth thinking about. I promise you that no more than you will I learn German for the single purpose of using this one book.

At this point I go round up your letter, and I see that all this time I have been passing by the big news it contained. A thing like that is a rude shock, there's no two ways about it. If one could resign from the church, you and I would have resigned ten years ago. But one cannot resign, one can only be excommunicated, and I would guess that as in my own case, you did not demand excommunication because there was no point to causing needless pain to numerous relatives. Anyhow, I hope you aren't prepared to retire forever from the soil of Zion. When I finally settle down in Utah in a place of my own, I will expect you to come visit me, and we can have your picture in the society section with a caption perhaps like this, "Mrs. Fawn M. Brodie, the well-known Mormon apostate who is now visiting Mr. & Mrs. Dale L. Morgan," etc.! O.K.? Anyhow, by that time I may be in your company, though it is true I don't have any vindictive avuncular church authorities in the undergrowth of my life.

Turning from persiflage to more serious things, I am sure you will be sorry to hear that Darel and Anna McConkey three weeks ago finally lost the long fight for their 9-months-old baby's life. The poor kid just didn't get a break from life. His heart was so greatly enlarged that at the time of his death it occupied four-fifths of the lung cavity. He was in oxygen all the time, the last two months of his life, and had been much of the time for two months before that, but nothing could save him in the end.

I had lunch with [LDS writer] Claire Noall on May 28. She dropped me a card in passing through two weeks before, and looked me up on her way back. It seems that she has twice rewritten her novel since I saw it, and her agent, who has faith in it, is trying to market it for her. She worked with Brewster Ghiselin at the U[niversity] of U[tah] during the school year, and feels that she learned much from him to improve her writing. She has completed her work for a Master's except for the thesis, and is embarking on a biography of Willard Richards for that. She hopes, but does not really expect, to have the MS done by the end of the year. She went to see [LDS church president] George Albert Smith and somebody else I forget, [George F.] Richards [president of the Quorum of the Twelve Apostles] perhaps, about getting unrestricted access to the church archives for writing her biography. It seems that her mention in your book had put the touch of the devil on her, and she had to do some convincing, but finally got full pledges of cooperation and no censorship! I asked Claire if there had been any reactions to your acknowledgments, and she said some, adding that she told people she was proud to be mentioned in such a scholarly work. From what she says, Levi Edgar Young[4] is displaying a much more liberal attitude toward the book than many others of the dignitaries.

This brings us back to the familiar subject of your book. There is a favorable paragraph about it in the first June issue of Christian Century, in case you haven't seen this, and I also saw a review of it in the current issue of New York History. The latter reviewer is the same fellow who wrote that piece on early Mormonism I showed you a year or more ago, and to some extent it reflects his convictions that he knows more about significant parts of your background than you do!

By the way, this Father Dwyer is not just a run-of-the-mill cleric. His doctoral thesis written at Catholic University in 1942, "The Gentile Comes to Utah," is one of the few first rate monographs in Mormon history that has been written, though I feel it gives inadequate attention to the economic background of the religious and social conflict it more particularly dwells upon. One can count on the fingers of one hand the works of equivalent stature in Mormon and Utah history. I understand that personally he is something of a conceited egg, but on the basis of this thesis he is a Grade-A workman. The Yale library no doubt has a copy if you want to look it up. I like one phrase in his bibliographical discussion, when he says that one Catholic historical work in Utah repeats the errors of an earlier one "almost verbatim."

I looked up Josiah Thorpe in the Union Catalog but he is not listed, so I suppose I will have to chase this guy down in Missouri libraries—when I get there. I have copied the [B. H.] Roberts Parallel [regarding the Book of Mormon] in odd moments at the office and have just finished it, so I return it with the other stuff in this envelope.

And that reminds me. Last week while looking at Mrs. Elizabeth Kane's *Twelve Mormon Homes*, published in 1874 and descriptive of the trip she made with [her husband] Thomas L. through Utah in 1873, I noticed that she mentioned (on p. 3) an encounter with a woman who told her positively that Joseph had revealed the principle of plural marriage to her 36 years before, and that she had become his wife. Mrs. Kane says the woman was now the wife of a high church member, but regrettably she does not give her name. If true (that is, if the recollection of the date is true, for there is little doubt about the incident itself), we have an interesting reference of 1837 on plural marriage.

I guess I'd better get started on a new chapter of my book. But let me first say that I seem to recall this Claire Stewart Boyer as a professional book reviewer in Salt Lake—the lecturer type, that is. You gave me some leaflets a while back, sent you by your mother, referring to these Sons of Aaron. I guess I'll have to dig up the dope about them when I get back to Utah.

All this literary gossip! Still, we have to dispose of it when it comes up. Suppose you write me next about yourself in the newest and most personal sense, how things went at the hospital, what the new accession to the family looks like, how you're feeling, and all those non-literary details which interest me. Also tell me if Dickie has realized what was coming in his life. I guess that preparation of an older child for a new birth is one of the most important jobs a mother has to do, to minimize as far as possible the psychological shock inevitably involved.

With very best wishes, now especially,

Dale

P.S. I omitted to thank you for the photos, which arrived safely some time ago. You may keep the Rocky Mountain Review, as I have another. Oh yes, and have you Stanley Ivins's[5] address?

[1] Albert E. Bowen (1875-1953), an LDS apostle since 1937, condemned Brodie's *No Man Knows My History* in an unsigned book review published in the LDS *Church News* for 11 May 1946.

[2] Harold B. Lee (1899-1973) was a colleague of Bowen in the Quorum of the Twelve Apostles. Named an apostle in 1941, he became LDS church president in 1972 and died late the following year.

[3] Meyer's book, *Ursprung und Geschichte der Mormonen, mit Exkursen uber die Anfang des Islams des Christentums*, published in 1912, was available only in German.

[4] Levi Edgar Young (1874-1963) was a member of the LDS church's First Quorum of the Seventy. He had taught history at the University of Utah, had twice been appointed president of the Utah State Historical Society, and was author of *The Founding of Utah*.

[5] Stanley Ivins, a Salt Lake City businessman, was an avid researcher of Mormon history, particularly polygamy. His correspondence with Morgan is housed in the Utah State Historical Society.

23. To FAWN BRODIE

Arlington, Virginia
19 August 1947

Dear Fawn,

So much stuff is piling up, that I think I had better send it all on to you to get it out from underfoot. This place is in such a constant mess these days that nothing is secure, and I am afraid matters are going to get a lot worse before they improve.

At [the] L[ibrary of]. C[ongress]. I've been engaged with a fascinating new field of research. I regret that I didn't get into it months ago, and now I will only be able to handle it on a cross section basis. That is, the impact of Mormonism on the American religious press, 1830-1844. It is a subject that merits a doctoral thesis, but I suspect that it will be many a long year before anyone has (1) enough interest; and (2) the time, patience, and money to follow up the complications the research involves. Just to construct a master bibliography of this press would be a heroic job in itself, and to locate and consult the files of these periodicals in libraries scattered all over the East is a job in its own right. I'll do what I can this fall, but I have no illusions as to the thoroughness of what I can accomplish, within the limitations of the time and money I will have at my disposal.

But, just for example, have a look at the item I found in the Evangelical Magazine and Gospel Advocate for April 9, 1831. Here is what we have been looking for, a contemporary account of that 1826 trial. True, it is not yet absolutely contemporary, not an 1826 newspaper report, which I hope eventually to lay by the heels, but one written within five years of the trial, and confirming and to some extent explaining the [William D.] Purple reminiscences and the trial record. I suspect that the author of this letter is the "young man named Benton" whom Joseph [Smith] mentions (Hist[ory of the]. Church I:87), though he would seem to be a Universalist rather than a Presbyterian. Also, this letter explains much more about the 1830 trial than we can gather from Joseph's own account; any resemblance between this account and Joseph's is purely coincidental.

(Incidently, I had a letter from Stan Ivins last night, saying that he had shown his findings to [Francis W.] Kirkham,[1] who had asked permission to use the material in the new edition of his book. He said Kirkham was glad to get the material, but seemed upset when he saw what it added up to. I am sending Stan a copy of this 1831 letter, too, but requesting him not to give it to Kirkham for the present, as I want to see if Kirkham faces up like a scholar to the facts you and [Stanely Ivins] have dug up, or whether his emotional loyalties override.)

And still on the subject of this letter, I inquire whether you tried to trace that 1830 trial as well as the 1826 one. I am under the impression you did, and that the records, if any, went up in smoke. Also, I damn well wonder what happened finally to Josiah Stowell. I have never heard anything of him after 1830. I wonder if he was alive in 1838 when Joseph made so bold as to assert in the Elder's Journal that he had done some digging for S[towell]. but soon prevailed on him to stop, &c. &c. Also, I would give a lot to know just what [Sidney] Rigdon was told and what he thought, and why, when he looked into the 1830 trials after his first encounter with Joseph.

Other stuff I send you (if you can read the wretched carbons) includes early interviews with Joseph and other interesting odds and ends, including, from the Vermont newspaper, what is the first long review of the Book of Mormon I have seen, antedating Alexander Campbell's by some four months. One of the communications by the "Clericus" incorporates the earliest letter about the Mormons I have seen in print, October 18, 1830.

I have been working weekdays in a hot study room in the main building at L[ibrary of]. C[ongress]., and on Saturdays and Sundays, theoretically by way of vacation, I have gone back to that problem that has obsessed me since the beginning of the year, what is said about the Mormons in the newspapers. I have now examined the Vermont newspapers for the 1830-34 period, anyhow, and the scattered New York papers down to the G's. The Vermont papers paid off with a story or part of a story from the New York Morning Courier and Enquirer which shows that my suspicion is well founded about the possibility of there being materials in the 1831 files, which L.C. does not possess. The section quoted form the Courier & Enquirer, which must be only part of a longer story, has all sorts of fascinating angles. From the reference to [William Wine] Phelps [an early Mormon convert] at the end, I suspect that the account was written from Canandaigua [New York], maybe even first published in a Canandaigua paper. But in this letter, who is the Ex-Preacher from Ohio, Rigdon? If so, this must be the earliest attribution in print of the Book of Mormon to Rigdon. Also note the reference to the "gingerbread factory." This and other things in the story make me suspect that the entire story in the Courier & Enquirer has some information about the earlier history of the Smith family.

Along with this stuff, I send you various items about Lucinda Morgan [wife of William Morgan, anti-masonic turncoat and martyr of the 1820s, who later became one of Joseph Smith's plural wives] which clear up some of the details about her history before she was swept up in the current of Mormon affairs. The Ohio Star is entirely correct, by the way, in saying [Martin] Harris [one of the three witnesses to the Book of Mormon] was a renouncing Mason. He and W. W. Phelps both had signed the so-called anti-masonic declaration of independence at Le Roy, N.Y., on July 4, 1829. Both were third degree Masons.

Before sending this off, I will write out for you a list of various corrections and modifications I would recommend for your book in its next printing or the ultimate revised edition; quite a lot of things have come to my attention of late, and I will note them down for you before I forget them, alas for the fallibility of human memory.

What I send you is merely error-in-detail. I disagree with you somewhat in some structural matters of interpretation, as for example the development of the first political and economic antagonism in Illinois, at Warsaw in particular, but this can wait until I have written my own version, and we can then thrash it out to our mutual satisfaction.

I am also sending my own publisher a list of corrections which will be about as long as the list I send you, in preparation for the second printing, though Lord knows when that will be. He writes me sadly about the dull times that have afflicted the book business for a year or more past.

Well, be a good girl. I'll see you about the middle of October, I imagine since I expect to spend ten days or two weeks in N.Y. before moving on north, and expect to clear out of Washington October 1. I hope the traveling weather is decent this fall. It's too bad you aren't a go-to-meetin' gal who could remember the weather in her morning prayers.

Dale

[1] Francis W. Kirkham, an LDS historian, had compiled in 1942 a collection of documents relating to the early years of Mormonism entitled *A New Witness for Christ in America*. After Morgan criticized his omissions (see Letter Number 27), Kirkham issued a second volume in 1951, based on material Morgan had called to his attention.

24. To MADELINE MCQUOWN

Windsor, Vermont
1 November 1947

Dear Madeline,

The above address is probably most familiar to you as the place where Solomon Mack [maternal grandfather of Joseph Smith] published his *Narrative*, about 136 years ago, but at the moment it happens also to be the place where I am bedded down for the night. Or at any rate, I am sitting on a bed there writing this, and in due course will claim the bed in its rightful function.

I have had quite a busy day, and I will write you about it while it is still fresh in memory. To bring you up to date first—after mailing your letter Wednesday morning I drove up to Burlington through a drizzle and heavy overcast, getting there about 11. I got a dim glimpse of Lake Champlain as I was approaching Burlington, but that was the last I saw of this famous lake, notwithstanding Burlington is a "lake port." I worked at the University of Vermont from 11 to 7 p.m., when I finished. I then ate at a Chinese cafe and hunted up a tourist room, finding an agreeable one. Next morning I drove across the mountains to Montpelier, still through that drizzly overcast; I ate lunch, got a haircut, worked in the State Library till it closed at 5, then hunted up a room again, had some dinner, and went to see a good-for-nothing movie called Second Chance. Friday I worked in the library until late afternoon, and would have liked to work Saturday morning also, but the necessity of getting to Woodstock so as not to be stymied by Sunday got me out of town late in the afternoon. I drove the 50-odd miles in about an hour and a half, in darkness the last half of the way, though the clouds had broken up earlier in the day. I wasn't much taken with Woodstock on my arrival there; the place seemed to be preoccupied with some kind of a kids' Hallowe'en festival, and a more lackadaisical town, from the tourist's viewpoint, I never did see. I put up at the hotel finally, which only confirmed me in my experience that tourist homes are infinitely superior to hotels, dollar for dollar.

Not to go into that subject exhaustively, I had breakfast at the White Cupboard Inn, a really lovely place to stay if you have what I suppose it costs to stay there, then headed for the courthouse. The County Clerk and I had a helluva time finding what I wanted, the court records concerning the counterfeiters of 1807; we finally turned up in the Supreme Court records of the county an account of the trail of Beniah Woodward, but the Abner Hayes business, as related by Fawn [Brodie], was not so readily disposed of. I finally found a lead, and the county clerk obligingly promised to search the files of writs in the vault, something that may take several days, and send me what I want in care of Fawn. So then the courthouse closed for the day, and without taking time for lunch, I backtrailed my route of the night before as far as Bethel and then turned east in quest of Joseph Smith's beginnings. I took some pictures, but have grave doubts how they will come out, despite perfect sunshine, because I did not adjust my light meter to black and white film after emptying it of that color film, and all the pictures I took this afternoon will almost certainly be overexposed. So let me write us both some descriptions we will want to have anyway.

I don't know whether you have seen the White River. It is really a beautiful stream running often over a series of stone ledges. The sky frequently is imprisoned in dark pools which ripple blue at the little rapids; at this season, at least, it is a placid and wholly lovely little river. On both sides the hills rise in a manner greatly reminiscent of the Provo and Weber [rivers in Utah], except of course that the hills do not give rise to mountains proper. There are great outcroppings of gray stone here and there, accented by the varied colors of lichen. Now, in November, the evergreens are the dominant note on the hillsides, set as they are amid the gray skeletons of the deciduous trees. The road winds down the valley, occasionally underpassing the railroad, and passing through the intermittent villages set in the widened valley bottoms.

I went to the most important place first, the old Smith farm. The road to this is located just beyond (in the direction I was going, i.e., east) South Royalton, which differs from the other villages in lying across the river from the road, reached by a narrow bridge. A little over a mile down the river from this bridge is the (somewhat) graveled road to the old Smith farm. This turns off almost at right angles from the main highway (State 14) and climbs sharply back into the hills. The road winds past farmlands, some of them fenced with piled gray stone, up into the hills for a little more than two miles, forking finally about half a mile below the old farm. I believe the left fork of this road goes only a few more hundred yards to some farm buildings; the right fork climbs up a hill and so arrives at the old farm.

I couldn't make out the dimensions of the old place from this cursory inspection without benefit of a guide, but the house itself, where the church cottage now stands, is situated on a lesser elevation rimmed about by gently rising hills. To the west these hills fall away in a kind of gap, so that the blue hills of the White River Valley give an accent of distance to this horizon.

The air today was winey and fresh, wholly delicious, the very smell of October in the hills. The rolling adjacent land seems still to be farmed after a fashion. I noticed that the soil was rocky still. I climbed over a barbed wire fence north of the place and climbed the higher of the hills looming above it until checked by a more formidable barbed wire fence I didn't think it worthwhile to climb, as I had altitude enough for the picture I wanted. I noticed that in this field above the old farm was a good deal of cutover land, with small stumps to give me an idea of some of the problems this land may have afforded when the original stand of timber was cleared off by the Smiths. Scenically the place was lovely even at this season, when the grays and russets and duns of November reign in the hills, for the hills still were carpeted by a brave fresh green of grass.

To return to the place, the [LDS] church has built a miniature Washington Monument behind the cottage to commemorate its prophet. There is a studious indirectness about all the signs around; not for the world has the church brought you up here to proselytize you, but you are welcome to visit the cottage, etc. The cottage, so called, is a pretty elaborate farmhouse, with roofs painted a startling green and walls painted so white as to look almost enameled. Another coat of paint was being applied today, the two painters and I being the only ones around.

I drove on back down to the main highway, then turned back up it to the road which intersects it at the South Royalton bridge. I turned up that road and drove five miles or so up it to Tunbridge, where the Smiths also lived at one time. This is located in the valley of the North Branch of White River, which is another such stream as the parent river. The widening of the valley in which Tunbridge is situated is a little reminiscent of Ogden Hole, in miniature, of course, and without the rugged backdrop of high mountains.

I here turned about and drove back down to State 14, then headed southeasterly for White River Junction. Sharon is another widening in the White River Valley four miles down from the road that leads up to the Smith farm. (The farm itself is located at the township boundary between South Royalton and Sharon; I'm not sure which side of the boundary line.) By now it was well past three, so I just kept right on going. I drove to White River Junction, then across the Connecticut to Hanover, a beautiful college town, thence south a few miles to Lebanon, thence to West Lebanon and on to Hanover again with the idea of staying all night there. The Hanover Inn had only regretful smiles, however, so I drove across the river to Norwich, Vermont, to try the Norwich Inn. There was nothing stirring there either, so I concluded to move on down US 5 until I had a chance to eat somewhere, then continue till I hit a likely tourist home.

Now, however, the semi-machine age caught up with me. It had been on my trail all day, as I had a helluva time starting the car at noon, and a helluva struggle everytime I tried to start it thereafter, even when the engine was warm. I didn't like the way it was behaving, but had been too busy to monkey with it.

As I got to the junction of US 5 and US 4 above the White River Junction, however—in fact, with the nose of the car poked out into the road, the engine stalled, and this time not all my skills or anathemas would start it again. I got a car behind me to push me across the road, then summoned help with the aid of a Shell service station there at the corner. I was towed to a garage a half-mile away, and a couple of mechanics went to work. They found that my points and condenser were virtually burnt up; they installed new ones, and the car practically exploded into life. So after an hour's delay I got started south again. But the semi-machine age is still with us. The gas pedal acts as peculiarly as hell. I noticed this even before leaving the garage, that the engine seemed to race when it should be idling. The fellow listened to it for a moment, then punched the gas pedal, and the car idled properly, indicating that the pedal had become merely stuck. But I have since discovered that it continues to stick. I drove thirty miles or so down the river to here, the first likely stopping place, and the car would even climb hills at 30 miles an hour with my foot off the pedal, which gives you an idea. I discovered that my tapping the pedal sharply with my foot, I could stop that racing effect, but next time I stepped on the gas, it was "stuck" that way all over again. I gassed up after reaching here, and had the service station fellow look at it, but he wasn't much help. He said the gas pedal linkage was well covered with grease and dirt, probably the cause of the sticking; he oiled the whole thing and hoped that would help, but it hasn't as yet. If the car will behave itself fairly decently until Monday, when I should find a Hudson place open somewhere along the line, I will be properly grateful.

I won't mail this letter until after I have had a look, or tried to have a look, at Whitingham tomorrow. So, being tired and dirty, I will now break off in favor of a bath and pick up tomorrow where I now leave off.

Whitingham, Vermont
Sunday, Nov. 2, 1 p.m.

This letter is picked up about ten yards from the Brigham Young stone. I have been talking to the owner of the property and have taken some pictures, and now I write this on the spot before rolling down hill again.

Whitingham is tucked away in the hills, a rolling upland country chiefly subsisted, I should imagine, by dairy farms. I understand there is a good deal of lumbering done in the neighborhood also. The old Young farm is reached by a road which joins the main highway, Vermont 8, almost at right angles in the tiny town center, a rocky, ill-kept and steep road which immediately climbs a hill, winding only slightly, to this eminence directly west of the town. A little to the west of north spread the waters impounded by the Whitingham

Dam, a beautiful blue sheet of water covering what in Brigham Young's time was the valley bottom of the Deerfield River.

The site of the old Young farmhouse even today is remarkably tumbled, with rocks outcropping everywhere. An old stone fence about 10 yards west of the Young monument is very old indeed and may well date to John Young's time. A scattered conifer or two grows on the property. Looking at it, you are at a loss to see how the Youngs made a living, for dairy farming was not then what it is today, and the land doesn't look productive enough for most crops. Today is wonderfully warm and sunny, with a fresh coolness in the air for all the world like October or even September in the mountains at home.

This is much wilder country than that where Joseph Smith was born, the land more tumbled and broken, to the degree that any eastern hill country can so be termed. Gray swaths of trees band the hillsides, set off by the fresh green of the conifers, for all the world like an aspen forest in Utah. Lovely country for a country home, in our modern thinking, at any rate.

The fellow who owns this property is Walter Hunt, Charlemont, Mass.

He bought the land, I understood him to say, about ten years ago. At any rate, he put up the cabin a hundred yards up the hillside about ten years ago, he said. He is, I should judge, about Dean Brimhall's age. He evidently likes this section very well for a weekend retreat. He says quite a lot of people come up here to visit the Brigham Young marker, Mormons mostly, from all over. It is not here, however, that the Church plans to erect its monument to Young. Instead, this is going to be on Town Hill, a prominent elevation lying over the horizon to the south of here. Hunt, who is an extremely pleasant and obliging fellow, doesn't know exactly what the dimensions of the old farm were, or whether the Youngs owned the higher hillside on which he has built his cabin; he thinks their property line ran along the road which separates this hill from the Young marker, the road on which I am now parked.

Well, I must get moving. The damned gas pedal is still misbehaving, and the car isn't happy except when it is going 50 miles an hour. I should imagine I will be in or near Boston by the time I mail this, as it is about 30 miles or so to Greenfield, Mass., and then about a hundred miles to Boston. I'll get out and get you a souvenir stone from the old Young property, then start down his hill and commence sailing.

Fitchburg, Mass.

Well, it's 7 p.m., and not to spin out this epic too much, I'm settled down for the night, and damned glad to be here alive and whole. A more nerve-wracking afternoon I never spent. It is all very well, this business of cars that will drive themselves, but not when they fight you and the brake. This afternoon has seen such colossal absurdities as that heavy car driving itself up a long hill at 45 miles an hour with my foot on the brake all the way to keep it from going even faster. On a country road this might be fun; in heavy traffic it is not. I have kept going only because I had doubts that any mechanics in the country I've gotten over have the experience to cope with the intricacies of a Hudson's throttle linkage. But the other side of Fitchburg my brakes gave way under the severe usage they've had today, and the last ten miles I've kept going only because there was no place to stop. I hope and believe my worries are now over, however, because two miles down the road I passed a Hudson Service place which ought to be open in the morning. With luck I'll get into Boston with a whole skin by noon tomorrow; from this tourist home where I now am, I'm 46 miles from there.

Except for the constant fight with the car all afternoon, I should have enjoyed the drive very much indeed. Massachusetts 2 is a magnificent highway across the most magnificent terrain I should imagine the state can offer, with some breathtaking summits. This is called the Mohawk Trail, whether with any good reason I don't know. Sometime I hope we can drive over it together under rather more pleasant circumstances. You would even like to eat where I did, at a Duncan Hines approved place in Shelburne Falls, for which today was the last day of its season. They scalped me with a 3-buck bill for the dinner, but as it was the first full dinner, or full meal of any description, I've had since yesterday, I had it coming to me. It began with assorted hors d'oevres, shrimp cocktail, pear and cheese salad, chicken broth, roast turkey with dressing, succotash and French fries, then a waffle with maple syrup, and finally ice cream; I turned down coffee, by this time having no room for it.

I hope there will be some word from you awaiting me in Boston. As for me, I'm pooped, and I am now going to sprawl out on this bed and read the morning papers and let the world go to hell as it may choose for a while.

Dale

25. To FAWN BRODIE

Rochester, New York
2 December 1947

Dear Fawn,

You beat me to the punch, in that your letter turned up at the post office today before I could write mine tonight. I am glad to have some word of you, but very sorry to learn that the flu has been hurling you around by the tail. Your letter of yesterday morning, I hope, inaugurates more enjoyable times for you.

The snowstorm in which I departed from Ithaca Saturday morning slowly gave way, and by the time I reached Canandaigua, the skies were mostly clear if plenty cold. I decided to keep right on going in the hope that I would be able to work the Rochester library Sunday, come back to Canandaigua Monday, and strike out for the west today. As it turned out, to my considerable surprise (even the Salt Lake library is not so provincial), the library was closed on Sunday, so I ambled back to Canandaigua Sunday afternoon, going via Mendon, worked at Canandaigua yesterday, drove to here at 10 last night, labored here today, and in the morning am heading for Cleveland, with a slight detour to see what can be seen of Niagara Falls.

From Canandaigua Saturday I drove via Palmyra. I think no one but you will know what I mean precisely when I tell you that the ghosts of my youth were trampling around like a herd of elephants. The Hill Cumorah, the Sacred Grove, and all the rest of it. The ultimate effect was comic, but even as I grinned, I was again a seven-year-old sitting on a tiny red chair which with others made a circle around a pretty Sunday school teacher to learn about the marvelous things that have come to pass in these last days. There is no shaking off the emotional impact of one's childhood experiences. (But I remember also that the Sunday school teacher's slip was showing, an observation which in my adult years I am inclined to think had some kind of erotic significance, one of my earliest erotic impressions. Maybe this shows how the devil was after me even at the age of 7.)

The Hill Cumorah rather surprised me. I had envisioned a more symmetrical geological formation, and had not looked for so narrow a ridge to be the "Mormon Hill" of local repute. It was less high, too, than I had anticipated. Also it was damned cold on top of the hill, and I am willing to bet you that if the Angel Moroni had appeared in December instead of September, Joseph would simply have pulled the covers tighter around his neck and told the angel to go find him another translator.

From any documentary point of view, my trip down into the Susquehanna country was a complete bust. I did not, of course, go back over the ground you did, but sought to find out what I could about the Colesville trial and whether Stowell was buried in the Harmony cemetery. The former effort was a complete bust, all trails leading me ultimately to the town clerk in Harpursville, who was not at all helpful, saying that a fire in 1895 burnt down records of earlier date. I endeavored to find out if anyone knew anything about Chamberlain, the judge of the 1830 trail, but the town clerk thought there were no descendants in the country and had apparently never heard the name. I have since discovered that there is a Chamberlain in Greene and another in Afton, so in due course I will write both to see if there is any relationship. I photographed the Stowell house in Afton where Joseph married Emma, and also photographed the gravestone at Harmony, using up all my white chalk in the effort to make the inscription legible; how these will come out, I don't know. When I can get three rolls developed, maybe in Cleveland, we'll see what we have. I had hoped to get back up to Afton to examine the grave stones in the cemetery there, but the weather being so cold and time pressing so hard, I decided against it, and from Harpursville took wing for Ithaca by NY 79, a most lovely road, even at this season of year. Or I might say, especially at this season of year.

But apart from documents, I feel that the Susquehanna expedition was well worthwhile in that it gave me a three-dimensional understanding of some years in Joseph's life, and in the segment it added to my mental mosaic of American landscapes. The Susquehanna Valley below Oakland is made depressing by the Erie Railroad right of way, but all the way above that, clear to the headwaters of the river, it is wonderful country at any season of the year. God, but this is a magnificent land we live in! If only man and his works, more especially the cities, were a little less squalid . . .

The work at Canandaigua was interesting. The grossly inaccurate Union list to the contrary notwithstanding, the Ontario Historical Society has a file of W. W. Phelps' *Ontario Phoenix* complete except for Jan. 5, 1831, from June 7, 1830, though unluckily it does not own the first two volumes of this paper. Phelps, it turns out, didn't have much to say about Mormonism, either while he was running the paper or after he left it. But I have now found out why he left. Characteristically, economic motives were a contributing factor to his joining the church in 1831. It seems (from a private letter of his I found at Albany in the Wayne Sentinel) that early in March, 1831, he went to Palmyra to inquire into Mormonism, and while he was there, some of his fellow anti-masons had a writ served on him for his debts, by which he was thrown into jail at Lyons until they should be paid. He seems to have been in jail for a month or six weeks before he was able to collect enough of what was owing him by his subscribers to get out of durance vile. After freeing himself, he came back to Canandaigua briefly, then set out for Kirtland. I found a curious letter he wrote his old paper from Independence later in the year, and enclose a copy of it. It is odd that he should have said nothing about his new religion—or were such references edited out by his old associates who were embarrassed by his religion? Early in 1832, the Phoenix, by then renamed the Freeman, printed his prospectus of the Evening and Morning Star, but when he sent them a copy, they merely recorded having received it, without remarking on it one way or the other.

The Ontario Historical Society has a wonderful file of the Ontario Repository from 1803, vol. 1, but unluckily almost the only issues lacking up to about 1830 are the volumes from April, 1828 to April, 1831. This is all the more to be regretted because in 1831 they reprinted a lot of stuff from the Painesville Telegraph, and from an oblique allusion by Phelps, it appears they had things to say about Mormonism earlier in 1831. There are only a few scattered issues at other libraries for the missing dates, including August 13, September 10, and September 17, 1828, and January 26, 1831, at Yale. Sometime maybe you would have a look at these and see if they bear on our problems.

I scanned the file from January, 1826 to the end of 1832, hoping it might have something on the 1826 trial, which it did not, or on the provenance of the Book of Mormon. The chief item of interest pertaining to the latter I also enclose.

At Albany I went entirely through the Palmyra file from 1817 up to the end of 1835, but I must admit some of the zest was taken from this through knowing that so careful a researcher as you had gone through it already, and there could be no major finds. However, in doing this, I did note a couple of inadvertences in the text of your book which you might note for that ultimate revised edition. For instance, that notice by Joseph Smith Sr. concerning Alvin's body appeared in the Sentinel not on September 25 but four days after the date of the exhumation, i.e., September 29, and it was published for seven issues altogether. Also, the Palmyra paper did not make mention of Jemima Wilkinson until after recording her death, so she might well have been unperturbed by anything said about her. Another thing, on reaching this region I find it said that Stephen A. Douglas attended the school in Canandaigua in 1831-33, not earlier, so if this is correct (of course I haven't checked it), your remark in your book is something of a non-sequitur.

I was going to add my citations to the Coe collection, but those papers are out in the car, and in this weather, I say the hell with it! It can wait till my next letter, with your kind permission.

Thanks again for all your kindness and your hospitality. I have missed both the kids. Tell Dick to print me something to enclose in your letter when next you write me.

Dale

P.S. The Arlington letter arrived—more details about the daughter born to the [undecipherable] of my last book.

26. To FAWN BRODIE

Fort Leavenworth, Kansas
24 December 1947

Dear Fawn,

It was gratifying indeed to have your letter awaiting me when I reached here Monday night. I like to think that there is indeed a "hole in the ground" out at Bethany now. Of course it would be an overstatement to say that I am as anxious as you to see your house go up, for how could anyone else possibly feel as strongly about it as you? But I take a very special interest in your home-building, and will be delighted indeed with real progress reports.

Opportunely, I have just received the color prints from the pictures I took last October, and so I am enabled to send you at this appropriate season the "October view from your front window" and the pictures of the greater part of the Brodie family (as constituted to date). All three pictures have some very pleasant memories associated with them, for me, and I am glad to have them.

Did you get your well sunk finally, and do you have a water suppy of your own now? All these details interest me very much, so keep me well posted.

This has been an instructive if somewhat wearing fall. For a couple of days I am taking an enforced rest at my sister's, being absolutely broke until some checks come through, but then I am going to start digging into things in this neighborhood. On the whole, this is a very strategic base of operations, with most of the sites of historic interest for me being in about a 40-mile radius. I want to visit the old Missouri River towns which for years have been familiar names in my ears—Weston, St. Joseph, and all the others—and of course the sites of Mormon interest in Jackson, Clay, Caldwell, and Daviess counties. I wrote Israel Smith before leaving Chicago Sunday morning, and it will be interesting to see what sort of welcome I get, if any. Otherwise there are a number of county archives I want to poke into, in addition to places to visit.

At Cleveland I worked almost exclusively in the newspaper collections, though I did copy that long letter by Eliza Snow to Isaac Streator. (Incidently if there is anything in that story Vesta Crawford told you of Eliza's having been "used by the mob" in Missouri, I'm willing to bet you it took place after that letter was written in late February. For all its feeling over the Mormon wrongs, there wasn't the accent of personal feeling that there would have been had Eliza known physical violence at first hand.) The newspaper research at Cleveland was very illuminating, but I regret that their files of the Painesville Telegraph, the only ones known for those years, are only 50 percent complete for 1836-38.

The Chicago Historical Society was very interesting also. You will recall that fellow, A. B. Deming, who got out a couple of issues of a paper called "Naked Truths about Mormonism." The Chicago Historical Society has some further affidavits collected by Deming which he didn't publish in the first two issues of his paper and which thus remained unpublished. In 1897 Deming sold them to a Chicago collector named Gunther, whose collections ultimately went to the Society. Among these was a statement by E. D. Howe, signed April 8, 1885, which is much more informative about his book and [Philastus] Hurlbut than his autobiography of 1878 was. He says that Grandison Newel, Orrin Clapp, Nathan Corning and others of Kirtland, Mentor, and Geauga County paid Hurlbut's expenses on that trip of investigation [into Joseph Smith's New York reputation] in 1833-34. After he came back, Hurlbut lectured about the countyside, and Howe heard him lecture in Painesville. "He finally came to me to have the evidence he had obtained published, I bargained to pay him in books which I sent to him at Conneaut, O[hio]. Before publishing my Book I went to Conneaut and saw most of the witnesses who had seen Spauldings Manuscript Found and had testified to its identity with the Book of Mormon as published in my book and was satisfied they were men of intelligence and respectability and were not mistaken in their statements. I published only a small part of the statements Hurlbut let me have." He says he was not acquainted with Hurlbut until H. came to him to have his evidence published, and adds that he "was good sized fine looking full of gab but illiterate and had lectured on many subjects." If he was indeed illiterate, this would seem to suggest that Howe must have put the affidavits into proper English unless, as has been doubted, the interviewed people wrote them. In a statement crossed out, Howe said he thought everybody would buy his book at one dollar a copy. The statement is in Deming's handwriting (and spelling), signed by Howe and witnessed by Deming, and one F. W. Regen, a grandson of Howe.

Deming also had half a dozen statements bearing on Hurlbut in 1836-37, which he may have kept unpublished because they weren't especially helpful to his anti-Mormon crusade—they had to do with accusations of theft made against Hurlbut at that time, and a case where Hurlbut brought a civil suit against a wealthy man whom he found in bed with his wife (the language is ambiguous as to whether this was not a put-up job between the Hurlbuts, a variant of the old badger game). Also Deming had a long interview with J. C. Dowen, who was the J[ustice of the]. P[eace]. in Kirtland during the Mormon years. This was very interesting, in the light of what we know. He says that he performed all the marriages in Kirtland to make them legal, then Joseph remarried the couples in a church ceremony, Joseph having no legal powers to marry people. He also says he excused Joseph from military service on the grounds that, as president of his church, he was of the same category as the Methodist minister. This, he says, pleased Joseph very much. But he sentenced Samuel Smith, something you will recall Joseph comments on in Doc[umentary]. Hist[ory]. [of the Church].

Quite as interesting as all this is an astonishing ledger Deming unearthed in Kirtland in 1885, the Stock Book of the Kirtland Bank. I had no time to examine this thoroughly or take any notes from it, but I did observe that Brigham [Young] owned 2000 shares of stock at $50 a share! This, on June 10, 1837, he turned over to O[liver]. Granger and J[ared]. Carter. On the same date Joseph and [Sidney] Rigdon turned over their shares to Granger and Carter, evidently part of the liquidation proceedings. I want to study this more thoroughly, this winter or next summer. The earliest dates in this ledger for the entries as to stock holdings are from October 18, 1836. Incidentally, Howe in his Statement says that Joseph in 1836 tried to borrow $100,000 from the Bank of Geauga, offering as security Kirtland lands valued at $300,000. Since the Bank of Geauga was capitalized at only $100,000, of course it turned him down, and it was soon after this that "Jo Smith claimed he received a revelation from God to start a Bank which would eventually 'swallow up all other Banks.' "

The Chicago Historical Society also has letters from Joseph to Emma written in June 1832 and January 1840, relating mostly to family matters, presented by Young Joseph in the 80's. Also a very interesting letter by Samuel Williams, commanding officer of the Carthage Greys, dated July 10, 1844, describing the happenings at Carthage jail. Williams says that when Joseph first arrived in Carthage and met with such an ugly reception, he "*actually fainted.*" In Doc. Hist. Joseph denies a rumor that he had "fainted three times," but this may be an evasion, of course; the Saints were adept enough at evasions.

While I was at Chardon I checked up on that item I showed you once in the 1834 Painesville Telegraph about the member of Zion's Camp who sued Joseph for wages after he got back. The spare court record is perfectly uninformative without the newspaper elucidation, but between the two you can get the whole story. The unregenerate in question was Dennis Lake. He won a judgment in the magistrate's court, but it was thrown out for lack of evidence when appealed to the Court of Common Pleas at Chardon.

At Detroit I worked for three days, 11 hours a day without intermission, in the [James] Strang MSS [Milo] Quaife generously placed at my disposal. I thus transcribed nearly everything pertaining to the larger history of Mormonism, but I was not able to touch a large quantity of documents pertaining primarily to the internal history of the Strangite church. I hope I can get back there next summer for this purpose. If Quaife should die, Lord knows what would happen to his MSS, and whether I could get access to them. I don't believe he has permitted any before me to use them as a whole, though he has supplied copies of individual documents to various people. He got back from Chicago in time to have a 15 minute talk with me my last day in Detroit. Although a generation older, he reminded me very much of Maurice Howe in his alert interest in things, the way he used his eyes and hands.

As to the Strang MSS themselves, they supplied some fine comic relief, and I enjoyed them very much. What a precious collection of rascals Strang surrounded himself with! The George J. Adams and John C. Bennett letters are priceless. Listen to Adams, for example, writing Strang from Wilmington, Delaware, on Nov. 1, 1849: "I think the Lord has a people in this Citty-, we shall see, but I pray God that He will keep all *Treacherous—Lecherous—Lying* and *Covenant Breaking Scoundrells.*—oh! James—When Shall we have rest—when Shall we be free—from the fangs of Lying Slanderous abuse, When Shall men Cease their phals accuseations [sic] against us—when Shall Ofenders be cut off,—You See as I antisipated all the power and Envy of Hell is let loose, is loet loose, at Me, Since I have arrisen to magnifiy my high and Holy calling, *Envy* the Child of hell, and *Ofspring* of peridition!!! they would Strike you through me,—James You know my virtue!—My Integrity—My goodness of heart, My high Sense of Honner.—thank God you know—my Mind and purity of purpose in all these matters—Touching wherein I have been accused—what have I ever done to any of *them* that they Should Oppose Me with such Malignity as they do—Oh! My god; Curse! Curse!! Utterly! Curse!!! them untill they repent—May they be cursed with Sickness—with Losses—and with Trouble and Sleepless—Nights—well let them go thank God we look for Better times." All this in relation to the smell of adultery that followed Adams everywhere he went.

Most interesting of all in the Quaife MSS was the original letter of appointment from Joseph to Strang. This is a remarkably clumsy forgery, and shows what a commanding presence Strang must have had to make headway despite it. Of course, the Nauvoo postmark and the smell of miracle helped a lot.

I was interested to hear about the new [Francis W.] Kirkham book, and not surprised at what you tell me. I think I was well advised to ask Stan Ivins to keep that 1831 letter under cover till Kirkham got his book out. Now we will fire on his position from still another flank.

Let's have a long letter about everything. Tell Dick I am glad to have a picture of him in color, especially with his happy smile, and I will see him and Bruce again some day—maybe next summer.

A happy holiday season to you all,

Dale

27. To FRANCIS W. KIRKHAM

Fort Leavenworth, Kansas
3 January 1948

Dear Mr. Kirkham:

Last week in Independence [Missouri] I bought a copy of the new edition of your book on the coming forth of the Book of Mormon [*A New Witness for Christ in America*], and I have read it with some interest. I am surprised that some of the slips of the pen from the previous edition have not been called to your attention, or have not themselves come to your attention, and for such value as a list may have for you, I will remark on some of these below.

What most impels me to write you however is my curiosity as to whether you are satisfied by the rebuttal you have made to the seerstone thesis set forth by Mrs. [Fawn] Brodie. I cannot believe that this represents the considered thought of church scholarship, and I am inclined to believe that much of the material you include came to light at such a late date that you were unable to weigh it properly. If no better rebuttal of the seerstone thesis can be made than this, objective scholarship is likely to regard it as established.

It strikes me that there are two critical weaknesses in your own theory, one in assuming that all the "glass-looking" and "seerstone" stories have originated in the affidavits gathered by [Philastus] Hurlbut; and second, in assuming that Joseph Smith's remark of 1831 invalidates anything David Whitmer and Martin Harris had to say in later years about the method of translation.

You will be interested, in the first instance, in an article reprinted from the *Wayne County Inquirer* (probably a Pennsylvania paper, but I have not investigated the point yet) in the *Cincinnati Advertiser and Ohio Phoenix* of June 2, 1830. These remarks were as follows: "A fellow by the name of Joseph Smith, who resides in the upper part of Susquehanna county, has been for the last two years we are told, employed in dedicating (sic) as he says, by inspiration, a new bible. He pretended that he had been entrusted by God with a golden bible which had been always hidden from the world. Smith would put his face into a hat in which he had a *white stone*, and pretend to read from it, which his coadjutor transcribed. The book purports to give an account of the 'Ten Tribes' and strange as it may seem, there are some who have full faith in his Divine commission. The book it seems is now published. We extract the following from the Rochester Republican." (Then follows the article, "Blasphemy," printed in your book. The Republican was, of course, the weekly edition of the Rochester Daily Advertiser.)

In view of the early date of this comment, it would be interesting to have you review the assumptions you make in your book, and see where you come out this time. In so reviewing your book, you will also have to give new authority to the disputed court record of 1826 and the [William D.] Purple reminiscences, for I have discovered a letter written from South Bainbridge in March, 1831, and printed in April, 1831, which discusses both the trial of 1826 and those of 1830; indeed, it interprets the Book of Mormon as simply an extension of the "glass-looking" for which Joseph had been tried four years earlier. Moreover, it harmonizes the discrepancies between the trial record and the Purple reminiscences by saying that although found guilty, because Joseph was a minor and on the theory that he would reform his conduct, he was not subjected to the penalty of the law on being convicted. Beyond giving you this general summary I do not wish to identify more closely the printed source and the contents of the letter in question, pending the writing of my own book later this year. I tell you this much because I am interested in seeing the best possible defense the Church can make to the seerstone hypothesis, and I cannot believe that either you or the Church will feel that your book serves adequately in this function.

With so much by way of larger comment, let me provide you with some correction and commentaries, in the event you get out still another edition of your book at some future time[:]

p. 16 and elsewhere, the advertisement by Joseph Smith, Sr., appeared in seven issues of the Sentinel, not three, and was first published September 29, not September 25, 1824.

p. 18 and elsewhere, "Delusions" was published in Boston, not New York, or at any rate I have never seen or heard of a New York edition. And [E. D.] Howe's book was Mormonism Unvailed, not Unveiled, or at any rate I have never seen a title page rendered as you have it. Also on this page, I do not think you can find substantial authority for saying that Hurlbut supplied anything to Howe's book but the affidavits. The expository material comes clearly out of Howe's own files, and he himself gives us warrant, in his signed statement in 1885, to think that Hurlbut contributed only the affidavits. In fact, he says he used only a small part of the affidavits Hurlbut gathered. The attribution of the book to Hurlbut has been primarily by the Mormons, who have wanted to give an apostate coloration to its entire contents, as indeed you do yourself in the present book, on occasion.

p. 19, first line, the date is 1838, not 1836; and among the titles you quote, I am under the impression you will find that the "Mormonism Unveiled" published in London in "1842" is the reprint without date of the romance originally published in this country 1855 as "The Prophets, or Mormonism Unveiled," attributed to Orvilla S. Belisle.

p. 20. The first edition of Mrs. Brodie's book is of course 1945.

p. 113. What is the basis of your statement that Joseph Smith's "Caractors" were similar to the characters found on the Rosetta Stone in 1816?

p. 118-9. The [Stephen R.] Harding letter was obviously written in 1867, not 1857, for he did not become governor until 1862 and was on good terms with the Saints on his first arrival in Utah. This bears on your further statement on p. 13 [blank in original] that Harding was a "lifelong" enemy of the Saints.

p. 139. Hurlbut's investigations took place after his expulsion but before the trial you speak of. Also they were not his own doings only; he was financed by a group of men living in and around Kirtland.

p. 141. Written in 1842?

p. 168. The article you quote is from the Wayne Sentinel.

pp. 169-70. The article you quote from the Hillsborough Gazette, which the copyist or printer has somewhat maltreated, you will find at length in the Morning Courier & New-York Enquirer for August 31 and September 1, 1831. It was written at Canan[d]aigua, August 15, 1831. The article as a whole would be devastating support of the adverse view of the character of Joseph Smith, Jr. and Sr., but it must be called into question because it brings [Sidney] Rigdon into the story in a manner no scholarship can accept. Whatever Rigdon was, he was not a money-digger in the 1820s. A large part of the second half of this article was reprinted in various New England and Ohio papers. If you quote the full story as found in the Hillsborough Gazette, this is only a fragment of the part that was generally circulated.

p. 182. You assert that [Ariel] Crowley finds the characters make "connected thought." What is this connected thought? It does not appear from your text.

p. 195. It strikes me that you should submit Emma Smith's statements about Joseph's illiteracy to the actual test of his writing. You will find in the Chicago Historical Society and Reorganized Church Libraries handwritten letters of 1832 which evidence a flair for words, a measure of eloquence, and a sufficient degree of schooling. I have not examined the personal diary you speak of, but I suspect that it too would invalidate Emma's memory.

p. 196. Will you not agree with me that all that can safely be concluded from Joseph Smith's remark in 1831 concerning the coming forth of the Book of Mormon is that at the moment he uttered it, he was not in a communicative mood?

pp. 211-12. Revelation to Harris or Emma?

p. 303. This is not the correct title of Corrill's history.

p. 307. Rigdon was back in Ohio by February 1, 1831.

p. 359-60. I am curious how you justify to yourself the inclusion of the matter quoted from the preface of Mrs. Brodie's book. Is this not what you object to in writings against the Mormons, an appeal to prejudice and to matters extraneous to issues of fact?

pp. 366-67. I would be curious to know how you feel that there is misrepresentation in how Mrs. Brodie has quoted or interpreted these statements, as against the way you feel she should have stated them. Or, put another way, in what manner is the reader likely to have been led astray by her reading instead of yours?

p. 376 and the question of seerstones in general. You nowhere squarely meet this question, and I would be interested to know what significance you give to seerstones in the history of the Church. What do you make of Brigham Young's notation in his journal, as cited by Mrs. Brodie? What of his demonstration before the regents of the University of the State of Deseret, as recorded by Hosea Stout? How do you interpret the seerstones and the use thereof as these crop up in the earliest annals of the church and certain of the revelations? What do you think of Brigham H. Roberts' remarks, as printed at least in the original version of the Comprehensive History? What seerstones remain in the possession of the Church today, and what is the official attitude taken toward their function, past use, and historical significance? All these things are of basic importance in a study of Mormon origins in general and the Book of Mormon in particular. It is certainly not possible to leave all these matters aside in an analysis of the claims made for the Book of Mormon.

pp. 384ff. Is it possible that no better method of defense can be found in dealing with the asserted court record than that you have adopted? Consider the arguments you adopt, Mr. Kirkham. You enter upon a legalistic treatment from a modern point of view of court proceedings in local courts, in a totally different social environment. It is your thesis that because the revised laws of New York State, printed in 1829, require the recording of certain facts not mentioned in the alleged record, and do not require the testimony of the defendant, this purported record of *1826* may be called in question. You even appeal to a "Manual for all counties and Town Officers" not published until 1837. Have you demonstrated that there was any prescribed methodology for the keeping of records by New York justices of the peace in 1826, or that there was any uniformity among justices of the peace in that year as to the manner of taking evidence or recording that evidence? What do you seriously make of the fact that j[ustice]. [of the] p[eace]. records are not found in the records of Chenango County, knowing as you must that j. p. records are almost never found with county records proper?

You print the Purple reminiscences, somewhat skirting the credit rightfully due Mrs. Brodie for bringing this information into the light of day, but you do not print the evidence she also found which went to establish Dr. Purple's credibility as a witness. Your treatment of the Purple material and the court record does credit to the integrity of your beliefs about your religion, but you will forgive my saying that it does not make very convincing objective history.

Returning to the alleged court record itself, it is a curious line of argument you adopt to show (a) that [Bishop Daniel S.] Tuttle himself did not maintain his belief in it; and (b) Funk and Wagnalls did not believe it. You make the first assertion despite the fact that Tuttle himself twice printed the document and gave an account of why he conceived it genuine, and never altered it in two successive editions of the encyclopedia [*Religious Encyclopedia*, edited by Philip Schaff] for which he had furnished the article, and on what grounds? Because he did not directly refer to it in his autobiography. A parallel to this, Mr. Kirkham, would be for you to write your autobiography now, and have it concluded that any statement you have made in your book or in your Improvement Era articles you no longer believed in becuase you didn't print it again in your book. Would you accept this method of investigation concerning your own life and writings? In the second instance, I should imagine that you are well aware that publishers do not interfere with the literary license of their authors as long as they stay within the bounds of fact—or more precisely, do not furnish fuel for libel suits. I have never heard of the Encyclopedia Britannica undertaking to tell its authorities what they should and should not put into their articles. I doubt that Funk and Wagnalls did anything of the kind, either. Mormon history is so large a subject, and anything that can be said about it in a few hundred words is so limited at best, that it is astonishing to have you find any significance in differences in the use and interpretation of facts, especially in view of the fact that when one writer redoes a job previously done by another, he is generally under the psychological compulsion to show he is indebted to the previous writer for nothing. These are indeed sad arguments to plead against the authenticity of the court record. Surely more solid arguments than these can be found to support the claims of the Church; this is hardly more than a grasping at straws.

I do not have the time just now to enter upon a discussion of your book in the large. It is an interesting and in many ways valuable book, but I think that the matters it "proves" are, generally speaking, those about which little controversy exists, and that it makes assumptions at critical points which are by no means supported by the evidence adduced. If you would be interested in a discussion of these matters, we can enter upon one when I finish my transcontinental researches in the spring. Although I cannot accept your logic on many points, I do respect your sincerity, the energy you have brought to your researches, and your effort to achieve a scientific basis for your religious convictions. There are not many Saints working in the field of Mormon history for whom one can feel this respect; the generality of the writers of history are content to lean on the researches of others, to the point where, if the Journal History were to be destroyed by some disaster, they would be utterly deprived of materials.

With best wishes,

Dale L. Morgan

28. To FAWN BRODIE

Fort Leavenworth, Kansas
25 January 1948

Dear Fawn,

I am getting ready to shove off again, Tuesday or at the latest Wednesday, so I'll send along the news before I take to the road. I expect to spend a day getting to Columbia, going via old Far West, Shoal Creek, Gallatin, etc., then after a couple of days in Columbia and one in Jefferson City, go on to St. Louis at the end of the week. After a week there, up to Springfield again, and on around to Fort Leavenworth via Nauvoo and the Mormon trail across Iowa to Council Bluffs. Once back here, I will shove off for the southwest, probably around February 15. Although I would like to revisit Chicago for a day or two and go up to Madison, I had better put that off to another time. I am rich in neither time nor money at the moment.

The work in Independence [Missouri] has been interesting in itself and for other reasons. Including the case of F. Brodie. Nothing was said about you at first [by officials of the RLDS church], but it was bound to come out finally, and it did, a day or two after I wrote you last. It was [S. A.] Burgess who brought up the subject. He commented on the fact that Utah admitted no one to its library, while they maintained an open policy. But, he said, they had been very much disappointed in you, and went on to add that you had misrepresented yourself and lied to them.

Naturally I had to take him up on this; whether I might want to or not, I must be your advocate in Independence, otherwise they will accuse me of dishonesty later. So I said that on the contrary I knew you well, that you were a person of great honesty and integrity, etc. It turned out that what he meant was that you had told them you were writing a very sympathetic book about Joseph and were much inclined to admire him. I then pointed out to Burgess that this was entirely true, that though your book came to adverse conclusions about the claims of the church, it was very sympathetic toward Joseph Smith the man, and that if he read all the reviews of the book, he would find that this was the impression it had made upon the reviewers. I added that you were one of the most objective persons about your writing that I had ever met, and were entirely willing to receive factual objections and weigh them judiciously. He said that they didn't want to advertise your book (!), and I said that was all the same to you: why didn't he write you about errors or misinterpretations as he viewed them. He said that would require almost another book, but that if he had a stenographer, he might consider doing something of the kind. So the discussion finally ended, as far as you were concerned, on that note, though it continued for some time about my own qualifications and background, not to say attitudes. One amusing remark in the conversation about you was that Burgess commented that in one of my letters to him several years ago I had spoken of having dinner with you. Some people, he said, would think that was improper, but he didn't! (This had to do with mistaken interpretations made from the written record.) Well, it was quite an afternoon, and wholly wasted as far as research was concerned. I didn't get one damned thing done, only this underbrush cleared away.

The following morning I had an interview with [RLDS president] Israel Smith to tackle him about the microfilms I wanted. He received me with neither warmth nor hostility. I opened the conversation by giving him the letter formally requesting the microfilming, then discussed the work I had sunk into this history, particularly my travels since summer. The first thing he said at all was that he had read my review of your book and had gained the impression I was strongly Mormon in my views. This nonplused me for a moment until I realized he meant pro-Utah church. I told him that I had avoided coming to any final conclusions until my research was done, but said I would be less than frank if I did not tell him that as far as the polygamy issue was concerned, I thought the Utah church had a better case than the Reorganized Church. He then went on to talk about the Utah church, how they made an awful liar out of their prophet, etc. He then spoke of some recent evidence he had found in Springfield, and eventually I found out what he was referring to. He said that [Andrew] Jenson's *Historical Record* says the Partridge girls were married to Joseph on May 11, 1843 (I think it was) by James M. Adams, and it seems that he had found a court record in Springfield showing that Adams was presiding over his court in Springfield on May 13. "Springfield is 125 miles from Nauvoo," he said. "Draw your own conclusions." He then complained that none of the Utah historians knew how to qualify a witness, etc.

But we ended on a pretty cordial note. He agreed to the microfilming of the periodicals I wanted done, and also offered to lend me his copy of the excerpted Memoirs of his father, and gave me a photographic copy of Joseph's letter to Orville Browning of June 27, 1844. His original sanction for the microfilming depended on its being done by the State Historical Society of Missouri, of which he is a trustee, but when I learned from them they had no facilities, and approached him about having it done by the Library of Congress instead, he readily agreed. Accordingly I wrote Dr. Evans a week ago, and hope it will go through without a hitch. With some lesser stuff, I want microfilmed Thompson's *Zion's Harbinger & Baneemy's Organ*, 1849-55, and the Hinkle-McLellin *The Ensign*, 1844-45, plus a book and a pamphlet published by Thompson.

I have seen a good deal of interesting stuff. It was not practicable to see the Book of Mormon MS, because this is kept in a K[ansas]. C[ity]. bank vault from which it may be removed only in the presence of the president *and* the presiding bishop, but I spent a day examining a negative photostat of the manuscript. On its internal evidence, I am disposed to think that this MS is wholly the second copy, from characteristic copyist's errors. However, on p. 138 there is what may be a constructive struggle at rendition of a dictated text. The MS was supposed to be in four handwritings, but I could identify only three in the original text. A fourth may have made some of the grammatical corrections which, Burgess tells me, were made sometime after publication of the 1830 edition and prior to the 1837 edition.

Another very interesting item was what appears to have been a part of the printer's copy of the Book of Commandments. There appears to be no doubt about it, and it is conclusive evidence that the B.C. as printed was not complete. This has been suspected, of course, for the B.C. ended in the middle of a verse and with a fully printed five sheets.

Well, I won't now go into all the stuff I have seen, but a lot of it, relating to the factions, is useful and valuable. Burgess also had Peter Whitmer's copy of the original quarto edition of The Evening and Morning Star, the first I have located. Incidently, I was fortunate enough to get from the Hedrickite headquarters on the Temple Lot a complete file of their reprint of the Star except for the last four pages of the first issue, contained in the reprint issue of July, 1911. Neither the original in the church's hands nor the reprint contains the Extra of July 20, 1833, disavowing "Free People of Color." I also got a copy of the Hedrickite reprint of the Book of Commandments; this was lucky, because at first they thought they had none.

I also examined with attention John Whitmer's history, including some crossed out material [Andrew] Jenson did not transcribe in the copy in Salt Lake City. From this it is evident that Whitmer stopped making entries originally in March, 1838, then about ten years later wrote the unpublished parts. Burgess was disposed to think the later part, which he says "is not history," was written after 1860, but I am willing to bet it was written about 1847-48 after the schism in the Strangite church led [William E.] McLellin and others in the Kirtland area to call upon David Whitmer to become the spearhead of a "true church."

One thing that interested me was that I found Burgess unexpectedly sensitive to the possibility that Emma may have married [Lewis] Bidamon for love. Without exactly saying anything, he intimated that there was more in this marriage than met the eye, and she had made a mistake. But if Emma was not in love with him, she gave a damned good counterfeit of it in a letter she wrote him in early 1850, directed to him at San Francisco. It seems that he had gone to California in the gold rush the previous summer, and the warmth of her letter made quite a contrast to Joseph's complaints in some of his letters about how she didn't put herself to the trouble of writing him. Pressed for time, I did not copy this letter, so I make a point of mentioning it to you in case you didn't see it yourself.

I haven't had a single peep out of [Francis] Kirkham on the subject of stones, and I wonder if I will. I wrote that letter with malice aforethought, both because I was annoyed at his condescending criticism of you, and because I want to put them on notice in Utah that I am interested in seerstones before I even show my face around there. After writing the letter to him, I made a lot more notes on the subject of money-digging and peepstones, in sources antedating [E. D.] Howe's book [*Mormonism Unvailed*], and it is interesting how much material there is, even in Kirkham's own book.

It was interesting to see Hiram Page's seerstone (but this is an olive-green color, not black as you call it in your book), and I wonder if I will get to see any others in Utah. Burgess peered through the stone at me, then said facetiously that he couldn't make it work—lack of faith!

Well, let's leave the Saints to take care of themselves, and think a little about the sinners. I've been wondering if you finally got your well driven through and now have a good supply of water of your own. It is turning out to be a very rough winter in your neighborhood, and I can hardly suppose that anything at all can be done in the way of building till spring gets a good toe-hold on the weather. The trouble is, you will die with impatience every week from now on, after waiting so long. The last few weeks are the worst. Ask Dick how it is just before Christmas.

I've maundered on so long in this letter that I am under the necessity of ending it so that the folks around here can get a little sleep, so we'll append a to-be-continued note. But thanks for the extract about Brigham [Young]. It is not news to me, but interesting to have a comment on the subject in a national journal of opinion. I enclose another of William Smith's varied stories about the origins of Mormonism, principally interesting right now for what it says about looking into hats. William's account of the Urim and Thummim is so brilliant I can't work up even a vague picture of what the whole was supposed to be like.

A cloudy groundhog day to you,

Dale

29. To FAWN BRODIE

Salt Lake City, Utah
20 April 1948

Dear Fawn,

I came home from the U[niversity] of U[tah] this afternoon, having finished the local phase of the work on my bibliography, and found in my mail box a letter dated April 14, signed by Joseph Anderson as Secretary to the First Presidency. (True to my promise, I mailed them a second letter this morning prodding them to answer my first letter, but as it turns out this was already in the mails.) The nub of this reply is that "an experience running over several years has persuaded us of the unwisdom of giving access to our manuscript records to people writing books, because that same experience has shown that people writing such books are rarely qualified to appraise accurately what they read, and too frequently, whether consciously or unconsciously, they misrepresent what they find. Such manuscripts will therefore not be available for general inspection nor use." The Historian's Office, being not a research library "but a private library, maintained and operated for the benefit of the Church," will afford me "access to printed materials which they have in the library, but this will not include the use of first and rare editions of books."

Or in other words, they will cooperate with me so far as my bibliography is concerned, but beyond that, to hell with me. So I say as cheerfully, to hell with them. I'll take them up on the bibliography, because I want that to be as complete as possible and because I want some information as to which, on the basis of titles in my bibliography, is "the greatest Mormon collection." But beyond that, I will write my book independently. Thank God I did the essential research for this book years ago, that is, the things wherein I am to any significant degree dependent on their collections.

Also in the mail this afternoon was the copy of Vermont Life, which I will file without bothering to read, since I have regarded

[Milton] Hunter [an LDS church authority and historian] as nothing but an ignoramus ever since I met up with his doctoral thesis, "Brigham Young the Colonizer," when this was serialized in the [LDS Deseret] News Church Section back in 1938-39. And likewise the copy of the Larson book, which I am glad to have, whatever its merits may prove to be.

On my return here I bought a copy of [Leland] Creer's new history, The Founding of an Empire, and I regret very much to report that it is the shoddiest kind of historical workmanship. Damn it all, I take some pride in my state and the caliber of work that is or should be done there. I should like Utah scholarship, quite apart from the Mormon factor, to be of the highest caliber. There is no reason why it shouldn't be. Creer in this work sidestepped the touchy Mormon problems for the first period (to about 1855, when his book ends), but that was all right with me, for he was writing a history of the State, not of the Mormons, and there is no necessity for those problems to be met frontally in such a work (cf. my own last book). But my God, his treatment of the fur trade, for instance, is slipshod in the extreme. Thus he quotes something from [Harrison C.] Dale's Ashley-Smith Explorations, then follows it with a quotation from a newspaper piece I wrote for the Writers' Project which presents later research wholly invalidating the quotation from Dale, then without seeing the slightest conflict between the two, he goes ahead in the old canon, etc. Hell! Worse still, he doesn't have the slightest feeling for primary sources. Anything is grist to his mill.

Still, there is some congenial company up on the hill. I enjoy talking to Dr. Chamberlain and Dr. Cottam; they have brains and the scientific spirit. Maybe it is not merely accidental that they are natural scientists.

The University itself I simply can't get used to. Everything is changed except the physical plant, and there are great changes in that, also. There isn't a single familiar face in the library, and very few among the faculty members. In some ways there is evidence of a more progressive spirit, but in others there is a depressing lack, as it seems, of function. I haven't yet been able to find out anything of interest about that so-called Humanities Foundation. Harold Folland is in charge of it, in a room in the library with presumed office hours Tuesday and Thursday from 10 to 1. But just try and find him there then! (Or any other time, so far as I can learn.)

More cheerful topic: It is making like spring here, and the last week has been very fine indeed. Tomorrow I am going to drive up to Logan to check the [Utah State] A[gricultural]. C[ollege]. library, and I anticipate a pleasant day's outing, whatever develops from the bibliographical search.

I was glad to hear that your contractor has finally stirred from his sloth, but sorry indeed to hear about Dick's accident. It is fortunate that the accident was no worse, and I hope that as time goes on some of the damage will be undone.

Thanks for remembering me about the [Latter-day Saints', Millennial] Stars. However, I already have a run from July 1844 through to December, 1855, and even for the missing volumes I wouldn't pay more than about $3.50 or $5—if I had the money. I doubt if I paid as much as $20 in all for the volumes I have, though of course that was back in 1941. The [Utah State] Historical Society has been working at filling in a file, but I believe they have most of these early volumes.

Incidently, I have turned up the answers to a couple of questions lately. When Sampson Avard joined the church, for example. Orson Pratt baptized him at Freedom (N.Y., evidently, but maybe Freedom, Pa., if there is such a place) in November, 1835, and immediately ordained him an elder. Avard previously had been a Campbellite and had preached among them. (Messenger & Advocate, Nov., 1835, p. 224.)

A second item of interest is that in the Journal of John Lyman Smith, which you drew upon in your book, there turns out to be some information on Sarah Cleveland. It seems that he [Smith] married a daughter, Augusta B., of John and Sarah Cleveland. In 1855, when enroute east on a mission, he called on them in Plymouth, which evidently was in Illinois but may have been in Iowa. So this shows they were living together at that date. To make things more interesting, John Smith was John Lyman Smith's father.

This shows once more how useful your book is. Had you had the advantage of your finished book when you started out to write it, how much more would you have derived from sources you turned to, for fragments of information that could have no meaning for you in the initial phase of the research would have meant a lot to you later on. I am the beneficiary of your work in this respect, and no doubt there will be someone to benefit from mine.

With all your other pursuits (and of course yourself as an object of pursuit), I hope you will still find time to keep plugging away at your book. It goes without saying it will be interesting, and I look forward to the time when it is finished.

Dale

30. To JOSEPH ANDERSON[1]

Salt Lake City, Utah
20 April, 1948

Dear Mr. Anderson:

Your letter of April 14, which was not delivered in the mails until this afternoon, of course answers in effect my second letter, mailed to you this morning.

I regret the position taken by the Church with respect to its archives. I feel that what amounts to a policy of suppression is a mistaken one, and ultimately will work out to the disadvantage of the Church. Although, as you say, people writing books may be "rarely qualified to appraise accurately what they read, and too frequently, whether consciously or unconsciously, . . . misrepresent what they find," this cannot be amended except by the appeal to the record. In the long run the record will correct itself. This is the principle on which all our concepts of the free press are founded; it is also the basis for all modern scholarship. So long as the Church permits access to its archives only when it can control the fruits of the scholarship, so long must it be content to be misrepresented and misunderstood. I do not question the right of the Church to adopt such policies, but I think that the position of the Church is fundamentally untenable, and sooner or later must be reversed.

I shall avail myself of your invitation to use the facilities of the Historian's Office, to the extent of inviting the cooperation of the Assistant Historians in checking my bibliography against the holdings of the Church. As your collections are so notable, I suspect that a number of titles which are unique outside your library, insofar as my researches have disclosed, may have a second existence in the Historian's Office; and the Church may have as many as 10 or 12 tracts or pamphlets I have found nowhere else. Much of this material is of little use to the historian who works in broad fields, but even pamphlets devoted to local controversies or doctrinal disputes have an ultimate interest, and I suspect that my bibliography will be found very interesting by members of the Church as well as scholars at large.

Since Mormon materials are so widespread and modern library facilities so flexible, I will not have to burden the Historian's Office in connection with research in printed sources for my history proper, which I shall write independent of the resources of the Church. I do not wish to lay the Church under any obligation it may feel unwilling to assume in connection with the writing of my book.

Sincerely,

Dale L. Morgan

[1] Joseph Anderson served as secretary to the LDS church's First Presidency from 1923 to 1972.

31. To JOHN SELBY[1]

Salt Lake City, Utah
26 July 1948

Dear Mr. Selby:

For the last month or so I have been working up the ambition to sit down and write you about my Mormon history, and your letter of the 22nd, arriving this morning, seems to provide the necessary energy, like a box of cornflakes or something.

The production of this book, or series of perhaps three books, has been in a condition of virtual suspended animation since I arrived back here from California at the beginning of April. My transcontinental researches, culminated with a broken cylinder in Berkeley in March, put me in a hell of a financial hole, and the last three months have been dedicated to the proposition of getting out of said hole. Thus except for some research in the form of obtaining some essential microfilms from the Library of Congress, New York Public Library, Harvard, and Yale libraries, the history has had to await the time when I could afford the luxury of working on it. This time is not going to arrive for another six weeks or so, because I have entered into a proposition with the State Department of Publicity and Industrial Development to do them a historic trails map of Utah; this is going to require four solid weeks of field research and another two weeks of putting the fruits of this research in shape for their draftsman. After that, however, except for an October visit to the Huntington Library at San Marino [California], made necessary by the declination of the Utah church to cooperate in the production of a history about it (the only library, and the only Mormon church in the entire country, by the way, which has not cooperated fully), I shall get to work on the first volume of the history and bring it to completion as rapidly as I can.

So this is the situation I have been intending to explore when I could get around to it. Everything considered, I believe that I had better ask for an advance on royalties so that I can spend my working time on the book instead of on the sundry kinds of hackwork that have taken up my time since April. I should like to have the first draft of the book done by the end of April, and the final draft done by the end of July.

But this of course is the first book, which brings up the second point requiring discussion. We have not got around to signing a contract for the Mormon history, but obviously we will have to if I am going to ask a royalty advance to enable me to get the book done within the reasonably early future. If such a contract is drawn up, I want it to encompass not only this first book of my Mormon history, but the entire work. I have felt that it would be advantageous not to try to market the history as a formidable three-volume work; rather, to write a series of three books which can be merchandised separately, but which when completed will comprise a closely integrated history in three volumes. Fortunately, the material falls naturally into such divisions—the first is concerned with the Mormon story down to Joseph Smith's death in 1844. The second opens with the struggle for power that took place among Joseph's followers, and closes with Brigham Young's death in 1877. The third volume brings the story down to our own time.

The underlying theme of the whole work is the social significance of the Mormons as a minority in American society, how the Mormons have influenced and been influenced by American life, how minority and majority come to terms with each other. Thus the Mormon story sheds a great deal of valuable light on numerous world problems today, and I believe that those who read my history will find that it imparts a useful point of view in evaluating some of these contemporary problems. As for myself, I have found my intensive study of the Mormon phenomenon a highly useful education—for my money, the Russians today are simply a nation of Mormons, embodying on a national scale the characteristics of the Saints during their intransigent period. (Not that the Mormons would be flattered to think so.)

But to get back to my main point, as it seems necessary for me to make some contractual arrangements, I want any contract to envision a total work of three volumes, though it is to be left to my discretion whether the work shall not be condensed into two instead. (From some points of view, except for thorough coverage of the subject, two volumes might be preferable to three. I could doubtless fill more, but here it is necessary to compromise what may be desirable historically with what is practicable commercially.)

If the firm [Rinehart & Company] is willing to draw up a contract along these lines, with the finished manuscripts to be delivered successively on August 1, 1949, August 1, 1950, and August 1, 1951, and if a substantial royalty advance can be made on the first book to enable me to give all my time to it, we will make a deal on this basis. Any questions of advances on the books to come can be left for determination after the first book is completed; I prefer not to spend a book before it has been written, and am only getting involved in such a proposition now because it seems the best of the several expedients open to me.

A further angle is Mrs. [Madeline] McQuown's book on Brigham Young. Naturally I don't want my own book to prejudice the success of hers in any way. She is working night and day right now to get the manuscript reduced to workable proportions so that you may have it for spring publication next year. You will know better than I whether it is advisable for you to take on two major books of similar nature. I believe both books will be memorable and it may be that each will help the other. I could take my book to another publisher if necessary, the mails having practically been infested with overtures, but I have felt a special obligation to Rinehart on this work and have wanted to give the firm first crack at it.

All this plain speaking covers all the angles, I believe. I will leave it to you to decide where we go from here, or at any rate, how we go from here.

Regards,

Dale L. Morgan

[1] John Selby was Morgan's editor at Rinehart & Company. He was also arts editor for the Associated Press.

32. To S. A. BURGESS

Salt Lake City, Utah
13 August 1948

Dear Mr. Burgess,

I received on Monday your letter of August 5, and since then I have been pondering how best to answer you. For it is not easy to answer you, just as it is not easy to answer any of the representatives of the several Mormon or L.D.S. churches with whom I have had discussions of one kind and another; it is not easy, because none of you can even agree very far among yourselves, and yet all of you I give credit for being honest and sincere, men of integrity who hold to their beliefs and their ways of thinking for the best of reasons, yet who hold beliefs which cannot be reconciled with each other. If I accept any part of what one of these men says, I am immediately challenged by some other among them. Whether one is regarded as "friendly" or not by one of these men depends upon the extent to which one accepts his views. And if one attempts to steer an impartial course among them, all of them are likely to regard him as "unfriendly."

Even you, who have shown yourself in our intercourse a gentle and generous nature, are not immune from what I might call these animosities, your basic assurance and insistence that you hold correct views. Thus while I was in Independence [Missouri], I mentioned to you my intention, when my book was completed, of submitting the draft of it for criticism by some responsible member of your church, as a means of repairing any gaps in my objectivity, although, I said, I could give no assurances that I would amend the book in any particular unless the objections brought to bear seemed to me reasonable and proper in the circumstances. You were at once antagonized by the reservation I had made, yet if you had paused to consider, you would have realized that anything else would be an abdication of my responsibility as author; in like circumstances, is it conceivable that if you had written a book on your church and submitted it to me for the critical benefit of my ideas about it, that you would have felt yourself bound to have the book reflect my ideas rather than yours? I think not. This of course was an emotional reaction at base, but it exhibits the difficulty of establishing ourselves entirely on common ground. Many things you say in the notes you now send to me are kindred to this.

A few weeks ago I was discussing some political questions with a friend, and I remarked then that we are only critical about the things we don't want to believe. I think this observation has a more general application, and certainly it applies to some of the things you say to me in this letter. For example, you talk at some length about polygamy, which of course is a subject about which your church has always been hyper-sensitive. It is common among the members of your church to bring to bear the question of legal proofs, evidence that would stand up in court, when the subject of polygamy is brought up. But your church members, even you yourself who have been educated in the law, only take such ground when the matter under discussion is one you do not wish to believe. For example, you say to me now, about Joseph Smith, "Considering only the esoteric aspects it appears true that he claimed at an early time of his life to have had some remarkable spiritual experiences. He tried to tell them to a neighboring preacher as well as to his father. The details and development of the Book of Mormon, the fact that such claim was made, is clear from newspaper and other accounts published at the time."

Perhaps I may be allowed to conclude from this that you are talking about the period down to 1830, say, down to the date of publication of the *Book of Mormon*. But the fact is, Mr. Burgess, that what you say is not true. I have made a most determined search for evidences that would support Joseph Smith's claims in this respect, the most thorough search, I believe, that anyone has ever made, and this evidence does not exist. I have examined all the surviving newspapers published in Palmyra and Canandaigua during the time of the Smith residence in that neighborhood, as well as fragmentary files of the papers published in the Susquehanna Valley—I spent months on this research—and in none of them is there anything to bear out Joseph Smith's later portrait of himself as a person who had had spiritual experiences of overwhelming import (that is to say, one to whom God the Father had shown himself). Mr. [Francis W.] Kirkham, who did much research in the same field, was not able to demonstrate anything in this respect either; on the contrary, the stories he found and published present quite another picture of the young Joseph Smith. If you had to go into a court and present a case for Joseph Smith that hinged upon establishing the fact that his spiritual claims were common knowledge during the seven years before 1830, not to speak of the period before that, you could present no evidence except that of an obviously interested witness, himself. And you could not establish that even he himself had set forth such claims as a public record before 1840. Whatever may be said about Mrs. [Fawn] Brodie's book, it must be said that she was absolutely within her province as historian in pointing out this fact. You will find in your Church History a presumptive reference to such a vision as early as 1835, in private conversation (and it is due Mrs. Brodie to say that she called attention to this), but the documents are unfortunately withheld, and one is not permitted to investigate the value and import of the document in question. I have made a most determined search to go beyond Mrs. Brodie's findings, a far more determined search than any members of any of the so-called Mormon churches has made, and I have found no evidence whatsoever—in newspaper, religious periodical, court record, or private journal—that the First Vision was talked about or even known among the church members before 1840.

Now, Mr. Burgess, you may say that I am unfriendly to Joseph Smith because, as a historian, I set up a yell for the facts when I come across any claim whatsoever in Mormon history, be it for or against the Saints. I am as willing to find things in Joseph Smith's favor as to find things against him; indeed, the only way I can do my job as a historian is to try to prove the case for as well as against, in any particular. But in the end I must sit in judgment, and the basis of my judgment has to be the facts at my disposal. I am under no illusion that anyone is ever absolutely objective about anything; the remark I quoted to you above, about people being critical only about those things they don't want to believe, applies as pointedly to me as to anyone else. But at least in the writing of history I try to take nothing for granted, and I have no emotional investment to persuade me to believe anything on one side or the other.

You may say to me that religious experience is of such nature that it does not necessarily reflect itself in the kind of facts that I, as a materialistic historian, must deal with. You may say this and I will have no quarrel with you. But religious experience in general, certainly Mormonism as it is proselyted, is not content with a purely metaphysical existence and meaning. It begins to "prove" itself by "facts," by material processes, correspondences, and relationships and to justify itself by these "facts." When religion removes from the metaphysical to the material plane, however, it subjects itself to material criteria. As it lays claim to "facts," so it becomes embodied in "facts," and those facts may be taken up and individually evaluated by even the most materialistic of historians without legitimate objection by the religion or its adherents. If you tell me that you know God lives, I have no argument with you. If you tell me that religious experience is the most rewarding experience of humankind, I do not necessarily argue with you, though the question is open to debate. But if you tell me that the Book of Mormon is "proved" by modern archaeological findings, or that the Book of Mormon explains the material objects dug up by modern archaeology more satisfactorily than any other hypothesis that has been advanced, I have every right to bring materialistic disciplines to bear on what you tell me—in other words, to argue with you—and it will not satisfy me to have you say, for example, that you have evidence these things are true because Joseph Smith once took up a human thigh bone from a mound and said that it was a part of a "prehistoric" man named Zelf.

Perhaps it is in point here to bring up the information about Brigham Young I tried to obtain from you, and which you, for good reasons as you now explain, felt it necessary and proper to withhold from me. The allegation you refer to is worth nothing in itself, of course. But for me it would have been a starting place. I should have inquired what the opportunities of the one making the allegation were for having correct information. I should have wanted to know where and when Brigham Young was asserted to have belonged to a love cult, what its nature was, what it was called, who if anybody was asserted to have been associated with him in this cult. I should then have set about establishing whether Brigham Young lived at such a place at such a time, whether the local histories or newspapers make mention of such a cult or such persons even as were asserted to have been involved, whether the census reports in the National Archives list such persons as living at such a place at such a time. And so on, to the extent that the source material would support researches. I tell you this merely in illustration of my point of view on source material, and of the responsibilities that rest upon anyone who comes into possession of suggestive material. This is the modern research discipline, Mr. Burgess; it is the basis for the writing of modern history. In view of the hard things you have to say about Mrs. Brodie, it will interest you to know that she too subscribes to this point of view. You are inclined to feel that she threw into her book everything that would damage Joseph Smith, and played down everything in his favor. It is too bad that you did not have the privilege of talking over her problems with her while she was writing her book, of obtaining some insight into the workings of her mind, and seeing what was rejected as well as what was accepted for the content of her book. This is not to defend the validity of everything that appears in her book; but practically nothing appears in her book that does not have evidence of some kind to pose at least the possibility of its being true, a supporting framework to justify its inclusion in the text.

Being human as we are, it is too easy for all of us to rest on certain easy assumptions while we become properly critical and scientifically objective about other things. I have no doubt that my own book too often will be defective in this respect. But it helps to remember our common frailility in this matter. For instance, Mr. Burgess, you have much to say in the notes you now send me about the asserted relationship of Joseph Smith and Mrs. Buell in the spring of 1839. You take your critical stand on the fact that "after two days travel towards Boone County we are asked to believe that Joseph Smith jr. escaping, turned his face West into [a] field of his enemies, rushed to Far West, committed adultery with a married woman, turned around and in two days from release was on Salt River??? History shows facts of transfer to Boone County, escape, and at Salt River in two days or second day later. Nothing is shown that he went near Far West." Now, I have not looked into these facts, but in reading what you say, several times adverted to in your notes, my curiosity is aroused to make me wonder who has said that Joseph Smith visited Far West after his escape. On examining Mrs. Brodie's book, I find that she has not said this. Nor is it established that Prescindia Buell was at Far West at the time of Joseph's escape, although it would appear probable that she was somewhere in Missouri. Your whole argument about the logic or illogic of Joseph's having visited Far West depends upon the prior assumption that in the period under discussion Mrs. Buell was in fact at Far West. Maybe she was; maybe you can even prove that she was. But you do not now present any evidence for the significant assumption upon which the validity of your entire argument depends.

It would take me a long while to comment individually on each of the numerous points you bring up. Some of your points are well taken; on others it is evident that you talk on the basis of insufficient evidence (for example, examine the title-page of Eliza R. Snow's biography of her brother; or see her signature to her manuscript autobiography in the Bancroft Library, which hardly supports your idea that she did not use the name "Smith" during her lifetime).

The question of seerstones I won't attempt to go into in detail right now, as my ideas and what I have found out will be spread before you in due course in the manuscript of my book. The same thing is true about the early Justice of the Peace record, or the trial in the Susquehanna Valley. As I said to you last winter, Kirkham's ideas are absolutely invalid and will have to be given up, for a description of the trial, published in April, 1831, triangulates with two different later sources, all far apart in place and time.

Incidently, let me correct you on one point. My great-grandmother Pratt was not Sarah but a later wife of Orson Pratt.

To leave the subject of your letter for the present, I wish to make a further inquiry about the imperfect copy of Parley Pratt's pamphlet of 1838, *Mormonism Unveiled,* which you showed me in January. At that time I supplied you with a typed copy of the title-page as I had found it on another copy. The question is which of the first three editions your imperfect is. I have discovered a single copy of the first edition in the Western Reserve Historical Society, and a couple of copies of the other editions in other libraries. There is at least one point of difference. The third edition is misnumbered "34" at the head of page 4. The first edition is corrected in its pagination, however. On inquiry at Harvard, I find that the second edition is also incorrectly numbered. It can therefore be determined whether your copy is first edition or not, although if not, I do not yet have further points of differentiations as between second and third editions.

I have worked periodically at this bibliography since my return to Utah, and when opportunity offers, I am now typing up a check-list to be checked against the holdings of such libraries as I could not visit in person, e.g., the State Historical Society of Wisconsin. When such libraries have reported as to their holdings, the final, chronologically organized bibliography will be typed up, and I shall see what can be done about getting the bibliography in print.

Sincerely,

Dale L. Morgan

33. To MARGUERITE SINCLAIR

Salt Lake City, Utah
17 February 1949

Dear Marguerite,

After separating from you last night I kept revolving in my mind the possibilities of a [Utah State Historical] quarterly built around the theme of pioneering by women. I believe a most effective volume could be made on this basis. Four possibilities occur to me for inclusion.

The first of course is the Wenner story. If printed as an integral part of this larger theme, it would be desirable to call Mr. Miller's introductory remarks to the Wenner memoirs not "A Short History of Fremont Island," but simply "Introduction."

The second is the Martha Spence Heywood journal, which would be the piece de resistance of the volume. I looked through this again after arriving home last night, and am more than ever persuaded of the importance and great human interest of this journal. It contains quite a full diary of the overland journey of 1850, thus making it of interest to collectors of overland diaries; it is one of the best documents of the women's side to Utah life that has come to light; it is a picture of polygamy by a plural wife that is most affecting in its simplicity and pathos; and it is or will be the first diary of pioneer life in Nephi [Utah] and the building of that community that has ever been published. If this journal is published, I think it imperative that it be edited by someone who will edit it as a labor of love, appreciating it for its distinction. I hesitate to become a candidate for the job, what with all my other obligations, but I should feel very badly if this were published with only a perfunctory editing by someone.

The catch about this journal is that I don't know where the original is. The Writers' Project copied it from a typewritten copy in the B.Y.U. library, the provenance of which was not indicated. If the Society seriously is to consider publishing it, you should immediately write Professor M. Wilford Poulson at B.Y.U., who may have been the one to dig it up, asking if he knows where the original is, and whose sanction should be had for its publication.

With these two documents can be published one or two more, depending on how your space runs. One of these is the life story of

Mary Ann Hafen, who as a six year old child was a handcart pioneer of 1860. LeRoy R. Hafen is her son, and if this autobiography is to be published, it would be a nice courtesy to invite Hafen to edit it for you. However, in the back of my mind is a vague idea that this autobiography may have been printed by the Hafen family. Perhaps I am wrong. But if you write Hafen, raising this possibility, you might inquire of him whether the document still is unpublished. If Hafen himself did not, for various reasons, want to edit the autobiography, Juanita [Brooks] would be a very good person to do so, as she was long very close to "Grandmother Hafen," and in fact Mrs. Hafen, without being named as such, was one of those described by Juanita in her 1934 Harper's article, "A Close-Up of Polygamy." Grandmother Hafen lived a long, full life and died so recently as about 1944 or 1945.

The fourth possibility for such a quarterly is the autobiography of Mary Minerva Dart Judd, who moved to southern Utah in the very early fifties, was involved in the life with the Indian missionaries (her husband being Zodak Knapp Judd) and the first efforts at cotton raising. If this is published, Juanita of course would be mandatory as the editor, having dug up the journal in the first place, and knowing more about the subject than any other living person. On space considerations this document may be preferable to Grandmother Hafen's autobiography. Or if all four documents could be published, you would have a varied and fascinating volume of the Quarterly.

In case there should be any hitch about the Martha Spence Heywood journal, a fine one in its place perhaps would be that of Eliza M. Partridge Lyman, which Juanita turned up for Huntington, and of which there is now a typed copy at B.Y.U. She had been Joseph's wife, later married [Amasa] Lyman, and her journal of Utah pioneering is as affecting in its way as that of Martha Spence Heywood.

Dale

34. To FAWN BRODIE

Salt Lake City, Utah
7 April 1949

Dear Fawn,

The very fact that you should write me at Hollywood Avenue shows how far behind I am on my correspondence, for I have been in a place of my own on 10th East ever since the first of the year. I guess one reason I have been so slow is my reluctance to admit how slowly my book itself is coming along. I seem to work all the time without ever having much to show for the time put in.

One reason, of course, is that a high proportion of my time goes into writing and research not immediately connected with my book. The University of Utah Press has appeared as a candidate for publisher of my enormous bibliography of Mormonism, 1830-1849, so I took time out from other pursuits to sort out my bibliographical sheets chronologically, and begin typing up a sample section of the bibliography. This has now been done to the end of 1836—with notes, requiring 21 pages to deal with the first 46 entries—and I have delivered this, with a title-page and six-page preface to the U of U for their consideration. Harold W. Bentley, the guy imported from Columbia a year ago to run their publishing activities, is in New York at the moment, and when he returns I expect an answer one way or the other. If he has the money, I think he will take it on, but the governor managed to cut the University's appropriation by half a million dollars, and it remains to be seen where this leaves Bentley and their press. When you see this bibliography, I think you will be as amazed as I was when the titles began to roll in on me. There are about 700 titles for the period 1830-1849, and literally dozens neither you nor I had ever heard of before I started this little job.

But this has required a vexing amount of work, because I had to type up a checklist for the whole thing, alphabetically by author, to send to various libraries I couldn't visit in person, and this in turn has turned up more titles requiring time and attention from me. At the moment the Library of Congress is making a final check in the Union Catalogue against a copy of the checklist, and I have suspended any work on the bibliography until this census work is done. If I get one penny out of that bibliography I will be amazed, but it is something I happened to get started on and then became responsible for, and I think it will be a lasting thing, and something of a revolutionary force in Mormon history, or at least the writing thereof.

I have also been concentrating on extracting as much information as possible from the various factions, as I suspect some of them may clam up on me once my first book is published. I believe you would be surprised to see what I have now, probably several hundred pamphlets relating to the factions. When I can afford the time, I mean to publish a series of bibliographical contributions on the publishing history of each of these. I have prepared a preliminary bibliography of the Cadmanite or Bickertonite Church of Jesus Christ (the one at Monongahela, Pa.) which I may offer this fall to the [Western] Humanities Review. I have managed to gather practically all the publications of this church, except their early hymn books, and also of the "Re-Organized Church of Jesus Christ" which split off from this in 1908 and is now nearly extinct. When I get through with this faction, I will bibliographically tackle the Strangite church, which however is a far more difficult proposition. Needless to say, the Utah and Reorganized Churches will be left to the last, and in fact I doubt that I will ever publish a bibliography of this sort for the Utah Church; it would have to be instead a continuation of my major bibliography from 1850, and I am just as willing that somebody else should cover the later era.

Eberstadt [Booksellers] in New York has just bought [Milo] Quaife's collection of Strang MSS, and it will be interesting to see who acquires them. I hope to God Coe does, or some other public institution. I spent three days in these papers in December, 1947, and extracted most of the information I wanted down to 1849, but I didn't have time to cover the MSS relating to Beaver Island, and had hoped to do this enroute east this spring. But I am in no position to set off for the east as yet, and am extremely doubtful of having things in shape before July, if then. Maybe by the time I do get east again, these things will be permanently located.

Stan Ivins is expecting to get off on a two-month trip to your parts about Saturday or Sunday, and we have been going over things he might look up for both of us. He is going to Independence [Missouri] first, and with a letter of authorization from the U of U, is hoping to be allowed to have some things microfilmed. Then to Jefferson City, Cedar Rapids, Chicago, and points east. He is going to have a look at the county records at Lyons, N.Y., to see if he can find record of the imprisonment for "juggling" of our Walters the Magician [a contemporary of Joseph Smith], of Reflector [newspaper] fame. I went to the [LDS] Genealogical Society today hoping to check the census returns of 1820 and 1830 at Sodus, and thus prove him a person of undoubted historicity, but they haven't filmed those records yet, and there was no Walters on the list of persons buried in cemeteries in that area.

The letter from this fellow Stokes is a curiosity. One of these days I am going to write an article on "Mormonism's Suppressed Books" which aside from discussing the half dozen or so which actually have been suppressed will also discuss the several dozens which by booksellers' folklore are supposed to have been suppressed. You can buy copies of Josiah Gibbs' book like any other Mormon book—if you are willing to pay the price asked for it these days. I myself have a copy which once belonged to B. H. Roberts and has some entertaining marginalia by him—didn't I show it to you once? The Gibbs book is all right in its way, but the only substantial thing it adds to Mormon history is to clear the Saints of complicity in the Gunnison Massacre of 1853—and this was reprinted a few years ago in the Utah Historical Quarterly. Gibbs' pamphlet on the M[ountain] M[eadows] M[assacre] is much more important.

I have been following [John A.] Widtsoe's radio series with a good deal of enjoyment, looking to the time when he will find us exploding some of these comfortable assumptions. And this reminds me of something else amusing. You recall the letter I wrote [Francis W.] Kirkham from Fort Leavenworth [Kansas] about your book, seerstones, etc. Well, he didn't reply immediately, but just before I left there for St. Louis, I got a letter from him saying he was coming east to Chicago for an insurance conclave and would like to talk to me. He arrived after I had set out, and tried again to catch me at St. Louis, but I was held up at Columbia by work and icy roads, and didn't get there until he had left. No more was heard from him for months thereafter, though once, late last spring, when I was in the Historian's Office, I saw him there. We had never "met," so I didn't say anything. But then last fall while I was out of town, he called my mother, saying he had just learned I was in town, and would like to see me. He didn't then call up for a couple more months; as it happened, I was out at the time, and he was going to call back but apparently did not. However, one day about six weeks ago I had lunch with Madeline [McQuown] at the Lion House, and just as we were getting up from our table, he came in with a tray. I nodded to him without reflecting that he didn't "know" me, and he nodded back, then said to Madeline, "Mrs. Morgan, I presume?" She disclaimed the honor, and we smiled pleasantly and parted. But this has amused me. Also I wonder what he will think about seerstones when he reads my book. Why, even Emma [Smith] tells of writing to Joseph's dictation while he sat before her, nothing between them, staring into "the stone" in the depths of a dark hat.

After our long, hard winter we have had a fine beginning on spring, at least ten days earlier than the season a year ago. I have thought of you often the last couple of weeks, wondering how you were enjoying the season at Bethany. I bought a book on North American trees a couple of months back, to fill in a long-standing vacancy in my common knowledge, and when I finally come to visit you, I am going to wander around identifying every tree you have on the place. Ornithology is agreeable too, but so much depends on the sound the bird makes and the quickness of one's eye that I will leave this department of knowledge to you.

Now, Sister Brodie, don't you fret about your new book. Your new subject has this importance, that it is about a national figure, not merely a regional one, as Joseph was. Your work with Joseph Smith was as notable as [Arthur] Schlesinger's on Andrew Jackson, but look who got the huzzas and the financial rewards. Jackson's role in national affairs, and the continuing significance his "revolution" has for American life accounts for this. This is true also of [Thaddeus] Stevens. You have a man of great national importance, central to an American revolution, and you may find ultimately that he will reward you better than Joseph did. Not that this can be guaranteed, of course, but don't be unmindful of the possibilities.

You might be interested to see the new book, Rocky Mountain Cities, which came out ten days ago and includes a piece on Salt Lake City I wrote for it in June, 1947. So far there have been no squawks by the Church here, but that may be simply because the apostles haven't got around to reading it. The Salt Lake Library squawked long and loud before the book came off the press, in re[gard to] the next to last paragraph. I had a conference with the librarian, which boiled down to this, that they would mend their ways and I would alter the paragraph. It turned out to be too late for the first edition, which made them very unhappy, but the change will be made in the second edition, if any. I will tell you about this at greater length when you have read the book, which by the way was published by W. W. Norton, which makes the sixth different publisher to put something of mine in book form. Tell Dean Brimhall[1] that my remarks about the [Salt Lake] Tribune in that article are in remembrance of a discussion we had several years ago about a speech by J. Reuben [Clark] to the woolgrowers here.

I have just sent the Saturday Review [of Literature] my copy for Virginia Sorenson's The Evening and the Morning, coming out April 22.[2] By all means read this, her first wholly satisfying novel and from any view point a highly distinguished one, with the exception of [Wallace] Stegner's Big Rock Candy Mountain, probably the best novel by any writer of Utah associations. I understand that it is autobiographical in a small way, that the small girl is more or less Virginia herself, and the grandmother founded to some extent on Virginia's own. Be this as it may, it is a damned fine novel, and one I would like to have written.

I understand Juanita [Brooks] is in town, but we have missed connections yesterday and today. She was named to replace Cornelia Lund on the [Utah State] Historical Society's Board of Control a few weeks back, in every way a good move, because Mrs. Lund simply was an axman for the D[aughters]. [of the] U[tah]. P[ioneers]. I think maybe Stanford [University] is going to take her MMM book but negotiations were in progress when I last heard from her several weeks ago, and I don't know what the upshot is. There were a number of bugs that had to be ironed out, in the contract, not the manuscript.

Happy Arbor Day!

Dale

[1] Dean R. Brimhall, a cousin to Fawn Brodie, had met Morgan at the Works Projects Administration. He was later named to the Board of Trustees of the Utah State Historical Society. His and Morgan's correspondence is housed at the University of Utah's Marriott Library, Special Collections division.

[2] During the 1940s and 1950s, LDS writer Virginia Sorenson authored several novels with Mormon themes, including *Little Lower Than the Angels*, *On This Star*, *Evening and the Morning*, and *Proper Gods*. Her correspondence has been published in *Where Nothing is Long Ago*.

35. To ELIZABETH LAUCHNOR[1]

Salt Lake City, Utah
19 August 1949

Dear Elizabeth,

This is between you and me and the lamp post, but I would like to ask you, acting for the [Utah State Historical] Society, to try and do something for me. There are things in the [LDS Church] Historian's Office I would very much like to be able to study in detail, things I haven't found elsewhere. As they are printed items, it may be that the Church would accede to a request by me to have them microfilmed, but because of the attitude the Church took officially toward my Mormon history, I don't want to be officially beholden to them. These are, however, items the Historical Society might very appropriately desire to own in microfilm form, hence I would appreciate it if you would write the Church Historian, Joseph Fielding Smith, formally asking on behalf of the Society microfilms of the items I list below. The letter might run something like this:

Dear Mr. Smith:

We wonder if it would be possible to make arrangements with the Church for the filming of certain rare pamphlets and periodicals which relate to the history of the various lesser churches which lived and died in the late forties and early fifties. We should like to obtain for our own files microfilms of some of these works, if possible, and perhaps it would be excellent insurance for the Church to improve upon this opporunity for having microfilms made for itself.

Voree Herald, vol. I, 1846 (or such issues as you may have of it).

Reuben Miller, James J. Strang, Weighed in the Balance of Truth, and Found Wanting. Burlington, Wis., 1846.

James C. Brewster, The Words of Righteousness to all Men. Springfield, Ill., 1842.

James C. Brewster, Very Important to the Mormon Money Diggers. Why do the Mormons rage, and the People imagine a Vain Thing? Springfield, Ill., 1843.

Lyman Wight, An Address by way of an Abridged Account and Journal of my Life from February 1844 up to April 1848, with an appeal to the Latter Day Saints.

Gladden Bishop, An Address to the Sons and Daughters of Zion. Kirtland, 1851.

We learn also that your file of the Nauvoo *Wasp*, the *Nauvoo Neighbor*, and the Salt Lake City *Mountaineer* were microfilmed several years since for the Huntington Library, and that the negative film remains in your possession. Would it be possible for us to obtain a print of these films for our own archives?

Sincerely, &c &c

And if hereafter you should be asked what in hell the Society wants with things like this, you could say that many queries come to the Society about such early publications from local historians in the various states, so that it has become desirable for the Society to obtain microfilms if possible. All of which is true enough, and will be even more true when my bibliography is published.

Dale

[1] Elizabeth Lauchnor served briefly as secretary/manager of the Utah State Historical Society between 1949 and 1950.

36. To STANLEY IVINS

Salt Lake City, Utah
29 August 1949

Dear Stan,

I have been closely examining the Walters [the Magician] stories in the Palmyra Reflector, and I observe something that has escaped my attention before. It has been assumed that those "Gold Bible" articles of 1831 were written by Dogberry[,] i.e., Abner Cole, and we went on this assumption in searching the criminal records at Lyons [New York]. But on examining them now, I see some reason to think that either the articles themselves or the specific reference to Walters' jail sentence may have been written by the Reflector's correspondent in Farmington, Ontario County [New York]. If this is the case, we may have been looking in the wrong records.

Just a day or so ago I wrote the County Clerk at Canandaigua asking him to search for the writ of ejectment concerning the [Joseph] Smith [Sr.] farm, hence I am reluctant to write him immediately again on a matter of Mormon research; maybe we would get better results if you were to write on this second query. You need not even mention that it is a Mormon matter, saying simply that you are seeking to establish the facts about a jail sentence for "juggling" apparently served in Ontario County sometime between 1820 and 1830 by one Walters, perhaps Luman Walters, then or later residing in the township of Sodus; can the facts concerning this jail sentence be obtained?

Dale

37. To FAWN BRODIE

Salt Lake City, Utah
8 September 1949

Dear Fawn,

My book is coming along slowly, a hell of a lot more slowly than I like to contemplate, but at least it is moving along and eventually will be published. I am trying to get it as far advanced by November 1 as possible, because I am now bending every effort toward returning permanently to Washington [D.C.], and would like to be there by Thanksgiving Day.

This decision to clear out of Utah has finally crystallized in the last month. Anything else is plain foolishness. Last year, about 60 percent of my income came from outside the state; the percentage will be higher this year, and after my book is published, any local income at all will be strictly accidental. When you combine this with the grave handicap of trying to write our kind of history without the resources of a great research library, the answer becomes plain enough. To write the kind of books I want to write, I must have an income to make me independent of local sentiment. Accordingly I have written the Library of Congress and the Civil Service Commission to see what I can stir up in Washington, and meantime I am pressing my book on toward completion as fast as possible.

All of which is preliminary to some questions I want to put [to] you. Your book [*No Man Knows My History*] makes an awkward precondition for mine, since you got into the subject much as I would have done had I written mine first, and I don't want mine to be a carbon copy of yours. So I have begun the story with the settlement of the Smiths upon the farm near Palmyra (incidentally, I am persuaded that they squatted there for two years before they began to buy it). In your book on pp. 10, 11 you say that the Smiths made 7,000 pounds of Maple sugar or syrup one season, and won the fifty-dollar bounty for top production in the county. I have not seen this in the sources, and wonder if you remember where you picked it up. It shows rather more industry in the family than the other sources testify to.

In cross-checking your book and my sources, I note a couple of slip-ups which you might correct in your copy for the eventual revised edition I am sure you will publish. On p. 18 your citation should be to the Palmyra Herald, and Canal Advertiser, July 24, 1822. The Wayne Sentinel story you cite has to do with money-digging in Vermont, all right, but it is not the one from which you quote. On p. 20, line 18, it is Joseph Capron, not Willard Chase, you are quoting from; and in the footnote on this page, Joseph exhibited his seerstone December 27, 1841, not 1842. On p. 26, Pomeroy Tucker as well as O. Turner is a non-Mormon authority who treats of Joseph early religious ideas.

Last week I had Francis Kirkham underfoot much of the time. I permitted him to study the fruits of my research from the contemporary newspapers and religious press, and he was struck with the fact that the First Vision was on vacation or something. I challenged him to find out some things in the [LDS] Church archives—what they have done with their seerstones, whether the original manuscript of Lucy Smith's history has a variant version of the First Vision instead of the quoted version printed, whether anything at all can be found in the contemporary Mormon diaries to support the First Vision, etc. He is a nice guy and honest according to his lights; and I have no doubt that another edition of his book will try more directly to grapple with the seerstone hypothesis. But since he told me he was convinced that the world would be better off if everyone in it belonged to the Church, we cannot expect wonders of objective scholarship from him.

A week ago I also had an unexpected letter from [LDS apostle John A.] Widtsoe asking for any pro and con references bearing on the question of whether the First Vision was invented in 1838. I replied that there was absolutely no evidence for it before 1840, said that the closed policy of the Church made it impossible to search for affirmative evidences, and placed the responsibility upon him for having such a search made. I am glad this came up in advance of the publication of my book, so that I will be on record as having challenged the Church to prove its claims. I suppose Widtsoe is publishing his radio addresses and that his expressed desire to publish all the evidence pro and con proceeds from this.

The Eberstadts in New York have acquired the Oliver Olney MSS, and Charles Eberstadt sent them out here for my use in my history, in return for which I will give him some notes on the content for their purposes in marketing the MSS. The papers are as fantastic as Olney's published pamphlet, extending between April, 1842, and February, 1843. One thing I get a kick out of. Commenting on the Joseph-Bennett-Mrs. [Orson] Pratt embroglio [over polygamy] and the accusations made against Bennett, Olney remarks that he knows nothing of his own knowledge, but report had it that Bennett was in clover up to his eye-brows with wives who felt themselves abused by the husbands! There is an entirely new slant on the early reverberations of plural marriage.

When I return the Olney papers, Eberstadt promises to send copies of material lately acquired which sounds even more extraordinary. "They relate at great length to the persecutions and are of the first interest. One outstanding document was a very full journal by a Mormon who became one of the Generals of the Nauvoo Legion (but not [Reuben] Miller or [John C.] Bennett) whose name excapes me for the moment (sounds like one of the Laws [William or Wilson]), and another important document was the epistle written by Joseph Smith from the Liberty jail. There are other interesting documents in this collection and the great problem to me was trying to identify the handwriting, for the epistle from the Liberty jail had much of the appearance of Joseph Smith's handwriting, although perhaps somewhat more refined, so that it might have been Hyrum's, and all of the other documents were close enough in character to indicate that the whole business was written by the same hand. Since Joseph and Hyrum and Lyman Wight and Parley Pratt and several others languished in the jail for some months, it seemed logical to me that if they were not in Smith's own hand they probably were copied in the jail by one of his associates."

It will be interesting to see those documents. Thank God there are Eberstadts in this world to counterbalance church libraries.

I hope you had a restful and zestful time at Santa Monica and have got back to Bethany recovered from your hard experience here. I have been looking for some word from you, and now you will have to buckle down to some correspondence. Incidentally, I mailed you yesterday a reprint of an article from the April [Western] Humanities Review.

Best wishes to Bernard and the boys,

Dale

38. To STANLEY IVINS

Alexandria, Virginia
14 January 1950

Dear Stan,

The [Oliver] Cowdery stuff arrived some days back. I didn't know Ray Kooyman had made three prints of one specimen of his handwriting, and since one is all I require, I am pleased to send you one back to retain in your own files.

I have delayed writing you for several weeks hoping to hear from the New York State Library on a point of some interest and maybe even importance. In going through the Evening and Morning Star for August, 1834, I was struck by Oliver Cowdery's letter to his brother Warren which makes it evident that some affidavits from the Susquehanna Country had been published months before *Mormonism Unvailed* appeared. If I draw the correct inference from Cowdery's language, these were first published in the Montrose *Susquehanna Register* and then picked up by the New York *Baptist Register*, published at Utica. No file is known for the former paper, but it appeared that the New York State Library might have the appropriate volume 10 of the latter. After long delay, they advise me to the contrary. But I have just discovered volume 8 of this paper in the Library of Congress, which makes it evident that what I want is volume 11. The State Historical Society of Wisconsin is credited with this volume, so I have just finished writing them, asking that a search be made for me and photostats made of anything found. I suspect that this will prove to be the Isaac Hale affidavit and the other stuff in Howe, but I am also hopeful that some of the affidavits only mentioned briefly or quoted briefly in Howe will here appear in full. I am even hopeful that some mention of the trial will appear, because Cowdery's history of the Church in the Messenger and Advocate was clearly provoked by these affidavits in the *Register*, and his remark about a trial in that country I suspect may have been made to answer these affidavits. Anyway, it will be interesting to find out.

This last week I have been giving a lot of concentrated attention to the pattern of revivalism in and around Palmyra, and what I have found amply confirms my conclusions based on my research in the Palmyra papers, that there was no revival at Palmyra after 1817 until the big revival of 1824-25, and that it is this revival Joseph antedates to 1820. Lucy and William Smith in their accounts fully corroborate this. And you will be interested in the enclosed fruits of my researches in the Methodist sources, which even include George Lane's own account of the revival. I have also been able to establish that 1824-25 was the only year, from the time the Ontario District was established in 1819, that Lane was its presiding elder. All the rest of the time he was in charge of the Susquehanna District, making his home in Wilkes-Barre.[1]

Returning to the Cowdery microfilm, no, this is not restricted. But as far as [Francis W.] Kirkham is concerned, I warmly recommend that you try to work out a quid pro quo arrangement. I very much want to know the content of the brief pamphlet James C. Brewster got out in 1843, *Very Important to the Money Diggers!* which I know from the brief look I got at it in the Historian's Office has something to say about the involvement of Hyrum Smith and the Beman family in New York in the early money-digging. Kirkham can get access to this pamphlet and make notes from it; O.K., challenge him to do so, and let us see what its bearing is on the last edition of his book. I tried to interest him in it myself last summer, with what success I don't know. But I hate to let any possible source of information go uninvestigated.

Israel Smith hasn't yet kicked through with any specimen pages from the Book of Mormon. I'll write him again and see if anything is forthcoming. I've felt somewhat better since the turn of the year, but without entirely shaking off this cold, Virus XYZ, or whatever it is, and this afternoon it feels as though it were ready for a return engagement. I hope you have things under better control at your end!

Dale

[1] Fifteen years later, Morgan's findings regarding the Palmyra revivals would be independently "rediscovered" and published by Wesley P. Walters. See Letter Number 48.

39. To MADELINE MCQUOWN

Washington, D.C.
18 December 1950

Dear Madeline,

As you see, this is a letter of the genuine, dyed-in-the-wool, aged-in-the-vat birthday persuasion. Also, to this point, this has been one of the damnedest birthdays in some time.

I worked until 1 A.M. last night, as I have for several weeks, so didn't climb out of bed until about a quarter to nine. When I opened my door to pick up the morning paper, I was amazed to find lying on it the card of Israel A. Smith, the president of the Reorganized [LDS] Church, with a scrawl on it to the effect that he had called at 8:30 and would come back at 9. Although I spent a lot of time and energy yesterday cleaning up the apartment, I myself didn't even reach the point of shaving. So I promptly retreated into the bathroom with all my clothes, and when I emerged in a condition to be seen, sure enough not only Smith but Francis W. Kirkham were seated in my front room looking with interest at the copy of Juanita's book [*The Mountain Meadows Massacre*] which I received yesterday afternoon from Stanford.

Well, it was quite a session, and they didn't leave so I could have breakfast until almost 11. It was all remarkably cordial; you would have thought I was a high priest under favorable consideration for elevation to the [Quorum of the] Twelve [Apostles]. Smith of course is extremely interested in my book, which is bound to affect the vital interests of his church one way or another, and Kirkham has been dying to see it published to find out what I will have to say about the trial of 1826. I told them once more what I have said many times, that before I deliver the book finally to Rinehart, I shall send copies of the manuscript to the presidents of the two churches. Not, as I said to Kirkham, that I owed this to the Utah church, which had not cooperated in any way, but that I owed it to myself, and I wanted the two churches to have the opportunity to express their point of view on the book in advance of publication so that I might take this into consideration, although the book was going to express my judgment on Mormon history, not theirs. Well, this was very well received by both; in fact, Kirkham regarded it as rather momentous news; he wrote it all down as a memorandum (1) I would finish the book; (2) I would send a copy to [LDS church president] George Albert Smith; (3) I would then deliver it to the printer. I showed them the photostat Eberstadt sent me in August of the John Whitmer license, and Israel Smith thereupon volunteered to send me a photostat of a still earlier example of Joseph's handwriting, on a Bible bought at E. B. Grandin's bookstore in Palmyra, I think he said on October 9, 1828, but which I believe was October 1829 instead. Something also was said about a History of the Hebrews Joseph had owned, whether of this period I didn't get straight; he remarked that at that time Joseph apparently did not realize that there was a distinction between Hebrews (I think he said) and Judah.

Among other pleasantries, I suggested that if they were going north, they might dig up and send to me the lost 116 pages of the Book of Mormon manuscript. I also told Smith why I had not pressed him for photostats of specimen pages of the Book of Mormon manuscript for study of the handwriting, which was because I had emphatically made up my mind that their copy was the secondary rather than the original copy, and pointed out to him the internal evidence of two of Joseph's revelations going to show that the first quarter of the Book of Mormon as it was finally published was not written until a time beginning in May, 1929. He was much struck with this and asked me please to write him a letter giving him the documentation I had given him verbally and [my] reference to the Book of Commandments. (In case you're having difficulty following me here, what I am getting at is that the evidence goes far to show that most of the rest of the book had been written before Joseph reconciled himself to the necessity of replacing the lost text.) I also told him frankly that I had demonstrated, conclusively I thought, that the revival which converted Joseph, or turned his thoughts to religion, occurred in 1824-25 rather than in 1820.

A piece of sad news from Smith is that S. A. Burgess, the kindly old fellow to whom I will always be indebted for courtesies shown me while visiting the Reorganized Church, died in November. I last heard from him in September in connection with my Strangite bibliography; he said then that he had had a serious heart attack a few months ago and was quite inactive now.

Well, with all this, it wasn't until 11 that I reached your birthday present. I thank you very much for it, my dear, and will take pleasure in reading it. I am all the more pleased with it because the jacket is a detail of one of the paintings I saw in the Corcoran show Friday. The original is perhaps more striking than the reproduction, because, as I recall, the original has a rather dark sky with an unearthly blue breaking out just above the skyline. The jacket seems to have cropped the painting so that this blue, which appears in consequence more normal, makes up all of the sky as represented. Anyway, it was a thoughtful present and one I am glad to have.

I haven't yet had an opportunity to study Juanita's book, but substantially it seems to have been published as I last saw it in manuscript, with, however, a more thoroughly worked out bibliography. It is evident either that Stanford has no staff to give its book a professional copyreading, or their copyreader is just about incompetent, for there are inconsistencies in style and such, here and there, which always get past the author and which it is the business of the copyreader to clean up before the printer gets the book. Juanita did not add to the acknowledgements as they were before, on the principle, I imagine, that she did not want to embarrass anybody who helped her in the light of the uncertainty she has been under of how the book will be received.

While on all this birthday-historical gossip, let me say that I don't exactly understand your recent question about the Deseret News and the [multi-volume] Journal History, and perhaps you had better re-phrase it. Maybe, on the other hand, you can find your answer in the following general information: The Journal History contains many typed transcripts from the Deseret News, sometimes appearing in the J.H. according to the date of publication of the News, sometimes according to the date of a certain happening, of a letter or document, or something else of the kind. Ordinarily, if the Church has the original letter itself, the J.H. would cite the original, or maybe the H[istory of]. B[righam]. Y[oung]. source, rather than the News source. However, there may be some cases where a piece of information is credited to the Deseret News, say, "7:234," with a parenthetic notation following: "(Original on file)." I can't answer you about any given case without knowing the exact case you are inquiring about and what my note on it was.

It is still cold here—by Washington standards, that is—with temperatures ranging from the middle twenties to the middle forties. Today is at least sunny, however.

I've been hellishly occupied with the Korns manuscript, involving nothing less than a translation of the Lienhard manuscript from the original German, a job so difficult that Darel [McConkey]'s German reading friends threw up their hands at it. I've been making progress nevertheless, having now translated one-seventh of it, some 6 typewritten pages. I'll tell you all about it later.

Meanwhile this must serve as my reverse-English birthday remembrance—and certainly my vehicle of appreciation. I will write again soon.

Dale

40. To STANLEY IVINS

Washington, D.C.
5 January 1951

Dear Stan,

After waiting long enough to avoid the appearance of unseemly haste in the matter, I have just written to Yale. For your information as a party of the second part, I enclose a copy of the letter. We will see if this siphon can be made to work!

I was much entertained by your account of your talk with [LDS Church Historian's Office employee A. William] Lund. Naturally he associates that pamphlet [*Very Important to the Money Diggers!*, by James C. Brewster] with me because nobody ever took the slightest interest in it before I examined it long enough for a bibliographical description of it in the spring of 1948, and of course I later tried to interest [Francis W.] Kirkham in it. You did very well in talking to Lund, making the right admissions and opening up some possibilities. Maybe he is just playing us for suckers, to see if we can swing Yale at will, but I hope not. Of course, their being willing to have Yale ask doesn't mean they have to say yes.

Especially amusing were Lund's remarks to you about me. What he was talking about, I suppose, is the Strangite bibliography. Last May I sent him a copy of the checklist on that, asking that he indicate which edition the church had of a couple of reprints, and also asking for the dimensions of a pamphlet of 1881. He never replied to that, and from the way he talked to you about "relenting," it is evident this just didn't so happen. Along toward fall as the bibliography was nearing completion, in a letter to Bill Mulder[1] of the [Western] Humanities Review I discussed the future study of the Hedrickites, and mentioned one difficulty that confronted me, the necessity of a page-by-page scanning of a couple of fairly early Hedrickite periodicals, and said if he knew anyone willing to take on so irksome a job for me, I would be very grateful. Mulder mentioned this to Albert Zobel who was interested enough to do it and sent his findings to Mulder, who relayed them to me. I wrote him my thanks and mentioned the three items in the Church holdings on which my Strangite bibliography was deficient, and said if he was ever in the library and wanted to look at the bound volume of Strangite pamphlets, I would be glad to have that information. I never had a reply to this letter, and your letter is the first even oblique information I have had that Zobel made any attempt to do anything about it. So I had to laugh at Lund's account of the incident. Actually, it makes no damned difference to me or the bibliography itself whether it is published with this information; the only real advantage it is to anybody is to the Church Library, to have their holdings fully reported. When I sent the Strangite bibliography in finally to Mulder in November, I told him that if he was in good odor at the Church Library and wanted to ask Lund for the information, he was welcome to do so, but as they had ignored my original letter, I didn't intend to press them further myself. So this was the background to your portentous interview with him! His remark about the Amelia Palace goes back to that Salt Lake City essay of mine. At the time it was published, he took exception to some things in that, and I discussed them casually with him, including the Journals of Discourses at the Salt Lake Library and the Amelia Palace. About this latter, I said that whether or not it had been built for Amelia, it was so called in casual conversation in Salt Lake City and later, hence my reference to it by that name was entirely proper. Apparently he is still rankled by the point!

A week before Christmas I was amazed to have call upon me one morning, even before breakfast, not only Francis W. Kirkham but [RLDS church president] Israel Smith himself. Both, of course, were interested in my history. I told them again what I have often said before, that before publication both Israel and [LDS church president] George Albert Smith will be given the opportunity to express to me their objection to any facts or conclusions the book may contain, although the book is of course mine and in the final analysis must express my point of view on their history, not theirs. Israel Smith thought this "fair enough," while Kirkham seemed positively amazed and wrote it all down as though he were going to tell George Albert this news personally. I added to Kirkham that I was extending this courtesy to the Utah church, not because I owed them anything, for they had not cooperated with me in any way as far as the history was concerned, but because I owed it to myself. It was on the whole a pleasant, even cordial session all round. Of course, it may be otherwise another time, when it is no longer possible to influence the shape my book will take. In talking with Smith, I told him why I had not pressed him further for photostats of specimen pages of the Book of Mormon manuscript, which was because that I had definitely concluded it was the secondary copy, which made it of little interest and no importance in whose handwriting it was written. I also discussed conclusions I had reached on the basis of certain of Joseph's revelations, which made it apparent that the earliest part of the Book of Mormon text as it now exists are the opening pages of [the Book of] Mosiah, and that the first quarter of the Book of Mormon as printed probably had not been written until most of the rest of the book had been written, certainly not before May, 1829. This made it unimportant whether or not the fragment in the possession of the Utah Church was in [Oliver] Cowdery's handwriting. All this apparently was news to Smith. He asked me to write him a letter setting forth what I had told him verbally, and quoting from the same revelations I had read from. I promised to do so. But as I would like a little information from him, I am now waiting on his initiative, so that I will have the advantage of this subtlety in our dealings. I showed him the photostat of the John Whitmer license, which was the earliest example of Joseph's handwriting I had seen. He then mentioned the Bible bought by Joseph and Oliver at E. B. Grandin's bookstore in 1828, I think he said October 4. Of course he must have meant 1829. He volunteered to send me a photostat of this inscription, and I said I should be glad to have it. So there we stand up to the present moment. How he and Kirkham happened to show up here together I didn't inquire and they didn't say. If he sends along the photostat and requests the documentation on the B[ook] of M[ormon], I will send him that, and at the same time ask him about the Missouri official documents.

I will send you my photostat of the Joseph Smith letter soon (it's his own handwriting), and also what I have of the Liberty Jail epistle. I find that the photostat of that [which] the Eberstadts sent me is not the whole, just some specimen pages of it. I learn from Eberstadt that not long since he made the Church Library a present of photostats of the [Albert P.] Rockwood material and some other miscellanea, by way of inducing them to give him a photostat of the last leaf of Reuben Miller's anti-Strang pamphlet of 1846, so the restrictions I laid upon you with regard to the Rockwood material no longer hold, although I haven't yet heard definitely that this has passed into the Coe collection. Incidently, did you see the rather amazing coincidence that the Rockwood narrative is mentioned in the F[ranklin]. D. Richards letter Eberstadt sent me just before Christmas?

Juanita [Brooks] writes me that she hears by the underground that by official policy the Church will ignore her book in all its publications, which doubtless will extend to the [Salt Lake] Tribune also. From her point of view this is at least better than a scathing public outburst against her. As far as reviewing her book is concerned, you need have no hesitancy on Juanita's behalf. She has a remarkably objective attitude and will receive anything you might say about the book in the spirit in which it is said. Whether you will want to review it in the [Western] Humanities Review of course is another matter. But if you do review it, pull no punches as far as Juanita is concerned; let her have the bad with the good.

At the last moment I held your Journals of Discourses here to take a few more notes, and this then got hung up because I have been involved in the damnedest chore I ever thought to tackle, translating from the original German the journal of a Swiss immigrant of 1846 who was a week ahead of the Donner party. This is to appear early this year in the U[tah]. H[istorical]. Quarterly as part of a memorial volume for my friend, the late J. Roderic Korns. I didn't know 20 words of German when I began, but my education has necessarily progressed by leaps and bounds since. But at the cost of an enormous expenditure of time, and under great pressure, for a deadline looms ominously over me. Your books will go off soon.

The Brimhall narrative Juanita mentions is one I myself gave her; I copied Fawn's copy back about 1944, and the 73 single spaced typewritten pages describes only the transcription I myself made; Fawn's was doublespaced and ran to more pages. Only 4 copies of the published book are known, as it is said for some reason to have been suppressed. There are two copyright deposit copies at the Library of Congress, one in the Church Library, and Dean Brimhall owns one. Auerback was reported to have one, but if so it didn't turn up in the auction. Last summer Dean Brimhall had 100 copies of the book reproduced by photolithographic process, and generously gave me one. He has disposed of them at $5 a copy. If you want one, write him here at 2000 F Street; perhaps he still has some. I recommended last summer to the Historical Society that they buy one; if they did, perhaps you can see it up at the Capitol. The relationship of the diary to all this I don't know, for Fawn hadn't seen the diary itself up to the time she left Washington in 1945; what she copied was the original manuscript of the book itself. Is this all clear?

I have just learned to my surprise that William Smith got out a paper at Palestine, Ill., in 1848, called Zion's Standard. I don't know how many copies were published or when it began or ended; I can't locate any copies at all. But it must have been extinct by early 1849 when [Isaac] Sheen's paper at Covington became William's organ.

By the way, Israel Smith told me that S. A. Burgess died in November of a heart ailment. This is sad news, for I rather liked the old fellow, who exhibited many courtesies to me over a number of years, and particularly while I was in Independence [Missouri] in January and February, 1948.

I've been sitting here at [the] L[ibrary of]. C[ongress]. writing on this for the past hour, and now I'd better get to work. A little belatedly, a happy new year to you.

Dale

[1] William Mulder was co-editor, with Harold Bentley, of the *Western Humanities Review*. He subseqently wrote *Homeward to Zion* (1957) and, with A. Russell Mortensen, compiled *Among the Mormons* (1958).

41. To FAWN BRODIE

Washington, D.C.
25 April 1951

Dear Fawn,

Like you, I have been enthralled by the fine comedy in progress out in Utah. Since the [Washington] Post did not know the inwardness of the story, it did not even publish the basic facts bearing upon it, and I had to wait impatiently till the Utah papers turned up at [the] L[ibrary of]. C[ongress]. to find out just what David O. [McKay] did about J. Reuben [Clark,[1] reassigning him second counselor in the First Presidency instead of first counselor]. Then I laughed indeed. It set me to wondering how it would have been received if David O. had decided to give the church the straight goods, and instead of the doubletalk you send me had said, "Brothers and Sisters, I know that I ought to love J. Reuben like a brother. But I ask you, how could anybody love him? I would prefer to throw him overboard entirely. But that wouldn't be the politic thing to do, and I am not prepared to face the consequences, so what I am doing instead is to kick him down to Second Counselor. Brothers and Sisters, this is the Spirit of the Lord speaking, and the spirit says that if J. Reuben doesn't take this well, the spirit of apostasy is in him and I warn you all to beware of him. Amen."

Of course I am completely unmoved, in the right way that is, by his accession to the presidency; my most positive feeling is that it could have been Joseph Fielding Smith, after all. I regret the death of George Albert Smith in itself, both because I think he was more of a true Christian gentleman than is common to the high places of the Church in these latter years, and because of the two men next in line in the succession. I think people respected without much liking Heber J. Grant; I think people liked and in a sense respected, though he was not a very forceful person, George Albert Smith. But how they feel generally about David O., I confess I do not know.

It occurs to me, by the way, that you should not delay longer in getting out the new edition of your book. By way of urging you on, I have written out a new title-page for you which you will find enclosed [see below], and I will leave the rest to you.

L'Affaire McKay is not the only funny business in Utah lately, though. I had a note from Stan Ivins yesterday with a beautiful tale. You may have heard that Samuel W. Taylor, who had that memorable piece in Holiday Magazine a couple of years back, has expanded it into a book, Family Kingdom. (I have a copy here from the S[aturday] R[eview of] L[iterature]; you can see it if you want.) This deals with his father, John W., one of the intransigent apostles who went right on practicing polygamy after the Church faced the other way, and by and large is a pretty good job, although it fights shy of digging very far into the inner developments in [LDS apostle] John W.'s estrangement and final excommunication back in 1906. Anyway, Stan writes: "Sam Taylor is in town publicising his new book. He thought he had cleared [it] with the Church, but, after it was printed, someone objected to his story of John W. Taylor's Conference reference to the reported unchastity of Tabernacle Choir members. So the Deseret Book will not display it and Auerbach's cancelled their 400 copy order and their autograph party. Sam is rather indignant about it all." Serves the guy right. Anybody who sets out to please the Church is going to find himself in these straits sooner or later. Better take what pleasure you can from fulfilling your sense of your own integrity as a writer.

Stan, by the way, was moving into a slightly larger place; his new address is 56 South Third East, Apt. 107.

Returning to David O., I have been wondering if you and I couldn't manage to bring about a re-merger of the Utah and Reorganized Churches. The method that occurred to me was for us to inviegle David O. and [RLDS president] Israel [Smith] into the same room, lock them up in it together, and neither let them out nor feed them anything but bread and water until one of them has had a revelation from God certified by the other as the real thing. If you want to undertake to deliver David O., I will see what can be done about producing Israel.

Dale

[Enclosure:]

No Man
Knows My History
The Life of JOSEPH SMITH
THE MORMON PROPHET
by
the niece of
DAVID O. MCKAY
PRESIDENT OF THE MORMON CHURCH
AUTHORIZED EDITION
New York Alfred A. Knopf
1951

[1] J. Reuben Clark was named counselor in the First Presidency of the LDS church in 1933 and an apostle the following year. He served as first couselor to LDS presidents Heber J. Grant and George Albert Smith from 1934 to 1951. Following David O. McKay's succession as church president in 1951, however, he was named second counselor, a change many viewed as a demotion.

42. To MADELINE MCQUOWN

Washington, D.C.
10 June 1951

Dear Madeline,

It is a Sunday all gray and green; it has been raining most of the day and now darkness is coming on. I've been alternately working at cleaning up the house, at writing, and a large miscellany of tasks. Just at this moment I am rattling around in the enormous emptiness of this apartment, for if anything is calculated to make a place emptier than the smell of biscuits in the oven, coffee ready to wash them down, and no one with me to dispose of them, I would like to know what it is. I don't like Sundays much, anyway, not right now. The improvement of my fortunes necessarily waits upon the functioning of the wheels of government, and they don't function at all on Sunday, not even to the extent of a mail delivery. I hope Sunday will come to have a different character before very much longer; you can be sure it is going to have such a character the minute I have the means. With warmth to be had in the world, I am going to have it.

But meanwhile it is a Sunday of large vacancy, and no way to get the devils out of me. . . . Last night I read a pocket version of another of [F. Scott] Fitzgerald's novels, this time The Beautiful and the Damned. I have read his novels in the reverse order they were written, so it probably is to his credit that I say each strikes me as worse than the last, with This Side of Paradise yet to come. The first half of The B & D struck me as a horrible performance, the kind of thing that wouldn't be published except as coming from a "successful" author. The last half was better, but the whole thing set me to wondering why Fitzgerald thought it worth writing. I should think its principal meaning and value to him was that it served him as a catharsis of all kinds of dislike and resentments attending the kind of life he was living then. Nobody and nothing is very appealing in the novel, yet the book is not informed by a very deep anger, either. Altogether, quite a curious book.

My neighbors are in action at sundry of the windows across the way. I have curiosities about a number of them, for I don't become casually acquainted as most people do, and thus am left to my own fantasies to explain things people customarily pick up by a kind of social osmosis. The apartment immediately across from this one is occupied by one or two fellows, I'm not quite sure which, who evidently are in the Navy, and one of these guys is a tooter of horns. The exact variety I don't know, perhaps a French horn, but every now and then I see him at his tooting, with his back to the window, sometimes with a couple of other tooters on hand too. What with my typewriter, the people in these buildings must have undergone quite a conditioning.

On the same floor as the above, front end of the building, is a gray haired woman I suppose to be in her forties, neither particularly attractive nor particularly unattractive. I've met her a couple of times on the walk and we have a nodding acquaintance, but I don't know who she is or what she does.

On the first floor of the building opposite is a young couple with a very small baby; they moved in just recently and I haven't seen much of them. At the moment another couple seems to be visiting them. On the same floor with them lives another young couple who also have moved in quite lately, and I couldn't describe them either except that the wife has reddish hair and carries herself rather slackly, a loose way of holding her shoulders and a rather sidling gait. In the basement apartment opposite a couple of working girls live and also apparently a man, but although they've been living there since early September, I'm damned if I can figure the menage out, whether the fellow is the husband of one of them, the brother, or what have you, as they seem to come and go more with each other than with him.

In this building, on my floor, live a rather odd couple. Originally I supposed they were mother and son, but it has become quite evident that they are man and wife. I don't know whether she is younger than she looks, he older than he looks, or both of them precisely as old as they look and the marriage consequently one of a not uncommon type. Both of them work. They have the only television set in the building, and their apartment is thus a mecca on weekends for the small fry who live in this building.

In the apartment under me live an air force sergeant, his wife, and their two small kids. I have seen him only infrequently of late and duty may have taken him off far enough to make it difficult to get home, or maybe he is on duty at ungodly hours of the day and night. When I talked to him last, some weeks ago, he had been busy hunting for a house. I had the impression when we all first moved in that his wife was pregnant, but if so she must have lost the child, for she is slimmer now with no baby in evidence.

On the same floor with them are some new arrivals I haven't yet sorted out, an older woman, a younger, and a small girl; it may be that the apartment belongs to the one in the middle, for I have the impression she is married and the others living with her. In the basement apartment is a young woman who has been here from the beginning. She has two quite small and attractive children, but whether she is divorced, widowed, or otherwise separated from her husband, I don't know. She works daytimes, and the children seem to be cared for by an older woman in the neighborhood who brings the kids back around 6 on weekdays. Of my neighbors who live in the other half of this building, 422 Condon, I know practically nothing, as they have their own entrance on the other side of the building and I never really cross paths with them.

Thus you see I know so little about all these people, merely what one picks up from casual visual observation, that I could almost write a novel about them, letting my fancy work upon them to explain who and what and why they are.

The biscuits and the coffee being ready, nothing better occurs to me than to eat them, though I am not especially hungry. I have had a certain amount of fever and a headache so that I find it difficult today to write to very good effect on my book.

* * * * * * * * * * * * *

All this was written yesterday, such as it is. Today I have two letters from you, and I am glad to have them. A little sorrowful, too, for how nice it would be to have letters from you written in this spirit without feeling that I have to twist your arm, figuratively, to induce you to write them. We all have our needs in this world, and one great need of mine is that people should feel something about me and have the urge to express this to me from no more complicated motive than the idea that it might help to make me happy. Sometimes wistfully, sometimes more urgently, this is something I have wanted for quite a long while now, and it lies back of much of the restlessness that periodically rides me.

I am very sorry for your mother as well as for you in the situation that presently exists. It is in many ways comparable with the situation that my grandmother has had to cope with since my grandfather's death, though she does have a degree of financial independence, the result of selling her home. You pay a price for everything in this world, and she had to pay a price for that: the place was too big for her alone, so that she could not take care of it at her age, and she is now as she has always been a fiercely independent person, so that her financial dependence upon her sons, from month to month, was extremely hard for her. By selling her home she got a certain amount of money of her own, but at the cost of a tearing up by the roots. She found it impossible to live with any happiness in California despite the presence of her sons there, and has been happiest, I think, since returning to Utah. She lives mostly with my mother, for it is quiet there and she also enjoys watching television (some months ago, last fall, Helen and Mother bought a radio-phonograph combination, and while they were at it they got a television combination too). Now and then she goes up to stay with her daughter for a few days or weeks, which gives her some change and also the sense of being able to relieve my mother, I suppose. On the whole, this is a more fortunate arrangement than anything that is immediately in sight for your own mother, and I shall certainly hope with all my heart that she can attain or be helped soon to a certain degree of security and ease of mind.

Your own letter makes better sense in what it has to say about your personal independence than the occasional disjointed things you have to say to me on this subject. Actually I believe you think and feel on two different levels, conscious and unconscious, about this, and they aren't always part and parcel of each other. You are yourself torn by these divergent stresses, and I am made to feel the effects of them too.

In other respects, though, your letters do not make sense, this talk about a job. You are not going to find a way out of your difficulties by putting yourself in a hospital at $21 a day, Madeline, and you should know this by now even in your moods of desperation. You had better be content to work at your book, for good and ill, for you can pace yourself with it as you cannot with a job. If you have a hundred dollar balance in the bank, you have to be realistic enough to refrain from writing $2,500 checks on that account, attractive as the idea of having $2,500 in currency may seem to you.

I will be glad to help you on your book [a biography of LDS church president Brigham Young] if you are as you say in a mood to be helped. Send along your manuscript or any part of it, and let me see what I can do, on any realistic terms, to help you move it along. You have resented my telling you so, but I have felt that you were utterly irrational in how you were trying to write it; it is as though someone who wanted to get to Salt Lake City from Ogden were to swim across the Great Salt Lake, walk on across the Salt Desert to Wendover [Nevada], and then ride the rails or hitch a ride in to Salt Lake City. It can be done that way if you are sufficiently determined to show someone that you can do it. But why must it be done that way? How about the possibilities of US 89 and US 91? You have wanted every kind of help from me so long as it did not require you to admit to yourself that I might contribute something to your book—as I did to Fawn's book, for example, or Nels Anderson's, or Juanita Brooks's, or any of half a dozen others. Better that I should send you whole files of documents for you to find yourself one note that you could use than that you should lay it on the line and show me what your problem was, your deficiencies in information, or what have you, and let me help you or not, as I might be able. As though an electronics manufacturer should be in need of certain critical components and forthwith order a carload of iron ore, lime, coking coal, and whatnot with the idea of producing what he wanted for himself without having to invoke the aid of intermediate industrial operations or specialized engineering services. And all this mainly to vindicate yourself before me. To show me that you can do it. Sure you can do it; I have been willing to grant you that from the beginning. But why isn't it possible to think a little in terms of *we*, without this rigid, controlling differentiation of thine and mine?

I'll refrain from writing about some other things in this letter, in view of the probability of which you inform me, your being in Salt Lake City, or Ogden, rather, by the time this gets out to California. Speaking of research and the Deseret News, were you aware that the Bancroft Library has a file of the News from 1865 to 1879, the last 12 years of Brigham's life, that is? For those years at least you need not travel all the way to Salt Lake City. When I was at Berkeley I talked with the Bancroft librarian, Helen Harding (now Mrs. Bretnor), who was very kind to me, having your case specifically in mind. There is a small elevator not normally open to use for the public which she said you could arrange to use, which would spare you climbing all those flights of stairs. Go talk with the Director, Dr. Hammond, or Mrs. Bretnor, mentioning me if you like, and I am sure you will be gratified by the results. Not that the Bancroft Library is exactly next door for you or anything. But it is a hell of a lot closer and more convenient than the Salt Lake Public Library just now.

I believe copies of Rod Korns' book will become available around the end of this month. You are to be sent one by Mrs. Korns or the [Utah] Historical Society, one or the other, so please let me know if and when one arrives. [A. Russell] Mortensen wrote me on the 1st that indexing was in progress, so by now I should think the printing itself has been done and the first work on the binding commenced. When this book is published, the first time you take a train east of Evanston [Wyoming] by daylight you will find that you have a new and engrossing interest in the terrain over the first 20 miles or so. This goes for me, too. I've only been through there once by train, and after dark at that.

Well, maybe for a change a few breaks will come our way. They don't roll the wrong way in perpetuity, and the law of averages is about due to catch up with us. Write and let me know what you will be doing the next couple of weeks, and where.

Dale

43. To MADELINE MCQUOWN

Washington, D.C.
18 January 1952

Dear Madeline,

This has certainly been a week to remember—but one to remember mostly for the wrong reasons. I'll make a beginning on a letter tonight, and perhaps mail it tomorrow if some of the dust has settled by then.

To begin with, on Wednesday morning I got a letter from Stanley Rinehart so nasty in its tone that I bridled all over. I had intended to send it on for you to read, but for reasons that will appear later, I had better hold to the original of it for the present. But this is what he had to say, except that I am running all his paragraphs together into one: "I have reviewed with considerable concern and disappointment the record on THE MORMONS. You have had this under way since January of 1945, and the contract was drawn in 1948. When you first asked us to help you get a Guggenheim Fellowship, you said that you had already been working on it for ten years, so that makes seventeen years in all. We have now received three chapters, so preliminary in nature that they give no indication of the projected book, and the volume of correspondence far outweighs this amount of manuscript. It seems to us grossly unfair for you to draw an advance and agree to a production schedule which called for the first volume two and a half years ago, and then make so little apparent effort to fulfill your commitment. I do think you should either complete the book or abandon it and return the advance. For the record, we are no longer committed to publication, but we would like either to read the manuscript or to have our money back."

Now, if Rinehart had written me gently that as I was having such great difficulty in meeting the commitment I had made, it would probably be better on both sides to drop the matter, and that they would like me to return the advance, I should have taken no offense whatever, embarrassing and difficult as this would have made things for me. But neither for $750 or any other sum do I give any man the right to insult or condescend to me. I received this in the morning, and not to be hasty about it, went on to [the] L[ibrary of]. C[ongress]. as usual, and thought it over all through the day.

What I finally decided to do was if humanly possible to free myself from all obligation to Rinehart and regain my freedom of action generally on this book. So that night I wrote to D. L. Chambers, the president of Bobbs-Merrill who has been extraordinarily kind and courteous through all our relations, and never ceased wishing that my Mormon book was on his list, proposing that we draw up a contract for the Jedediah Smith biography, to be delivered January 1 of next year. I conditioned this upon Bobbs-Merrill's making an immediate advance of $750 on that book, and frankly told him what I wanted it for, to regain my liberty with respect to the Mormon book; I also told him I would give him an option upon that book, or if he like, sign a contract with him for it, with the understanding that it would be delivered after the Smith biography. I asked him to give me a reply, if possible, by this coming Monday, and you have no idea how much I hope the check will be forthcoming so that I can write Rinehart at once to tell him that I am returning his money and relieving him of all anxiety about it. This is the reason for holding his letter here; his concluding remark is my legal release from any obligation to Rinehart provided he gets his money back.

I have many times regretted that I committed myself on this book when as it proved the circumstances of my life were such that I was not able to make good on the commitment; and as I have not been willing to throw a text together to satisfy a merely legal obligation, I have been in a cruel situation. If this works out as I hope it will, it will all be for the best, for the Smith biography can be written realistically within a time limit, and the Mormon book need go to the printer only when I am satisfied with it finally.

I told Chambers that I would hope to have a rough draft of the book by summer, that I would hope to get over some of the Smith trails in the West in July, get down into Mexico for a foray into the Mexican archives by autumn, and polish the book for delivery by the end of the year.

But now there are wider and wider ripples flowing out from my numerous predicaments, and for this we have to go back again.

Thursday morning I went in to the Episcopal hospital for a second and far more thorough examination of my eyes as they were tested for refraction. The doctor told me that mine were the type of eyes that were prone to retinal detachment, and if I should ever have any of the symptoms, flashes of light, or the sense of a veil before the eyes, I should have an oculist look at them immediately. He tested both eyes at great length, and finally told me it was impossible to bring my eyes into perfect balance, but that he could sharpen the vision of the left eye more satisfactorily. He didn't have much to say about my right eye, and I am not sure that he fully grasped or observed from testing the peculiarity I stumbled upon Monday, that this eye has much better long vision, but much worse close vision. Anyway, I told him that I felt there had been considerable improvement in the condition of my eyes in the last week, and certainly a vast improvement over the state they were in through December. He thought it would be best to go on with my present glasses for a while, to see if the improvement continues; so barring something unexpected, I shall sit tight on the matter of new glasses for the next month.

This gave me something to think about, too, as you can well imagine. I may go to the end of my days without ever experiencing a first class crisis in my eyesight; but also I have now been placed upon warning that something could happen to one or another of my eyes at any time. If that actually should happen, it would probably bring an effective end to me as a writer of history, and I would have to branch out into another sphere of writing which did not so largely depend upon the intake of facts. The only intake I have is my eyes; I couldn't get by as [Francis] Parkman did. But since this danger does exist, I would very much like to get this [Jedediah] Smith biography and the three Mormon books down in type, and the sooner the better, so that all that I have put into them for so long will not be in danger of waste and loss.

Under these circumstances, I have just about determined (if the Smithsonian thing should fall through within the next couple of weeks, as I gloomily am prepared to anticipate) to write to [A. Russell] Mortensen to see if we can somehow come to terms for a half-time job which would pay my bills and give me some freedom for my own writing through the rest of this year. He might be able to find the funds for such a job where he could not for a full-time job. Also, he might not; and I haven't yet had word from him whether or not he has been able to swing that supplementary check he hoped he could put through after the first of the year.

Of course, if the Smithsonian thing should come through, I will grab it, and hang on if I can at least for a year or two, for it would give me money, sick leave if necessary, the means of taking out health insurance, and such other things as I must try to bear in mind now.

If, if, if. You see how many ifs there are floating around in the air this Friday night in January. By God, I sure could use a Saturday mail box full of good breaks for a change, a check from Mortensen, an affirmative answer from Chambers, a job offer from Smithsonian. I would settle for the first two of these, or, for that matter, the second alone.

This letter so far is mainly a catalog of disaster, but I have something rather nice to tell you also—nice, that is, for its bearing upon the kind of people persons can be. When Bob and Jean Curtis were out here last week, Jean noticed in my bookcase the lipreading text, and brought up the subject of the problems it entailed for me, and the kind of help I had to have. One day this week Bob asked me if I wouldn't bring the book into [the] L[ibrary of]. C[ongress]. and let him work with me on it an hour or so a day. No, this was the last part of last week. I put him off, telling him he didn't know what he was getting himself into, and that someone who was working on a Ph.D. thesis couldn't afford to be so prodigal of his time; also that it would be exceptionally trying for both of us right now because of

[the] blurring trouble I have been having with my eyes. I had supposed this ended the matter, but he was persistent and came back to the subject Thursday morning after I reached L.C. from the hospital. If I wanted, he said, I could repay him with a portrait of his wife. I was genuinely touched, for both ways that was a very nice compliment. So I agreed, and we made a beginning with a half hour's work this afternoon in a study room at L.C. It did not go too well, for besides being long out of practice on close application of that kind, the slight degree of blurring, a little like looking in a wavy mirror, made it the more difficult to concentrate upon his lips. But we will hope that there is some improvement all round. He took the lipreading text home tonight to read all the preliminary matter the teacher is supposed to know, and next week I will supplement with mirror work this active drill with him.

The coffee hour: Saturday morning.

This letter thus far has been about my own concerns. I have not exhausted the topic by any means, and will come back to it in due course, but I want to give some space now to you and your more personal concerns.

The last week or more certainly must have been hard on you, with the storms cutting you off from any normal contact with Utah, and your mother's situation so much a source of worry to you. Surprisingly your airmail letters have come through pretty fast; be glad that you aren't an airmail pilot this month.

It surprises you that your mother, "in spite of everything," should turn to you in her present distress. But insofar as I know her three children, it does not surprise me. The very qualities of independence and self-sufficiency in you which in times past may have made relations with your mother more difficult are the qualities she is bound to turn to in her present situation. So also the sense of responsibility you have, to yourself and the people who make up your world. In the easy times such people may be a frequent annoyance in being so little amenable to one's will. But come the hard times and the end of something solid to hold to, the values shift a good deal and are seen in quite different perspective.

I will wait anxiously for further word about her physical condition, what will be possible for her and thus for you. If it should be practicable for her to move down to the coast for a few months, and not practicable for you to stay in Ogden very long, would it be feasible for her to rent the house in Ogden? That would give her some income to enable her to feel that she was paying her own way—something that can mean a good deal in this tough world we live in. But you will have to cope with this situation as its imperatives unfold.

What you say about the recent shift in some of your attitudes, and your emergence from the kind of despondency which gripped you through much of last year, is of course very interesting to me, but no surprise. I have really discussed these questions frontally with you only once, before the fire one winter day at the place on 10th East Street. I told you then of my belief in the incredible resilience and toughness of life, and pointed out the application in your own life. Literarily, you can within the space of a single paragraph reduce all civilization to smoking ruins and wipe out all life. But just consider, I said, what you yourself had lived through, all the difficulties you had surmounted, the handicaps you had overcome. On a strictly logical basis, some medical man might have written you off long ago. But you have a tremendous will to exist, a tenacious hold upon life, a knowledge of your limitations, and what you can do within those limitations, an acquired skill in pacing yourself. You have come triumphantly through all these trials, and people doctors would have given a life expectancy of another half century or so have been dying every day, as witness the obituary columns in any morning's newspaper. In short, you were yourself the best possible answer to this kind of morbidity, a living example of the resistance of life to its extinguishment. This discussion rather fully expressed my point of view on the matter, and otherwise I have been content to remark from time to time that it is just the time one happens to live in that seems most unendurable. There have been some very bad things abroad in the world; there are plenty abroad at this very moment. But also prophets of doom have been speaking their piece from the beginning of recorded history; and on the plane of day-to-day life, one only has to work with the materials of Mormon history as you and I have done to see that the abrasions of daily life have been much worse in times past than they are for you and me today. We don't have to be satisfied with our lot in life, but it helps, as you observe to me, to retain a certain perspective about it.

Now let me go on to various questions you have put [to] me lately. First, about the [John D.] Lee journals. You are certainly not to suppose that Juanita [Brooks] has sent me the highlights of these journals. She sent me a couple of extracts that interested her, and which I passed on to you, relative to Lee and Young and the M[ountain] M[eadows] M[assacre]. She also sent me some extracts from 1848-49 bearing on the beginning of the State of Deseret. For the rest, I know no more about the contents of the journals than you. But the extracts she sent me from 1848-49 show that the diary for this period is comparable in importance with the 1846-47 diary [Charles] Kelly printed [in 1938], which means of course that it is in a class by itself. But nothing can be done about this except as it can be done through Huntington. I had occasion to write them about something earlier in the week, and I took advantage of the opportunity to inquire impersonally about the status of the Lee journals. Depending upon what they answer, you may be able to follow up, but we will reserve discussion of that until we see what the situation is.

Since I recently threw a long accumulation of papers together in a large box, I cannot without long searching repeat the description of the Lee journals I sent you before. But as I recall, they consist first of a diary with some gaps kept from mid-1848 to mid-1849, a diary from December, 1857 to June or July, 1861 (with a gap in it largely filled by the fragmentary diary of 1859 Kelly printed). Then three diaries which I believe cover the entire period from 1866 to 1875 or 1876. Huntington also has Rachel Lee's diary for the period 1856-1860.

The diaries in the [Church] Historian's Office were not microfilmed, but were transcribed by hand, by descendants of Lee. This diary Juanita describes as follows in the bibliography to her book: "On the flyleaf of this is written, 'John D. Lee's Journal bought in St. Louis, May 29, 1844. No. 4.' The first entry is dated May 28, and it gives an account of Lee's boarding the ship on the Mississippi to go on a mission. . . . It is written in a small, fine hand, and is decorated in places with geometric drawings and embellished acrostics. The daily entries tell his experiences as a missionary, his return to Nauvoo upon hearing of the death of Joseph Smith, and his subsequent activities. The last section of the little volume is a day-by-day account of his mission with Howard Egan for the battalion money. The last date in this book is November 18, 1846." In other words, the last part of this diary directly precedes the diary Kelly printed.

The other diary at the H[istorian's]. O[ffice]., according to Juanita's description, is inscribed, " 'John D. Lee Record. A book Containing an Inventory of all the Camps of the Saints! Also the circumstances connected with the Exodus from Nauvoo, The City of Joseph, West through the Wilderness in search of Home and Place of rest by John D. Lee Young. 1846.' This record gives details of the preparations for the exodus of the Mormons, the organization of companies, the purchase of supplies, and the securing of wagons and equipment." Juanita later sent me a fuller account of this diary which I passed on to you; I think she said it consists of a summary narrative of the events of late 1844 and early 1845, and I believe diary entries for a part of 1846.

A third diary at the H.O. is the "Journal of the Iron Mission, 1850-52." This too was copied by the Lee family, and it is the one [A. Russell] Mortensen recently obtained permission to print in the [Utah Historical] Quarterly.

Besides all these, there are two diaries describing Lee's missionary activities in Tennessee between January, 1841, and January, 1842. Juanita dug these up in her collecting program. She obtained merely a typewritten copy of the first of these, of which she gave me the copy you saw while I was living on 10th East, and managed to photostat the second one. This latter photostat is at . . . [The remainder of this letter is missing.]

44. To STANLEY IVINS

Salt Lake City, Utah
9 June 1953

Dear Stan,

I just this moment got a note from Fawn [Brodie] enclosing one from a fellow named Edward Bowditch from the Harvard Club in N.Y. He has been reading her book [*No Man Knows My History*] and says, "On pp. 170-174 you speak of the four egyptian mummies bought by the church and the papyri [once in the possession of Joseph Smith] which have been destroyed. Did you ever see the evidence in the files of the curator of Egyptology of the Museum of Fine Arts in N.Y. which might prove that all of the papyri were not destroyed in the Chicago fire? I think they would be of interest to you."

If you have the time, and if this reaches you in time, maybe it would be worthwhile to pay them a visit and find out what this is all about.[1]

Regards,

Dale

[1] These papyri were later "rediscovered" in the mid-1960s and donated to the LDS church. See also Letter Number 48.

45. To FAWN BRODIE

Berkeley, California
2 May 1955

Dear Fawn,

Let me make you a present of a photostat which will interest you considerably. I've been trying to run this thing down for some years, but have only now made connections on it. There was something in the Evening and Morning Star which gave me cause to think the Isaac Hale affidavit had been printed in advance of its appearance in [E. D.] Howe's book [*Mormonism Unvailed*], and now we have the whole story. I suppose it appeared in the Montrose paper the last week of March or first week of April, 1834, but no files of that paper are known for the critical period.

What I have wanted to demonstrate here was that Hale made his statement without any leading questions being put him, and without any prompting from [Philastus] Hurlbut. Howe was circumspect here, I think, although his own purpose and "prejudice" is obvious. And Hurlbut did not figure in the final making of an affidavit, though we don't get clear of him entirely, not knowing what he wrote Hale in the first instance, and what Hale's response was.

The extent of Hurlbut's own contribution to Howe's book has been long debated. If he actually wrote anything in it, I think it was merely the running analysis of the content of the Book of Mormon. He turned over the affidavits and such he had gathered, but the main text, I am sure, was written by Howe. It ties into Howe's back files of the Telegraph, and goes forward beyond the Hurlbut time to include an account of the Zion's Camp episode, the style of this being part and parcel with the rest of the contemporary history. Evidently Howe preferred to play down Hurlbut and the part he had played in assembling the affidavits, etc., for the things he cut from the photostat text I now send you are mainly related to Hurlbut's previous letter of inquiry. Anyway, it's nice to have these things come out of the corners.

Yesterday Francis W. Kirkham walked in on me and visited for an hour or so. He is in some farm bureau insurance business now, but was down here visiting three children who live in the area. He didn't have anything very interesting to say, unfortunately, seeming more concerned about taking notes on what I had to say, including such commonplaces as the lack of intellectual curiosity in the Mormon generation that has come of age since the war, etc., etc. He did remark that his books hadn't done notably well, perhaps because he lacked promotional ability. He did comment though on the tendency of church members to buy books by Authority, meaning the authorities of the church, of course. It appears that the Deseret Book Store has bought out Zion's Printing & Publishing Company, or whatever the name of that Independence outfit is, and consequently fell heir to a considerable number of copies of his books, so that they had a conference sale on these. Sales results he didn't know.

Having permitted him to pick my brains in the interest of his books before, I chose to say nothing this time about the Isaac Hale stuff, and did not get the photostat out of my desk to let him see it.

Fred Rosenstock, the Denver bookseller, was through here three or four weeks ago, having stopped off enroute in Provo to visit [LeRoy] Hafen, [M. Wilford] Poulson[, a professor of psychology at BYU], and other friends. It would seem that Poulson is happier than in some years, for [S.] Lyman Tyler, the young fellow who was named Director of Libraries at BYU a year ago, likes Poulson and vice versa; he hired Poulson to arrange and catalogue the Mormon collections there at BYU and has otherwise made life seem worth living. I think he said Poulson was now 75; can this be correct? Anyway, it appears that he is in very good health right now, and that he anticipates a visit to Bancroft sometime in the not too distant future. I wonder if he ever will do what he has contemplated, publish Strang's diary with proper notes. He contemplated doing a lot of things after retirement on Social Security, when, without actually saying so, he was free from reprisal for honest comment on facts. I don't remember whether I ever discussed this with you, but M[ilo]. M. Quaife actually butchered Strang's diary. He did not decipher the coded sections, put the pages together in the wrong order, transcribed incorrectly, etc., etc. The coded passages are remarkable, for they show Strang as a young man gripped by the Napoleonic achievement, an atheist, one with ambitions to set up a personal empire in America, etc., etc! If we had a secret diary kept by Joseph Smith for the same period, we might find some very similar inner thoughts.

I continue as busy as ever on this Navaho project, on the Bancroft job, and on the preliminary work for the Rand McNally book, to say nothing of a couple of jobs for the Eberstadts stacked up in my front room and demanding attention. Probably I will have to participate in some Navaho field work in July or August; and sometime during the summer I hope to get to Washington for a week or two. The centennial atlas text has to be ready October 1, and I hope to have the text of my book of Ashley documents ready by December. Rosenstock's Old West Publishing Company will probably publish it, the printing to be done by Lawton Kennedy, the outstanding San Francisco printer who did the Jedediah Smith map book. It will be a limited edition of about a thousand copies, and will yield a personal return of about as many dollars, which is better than one generally expects from a documentary book. After that is done, I'll concentrate my attention on the Mormons again.

I am glad for all the news of the Brodies. It is an age since I saw you all, and even now, heaven knows when I'll stretch my legs in your company again. Unless you all wander up this way and have dinner with me. You must continue full steam ahead on your book, knowing as I do that it will be a damned good book when you are through with it. I am somewhat surprised that Bernard has a new book under way, being under the impression he knew too much these days to be permitted to write books. But he ought to be full of news and views on air power, and I shall look forward to this new work of his.

The news of your father's physical toughness is a pleasant surprise; may he hold out forever. Some similar good news has come from Ogden, where Madeline's mother has far exceeded the expectations of her doctor, who at best thought she might be in for a life of permanent invalidism. Still her health is exceedingly precarious; these things are stacking up on her heart, and a time will come with her as it did with Maurice Howe when the overload becomes too great. So Madeline is frightened by any telegram that is sent her these days. She and Tom have been hunting for a house in the Berkeley area, out of the fog belt, but so far without success.

To get away from the constant pressure of print on my eyes, I have taken up with art again. The last six weeks I have been going occasionally to a life class over in San Francisco and to another here in Berkeley, drawing in pastel at the former, where the poses are longer, and in charcoal at the latter. The first drawing of the kind since before I went to Washington in 1942. I am somewhat out of practice, but I find the skills come back more rapidly than I looked for. I have somewhat a guilty feeing when I play hookey from work, but I feel guilty before my eyesight if I work all the time, too, so what the hell, I'll choose the lesser guilt and have some fun besides. I mean to do some landscape painting in oil, too, but Sunday is the only chance for that at present, and the last three weeks our Sundays have been cold and rainy. Ergo, no landscape painting.

I am, dear Sister Brodie, your bro. in the bonds of faith,

Dale

46. To FAWN BRODIE

Berkeley, California
19 September 1957

Dear Fawn,

I got your [1830 first edition] Book of Mormon off by registered mail yesterday; it is pure inertia that it hasn't been returned to you long since, and it is for the good of my immortal soul that I should be prodded into doing so. Or my conscience, or whatever.

Still, hanging on to the book got me a letter out of you, so maybe I am justified after all. You must be as busy from one day to the next as I am, and found the same havoc wrought in your correspondence. We are the losers by it, too, for when we live at a distance and opportunities for visits in the flesh are of rare occurence, letters must be our recompense and solace.

So I was glad for all the news of your family and yourself. What a fine, promising lot of kids you have, and how things have changed since I first made Dick's acquaintance, pushing a wine bottle around on the floor of your apartment on Wisconsin Avenue! Somehow time keeps squeezing us along the path we must go.

But meanwhile you have finished a new book, at the cost of what pains I am only too aware, and I hope it will be moved right along into print; I have no doubts as to the quality of the book, having seen you once around the course with Joseph Smith. If Knopf sent or sends the book out to a revisionist critic, and gets a flaming response, all the better. For controversy is what sells books, and don't think Knopf has gone all this time without finding it out!

Currently I have on hand from the Saturday Review a book being published next week by Chicago, Thomas O'Dea's *The Mormons* (the guy stole my title, confound him). This is the first thoughtful book about the Mormons that has been published since yours came out, and I think it will interest you. He has been markedly influenced by your book, but he also offers a somewhat different analysis of the Book of Mormon. Of course this is not a book of rigorous scholarship, but a rather generalized work which approaches Mormonism temperately on the philosophical and sociological plane, no more well written than you would expect a university press book to be. But as I said, thoughtful at least, which is more than one can say for most books about the culture from which we sprang.

I was up in Utah for two weeks in August, and brought back with me a new little work by George B. Arbaugh somewhat gaudily titled *Gods, Sex, and Saints*, a 61-page pamphlet published by Augustana College where he now holds forth. This is about what you would expect from him, with all the merits and otherwise of his *Revelation in Mormonism.*

I am reminded to say, too, that O'Dea remarks that the Church republished in pamphlet form that blast in the Deseret News Church Section; this was news to me if not to you.

The New Yorker surprised me at least with its review, for the book was published as long ago as December! In fact, I have been involved with so many other things that the book seems only a faint memory now. My book of Ashley documents, called *The West of William H. Ashley*, is about ready to go to the printer, and it will be followed almost at once by a related volume of Robert Campbell documents and a 49er Journal. With these three books of documents off my hands, I expect to get back to some plain narrative history, especially my major obligation, the Mormons. But time has come hard this summer and will come harder this fall because of Navajo necessities. We have been involved with the documentation to work out a conflict with the pueblos of Laguna and Acoma, and this in turn leads straight into our historical report on the southeastern quadrant of the Navajo claim. Our objective is to have a draft of the whole historical report done by January 1, but don't bet any money on it. My next job is to digest an incredible volume of documents we have assembled pertaining to the San Juan country, and this will swallow up all the time I can find. Such is the irony of life, this Navajo work pays me double what the Bancroft job does, but I have been transfixed on Bancroft necessities, too, the need to get the library off the hook on the Guide to the Manuscripts which has been kicked around since 1947. So I haven't been in a position to go on leave from that job, and have just had to pile a half-time job on top of a full-time job. Making some money along the way, but a wearing process, and I am not going to do it indefinitely. Life, as the philosopher says, is too short.

Madeline [McQuown] made a long, slow recovery from the very bad siege she had last summer, and she is limited in ways she was not before. But she is a woman of great courage and perserverance, not suited to this wretched Bay Area climate, alas, but unable to get away from it. She and Tom have been making an exhausting search for housing they can buy amid the impossible snarl of red tape and prohibitory regulation that governs loans and purchases of real estate, and I hope to high heaven that something is about to be settled about this. We saw last weekend a very interesting place in Walnut Creek, about 15 miles east of Berkeley, and probably as dry and sunny a location as this foggy area provides. But whether they can swing the deal remained to be worked out. Perhaps they will be down this weekend with further news, good, I hope.

Don't you ever get up this way? I'd like to do the honors, also show you the various LeConte Stewart oils and pastels I have bought, including a lovely November scene in Liberty Valley I purchased from him in August, an 18 x 24 canvas I am currently having framed. You will have to try to make it up here soon, so we can have a real visit.

With best regards,

Dale

47. To FAWN BRODIE

Berkeley, California
21 August 1967

Dear Fawn,

All my friends and relatives are complaining of me, and not without good reason. I get up in the morning and vow faithfully, "Today I will write Fawn, and my sister Ruth, and my brother Bob, and my uncle Hal, and Dan and Sandra Howe, and Dan's mother, and Anna McConkey, and Floyd Risvold, and Robert Greenwood (and so on down the line)." And the sun goes down, and the moon too, and I wind up in bed, and I haven't managed to write any of those letters.

So now I have your note of the 14th, which made a slow passage through the mails, and it shows you a true heroine, not one word of reproach for unpardonable neglect. Accordingly, I sit down at my typewriter immediately on getting back to B[ancroft]. L[ibrary]. from lunch, and try to justify my continued standing in the fellowship of amiable souls.

Last Christmas, so sorely beset was I that I didn't even get my customary Christmas letters off to my friends, and of course that has complicated my life since, for all these friends, and especially you, deserve something special to atone for this neglect. I did hand onto the University Librarian, Coney, your memorandum about your [Richard] Burton collection, and I hope something came of that, though I knew that a considerable degree of duplication existed, in that the University Library bought many of the books as they were published, even in Burton's day. I was going to say then that I didn't feel you needed to sweeten the deal in any way by throwing in your personal papers relating to N[o] M[an] K[nows] M[y] H[istory], for these were deserving of separate and individual disposition.

One trouble has been that I am still engaged in a major effort to catch up on all the time and effort that got diverted for a number of years to Navajo matters, while my books gradually jammed up behind. I have been attacking this logjam to the extent of getting out three or more books a year for the last several years, mainly works of documentary character that I could work at in a disconnected way, and though I have made progress, I am still about ten books away from getting current. Meanwhile I took on the job of editing the annual Lakeside Classic that [Milo] Quaife used to do; I did the 1965 book on the Minnesota Sioux uprising of 1862, the 1966 book, Laura F. Judd's reminiscences of Honolulu, 1828-1861, and I have just sent off the index for the 1967 book, Jeremiah Lynch's Three Years in the Klondike. These books had some side values, in that they brought me expense-paid visits to Minnesota in 1964 and to Hawaii, the Yukon, and Alaska last year. My primary interest, though, was in making conceivable and workable retirement from B.L. when I reach the minimum retirement age three years hence, with the object of spending all my time on research and writing thereafter. I am not going to do the 1968 classic, some work or other dealing with early Illinois history which Paul Angle will probably handle for them. But this has not taken any pressure off yet. Eleanor Harris and I will shortly have out at Huntington the massive William Marshall Anderson journals of 1834, in press there for more than a year. I am turning over to the printer, Lawton Kennedy, tonight the massive California recollections, 1849-1857, of Howard C. Gardiner; and next week I expect to wind up work on a somewhat shorter book, From Hudson Bay to the Great Salt Lake: The Journal of Joseph Burke in the Canadian and American West, 1843-1846. (Made up principally of letters Burke wrote to Sir William Hooker while acting as a botanical collector, letters preserved in the Royal Botanic Garden at Kew, England.) By October I hope to give Knopf the overdue manuscript fashioned from the diary of William B. Lorton, the finest Forty-niner diary I have ever laid eyes on. There are a couple more things to be done by Christmas, and by spring I want the companion book to my giant Ashley book, one centering upon Robert Campbell and to be called the Rockies and the Yellowstone, ready to go. I have meanwhile done most of the preliminary labor on my long-deferred bibliography on Mormonism, 1830-1849, but have sat on that all this year, rather hoping that U[niversity of]. C[alifornia]. might untrack itself and so amend its sabbatical leave setup as to include me and similar specialists. With [California governor Ronald] Reagan's war on the finances of the University, though, heaven knows when such a step may be taken. I have about another year of working with basic documentary texts before I can tackle things like my general work on the fur trade and my long deferred general work on the Mormons.

Meanwhile, of course, we get older and creakier. Some tests begun in 1965 finally arrived at a finding that I am a mild diabetic, and for the past year I have been cooperating in a diabetic research program undertaken by the Kaiser people in cooperation with the U.S. Public Health Service. What this mainly involves is watching what I eat (avoiding sugar as much as possible) and gulping a pill with breakfast and dinner. The pill seems to go on poorly with alcohol, so I am circumspect about cocktails and dinner wine, to avoid blackout reactions.

It was in my mind's eye to write you months ago to share the amusement you too must feel over how the two of us (and some others) are reflected in the pages of the new independent Mormon journal, *Dialogue*, being published at Stanford. We were well-meaning, and all right in our day, but of course the new generation of Church-oriented historians are more solidly grounded and have a greater maturity. Old Lady Brodie, how are you doing these days?

And more recently I am sure you shared my sorrow in learning of Stan Ivins' death a few weeks ago. I always saw Stan when in Salt Lake, most recently last October, and he seemed positively ageless to me, practically unchanged from the first time I met him, which I believe was in Salt Lake in the Spring of '45, when we visited Utah at the same time. Stan complained of getting old, but it still seems incredible that he was past the age of 75 at his death. He nobly willed his library to the Historical Society, in case you had not heard.

Well, I have been a long while getting there, or back to there, but let me now take up your letter of the 14th. As it happens, Madeline has been working determinedly on her MS [a biography of Brigham Young] despite all physical handicaps the past two years, and from December to July had an apartment in Berkeley to enable her to work at the Bancroft. Her book is now substantially complete, but is so massive a production—it may yet have to be a two volume work—that she has been making a violent effort at compression. I have not read any of it, as she has prefered to work independently and show it to me only when prepared to let loose of it, but she has done an amazing research job, and clearly the book will be an event. She has discussed it with Angus Cameron of Knopf, but has not made up her mind about a publisher, and in fact has been unwilling to sign a contract until it was finished, the limits of her strength being what they are. As a matter of fact, I have roundly criticized her for working beyond the limits of her strength, not being willing to discipline herself by working only so many hours a day—sometimes she should not work at all—and thereby pushing far beyond her physical capacity. She has obstinately, almost compulsively, gone her own way, but has paid a penalty the past six weeks, with exhaustion and the usual difficult summer climate in San Jose raising hob with her heart. She had hoped to finish the book by mid-August and go off to visit a friend in France during September, but her doctor put his foot flatly down last week. He wanted her to go to a dry climate closer to home, so she said Saturday, when she dropped by, that she would head this week for Salt Lake or Ogden, to remain perhaps til October. And meanwhile, she said mutinously, get the book finished.

In the face of all this, I don't presume to advise you. I imagine Madeline's viewpoint is about the same as mine on my Mormon history; anybody can write what he pleases on Brigham, that won't be her book. I might be inclined to advise you to wait and see where she comes out at finally, what her standpoint is on Brigham, and what might be left for someone else to say. But this is something you will have to decide for yourself.

I have admired your [Richard] Burton book [*The Devil Drives*] without having had an opportunity to read it yet, only to glance through and sample it. I sent a copy to my sister, whom you may remember, as a birthday present ten days ago, knowing she would find many reasons to savor it. So far I have seen only the Time review, which of course was not a review of the book but an account of the man Burton (and therefore publicity, primarily), and the enclosed account in the Book of the Month Club News. I don't know what the man is talking about in comparing you with Lady Burton, and doubt if he could explain himself.

Maybe with the long letter, I will be restored to good standing with you at least, in which case, let me hear all about the Brodies, Bernard, Fawn, Dick, Bruce, Pam—how the world is treating them, and how they are treating the world. I would be glad to see you again, and who knows, maybe one of these days we will manage it.

With best regards,

Dale

P.S. After 13 years on the south side of the campus, on September 1, I am moving to the north side, 1634 La Loma Avenue, Berkeley, 94709. This is the upper half of a duplex, with a fireplace, an interesting view of the Bay, and two bedrooms, one of which will be converted into a library and for a few weeks will give me the illusion of having more space. I am all but suffocated in books and papers on Benvenue!

48. To WESLEY P. WALTERS[1]

Berkeley, California
27 November 1967

Dear Reverend Walters:

I am most obliged to you for your courtesy in sending me a copy of your monograph on the Palmyra revivals [*New Light on Mormon Origins*]. You have done a most excellent job of scholarship, backed up by a temperate presentation of your findings, and I am in almost complete agreement with you.

The historicity of the First Vision is of course crucial in any interpretation of the character and history of Joseph Smith. If he had no vision of the kind to which he afterward laid claim, then there is no reason to conceive of him as one given to delusions, and most of the psychologizing about Joseph Smith that has cluttered up the literature is wholly beside the point.

In the summer of 1947 I found the George Lane account of the Palmyra revival in the *Methodist Magazine*, and the further point that 1824-1825 was the only year Lane ever officiated in the Palmyra area. To this extent I was ahead of you; but in your monograph you have gone far beyond the point I had to leave off, inquiring into Presbyterian and Baptist records as well as the Palmyra papers I searched in Albany in the fall of 1947; again I congratulate you on a fundamental and well-done job.

One point I would stress is that the year 1823 was early established in Mormon history as the crucial year for the first revealment of the golden plates, and of course this date exerted a powerful influence in antedating the concept of the First Vision. If Joseph Smith was associating with angels from 1823 on, he had a direct conduit to heaven, so why would he have been messing around with other religions in 1824-1825 and wondering whether any of these was "correct" . . . ? It is perfectly clear, and you have laid out most of the relevant considerations, why his history had to be rewritten over a period of years to answer to Joseph Smith's changing necessities.

I am sorry to say that I know nothing of the present whereabouts of Lane's diary, which would be a welcome find, even though it added nothing to his narrative in the *Methodist Magazine*.

I also note with interest that you say the records of the Western Presbyterian Church at Palmyra covering the 1824-1825 period have been missing since 1930. Could you elaborate upon that item of information? Is there any suggestion that the volume in question might have been stolen in that year of the Mormon centennial?

Your remark to the effect that [Brigham Young University religion professor] Hugh Nibley has photographs "of the papyri fragments remaining from the Book of Abraham scroll" is certainly a fascinating one. You say, "We have the index numbers but do not know to what collection they refer," and I assume by this that the papyri are not in the possession of the church itself. The [Jerald and Sandra] Tanners [LDS critics] recently publicized Joseph Smith's "Egyptian dictionary," which is in fact held by the church, and I cannot believe there has been any confusion of identity between this and the papyri.

Sincerely,

Dale L. Morgan

[1] Wesley P. Walters, a minister in the United Presbyterian Church, published in 1967 a brief analysis of Joseph Smith and revivalism in New York. His research, much of which duplicated Morgan's own, subsequently became the focus of a concerted response from LDS scholars.

49. To FAWN BRODIE

Berkeley, California
24 December 1969

Dear Fawn,

Here I am, exhibiting my customary efficiency. If the U.S. mails are equally efficient, you may get this for Christmas 1970. This has been an eventful year in many respects. My mother died June 19, which was a mercy, for a succession of small strokes had cut her down since last December. (She was 75 on May 1.) I came to S[alt]. L[ake]. for a niece's wedding on June 16, went on to Denver from there, and was summoned back to Salt Lake for the funeral.

I was in Washington [D.C.] in July and again in late October and early November, working again on a long term project begun in

1965, when I asked Louise North to marry me. (Max died of cancer in 1964. She is an old friend of 23 years' standing—from O[ffice of] P[rice] A[dministration] days—and has two daughters, now aged 21 and 17. We have developed a very close and warm relationship, satisfying in all respects, but some problems remain, mostly, I think, from putting together two such widely separated lives. (I don't think she can ever be happy away from her hilltop home at Accokeek, Md., opposite Mt. Vernon, and she also is doing well in the gov[ernmen]t job (H[ousing and] U[rban] D[evelopment]) she took two months after Max died.) Maybe I can work things out next year, we'll see. I have also applied for another Guggenheim; the odds may be against it, but this would help mightily. I might also retire from [the] U[niversity of] C[alifornia] at age 56 a year hence. Again, *we'll see*. Will have another large gold rush book out in Jan[uary], and hope to clean up five or six more books in 1970 to clear the decks for (a) my big fur trade history; and (b) the Mormon history.

And how about the Brodie clan?

Dale

50. To FAWN BRODIE

Berkeley, California
13 May 1970

Dear Fawn,

I am chagrined to have your note today on the subject of the Guggenheim—that is, I am irked at myself, for I had wanted to tell you myself, before the public announcement was made on April 13, a month ago. And this because the most memorable thing about my original Guggenheim fellowship was your pleasure in it. I shall never forget that. You had invited me to dinner in your apartment on Wisconsin Avenue; it was the week of President Roosevelt's death, just a day or so after, and that dominated the conversation for quite some time after I arrived. Eventually I got around to telling you of the word from the Foundation, and it both surprised and moved me how your eyes filled in your pleasure over the news, how you called out to Bernard in the next room to share the news, and how you reproached me, "Why didn't you say something!" In a sense, you were more moved emotionally by the word than I was myself; it was a measure of the fine, warm friendship we had developed, and the memory has stayed with me ever since, fresh and fragrant, and a token of the kind of person you are.

Well, I didn't quite get to that letter, and this despite the fact that I had more or less been waiting on that news, good or bad, since February, as a preliminary to answering your most interesting letter about your January trip to Utah. (And now what have I done with that letter? It is buried somewhere on or within this desk at Bancroft.) I had some intimation at the beginning of March that I might well receive the fellowship, in that they wrote me for a budgetary statement, how much money I was asking for, how much allocated to travel, living expenses, and so on. In my innocent way, I had failed to realize what had happened to fellowship grants since the Act of 1954, and supposed they would merely hand out what they could afford, perhaps (in view of inflation) double the $2,000 which just about bankrupted me the first time. When I wrote it all out, specifying where I was going, air travel costs, per diem expenses based on current U[niversity of] C[alifornia] per diem allowances, etc., I ended up by asking for $9,130 altogether, including $1,400 in air fares and $1,000 for photostats, microfilms, etc. (Also not including $2,500 I would put in myself, what with not being entitled to sabbatical leave.) I came out pretty well, the grant is in the amount of $9,000. And in accordance with my request, it will take effect about May 1 of next year, which will give me time to finish some books in progress and get some accumulated Bancroft jobs off my neck. Sometime between now and the end of the year I will make up my mind whether to retire from B[ancroft]. L[ibrary]. when entering upon the fellowship, or to ask for a leave of absence without pay for 12 months. (Including accumulated vacation time, that would permit me to work on the book exclusively till mid-July, 1972.) Perhaps I could make a pitch to the Chancellor for a special grant of a sabbatical even though I am not a member of the Academic Senate. But that raises the question whether I wanted to commit myself to coming back to U.C. for at least a year when the leave ends. I don't know the answers yet, and meanwhile I am keeping my own counsel on campus.

As even this much will have made clear, all my plans revolving around the Guggenheim are of the contingent order, for a great deal depends on what I work out with Louise [North]. So let me bring you up to date on that, too. I believe I told you that we made a fundamental break-through in our relationship last June, and ever since that relationship has become closer, warmer, and more endearing. Louise has not agreed to marry me yet, but it is clear to both of us that it has nothing to do with me as a person, but rather concerns something unresolved within herself. As a matter of fact, I think 90 percent of it is the distance involved, our widely separated lives; if Bancroft were in a Washington [D.C.] suburb, or Accokeek [Maryland] were a Berkeley suburb, I think we would get things settled in very short order. Various things militate in Louise. She is a very independent person, for one thing, and she values her independence. She has two girls of college age, one with a year to go, one entering college this coming fall, and is not prepared to have someone else assume the financial burdens involved in putting them through school. Again, the aunt who reared her lies in a rest home in Florida; the last of her personal resources will soon be expended, and Louise and her brothers will have to take on these very heavy expenses. So Louise is not prepared to have someone else assume that part of her burden, either. Moreover, she likes her job with H[ousing and] U[rban] D[evelopment] and has done very well in it; she is head of her own small Community Relations branch. Thus she likes both the work and the people, and not just the independence, financial and psychological, that the job affords her. Up to now, there has been no question of uprooting her, either. If she were capable of living anywhere else than on the hilltop of Accokeek in the house she and Max built, knowing every stick and stone, feeling absolutely at home there as nowhere else—as I say, if she were even capable of leaving there, she was not prepared to do it before her youngest, Lisa, graduated from high school, which will be a month hence. Louise will be living in a changed world from this time forth, even as early as this summer, for as soon as she graduates, Lisa is going with a high school group on a trip to West Germany, Italy, Greece, and Turkey. She will be back in late July, but a month later she will leave for Ann Arbor [Michigan], and after that Louise will be alone as she has been at no time since her marriage 25 years ago. Will she be prepared to leave Accokeek a year from now, move to California, say, and find a new job out here? I'm not ready to bet on it.

The crux in all this is that now for the first time it is really possible for me to do the uprooting. Since last December it has been technically possible for me to retire from Bancroft, though I am only too aware that what I could now draw down in the way of retirement income will scarcely even equal the widow's annuities Louise will lose in a remarriage. To retire or not to retire, this is a fundamental question I must settle in the next year. I don't lack in confidence that I can earn enough money, working full time at my own books, to compensate for a job. But this is not just a gamble involving myself; it involves the lives of three others: the name of the game is responsibility. Perhaps, then, what I should do is look at long range for a job in the Washington area, to take on at the end of the Guggenheim. But there is no logic in that unless Louise marries me. And one inhibition in the matter of marrying me is her feeling of wrongness that *I*, not she, should do the uprooting. There are, in short, ethical problems involved in our widely separated lives, and it is these above all that require to be solved.

I went to Washington on March 20 for ten days, to celebrate Louise's 52nd birthday on one weekend, and Easter the next. The eldest daughter, Lynn (who with her roommate visited me for three days out here before New Year's) also came home from Ann Arbor for the birthday weekend, and, as usual, we all had a very good time together. I told Louise beforehand that I was not going to press her about marriage on this visit, in view of the enforced separations we must accept over the course of the next year. I intend going east again toward the end of June, or in the early part of July, and neither will I press her very hard then. October is a different matter, though. I intend to spend two weeks in Washington in October, and I think it would be an excellent idea to start off the whole thing with a wedding. I then contemplate that Louise and the girls shall come to Berkeley for two weeks at Christmas; and that when the spring break comes at Ann Arbor, in mid-March, they all three shall go to Hawaii with me for a week while I research some aspects of the Northwest Coast fur trade. (This was written into the Guggenheim, and funded thereby, but it will be convenient to do this in advance of technically embarking on the fellowship.) Then I will pull out of Berkeley on May 1, next year, research the libraries in Oregon, Washington, and western Canada, preliminary to showing up in D.C. on May 29 to fly to Europe with Louise. The girls will get out of school at the end of April, so it is my idea to send them on ahead, to knock about on their own for a month. I want Louise to take a three months' leave of absence without pay, a month of knocking around western Europe, and two months of working in England. (She objects that she wouldn't have a job to come back to if she took three months off; and there is a problem there, her branch consisting of herself, an assistant, and a secretary. Still, I am a persistent man, and as I told Louise, you never know what is possible till you try.) I would then return to the U.S. in the fall of 1971, spend most of the autumn working in libraries in New England and eastern Canada (hopefully joined by Louise on weekends; she could fly up from Washington). Then settle in for nine months or so in the Washington area, to write as much as possible of this big book.

Well, that's the program, but it is going to take one hell of a lot of working out, and first things first, Louise makes the final personal commitment this fall. After that, we mutually agree on the objectives and the probable best solutions. Stick around for awhile and see what develops! I enclose a couple of snapshots I made of Louise last summer (one an enlargement from movie film) so you will have a little more the sense of knowing her, until the day comes that you meet her.

It so happened that the telegram from the Guggenheim Foundation was relayed to me while I was in Washington, a further poignant reminder of that April day 25 years ago, about which I told Louise. This also set me to thinking about your Jefferson book [*Thomas Jefferson: An Intimate History*], a most interesting project. You do not mention it in your latest letter, but if you propose to go ahead with that, why not propose it to the Guggenheim people? The only complication I can think of is the UCLA one, if taking or obtaining leave would present any problems. Meanwhile, it is a pleasure to learn of the revised edition of *your* J[oseph]. S[mith]. [i.e., *No Man*

Knows My History]. *My* J[edediah]. S[mith]. is also up for revision, during this year, hopefully. Or failing that, during the Guggenheim year. I am only waiting upon the release of a newly-discovered document of major import, Jedediah's journal of his *first* journey to California, 1826-1827, the finding of which in St. Louis is an incredible story. I have a copy of it, but cannot make use of it yet, and in fact the whole business is a deep, dark secret for the moment.

We have had plenty of [student] upset up here to match any you have had down there, naturally. Berkeley was where the style was set, six years ago. My background is such that I have only a very limited sympathy for some of the student activism I have seen, the last couple of years. That is, I am utterly opposed to mobs and mob action, not only in Missouri and Illinois, but in the South, Chicago, New York, Washington, California, or anywhere else. Also the rabblerousing that is involved, the baiting and the rockthrowing, anti-intellectual conduct at its worst, at best to be equated with the tantrums of children, and the childlike egocentrism which wants everything delivered on a platter here and now. (Did you reflect on an observation in the second article on Nepal in the last New Yorker? It was remarked that most Everest climbers are 35 and up. Younger people are temperamentally not suited to the day by day slogging without any very spectacular or even obvious progress toward an objective.) I have seen plenty of roving mobs on this campus, and the fact that the mobs are composed of college students instead of the Great Unwashed makes them only the more offensive in my eyes. Granted, we are urgently in need of change. But change that will in itself have some prospect of permanence, by change in our society, our institutions. I reflect too on a story in this morning's paper about this week's agitation for a "reconstitution" of the University by a "restructuring" of classes. A psychology prof was all for it, which perhaps says something about the slippery nature of most social or near-social sciences. A math professor held other ideas. In math, you either do the work or you do not, pretty names put upon it do not change the fact, or the necessity of doing the work. It is this necessity of doing the work, as against instant results, that so many young people find repugnant about social action. Nor was I much impressed last week with the ideas brought forth by a group that called itself a Social Coalition. They proposed that "observers" be sent to every class on campus, to be sure that "right things" were being taught in the right way. So who is going to appoint these political commissars, and whose is the privilege of deciding the rightness of it all? I find this all very sad, and infinitely depressing, all emotion and no gumption.

I am pleased to have the more personal news, the June trip in prospect for Europe for you and Bernard, Pam, Bruce, and Dick. Paradoxically, I think Dick might find Utah a rather stimulating environment if he can look upon the Mormons and Mormon society in transition with a lively sense of curiosity combined with emotional detachment. There is enough parochialism there, but I find parochialism everywhere I turn, these days.

Let me hear from you again, I would love a fuller report on the Utah scene of January and the complex feelings you must have had, being coincidently there at such a time.[1] And one of these days maybe we can talk out such things in our proper persons again.

Dale

[1] Brodie's uncle, LDS church president David O. McKay, had passed away at the age of ninety-six in Salt Lake City on 18 January 1970.

THE HISTORY

None of Dale Morgan's works was more important or frustrating to him than his projected three-volume history of the Mormons. He began research in the 1930s and worked regularly through the early 1950s, trying to finish his "definitive history" of Mormonism. At his death in 1971, "The Mormons" remained among the unfinished business left behind. There were four completed chapters and two appendices he had intended to submit to his publisher. An additional three chapters survived in rough draft form.

It is a singular tragedy for Mormon historiography that Morgan did not finish what would have been his masterpiece. He probed more deeply, with a keener eye, into more relevant primary and secondary source materials than anyone had previously. Few had been as thorough, ambitious, honest, or had worked under a more serious disability. His thoughtful approach revealed new and sometimes controversial insights into the genesis of Mormonism. Among other things, his pioneering work dated the Palmyra, New York, revivals which prompted Joseph Smith to seek answers through prayer not in 1820, but in 1824-25. He also provided a carefully conceived naturalistic explanation for the production of the Book of Mormon. His pathbreaking analysis, given its place in the development of Mormon historiography, is remarkable and underscores the loss his death represented. While some readers will disagree with his conclusions, most will be impressed by the scope of his researches and the depth of his investigations.

In editing the following seven chapters and two appendices for publication a fine line has been travelled. All typographical, spelling, and grammatical errors have been corrected, but the source material Morgan quotes verbatim has been left without change. The first four chapters and the appendices were in final form and did not require significant editorial decisions. The endnotes have also been left generally as Morgan wrote them with almost no attempt to update or revise them.

Chapters 5 to 7, however, did not avail themselves to such ease in editing. Where several drafts of a section were present, that draft which appeared to be the latest or most complete, or which fit most evenly into the text of the chapter, was favored. When the final selections were made and placed in order, they meshed together with a high degree of cohesiveness. It is thus often difficult to detect the editing when reading the "rough draft" chapters, although in a handful of instances necessary transitions have been added.

Originals of the first four chapters and the first appendix are housed at the University of Utah's Marriott Library, Special Collections division, in the Madeline R. McQuown Collection. Original drafts to chapters 5 through 7 and the second appendix are to be found in the Bancroft Library at the University of California, Berkeley, in the Dale Lowell Morgan Collection.

THE CALLING OF A PROPHET

The new place was two miles out the Stafford Road, just beyond the Palmyra township line in what was soon to become known as Manchester. Overgrown with great oaks, maples, beeches, and basswood, through which the sun struck here and there into fragrant growths of sassafras and wild tangles of raspberry briars, the hundred acres were part of the Everson land, owned by non-resident heirs who left it neglected.[1] No one in Palmyra cared who lived there.

In this late autumn of 1818 there were ten Smiths, small and large, to take up residence on the farm. The tall and supple Joseph Smith, Senior, and Lucy, his wife, had six sons and daughters, with a last straggler yet unborn, a girl who would be named for her mother. The strapping eldest boy, Alvin, was twenty, and the children ranged on down through Hyrum, Sophronia, Joseph, Samuel, William, and Catherine to Don Carlos, who was two. The third son and fourth child, Joseph, Junior, was just short of thirteen and had first seen the light of day December 23, 1805, when amid their many peregrinations the Smiths had been briefly resident at Sharon, Vermont. All of the Smith children were tow-haired and blue-eyed; their paternal grandfather, Asael Smith, who had once predicted that a prophet would be raised up in his family,[2] might well have been baffled had his eight grandchildren been ranged before him and he required to denominate the prophet from among them.

Two years had elapsed since the family turned their backs on Vermont's stony hills and close-hemmed valleys to seek out a country of more promise. Three successive crop failures had given them their bitter fill of that land all granite and frost, the last year on the farm at Norwich sufficient to convince even the stubborn Joseph that Vermont was not for him. A foot of snow had fallen in June; snow fell even in July and August, at the height of summer, and a killing frost on September 10 cut down such hardy crops as had survived. The year 1816 has ever since been remembered as "eighteen-hundred-and-froze-to-death," and on all the roads that fall, west across the Green Mountain to the valley of the Hudson and beyond, dust bellied up in sullen clouds about the wagons of those who, like the Smiths, had abandoned hope in New England.[3]

Joseph had lost his own farm long ago, and the farm at Norwich had offered only a tenant's living, but even so, the uprooting had not gone easily. As he took the long road west, going in advance to find a place where the family might make a fresh beginning, he must have reviewed sorely in his mind the years of obstinate, fruitless struggle while the friends of his boyhood who had let themselves be carried off by the Genesee fever which had raged in New England these twenty years had been clearing prosperous farms and otherwise establishing themselves in vigorous young towns scattered across western New York. At the age of forty-five, he was a failure, a thought which must have bit into his pride even as he justified himself. From 1638, when Robert Smith settled at Topsfield, Massachusetts, down to Joseph's own time, the Smiths had been solid and substantial people, at one with the God-fearing and prosperous. Joseph's father, Asael, a man of independent mind who had found the settled world of Topsfield too confining, had gone into upper New England, first to New Hampshire and subsequently to Vermont, where he, too, wherever he went, was a man competent to build a world for himself.[4]

Joseph, Senior, had grown to manhood full of promise, a six-foot two-inch fellow powerful of limb and fond of wrestling, who, in his youth, like an earlier Jacob, had met one man only whom he could not throw.[5] He had begun life farming his father's farm on shares, confident of making his place in the world. But from the January day in 1769 when he took Lucy Mack to wife, his life had been wrenched and malformed by misfortune. The hopeful farm at Tunbridge. The catastrophic venture in storekeeping at Randolph, which had thrown him into the arms of the poverty that had held him cold and close ever since. Farms at Royalton and Sharon, at Tunbridge again, again at Royalton—just living enough, when eked out with the slender income from teaching school, to keep his ever-enlarging family clothed and fed. Twist and turn as he would, he could not get on in life, neither during the interval across the Connecticut River at Lebanon nor during the three gaunt years on the farm at Norwich.[6] The Vermonters are wont to say that their climate consists of nine months of late fall; this was Joseph's experience and he could be glad to have seen the last of such a land.

Like the son who bore his name, to this day the elder Joseph Smith remains something of an enigma. Imagination and ambition were never beaten out of him but these were qualities which did not make any more endurable the drudgery of the farm. From the uncompromising realities of his life he took refuge in dreams. Lucy Smith remembered a number of visions her husband had had over the years, all of them, in her recollection, pointing up some religious moral. But she was more attracted by formal religion than he; at various times he could be a Methodist and a Universalist but was never permanently converted to any formalized belief;[7] Lucy said of him that "he would not subscribe to any particular system of faith, but contended for the ancient order, as established by our Lord and Saviour, Jesus Christ and his Apostles."[8] Joseph's daily life was more vividly colored, however, by that common heritage of his society, the tenuous but ineluctable realities of magic, witchcraft, and demonology the *Mayflower* and the *Arbella* had disgorged so long ago into the gray mists of Massachusetts shore. Good fortune or bad, as Joseph well understood, was not an affair of Providence only; man had to contend with the dark world of the supernatural, penetrable or governable only by the most potent of ritual and incantation.[9]

The senior Smith brought much to the making of a prophet; his stalwart body, his hatred of the farm, his skeptical views on denominational religion, his love for the strange and the marvelous, his inventive fancy, his will to rise above the circumstances of his life. His wife Lucy, too, had a contribution that was not less vital. Shrewd, strong-willed, warm-hearted, garrulous, passionately devoted to her family, credulous and even superstitious, on the homeliest of terms with God, who manifested his mind and will to her in dreams and "providences," Lucy was to see all these characteristics abundantly reflected in her third son—and ultimately in the church he founded. Although the Macks were born of no such settled tradition as the Smiths, they embodied many diverse energies at work in American society which were to be intimately bound up in the life of the Mormon prophet. Lucy's father, Solomon Mack, after many ups and downs as soldier, tradesman, farmer, privateer, and commercial fisherman, in his rheumy old age had been converted to the Word and written a chapbook which he hawked about the Vermont country-side, riding painfully in a woman's side saddle.[10] The eldest of his sons, Jason, had become a preacher by the time of his twentieth birthday, a Seeker who believed that by prayer and faith the gifts of the Gospel, as enjoyed by the disciples of Christ, might be attained. Buying a tract of land in New Brunswick, Jason settled upon it a community of thirty impoverished families to whom he gave the rest of his life. The second son, Stephen, turned his attention to business. At the time of Lucy's marriage he was already partner in a flourishing store at Tunbridge, and he was to make a comfortable fortune in Detroit and Pontiac. The third of Solomon's sons was happily characterized by his sister as rather worldly minded, though "not vicious," but possessed of "a very daring and philanthropic spirit." The fourth son was content simply to remain in New Hampshire and till the family farm the rest of his days, while gathering to himself "field, flock, and herds."[11]

Chance brought the elder Joseph Smith to Palmyra, 220 miles west of Albany and half as far east of the thriving young town of Buffalo. He stayed because he liked the looks of the place, with its rich farms set amid the green drumlins studding the low Ontario plain and the flourishing village at the heart of the township. No doubt, he would better have continued west into Ohio or Indiana, where lands were still to be had at a dollar or so an acre. But Joseph had no liking for the ax and little more for the plow, and was not the man to immure himself in a lonesome clearing at the outer reaches of civilization. Palmyra was a settled place already a generation old, lacking in neither amenity nor opportunity. Its prosperous business establishments included a wagon and sleigh-making concern; a saddle and harness shop; two cabinet factories; a copper, tin, and sheet-iron manufactory; a sign-painting and gilding firm; a coopering business; two tailoring establishments; a tannery; a boot and shoemaking shop; a store vending paints, oils, dye-stuffs, drugs, medicines, snuff, and other notions; and no less than five general stores. There was even a bookstore, and within the year the town would have its own newspaper, in which all of these concerns might seek the patronage of the public.[12]

Joseph rented a small frame house on Vienna Street near the eastern outskirts of the village,[13] and there, after being joined by his family, he and Lucy opened a "cake and beer shop." Their resources were too limited ever to permit them space in the columns of the village paper, but if a sign that creaked to every vagrant breeze was insufficient advertisement, the handcart Joseph built to peddle Lucy's gingerbread, pies, boiled eggs, and root beer about the streets soon made their wares familiar to all the town.[14] Not without a touch of malice, a contemporary observed that Joseph, with his "tongue as smooth as oil and as quick as lightning," followed "a branch of the 'American System'—the manufacture of gingerbread and such like domestic wares [in which] he was a considerable speculator, having on hand during a fall of price no less than two baskets full;" and it was suggested that the Smiths, in consequence of the amount of molasses they used, were against the tariff on that article.[15] The slender income from the shop the family augmented with the sale of oil cloth coverings for tables and stands, painted by Lucy herself, and with proceeds from the day labor of Joseph and his sons at carpentering, coopering, and as harvest hands in the country roundabout.[16]

The fact remained that the location at Palmyra had not been fortunate. Joseph and Lucy had arrived in the village with few belongings but their children, in no wise situated to bargain for a piece of land, and by the following summer it was too late to buy on any advantageous terms, for De Witt Clinton had shepherded through the state legislature the long-dreamed-about Erie Canal project, the generation's greatest work of internal improvement. Ground was broken July 4, 1817, and, though it was 1822 before canal boats moved produce out of Palmyra and 1825 before the state finally joined the Hudson to Lake Erie, land prices along the line of the canal did not wait to mount upon a dizzy upward spiral. Land having soared out of reach, sometime in the fall of 1818 Joseph and Lucy moved their brood out the Stafford Road to take up squatter possession of the hundred-acre tract that was to be their farm.

The new place was better, but just barely better, than living in town. Liable to eviction at any time, the Smiths had small incentive to work the land. Any improvements they might make would only go to increase the value of the property to their own disadvantage should they ever be situated to bargain for its purchase. Beyond clearing a few acres, enough to provide space for a small log house and garden, they did nothing with the land, making their living instead by tapping maple trees, retailing cordwood to the villagers, manufacturing and selling black-ash baskets and birch brooms, laboring at well digging and carpentering or as harvest hands, and still peddling, on holidays and at times of militia muster, gingerbread cakes and beer.[17]

In one way or another—principally, it would seem, through the energetic efforts of Alvin—the family scraped together enough money to contract with the owners of the property for its purchase. Very little is known about the terms. Land in the general vicinity had sold ten years earlier at around five dollars an acre, and ten years later values had advanced to the neighborhood of thirty-five dollars.[18] Perhaps the price approached twenty dollars an acre, spread over a period of ten years or so, though William Smith reported that the farm was "articled for, to be paid in yearly installments of $100 each."[19] William also said, replying to the reproaches of their neighbors as to the shiftlessness of the family, that clearing the land presented great difficulties, sixty acres of it being as heavily timbered as any land he had ever seen, their labors made the heavier by the 1,200 to 1,500 sugar maples which had to be attended to each spring when the sap began to rise.[20] Down to the time they contracted to buy the property, the family was content to live in the log house put up in 1818, described as "a small, one-story, smoky" dwelling divided in two rooms below, with a low garret above, likewise divided in two apartments. To this structure a bedroom wing of sawed slabs had been added later. In their new security, the Smiths began to build a small frame house, converting the original home into a barn, though it does not seem that the new house was ever wholly completed during the period of their residence.[21]

By their neighbors the family was regarded sometimes with tolerance and even liking, sometimes with amiable contempt. Their poverty was an annoyance to those who could lay it to bad management or pure shiftlessness, and the increasing propensity of the elder Joseph for the marvelous gained him nothing in popular esteem. Puffing upon her old clay pipe, Lucy was a welcome visitor in the kitchens of her neighbors, a good hand with the stick, and on occasion called in to help out with family washings. Joseph and his sons were known now and then to tap a keg of cider or something harder, but as one acquaintance remarked philosophically in later years, "everybody drank them times." Except for a few weeks each winter when school was kept, the younger children were allowed to run wild, while the two eldest sons, Alvin and Hyrum, increasingly had to pitch in with their father in providing a living for the family. Alvin was regarded as the hardest worker, but Hyrum and Sophronia were the children most smiled upon.[22]

The third son, Joseph, to whom it fell in the end to fulfill his father's faith that the family was meant to occupy a station in life "above the generality of mankind," did not display any precocious earmarks of greatness. To those who later came inquiring about extraordinary incidents which must have attended his childhood, his mother could reply only that apart from an infection which for a time threatened the amputation of one leg, "nothing occured during his early life, except those trivial circumstances which are common to that state of human existance."[23] His contemporaries remembered him as a dull eyed boy inexpressive of countenance and somewhat taciturn, like his father a skilled wrestler, goodnatured, and possessed of both a facile tongue and a lively and original imagination.[24] The schooling he had received enabled him to read without much difficulty and write an imperfect hand, and it is said that he had "a very limited understanding of the elementary rules of arithmetic," but these were, in Orson Pratt's words, his "highest and only attainments."[25] Orasmus Turner, who with other devils in the office of the *Palmyra Register* delighted in blackening Joseph's face with printers ink when the boy came by for his father's paper, later recalled him to have "a little ambition; and some very laudable aspirations; the mother's intellect occasionally shone out in him feebly, especially when he used to help us solve some portentous questions of moral or political ethics, in our juvenile debating club, which we moved down to the old red school house on Durfee street, to get rid of the annoyance of critics that used to drop in upon us in the village; and subsequently, after catching a spark of Methodism in the camp meeting, away down in the woods, on the Vienna road, he was a very passable exhorter in evening meetings."[26]

This language describes Joseph more particularly between his seventeenth and twentieth years, the debating school having been established in January 1822,[27] whereas the revival which awakened him to a passing concern with Methodism blazed up in the Palmyra churches late in 1824.[28] Although in his autobiography Joseph presents himself in quite another light, there is no reason to think that religion much engaged him before the fall of 1824, and his mother's remark, in however curious a context, that up to the age of eighteen he had never read the Bible through,[29] may be given full credence. The penetrating anxieties of the revival of 1824-25 gave rise in him to a more pressing interest in religion, and Pomeroy Tucker is our warrant that Joseph became familiar with the Bible so as to quote from it and elaborate a text with great assurance, his interpretations of scriptural passages always original and unique.[30]

Joseph's own history of these years, and particularly his account of the experiences upon which are founded the claims of his church to a divine calling, must wait upon another chapter, when it will become apparent how at variance is his narrative with facts readily developed from other sources which have less of self-interest to serve. But let us here contemplate the religious tradition in which he grew up.

When De Witt Clinton, as one of the state canal commissioners, rode in 1810 along the line of the proposed Erie Canal, he talked with an old woman living near Oneida Lake who informed him that she belonged to "the church," but what church she could not tell.[31]

Diverting as Clinton found this item for his journal, it encompased both the genius and the dilemma of American churches, for the faith whereof the woman spoke had no confession other than her Bible, no ministry beyond her daily walk, no edifice but her heart. Joseph's grandfather, Asael, was a communicant of the same church. In 1799, addressing the theme of religion for the benefit of his posterity, he was principally concerned to instruct them to "search the Scriptures and consult sound reason" in all that pertained to Deity. Not in the outer formalities, he declared, but in the hidden things of the heart lay the surest hope of salvation.[32] In his eccentric fashion, Solomon Mack exhibited another aspect of this conviction; his conversion was effected in his old age by firey lights in the night and mysterious voices calling him by name, terrifying him until he understood that the Lord had taken this direct means to call him to redemption.[33]

Lucy Smith, though caught up by the prevailing anxiety to feel "a change of heart," could not deliver herself from the impasse resulting from the disintegration of Protestantism into its racking schisms: "If I remain a member of no church, all religious people will say I am of the world; and if I join some one of the different denominations, all the rest will say I am in error. No church will admit that I am right, except the one with which I am associated. This makes them witnesses against each other, and how can I decide in such a case as this, seeing they are all unlike the Church of Christ, as it existed in former days!" As for the elder Joseph, he finally threw up his hands in the conviction that "there was no order or class of religionists that knew any more concerning the kingdom of God than those of the world."[34]

Neither Joseph's parents nor his grandparents were avowedly irreligious, but all, by formal definition, were unchurched. In this as in the rationalism that pervaded their thinking, they reflected in all fidelity the state of contemporary religion. Save only in New England, where Congregationalism for two hundred years had struggled obstinately to preserve its condition of blessed matrimony with the state, no church the length and breadth of the land had been able to maintain itself in privilege and keep a firm grasp upon its membership. As immigrants poured across the Atlantic from England, Scotland, Ireland, Holland, France, and the Rhineland, the churches which were the most yeasty ferment of the Reformation came with them. There was little stability in these churches, and even the tightest bonds of fellowship grew slack in the social climate of the New World. With a vast frontier open to the west and society always in flux, the American community was not stable and could not be made so. Nowhere was this instability more immediately reflected than in the churches. Of ministers there were never enough, from Anglican bishops to Methodist circuit-riders; and had there been, no church proved supple beyond its rivals in adjusting its institutions to the difficulties and the challenge inherent in the new order of society. Everywhere the people slipped out of the grasp of the churches, many of them, in truth, having been held but by the collar. Yet break-up did not degenerate into entire disintegration. The Great Awakening of 1740-60 which called men back to devotion in new agony of soul, blew its sonorous trumpets through all the colonies, and reinvigorated all the churches. Revivalism was made respectable, and presently it came to grips with the rationalism which for a time promised to make away with religion entirely. The first generation after the American Revolution saw a war for the souls of men carried to the most distant back-woods.[35]

Other forces were at work within the churches themselves. The doctrine of the universal priesthood of all believers, with its theses of the equality of every man before the Lord and the right of every man to approach the Lord on his own authority, was one of the most seminal of the ideas that came out of the Reformation, and it accorded happily with the individualism, political and economic, which was a basic characteristic of American society. But like many other coinages, the idea lent itself readily to debasement. Zealots with the most startling claims began to trouble the religious scene.

There were the merely apocalyptic, like Nimrod Hughes down in Abingdon, Virginia, who, when Joseph Smith was not yet six years old, announced by direct revelation from heaven that on June 4, 1812, one-third of mankind would be destroyed. Nimrod was neither the first nor the last to give such notice of the approaching end, the winding-up scene having been imminently looked for in America with hardly less of satisfaction than of apprehension since Cape Cod gave shelter to the *Mayflower*. There were others, only too glad to pass by the threatened unpleasantness, well persuaded that the Millennium had already begun, like McDonald, the bald-headed tailor of Bowling Green, Kentucky, who in 1822 came to the realization that he himself must be Jesus Christ, and, fortified by reassurances he found in the Bible, began expounding the happy doctrine of living forever. Christ had many such incarnations, sometimes embodied in the fleshly tenements of a woman, like the gentle Ann Lee, who in 1774 had brought to America from England her Shaking Quakers, or like Jemima Wilkinson, the lustrous-haired Universal Friend, over on Keuka Lake only a few rifle shots away from the Smith farm. Even God the Father was occasionally discovered incarnate, as in the person of Joseph Dylks, the Leatherwood God, who in 1828 put an Ohio community into an uproar with his doctrine that he was the Father, Son, and Holy Ghost united in one supernal personage. Cry out as the newspapers might against these "wretched fanaticisms," they had a way of proliferating until it seemed at times that the whole continent was on its way to becoming a vast lunatic asylum. No idea was too absurd, no person too squalid, to compel belief. A club-footed prophet, Issac Bullard, may serve to represent his kind. In the summer of 1817 he wandered into Vermont from Lower Canada to gather himself a following of "Pilgrims" near Woodstock, a few miles south of the neighborhood so lately abandoned by Joseph and Lucy Smith. Commissioned by God to plant the church of the

Redeemer "in the wilderness, and among the heathen," in his dusty beard and bearskin girdle, Issac set out at the head of his sixty followers west across the mountains into New York, down through Ohio to Cincinnati, and on down the Ohio and Mississippi rivers to the Arkansas, where the prophet died and the remnant of his following scattered.[36]

Hardly a state in the Union lacked some such exemplar of the Christian life. If established churches turned away from the Bullards in disgust, it was to defend themselves in turn from Universalists, deists, and still worse those who mocked them in their revivals and denounced their brimstone theology. Against such critics, they were not defenseless; the revivalists, with their rare gift for evoking the very sound and sight of the damned shrieking in hell, from the middle twenties roamed back and forth across western New York and upper New England, ravaging the souls of all who heard them. It was against this smoking background that Mormonism was to take form; nor was Mormonism strangest among the "isms" spawned by the "burnt-over district;" on the pages of history Joseph Smith's church is jostled by spiritualism, Perfectionism, and Millerism, its toes stamped upon by Anti-Masonry, its ribs bruised by the bony elbows of Abolitionism, its throat parched by the arid winds of the Temperance crusade.[37]

In this milieu young Joseph grew to manhood. Yet, during the years of his boyhood, there were things about his environment far more inflammatory to the imagination than the narrow road and the straight gate. For seven years after the great revival of 1816-17 Palmyra lived at peace with God, the Smiths themselves not even church-goers. It was not the mysteries of the Kingdom of God but the mysteries of antiquity that engaged the attention of boys growing up in Palmyra. No one had yet unriddled the conundrum of America's past, not even so much as the monumental structures left by the mound-builders. No one had convincingly explained where the Indians had come from, though the profoundest ingenuities of the antiquarians had been expended on the problem. It had been suggested, though not received with any great credence, that the Americas had been peopled by Scythians who in some long time past had crossed into Russian America across the Straits of Bering. A more popular view was that the Indians were the descendants of the ten tribes of Israel. Romans, Phoenicians, Egyptians, ancient Greeks—all made claims upon the credulity of the public mind.

News items intermittently picked up by the Palmyra paper exhibited both the general interest in the matter and the baffling character of the information brought to light. A Roman coin believed to date from 150 years after Christ had been found in digging a cellar in Tennessee. Plates of brass thought to be cartouche boxes and the blade of a large knife had been found with skeletal remains in the course of excavations made for the Erie Canal. A stone tablet enigmatically inscribed in Latin had turned up in Pompey, New York. Farther afield, there were recurring stories of white

Indians living in the remotest recesses of the Rocky Mountains, where mammoths were said to roam as well.

If there was an element of doubt about such advices, as being mere newspaper stories, there was no question that a vanished people had once overspread eastern America. The mounds this lost race had built were being dug into by wandering antiquarians from western New York to the Mississippi. So far back as 1810 De Witt Clinton, who like many gentlemen of the age shared Thomas Jefferson's interest in antiquarian pursuits, had taken note of three mounds in the vicinity of Canandaigua—mounds overgrown by trees which, judging from their annual rings, he estimated to be from 150 to 300 years old, and second growth at that. Other mounds in the Muskingum Valley of Ohio were surmounted by trees which on the same evidence he could believe to be a thousand years old.[38] Nobody was willing to conceive that such mounds were the work of the Iroquois. Typically, in 1817 a writer declared that this country, which had every mark of having been for centuries a desolate wilderness, at one time had been thickly inhabited "by a warlike people, who had made much greater advances in the arts of civilized life, than any of the aboriginal inhabitants of North America, who have been known since its discovery by Europeans."[39] Such a view prevailed through another generation. Not long before log cabins and hard cider preempted his attention, William Henry Harrison was converted to the romantic thesis that the final extirpation of this mysterious people had taken place on the banks of the Ohio, where a feeble band, the "remnant of mighty battles fought in vain," had, he was pleased to fancy, there collected "to make a last effort for the country of their birth, the ashes of their ancestors and the altars of their gods."[40]

It was General Harrison's conceit that the scene of final doom had been enacted in the Ohio Valley, but in western New York, where the mounds were fewer and much less imposing than in the West, it seemed more logical to the settlers that the last clashes of arms had taken place on the very ground where their farmhouses stood. In the vicinity of Palmyra, many of the high mounds of glacial debris were also pronounced to be the work of human hands, a conclusion made all the more plausible in that many of the drumlins were capped by pallisaded forts. It would be some years before the antiquarians could demonstrate that these log fortifications dated only from the historic Iroquois period, and in the years of Joseph Smith's growing up, opinion was general that they remained from the last wretched struggles of that doomed race of antiquity.

The fascinating possibilities of this vanished civilization were not lost on the people living in and around Palmyra. Faced with extermination, the ancients must have hidden away their valuables to preserve them from their merciless enemies. Obviously, these riches lay buried still, the prize of those souls able to find them.

In taking up the quest for buried treasure, which was to give him a first gratifying and then perilous celebrity, and bring him out finally upon a high plateau of eminence as prophet, seer, and revelator to a new religion, Joseph Smith displayed not originality so much as a striking ability to compel belief. Desultory digging had been carried on in western New York for a half-generation or more,[41] and the urge to dig in the earth in search of treasure was of greater antiquity still, as old and as widespread as the human race. The feverish digging that distinguished the early twenties in and around Palmyra was, moreover, only a local form taken by a contagion that broke out epidemically across hundreds of miles of country, from the valley of the Connecticut to that of the Susquehanna.

Though the evidence is too slender to justify a firm conclusion, Vermont appears to have been the place of prime infection, the lore of the money-digger and the rural diviner carried from its rocky hills west and south wherever emigrating Vermonters settled—in the Susquehanna Valley, about the Finger Lakes, in the Genesee country, in the Western Reserve of Ohio. The infertile mountain farms held insufficient of wealth to recompense the grueling labor they never ceased to demand. Not honest effort but miracle was the best hope of the farmer; and it is the authentic tones of the Vermonter one hears when the elder Joseph Smith pointed out to one of his neighbors at Palmyra the large stones embedded in the ground of his farm—rocks in appearance, but only in appearance; in reality nothing less than chests of money raised to the surface of the earth by the heat of the sun.[42]

It may be that the elder Joseph had done some treasure-hunting before leaving Vermont;[43] as to this, a Palmyra editor in 1831 was unable to say, but did print it as "a well authenticated fact that soon after his arrival here, he evinced a firm belief in the existence of hidden treasures, and that this section of the country abounded in them. He also revived, or in other words propagated the vulgar, yet popular belief that these treasures were held in charge by some *evil* spirit, which was supposed to be either the DEVIL himself, or some one of his most trusty favorites."[44] That the senior Joseph did much to launch his son upon his troubled career as a diviner and peepstone seer, that his unbounded extravagance of statement as to the wonders his son could see contributed largely to his celebrity, is clear from all accounts; the more fantastic stories of Joseph's early powers and the marvels he discerned are to be traced back to the wagging tongue of his father.[45]

All the influences that worked upon Joseph Smith to make him what he became are difficult now to separate out of the matrix of his history. The social environment was favorable, the whole climate of opinion and belief in which so much more was possible of growth than in another time and place. There was some compulsion working upon him from within the family, the rich lore they had carried with them out of Vermont, and the pressure of their continuing poverty, the more irksome because of their conviction that their rightful state in life was above the common level. Lacking in education and opportunity, which might have afforded him some conventional outlet for the energies that drove him, Joseph was all the more inclined to reach out for the rewards that the career of the diviner promised him.

Perhaps Joseph the Seer will be more readily understood if we turn aside for a moment to consider his exact analogue, a boy who turned up among his followers in Utah a generation later.

William Titt, like Joseph himself, belonged to the disinherited. He exhibited the same sense of insecurity, the same hunger for attention, the same desire to please, the same wayward imagination. His mother dead, and unable to get along with his stepmother, about the year 1857, as a boy perhaps twelve years old, he was sent from Great Salt Lake City down to a town in southern Utah to make his home with the gentle Thomsonian doctor, Priddy Meeks. The boy, Priddy tells us, was born a natural seer, but no one knew it until he came to live in the Meeks family. Priddy was inclined to think that the Lord overruled William's coming, for though he himself had "the knowledge of the science of seer stones" and was gifted in knowing one when he came upon it, he was never able to see in such a stone. William, as it developed, could see into them readily, "and did a great deal of good by finding lost property and by telling people how their kinsfolks were getting along, even in England. He would satisfy them that he could see correct by describing things correctly." Sometimes, of course, William fell into pitfalls which Joseph Smith had run afoul in his time—"when it came to things that the devil did not want the truth to come out the devil had power to make false appearances, and William would miss the truth. William being young and limited in experience he was not able to compete with the devil at all times, and they [individual devils] undertook to destroy him and they told him if it had not been for old Meeks they would have destroyed him." Priddy was convinced that it was because of William's gifts that the devils sought to destroy him.

Some of William's sore trials, beset by these devils, Priddy describes at length. There was the time three devils came into the house and caught the boy around the body, nearly squeezing him to death. Priddy called in two of the brethren to join him in laying on hands, that these foul spirits might be rebuked. William began cursing them, and the brethren were taken aback, knowing that William did not swear, but Priddy urged them on. Sure enough, they had hardly laid hands on him than William cried, "There goes one devil out of the door; there goes another, and there goes another," whereupon he became rational again. Another case: Priddy got his wood only at the cost of considerable labor, in which William had to join, and it so happened that when they went for wood, these three devils would meet the two of them, tormenting the boy so badly that on one occasion they had to go home without their wood. Although he himself could not see the devils, Priddy knew they were there, for the skin would crawl and draw all over him, and his hair stand up "like a scared hog's bristles." The last time these devils came to trouble William, Priddy relates, the boy "was upstairs in bed after night. He said he saw them all three coming slowly as though they were doubtful. They approached close by and one said, 'I do not intend to have my trip for nothing. I will go and attack that yearling in the yard,' and in the morning I found that yearling on the lift and it died, and I took the hide off and hung it on the pole. When William saw the hide off he said, 'Do you know what killed that yearling calf?' I said, 'Poverty, I guess.' 'No,' said he. 'It was one of these devils for he told me was going to attack that yearling last night.' If he had not told me that, I should never have known what killed it."[46]

Though one may smile, albeit with a degree of tenderness, at the ingenuousness of the kindly practitioner of botanic medicine, what Dr. Meeks tells us of the seer who lived in his own family is illuminating in its bearing on the truism that the magician on any level is always the creation of his environment. In a recent work dealing with magic and religion, Arturo Castiglioni makes this point, and he goes on to say that the magician's voice in reality is nothing but the echo of the voice of the hopes and desires of the crowd, created by collective suggestion. The essential quality in the magician, Castiglioni remarks, is his ability to provoke, in himself and others, the peculiar state of mind the exercise of magic demands. On both sides faith is indispensable. Men with a critical and developed spirit, who are in any way inclined to doubt themselves, are never true magicians, while the group for whom the magician practices, "imbued with faith and will, solely animated by desire for the success of the awaited magic action, is divested, from the beginning, of all critical faculty and rational action that might impede suggestion or render it difficult. Any occurence, no matter how simple or insignificant, is interpreted according to promise and expectation, and the impression it creates is proportionate to the organization, preparation, and numerical size of the group." Within certain limits, belief in the magician must be absolute; failures never attributable to him or his art, but to hostile forces, errors committed by others, or a false interpretation of the orders received. The rituals and incantations—all the professional paraphernalia of the magician—have the extremely important function of preparing the atmosphere, concentrating the attention, allaying criticism, exciting the emotional faculties of the onlookers and imbuing them with faith in the anticipated feat.[47]

With the minor adjustment that any abstract analysis requires in being fitted to a concrete situation, these remarks are notably applicable to Joseph Smith—not merely during the years when he fulfilled the function of the magician in the lowly calling of rural scryer, but later as well, when he had become the oracle of God. That correspondence will become more fully apparent as this narrative progresses, but Joseph's fantastic employment of his youth was in no sense incidental to what he finally became; it was, in fact, absolutely pivotal. Had Joseph Smith not taken up with peepstones, there would be no Mormon church today.

A STONE IN A HAT

The precise by-path by which Joseph Smith reached the high-road of his calling has been obscured by the dust of time, but from the perspective of 1830, the Palmyra *Reflector* considered that he had followed in the steps of a local conjurer, "Walters the magician."

A vagabond fortune-teller who lived at Sodus and had once been committed to the county jail for "juggling," Walters was said to have been paid three dollars a day for the services he rendered to the early seekers after buried treasure. With his rusty sword, his peepstone, his stuffed toad, and other paraphernalia no less impressive, Walters carried a copy of Cicero's *Orations* in Latin, from which, said the *Reflector*, "he read long and loud to his credulous hearers, uttering at the same time an unintelligible jargon, which he would afterwards pretend to interpret, and explain, as a record of the former inhabitants of America, and a particular account of the numerous situations where they had deposited their treasures previous to their final extirpation. . . . Walters assembled his nightly band of money-diggers in the town of Manchester, at a point designated in his magical book, and drawing a circle around the laborers, with the point of an old rusty sword, and using sundry other incantations, for the purpose of propitiating the spirit, absolutely sacrificed a fowl, ('*Rooster*') in the presence of his awe-stricken companions, to the foul spirit, whom ignorance had created the guardian of hidden wealth; and after *digging* until day-light, his deluded employers retired to their several habitations, fatigued and disappointed."[1]

There were, in the neighborhood, other practitioners of the necromantic arts.[2] From all of them Joseph may have derived instruction, but with his lively fancy, his abounding faith in himself, and above all his will to be foremost, he soon had a peepstone and a clientele of his own. Before he was done, he all but obliterated his rivals from Palmyra's collective memory.

How Joseph found his peepstone, or as Mormon annals call it in dignified reproof, his "seerstone," was related by his father in 1830 to two curious callers. Some years before, he said, his son had happened upon a man who looked into a dark stone and told people where to dig for money and other things. "Joseph requested the privilege of looking into the stone, which he did by putting his face into the hat where the stone was. It proved to be not the right stone for him, but he could see some things, and among them, he saw the stone, and where it was, in which he wished to see." The place where he saw the stone was not far from their house; and, under pretense of digging a well, they found water and the stone at a depth of twenty or twenty-two feet. After this, Joseph spent about two years looking into this stone, telling fortunes, where to find lost things, and where to dig for money and other hidden treasures.[3]

Joseph clung to this seer stone the rest of his life, even after his first employment of it had become a memory to be curtained off by his will, and as late as 1841 he exhibited it to some of his followers. "Every man who lived on the earth," Joseph said to them, "was entitled to a seer stone, and should have one, but they are kept from them in consequence of their wickedness, and most of those who do find one make evil use of it."[4] The persistence of peepstones among the early Saints, and also this view of them, was attested by Priddy Meeks, who has explained that "seer stones, or peepstones, as they are more commonly called" were the connecting link between the visible and the invisible worlds. "It is not safe," he stipulates, "to depend on [a] peepstone in any case where evil spirits have the power to put false appearances before [the seer] while looking in a peepstone. If evil influences will not interfere, the verdict will be as true as preaching. That is my experience in the matter; also the Patriarch, Hiram Smith, the brother of the Prophet Joseph Smith, held the same idea, but stated that our faith was not strong enough to overcome the evil influences that might interfere, but seemed to think that [that] time would come. . . . I believe a peepstone is of the same piece with the Urim and Thummim, if we understand it."[5]

Joseph's own stone was found, as his father was to say, during the digging of a well on the Chase farm in Manchester, sometime in the year 1822.[6] Willard Chase, working with Alvin and Joseph Smith at the digging, says that when they reached a depth some twenty feet below the surface of the earth he

> discovered a singularly appearing stone, which excited my curiosity. I brought it to the top of the well, and as we were examining it, Joseph put it into his hat, and then his face into the top of his hat. It has been said by Smith, that *he* brought the stone from the well; but this is false. There was no one in the well but myself. The next morning he came to me, and wished to obtain the stone, alledging that he could see in it; but I told him I did not wish to part with it on account of its being a curiosity, but would lend it. After obtaining the stone, he began to publish abroad what wonders he could discover by looking in it, and made so much disturbance among the credulous part of [the] community, that I ordered the stone to be returned to me again. He had it in his possession about two years. I believe, some time in 1825, Hiram Smith (brother of Joseph Smith) came to me, and wished to borrow the same stone, alledging that they wanted to accomplish some business of importance, which could not very well be done without the aid of the stone. I

> told him it was of no particular worth to me, but merely wished to keep it as a curiosity, and if he would pledge me his word and honor, that I should have it when called for, he might take it; which he did and took the stone. I thought I could rely on his word at this time, as he had made a profession of religion. But in this I was disappointed, for he disregarded both his word and honor. . . . [O]n [my] going to Smith's [in the fall of 1826] and asking him for the stone, he [Hyrum] said, "you cannot have it;" I told him it belonged to me, repeated to him the promise he made to me at the time of obtaining the stone; upon which he faced me with a malignant look, and said, "I don't care who in the Devil it belongs to, *you* shall not have it!" . . . In April, 1830, I again asked Hiram for the stone which he had borrowed of me; he told me I should not have it, for Joseph made use of it in translating his Bible. I reminded him of his promise, and that he had pledged his honor to return it; but he gave me the lie, saying the stone was not mine nor never was.[7]

Pomeroy Tucker remembered this remarkable stone to have had a peculiar shape resembling that of a child's foot,[8] and William D. Purple, who saw the stone in 1826, said that it was "about the size of a small hen's egg, in the shape of a high-instepped shoe. It was composed of layers of different colors passing diagonally through it" and was very hard and smooth.[9] Descriptions of the stone vary with individual memories, but Hosea Stout had seen it within a few hours when he wrote in his diary on February 25, 1856, that it was apparently "a silecious granite dark color almost black with light colored stripes some what resembling petrified poplar or cotton wood bark . . . about the size but not the shape of a hen's egg."[10] Joseph's own wife remembered it as "a small stone, [which was] not exactly, black, but was rather a dark color."[11] These descriptions are consistent except that Tucker describes the stone as "of a whitish, glassy appearance, though opaque, resembling quartz." It may be that Tucker confused the first stone with the one Joseph used later.[12] The church Joseph Smith founded has not cared to exhibit either stone with the other relics of its early history, and these contemporary descriptions must suffice.

The remarkable occupation which Joseph called "glass-looking"[13] has a history old if not always honored. To recover the lost, divine the unknown, and reveal the future, the ancient Greeks employed magic mirrors, sacred springs, and even pure water in a goblet. Round pieces of rock crystal and other stones of strange shape or color were used by scryers in Europe at least from the second century, and three hundred years before Joseph's time, a "cristal stone wheryn a chylde shall loke, and see many thyngs" was an object of curious note in England.[14] Divining rods, which usually were forked twigs cut from witch hazel, willow, peach, or some other favored tree, have a similar antiquity, dating back to the times of the Medes and the Persians, but the employment of rhabdomancy specifically for locating mines and buried treasure seems to have developed about the fifteenth century in the Harz Mountains of Germany. The practice was brought to Cornwall by German miners in Elizabethan times, and became general in England and western Europe during the next century.[15] The evolution of practice and belief in America has not been the subject of a scholarly investigation,[16] but the matured folklore as it found expression at the backwoods level was graphically described in the Palmyra *Reflector* early in 1831:

> Mineral rods and balls, (as they were called by the imposter who made use of them,) were supposed to be infallible guides to these sources of wealth—"*peep stones*" or pebbles, taken promiscuously from the brook or field, were placed in a hat or other situation excluded from the light, when some *wizard* or *witch* (for these performances were not confined to either sex) applied their eyes, and nearly starting their balls from their sockets, declared they saw all the wonders of nature, including of course, ample stores of silver and gold.
>
> It is more than probable [said the *Reflector* in the skeptical tradition to which it was dedicated] that some of these deluded people, by having their imaginations heated to the highest pitch of excitment, and by straining their eyes until they were suffused with tears, might have, through the medium of some trifling emmision of the ray of light, receive[d] imperfect images on the *retina*, when their fancies could create the rest. Be this however as it may, people busied themselves in consulting these blind oracles, while the ground nightly opened in various places by men who were too lazy or idle to labor for bread in the day time, displayed a zeal and perserverance in this business worthy of a better cause.[17]

To probe the mysteries of his own stone, Joseph placed it in the depths of a battered white stovepipe hat and buried his face in the hat.[18] The wonders developed were many—chests of money, bars of gold and silver, lost property of all kinds, and even spirits of malevolent disposition. William Stafford and Rosewell Nichols were two neighbors who listened in fascination to stories of "keys, barrels and hogsheads of coined silver and gold—bars of gold, golden images, brass kettles filled with gold and silver—gold candlesticks, swords, &c &c." Nearly all the hills in this part of New York, it was impressed upon them, had been thrown up by human hands. In these hills were large caves containing gold bars and silver plates[19]—and spirits in ancient dress, in whose charge these treasures remained. One evening, William Stafford relates, the senior Joseph came to see him

> and told me, that Joseph, Jr. had been looking in his glass, and had seen, not many rods from his house, two or three

> kegs of gold and silver, some feet under the surface of the earth; and that none others but the elder Joseph and myself could get them. I accordingly consented to go, and . . . repaired to the place of deposit. Joseph, Sen. first made a nice circle, twelve or fourteen feet in diameter. This circle, said he, contains the treasure. He then stuck in the ground a row of witch-hazel sticks, around the said circle, for the purpose of keeping off the evil spirits. Within this circle he made another, of about eight or ten feet in diameter. He walked around three times on the periphery of this last circle, muttering to himself something which I could not understand. He next stuck a steel rod in the centre of the circles, and then enjoined profound silence upon us, lest we should arouse the evil spirit who had the charge of these treasures. After we had dug a trench about five feet in depth around the rod, the old man by signs and notions, asked leave of absence, and went to the house to inquire of young Joseph the cause of our disappointment. He soon returned and said, that Joseph had remained all this time in the house, looking in his stone and watching the motions of the evil spirit—that he saw the spirit come up to the ring and as soon as it beheld the cone which we had formed around the rod, it caused the money to sink. We then went into the house, and the old man observed, that we had made a mistake in the commencement of the operation; if it had not been for that, said he, we should have got the money.[20]

The spirits in whose charge the treasures had been left were pertinacious in the discharge of their trust. Joseph Capron describes another unavailing effort to outwit them, after Joseph's peepstone discovered, near Capron's house in Manchester, a buried chest filled with gold watches. A number of large stakes were driven in a circle, several rods in circumference, around the place where the treasure was deposited, after which, a messenger having brought from Palmyra a polished sword, Samuel F. Lawrence, with sword in hand, marched around and around to frighten off the devil. Meanwhile the rest of the money-diggers dug for the watches, working until they were exhausted. But despite their earnest labors, their bulwark of stakes, and their formidable defender, the devil came off victorious and carried away the treasure.[21]

What made the seeking so peculiarly difficult was the facility with which the treasures moved around the earth. It was the opinion of Joseph, Senior, as we have seen, that the heat of the summer sun could pull chests of money up through the earth to the surface of the ground, but magic also could affect this subterranean movement, and with far greater celebrity. Often the treasures were wisked away from the diggers at the very moment of seeing triumph. No lesser authority than Brigham Young preserved for us the memory of such a happening. He once told a Mormon congregation:

> Or[r]in P. Rockwell is an eye-witness to some powers of removing the treasures of the earth. He was with certain parties that lived near by where the plates were found that contain the records of the Book of Mormon. There were a great many treasures hid up by the Nephites. Porter was with them one night where there were treasures, and they could find them easy enough, but they could not obtain them. . . . He said that on this night, when they were engaged hunting for this old treasure, they dug around the end of a chest for some twenty inches. The chest was about three feet square. One man who was determined to have the contents of that chest, took his pick and struck into the lid of it, and split through into the chest. The blow took off a piece of the lid, which a certain lady kept in her possession until she died. That chest of money went into the bank. Porter describes it so [making a rumbling sound]; he says this is just as true as the heavens are. I have heard others tell the same story. I relate this because it is marvelous to you. But to those who understand these things, it is not marvelous.[22]

Marvelous or not, in this treasure-seeking it invariably turned out that some mistake had been made, or that some uncontrollable spirit or impenetrable enchantment met with. Once only, in Palmyra's remembrance, were the Smiths' efforts clearly rewarded. The scene of this exploit, the hill called "Old Sharp," is still pointed out. One day the elder Joseph came with one of his sons to tell William Stafford that Joseph had discovered some treasures which could be procured in one way only. It would be necessary to take a black sheep to the ground where the riches lay concealed, and after cutting its throat, lead it around a circle while bleeding. Thus the wrath of the evil spirit might be appeased and the treasures obtained.[23] Stafford had a black wether both large and fat, but though promised a four-fold share in the treasure, he was unconvinced of the necessity for the sacrifice of this wether until it was pointed out to him that because the treasures were to be obtained through the *black* art, none but a *black* sheep would do.[24] "To gratify my curiosity," Stafford says, "I let them have . . . [the] sheep. They afterwards informed me that the sheep was killed pursuant to commandment; but as there was some mistake in the process, it did not have the desired effect." There remained the mutton, gratefully received on the Smith table, which in Stafford's view signalized this as "the only time they ever made money-digging a profitable business."[25]

In later years Joseph found it expedient to ignore the tales by his old neighbors at Palmyra. His followers have improved upon his example.[26] Their prophet gave them a sufficient history of his youth to run a church on, and they have never been willing to go back of that history. It has been easier to believe there was no one of any integrity in the whole town of Palmyra than to open the door upon doubt. Even the most responsible of the Mormon historians, B. H. Roberts, simply waved aside the universal testimony of Palmyra concerning their old neighbor—mere idle stories, dark insinuations, anything to discredit the prophet.[27] It may be, as Joseph once maintained, that he engaged in his glass-looking only at the importunities of others,[28] and it is certainly true that the more extravagant stories of what he could see in his stone issued from other members of his family. But the picture of Joseph, his family, and their friends as indefatigable searchers after buried treasure, limned in contemporary newspapers and the recollections of their neighbors, stands forth clearly after every discount has been made for malice and dislike.[29]

During the two years after the finding of the seerstone, the fortunes of the family progressed only from bad to worse—whether an effect or a cause of the unremitting treasure-seeking it is impossible now to say.[30] The loss on November 19, 1823, by what would appear to have been acute appendicitis, of the eldest son, Alvin, not only cost the family their most energetic wage earner but soon made them the butt of a cruel wit directed, it is obvious, at their nocturnal excavations. It was bruited about that body-snatchers had made off with the corpse, and in September 1824 the elder Joseph had the grave opened to establish that Alvin lay undisturbed, a fact he publicized with a pathetic notice in the village paper which attributed the reports in circulation more to "a desire to injure the reputation of certain persons than a philanthropy for the peace and welfare of myself and friends."[31]

The same day Joseph had his son's grave opened, September 25, 1824, the Methodists began a historic two-day camp-meeting in Palmyra. The town had been smoldering with religious unease since early in the spring, and now it caught fire. Through the fall of 1824 and the winter and spring of 1825 a powerful revival raged, catching up the Smiths with the other townsfolk, and eventually bringing Lucy and some of the elder children into the bonds of Christian fellowship. Joseph and his father hesitated on the fringe of conversion, half persuaded by the arguments of the Methodists, but finally turned their backs upon this opportunity for salvation.[32] It seems likely that for some months the hectic treasure-seeking was neglected, for the revival plunged the community into anxious preoccupation with thir state and standing before the Lord, and the Palmyra *Reflector* speaks of a time anterior to the first rumors about the golden plates "when the money-digging ardor was somewhat abated;"[33] moreover, Willard Chase has said that for a time he reclaimed the peepstone from Joseph, apparently in 1824.[34] But this is an interregnum only; late in the summer of 1825 an old Vermonter by the name of Josiah Stowell, who made his home in the Susquehanna Valley, heard from his son at Palmyra of the wonders Joseph could see in the stone, and journeyed north to talk with the seer. Sending Hyrum to borrow the peepstone from Willard Chase,

Joseph gave the old man so convincing a demonstration of his powers—first describing Stowell's house and out-buildings at Bainbridge, and then descrying the whereabouts of buried money which so much engrossed the old man—that Joseph was engaged upon the spot. He and his father were assured, as a minimum, of a wage of fourteen dollars a month for labor through the winter on Stowell's farm; Joseph would have the opportunity of going to school while there, and he and his father would receive a share amounting to two-elevenths of all the treasures that should be brought to light.[35]

Since the money-digging he did for Josiah Stowell is the sole activity of the kind to which Joseph ever made anything resembling forthright confession, it is instructive to see what his autobiography makes of the episode. All he has to say, actually, is that he "hired with an old gentleman by the name of Josiah Stowell, who . . . had heard something of a silver mine having been opened by the Spaniards in Harmony, Susquehanna county, state of Pennsylvania; and had, previous to my hiring, been digging in order, if possible, to discover the mine. After I went to live with him, he took me, with the rest of his hands, to dig for the silver mine, at which I continued to work for nearly a month, without success in our undertaking, and finally I prevailed with the old gentleman to cease digging after it."[36]

In the autobiography of any but a prophet of God, the experiences Joseph thus lightly passes over would provide one of its most fascinating chapters. Just why Stowell was seeking Joseph was more clearly set forth in 1835, with Oliver Cowdery serving him as spokesman. Some forty miles south of Stowell's home at Bainbridge, in the township of Harmony, just below the Pennsylvania border, Cowdery explained, there was said to be "a cave or subterraneous recess" of some kind. "A company of Spaniards, a long time since, when the country was uninhabited by white settlers, [had] excavated from the bowels of the earth ore, and coined a large quantity of money: after which they secured the cavity and evacuated, leaving a large part still in the cave, purposing to return at some distant period. A long time elapsed and this account came from one of the individuals who was first engaged in this mining business. The country was pointed out and the spot minutely described." Enough was credited of the Spaniard's story to excite belief in many "that there was a fine sum of the precious metal lying coined in this subterraneous vault," and among those so persuaded was Stowell.[37]

Active digging in search of this treasure seems to have begun in 1822, only to be suspended when the seer who directed operations informed the seekers that the enchantment resisting their efforts could not be dissolved except through the death of one of their number. Providentially, as it was thought, one of the band of treasure-hunters was murdered early in 1824,[38] but from some cause, the diggers were no better able than before to locate the object of their search, and the work had reached a standstill when Stowell heard of Joseph's singular powers and came to seek his aid.

Stowell and the two Smiths arrived back in the Susquehanna country late in October 1825. A few days later the parties concerned drew up a curious document to apportion the anticipated rewards of their labors. Among other things it provided:

> That if anything of value should be obtained at a certain place in Pennsylvania near a *Wm*. Hale's, supposed to be a valuable mine of either Gold or Silver and also to contain coined money and bars or ingots of Gold and Silver, and at which several hands have been at work during a considerable part of the past summer, we do agree to have it divided in the following manner, viz.: Josiah Stowell, Calvin Stowell and Wm. Hale to take two-thirds, and Charles Newton, Wm. I. Wiley, and the Widow Harper to take the other third. And we further agree that Joseph Smith, Sen. and Joseph Smith, Jr. shall be considered as having two shares, two elevenths of all the property that may be obtained, the shares to be taken equally from each third.

Generously, the agreement also provided that three men who had dug unavailingly prior to this time should be considered equal sharers in the mine after all the coined money and bars or ingots obtained had been removed. This agreement was drawn up at Harmony on November 1, 1825, doubtless at the home of Issac Hale, who signed it as witness.[39]

Hale was one of the most famous hunters in the Susquehanna country, his celebrity attested even on the worn stone that marks his grave today in the little cemetery south of Oakland, Pennsylvania, but it was game rather than buried treasure that took him so often into the hills. A one time Vermonter, he had at first a lively interest in Stowell's project and willingly boarded the treasure seekers at his home, but soon decided that it was all nonsense. In a statement a few years later he declared:

> I first became acquainted with Joseph Smith, Jr., in November, 1825. He was at that time in the employ of a set of men who were called "money-diggers;" and his occupation was that of seeing, or pretending to see by means of a stone placed in his hat, and his hat closed over his face. In this way he pretended to discover minerals and hidden treasures. His appearance at this time, was that of a careless young man—not very well educated, and very saucy and insolent to his father. Smith, and his father, with several other (money-diggers) boarded at my house while they were employed in digging for a mine that they supposed had been opened and worked by the Spaniards, many years since. Young Smith gave the (money-diggers) great encouragement, at first, but when they had arrived in digging, to hear the place where he had stated an immense treasure would be found—he said the enchantment was so powerful that he could not see. They then became discouraged, and soon

> after dispersed. This took place about the 17th of November, 1825; and one of the company gave me his note for $12.68 for his board, which is still unpaid.[40]

In his autobiography Joseph passes delicately over the outcome of this treasure-seeking, saying only that after working unsuccessfully for nearly a month, he prevailed with Stowell to cease digging. So far as it went, this was indeed the case. But if Joseph returned with Stowell to spend the winter working upon the latter's farm at Bainbridge, and attending school there, he was not done with glass-looking. Throughout the winter, the scenes familiar to Palmyra were reenacted with a fresh cast of characters—digging for money buried on Bend Mountain, seeking after gold on Monument Hill, tramping through the night in quest of a salt spring. Joseph could translate Indian pictographs without the smallest hesitation; and if an inquirer would know what miscreant had made off with money missing these sixteen years, Joseph could inform him. (It turned out to be the person suspected all along.) Besought to say where a chest of dollars lay buried in Windsor, Joseph looked into his stone to find out, and even marked out its dimensions with leaves on the ground. As had happened at Palmyra, the diggers came near seizing this treasure, only to have it sink into the ground.[41]

By now Joseph was a grown man, at the threshold of his majority. A lithe six feet in height, blonde hair darkened to light brown, his blue eyes curiously mild, even innocent, in his pale, expressionless face, he was a figure to bring a second glance from any woman. At Palmyra his name had not, so far as his contemporaries have left record, been coupled with that of any girl, but in Bainbridge there were curious eyes to note that he was keeping company with the Stowell girls, and malicious tounges to find fault with his association with Eliza Winters, to the point of saying, even, that he had attempted to seduce her.[42] Presently it became apparent that it was not these girls but Issac Hale's second daughter, the tall, dark, hazel-eyed Emma, who had caught his eye.

The courtship proceeded under difficulties, for Hale had come to the blunt opinion that Joseph was a lazy whelp who would never be good for anything. Emma herself must have been troubled what to make of this young man so unlike anyone else she knew, and was disturbed by her father's contempt for him. But in her twenty-second year Emma was still unmarried, the specter of spinsterhood following her ominously about, and her heart took no heed of his prospects. Perhaps she would have married him that spring. Late in the winter, however, Joseph's wooing was brought up short. Charging him with being "a disorderly person and an imposter," Josiah Stowell's sons haled him before a magistrate, thereby plunging him into the first great crisis of his career.

The trial took its painful course in Bainbridge March 20, 1826, before Albert W. Neely, a pioneer merchant who also served the town in the capacity of justice of the peace. Joseph unhesitatingly admitted to possession of his peepstone, and exhibited it to the court; he also admitted to its uses, but maintained that he had largely given up looking through the stone, having found it injurious to his eyes. Far from soliciting such business, he said deprecatingly, he had always rather declined having anything to do with it. Stowell himself testified to the glass-looking Joseph had done for him, but denied that the seer had either pressed his services upon him or deceived him in their use. When the justice asked incredulously, "Deacon Stowell, do I understand you as swearing before God, under the solemn oath you have taken, that you *believe* the prisoner can see by the aid of the stone fifty feet below the surface of the earth, as plainly as you can see what is on my table?", Stowell answered stoutly, "Do I believe it? No, it is not a matter of belief. I positively know it to be true!" Stowell's hostile sons described how Joseph had undertaken to locate, through the use of his dark stone, the chest of dollars reputedly buried in Windsor, and a "palpable deception" by which he had undertaken to demonstrate the qualities of his white stone. Stowell's hired man, however, was as convinced as his employer of Joseph's rare powers, and said so bluntly.[43]

It was an awkward decision for the justice to make; apart from this aberration, Josiah Stowell was a respected member of the community, and a pronouncement of guilty must be a verdict upon the intelligence of the old man. In the fact that Joseph was still a minor, nine months short of his twenty-first birthday, the justice seems to have found a way out of the dilemma. He pronounced Joseph guilty, but, as it appears, saved the situation by placing him on probation with a stern warning to end his conduct.[44]

The fact of the trial, as much as its outcome, must have shaken Joseph Smith to his center. During the three years he had communed with his stone in the depths of his white stovepipe hat, he had enjoyed an awe and consideration no other youth of his age could command, and had experienced the strange, intoxicating power of being able to move men as he would. The experience had been astonishing and gratifying, lifting him out of the ruck of common humanity. But it had ended by bringing him to this contretemps: what had happened in Bainbridge could happen again, in Palmyra or anywhere he went. In December he would reach his majority, and his youth would not serve him again if brought to the bar of justice.

It must have been with a feeling as of a world come apart at the seams that Joseph returned, without Emma, to take up once more at Palmyra the depressing burden of the farm.

PORTRAIT OF A PROPHET AS A YOUNG MAN

Quite another picture of his early life than this so painstakingly pieced together was painted by Joseph Smith when, as a prophet of the living God, he undertook to minister to the hunger of his followers for a stirring legend of his youth. His history of the years that shaped him for his high calling is a thing all light and splendour, filled with the terror and the wonder implicit in all intercourse with God.

Joseph's account of his visions may be likened to a mural rendered on two panels. The "First Vision" depicts the appearance to Joseph Smith in his fifteenth year of no lesser personages than the Father and the Son to instruct him that the churches of his day were all corrupt and that he must hold himself apart from them. The "Vision of the Angel Moroni" is a companion piece delineating the appearance to Joseph three and a half years later of an angelic messenger sent to reveal to him his great calling as a prophet and rest upon him the responsibility for placing before the world an ancient record, the Book of Mormon.

This mural from the early 1840s has been cherished by Joseph's followers, who have brought the unconverted from afar to admire it and multiplied reproductions to scatter abroad to the world. Even iconoclasts, impressed by the boldness of the conception and the glowing detail, have so far accepted Joseph's masterpiece, placing upon it bizarre hypotheses as to the wellsprings of his personality.

When this remarkable work is more minutely examined, however, its luminous surface takes on a singularly different aspect. Here the brush-work in the underpaint has left ridges in the overpaint; there the top surface was so thinly painted as to have become semi-transparent under the clarifying action of time. Scholarship brought to bear, like the action of x-rays or ultra violet light, brings into shadowy definition the surfaces painted over, which at once are striking in revelation of the intent of the artist, the painful evolution of his conception, and his progressive manipulation of reality in the service of his art. It becomes apparent that the two panels of this mural were originally to have been one, that elements from the original conception were altered and recombined to form a new design altogether, that it is indeed legend and not history with which we have to deal in taking up Joseph's account of his youth.

Let us examine first the finished work, this epic of his early life.

Sometime in the second year after the removal of the Smith family from Palmyra to Manchester, so Joseph's recital of his First Vision begins,[1] in the spring of 1820, there commenced in his neighborhood an unusual excitement on the subject of religion. Beginning with the Methodists, it became general among all the sects, until the whole region was aroused, some contending for the Methodist faith, some for the Presbyterian, and some for the Baptist. Amid this war of words and tumult of opinion, Joseph, being then a boy in his fifteenth year, could not come to any certain conclusion as to which of the churches might be right. His mother, his brothers Hyrum and Samuel, and his sister Sophronia were proselyted to the Presbyterian faith, but his own inclination was towards the Methodists.

In his perplexity, he was one day struck with the force of a passage in James: "If any of you lack wisdom, let him ask of God, that giveth to all men liberally, and upbraideth not, and it shall be given him." Never, he says, "did any passage of Scripture come with more power to the heart of man than this did at this time to mine," and on the morning of a beautiful, clear day, early in the spring of 1820, he retired to the woods and knelt down in prayer. Scarcely had he done so than he was seized by some power which entirely overcame him, binding his tongue so that he could not speak; thick darkness gathered around, and it seemed to him that he was doomed to sudden destruction. Exerting all his powers, he called upon God to deliver him out of the power of this enemy, "and at the very moment when I was ready to sink into despair and abandon myself to destruction—not to an imaginary ruin, but to the power of some actual being from the unseen world, who had such marvelous power as I had never before felt in any being—just at this moment of great alarm, I saw a pillar of light exactly over my head, above the brightness of the sun which descended gradually until it fell upon me." Miraculously delivered from the enemy which had held him bound, he saw standing above him in the air two personages having a brightness and a glory beyond description. One of them spoke to him, calling him by name, and said, pointing to the other, "This Is My Beloved Son, Hear Him!"

Mindful of his object in going to inquire of the Lord, Joseph, as soon as he was able to speak, asked these glorious personages which of the sects was right, which he should join. He was answered that he must join none of them, for they were all wrong, and the personage who addressed him, clearly the Savior himself, said that all the creeds were an abomination, that their professors were corrupt in His sight: "They draw near to me with their lips, but their hearts are far from me; they teach for doctrines the commandments of men: having a form of godliness, but they deny the power thereof." He again forbade Joseph to join with any of the sects, and told him many other things which the prophet never saw fit to reveal. When the boy came to himself again, he was lying on his back, looking up into heaven. Recovering his strength in some degree, Joseph went on home to tell his mother somewhat inadequately, it will be agreed, that he had found out for himself that Presbyterianism was not true.

Some days later, happening to be in company with one of the Methodist preachers active in the revival, Joseph gave him an account of the vision. Great was Joseph's surprise when the story was not only treated lightly but with great contempt, as being of the devil. The minister assured him that there were no such things as visions or revelations any more, all of which had ceased with the apostles. Thus Joseph soon found that his story excited a great deal of prejudice against him among professors of religion and was the cause of great persecution: "Though I was an obscure boy, only between fourteen and fifteen years of age, and my circumstances in life such as make a boy of no consequence in the world, yet men of high standing would take notice sufficient to excite the public mind against me, and create a bitter persecution; and this was common among all the sects—all united to persecute me." However strange his story, Joseph insisted that he, like Paul, had seen a vision, and all the persecution under heaven could not make it otherwise: "I had actually seen a light, and in the midst of that light I saw two personages, and they did in reality speak to me; and though I was hated and persecuted for saying that I had seen a vision, yet it was true; and while they were persecuting me, reviling me, and speaking all manner of evil against me falsely for so saying, I was led to say in my heart, Why persecute me for telling the truth? I have actually seen a vision, and who am I that I can withstand God, or why does the world think to make me deny what I have actually seen? For I had seen a vision; I knew it, and I knew that God knew it, and I could not deny it, neither dared I do it, at least I knew that by so doing I would offend God, and come under condemnation."

This, in bold outline, is Joseph's "First Vision." Before we leave it to inspect his "Vision of the Angel Moroni," let us rig some cross-lighting and take a penetrating second look, for the underpaint is by no means obscured by the paint Joseph subsequently splashed on with so much assurance, for it readily becomes apparent that the idea of a visitation from the Father and the Son was a late improvisation, no part at all of his original design.

Not to belabor our metaphor, Joseph told two distinctly different stories to account for his having become a prophet of God. The First Vision is the last of these, entirely unknown to his followers before 1838, when he began to write a formal autobiography; and was not published in any form until late in 1840, and not by Joseph himself until the spring of 1842. Prior to that time, as early as 1834-35, Joseph had published in the church periodical a history of his life having an astonishingly different import,[2] and that history is the defiant underpaint of our metaphor.

According to that earlier version of his novitiate, Joseph's interest in religion was first awakened during the visit to Palmyra of a Methodist minister, the Reverend Mr. George Lane. This event took place, not in 1820, as his autobiography declares, but three years later, in Joseph's seventeenth year.[3] Elder Lane being "a talented man possessing a good share of literary endowments, and apparent humility," there was a great awakening in Palmyra, with large additions made to the Methodist, Presbyterian, and Baptist churches. "Mr. Lane's manner of communication," it is explained, was peculiarly calculated to awaken the intellect of the hearer, and arouse the sinner to look about him for safety—"much good instruction was always drawn from his discourses on the scriptures, and in common with others, . . . [Joseph's] mind became awakened."[4]

For a time the reformation seemed to move on harmoniously, but after "those who had expressed anxieties, had professed a belief in the pardoning influence and condescension of the Savior," the various denominations began a general struggle for proselytes, and the cry, "I am right—you are wrong," was heard. In this strife for followers, Joseph's mother, one sister, and two brothers were persuaded to unite with the Presbyterians, which gave Joseph cause for still more serious reflection. Strongly solicited to unite with several of the denominations, but seeing the apparent proselyting disposition manifested with equal warmth by all, the future prophet hesitated. "To profess godliness without its benign influence upon the heart, was a thing so foreign from his feelings, that his spirit was not at rest day nor night. To unite with a society professing to be built upon the only sure foundation, and that profession be a vain one, was calculated, in its very nature, the more it was contemplated, the more to arouse the mind to the serious consequences of moving hastily in a course fraught with eternal realities. To say he was right, and still be wrong, could not profit; and amid so many, some [churches] must be built upon the sand."

What was he to do? If he went to one church he was told they were right and all others wrong. If to another, the same was heard, all professing to be the true church, but none having satisfactory evidence to support its claims. A proof from some source was wanting, and that source could only be the Lord, who long ago had said that to him who knocks, to him it shall be opened, and that whosoever will, may come and partake of the waters of life freely. Therefore, while this excitement continued, Joseph called upon the Lord in secret "for a full manifestation of divine approbation, and for, [what was] to him, the all important information, if a Supreme being did exist, to have an assurance that he was accepted of [God]." On the evening of September 21, 1823, Joseph's mind being "unusually wrought up on the subject which had so long agitated his mind—his heart was drawn out in fervent prayer, and his whole soul was so lost to everything of a temporal nature, that earth, to him, had lost its [charms] and all he desired was to be prepared in heart to commune with some kind messenger who could communicate to him the desired information of his acceptance with God." For hours he prayed, and finally all the wishes of his heart were granted. As though the house were filled with consuming and unquenchable fire, a radiant messenger appeared to him, come from the presence of God to tell him that his sins were forgiven, his prayers heard.

But all at once, and disconcertingly, this picture blurs and its lineaments are strangely altered. The scene has ceased to be God the Father appearing in glory to Joseph in the woods but has become the Angel Moroni appearing to him in his bedchamber. The time is not the spring of 1820 but the early autum of 1823. In fact, this is not Joseph's First Vision at all, but his Vision of the Angel Moroni, with Joseph not merely oblivious of the fact that he had once been visited of the Father and the Son, but, worse yet, concerned to know whether a supreme being ever existed.

The facts are the same in the two accounts, right down to their discordant result: A revival had occured in the neighborhood of Palmyra which had begun among the Methodists and spread to the other denominations; the Smith family in general and Joseph in particular had been aroused; Joseph's mother and sister had joined the Presbyterian church; and he himself, too much troubled by doubts about all of the denominations to join with any, had been led to seek in prayer the assurance and firm guidance that God alone could give. The discordance between the two accounts is not a mere matter of dates; it results from an enlargement of the original conception. The considerations which led Joseph to enlarge his story in this fashion will be weighed later in this chapter, when the facts have been more fully developed, but it is clear that no man in his church, not even Joseph himself, suspected in 1835 that he had been visited in his youth by the Father and the Son. No one dreamed that his history included an event of such overwhelming import until, Joseph having wrought further upon the divinity of his calling, Orson Pratt carried the story to the world late in 1840.[5]

Contemporary publications (such as those reprinted in Appendix B) illustrate the understanding of the early Mormons that their church dated from no earlier an event than the appearance of an angel to Joseph Smith in 1823. The pronouncement by the Father and the Son that all churches before Mormonism were corrupt, which has yielded such aid and comfort to the modern church, is an argument so obviously useful that it is impossible to conceive that the early missionaries would not have employed it had they known of it.[6]

Lucy Smith alone, by incorporating into her *Biographical Sketches* through direct quotation her own son's account of the First Vision, provides any evidence that the tale of the First Vision was ever countenanced within Joseph's own family; and even she, writing to her brother in January 1831 to urge upon him the divinity of her son's claims, thought only to tell him that "Joseph, after repenting of his sins and humbling himself before God, was visited by an holy angel" who gave him commandments inspired from on high and the means to translate the Book of Mormon.[7] That Lucy should have failed to mention such a vision in 1831, and preserved no independent recollection of it in 1845 when dictating her autobiography, does not make her the best of witnesses in her son's behalf. The prophet's younger brother, William, never showed himself able to conceive of Joseph's visions in any terms but a vision of the Angel Moroni.[8] Finally, it is significant, all the more significant in view of the unrelenting persecution Joseph would have us understand came upon him in his youth, that the folklore relative to his early life, an admirable index to the public mind if not a storehouse of exactly determinable event, at no time ever pictured Joseph as being, in the idiom of the day, "a miserable fanatic" given to delusions; he has always been, in Palmyra's collective memory, the moneydigger and seer in peepstones.[9]

We can now look more closely, and frankly with more interest, at the second of the panels that makes up Joseph's great mural,the Vision of the Angel Moroni. This second of his visions, as his autobiography would have us believe, or his first, as he originally gave the Saints to understand, led directly to the writing of the Book of Mormon and so to the founding of his church. Here again his original conception underwent radical revision as his brush worked upon it. The alterations and the substitutions could not be hidden from the critical eye, but it was the only surface Joseph had to work on, and he made it do.

The autobiography relates that between the time of the first vision and the autumn of 1823, Joseph continued to pursue his common vocations in life, all the while "suffering severe persecution at the hands of all classes of men, both religious and irreligious," because he remained unshaken in his affirmation that he had seen a vision. Having been forbidden to join any of the religious sects of the day and being of very tender years and persecuted by those who, said the prophet with melting heart, ought to have been his friends and treated him kindly, or if they supposed him deluded to have endeavored in a proper and affectionate manner to reclaim him, he was left to all kinds of temptations and mingling with all kinds of society, frequently falling into many foolish errors, and "displayed the weakness of youth and the corruption of human nature, which I am sorry to say led me into divers temptations, to the gratification of many appetites offensive in the sight of God."[10]

Feeling condemned by his weaknesss and imperfection, and desiring to know his state and standing, Joseph was moved on the night of September 21, 1823, to seek a second manifestation from God. As he was in the act of calling upon the Lord, a light appeared in his room, which increased until the room was lighter than at noonday, and in the brightness Joseph saw a personage, his aspect "glorious beyond description, and his countenance truly like lightning." This personage informed the youth that his name was Moroni, that he was a messenger sent to tell of the work God had for him to do, in consequence of which his name should be had for good and evil among all nations, kindreds, and tongues. Hidden in a nearby hill, declared the angel, was a book engraved upon golden plates, a record giving an account of the former inhabitants of this continent, and the source from whence they sprang; it contained the fullness of the everlasting gospel, as delivered by the Savior to the ancient inhabitants, to whom he had appeared for this purpose after his resurrection. Deposited with the golden plates were two stones, set in silver bows and fastened to a breastplate—the instrument anciently called the Urim and Thummim, the possession and use of which had distinguished "seers" in times long past. God had prepared these stones for the express purpose of translating the history recorded upon the plates, and Joseph was to be the translator.

Nor was this all. Solemnly the angel quoted the words of Malachi concerning the coming of a messenger who should prepare the way for the Messiah; the prophetic language of Isaiah about a rod which should come forth out of the stem of Jesse,[11] the promise in Acts that the Lord God should raise up a prophet to be heard in all things under the penalty of being destroyed; and last of all, the dread poetry of Joel:

> And it shall come to pass afterward, that I will pour out my spirit upon all flesh, and your sons and your daughters shall prophesy, your old men shall dream dreams, your young men shall see visions: And also upon the servants and upon the handmaids in those days will I pour out my spirit. And I will shew wonders in the heavens and in the earth, blood, and fire, and pillars of smoke. The sun shall be turned into darkness, and the moon into blood, before the great and the terrible day of the Lord come. And it shall come to pass, that whosoever shall call on the name of the Lord shall be delivered: for in Mount Zion and in Jerusalem shall be deliverance, as the LORD hath said, and in the remnant whom the LORD shall call.

All these things, said the angel, were soon to be fulfilled, and he admonished Joseph again about the golden plates. When he should come into possession of them, he should show them to no one, nor the breast plate with the Urim and Thummim—to none but by command, under penalty of being destroyed. As the angel spoke of the plates, the vision was opened so that Joseph could see the place where they lay buried, and so distinctly that he knew the place when he visited it in the flesh.

Now the light began to gather about the person of Moroni until the room was again dark, save immediately around the angel, when Joseph saw, "as it were, a conduit open right up into heaven, and he ascended until he entirely disappeared, and the room was left as it had been before this heavenly light made its appearance." Joseph lay musing on the singularity of what had passed, when on a sudden he was startled to find the radiance returning. The angel reappeared at his bedside and again related his message, without the smallest variation, except that when done he advised the youth of great judgements that were coming upon the earth, desolations by famine, sword, and pestilence. The angel disappeared only to reappear a third time, and a third time relate his message, thus establishing beyond any possibility of doubt the divine character of what had transpired.[12] Before taking his final leave, the angel warned Joseph that Satan would tempt him, through the indigent circumstances in which the Smiths found themselves, to get the plates for the purpose of enriching himself. Should Joseph hold any object in view other than to glorify God, should he be influenced by any motive other than that of building His kingdom, he would fail in obtaining the plates.

This series of interviews with Moroni terminated only with cockcrow. As the gray light of dawn replaced the radiance which had filled Joseph's bedchamber, he arose and proceeded about his daily labors. He found, however, that his strength was strangely exhausted. His father, laboring alongside him in the field, told him to go home, but on starting for the house, in attempting to cross the fence, Joseph fell helpless to the ground. After a time, he was aroused by a voice calling him by name and, on looking up, for the fourth time beheld the angelic messenger, standing over his head surrounded with light. Once more the angel rehearsed the story, then commanded the boy to go to his father and tell him of the vision and the commandments laid upon him.[13] "I obeyed," Joseph says; "I returned to my father in the field, and rehearsed the whole matter to him. He replied to me that it was of God, and told me to go and do as commanded by the messenger. I left the field, and went to the place where the messenger had told me the plates were deposited; and owing to the distinctness of the vision which I had had concerning it, I knew the place the instant that I arrived there."

The place of deposit was a high, narrow ridge with an abrupt north face, rising several miles southeast of the Smith farm along the mail road between Palmyra and Canandaigua—"a hill of considerable size," Joseph described it, "the most elevated of any in the neighborhood." On the west side of the hill, near its top, under a stone of considerable size, he found the plates, deposited in a stone box, and with them the Urim and Thummim and the breastplate. On attempting to remove these objects, Joseph was forbidden by the messenger, who told him that the time for bringing them forth was yet four years distant. But he was instructed to return to the place in one year precisely, when the messenger would again meet with him; in this way they should continue until the time arrived for obtaining the plates. Accordingly, on each succeeding September 22 down to the year 1827 Joseph returned to the place of deposit, met the messenger, "and received instruction and intelligence from him ... respecting what the Lord was going to do, and how and in what manner His kingdom was to be conducted in the last days."

Thus is the resplendent second of the two panels which comprise the mural of Joseph's visions. Together they have a rare charm and simplicity, the mighty questions of eternity dextrously reduced to finite understanding. Yet the second of these paintings, like the first, affords abundant evidence of the labor the artist expended upon it to produce his effort. The "Vision of the Angel Moroni," even as the "First Vision," rewards a thoughtful second look.

Let us consider, in particular, the difference in mood between the legend of his life as Joseph delineated it in 1834-35 and that legend as he refurbished it in 1838. The earlier version of the events which led to the founding of his church was written under the long shadow cast by his money-digging past, accounts of which were rife in the very country to which the Mormon missionary efforts were being most insistently addressed.[14] Apology and explanation to set the facts at defiance color the whole of this first official history of the coming forth of the Book of Mormon. By the time Joseph came to dictate his autobiography, he had survived not merely that small crisis but upheavals of proportions so seismic as to have all but destroyed him. The burden of his theme reflected both this change in his fortunes and the hardening of his spririt: now his theme was not apology but indictment. Not his own frailties but the stony heart of mankind stood arraigned.

Nowhere is the shift in emphasis more evident than in the two pictures Joseph gave to his church of his life before the Angel Moroni came into it. His matured account of these years we have already seen; it presents a picture of an obscure, inoffensive boy hounded by persecution and misrepresentation solely because he had dared to tell the world that he had had a vision—a boy who may have become somewhat wayward, but only because of these dire circumstances. But three and a half years earlier, Joseph, in the church periodical, had been principally concerned to defend himself against accusations of "gross and outrageous violations of the peace and good order of the community," implicit in the widespread tales of his money-digging. He admitted having in his youth fallen into many vices and follies, chiefly "a light, and too often vain mind, exhibiting a foolish and trifling conversation," but this "uncircumspect walk and unchaste conversation" was, he declared, all and the worst his accusers could substantiate against his moral character; and he wanted it understood that he did not pretend to be any "other than a man 'subject to passion,' and liable, without the assisting grace of the Savior, to deviate from that perfect path in which *all* men are commanded to walk!"[15]

The reorientation, not to say vindication, of himself in relation to his visions becomes, on close inspection, the principal end Joseph had in rewritting his history. The First Vision itself is a conception investing him with an ineffable dignity, for in all recorded history, to what other men have the Father and the Son appeared? And how much more imposing the revised version of the words spoken to Joseph by Moroni than the version so thoughtlessly quoted to the church in 1835! The autobiography pictures Moroni as telling a great prophet of his destiny, that prophet foretold by Malachi, Isaiah, and

Joel, whose words men shall heed under penalty of being destroyed. Far more modest is the language of Moroni as recounted in 1835. The only scripture Moroni had thought to mention was, embarrassingly, the reminder given by Paul to the Corinthians, that God was wont to choose the foolish things of the world, the base things, the things which were despised, to confound the things which were mighty. It is not surprising that Joseph, as time went on, searched the Bible for scripture less tactless in its application, more befitting the man he had become.

There are other things to be observed in the language of Moroni as Joseph gave it to the world in 1835. According to God's covenant made with his ancient saints, Moroni said, it was necessary that his chosen people, the house of Israel, come to a knowledge of the gospel, their own Messiah, whom their fathers had rejected, and be gathered with the fullness of the Gentiles to rejoice in one fold under one shepherd. Joseph, said Moroni, had been chosen to be the instrument in the Lord's hand "to bring to light that which shall perform his act, his strange act, and bring to pass a marvelous work and a wonder. Wherever the sound shall go it shall cause the ears of men to tingle, and wherever it shall be proclaimed, the pure in heart shall rejoice, while those who draw near to God with their mouths, and honor him with their lips, while their hearts are far from him,[16] will seek its overthrow, and the destruction of those by whose hands it is carried. Therefore, marvel not if your name is made a derision, and had as a by-word among such, if you are the instrument in bringing it, by the gift of God, to the knowledge of the people."

In this language Joseph was justified and defended against aught that might be said of him, and the major purpose of this first history of his life was served, the Saints given a shield and buckler for the defense of the faith. But we are not done with this early version of the Vision of the Angel Moroni, for Joseph could not rest content with the role in which it cast him.

It will be remembered that the autobiography explains how the angel, on telling Joseph of the golden plates, informed him that the time was not yet ripe to obtain them, that he must wait four years during which he must prove himself worthy. This was by no means the story as Joseph originally gave it to the church; on the contrary, he was to have had the plates immediately, and it was only his own baseness of heart, or at any rate his own frailty, that prevented it.

Moroni having explained that he should have the golden plates on condition that he proceed with "an eye single to the glory of God," Joseph set out the morning after the visitation to find the places where the plates lay hid. As he walked along, we are told, two different considerations began to war in his mind, "as though two invisible powers were influencing, or striving to influence his mind," his dependence upon and need to serve the Lord with a whole heart, against the prospect "of obtaining so desirable a treasure—one in all human probability sufficient to raise him above a level with the common earthly fortunes of his fellow men,[17] and relieve his family from want, in which, by misfortune and sickness they were placed."

When at last the treasure lay exposed to his gaze, Joseph would have taken it from its stone receptacle, but "a shock was produced upon his system, by an invisible power, which deprived him, in a measure, of his natural strength." This happened a second time, and a third, until at last he cried out, "Why can I not obtain this book?"

He was answered, "Because you have not kept the commandments of the Lord." The angel again stood in his presence, and he was shamed in the realization that he had failed to remember the great end for which the plates had been kept. Instant contrition swept him. He gave himself up to god in prayer, and as he prayed, the darkness began to disperse from his mind. The heavens were opened, the glory of the Lord rested upon him, and he was shown a vision of the prince of darkness, surrounded by his innumerable train, so that he might never forget the two powers that warred for his soul. The plates, he must never forget, were deposited, not "for the sake of accumulating gain and wealth for the glory of this world: they were sealed by the prayer of faith, and because of the knowledge which they contain . . . the fullness of the gospel of Jesus Christ, as it was given to the people on this land." Before the plates could be permitted to come into his hands, he was told, he must be tested for worthiness. When it became known what the Lord had shown him, the workers of iniquity would seek his overthrow, circulate falsehoods to destroy his reputation, and even seek his life. But if he should prove faithful and keep the commandments of the Lord, he should be preserved to bring forth this remarkable work and wonder.

From that time to September 1827, so Joseph told his church in 1835, "few occurences worthy of note transpired." If, as his autobiography maintains, he made annual pilgrimages to the place where the plates were hidden to be met and instructed by the messenger sent by the Lord, it was not among the things, in 1835, regarded as worthy of note. It had only to be added, for Joseph's narrative had now come around full circle to the point of beginning, that so far from being "a lazy, idle, vicious, profligate fellow" who had dug down all the mountains of Susquehanna County, as his traducers declared, the prophet had always been "an honest, upright, virtuous, and faithfully industrious young man." Opinions to the contrary could be influenced by no other motive than to destroy his reputation, even as the Angel Moroni had foretold.[18]

Strangely, although the discordances between Joseph's several versions of his visions have not gone unnoticed, no serious effort has ever been made to set his history of the visions within the framework of the religious history of his time. Although there is much subjective content in the visions, both of the Father and the Son and of the Angel Moroni, Joseph hinged them on reality, drawing upon the troubled memories of the revivals to give them the impact of truth. Thereby he also gave the visions an objective content by which they may be absolutely evaluated.

It so happened, whether from chance or some particular susceptability, that Palmyra was a seed-ground for all the great revivals which swept western New York in the late eighteenth and early nineteenth centuries. At the time of the celebrated awakening at the turn of the century, which has come down in history most vividly for the pathological intensity it reached in the West,[19] almost the earliest response in New York was in Ontario County, where, as a minister of the time took glad note, "the seriousness" began in Palmyra.[20] The revival so commenced spread like fire in stubble and raged until 1801, but, as usually was the case when religious emotion burned too long and furiously, there followed a prolonged period of spiritual darkness.

The embers were not again quickened into flame until 1816, the year the Smiths migrated to Palmyra. The cold breath of "the year without a summer" had blown chill upon the necks of the Yorkers, and the clergy made haste "to improve the providence, by impressing the minds of the people with a sense of their entire dependence on God, [who] could easily deprive them, not only of the comforts, but even of the necessaries of life."[21] By September the commencement of a glorious work was reported from Palmyra, many rejoicing in hope, multitudes inquiring the way to salvation, and before the revival spent itself, the Presbyterian church alone in Palmyra could list 120 converts who had found hope of a saving acquaintance in Christ.[22]

Powerful as was this revival, it was not sustained beyond the spring of 1817. The abnormal cold of 1816 had been exorcised by the praise of God, and by the summer of 1817 religious disquiet could give place to expansive talk about the Erie Canal, long dreamed of but now actually to become a reality. The atmosphere of soaring optimism was never conducive to the anxiety of soul which found its characteristic catharsis in the revivals, and it is in no way surprising that the Palmyra newspaper, which from 1817 faithfully chronicled isolated revivals in Massachusetts, Vermont, and New York, had no news of religious moment from any nearby locality until word came to hand in January 1822 of "a most extraordinary change within two or three weeks past" at Lyons, twenty miles to the north.[23] In Palmyra itself the editor had to be content with lesser things, "a happy change" lately observed among the townsfolk, with young gentlemen actually to be met with in the sanctuary on Sundays, and young ladies seen to grace the church with their presence.[24] Though the moral tone of the community continued to improve under the influence of a debating society established for young people, and a society rigidly bent upon the suppression of vice and immorality,[25] through all these years no precious drops from the Throne of Grace fell in Palmyra. The village delayed until 1824 to begin a third memorable seeking after the word.

In other words during all these years, when by the necessities of Mormon history Palmyra should have been in continual spiritual torment, its religious life all of a color to grace under the last of the revivalists, the townsfolk were going about their daily labors untroubled by the awful probability that they were children of Wrath and in danger of hell. Not in 1820 as the First Vision would have it, not in 1823 as the Vision of the Angel Moroni would have it, but in 1824 began the revival which has left its indelible impress upon Mormon history.

Decisive in fixing the accounts by Joseph Smith and his family within the framework of contemporary event is the memory that has come down to us of the Reverend George Lane, chief architect of the revival. Lane, prior to the fall of 1824, had never ridden the circuits of the Ontario District, and he was never to ride them again. During the five years previous to this time he had been stationed in the Susquehanna District, hundreds of miles to the south, Jonathan Huestis and Abner Chase meanwhile looking after the spiritual welfare of the brethren in the Ontario District, and after this great year of revival, Lane left the itinerancy to become a local preacher at Wilkes-Barre.[26] From Lane's career only, and without reference to the abundant supporting evidence, it can be established that the revival which awakened Joseph to the importance of religion took place from four to five years after the Father and the Son appeared to him, and from a year to a year and a half after the Angel Moroni came to his bedside to reveal his momentous calling.

George Lane's impassioned preaching, Oliver Cowdery has noted, was "peculiarly calculated to awaken the intellect of the hearer, and arouse the sinner to look around him for safety."[27] This was a view fully shared by Lane's associates in the ministry, who have said that his prayers were characterized by deep agony of soul and firm confidence in God, his sermons by a thorough acquaintance with the scriptures and with the human heart, so that "sometimes under his powerful appeals vast congregations were moved like trees of the forest before a mighty wind. Many a stout-hearted sinner was broken down, and cried aloud for mercy under his all but irresistable appeals."[28]

This work at Palmyra to which he set his hand had already been underway for some months, having commenced in the spring of 1824.[29] How ripe the field was for the harvest is revealed by a communication in the *Wayne Sentinel*, published ten days before Lane rode into town: "The love of God has been shed abroad in the hearts of many, and the outpouring of the Spirit seems to have taken a strong hold. About twenty-five have recently obtained a hope in the Lord, and joined the Methodist church, and many more are desirous of becoming members. He that hath ears to hear, let him hear; God invites all to come—to repent and be saved. Sinners, recollect that you are, as it were, suspended by the brittle thread of life, over the rolling billows of that lake of fire and brimstone where flames are never quenched. The son of man cometh when no one knoweth it, and those who continue in their wicked career, will sooner or later be precipitated into Hell!"[30]

To such a labor Lane gladly addressed himself. "There was a great awakening," Oliver Cowdery tells us, "and much enquiry for the word of life." William Smith, who alone among the elder Smith children perserved some detachment about the excitement, and offered himself as a convert to no church, adds that great numbers were converted as the excitement extended from the Methodists to the Baptists, and from them to the Presbyterians.[31] Joseph's own autobiography declares that "great multitudes united themselves to the different religious parties," and Lane himself has said that the work broke out from the village like a mighty flame and spread in every direction. By December, when he left Palmyra finally, he could count in the village and its vicinity upwards of 150 who had joined his society, besides a number who joined other churches, and many who had not yet joined any church.[32]

The fires burned at white heat throughout the winter. In January 1825, the Rochester *Religious Advocate* counted more than 200 hopeful subjects of divine grace in Palmyra, Macedon, Manchester, Phelps, Lyons, and Ontario. "This is a powerful work," the *Advocate* rejoiced; "it is among old and young, but mostly among young people. Many are ready to exclaim, 'what hath God wrought!' "[33] By the first week in March the *Wayne Sentinel* could print the extraordinary intelligence that "in Palmyra and Macedon, including Methodist, Presbyterian and Baptist churches, more than 400 have already testified that the Lord is good. The work is still progressing. In the neighboring towns, the number is great and fast increasing. Glory be to God on high; and on earth, peace and good will to all men."[34] It was April before "this very powerful revival in Palmyra" showed signs of subsiding.[35]

Lucy Smith had always been attracted by formal religion, and more, perhaps, than anyone in her family, she was stirred by the awakening. Being, as her son William says, "a very pious woman and much interested in the welfare of her children, both here and hereafter, [she] made use of every means which her parental love could suggest, to get us engaged in seeking for our souls' salvation. . . . She prevailed on us to attend the meetings, and almost the whole family became interested in the matter."[36] It was to the Presbyterian church, the oldest and the most numerous in Palmyra, that Lucy and the elder children were drawn. Unfortunately, it was the minister of this denomination, the Reverend Benjamin B. Stockton, who had preached Alvin's funeral sermon a year or so before and been so intemperate in his language as to intimate strongly that Alvin, not being a church member, had gone to hell.[37] This had enraged the elder Joseph, and though Lucy says that to gratify her he attended two or three meetings, he then "peremptorily refused going any more, either for my gratification, or any other person's."[38]

Whether because he shared his father's feeling or because he had been deeply impressed by the Methodist circuit rider, Joseph also resisted the general movement of his family into the Presbyterian fold. There is no doubt that he had been aroused under Lane's preaching to "look about him for safety"; it is to Lane that Oliver Cowdery, speaking for Joseph, accorded the credit for the providence that his mind "became awakened." Joseph himself says that he "became somewhat partial to the Methodist sect," and "felt some desire to be united with them."

In this general chorus of agreement the non-Mormon sources join. Orasmus Turner remarks that Joseph caught "a spark of Methodism in the camp meeting, away down in the woods, on the Vienna road," to the point of becoming a passable exhorter in the evening meetings, while Pomeroy Tucker says that Joseph went so far as to join the probationary class of the Methodist church and make some active demonstrations of engagedness, though his convictions were "insufficiently grounded or abiding to carry him along to the saving point of conversion," and he soon withdrew.[39]

Tucker's further remark, that the final conclusion announced by Joseph was that "all sectarianism was fallacious, all the churches on a false foundation, and the Bible a fable," may be received as gratuitous, but there is nothing inherently improbable in it. Within a few years after 1825 Joseph was apologizing for his "former uncircumspect walk, and unchaste conversation,"[40] and his skeptical cast of mind is evidenced as well by the fact that he was finally converted to no church as by a conversation his mother's memory preserved. When she persisted with him on the subject of religion, he said to her, "Mother, I do not wish to prevent your going to meeting, or any of the rest of the family's; or your joining any church you please; but, do not ask me to join them. I can take my Bible, and go into the woods, and learn more in two hours, than you can learn at meeting in two years, if you should go all the time."[41]

The exact date Joseph turned his back on the high promise the revivals had held out to him can only be guessed,[42] but most probably by the early summer of 1825 he had withdrawn altogether from the embrace of the Methodist church. When he went off to the Susquehanna country that fall, he could take up his glass-looking again with an untroubled heart.[43]

Joseph had not easily been persuaded to yield up the details by which the integrity of his account of himself may be appraised. To importunate followers in 1831 he said shortly that "it was not intended to tell the world all the particulars of the coming forth of the Book of Mormon; and . . . it was not expedient" for him to relate these things.[44] Joseph would best have held to that ground. The progressive enlargement of his story, climaxed finally in the breathtaking vision of the Father and the Son, involved him in difficulties that ended by setting reality at complete defiance. He committed himself very early to the thesis that he had been visited by an angel in 1823. When Joseph shifted his ground in 1834-35, drawing upon the troubled emotions of the revivals to give verisimilitude to his account of his visions, the revival of 1824-25 was wrenched out of its proper context and dated back to 1823, for it was logically impossible that Joseph's awakening to religion should have been delayed for months after the Angel Moroni appeared to him. From this position it was only a step to the final ground he occupied, the revival moved back in time three more years, and his sanction found in the Father and the Son themselves.

How is it possible that Joseph's followers accepted all that he chose to tell them, never doubting, deaf to inconsistency and blind to impossibility? A Mormon authority has given an answer of a kind: "Our fathers and our people in the past and now, were and are uncritical. They have been and are now—and to their honor be it said—more concerned with the fact of the divine origin of the Book of Mormon and the great work it introduced than [with] the *modus operandi* of its translation. Overwhelmed by a divine testimony of its truth they have paid little attention to the precise manner by which it was brought forth."[45] It was emotionally impossible for the Saints to challenge the integrity of their prophet, in the matter of his early life or anything he chose to tell them. If deceived in anything, it might be that they were deceived in everything. The whole power and discipline of their faith conditioned them to belief. Yet their own responsibility in the make of their prophet, in the proliferation of his legend, is not to be dismissed. Their hunger for miracle, their thirst for the marvelous, their lust for assurance that they were God's chosen people, to be preserved on the great and terrible day, made them, hardly less than Joseph, the authors of his history. His questionable responsibility is the faithful image of their own.

Since Joseph placed his record of his visions before the world, the visions have been argued unceasingly. It is idle to argue over them any longer. His story of the visions is not a record of genuine event, objective or subjective, but a literary creation, of which we have both the trial draft and the finished work, revealing Joseph's mind and personality only as any literary work reveals any writer. The subtleties of his personality are better weighed on a later page, when the evidence of his entire life may be passed in review, but the visions themselves cease to have any significance as history. It is impossible to grant them any standing, to accept them as an adequate accounting of Joseph Smith's youth, a history standing fierce in contradiction against what has been remembered about him by those who knew him so well.

Yet, as a literary creation, Joseph's visions have a continuing fascination. All his life long he appropriated freely from the intellectual currency of his age, validating his borrowings with the seal of his own extraordinary mind and will. If he laid claim to visions, this was no more than Elias Smith had done, with his glory seen in the forest at Woodstock and his transcendant vision of "the Lamb upon Mt. Sion."[46] Again, there was John Samuel Thompson, the Universalist minister who had held forth in the Palmyra Academy while the revival raged in 1825—to him Christ had descended from the firmament "in a glare of brightness, exceeding ten fold the brilliance of the meridian Sun . . . saying: 'I commission you to go and tell mankind that I am come; and bid every man to shout victory.' "[47]

Admittedly, Thompson's vision was only a dream, but to Asa Wild, of Amsterdam, New York, the Lord God Jehovah had appeared to reveal the imminence of the Millennium and the great cataclysms which were at hand, including wars, massacres, famine, pestilence, and earthquakes. Every denomination of professing Christians, God had instructed Asa, had become extremely corrupt, many having never had any *true* faith at all, being guided only by depraved reason; the severest judgements were to be inflicted on the false and fallen professors of religion.[48] Even the Presbyterian ranter, Charles G. Finney, could tell of a walk in the woods which had led to his conversion—his anguish of heart, his solitary prayers before the Lord, the great peace that came upon him, and the apparition afterwards in his room, as of the Lord Jesus Christ met face to face.[49]

If God had not appeared to Joseph in 1820, or the Angel Moroni in 1823, this was, Joseph could come to appreciate, an oversight only. It was an oversight which, after due consideration, he did not hesitate to amend.[50]

THE GOLDEN BIBLE

Sometime in late 1826 the Smiths lost their farm. They had been unable to meet their payments and lacked a thousand dollars of completing the purchase when the land agent in Canandaigua foreclosed the property and sold it to Sheriff Lemuel Durfee. Although Durfee permitted the Smiths to remain in possession, in consideration of a small annual payment sufficient to pay the interest on the balance,[1] the family was heartbroken—their long ordeal by poverty suffered to no purpose.

Despite this black turn in the fortunes of the family, Hyrum took Jerusha Barden to wife early in November;[2] their marriage seems to have given Joseph courage to return to Harmony and press his suit with Emma Hale. His mother relates how one day he called her and his father aside and said, "I have been very lonely ever since Alvin died, and I have concluded to get married; and if you have no objections to my uniting myself in marriage with Miss Emma Hale, she would be my choice in preference to any other woman I have ever seen." They not only gave him their blessing but urged him to bring Emma back with him and make their home with the family. Accordingly, Joseph set off for Pennsylvania.[3]

As always, he was welcome at Josiah Stowell's, but when he rode down the river to the Hales to ask Emma's hand, Issac, her father, was abrupt in refusal, giving among other reasons that Joseph was a stranger and followed a business he could not approve of.[4] But Emma was both compliant and of age, and when Joseph proposed that they elope, one Sunday morning while her father was at church, she gladly mounted his old horse. The next day, January 18, 1827, at the home of Squire Tarbill in Bainbridge, they became man and wife.[5] It was not expedient to remain in Bainbridge, for Hale was a man of quick temper and stubborn will, so Joseph set off with his bride for his father's home, arriving before the month was out, "in good health and fine spirits."[6]

Little information has survived to indicate what Emma thought of the strange surroundings to which she was brought. In Harmony the Hales had always been among the most respected members of the community, and if not affluent, at least beyond the immediate reach of hardship. It was far otherwise with the Smiths in Manchester, and the only special distinction to which her husband laid claim could not have made Emma entirely happy. She must have often been homesick; there is at least one remembrance of her weeping, saying that she had been deceived and had got into a hard place.[7] Yet the marriage on which she entered was to be the great experience of her life, standing up under stresses that would have shattered a relationship of lesser quality; whatever there was about her husband that she found unaccountable and disquieting, she had given herself to him irrevocably.

At some cost to her pride, but impelled by their need, Emma eventually wrote her father to inquire whether she could obtain the property she had left behind: her clothing, some furniture, and a few cows. In reply she received a formal assurance that her belongings were safe and at her disposal.[8] Doubtless with some trepidation, she and Joseph set out in August for Harmony, taking Peter Ingersoll with them to help in moving her things. At sight of the runaways, Hale burst into tears. "You have stolen my daughter and married her," he said to Joseph. "I had much rather have followed her to her grave. You spend your time in digging for money—pretend to see in a stone, and thus try to deceive people." Joseph wept in turn, Peter Ingersoll says, and "acknowledged he could not see in a stone now, nor never could; and that his former pretensions in that respect, were all false. He then promised to give up his old habits of digging for money and looking into stones." It was a rare moment of self abasement in Joseph's life. Much mollified, Hale told his son-in-law that if he would move to Harmony and work for a living, he would help Joseph establish himself, an offer Joseph gratefully accepted.[9]

Thus in a moment there opened up for Joseph the offer of a new life, a place he might make for himself in the world with strict regard to the traditional virtues of sobriety, thrift, and honest toil. In the affecting presence of his father-in-law, his wife clinging to his arm, it had been easy to turn his back upon his past. But back in Manchester the values shifted again. Throughout his life his father had labored at farming and it had profited him nothing. Joseph had never been able to regard himself as a son of the soil; against the constricted life of the farm he had already been in rebellion five years and more. Moreover, for all that moment of weakness before his father-in-law, Joseph could not so meanly regard his powers of second sight. He may or may not have believed unreservedly in his gift, but an irreducible minimum of belief he held all his life is exemplified by the tenacity with which he clung to his seerstone.

Above all, in promising Isaac Hale that he would give up his glass-looking, Joseph had not reckoned with the necessities of his family, who could neither understand nor condone his promise, insisting that he "resume his old practice of looking in the stone." Peter Ingersoll, who claims to have been Joseph's confidant at the time, tells us of the importunities of the family and the seer's troubled indecision over what he should do.[10] The family's faith in Joseph at no time had ever wavered, and he could not be unmoved by the straits in which he saw them. Now perhaps as never in their lives they looked to him to retrieve their shattered fortunes; he had even given them reason to think that this very fall they should obtain certain strange treasure which had engrossed them for years. The farm gone, their status upon it little better than that of squatters, they had no other hope than what he represented.

His irresolution did not last long. Turning his back upon the fair prospect Issac Hale had held out to him, he cast his lot with his family. The news spread at once through Palmyra in the shape of a heart-stopping rumor. After so many years of staring into his stone, white hat held close against his face while his eager followers dug up the countryside, Joe Smith—said this clamorous rumor—had done it. He had found in the side of a hill not three miles distant from his home a book written upon plates of gold, a treasure of incalculable value. Any skeptics were confounded the first time the elder Joseph walked into the village thereafter. The town loafers spiked his cider with whiskey, got him drunk, and extracted the whole dazzling story from him.[11]

Whatever the pressure of need which brought it to dramatic climax, Joseph Smith's story of the golden plates was no invention of casual provenance. It has a complex history which traces its origins back almost to the inception of his money-digging, and in a sense goes back in time further still, to the firm belief in *genius loci* his father had brought with him from Vermont. The most diverse influences operated to shape the story, and over a long period of time it seems to have undergone many mutations, never twice told the same, even after a church had grown out of it and Joseph had set one version down in print for the benefit of that church. Yet in outline the story can be developed without much difficulty, and its basis in reality established.

The circumstances which immediately gave rise to the tale of these fabulous plates clearly was Joseph's interest in the antiquities. His mother has perserved an arresting memory of his imagination as it worked upon the ancient Americans; he was given, she says, to regaling the family with "some of the most amusing recitals that could be imagined," describing "the ancient inhabitants of this continent, their dress, mode of travelling, and the animals upon which they rode; their cities, their buildings, with every particular; their mode of warfare; and also their religious worship . . . with as much ease, seemingly, as if he had spent his whole life with them."[12]

The idea of a buried record which should have preserved the history of this vanished people followed logically—a book to give "an account of the ancient inhabitants (antediluvians) of this country, and where they had deposited their substance, consisting of costly furniture, etc., at the approach of the great deluge."[13] The record itself could be fashioned of nothing but gold, or Joseph would have violated every convention of the scryer.

It seems likely that it was in September 1823 that Joseph first intimated to the family that such a record existed. The recurrence of month and year in many different accounts, and the fact that the eldest brother, Alvin, who died in November 1823, figures large in the story, is sufficient reason to think so.[14] That Joseph's peepstone played an important part in the events is clear, but its precise role is difficult to describe. Perhaps it was Joseph's means of communication with the spirit which came to dominate the drama; or perhaps its clouded depths first revealed the existence of the treasure.[15]

The spirit who entered so decisively into the story is said to be the same spirit Walters the magician once attempted to propitiate with the sacrifice of a fowl. An imposing personage, the spirit was difficult to describe. A "little old man with a long beard" in one account, in another he was a very large, tall man dressed in an ancient suit of clothes covered with blood.[16] Now he appeared "like a Spaniard, having a long beard down over his breast, with his throat cut from ear to ear and the blood streaming down";[17] at another time he had something of the aspect of a Quaker, being dressed in the plainest of clothes.[18] In this same description he was identified as "the spirit of one of the Saints that was on this continent, previous to its being discovered by Columbus,"[19] and not long after, so far from being a mere spirit, he was recognized to be an actual angel of the Lord.[20]

Although this spirit, in whatever form, had revealed to Joseph long before 1827 that the record it so closely guarded should come into his hands, it was exacting about the conditions, Joseph being given to understand that the prescribed rituals must be adhered to without the smallest deviation.[21] He was required to dress himself in black clothes and ride to the place of deposit on a black horse with a switch tail.[22] Having arrived at the appointed place, he should demand the book in a certain name,[23] and after obtaining it, go directly away, neither laying the golden record down nor looking behind him. Joseph's father, it seems, found the requisite articles, and Joseph rode off into the darkness on his eerie mission. He found the place of deposit without difficulty, a stone box of strange workmanship, and was able to open it and take up the treasure that lay within. But in an incautious moment, impressed with the other treasures the vault contained, he laid the record down. Instantly the spirit appeared to buffet him with much violence as to send him reeling, and to inform him that because of his failure to abide by his instructions, he should not be permitted to carry away the precious record. When Joseph inquired timidly if he might be allowed to get the plates at another time, he was told to come back in one year, bringing his eldest brother back with him; they would then be given into his keeping.[24]

The mention of Alvin in this connection is not the least interesting feature of the legend. Lucy Smith says that Alvin displayed, if possible, a greater interest in Joseph's story of the plates than any other member of the family, so much so that for a long time after his death they could not bear to hear anything said on the subject.[25] That Alvin would have been inclined to credit such a story is also evident from the remembrance of him perserved at Palmyra; he shared fully the faith of his father, Hyrum, and Joseph in the strange powers of peepstones, and even experimented with one himself.[26]

The unlucky circumstance of Alvin's death cast down all the hopes of the family. When September 22, 1824, came around, far from Alvin's being able to participate in the obtaining of a choice treasure from out of the earth, his father was having to make up his mind to the unpleasant necessity of disinterring Alvin himself. The spirit shook his head over this second failure to observe the conditions required of him, but held out some hope to Joseph that he would yet succeed. He should wait another year, and again return to where the plates were hidden, bringing a man with him. To Joseph's question who this man should be, the spirit would say only that Joseph would know him when he saw him.

According to Willard Chase, Joseph was disposed to think that Samuel T. Lawrence was the appointed individual, and so advised him, taking him to a singular-looking hill in Manchester and pointing out where the treasure lay buried. Subsequently, however, he changed his mind and declared that he had been mistaken; Lawrence was not the right man nor had he told him the right place. Two years went by,[27] and then, as Joseph's father told the tale, his son came to realize that the designated person was not a man but a woman; it was, in fact, none other than Emma Hale. Not again to be thwarted, Joseph courted and married Emma and brought her home to Manchester. With her help it was impossible that he should not at last obtain the plates. Once they were in his possession, Joseph would translate them with the aid of his stone; the translation would be published; and as the glorious consumation of the whole affair, from the profits of the work, the Smiths should be enabled "to carry into successful operation the money-digging business."[28]

In general, the story of the golden plates as thus outlined seems to have been known in Palmyra by the early summer of 1827, though the prominent role given Emma may have been an afterthought. Willard Chase says that the elder Joseph related to him a story of the kind in June 1827 and held then the expectation that his son would succeed in getting the plates in September. In her own way, Joseph's mother refers to the same expectation. She says that not long after Joseph brought Emma back to Manchester as his bride, he came home one night looking much exhausted, saying that as he was passing by the Hill Cumorah the angel had stopped him to remind him that he had not been enough engaged in the work of the Lord, that the time had come for the record to be brought forth, and he must be up and doing.[29] If, as there is every reason to think, the legend had so far matured by the summer of 1827, it may be appreciated how grave were the embarrassments of Joseph's position in the light of the promise he had made to Issac Hale, and why, finally, he took his courage in both hands and wedded his life to the legend.

With characteristic unconcern for the details, all that Joseph Smith ever placed on record about the circumstances under which he came into actual possession of the golden plates is that he went at the appointed time to the hill where they lay buried and received them from the heavenly messenger, being charged to look after them carefully under penalty of being cut off.[30] His mother is much more generous with details. At this time, late September of 1827, Josiah Stowell and Joseph Knight, from the Susquehanna country, were visiting the Smith home. Lucy maintains that they had come north out of concern for her family; Martin Harris says tactlessly that Stowell was "at old Mr. Smith's, digging for money."[31] Be this as it may, about midnight on September 21 Joseph flustered Lucy by coming to her and asking if she had a chest with a lock and key. In view of the close quarters at which the family had to live, it might be supposed that Joseph should have known that answer without asking the question; nevertheless, he alarmed his mother, as she had more than an inkling of why he wanted it and could not supply the deficiency. Joseph calmed her fears, telling her that he would make out all right, and a moment later he left the house with Emma, the two of them rattling off in the horse and wagon which belonged to Joseph Knight.[32]

The Mormon prophet was never very communicative as to just what happened that night, and his wife could not be sure that anything at all had happened,[33] but Willard Chase, who claims to have had the story from Joseph a week or two later, says that Joseph "arose early in the morning, and took a one-horse wagon, of some one that had stayed over night at their house, without leave or license; and, together with his wife, repaired to the hill which contained the book. He left his wife in the wagon, by the road, and went alone to the hill, a distance of thirty or forty rods from the road; he said he then took the book out of the ground and hid it in a tree top, and returned home."[34] Without much variation, this is the story Joseph told Martin Harris, with the additional detail, however, that while he was obtaining the plates, Emma knelt down and prayed. The book of gold he had hidden "in an old black oak tree top which was hollow."[35]

On this mission Joseph and his wife were gone all night, not returning until long after sun-up, by which time Knight had fully decided that some rogue had made off with his property. When at length her son returned, Lucy says she trembled with fear, lest all might have been lost in consequence of some failure "in keeping the commandments of God." Joseph reassured her: "Do not be uneasy Mother, all is right—see here, I have got a key." This "key," she found on taking it into her shaking hands, consisted of "two smooth three-cornered diamonds set in glass," the glasses being set in silver bows connected with each other in much the same way as old fashioned spectacles, no less a marvel than the Urim and Thummim.[36] He took them from her and left her, having said nothing whatever about the golden plates. But she would not be left in doubt that after all these years he had at last succeded in obtaining this singular record, for in a few moments he returned to ask her about having a chest made. "I told him," Lucy says, "to go to a certain cabinet-maker, who had made some furniture for my oldest daughter, and tell him that we would pay him for making a chest, as we did for the other work . . . namely, one half in cash and the other in produce. Joseph remarked that he would do so, but that he did not know where the money would come from, for there was not a shilling in the house."[37]

This episode of the chest is by no means least curious among all such events. It has even been speculated whether Joseph was at first wholly serious in his claim to have gained possession of the plates: did he need a chest in which to keep a rare treasure, or did he claim possession of the treasure as an expedient for obtaining a chest he lacked money to buy? Willard Chase tells us that before Joseph got the plates, he came to him, as a skilled cabinet-maker, requesting that he make a chest. He intended shortly to move to Pennsylvania, he said, and before leaving expected to get the book of gold; he needed the chest so that he could keep the treasure under lock and key. Chase was given to understand that if he would make the chest, he should share in the treasure. Although Chase had done some digging by night, he was not much impressed by Joseph's proposition, and suggested that the latter bring the golden book to him; he himself would keep it locked up. Joseph dismissed this idea as out of the question; he was commanded to keep the record for two years, without letting anyone other than himself look upon it. "I told him," Chase affirms, "to get it and convince me of its existence, and I would make him a chest; but he said, that would not do, as he must have a chest to lock the book in, as soon as he took it out of the ground. I saw him a few days after, when he told me that I must make the chest. I told him plainly that I could not, upon which he told me that I could have no share in the book."

Chase was left to wonder about Joseph's motives, for ten days or so after that fateful September 22, Joseph came over to relate the story of how he had obtained the plates. Was he still hoping to cajole the cabinet-maker into giving him what he wanted? Chase heard later that Joseph had told one of the neighbors that "he had not got any such book, nor never had such an one, but that he told the story to deceive the d——d fool, (meaning me,) to get him to make a chest."[38]

Many contradictory stories were now afloat. Had Joseph lied in the first place to get himself a chest made? Or was he lying when he denied having the plates? Very few in Palmyra could make up their minds what to believe. But those few could not be deceived. The men who dug fruitlessly at Joseph's direction over so many years had implicit faith that he had at last come up with something worth naming, and with furious determination, they set about making him share in his find. It was their contention, Martin Harris says, "that they had as much right to the plates as Joseph had, as they were in company together. They claimed that Joseph had been traitor, and had appropriated to himself that which belonged to them."[39]

So resounding was the uproar which followed that it has left its impress even on Joseph's almost impervious autobiography. The most strenuous exertions, he says, were used to get the plates from him. "Every stratagem that could be invented was resorted to for that purpose. The persecution became more bitter and severe than before, and multitudes were on the alert continually to get them from me if possible."[40] One of his neighbors remembered that on one occasion Joseph was ducked in a pond;[41] Joseph himself says that things came to such a pass that several times he was shot at, narrowly escaping.[42] If Joseph had a sense of irony that was even vestigial, he must have been struck with the predicament into which he had got himself, forced into the most strenuous efforts to hide a treasure the very existence of which is hard to credit. He had, in truth, taken by the tail a bear he was never afterward able to let go.

That turbulent fall of 1827 comes down to us graphically in the narrative of Joseph's mother. Her husband, Lucy says, learned within a few days after Joseph came into possession of the golden plates that ten or twelve men had gathered together with Willard Chase at their head, for the purpose of uncovering Joseph's find.[43] These men had actually sent sixty or seventy miles for a conjuror of rare accomplishment to divine for them where the treasure lay hid. The name of this conjuror has not been preserved, which is unfortunate, because Brigham Young declares that the man, whom he knew personally, was "possessed of as much talent as any man that walked on the American soil"—a fortune-teller, necromancer, astrologer, and soothsayer with a particular gift for language, insomuch that to those who loved swearing it was music to hear him.[44]

Impressed by the appearance on the scene of a wizard of such formidable attainments, the elder Joseph hastened home to inquire of Emma if she knew whether his son had taken the plates from their place of deposit, or if she could tell him where they were. Emma was remarkably vague upon the subject in view of the fact that she had accompanied Joseph on that historic night; she did not know where the plates were, or even whether Joseph had removed them from their ancient hiding place.

The elder Joseph insisted upon the danger, so Emma set off in search of her husband, who was engaged in digging a well in the adjacent village of Macedon. Lucy explains that Joseph kept constantly about his person the "key" he had displayed to her, the Urim and Thummim, through which "he could in a moment tell whether the plates were in any danger. From "an impression" he had had, Joseph came up out of the well just as Emma rode up. Informed what had transpired, he looked in the Urim and Thummim and saw that the golden record was safe but nevertheless decided it was advisable to return home.[45]

When they got there, they found the elder Joseph pacing the ground in anxiety. His son calmed his fears, saying, "Father, there is no danger—all is perfectly safe—there is no cause of alarm." After taking a cup of tea and dispatching to find a chest with a good lock and key, Joseph started off to where the golden record was secreted, three miles away. Taking up the plates, he set out through the woods for home.

He arrived bruised and breathless, with a tale of having been thrice attacked along the way by men who sought to wrest his treasure from him; he had fought them all off and had managed to bring the plates home safe.[46] His father, Josiah Stowell, and Joseph Knight went out in search of his assailants, but in vain; no sign of the miscreants was to be found. Hyrum came on the gallop with a chest, and in it Joseph placed "the record," which meantime had been veiled from the profane eyes of the family by the linen tow frock in which he had carried it home.

Joseph's father never required a spur for his imagination, and out of the slender basis in fact the events of the afternoon provided—Joseph's coming home with the plates, his story of having been attacked along the way, and the injury to his person—he contrived an imposing elaboration of Joseph's legend. According to this burgeoning odyssey, the spirit which had given the plates into Joseph's keeping had repented of its action and made a desperate effort to regain possession. "In sheer spite," as the Palmyra *Reflector* heard the story, "this rogue of a spirit" raised a whirlwind which flung trunks and limbs of trees about Joseph's ears, and bruised him severely in the side. As LaFayette Lapham heard the tale in his turn, devils beset Joseph with hideous yells all the way home, and not content with that, "as he was going over the fence, one of the devils struck him a blow on his side, where a black and blue spot remained three or four days." Perhaps the afternoon was stormy; perhaps Joseph was struck by a lashing limb and injured slightly. Whatever the difficulties with which he had to contend, legend and history can agree that he got home safe with something under his arm which the family accepted as being the golden plates.[47]

If Joseph is regarded as a competent witness in his own behalf, he put away in Hyrum's clapboard chest that afternoon a record "engraven on plates which had the appearance of gold, each plate . . . six inches wide and eight inches long and not quite so thick as common tin. They were filled with engravings, in Egyptian characters and bound together in a volume, as the leaves of a book with three rings running through the whole. The volume was something near six inches in thickness, a part of which was sealed. The characters on the unsealed part were small, and beautifully engraved. The whole book exhibited many marks of antiquity in its construction and much skill in the art of engraving."[48] What it was that Joseph kept under lock and key, if not a record of this description, is difficult to say. Peter Ingersoll claimed that Joseph told him the treasure was nothing more than a few quarts of sand, washed beautifully white by the rain, which he had found in the woods and brought home in his frock.[49] Martin Harris, who many times "hefted" the chest in which the plates were kept, says that he "knew from the heft that they were lead or gold," and he knew too that Joseph had not credit enough to buy so much lead. The metallic character of the plates was also evident from the fact that one witness "heard them jink" when they were placed in a box prepared for them.[50] That the plates were thus not a *pure* figment of Joseph's imagination, despite the fact that no one was ever permitted to examine them, is manifest. They evidently had both mass and weight, for Joseph told Willard Chase they weighed between forty and sixty pounds, and Martin Harris agreed.[51]

On first bringing home the plates, Joseph hid them under the hearth in his father's home. The house which had so long been under construction was still unfinished, and it was impossible to regard this hiding place as a secure one, for Joseph's old money-digging associates were nothing if not persistent. "The wall being partly down," says Martin Harris, "it was feared that certain ones, who were trying to get possession of the plates, would get under the house and dig them up." Accordingly, Joseph took the plates out again and hid them under the floor of the old log-house across the road, once their home and now used by the family as a cooper's shop. Perhaps, as his mother would have us believe, Joseph was warned by the Urim and Thummim of the deadly peril to which the plates were exposed; perhaps, as Martin Harris heard from him later, he was warned by an angel; at any rate, Joseph tore up the floor of the shop, took the plates from the box, and hid them in a quantity of flax. He then nailed up the box and replaced it under the floor.[52] The desperate money-diggers had now enlisted the aid of Willard Chase's sister, Sally. In her green glass, Lucy informs us, "she could see many very wonderful things," including the place where the treasure lay hid. Sally saw well enough; that night, when "the mob" came to ransack the Smith farm, they tore up the floor of the cooper's shop and "shivered in pieces" the empty box Joseph had hidden under it. The plates themselves, by some fortunate chance, went undiscovered.[53]

It was at this difficult moment, without a shilling to his name, helpless to avail himself of the offer made to him in August by his father-in-law, his days turned into nightmare by the very men whose deference he had so long commanded, that Joseph found a stout supporter who became the single most decisive force in shaping his strange career. As in the early stages of a forest fire, when a slight dew, a small shift of wind, or an obstructing stone, may suffice to abort the fire, any of a dozen small adversities might have extinguished Joseph's incipient church in its first precarious months. The erratic enthusiasm Martin Harris brought to Joseph's tale of the golden plates was the fitful wind which fanned the smoldering spark of Mormonism into flame; and the money that was forthcoming from him over the next two and a half years was the tinder on which the fire fed until its hungry growth crowned in the inflammable popular will for a new revelation.

Harris was at this time a man in his forty-fifth year. His father had been one of the early settlers of Palmyra, and he himself had grown up as one of the wealthier farmers of the community, having amassed a competence said to have approached ten thousand dollars. As had been the case with Josiah Stowell, however, Harris's farm could not provide a sufficient outlet for his energies; there was in his spirit something wayward which the passing years found ever more difficult to confine.

This restlessness had been fully evidenced in his seeking after the things of God. At various times he had been a Quaker, a Universalist, a Restorationer, a Baptist, and a Presbyterian. He had an unstable, violent temper, and yet withal a certain Christian meekness which emerged at unexpected moments. There were many paradoxes in his nature, above all a shrewd, almost naive practicality that was perpetually at war with his uncritical appetite for the marvelous. John A. Clark, an Episcopalian minister of Palmyra, says of him that he "had always been a firm believer in dreams, and visions, and supernatural appearances, such as apparitions and ghosts," and seemed at this period "to be floating upon the sea of uncertainty" in his religious views, his extensive knowledge of the scriptures united with a most disputatious turn of mind.

His wife declares that "about a year previous to the report being raised that Smith had found gold plates, he became very intimate with the Smith family, and said he believed Joseph could see in his stone any thing he wished."[54] This is substantially what Harris himself says. He relates how, after Joseph had had his peepstone for some time, he questioned Joseph about it. The seer proposed to bind the stone on his eyes and run a race with him in the woods, but Harris was seemingly not inclined to exercise of this description. A few days later, at the Smith home in Manchester, Joseph gave him a conclusive demonstration of his powers. While sitting on the bars, Harris says, he was picking his teeth with a pin. "The pin caught in my teeth, and dropped from my fingers into shavings and straw. I jumped from the bars and looked for it. Joseph and Northrop Sweet also did the same. We could not find it. I then took Joseph on surprise, and said to him—I said, 'Take your stone.' I had never seen it, and did not know that he had it with him. He had it in his pocket. He took it and placed it in his hat—the old white hat—and placed his face in his hat. I watched him closely to see that he did not look to one side; he reached out his hand beyond me on the right, and moved a little stick, and there I saw the pin, which he picked up and gave to me. I know he did not look out of the hat until after he had picked up the pin."[55]

From a seer so rarely gifted, anything might be expected, but when the rumor of the golden plates first reached his ears, Harris wondered only whether the money-diggers had not "dug up an old brass kettle, or something of the kind." On going into Palmyra next day, he found the village profoundly stirred by the report of Joseph's find. Harris indicates that there was already some tendency to refer to the plates as a "golden bible," but this may be the particular color his own habit of mind applied to the story as he reflected upon it in later years. In any event, he became curious enough to decide that he would ride over to the Smith home and see what lay back of the floating stories.

Before he had done so, Joseph's mother came to see him. She advised him of Joseph's bringing home the plates and said that her son had sent her over to request that Harris come and talk with him. For some reason he does not make clear, Harris resisted her importunities, but sent her home in his carriage accompanied by his wife and daughter. When his womenfolk returned, he questioned them at length. Yes, they told him, for a certainty Joseph had found something; it was kept in a glass box; both had lifted the box and found it very heavy. Perhaps Mrs. Harris reported the colloquy Joseph's mother says she had with her son: "Joseph," she had said, "can you look full in my eye, and say before God, that you have in reality found a Record, as you pretend?" And he answered indifferently, "Why, yes, Mrs. Harris, I would as soon look you in the face, and say so as not, if that will be any gratification to you."[56]

Harris was inclined to dissemble his interest, but a day or so later he rode over to the Smith farm. Joseph was away when he arrived, but this suited Harris very well; he proceeded to catechize the other members of the family separately, to see whether their stories agreed. Their stories did agree, and when Joseph came home, Harris eagerly drew him aside. Joseph described the plates that he had found "by looking in the stone" and informed Harris that "the angel told him he must quit the company of the money-diggers. That there were wicked men among them. He must have no more to do with them. He must not lie, nor swear, nor steal. He [the angel] told him to go and look in the spectacles, and he would show him the man that would assist him. That he did so, and he saw myself, Martin Harris, standing before him. That struck me with surprise. I told him I wished him to be very careful about these things. 'Well,' said he, 'I saw you standing before me as plainly as I do now.' I said, if it is the devil's work I will have nothing to do with it; but if it is the Lord's, you can have all the money necessary to bring it before the world. He said the angel told him, that the plates must be translated, printed and sent before the world. I said, Joseph, you know my doctrine, that cursed is every one that putteth his trust in man, and maketh flesh his arm; and we know that the devil is to have great power in the latter days to deceive if possible the very elect; and I don't know that you are one of the elect. Now you must not blame me for not taking your word. If the Lord will show me that it is his work, you can have all the money you want."

On this impressive note the interview ended. Harris went on home, and before retiring he prayed God to instruct him as to the course he should pursue. The "still small voice spoken in the soul" gave him the answer. The book was the Lord's work, and he was under a covenant to bring it forth.[57]

More than any other person, Martin Harris seems to have been responsible for the fact that Joseph's concept of the golden plates came to have a religious content. It is clear from other sources that Harris did not view the golden bible with the eye of the spirit exclusively; he got the village silversmith to give him an estimate of the value of the plates, taking as a basis Joseph's account of their dimensions;[58] and he listened raptly when Joseph's mother expatiated on the profits the work might bring, not merely from sales of the translation to be published by Joseph, but from public exhibition of the plates, the price of admission to be twenty-five cents.[59] To be enriched for doing the work of the Lord suited the inclination of Harris exactly.

Nevertheless, the fact that the book was the work of God, that he, Martin Harris, was an instrument in the hands of the Lord, was the consideration which moved him most powerfully. In this fact Joseph could find matter for meditation. Men could be moved by their religious beliefs as by no other means, for religious faith dignified and enobled what it touched. A man who gave him five dollars to search out in his peepstone the whereabouts of a lost cow was discontent and wanted his money back if the cow could not be found. A man who gave him fifty dollars to do the work of the Lord rejoiced in his soul over his own generosity and counted the money well spent. Joseph seems to have been quick to see the implication of this truth, and ordered his life accordingly. Not folk magic but religion should henceforth be his sphere, his plates of gold found to comprise, in all truth, a golden bible.

The lives of Joseph's family not less than his own were reshaped by this decisive new direction given his life, their very memories remolded to its necessities. The stories they told in later years about the intercourse of Joseph with angels and devils were not fabricated out of whole cloth. Their memories had a content of the supernatural that was inextricably a part of their daily life, and this they were able to accommodate to the great legend in which Joseph involved them. In the process of accommodation they may have had some troubled moments, wondering in their hearts whether their early life had been quite as Joseph represented it to the world, but the rationalization required of them was not, after all, very difficult. It was not for them to say how God should bring his purposes to pass. If, over the years, Joseph had made spirits rather than angels their familiars, perhaps God in his wisdom had made the truth appear in such a light until the world was ready for it. With the wisdom of hindsight they could rearrange their memories, perceive what was reality in the seeming reality, and substitute the reality for the seeming. No one need doubt the accent of Lucy's letter to her brother Solomon so early as January 1831. Her son, Joseph, she was able to say earnestly, had been visited by a holy angel who gave him "commandments which inspired him from on high," and he had been given at the same time means to translate a golden record and bring its saving message to the world. "I feel to thank my God," she cried devoutly, "that he hath spared my life to see this day."[60]

A SEALED BOOK

It was not without some misgiving that Joseph Smith returned to the Hale home in Pennsylvania in December 1827. Amid the difficulties and dangers of his situation in Palmyra, the very name of Harmony had fallen sweetly upon his ear, but the angle of view changed as soon as Joseph got safe out of Palmyra with his wife. It was impossible for him to abide by the agreement Emma's father supposed they had reached in August, and to put a good face upon the altered circumstances might tax all his ingenuity. Joseph may have hoped his father-in-law would be sufficiently mollified with his promise that there should be no more peeping for moneydiggers, no more flitting about the hills in the dark of the moon. Perhaps, even, though this bordered on wishful thinking in view of Isaac Hale's skeptical case of mind, Joseph had hoped that the old man could be convinced of the reality of his golden plates. There was this in Joseph's favor, at least: the scars of Hale's first estrangement from his daughter were not yet healed, and he would be slow to alienate her forever.

That such considerations sustained Joseph through the awkward explanations which followed his arrival at Harmony can hardly be doubted. Isaac has said that Joseph made the effort to convert him to the wonderful tale of the golden plates. By way of convincing the old man that the story was not mere moonshine, Joseph took him into his chamber and exhibited the glass-box brought from Palmyra. This, he declared, contained the marvel. If Hale had any doubts, he might heft the box and satisfy himself in the matter.

Joseph's impenetrable self-assurance was enough to give anyone pause, and Isaac Hale must have been tempted to accept this tale at full value, for if Joseph actually had come up with something from out of the earth, it put a very different face on his past history, and to be able to respect Emma's young man meant a great deal to him. But the sharp-eyed old bear-hunter was no swallower of marvels after the order of Martin Harris, and this business had too much the aspect of a piece of legerdemain. Who, the old man demanded, would be the first person permitted to view these mysterious plates? When Joseph replied in his opaque way that this privilege had been reserved to his own unborn son, Hale snorted his disbelief. If anything of the kind was to be kept in his house, he said bluntly, he should certainly examine it. From that time the plates were understood to be hidden in the woods.[1]

Notwithstanding, Isaac Hale set off to Joseph a 13 1/2-acre tract at the northeastern corner of his farm and provided a dwelling for good measure, an unfinished building he had been using to dress deerskins.[2] But until this structure could be hauled into place and transformed into a home, Joseph and Emma would stay on under his own roof.

Thus it happened that Joseph began his translation of the golden plates in a garret of the Hale home. Of this extraordinary undertaking his autobiography says only that immediately after his arrival at Harmony he commenced copying the characters off the plates. "I copied a considerable number of them, and by means of the Urim and Thummim I translated some of them, which I did between the time I arrived at the house of my wife's father, in the month of December, and the February following."[3] More interesting and illuminating are the recollections of these months preserved by others.

The memorable labor of translation commenced in December 1827. From the very beginning it was attended by the same elaborate mystification that had so long characterized Joseph's practice as a seer in peepstones, and this was to be expected, for the translation of the golden plates was a culmination of, rather than a break with, Joseph's highly flavored past. That the Book of Mormon constituted a new beginning—itself the author of a prophet, seer, and revelator—was not understood at once, and the unabashed hocus-pocus in which Joseph indulged himself, the sustained sleight-of-hand performance he put on through the next eighteen months, was inherent in the situation, for his book had to be a marvel greater than any with which he had ever favored his following.

To this time, in all his peeping, Joseph had required only his stone, his battered white hat, and proper deference in those who besought him to exercise his gift. Eventually he would learn that the first two even of these could be dispensed with. But to produce his greatest marvel, the seer added to his stage properties not only a book of golden plates but a magic set of spectacles, articles elegant in conception and imposing in effect, if somewhat of a kind with the surpassing fine clothes created for the king in the fairy tale. Joseph was to demonstrate that he could conjure with plates and spectacles as the tailor with the clothes of the king. But not on the day-to-day level, and certainly not at once.

He commenced, therefore, by nailing up a blanket in the Hale garret. His scribes, the troubled but compliant Emma and her awe-struck younger brother Reuben, Joseph seated at a table on one side of the blanket, while on the other side he carried forward the mysterious labors of the translation, pronouncing aloud the sense his magic contrivance, the Urim and Thummim, made of the strange characters in which the golden plates were inscribed.[4] As he gained confidence and improved in facility, Joseph was able to dispense with the blanket, and the greater part of the Book of Mormon was dictated without benefit of the privacy it afforded. But when he gave up the blanket, he had to give up golden plates and Urim and Thummim too. During the first few weeks his magical apparatus was essential to the impression he was concerned to make.

Although Joseph later returned to his stone, burying his face in his hat and dictating without regard to the absence or presence of the golden plates, his concept of the Urim and Thummim remains a significant point of departure in his history, one of the earliest examples of a gift that would be of prime importance to him, the ability to seize upon biblical ideas and shape them to his needs. All that was known from the Bible with respect to the Urim and Thummim was that they constituted a means of communication with God, who had required Aaron, before coming in to him, to gird himself in a "breastplate of judgment" in which he should place "the Urim and Thummim."[5] The concensus of biblical scholars, that the Urim and Thummim were two stones which by some alteration in brilliancy reflected the mind and will of the Lord, was one to delight every peepstone seer, and Joseph had no qualms about filling up the gaps in Divine Writ with the homely details. The Urim and Thummim, he explained, was a device made up of two stones set in silver bows and fastened to a breastplate. Seers in ancient or former times had owed their powers to possession of this instrument, and God had prepared it for the express purpose of translating the golden plates.[6]

Joseph's Urim and Thummim has always been characterized as a kind of spectacles, but the descriptions that owe to Martin Harris make it evident that the instrument could not have been employed as such. The whitish stone lenses, Harris tells us, were approximately the size of ordinary spectacle lenses, but the bow which joined them, being some four inches in length, made it impossible to look into more than one stone at a time; with one lens held to the eye, the other would have projected well beyond the opposite ear.[7] Functionally the Urim and Thummim served no purpose that was not served equally well by Joseph's seer stone, but the device was justified in Joseph's eyes by the effect it produced on his disciples. "I never dared to look into them by placing them in the hat," Harris said of these magical stones more than thirty years later, "because Moses said that 'no man could see God and live,' and we could see anything we wished by looking into them; and I could not keep the desire to see God out of my mind. And besides, we had a command to let no man look into them, except by the command of God, lest he should 'look aught and perish.' "[8]

Notwithstanding the magical apparatus at his disposal, Joseph found the road to authorship as rocky as it has generally proved to be for writers less fortunately equipped. For all his declaiming before the Palmyra debating society and his leading out in the Methodist class-meetings, for all his discourses to the Smith family on the lives and times of the ancients, dictating a book that could be received as living history was an undertaking close to the limits of his abilities. Even getting started was desperately hard, as is suggested by the curious language of Joseph's autobiography. Between December 1827 and February 1828, this account says, he copied a considerable number of the characters off the plates, and by means of the Urim and Thummim "translated some of them."[9] More than once, it would appear, Joseph despaired of ever being able to produce the work on which so much depended, and there is some evidence of a passive resistance in Emma which must have contributed to the general bleakness of his mood. On one occasion he went to Emma's uncle, Nathaniel Lewis, to ask whether he should keep on with the translation; though still insisting that God had commanded him to translate the record, he was, he said, afraid of the people.[10] Lewis declined to advise him in so delicate a matter, but as late as February, when Martin Harris came to Harmony to see how the translation was progressing, Joseph was prepared to abandon the whole project. After listening to the prospective "Author and Translator" plead his justification, the opposition of his wife and others, Harris waved such frivolities aside. "I have not come down here for nothing," he said shortly, "and we will go on with it."[11] Perhaps as much as anything, Joseph had needed to have someone else assume the moral responsibility for going ahead. But it may be that the look Harris bent upon him made Joseph realize for the first time the extent of his own involvement in his legend. It came down to this: He had to produce a book that would satisfy Harris or sooner or later he would answer to a magistrate for obtaining money under false pretenses. No matter how good or how bad the book, from this moment Joseph did not lack incentive to write it.

For all his brave words, Martin Harris could not but have been shaken to find in Jospeh such little constancy to the great cause, while he himself was prepared to mortgage his farm to finance publication of the book. Swift to retrieve his mistake, Joseph proposed that Harris carry to New York a sheet of characters transcribed from the golden plates, and secure opinions on them from the foremost scholars of the day. This was a means of dealing with his followers Joseph would find useful to the end of his life. In a perilous situation, set people to doing something: It kept them occupied, enlisted their loyalties, and served to identify their interests with his own.

Although in the weeks since he had left Palmyra Joseph might have made conspicuous progress with the translation, he had at any rate acquired a fund of fascinating information about his golden plates. They were made, as Joseph explained to the rapt Harris, of a sealed and an unsealed portion. The contents of the sealed plates were not to be revealed to the world until some time expedient in the judgment of God; the other part of the record had been given to Joseph to translate. The unsealed portion recounted the history of Lehi, a Hebrew prophet in Jerusalem, and his family who had been warned by the Lord to flee the Holy City just before its fall six centuries before Christ. In America the descendants of these wanderers had split into two warring peoples, a white-skinned and delightsome folk, the Nephites, and a savage race, the Lamanites, cursed by the

Lord with a dark skin. The Nephites were the authors of those great moments of American antiquity which for so long had baffled the learned and engrossed the common folk. But they had fallen into evil ways; the Lord had turned his face from them; and after a thousand years they had been exterminated in a series of mighty battles. By the thousand and the ten thousand their armies had been given up to slaughter, their battlefields still marked by great mounds the length and breadth of the Mississippi Valley where the dead had been heaped high and covered by the victors with a shallow blanket of earth. The last remnant of this once great people had been brought to bay in western New York where the scene of final doom had been enacted.

Foreseeing the fate of the stubbornly iniquitous Nephites, their last great leader, the prophet-general Mormon, had prepared the golden plates upon which the story of his people might be preserved, and these plates had been hidden away by Mormon's son, Moroni, the last survivor of his race, about the year 420 A.D. The spirit who had finally delivered this remarkable record into Joseph's hands was none other than the Angel Moroni. And it was Joseph's great privilege, with Harris's backing, to translate and publish to the world this fabulous history, a work which resolved the mysteries of American antiquity and would be found equal in authority with the Bible.

The characters transcribed from the golden plates Joseph gave to Harris had not, surprising as it might seem in view of the history Joseph was writing, the slightest resemblance to Hebrew. The language, Joseph explained, was a "reformed Egyptian;" being small, the plates were better suited to the compact characters of this language than to the mother tongue. Had Harris been disposed to find flaws in this logic, Joseph could have pointed out that no longer ago than last summer the Palmyra paper had printed a story reporting that affinities had been found between the Egyptians and the ancient Mexicans, clear evidence of the persistence of Egyptian cultural influences in the New World.[12]

It is probable, however, that Harris was charmed to learn that Joseph's golden plates were inscribed in Egyptian, "reformed" or otherwise, for investigations being carried on in the Egyptian antiquities just then had excited the interest of the whole civilized world. To describe his characters as "reformed Eqyptian" was, however, prudent of Joseph, for, as he must have been aware, Thomas Young and Jean Francois Champollion had lately worked out an alphabet from the Rosetta Stone and were on the verge of opening up the dustiest recesses of Egyptian antiquity.[13] Joseph might have been more circumspect still had he been scholar enough to know that until well after the time of Christ Hebrew had had a consonantal alphabet and could be written quite as compactly as any form of Egyptian.

Gratified to have a part in bringing such a marvel before the world, and no doubt still more gratified at the prospect of obtaining ammunition to silence his wife and the neighbors who for three months had made him a butt of their wit, Harris set off to lay siege to the savants of New York. Arriving in the metropolis, he went to see Dr. Samuel L. Mitchill, vice-president of Rutgers Medical College, whose learning spilled over into so many fields as to have given him the reputation of a living encyclopedia. Not less than Mitchill's eminence as a scholar, it must have been the doctor's well known interest in the American antiquities which brought Harris rapping on his door; Mitchill had espoused the theory that the fortifications, mounds, and other ancient structures of the Mississippi Valley and the Great Lakes area had been raised by colonies of Australasians or Malays who had landed on the west coast of North America and penetrated across the continent; this people, he conjectured, had later been all but exterminated by ferocious hordes of Tartars who had crossed over into America from northeastern Asia.[14] The doctor received Harris courteously but, "chaos of knowledge" though he was, could make nothing of the strange characters shown him.[15] The good doctor politely sent Harris on to his friend, Charles Anthon, a member of the faculty of Columbia College, who was to achieve distinction as a Greek and Latin scholar and whose linguistic interests at this time evidently extended to all the antiquities.

Anthon said later that the transcript brought him by this "plain, and apparently simple-hearted farmer" consisted of "all kinds of crooked characters disposed in columns, and had evidently been prepared by some person who had before him at the time a book containing various alphabets. Greek and Hebrew letters, crosses and flourishes, Roman letters inverted or placed sideways, were arranged in perpendicular columns, and the whole ended in a rude delineation of a circle divided into various compartments, decked with various strange marks, and evidently copied after the Mexican Calender by Humboldt."[16] What has been preserved among the Saints as the "Anthon transcript" does not conform to this description, nor is the evidence satisfactory that the extant transcript is that which was taken to Anthon. But there is no reason to suppose that the sheet of "Caractors" usually referred to as the "Anthon transcript" was not prepared by Joseph Smith as a representation of the characters found on the plates, and it may be critically discussed in this light.[17]

Precisely what took place between Harris and Anthon has vexed Mormon history from the moment Anthon showed his visitor to the door. The substance of the discussion, as first given out among Joseph Smith's followers, was that Anthon thought the characters very curious, but admitted his inability to decipher them, so that Harris came home with the joyful intelligence that none but Joseph himself "was learned enough to English them."[18] Harris's version, as related second hand by Joseph Smith fourteen years later, was that Anthon pronounced the characters to be "Egyptian, Chaldaic, Assyric, and Arabic," and stated that the translation was correct, "more so than any he had before seen translated from the Egyptian," after which he wrote out a certificate "certifying to the people of Palmyra that they were true characters, and that the translation of such of them as had been translated was also correct."[19] As Harris was leaving, according to Joseph's account, Anthon bethought himself to inquire how the young man who wrought this translation had found the golden plates. On being informed that an angel of God had made known their existence, Anthon tore up the certificate, saying that there was no longer such a thing as ministering by angels. He then told Harris to bring in the plates, and he would translate them himself. When Harris replied that part of the plates were sealed, and that he was forbidden to bring them, Anthon put an end to the interview, saying shortly, "I cannot read a sealed book."[20]

Later, when the Mormons began to use his name in contending for the truth of the Book of Mormon, the annoyed Anthon branded the story that he had pronounced the characters to be "reformed Egyptian" perfectly false. Anthon's account of the interview is interesting not only in itself but for what it reveals of Joseph's conception at a stage in its evolution still very early:

> Some years ago, a plain, and apparently simply-hearted farmer, called upon me with a note from Dr. Mitchell of our city, now deceased, requesting me to decypher, if possible, a paper which the farmer would hand me. . . . Upon examining the paper in question, I soon came to the conclusion that it was all a trick–perhaps a *hoax*. When I asked the person, who brought it, how he obtained the writing, he gave me the following account: A "gold book," consisting of a number of plates of gold, fastened together . . . by wires of the same metal, had been dug up in the northern part of the state of New York, and along with it an enormous pair of "*gold spectacles*." These spectacles were so large, that, if a person attempted to look through them, his two eyes would have to be turned towards *one* of the glasses merely, the spectacles in question being altogether too large for the breadth of the human face. Whoever examined the plates through the spectacles was enabled not only to *read* them, but fully to *understand* their meaning. All this knowledge, however, was confined at that time to a young man, who had the trunk containing the book and spectacles in his sole possession. This young man was placed behind a curtain, in the garret of a farmhouse, and, being thus concealed from view, put on the spectacles occasionally, or rather, looked through one of the glasses, decyphered the characters in the book, and, having committed some of them to paper, handed copies from behind the curtain, to those who stood on the outside. Not a word, however, was said about the plates having been decyphered "by the gift of God." Every thing, in this way, was effected by the large pair of spectacles. The farmer added, that he had been requested to contribute a sum of money toward the publication of the "golden book," the contents of which would, as he had been assured, produce an entire change in the world and save it from ruin. So urgent had been these solicitations, that he intended selling his farm and handing over the amount

> received to those who wished to publish the plates. As a last precautionary step, however, he had resolved to come to New York, and obtain the opinion of the learned about the meaning of the paper which he brought with him, and which had been given him as a part of the contents of the book, although no translation had been furnished at the time by the young man with the spectacles. On hearing this odd story, I changed my opinion about the paper, and instead of viewing it any longer as a hoax upon the learned, I began to regard it as part of a scheme to cheat the farmer of his money, and I communicated my suspicions to him, warning him to beware of rogues. He requested an opinion from me in writing, which of course I declined giving, and he then took his leave, carrying the paper with him.[21]

In a letter published some years later, Anthon gave substantially the same account, with one major discrepancy, however. He said on being requested to give an opinion of the transcript in writing, he "did so without any hesitation, partly for the man's sake, and partly to let the individual 'behind the curtain' see that his trick was discovered. The import of what I wrote was, as far as I can now recollect, simply this, that the marks in the paper appeared to be merely an imitation of various alphabetical characters, and had, in my opinion, no meaning at all connected with them. The countryman then took his leave, with many thanks, and with the express declaration that he would in no shape part with his farm or embark in the speculation of printing the golden book."[22]

Whatever the details of the interview, Harris returned home with his faith in Joseph's golden book fully established. A scholar like Anthon had admitted that he could not translate the characters, whereas Joseph could. Clearly, it was presumptuous of Anthon to seek to dissuade Harris of the fruits of a promising speculation, to say nothing of what might come of the plates themselves. Most significant of all was Anthon's abrupt remark that he could not read a sealed book. For in the twenty-ninth chapter of Isaiah, Harris could find a passage written as if for his special benefit: "And the vision of all is become unto you as the words of a book that is sealed, which men deliver to one that is learned, saying, Read this, I pray thee: and he saith, I cannot; for it is sealed. And the book is delivered to him that is not learned, saying, Read this, I pray thee: and he saith, I am not learned."

Not less than Harris, Joseph was impressed with this remarkable coincidence, and he took pains to improve upon the scripture when he incorporated it with many other borrowings into his Book of Mormon; from a simple figure the passage became explicit prophecy:

> it shall come to pass that the Lord God shall say unto him to whom he shall deliver the book: Take these words which are not sealed and deliver them to another, that he may

> show them unto the learned, saying: Read this, I pray thee. And the learned shall say: Bring hither the book, and I will read them. . . . And the man shall say: I cannot bring the book, for it is sealed. Then shall the learned say: I cannot read it. Wherefore it shall come to pass, that the Lord God will deliver again the book and the words thereof to him that is not learned; and the man that is not learned shall say: I am not learned. Then shall the Lord God say unto him: The learned shall not read them, for they have rejected them, and I am able to do mine own work; wherefore thou shalt read the words which I shall give unto thee.[23]

In later years, after the Book of Mormon had been published, Harris visited Anthon again, pressing upon him a copy of the new scripture with an insistence that affronted the scholar.[24] No doubt Harris anticipated that Anthon would be impressed with their joint participation in the fulfillment of prophecy. As for himself, he had become the perfect believer. Of Joseph's commission, he told John A. Clark after returning to Palmyra, he had no more doubt than of the divine commission of the apostles. The very fact that Joseph was an obscure and illiterate man showed that he must be acting under divine impulses, and he proposed to sustain him though it consumed the whole of his earthly substance.[25] As soon as he could arrange his affairs, Harris set out for Harmony, arriving early in April prepared to serve as Joseph's scribe until the great book should be completed.[26]

Relieved though Joseph may have been to have Harris return in such a frame of mind, his coming was not happiness unalloyed, for Lucy Harris had badgered her husband into bringing her with him. No sooner had she reached Harmony than she announced that she had come to see the plates and would never leave until she had done so. She began ransacking every nook and corner, chests, trunks, and cupboards, and when she had finished with the house, she extended her search to the surrounding woods, all the while assuring the neighbors that Joseph was an impostor who had no other object than to strip her and her husband of all the property they possessed.[27] When, after two weeks, she gave up the search and returned to Palmyra, the peace that settled on Joseph's domicile must have been like waking from a nightmare.

The writing now commenced in earnest. How much of the book had been written between December and April there is no way of knowing, but between April and June 1828, Harris filled no less than 116 foolscap pages with Joseph's dictated words. Isaac Hale thought the whole performance fantastic nonsense, for the manner in which Joseph "pretended to read and interpret," he said later, "was the same as when he looked for the money-diggers, with the stone in his hat, and his hat over his face, while the Book of Plates was at the same time hid in the woods!"[28] Even Joseph's scribes had moments when they wondered if they had taken leave of their senses. Yet the seer's imperturbable mien and the grave flow of his language, setting forth a story they could not believe him capable of creating out of whole cloth, were deeply impressive. Not only Harris but Joseph's own wife became persuaded of the reality of what they were about.

Emma said later that the first 116 pages of the manuscript were translated with the aid of the Urim and Thummim, the remainder of the book—which is to say, virtually all that was finally published—being translated through the medium of the seerstone.[29] It is the stone, however, rather than the Urim and Thummim, which figures in the reminiscences of Emma and Martin Harris; it may be that the Urim and Thummim, like the plates themselves, were understood to be hidden in the woods. Emma remembered how she wrote for her husband, day after day, "often sitting at the table close by him, he sitting with his face buried in his hat, with the stone in it, and dictating hour after hour with nothing between us."[30] Harris recalled that occasionally, when the labor of translation became irksome, he and Joseph would relax by strolling down to the bank of the Susquehanna and throwing stones into the river. Once, he says, he found a stone resembling Joseph's seerstone, and substituted it for the genuine article. But when they resumed their labor, Joseph was silent, "unusually and intently gazing in darkness," until at last he cried, "Martin! What is the matter? All is as dark as Egypt!" Betrayed by his countenance, Harris explained what he had done, and why—"to stop the mouths of fools, who had told him that the Prophet had learned those sentences and was merely repeating them." The seerstone, as Harris insists, "differed in appearance entirely from the Urim and Thummim that was obtained with the plates."[31]

Joseph's increasing assurance and mastery of his medium was evidenced in the independence he now displayed of the blanket, essential as it had been to him in the beginning. The independence was not absolute, however, for Harris is quoted as having said that at times Joseph "would sit in a different room, or up stairs, while the Lord was communicating to him the contents of the plates," and at least once the presence of the Lord was so great that a screen had to be hung up between the translator and his scribe.[32] E. D. Howe nevertheless struck upon an important point when, six years later, he commented: "The plates . . . which had been so much talked of, were found to be of no manner of use. After all, the Lord showed and communicated to him every word and letter of the Book. Instead of looking at the characters inscribed upon the plates, the prophet was obliged to resort to the old 'peep stone' which he formerly used in money-digging. This he placed in a hat, or box, into which he also thrust his face. Through the stone he could then discover a single word at a time, which he repeated aloud to his amanuensis, who committed it to paper, when another word would immediately appear, and thus the performance continued to the end of the book."[33]

The mode of translation as Howe pictures it is also the way it was described by two of Joseph's special witnesses to the Book of Mormon, and it is evident that Joseph gave his associates to understand that when he had placed his stone in his hat and clapped his hat to his face, sentences appeared before his eyes which he read aloud to his scribes. Martin Harris reports that when he had taken down the dictated words, he would say, "Written," and if correctly written, the sentence would disappear from before Joseph's eyes, another appearing in its place; if not, the sentence remained until corrected.[34] David Whitmer, speaking of a later stage in the writing, similarly comments that Joseph "would cover his face with a hat, excluding all light, and before his eyes would appear what seemed to be parchment, on which would appear the translation, in English, which Smith would read to his scribe, who wrote it down exactly as it fell from his lips. The scribe would then read the sentence written, and if any mistake had been made the characters would remain visible to Smith until corrected, when they faded from sight to be replaced by another line."[35] Thus Joseph's early converts were persuaded that there was no possible mistake in translation, a grave liability of the Bible; the Book of Mormon was the pure word of God set down in all its plainness and power.

This conviction afforded great comfort to the early converts to the church, but criticism leveled against the Book of Mormon over the years with respect to its borrowings from the King James Bible, its defects in style and grammar, and the revisions made in it after publication, which could not be explained away as mere correction of typographical error, eventually led the church to jettison these claims and the stories owing to Joseph's intimates.[36] The defects of the book having to be admitted, it was argued that the translation could not have been a merely mechanical process, but required "the utmost concentration of mental and spiritual force possessed by the prophet, in order to exercise the gift of translation through the means of the sacred instruments provided for that work," but beyond this, the book had to be written "in such language as the prophet could command, in such phraseology as he was master of and common to the time and locality where he lived. . . . This view of the translation of the Nephite record accounts for the fact that the Book of Mormon, though a translation of an ancient record, is, nevertheless, given in English idiom of the period and locality in which the prophet lived; and in the faulty English, moreover, both as to composition, phraseology, and grammar, of a person of Joseph Smith's limited education; and also accounts for the sameness of phraseology and literary style which runs through the whole volume."[37]

These admissions, both as to the imperfections of the book and their peculiarly personal character, were not made by Joseph Smith or by others during his lifetime. Indeed, he always declared the Book of Mormon to be "the most correct of any book on earth" and never formally acknowledged that anything but the power of God had entered into the writing. Not understanding the phenomena of translation, his early believers attributed any faults in the published book to defects in the original record, and although between first and second editions Joseph corrected certain deficiencies as to grammar and diction, he left his followers to infer that such changes were mere correction of typographical error rather than any failing on his part. If the Book of Mormon were to be the most correct of any book, then, it followed, Joseph's translation would have to be of equal stature.[38]

INTIMATIONS OF A CHURCH

By June 14, 1828, Joseph Smith and Martin Harris had brought into being something over 116 foolscap pages of manuscript. As the history grew in size, Harris's excitement and self-importance swelled in proportion, and he began to badger Joseph to be allowed to take the manuscript home and exhibit it to his family. Joseph put him off time and again, but finally yielded when Emma's labor began and the work had to be suspended for a season.[1]

Promising that he would show it to none but those Joseph had sanctioned, Harris set off for Palmyra with the precious manuscript. For two weeks, Joseph hardly had a moment's peace. Emma's child was born June 15, a son as Joseph had foretold, but still-born, and the mother herself for days hovered between life and death.[2] It was not until she began to mend that her distracted husband could begin to think again about his book. The more he thought about it, the more worried he became, for after three weeks Harris had not returned and the mail brought no word from him. Finally, urged by Emma, Joseph took the stage for Palmyra.

Arriving at his parents' home after a fatiguing journey, Joseph sent peremptorily for Harris. Harris responded to this summons with something less than his usual alacrity, and when he dragged into sight, it was to bury his face in his hands and cry out in anguish, "Oh, I have lost my soul! I have lost my soul!" Joseph sprang from his seat. "Martin! Have you lost that manuscript? Have you broken your oath?" "Yes, it is gone," Harris replied, "and I know not where."

"Oh, my God!" Joseph cried, clenching his hands. "All is lost! All is lost! What shall I do? I have sinned–it is I who tempted the wrath of God. I should have been satisfied with the first answer which I received from the Lord; for he told me that it was not safe to let the writing go out of my possession." He wept and groaned, and walked the floor continually. All the family, Lucy Smith says, were in the same frame of mind; "sobs and groans, and the most bitter lamentations filled the house;" but Joseph was the most deeply affected, for he alone fully "understood the consequences of disobedience."[3]

Shamefacedly Harris explained what had happened. He had brought the manuscript home and shown it first to his wife and family, and then to any and all who came desiring to see it. Then, suddenly, it had vanished from the drawer in which he kept it. His wife denied knowing anything about it; he had searched for it in vain, and it would appear that she had continued in her professions of silence even when he administered a judicious beating to her. No one else, however, had so excellent a motive for making off with the manuscript, but Joseph dared not assume that her motives were so transparent. Theoretically it should only have been necessary to start again at the beginning, the method of translation being such that he would be able to reproduce the text in its entirety. But though his family and Harris might hope that in this way he would retrieve the situation, no one knew better than Joseph how impossible it was to reproduce word for word the text he had dictated to Harris. Well might he feel that all was lost, that this was a deep-laid plot to bring him low. Later he would explain that those who had gained possession of the manuscript designed to alter the words he had dictated so that they would read contrary to what he had translated and caused to be written. True, he could, if he chose, abandon the book and Harris would have no legal recourse. But Joseph's conspicuous progress with the book during the spring had given him confidence and incentive; to give it up was the last thing he desired. In deep gloom he set out for home. "We parted," his mother remembers, "with heavy hearts, for it now appeared that all which we had so fondly anticipated, and which had been the source of so much secret gratification, had in a moment fled, and fled for ever."[4]

Too ebullient to be cast down for long, soon after his return Joseph hit upon a way out of his difficulties. It was an expedient which gave a final decisive turn to his life. In his book he had not hesitated to speak in the name of the Lord, and in this present crisis he went one step further. Others before him had laid claim to revelation, and there was no lack of precedent. In this turmoil of spirit it is quite possible that he also believed in the revelation he now dictated to Emma:

> The works, and the designs, and the purposes of God, can not be frustrated, neither can they come to nought, for God doth not walk in crooked paths; neither doth he turn to the right hand nor to the left; neither doth he vary from that which he hath said. . . . Remember, remember that it is not the work of God that is frustrated, but the work of men: for although a man may have many revelations, and have power to do many mighty works, yet, if he boasts in his own strength, and sets at nought the counsels of God, and follows after the dictates of his own will, and carnal desires, he must fall and incur the vengeance of a just God upon him.
>
> Behold, you have been intrusted with these things, but how strict were your commandments; and remember, also, the promises which were made to you, if you did not transgress them; and behold, how oft you have transgressed the commandments and the laws of God, and have gone on in the persuasions of men: for behold, you should not have

> feared man more than God, although men set at naught the counsels of God, and despise his words, yet you should have been faithful and he would have extended his arm, and supported you against all the fiery darts of the adversary; and he would have been with you in every time of trouble.
>
> Behold . . . thou wast chosen to do the work of the Lord, but because of transgression, if thou art not aware thou wilt fall, but remember God is merciful. Therefore, repent of that which thou hast done, and he will only cause thee to be afflicted for a season, and thou art still chosen, and wilt again be called to the work: and except thou do this, thou shalt be delivered up and become as other men, and have no more gift.
>
> And when thou deliveredst up that which God had given thee sight and power to translate, thou deliveredst up that which was sacred, into the hands of a wicked man, who has set at nought the counsels of God, and has broken the most sacred promises, which were made before God, and has depended upon his own judgment, and boasted in his own wisdom, and this is the reason that thou hast lost thy privileges for a season, for thou hast suffered the counsel of thy director to be trampled upon from the beginning.

It is apparent that Joseph did not perceive all the implications of this point of departure from his past life, for the concluding passage of the revelation did not look beyond the completion of his book:

> Nevertheless, my work shall go forth and accomplish my purposes, for as the knowledge of a Savior has come into the world, even so shall the knowledge of my people, the Nephites, and the Jacobites, and the Josephites, and the Zoramites, come to the knowledge of the Lamanites, and the Lemuelites and the Ishmaelites, which dwindled in unbelief, because of the iniquities of their fathers, who have been suffered to destroy their brethren, because of their iniquities, and their abominations: and for this very purpose are these plates preserved which contain these records, that the promises of the Lord might be fulfilled, which he made to his people; and that the Lamanites might come to the knowledge of their fathers, and that they might know the promises of the Lord, and that they may believe the gospel and rely upon the merits of Jesus Christ, and be glorified through faith in his name; and that through their repentance they might be saved: Amen.[5]

Catastrophe though the loss of the manuscript may have been, there were compensations. The child of Emma's who was to have been the first person to see the plates had been born dead, but Joseph was relieved of any embarrassment upon this score through being enabled to point to the transgression of Martin Harris. He let it be known that for a season both plates and Urim and Thummim had been taken from him, and meanwhile, as he relates in his autobiography, he went to laboring with his hands upon his farm, in order to provide for his family.[6] His mother tells us that although it was not until that day of recurring wonders, September 22, after much supplication to God, that Joseph received back the Urim and Thummim, the angel who delivered this instrument seemed much pleased with him and told him the Lord loved him for his faithfulness and humility.[7]

Joseph himself has left almost nothing on record about his labors upon his book during the fall and winter of 1828-29, but when his parents came to Harmony for a visit in February 1829, they learned that he had resumed translating, with Emma as his scribe. More important still, he signalized the occasion of their visit by the second of his revelations, addressed rather abstractly to his own father:

> Now, behold, a marvelous work is about to come forth among the children of men, therefore, O ye that embark in the service of God, see that ye serve him with all your heart, might, mind and strength, that ye may stand blameless before God at the last day: Therefore, if ye have desires to serve God, ye are called to the work, for behold, the field is white already to harvest, and lo, he that thrusteth in his sickle with his might, the same layeth up in store that he perish not, but bringeth salvation to his soul, and faith, hope, charity, and love, with an eye single to the glory of God, qualifies him for the work.
>
> Remember temperance, patience, humility, diligence, etc., ask and ye shall receive, knock and it shall be opened unto you: Amen.[8]

Chiefly remarkable in this revelation is what it reveals of the continued drift on Joseph's part toward a definitive partnership with God. Both its language and ideas are largely borrowed from the Bible,[9] and the origin of the passages shows how impressed Joseph had been with Martin Harris's interview with Charles Anthon and what it had developed concerning sealed books, the learned, and the unlearned.[10] But his second revelation had followed his first by only seven months, and now he was prepared to use revelation as a moving force as need might require. His third revelation, which would come a month after his second, would show that his command of the language and his self-assurance in the employment of it were nearly complete. A church was becoming implicit in all that Joseph said and did.

Martin Harris sometime during the winter of 1828-29 had returned to Harmony to take up again his labors as Joseph's scribe. It would seem that Harris had not been permanently subdued by his transgression of the preceding summer, for Joseph's father-in-law says that as time went on, he began to pester Joseph for a view of the plates. "Martin Harris informed me that he must have a *greater witness*, and said that he had talked with Joseph about it—Joseph informed him that he could not, or durst not show him the plates, but that he (Joseph) would go into the woods where the Book of Plates was, and that after he came back, Harris should follow his track in the snow, and find the Book, and examine it for himself. Harris informed me afterwards, that he followed Smith's directions, and could not find the Plates, and was still dissatisfied."[11] Joseph's first revelation of far-reaching implications was in response to this situation, but it has an importance far beyond the immediate purpose it served. In this revelation, for the first time, a church is foreshadowed. Later Joseph was to repent of this revelation and rewrite it from beginning to end, the Lord having been much too explicit on some points and insufficiently informed on others. But in this month of March 1829 the Lord intoned:

> Behold, I say unto you, that my servant Martin [Harris] has desired a witness from my hand, that my servant Joseph has got the things of which he has testified, and borne record that he has received of me.
>
> And now, behold, this shall you say unto him:—I, the Lord am God, and I have given these things unto my servant Joseph, and I have commanded him that he should stand as a witness of these things, nevertheless I have caused him that he should enter into a covenant with me, that he should not show them except I command him, and he has no power over them except I grant it unto him; and he has a gift to translate the book, and I have commanded him that he shall pretend to no other gift, for I will grant him no other gift.[12]
>
> And verily I say unto you, that wo shall come unto the inhabitants of the earth, if they will not hearken unto my words, for, behold, if they will not believe my words, they would not believe my servant Joseph, if it were possible that he could show them all things. O ye unbelieving, ye stiffnecked generation, mine anger is kindled against you! Behold, verily I say, I have reserved the things of which I have spoken, which I have intrusted to my servant, for a wise purpose in me, and it shall be made known unto future generations: But this generation shall have my words, yea and the testimony of three of my servants shall go forth with my words unto this generation; yea, three shall know of a surety that these things are true, for I will give them power, that they may behold and view these things as they are, and to none else will I grant this power, to receive this same testimony among this generation. And the testimony of three witnesses will I send forth and my word, and behold, whosoever believeth in my word, them will I visit with the manifestation of my Spirit, and they shall be born of me, and their testimony shall also go forth. . . .
>
> And now I speak again concerning the man that desireth a witness: behold I say unto him, he exalteth him-

> self and doth not humble himself sufficiently before me, but if he will go out and bow down before me, and humble himself in mighty prayer and faith, in the sincerity of his heart, then will I grant unto him a view of the things which he desireth to know: and then he shall say unto the people of this generation, behold I have seen the things and I know of a surety that they are true, for I have seen them, for they have been shown unto me by the power of God and not of man. And I command him that he shall say no more unto them, concerning these things, except he shall say, I have seen them, and they have been shown unto me by the power of God.
>
> And these are the words which he shall say.—But if he deny this he will break the covenant which he has before covenanted with me, and behold he is condemned. And now except he humble himself and acknowledge unto me the things that he has done, which are wrong, and covenant with me that he will keep my commandments, and exercise faith in me, behold I say unto him, he shall have no such views, for I will grant unto him no views of the things of which I have spoken. And if this be the case, I command him that he shall do no more, nor trouble me any more concerning this matter.
>
> And if this be the case, behold I say unto you, Joseph, when thou hast translated a few more pages thou shalt stop for a season, even until I command thee again; then thou mayest translate again.

Altogether, this revelation was a remarkably sophisticated document. Harris was given to understand that he would be permitted to view the plates only if he were not under transgression, so that it was his own fault if thereafter he should not succeed in his object. On the other hand, if he did see the plates, he was forbidden to say anything about them except that he had seen the plates and they had been shown him by the power of God. In either event, he was not to heckle Joseph further, the seer being authorized to cease work entirely if Harris did not behave himself.

But there was much more that was remarkable about this revelation. It did not contain any of the resounding intimations of things to come with which Joseph later inflated it. It did not tell Joseph that hereafter he should be ordained and go forth and deliver God's words unto the children of men. It did not tell him that the three witnesses should be "called and ordained," nor say that "from heaven" God would declare unto these witnesses the truth of "these things." It did not assert that "this [was] the beginning of the rising up and the coming forth of my Church out of the wilderness—clear as the moon, and fair as the sun, and terrible as an army with banners." Joseph was not told that he must wait yet a little while, being as yet unordained. All this and much else Joseph wrote into the revelation later, when he had become a prophet whom it was seemly the Lord God should have given some prevision of the future. But this, at least, the Lord did say to Joseph that March day in 1829, and out of it a church was formed:

> If the people of this generation harden not their hearts, I will work a reformation among them, and I will put down all lyings, and deceivings, and priestcrafts, and envyings, and strifes, and idolatries, and sorceries, and all manner of iniquities, and I will establish my church, like unto the church which was taught by my disciples in the days of old.
>
> And now if this generation do harden their hearts against my word, behold I will deliver them up unto satan, for he reigneth and hath much power at this time, for he hath got great hold upon the hearts of the people of this generation: and not far from the iniquities of Sodom and Gomorrah, do they come at this time: . . . Behold I tell you these things even as I also told the people of the destruction of Jerusalem, and my word shall be verified at this time as it hath hitherto been verified.

How much of the Book of Mormon was written during the period when Joseph first resumed work on it, Emma and Harris serving as scribes, is not known, though Harris many years later asserted that he had taken down nearly a third of the text that was finally published.[13] The exasperation to which Joseph gave vent in his revelation shows, nevertheless, that Harris was not an ideal scribe, and it was a stroke of unexpected good fortune that the Lord a few weeks later sent a more tractable instrument to replace him.

Oliver Cowdery, a dark-haired, thin-faced, serious-eyed young man destined to play a prominent part in the completion of Joseph's book and the founding of his church, surprisingly sought out Joseph at Harmony the first week in April 1829. Like Joseph, he was a native Vermonter, and was nearly of an age with him. Perhaps neither of them knew it, but they were blood relatives, Cowdery being a third cousin of Joseph's mother.[14] Much was similar in their backgrounds, for Wells and Poultney, Vermont, where Cowdery spent the first nineteen years of his life, had not been unfavored with dowsers, scryers, prophets, and revelators. About 1799 one Winchell or Wingate, a practitioner with divining rods, had made his appearance at Wells, staying for a time, it is said, with Cowdery's father. By the spring of 1800 Winchell had gathered about himself a considerable number of believers in the hazel rod, and that summer and fall there was much digging after money, precisely after the fashion later so popular at Palmyra. Winchell and his rod were taken up by a local dissenter, Nathaniel Wood, of Middletown, and by the fall of 1800 dozens of the townsfolk had put hazel rods to use as a medium for divine revelation, calling them "St. John's" rods. The excitement climaxed in a determination that God's judgment would be visited upon the wicked Gentiles on January 14, 1801, when destroying angels would pass through the community and slay a portion of the unbelievers, this work of destruction to be completed by an earthquake that would follow the same night. The dreadful day passed without untoward event, however, and the Wood family soon after removed to New York, some among them eventually going on to Ohio, where one of the sons became state governor.[15] These exciting events had occurred five years before Oliver Cowdery was born, but the countryside roundabout Wells, Poultney, and Middletown had remained pitted by the excavations of the money diggers, and he had grown up within a tradition which predisposed him to accept Joseph Smith's claims, he himself being an experimenter with forked rods and peepstones. About 1825 he had moved to western New York, and in the winter of 1828-29 was employed as a school teacher in Manchester, some of the younger Smith children being among his students.

David Whitmer, who was of nearly the same age as Cowdery and Joseph, and who was to become the brother-in-law of the one and a witness of the other, says that he made a business trip to Palmyra from Fayette in 1828 and discussed with Cowdery and others the story of the golden plates. He himself supposed the tale mere idle gossip, but Cowdery admitted to a belief that there was some truth in the story and announced his intention of investigating it.[16] In the course of "boarding 'round," Cowdery came to stay with the Smith family, and, according to Joseph's mother, gained the elder Joseph's confidence "so far as to obtain a sketch of the facts relative to the plates. Shortly after receiving this information, he told Mr. Smith that he was highly delighted with what he had heard, that he had been in a deep study upon the subject all day, and that it was impressed upon his mind, that he should yet have the privilege of writing for Joseph." In short, he determined to accompany Joseph's younger brother Samuel to Harmony as soon as school should close and, from this time on, was "so completely absorbed in the subject of the Record, that it seemed impossible for him to think or converse about anything else."[17]

They set out late in March, stopping off en route at the Whitmer farm near Seneca Lake, where Cowdery promised the Whitmer family that he would soon write them the truth of the matter. "After he got there," David Whitmer adds, "he . . . wrote to me telling me that he was convinced that Smith had the records, and that he [Smith] had told him that it was the will of heaven that he [Cowdery] should be his scribe to assist in the translation of the plates."[18] Cowdery himself has related, more grandly but rather more vaguely, that he arrived at Joseph's home near sunset on April 5, 1829, and "on Tuesday, the 7th, commenced to write the book of Mormon. These were days never to be forgotten—to sit under the sound of a voice dictated by the *inspiration* of heaven, awakened the utmost of gratitude of this bosom! Day after day I continued, uninterrupted, to write from his mouth, as he translated, with the *Urim* and *Thummim*, or, as the Nephites would have said, 'Interpreters,' the history, or record, called 'The Book of Mormon.' "[19] Still later, even after a rift had opened between the two men, Cowdery wrote, "Although favored of God as a chosen witness to bear testimony to the divine authority of the Book of Mormon, and honored of the Lord in being permitted, without money and without price, to serve as a scribe during the translation of the Book of Mormon, I have sometimes had seasons of skepticism, in which I did seriously wonder whether the Prophet and I were men in our sober senses when we would be translating from plates through 'the Urim and Thummim', and the plates not be in sight at all. But I believed both in the Seer and in the 'Seer Stone,' and what the First Elder announced as revelation from God, I accepted as such, and committed to paper with a glad mind and happy heart and swift pen; for I believed him to be the soul of honor and truth, a young man who woud die before he would lie. . . . I felt a solemn awe about me, being deep in the faith, that the First Elder was a Seer and Prophet of God, giving the truth unsullied through 'Urim and Thummim,' dictated by the will of the Lord, and that he was persecuted for the sake of the truth which he loved."[20]

Grateful for this first of the many humble converts who were to make possible the church he brought into being, Joseph rewarded Cowdery with a revelation from God which went so far as to promise the scribe "a gift . . . to translate, even as my servant Joseph," records containing much of the gospel having been kept back because of the wickedness of the people. "I command you," the oracle continued, "that if you have good desires, a desire to lay up treasures for yourself in heaven, then shall you assist in bringing to light, with your gift, those parts of my scriptures which have been hidden because of iniquity. And now behold I give unto you, and also unto my servant Joseph, the keys of this gift, which shall bring to light this ministry; and in the mouth of two or three witnesses, shall every word be established."[21]

These rash promises Joseph shortly had cause to repent of, for Cowdery was soon yearning to start translating himself, and God had to intervene. Verily, verily, the Lord said unto Oliver, he should receive a knowledge of whatever things he asked in faith, including "the engravings of old records, which are ancient, which contain those parts of my scripture of which have been spoken, by the manifestation of my Spirit. . . . Now, behold this is the Spirit of revelation:—behold this is the spirit by which Moses brought the children of Israel through the Red sea on dry ground: therefore, this is thy gift; apply unto it and blessed art thou, for it shall deliver you out of the hands of your enemies. . . . Remember this is your gift. Now this is not all, for you have another gift, which is the gift of working with the rod: behold it has told you things: behold there is no other power save God, that can cause this rod of nature, to work in your hands, for it is the work of God; and therefore whatsoever you shall ask me to tell you by that means, that will I grant unto you, that you shall know."[22]

Even this revelation did not suffice. Before the month of April was out, God had to put his foot down absolutely:

> Behold I say unto you my son, that, because you did not translate according to that which you desired of me, and did commence again to write for my servant Joseph, even so I would that you should continue until you have finished this record, which I have intrusted unto you: and then behold, other records have I, that I will give unto you power that you may assist to translate.
>
> Be patient my son, for it is wisdom in me, and it is not expedient that you should translate at this present time. Behold the work which you are called to do, is to write for my servant Joseph; and behold it is because that you did not continue as you commenced, when you begun to translate, that I have taken away this privilege from you. Do not murmur my son, for it is wisdom in me that I have dealt with you after this manner.
>
> Behold you have not understood, you have supposed that I would give it unto you, when you took no thought, save it was to ask me; but behold I say unto you, that you must study it out in your mind; then you must ask me if it be right, and if it is right, I will cause that your bosom shall burn within you; therefore, you shall feel that it is right; but if it be not right, you shall have no such feelings, but you shall have a stupor of thought, that shall cause you to forget the thing which is wrong; therefore, you cannot write that which is sacred, save it be given you from me.
>
> Now if you had known this, you could have translated: nevertheless, it is not expedient that you should translate now. Behold it was expedient when you commenced, but you feared and the time is past, that it is not expedient now; for, do you not behold that I have given unto my servant Joseph sufficient strength, whereby it is made up? and neither of you have I condemned.
>
> Do this thing which I have commanded you, and you shall prosper.[23]

Thus finally Cowdery was shaped into an instrument suited to Joseph's need. No more is heard of those precious ancient records he was to bring before the world, for Joseph's church was now fast ripening in his mind, and he would find other means of rewarding Cowdery for his steadfastness and his untiring labor. Meanwhile, however, these revelations had become increasingly bold in their language, and Joseph had shown himself increasingly inclined to revelation to smooth the path. The first of the revelations to Cowdery had begun with much the same language employed in the revelation to Joseph's father in February, and which was repeated time and again during the next three months: "A great and marvelous work is about to come forth unto the children of men. . . . Behold, the field is white already to harvest, therefore whoso desireth to reap, let him thrust in his sickle with his might . . . if you will ask of me you shall receive; if you will knock it shall be opened unto you." But that first revelation to Cowdery, with all else it had contained, had included the concept that the bringing forth of the Book of Mormon was in itself a ministry:

> Behold I give unto you, and also unto my servant Joseph, the keys of this gift, which shall bring to light this ministry; and in the mouth of two or three witnesses, shall every word be established.
>
> Verily, verily I say unto you, if they reject my words, and this part of my gospel and ministry, blessed are ye, for they can do no more unto you than unto me; and if they do unto you, even as they have done unto me, blessed are ye, for you shall dwell with me in glory: but if they reject not my words, which shall be established by the testimony which shall be given, blessed are they; and then shall ye have joy in the fruit of your labors. . . . Fear not little flock, do good, let earth and hell combine against you, for if ye are built upon my Rock, they cannot prevail. Behold I do not condemn you, go your ways and sin no more: perform with soberness the work which I have commanded you: look unto me in every thought, doubt not, fear not: behold the wounds which pierced my side, and also the prints of the nails in my hands and feet: be faithful; keep my commandments, and ye shall inherit the kingdom of heaven: Amen.[24]

It is obvious where all this was trending, and Joseph and Oliver stepped across the dividing line in mid-May 1829. No men in their sober senses, Oliver Cowdery says, could translate and write the directions given to the Nephites from the mouth of the Savior as to the precise manner in which men should build up his church, "especially, when corruption had spread an uncertainty over all forms and systems practiced among men, without desiring a privilege of showing the willingness of the heart by being buried in the liquid grave." He and Joseph waited only for the commandment to be given, "Arise and be baptized." They had not long to wait, for on a May day as they walked in the woods, "as from the midst of eternity, the voice of the Redeemer spake peace to us, while the vail was parted and the angel of God came down clothed with glory, and delivered the anxiously looked for message, and the keys of the gospel of repentance . . . His voice, though mild, pierced to the center, and his words, 'I am thy fellow-servant,' dispelled every fear . . . as he said: 'Upon you my fellow servants, in the name of Messiah I confer this priesthood and this authority, which shall remain upon earth, that the sons of Levi may yet offer an offering unto the Lord in righteousness.' "[25] Cowdery's own account, thus stripped to essentials, is full of cloudy glory and somewhat deficient as to detail.[26] Joseph himself, working some years after the event, writes that Cowdery and he were "forced to keep secret the circumstances of having received the Priesthood and our having been baptized, owing to a sprit of persecution which had already manifested itself in the neighborhood. We had been threatened with being mobbed from time to time, and this, too, by professors of religion. And their intentions of mobbing us were only counteracted by the influence of my wife's father's family (under Divine providence), who had become very friendly to me, and who were opposed to mobs, and were willing that I should be allowed to continue the work of translation without interruption; and therefore offered and promised us protection from all unlawful proceedings as far as in them lay."[27]

The services done him Joseph repaid in the coin he now minted so freely, and which was received at so gratifyingly high a valuation, the word of the Lord. Revelations came for David, John, and Peter Whitmer, Jr., declaring as usual the great and marvelous work about to come forth unto the children of men, the field white to the harvest and the sickle to be thrust in. All the brothers were instructed to declare repentance unto the people and bring souls to Christ, but David was also promised that if he should ask the Father in the name of the Son, having faith, he should receive the Holy Ghost and stand as a witness of things to be seen and heard: in short, with Oliver Cowdery and Martin Harris he should be one of the promised special witnesses to the truth of the Book of Mormon.[28]

As the long and arduous labor on the Book of Mormon approached its end, Joseph had to come to grips at last with the problem of authenticating the golden plates from which this precious record had been translated. In March, before the coming of Oliver Cowdery to Harmony, a revelation through Joseph to Martin Harris had promised that the testimony of three should go forth, "Yea, three shall know a surety that these things are true," and this promise appeared as a prophecy in the Book of Mormon itself. It may be that Joseph originally had intended that he himself should be one of the witnesses; and a conditional promise had been made to Harris, but the context of the revelation was such that Harris could be judged as being in transgression, and Joseph did not feel bound to include him among his special witnesses. After the coming of Cowdery, he too was granted a hope of seeing the plates, though in language so phrased that Joseph need not feel embarrassed by it, for God said only that as respecting this "knowledge concerning the engravings of old records, which are ancient . . . behold I will tell you in your mind and in your heart by the Holy Ghost, which shall come upon you and which shall dwell in your heart."[29]

In the case of both Harris and Cowdery, Joseph had so hedged about the viewing of the plates with the necessity of faith as to make it a reflection upon either should he not be shown them finally. When Joseph, after reaching Fayette, decided that David Whitmer should also be one of his witnesses, the revelation made the point again, but more gently: "It shall come to pass, that if you shall ask the Father, in my name, in faith believing, you shall receive the Holy Ghost, which giveth utterance, that you may stand as a witness of the things of which you shall both hear and see."[30]

It may be that Joseph announced finally his authorization to exhibit the plates to three witnesses aside from himself with a special revelation, though it is a suspicious circumstance that this revelation was not included in the Book of Commandments but was first given to the world in 1835.[31] And according to the story Joseph's own mother tells, it was more or less by accident—or rather, her own innate kindness—that Harris figured in the episode at all.

As soon as the translation was finished, she says, Joseph sent his parents word to this effect, asking that they come immediately to Waterloo. "The same evening, we conveyed this intelligence to Martin Harris, for we loved the man, although his weakness had cost us much trouble. Hearing this," Lucy writes, "he greatly rejoiced, and determined to go straightway to Waterloo to congratulate Joseph upon his success. Accordingly, the next morning, we all set off together, and before sunset met Joseph and Oliver at Mr. Whitmer's." The following day, after morning prayer, "Joseph arose from his knees, and approaching Martin Harris with a solemnity that thrills through my veins to this day, when it occurs to my recollection, said, 'Martin Harris, you have got to humble yourself before your God this day, that you may obtain a forgiveness of your sins. If you do, it is the will of God that you should look upon the plates, in company with Oliver Cowdery and David Whitmer.' "[32] A few minutes later, the four men retired to a grove, a short distance from the Whitmer house, and there they had the supernal experience that had been promised them. They returned after a time to draw up the Testimony of Three Witnesses which has since been printed in each edition of the Book of Mormon:

> Be it known unto all nations, kindreds, tongues, and people, unto whom this work shall come, that we, through the grace of God the Father, and our Lord Jesus Christ, have seen the plates which contain this record, which is a record of the people of Nephi, and also of the Lamanites, his brethren, and also of the people of Jared, which came from the tower, of which hath been spoken; and we also know that they have been translated by the gift and power of God, for his voice hath declared it unto us; wherefore we know of a surety, that the work is true. And we also testify that we have seen the engravings which are upon the plates; and they have been shewn unto us by the power of God, and not of man. And we declare with words of soberness, that an Angel of God came down from heaven, and he brought and laid before our eyes, that we beheld and saw the plates, and the engravings thereon; and we know that it is by the grace of God the Father, and our Lord Jesus Christ, that we behold and bear record that these things are true; and it is marvellous in our eyes: Nevertheless the voice of the Lord commanded us that we should bear record of it; wherefore, to be obedient unto the commandments of God, we bear testimony of these things.—And we know that if we are faithful

in Christ, we shall rid our garments of the blood of all men, and be found spotless before the judgement seat of Christ, and shall dwell with him eternally in the heavens. And the honor be to the Father, and to the Son, and to the Holy Ghost, which is one God. Amen.

OLIVER COWDERY,
DAVID WHITMER,
MARTIN HARRIS.

Oliver Cowdery has left no independent account of this episode, and it was not until near the close of his life that Martin Harris had much to say about it either, though it was freely said that "an angel" had shown them the plates.[33] When, in January 1859, Joel Tiffany questioned Harris on this score, all he would say was, "I am forbidden to say anything how the Lord showed them to me, except that by the power of God I have seen them."[34] Later, he was more free with details. To the Saints who hung upon his words, he explained that the angel who appeared to him stood on the opposite side of a table "on which were the plates, the interpreters, etc., and took the plates in his hands," turning them over like the pages of a book, meanwhile declaring that the Book of Mormon had been correctly translated "by the power of God and not of man."[35] Just before his death, however, he informed an inquirer that he had seen the plates "only in a visionary or entranced state," which agreed with what John A. Clark had heard a generation before.[36]

The earliest account of the experience by David Whitmer is that "he was led by Smith into an open field, on his father's farm near Waterloo, when they found the book lying on the ground; Smith took it up and requested him to examine it, which he did for the space of half an hour or more, when he returned it to Smith, who placed it in its former position, alleging that the book was in the custody of *another*, intimating that some Divine agent would have it in safe keeping."[37] In an interview, in 1878, Whitmer related:

> The angel showed us (the Three Witnesses) the plates, as I suppose to fulfill the words of the book itself. Martin Harris was not with us at this time; he obtained a view of them afterwards (the same day). Joseph, Oliver and myself were together when I saw them. We not only saw the plates of the Book of Mormon, but also the brass plates, the plates of the Book of Ether, the plates containing the records of the wickedness and secret combinations of the people of the world down to the time of their being engraved, and many other plates. The fact is, it was just as though Joseph, Oliver and I were sitting just here on a log, when we were overshadowed by a light. It was not the light of the sun nor like that of a fire, but more glorious and beautiful. It extended away round us, I cannot tell you how far, but in the midst of this light . . . [a few feet distant] there appeared, as it were, a table with many records or plates

> upon it, besides the plates of the Book of Mormon, also the sword of Laban, the directors—i.e., the ball which Lehi had, and the interpreters. I saw them just as plain as I see this bed (striking the bed beside him with his hand), and I heard the voice of the Lord, as distinctly as I ever heard anything in my life, declaring that the records of the plates of the Book of Mormon were translated by the gift and power of God. [Questioned whether he saw the angel at this time:] Yes, he stood before us.[38]

Whitmer did, however, add this qualification subsequently: "Of course we were in the spirit when we had the view, for no man can behold the face of an angel, except in a spiritual view, but we were in the body also, and everything was as natural to us, as it is at any time. Martin Harris, you say, called it 'being in vision.' We read in the Scriptures [that] Cornelius saw, in a vision, an angel of God, Daniel saw an angel in a vision, also in other places it states they saw an angel in the spirit. A bright light enveloped us where we were, that filled at noon day, and there in a *vision*, or in the *spirit*, we saw and heard just as it is stated in my testimony in the Book of Mormon."[39]

Notwithstanding God had declared in March that three only in this generation should be privileged to "know of a surety" that his servant Joseph "has got the things of which he has testified,"[40] so successful was Joseph's experience with his Three Witnesses that some days later he procured an additional testimony from eight more witnesses. Joseph, Oliver, and the Whitmers, Lucy Smith says, came to Manchester on a visit to make some arrangements for getting the book printed. "Soon after they came, all the male part of the company, with my husband, Samuel, and Hyrum, retired to a place where the family were in the habit of offering up their secret devotions to God. They went to this place, because it had been revealed to Joseph that the plates would be carried thither by one of the ancient Nephites. Here it was, that those eight witnesses, whose names are recorded in the Book of Mormon, looked upon them and handled them."[41]

> Be it known unto all nations, kindreds, tongues, and people, unto whom this work shall come, that Joseph Smith, Jr. the Author and Proprietor of this work, has shewn unto us the plates of which hath been spoken, which have the appearance of gold; and as many of the leaves as the said Smith has translated, we did handle with our hands; and we also saw the engravings thereon, all of which has the appearance of ancient work, and of curious workmanship. And this we bear record, with words of soberness, that the said Smith has shewn unto us, for we have seen and hefted, and know of a surety, that the said Smith has got the plates of which we have spoken. And we give our names unto the world, to

witness unto the world that which we have seen: and we lie not, God bearing witness of it.

CHRISTIAN WHITMER	PETER WHITMER, Jr.
HIRAM PAGE	HYRUM SMITH
JACOB WHITMER	JOHN WHITMER
JOSEPH SMITH, Sen.	SAMUEL H. SMITH

In its curious mixture of the vague and the specific, this testimony of the Eight Witnesses has comforted both believers and disbelievers ever since. The faithful point triumphantly to the concreteness of the testimony, "we did handle with our hands," "we have seen and hefted." The skeptical dwell upon the shortcomings of the document, with respect to time and place, and the lack of supporting detail, either in the testimony itself or in independent statements by the witnesses. As three of the eight were Smiths, four were Whitmers, and the fifth a Whitmer by marriage, neither have there been wanting those to echo Mark Twain: "I could not feel more satisfied and at rest if the entire Whitmer family had testified."

It is understood from Mormon sources that there was no angelic visitation attendant upon this final showing of the plates, Joseph Smith himself having done the honors, but the only purported description of the event, which believers dismiss as "mere drivel," is that by Thomas Ford:

> It is related that the Prophet's early followers were anxious to see the plates; the Prophet had always given out that they could not be seen by the carnal eye, but must be spiritually discerned; that the power to see them depended upon faith, and was the gift of God, to be obtained by fasting, prayer, mortification of the flesh, and exercises of the spirit; that so soon as he could see the evidence of a strong and lively faith in any of his followers, they should be gratified in their holy curiosity. He set them to continual prayer, and other spiritual exercises, to acquire this lively faith by means of which the hidden things of God could be spiritually discerned; and at last, when he could delay them no longer, he assembled them in a room, and produced a box, which he said contained the precious treasure. The lid was opened; the witnesses peeped into it, but making no discovery, for the box was empty, they said, "Brother Joseph, we do not see the plates." The Prophet answered them, "O ye of little faith! how long will God bear with this wicked and perverse generation? Down on your knees, brethren, every one of you, and pray God for the forgiveness of your sins, and for a holy and living faith which cometh down from heaven." The disciples dropped to their knees, and began to pray in the fervency of their spirit, supplicating God for more than two hours with fanatical earnestness; at the end of which time, looking again into the box, they were now persuaded that they saw the plates.[42]

The Book of Mormon was completed finally sometime in July or August 1829; it was copyrighted as early as June 11, 1829, but only by deposit of title-page. Negotiations were entered into with E. B. Grandin, publisher of the *Wayne Sentinel*, for the printing of 3,000 copies, Martin Harris agreeing to stand security for the $5,000 which was the estimated cost. Grandin appears to have been reluctant to see Harris victimize himself through such a project,[43] and accordingly Joseph, Harris, and some others rode to Rochester to see about having the book printed there. Thurlow Weed, later one of the great political bosses, but in 1829 only the publisher of a party organ, the *Anti-Masonic Inquirer*, refused to be interested, but Joseph and his associates persisted and succeeded in securing from another Rochester publisher, Elihu F. Marshall, a tentative agreement to publish the book. With the aid of Joseph's mother, the contract provided that Harris was to put up one-half of the money and the rest was to be paid by Joseph and Hyrum. If her memory is to be relied on in this, the two Smiths must have contemplated paying their share out of profits to be realized after the book was published, for the Smith family had fallen upon such evil times, financially, that there is no possibility that they could have put up the requisite capital in advance; dispossessed from their old farm, all of them, with the exception of Joseph, now living in Hyrum's crowded little home.[44]

Having learned a lesson from his earlier experience with Harris, Joseph now, as his mother says, received a commandment:

> First, that Oliver Cowdery should transcribe the whole manuscript. Second, that he should take but one copy at a time to the office, so that if one copy should get destroyed, there would still be a copy remaining. Third, that in going to and from the office, he should always have a guard to attend him, for the purpose of protecting the manuscript. Fourth, that a guard should be kept constantly on the watch, both night and day, about the house, to protect the manuscript from malicious persons, who would infest the house for the purpose of destroying the manuscript.[45]

All these things, she adds, were strictly attended to, and Joseph meanwhile returned to Harmony where Emma had patiently remained all this while.

Typesetting on the book began in August 1829 and the slow labor of printing on the primitive hand press on which the *Wayne Sentinel* itself was issued was not finished until March 1830. The intervening months, however, were by no means without event. According to David Whitmer, the elders of the incipient church as early as August 1829 began to preach the gospel. "The Book of Mormon was still in the hands of the printer, but my brother, Christian Whitmer, had copied from the manuscript the teachings and doctrine of Christ, being the things which we were commanded to preach." For eight months before the church was formally organized, they preached, baptized, and confirmed,[46] and this was a phenomenon to excite both the wonder and the risibility of the citizens of Palmyra. Pranksters were not lacking, and Joseph's own brother in law, Calvin Stoddard, who lived a few miles away in Macedon, was set to frantic preaching of the new faith by an Angel of the Lord who came knocking on his door one dark night with a thunderous command to preach "the gospel of Nephi" next day under penalty of having his ashes scattered to the four winds of heaven.[47] "The experiment," Pomeroy Tucker recalls, "was a complete success . . . Early the next morning the subject of this 'special call' was seen upon his rounds among his neighbors, as a Mormon missionary, earnestly telling them of the 'command', he had received to preach. Luminous arguments and evidences were adduced by him to sustain the foundation of his belief in this his revealed sphere of duty!"

The newly established Palmyra *Reflector*, espousing as it did Alexander Pope's dictum, "Know then thyself, presume not God to scan! The proper study of mankind is man," could not resist making sport of such game, and throughout the fall enlivened its columns with a succession of ironical digs at the book, its believers, and the religious community generally. All this the Smiths endured as patiently as might be, but the editor of the *Reflector*, a certain Esquire Cole, writing in the December 9, 1929, issue, fairly startled them with an announcement concerning the "Gold Bible." As the work bearing this cognomen was now in press, as there was much curiosity locally concerning it, and as the work itself would not be ready for delivery for some months to come, said the *Reflector*, "at the solicitation of many of our readers, we have concluded to commence publishing *extracts* from it." As good as its word, in its issues of January 2 and 13, 1830, the *Reflector* published a long extract from the first chapter of Joseph's book.

Consternation reigned in the Smith household at this development. Notwithstanding what Cole had said about publishing extracts merely, they were appalled to think that he proposed to furnish his subscribers with "the principal portion of the book in such a way that they would not be obliged to pay the Smiths for it." In his paper, Lucy remembers with more heat than strict justice, Cole "had thrown together a parcel of the most vulgar, disgusting prose, and the meanest, and most low-lived doggerel," in juxtaposition with the pilfered portion of the book of Mormon. In no wise conciliated by Cole's observation that he had so far discovered in the book nothing treasonable or having "a tendency to subvert our liberties," or his advice to those members of the community who professed liberal principles not to give themselves to much uneasiness "about matters that so little concern time," Lucy says that the Smiths were shocked at such a perversion of common sense and moral feeings, "as well as indignant at the dishonest course which Mr. Cole had taken, in order to possess himself of the work."[48]

Forthwith Hyrum hied himself around to the printing office to forbid Cole's publishing another word. The lawyer, a gamecock of a man, defied him up and down, and thus it became necessary to bring Joseph from Pennsylvania and threaten Cole with the pains and penalties of the law. Meanwhile, in his issue of January 22, Cole printed a third abstract from the sacred work, and he only desisted finally when Joseph threatened him with suit for violation of copyright.[49]

By no means was this the only crisis which had to be met while the printing of the book was in progress. According to Joseph's mother, the inhabitants of the surrounding country, seeing that the work still progressed, became uneasy and called a mass meeting on the subject, at which it was resolved to boycott the book when finally published. A committee then awaited upon Grandin and informed him of the resolutions passed, and explained to him "the evil consequences which would result to him therefrom," at the same time advising Grandin to cease work on the book "as the Smiths had lost all their property, and consequently would be unable to pay him for his work, except by the sale of the books. And this they would never be able to do, for the people would not purchase them." It became necessary, Lucy adds, to send for Joseph; he then went at once with Martin Harris to Grandin, and "succeeded in removing his fears, so that he went on with the work, until the books were printed."[50]

This curious episode is almost the only real evidence that Lucy may have been right in saying that the original contract for the publication of the book provided that Joseph and Hyrum were to have assumed half the cost while at the same time reserving to themselves half of the profits, for when Grandin demanded payment in full before he would complete the printing and the binding, Joseph had no recourse except to figuratively twist Martin Harris's arm to obtain the necessary funds. Consequently, a revelation, "A commandment of God and not of man to you, Martin, given (Manchester, New York, March 1830,) by him who is eternal," terrified Harris with the threat of God's punishment, endless and eternal. On the last great day of judgment, God would visit the inhabitants of the earth, "judging every man according to his works, and the deeds which he hath done. And surely every man must repent or suffer. . . Wherefore, I command you by my name, and by my Almighty power, that you repent: repent, lest I smite you by the rod of my mouth, and by my wrath, and by my anger, and your sufferings be sore: How sore you know not! How exquisite you know not! Yea, how hard to bear you know not!" Misery should be his lot if he slighted these counsels, "Yea, even destruction of thyself and property. Impart a portion of thy property; Yea, even a part of thy lands and all save the support of thy family. Pay the printer's debt. Release thyself from bondage." The way thus opened up, and Joseph's new revelation was offered for sale in late March 1830.[51]

THE BOOK OF MORMON

Any analysis of the Book of Mormon, whether the evolution of its text or the sources of its ideas, is complicated by the circumstances under which the first quarter of the book was lost and eventually replaced. There is good reason to think that the earliest portions of the text as it now exists are the opening paragraphs of the Book of Mosiah, and that the books which precede Mosiah were not written until much later, possibly not until the late spring of 1829, when most of the book had been completed.

It has been assumed that the 116 pages Martin Harris lost comprised all of the manuscript which had been written to that time. That this assumption is mistaken, that some few pages, at least, had been written beyond that point, is shown by a revelation of May 1829, which gave instructions for replacing the lost portion of the manuscript: "You shall translate the engravings which are on the plates of Nephi, down even till you come to the reign of king Benjamin, or until you come to that which you have translated, *which you have retained.*" The language of this revelation is employed again in Joseph's special foreward to the first edition of the Book of Mormon: "The Lord said unto me . . . thou shalt translate from the plates of Nephi, *until ye come to that which ye have translated, which ye have retained.*"[1] (The italics in each case are mine.)

The Book of Mormon itself provides the only evidence as to the character of the lost Book of Lehi and other books replaced with those of 1 and 2 Nephi, Jacob, Jarom, and Omni. 1 Nephi 1:16 declares, "I, Nephi, do not make a full account of the things which my father hath written, for he hath written many things which he saw in visions and in dreams; and he also hath written many things which he prophesied and spake unto his children, of which I shall not make a full account." Again, 1 Nephi 6:1 says, "I, Nephi, do not give the genealogy of my fathers in this part of my record; neither at any time shall I give it after upon these plates which I am writing; for it is given in the record which has been kept by my father." Further, 1 Nephi 19:2 speaks of that book which contained "the record of my father, and the genealogy of his fathers, and the more part of all our proceedings in the wilderness." There is also, in addition to this account of the Book of Lehi, a single indication as to the contents of the orignial Book of Nephi which in the trial draft of the Book of Mormon followed the Book of Lehi. 1 Nephi 19:4 explains,

"I, Nephi, did make a record upon the other plates, which gives an account, or which gives a greater account of the wars and contentions and destructions of my people;" the later version—the one finally published—restates this summary but adds, "Nevertheless, I do not write anything upon [these] plates save it be that I think it be sacred."

The fact that the revelation solving Joseph's problem in connection with the lost portion of the original manuscript was not given until May 1829 is the best of evidence that he did not begin all over again when, in the summer or fall of 1828, he resumed work on his book.[2] The existing manuscripts of the Book of Mormon itself are of no service in the critical examination of these questions, for the only complete copy of the manuscript, in the possession of the Reorganized LDS church at Independence, Missouri, is clearly a secondary copy, evidenced not only by the character of the written text, the mistakes of which are those normal to any copyist, but also by the numbering of the folios and the juncture of the two portions of the manuscript. The fragments of what supposedly is the original manuscript of the Book of Mormon, preserved by the Utah LDS church, are withheld from study even in photographic reproduction, but the pages thus preserved are known to consist only of a few leaves from the opening chapters of the book, and thus are of no service in studying the missing sections of the manuscript which are of most critical interest, particularly the Mosiah text whose priority is evident at once.[3]

The Book of Mormon evolved naturally from the circumstances of Joseph Smith's growing up, the world he lived in, his interests and his needs. It is not possible to say at just what moment and under what circumstances the idea that he might undertake the writing of a history of ancient America crystallized in his mind. Perhaps, as some in Palmyra later thought, the magician Walters, flourishing his copy of Cicero in the faces of the money-diggers, directly suggested the idea of such a book and it remained latent in Joseph's mind until it ripened under the exigencies of 1827. Perhaps the book slowly took shape in his mind over a period of four or five years. Or the idea may have come as a sudden inspiration, the catalytic agent being a casual notice in the Canandaigua paper of a pamphlet published in 1827 by a Tuscarora Indian which purported to set forth "the Ancient history of the Six Nations," including their creation myths and a "real account of the settlement of North America, and their dissensions."[4] The cultural environment was, however, so rich in sugggestion that the idea may have occurred to him independently. We will never be quite sure, for Joseph himself would never acknowledge that anything but the power of God entered into the writing of his book, and very little independent information concerning it exists.

Still, it is illuminating to see how suggestive the environment was, and to consider certain ideas which may have influenced not only the character of the Book of Mormon but the decision to write it. Nor must it be forgotten that Joseph was not the first in his family to undertake the writing of a book; Solomon Mack's little autobiography was one of the few claims to distinction which his family, during the years of Joseph's growing up, had possessed. While the paucity of information about Joseph Smith's early life is such that it cannot be proved that he had read any particular book, parallels between the book he eventually published and a popular historico-religious treatise of this decade are too striking to pass without comment. Pastor of a church in Poultney, Vermont, a few miles west of the area from which the Smith family migrated to New York in 1816, Ethan Smith published in 1823 a painstaking contribution to the theory that the American Indians were of Israelitish descent, and this book, *View of the Hebrews; or the Tribes of Israel in America*, was so well received as to have been reprinted in an enlarged edition two years later.

View of the Hebrews, like the Book of Mormon, espoused what in the 1820s was incomparably the most popular view of the origin of the American Indians, the theory of Hebrew descent. Ethan Smith conceived the Indians to be the remnant of the lost ten tribes of Israel; his young contemporary, whether from pure creative impulse or from a judicious appreciation of the dangers of getting beyond his depth,[5] was content to present the Indians as the descendants of a few families who had come to America independently (though later he gratified the curiosity of his followers as to the Ten Tribes to the extent of explaining that they had taken up their residence in the vicinity of the North Pole[6]). Otherwise Ethan and Joseph Smith were in cordial agreement with respect to the pre-Columbian history of the Americas. "It is highly probable," the Vermont minister theorized in words that anticipate the Book of Mormon in detail, "that the more civilized part of the tribes of Israel, after they settled in America, became wholly separated from the hunting and savage tribes of their brethren; that the latter lost the knowledge of their having descended from the same family with themselves; that the more civilized part continued for many centuries; that tremendous wars were fought frequently between them and their savage brethren, 'til the former became extinct. This hypothesis accounts for the ancient works, forts, mounds, and vast enclosures, as well as tokens of a good degree of civil improvement, which are manifestly very ancient. . . . These partially civilized people became extinct. What account can be given of this, but that the savages extirpated them after long and dismal wars?"

This theory, so congenial to the sentiments of a religious community which regarded the Bible as the ultimate frame of reference in which all human knowledge must be set, Ethan Smith supported with quotations from Humboldt and contemporary American antiquarians as to the existence in the New World of ancient fortifications, temples, and whole cities, and he argued at length the cultural evidences that the American Indians and the Ten Tribes were one. For three hundred years, ever since the discovery of America, those of scholarly bent and pious inclination had dissected the folkways and beliefs of the Indians for proofs of their Israelitish descent. The languages of the Indians, in actuality as widely dissimilar as those of the peoples of Europe or Asia, were listened to for Hebrew affinities and roots; ideas of a Great Spirit which the red men had picked up from intercourse with the whites were identified as a survival of Jewish monotheism; while the taboos, ritual purifications, and sacrifices, which have proved to be common to all primitive peoples everywhere, in this generation seemed conclusive proof of the identity of the Indians with ancient Israel. Ethan Smith dwelt upon the existence among the Indians of inspired prophets and gifts of the spirit, and did not fail to point out the similitude to the Urim and Thummim of the breastplate of an Indian medicine-man, "made of a white conch-shell with two holes bored in the middle of it, through which he puts the ends of an otter skin strap, and fastens a buck horn button to the outside of each, as if in imitation of the precious stones of the Urim."

View of the Hebrews made much of the destruction of Jerusalem, the scattering of Israel, and its promised gathering "in the last days," themes which are central to the Book of Mormon. Both books quoted extensively and almost exclusively from Isaiah, anticipating the literal fulfillment of Isaiahic prophecies; both conceived the American nation as the instrument by which Israel in America should be saved in the last days; and even the Book of Mormon's conception of a ministry performed by Christ in the New World is implicit in Ethan Smith's view of Quetzalcoatl, the dominant figure of Aztec mythology, as a "type of Christ."

As if these textual correspondences were not striking enough, *View of the Hebrews* reads almost like a manual of instruction for intending prophets, seers, revelators, and translators. If the Indians were of Israel, Ethan Smith declared, some decisive evidence of the fact would soon be exhibited. Suppose a leading character in Israel "should be found to have had in possession some biblical fragment of ancient Hebrew writing. This man dies, and it is buried with him in such manner as to be long preserved. Some people afterwards removing that earth, discover this fragment, and ascertain what it is—an article of ancient Israel. Would such an incident . . . be esteemed of some weight?" Ethan Smith could not—nor has anyone since been able to—furnish evidence so decisive for his thesis, but he related a story he had lately heard about an old Indian at Stockbridge, Massachusetts, who was reported to have given information "that his fathers in this country had not long since had a book which they had *for a long time preserved*. But having lost the knowledge of reading it, they concluded it would be of no further use to them; and they buried it." Such things seemed now to be turning up; he himself had just barely failed to establish the whereabouts of certain parchments said to have been dug up in Pittsfield, reliably reported to be written in Hebrew. Ethan Smith was confident that some such discovery soon would be authenticated, and his reflections upon the significance of such a find for the redemption of the Indians are fully echoed in the Book of Mormon: "When God's bowels shall yearn for Ephraim, earnestly remembering him still, and about finally to restore him, it will prove that he has not been unmindful of that providential train of evidence, which must eventually identify a people long outcast and lost from the knowledge of the literary and civilized world, with his ancient beloved children of Abraham."[8]

As impressive as are the parallels between *View of the Hebrews* and the concept and content of the Book of Mormon, we need not insist upon them. It is more important that the ideas common to the two books should have been the common property of their generation. That this should be the character of Joseph's book, that it should exemplify as truly as *View of the Hebrews* a state of mind and a complex of ideas, the concepts of its time embedded in its pages like so many oysters in a stratum of limestone, is more significant in the evaluation of the Book of Mormon than any question of literary derivation, however decisive its bearing may be upon what the book claims to be. For, painful as such a finding may be to the sensibilities of those to whom the historicity of the Book of Mormon is a matter of the greatest importance, Joseph's book is a great deal more useful to a student of the intellectual preoccupations and the folkways of New York State in the third decade of the nineteenth century than to a scholar who would reconstruct the pre-Columbian history of America. In contrast to the often fascinating correspondences archaeologists have discovered between the Bible record and the early civilizations of the Near and Middle East, during a century of intensive excavation in the New World the Book of Mormon has neither pointed to, accounted for, nor been illuminated by any find, while its central idea, the Hebraic origin of the American Indians, has been wholly exploded, and is given credence today nowhere outside Mormon seminaries.[9] Yet from the beginning, the basis of the appeal of Joseph's book was that it constituted a record of the New World comparable in every respect to the biblical account of the Old. But if the materials directly borrowed from the Bible—its prophets, kings, and judges; its wrath and goodness of God; its silks, fine-twined linens, chariots, and implements of brass and steel—were sifted out of the Book of Mormon, what remains would mirror only Joseph's own milieu, extending even to treasures hid up in the earth and made "slippery" by "sorceries, and witchcrafts, and magics."[10]

The story Joseph undertook to tell was that of a people who had come to America from Jerusalem six centuries before Christ. These wayfarers split into two warring races, the "white and delightsome" Nephites, and the savage and murderous Lamanites. The Nephites were greatly favored of God, and built up a great civilization, but eventually fell into transgression, and their abominations and wickedness were such that God turned his face from them. In a long series of wars, climaxed by many bloody battles in which their armies were slaughtered by the thousand and ten thousand, the wayward

Nephites finally were exterminated by the Lamanites. That their history might be preserved, it had been engraved upon golden plates which, about the year 421 A.D., had been hidden away in the Hill Cumorah, not to come forth until the Lord in his wisdom should provide.

As a work of speculative ethnology, the Book of Mormon undertook with considerable ingenuity to unriddle the mystery of America's past. It was the Nephites, readers of the book were to learn, who had built the walled cities, temples, towers, and pyramids which had so long deeply impressed visitors to Mexcio. Driven northward by their relentless enemies, the Nephites had built the great mounds of the Mississippi and Ohio valleys, and finally in western New York had been overwhelmed amid their last defenses. Thus was solved the mystery of the mound builders. All this was well calculated to appeal to men of reason, for except that it gave a new name to the Mound builders there was nothing in the least original about it. For their iniquities, the Lamanites were cursed by the Lord with dark skin; "their heads [were] shaved that they were naked;" they were girded with a "leathern girdle about their loins;" and were given to painting their faces with vermillion. An idle race, full of mischief and subtlety, they dwelt in the wilderness and subsisted upon beasts of prey. That the Lamanites were thus the ancestors of the Indians was perfectly apparent.

Had Joseph been content to keep his story within the bounds of so simple a framework, it would probably never have been published. Indeed, it is doubtful whether it would ever have been written. Primarily, it was the character of the Book of Mormon as a work of religious import which induced Martin Harris to finance the writing and which enabled Joseph to command the labors of the succession of scribes without whom there could have been no book, though Joseph's bible has some internal admissions that as first conceived it did not concern itself entirely with sacred history, being more characteristically "an account of the reign of the kings, and the wars and contentions" of the people.[11]

From the very beginning, however, Joseph wedded his book firmly to the Bible, which became the inexhaustible well from which he drew ideas, incidents, material, culture, and even language. The deadly style of Chronicles had of course been the literary stock-in-trade of every village editor since the Revolution, and it was a rare political campaign in which the air did not resound with "beholds," "it-came-to-passes," and "false prophets ravening amongst the people."[12] And there would be occasion for surprise if Joseph had not already tried out this idiom before the juvenile debating club in the old red schoolhouse in Palmyra. Although his adoption of the idiom of the King James Bible for his narrative, which lent itself readily to wholesale borrowings from the King James text, has become one of the major embarrassments of the Book of Mormon, contributing largely to a revision of Mormon critical thinking about it, it is quite certain that Joseph could neither have written nor won acceptance for the divinity of a book phrased in any other idiom.

The tale which, with its mingled qualities of the familar and the strange, Joseph's scribes wonderingly set down on paper commenced in Jerusalem during the reign of the king Zedekiah, six hundred years before Christ. It was given the patriarch Lehi, even as his sorrowing contemporary, Jeremiah, to foretell the imminent destruction of the Holy City. When Lehi was scorned, reviled, and threatened, the Lord commanded him to leave the accursed city and flee into the wilderness. It being wisdom in the Lord that he should carry with him a record of his forefathers, Lehi sent his sons back to Jerusalem to obtain from his kinsman Laban certain brass plates on which this genealogy was engraved. After many difficulties, the resolute younger son Nephi slew Laban with his own sword and carried off the plates. Joined by Laban's servant Zoram, and by the patriarch Ishmael and his family, which included a convenient number of unmarriaged daughters, the little party launched upon their arduous journey. After some years of wandering, they reached the shores of a distant sea where by the help of God they built a vessel in which to voyage to a new world.

Thus briskly Joseph set his narrative to marching, though how much literary skill his opening chapters exhibited, and how he may have fumbled with either the theme itself or the language in which he developed it, is impossible now to say, for the first quarter of the book as it was originally composed was lost and eventually rewritten from a different angle of view. It would appear that the first draft was less pretentious than the version finally published, and that it partook rather more of profane history—"an account of the reign of the kings, and the wars and contentions" of the people, though containing also a liberal admixture of "many things which [Lehi] saw in vision and in dreams; and . . . many things which he prophesied and spake unto his children."

This mention of the visions of Lehi is more than provocative, and an analysis of them, had the text survived, might have been revealing. For like any novelist, Joseph may have converted the stuff of his own life to the service of his art. Emma herself must have been struck with some of the parallels between Joseph's own family and the central personalities of his book. The patriarch Lehi was, in the words of his wife Sariah, "a visionary man," a view of the elder Joseph Smith to which Lucy Smith distinctly inclined; and during the time Lehi remained in the wilderness, while pausing in a valley called "Lemuel" in remembrance of his stiff-necked, irascible second son,[13] Lehi was vouchsafed a vision of the gospel and of Babylon which anticipated in remarkable detail a dream Joseph Smith, Senior, had had 2,400 years later.[14] Quite as extraordinary were the resemblances between the two sons, for both Nephi and Joseph, Junior, were born of goodly parents, large of stature, taught somewhat in the learning of their fathers, visited with many afflictions in the course of their days yet highly favored of the Lord, and possessed of a great knowledge of and thirst after the mysteries of God. (Both also, the unkindly might observe, appeared to be given to the making of records with their own hands, according to their own knowledge.)

Lehi was, however, less fortunate in his family than the elder Joseph, for though occasionally the inflammable William stirred up strife among the Smith sons, none among them was possessed of so evil a genius as Lehi's wayward and truculent eldest sons, who were in almost continual rebellion against the Lord, a sore trial to the tractable Lehi. Notwithstanding, in their strange craft (which Joseph never undertook to describe other than to say that it was "constructed after the manner which the Lord had shown . . . wherefore, it was not after the mannner of men"), Lehi and his strife-torn following succeeded in voyaging to what they, even as the stump orators of Palmyra and Harmony, "did call . . . the promised land." There they found "beasts in the forests of every kind, both the cow and the ox, and the ass and the horse, and the goat and the wild goat, and all maner of wild animals, which were for the use of men." This abundance Joseph drew uncritically from the wealth of the Bible; had he been better educated, he might have been more circumspect, for the well-informed even among his contemporaries knew that save perhaps the "wild goat," all these animals had been introduced into America by the dons and hidalgos who sailed in the wake of Columbus.

Fair as was the new land, it soon was as embattled as the old. The willful Laman and Lemuel drew the sword against their kinsmen, obliging Nephi and such others as remained faithful to seek refuge in the wilderness. Cursed with "a sore cursing, because of their iniquity," the Lamanites saw their own flesh turn dark, and commenced with the Nephites a thousand-year-long strife which could end only in the entire extinction of the one people at the hands of the other. Since it was only too evident that the savages rather than the civilized peoples of ancient America had emerged victorious from the age-long warfare, it was incumbent upon Joseph to explain. Here the religious turn his book had taken provided an answer: The Nephites had come to their untimely end because they had turned their faces from God—they had sunk under the weight of their own abominations and wickedness.

Joseph's narrative, however, soared far beyond this simple necessity of plot. The promise inherent in the biblical prose of his story and its beginning in doomed Jerusalem, Joseph's book made good in truly original fashion. "Other sheep have I," Christ had said, "which are not of this fold." Those sheep, Joseph reasoned, were the American aborigines, and his book built up to the climactic drama implicit in the appearance of the risen Redeemer to his believers in the New World after he had taken final leave of his disciples in the Old. The final debacle which had overtaken the Nephites Joseph dismissed in as small space as possible, the events of the final four hundred years of Nephite history being compressed into forty pages.

Undoubtedly the most anachronistic feature of the book was the introduction into it of Christian themes. Through revelation, the Nephites were made conversant, centuries before Christ, with all the details of his ministry. Long before the time of Christ, the Nephites, as Joseph developed their story, believed in him as the Redeemer, worshipped in his name, and even sought to be reconciled to the Father through an atonement yet to be made. Assuming Joseph's authorship, what could have motivated him in this turn he gave to his narrative? It may be that in his own fashion he was simply trying to present his Nephites as a people more favored of the Lord than any other who ever lived. But it may also be that Joseph's well of invention ran dry when called upon to flow sufficient detail as to make green a thousand years of history. This expedient greatly simplified the task by enabling Joseph to fill out the book from the interminable religious disputations to which he had been exposed in church and out these many years. As Alexander Campbell was soon to observe, "This prophet Smith, through his stone spectacles, wrote on the plates of Nephi, in his book of Mormon, every error and almost every truth discussed in New York for the last ten years. He decides all the great controversies–infant baptism, ordination, the trinity, regeneration, repentance, justification, the fall of man, the atonement, transubstantiation, fastng, penance, church government, religious experience, the call to the ministry, the general resurrection, eternal punishment, who may baptize, and even the question of freemasonry, republican government, and the rights of man."[15]

The Book of Mormon has been likened to a novel, one of the early examples of frontier fiction.[16] Actually, it belongs to a genre much more rare, fictional history written to be read as real history. The Book of Mormon is directly modeled upon the Bible and reflects the fulfillment of an inspiring design that the red men might be brought to a knowledge of their fathers, believe the gospel, be glorified through faith in Jesus Christ, and at last, through repentance, be saved. The religious significance with which Joseph invested his history was of the greatest importance in the shaping of both the book and his own career. Bringing the red men to a saving knowledge in Christ, after all, had been a preoccupation of the American conscience from the time of John Eliot, although the zeal to save the souls of the Indians increased at about the square of the distance from the frontier. Joseph's history was calculated to gratify both the pious and the intellectual curiosities of the age, and to suppose that he was unaware of this would be to grossly underrate his intelligence. It is even possible that the utility of the Book of Mormon for proselyting the Indians was Joseph's initial moral justification for writing it; it certainly became the basis for the elaborate rationalization by which eventually he came to the conviction that both his book and its author were divinely inspired.

That no part of the book's conception was conspicuously original only strengthened its appeal and was strikingly characteristic of

Joseph's subsequent practice in the role of prophet, seer, and revelator, for the distinguishing feature of Joseph's church was not to be the novelty of its doctrines but the authority with which it seized upon the floating ideas of its generation. What gave Joseph's book vitality, however, was not intellectual content but the emotional impact which followed from its identification with the Bible. Joseph had neither the wit nor the learning to write a book parallel to the Bible which men would be able to receive as being of equal standing, but he did possess a boundless ingenuity, a certain plasticity of mind, and a verbal facility which are worthy of all admiration, whatever the defects of the work they combined to produce. The Bible gave him both his frame of reference and the warp into which he wove the blood-and-thunder adventures, platitudinous moralizing, family memories, revivalist sermons, political alarms, speculative ethnology, backwoods folklore, and all the other curious threads which make up the woof of his narrative.

The eminently personal character of the Book of Mormon extends far beyond its incidental revelation of Joseph's lack of learning. In a sense it is a truer autobiography than the formal account he later gave the world, for quite unconsciously it mirrors his mind, both its quality and the character of its ideas and interests. The absorption of his society in the mystery of the moundbuilders and the origin of the American Indians, its rapt interest in folk magic, the periodic interruption of its religious anxieties and ecstasies, its naive assurance in the divinely ordained future of America, all are presented in Joseph's book with as much assurance as the cracker-barrel sage of any village store. If all this, which gave flesh and blood to a fictional history designed to be read as living history, was received with conviction, it was because he brought to it an elemental simplicity which returned all controversies to the ultimate authority of the scriptures.

In significant ways the Book of Mormon has shaped the evolution of Mormon thought. It has made uncompromising fundamentalists out of believers, who are bound to a monolithic view of the Bible which can admit nothing to higher criticism, and who must dismiss as mere speculation scientific discoveries which stand against a literal interpretation of the scriptures. It has also given them a curious sense of inferiority which has emerged throughout its history in the characteristic form of aggression, a natural resentment felt because of the basic necessity for apology the marvelous phenomena attendant upon the coming forth of the Book of Mormon has always imposed.

It has been claimed for the Book of Mormon that it contains the gospel in its fulness, the word of God brought down through time uncorrupted, whereas from the Bible "many precious parts" have been lost. These claims, however, are not now often heard, for its believers can point to no great truths it contains that are not found in the Bible,[17] and its importance now is held to be that it "confirms" the truth, inspiration and authenticity of the Bible, making it "more valuable than a thousand Rosetta Stones." The controversies which it addressed are dead; its naive speculations as to American ethnology and archaeology have been shown to be idle. If the Book of Mormon remains for Mormonism what Joseph called it, "the keystone of our religion," it is only in the circumstances of its coming forth, a kind of artifact, not for any truths it contains. But it will continue to be interesting, both for what it reveals of Joseph's mind and as a kind of concretion of its age.

APPENDIX A

Joseph Smith on Trial in 1826

One of the questions of most critical importance for the beginnings of Mormonism is whether or not Joseph Smith was tried in March 1826, Chenango County, New York, on charges of being "a disorderly person and an imposter." Although reference to such a trial has been made in the literature, it is only since the publication in 1945 of Fawn M. Brodie's biography of Joseph Smith, *No Man Knows My History*, that it has become recognized as of major importance.

In behalf of the church, the alleged court record of 1826, which if valid would give Joseph Smith an ante-Mormon history entirely at variance with his later claims as a religious leader, was attacked by Albert E. Bowen, a member of the church's Quorum of the Twelve Apostles, in an unsigned review of Brodie's book published in the *Deseret News*, May 11, 1946. Bowen objected:

> The author produces no court record at all, though persistently calling it such. . . . She carefully avoids saying that it was found among the records of the court, though she clearly intended that the casual reader would assume that it was. . . . Why didn't she produce it instead of a secondary source, on its face discredited? A justice's court is not what the lawyers call a court of record, the testimony of witness is usually not taken down nor preserved as a part of the record in the case. This alleged record is obviously spurious because it has Joseph testify first, giving the defense before the prosecution has made its case. Indeed there is no record that the prosecuting witness testified at all, nor that any witness was sworn [sic]. Joseph didn't have to testify against himself at all, but here he is doing it before there is any proof against him. Then the recital is that the court "finds the defendant guilty." Of what? He was charged with being "a disorderly person and an impostor." Which was he guilty of? . . . More wonderful still, the record does not tell what the judgment or sentence of the court was. The really vital things which a true record must contain are not there, though there is a lot of surplus verbiage set out in

> an impossible order which the court was not required to keep.
>
> This record could not possibly have been made at the time as the case proceeded. It is patently a fabrication of unknown authorship and never in the court records at all.

Francis W. Kirkham also reacted to the challenge implicit in this court record and in the *Improvement Era*, March 1947, pp. 182ff., branded it a forgery, "written by a person totally unfamiliar with court procedure." Contemporary justice of the peace records, Kirkham maintained, "contain only the names of the plaintiff, the defendant, the statement of the case, the date of judgment, the amount of judgment, the cost and fees." And he concluded, "No record exists and there is no evidence to prove one was ever made in which [Joseph Smith] confessed in a justice of the peace court that he had used a seer stone to find hidden treasures for purposes of fraud and deception."

These conclusions Kirkham incorporated into a new edition of his *A New Witness for Christ in America* (Independence, Missouri, 1947). Meanwhile, Brodie had uncovered in southern New York an account of the 1826 trial written by a reputable eyewitness, Dr. William D. Purple; and Stanely S. Ivins of Salt Lake City discovered what purported to be a transcript of an agreement concerning the Smiths' money-digging in Pennsylvania, as well as fresh information on the provenance of the court record itself. These documents, placed at the disposal of Kirkham, were included in a last minute supplement to his book. The facts developed clearly controverted his argument, so to rebut them he dwelt on inconsistencies between the court record and the reminiscent account of the trial, arguing also that pages "claimed to be taken from a forty-five-year-old book are not valid evidence until the book and the pages are identified." In the absence of any contemporary evidence of such a trial, he declared, there was no reason to think it had ever taken place; the record was a forgery; and reminiscences of Joseph Smith as a money-digger were nothing but folklore springing up in the wake of an anti-Mormon book, *Mormonism Unvailed*, published in late 1834.

The attacks made upon the court record by these spokesmen for the church had an essentially legalistic basis. While such objections may quite properly be made, it does not follow that a justice of the peace court in rural New York in 1826 proceeded with the nicety of a supreme court session, or that it did not exhibit any unorthodoxy, according to the custom of the neighborhood or the temperament and practice of the justice. Moreover, this negative attitude toward the purported record ignores the question of internal evidences. If the persons named as figuring in the trial can be consistently identified, the court record cannot be dismissed out of hand as a cheap fabrication. In here reprinting it, that annotation has been performed.

The value of the court record is clearly heightened by the discovery of Dr. Purple's reminiscences, which not only corroborate but explain and illuminate it. The chief lack in the pattern of evidence has been a contemporary allusion to the trial. That lack I am fortunately able to supply, a letter published April 9, 1831, which is corroborative of both the other documents and in its provenance as far removed from either of them as they are from each other.

The documents as here reprinted come from secondary sources. It is to be hoped that this emphasis placed upon their importance may serve in bringing the originals to light: the justice of the peace record from which the pages were cut, the excised pages themselves, and the articles of agreement drawn up in 1825.

The Money-Digging Agreement, 1825

The following document, as reprinted from the Susquehanna *Journal* of March 20, 1880, was discovered by Stanley S. Ivins in the Salt Lake City *Daily Tribune* of April 23, 1880. Although the story ties in directly with the accounts of the 1826 trial, the articles of agreement are not necessarily adverse to the claims of the church, Joseph Smith himself having admitted that in the fall of 1825 he engaged in money-digging activities at the instance of Josiah Stowell.

The earliest Mormon account of this episode was by Oliver Cowdery, writing in Joseph Smith's behalf in the *Latter Day Saints' Messenger and Advocate*, Oct. 1835. Employed as a common laborer by a gentleman from Chenango County, Cowdery explained that Joseph Smith

> visited that section of the country; and had he not been accused of digging down all, or nearly so, the mountains of Susquehannah, or causing others to do it by some art of nicromancy, I should leave this for the present, unnoticed. You will remember, in the mean time, that those who seek to vilify his character, say that he has always been notorious for his idleness. This gentleman, whose name is Stowel, resided in the town of Bainbridge, on or near the head waters of the Susquehannah river. Some forty miles south, or down the river, in the town of Harmony, Susquehannah county, Pa. is said to be a cave or subterraneous recess, whether entirely formed by art or not I am uninformed, neither does this matter; but such is said to be the case,—where a company of Spaniards, a long time since, when the country was uninhabited by white settlers, excavated from the bowels of the earth ore, and coined a large quantity of money; after which they secured the cavity and evacuated, leaving a part still in the cave, proposing to return at some distant period. A long time elapsed and this account came from one of the individuals who was first engaged in this mining business. The country was pointed out and the spot minutely described. This, I believe, is the substance, so far

as my memory serves, though I shall not pledge my veracity for the correctness of the account as I have given.—Enough however, was credited of the Spaniard's story, to excite the belief of many that there was a fine sum of the precious metal lying coined in this subterraneous vault, among whom was our employer; and accordingly our brother was required to spend a few months with some others in excavating the earth, in pursuit of this treasure.

In what it details of a mine and money coined therefrom, this account by Oliver Cowdery is fully in accord with the agreement hereafter reprinted. Joseph's own account of his association with Josiah Stowell implies that he worked as a mere day laborer for a wage of fourteen dollars a month, and this is Cowdery's assertion also. The agreement that follows has nothing to say of such an arrangement, which it is conceivable may have applied to actual work on Stowell's farm; instead, it provides that Joseph and his father were to be given two-elevenths of all the wealth that might be found, for services that remain unspecified but may readily be inferred.

Yellowstone Valley, Mt.
Apr. 12, 1880

Eds. Tribune: Knowing how interested you are in any matter pertaining to the early history of our Church, I enclose a slip cut from the Susquehanna, (Pa.) *Journal* of March 20, which will throw some light on the subject. The *Journal* is published near the scene of our martyred Prophet's early exploits.

Respectfully Yours
B. Wade

The following agreement, the original of which is in the possession of a citizen of Thompson township, was discovered by our correspondent, and forwarded to us as a matter of local interest.

The existence of the "buried treasures" referred to was "revealed" to Joe Smith jr., who with his father the Prophet, at that time resided on what is now known as the McCune farm, about two miles down the river from this place, and upon the strength of which revelation a stock company was organized to dig for the aforesaid treasure. After the company was organized, a second communication was received by Joseph, jr., from the "other world," advising the treasure seekers to suspend operations, as it was necessary for one of the company to die before the treasure could be secured.

Harper the peddler, who was murdered soon after, near the place where the Catholic cemetery in this borough is now located,[1] was one of the original members of the company, and his death was regarded by the remainder of the band as a Providential occurence, which the "powers" had brought about for their special benefit. The death of Harper having removed the only obstacle in the way of success, the surviving members recommenced operations, and signed an "agreement," giving the widow Harper the half [sic] of one-third of all the treasures secured. The following is the agreement, written by the old humbug, Joseph Smith, himself:

ARTICLES OF AGREEMENT

We, the undersigned, do firmly agree, & by these presents bind ourselves, to fulfill and abide by the hereafter specified articles:

First—That if anything of value should be obtained at a certain place in Pennsylvania near a Wm Hale's, supposed to be a valuable mine of either Gold or Silver and also to contain coined money and bars or ingots of Gold or Silver, and at wich several hands have been at work during a considerable part of the past summer, we do agree to have it divided in the following manner, viz.: Josiah Stowell, Calvin Stowell and Wm. Hale to take two-thirds, and Charles Newton, Wm. I. Wiley, and the Widow Harper to take the other third. And we further agree that Joseph Smith, Sen. and Joseph Smith, Jr. shall be considered as having two shares, two elevenths of all the property that may be obtained, the shares to be taken equally from each third.

Second—And we further agree, that in consideration of the expense and labor to which the following named persons have been at (John F. Shephard, Elihu Stowell and John Grant) to consider them as equal sharers in the mine after all the coined money and bars or ingots are obtained by the undersigned, their shares to be taken out from each share; and we further agree to remunerate all the three above named persons in a handsome manner for all their time, expense and labor which they have been or may be at, until the mine is opened, if anything should be obtained; otherwise they are to lose their time, expense and labor.

Third—And we further agree that all the expense which has or may accure until the mine is opened, shall be equally borne by the proprietors of each third and that after the mine is opened, the expense shall be equally borne by each of the sharers.

Township of Harmony, Pa., Nov. 1, 1825
In presence of

Isaac Hale	Jos. Smith, Sen.	Calvin Stowell
Chas. A. Newton	P. Newton	Jos. Smith, Jr.
David Hale	Isaiah Stowell	Wm. I. Riley.[2]

The place where treasure was supposed to lie buried was on the place now owned by J. M. Tillman, near the McKune farm, then the property of Wm. Hale. Excavations were also made on Jacob Skinner's farm, some of which remain well marked to-day. It was while pursuing this unsuccessful search for treasures that Prophet Smith pretended that he unearthed his famous "tablets."

(Brother Wade may have made a mistake in directing his letter to the proper Church journal. If he has, Granny [the *Deseret News*] has our permission to copy the above by giving *The Tribune* proper credit.)

The 1826 Court Record

As published by Fawn Brodie, the record of the trial at Bainbridge, New York, on March 20, 1826, was derived by an article on Mormonism contributed by Daniel S. Tuttle, Methodist Episcopal Bishop for Utah, to the *Religious Encyclopedia or Dictionary of Biblical, Historical, Doctrinal, and Practical Theology Based on the Real Encyclopedia of Herzog, Plitt, and Hauck*, edited by Philip Schaff, and published by Funk & Wagnals, New York, 1883, vol. 2, p. 1576. Bishop Tuttle evidently thought this to be the first publication of the document, but Stanley Ivins has demonstrated its appearance in print ten years earlier.

The record was evidently first printed in an English periodical, *Fraser's Magazine*, Feb. 1873, vol. 7 (New Series), pp. 229-30, as a part of the text of an article entitled, "The Original Prophet," printed over the signature "C. M." From this source it was immediately reprinted in an American periodical, *The Eclectic Magazine*, April 1873, vol. 17 (New Series), p. 483. The author of the article was presumably Charles Marshall, who contributed other articles to *Fraser's Magazine* on the basis of a visit to Utah he made in 1871. In printing the court record, Marshall said of it, "The original papers were lent me by a lady of well-known position, in whose family they had been preserved since the date of the transactions."

This "lady of well-known position" was identified by Bishop Tuttle when he again printed the court record in the *Utah Christian Advocate* for January 1886: "The Ms. was given me by Miss Emily Pearsall who, some years since, was a woman helper in our mission and lived in my family, and died here. Her father or uncle was a Justice of the Peace in Bainbridge Chenango Co., New York, in Jo. Smith's time, and before him Smith was tried. Miss Pearsall tore the leaves out of the record found in her father's house and brought them to me." Tuttle's *Reminiscences of a Missionary Bishop* (New York, 1906), p. 272, notes that Miss Pearsall had come from Bainbridge to Salt Lake City in 1870 to assist her church as a "Sister" or "Woman missionary," that she died after two years' faithful service, and that she was buried in Mount Olivet Cemetery. More precise vital statistics are provided by a *History and Genealogy of the Pearsall Family in England and America*, edited by Clarence E. and Hattie May Pearsall and Harry L. Neall (San Francisco, 1928), vol. 2, pp. 1,143 and 1,151, from which it appears that Emily was born January 25, 1833, and died November 5, 1872. Her father's sister, Phoebe Pearsall, married Albert Neely, who as will be seen from the reminiscences of Dr. Purple, presided over the 1826 trial.

The version of the court record printed in the Schaff-Herzog encyclopedia, and reprinted by Brodie, did not include the costs which follow the finding of the court. Otherwise, except for small typographical variations, all printed versions are alike. The text now reprinted is that of the *Utah Christian Advocate*, with some corrections in brackets illustrating variations found in the published version of 1873:

> *Exact copy trial and conviction of Joseph Smith author of Book of Mormon March 20, 1826, Bainbridge, New York.*
>
> PEOPLE OF STATE OF NEW YORK,
> VS.
> JOSEPH SMITH.
>
> Warrant issued upon written complaint upon oath of Peter G. Bridgman[3] who informed that one Joseph Smith of Bainbridge was a disorderly person and an Impostor. Prisoner brought before court 20 March. Prisoner examined, says, that he came from town of Palmyra, and, had been at the house of Josiah Stowels in Bainbridge most of time since, had small part of time been employed in looking for mines,—but the major part had been employed by said Stowell on his farm, and going to school. That he had a certain stone, which he had occasionally looked at to determine where hidden treasures in the bowels of the earth were, that he professed to tell in this manner where gold mines were a distance under ground, and had looked for Mr. Stowell several times and informed him where he could find those treasures, and Mr. Stowel had been engaged in digging for them—that at Palmyra he had pretended to tell by looking at this stone, where coined money was buried in Pennsylvania, and while at Palmyra he had frequently ascertained in that way where lost porperty was of various kinds; that he has occasionally been in the habit of looking through this stone to find lost property for 3 years, but of late had pretty much given it up on account of injuring his Health, especially his eyes, made them sore—that he did not solicit business of this kind, and had always rather declined having anything to do with this business.
>
> Josiah Stowel sworn, says that, prisoner had been at his house, something like 5 months, had been employed by him to work on farm part of time—that he pretended to have skill of telling where hidden treasures in the earth were by means of looking through a certain stone—that Prisoner had looked for him some times once to tell him about money buried on Bend Mountain in Pennsylvania, once for gold on Monument Hill, and once for Salt Spring[4] and that

he positively knew that the Prisoner could tell and possessed the art of seeing those valuable treasures through the medium of said stone—that he found the digging part at Ben and Monument Hill, as prisoner represented it—that prisoner had looked through said stone for Deacon Attlton [Attleton or Attelon][5]—for a mine did not exactly find it but got a (piece) of oar which resembled gold, he thinks; that Prisoner had told by means of this stone where, a Mr. Bacon[6] had buried money, that he and prisoner had been in search of it; that prisoner said that it was on a certain Root of a stump 5 feet from surface of the earth, and with it would be found a tail feather that said Stowel and prisoner thereupon commenced digging, found a fail feather, but money was gone, that he supposed that money moved down—that prisoner did not offer his services; that he never deceived him,—that Prisoner looked through stone and described Josiah Stowels house and out houses, while at Palmyra at Simpson Stowels[7] correctly, that he had told about a painted tree with a man's hand painted upon it by means of said stone; that he had been in company with prisoner digging for gold, and had the most implicit faith in Prisoners skill.[8]

Horace Stowel[9] sworn, says he see Prisoner look into that strange stone, pretending to tell where a chest of dollars were burried in Windsor a number of miles distant, marked out size of chest in the leaves on ground.

Arad Stowel[10] sworn, says that he went to see whether Prisoner could convince him that he possessed the skill that he professed to have, upon which prisoner laid a Book open upon a White Cloth, and proposed looking through another stone which was white and transparent; held the stone to the candle, turned his back to book and read, the deception appeared so palpable that went off disgusted.

McMaster,[11] sworn, says he went with Arad Stowel, to be convinced of Prisoner's skill, and likewise came away disgusted, finding the deception so palpable. Prisoner pretended to him that he could discern objects at a distance by holding this white stone to the sun or candle; that prisoner rather declined looking into a Hat at his dark-colored stone as he said that it hurt his eyes.

Jonathan Thompson,[12] says that Prisoner was requested to look Yoemans[13] for chest of money—did look and pretended to know where it was, and that Prisoner, Thompson and Yoemans went in search of it; that Smith arrived at Spot first, was in night, that Smith looked in Hat while there and when very dark, and told how the chest was situated—after digging several feet struck upon something sounding like a board or plank—Prisoner would not look again pretending that he was alarmed, the last time that he looked on account of the circumstances relating to the trunk being buried came all fresh to his mind, that the last time that he looked, he discovered distinctly, the two Indians who buried the trunk, that a quarrel ensued between them and that one of said Indians was killed by the other and thrown into the hole beside of the trunk, to guard it as he supposed—Thompson says that he believes in the prisoners professed skill, that the board he struck his spade upon was probably the chest but on account of an enchantment, the trunk kept settling away from under them while digging, that notwithstanding they continued constantly removing the dirt, yet the trunk kept about the same distance from them, Prisoner said that it appeared to him that salt might be found in Bainbridge, and that he is certain that Prisoner, can, divine things by means of said Stone and Hat; that as evidence of fact—Prisoner looked into his hat to tell him about some money Witness lost 16 years ago, and that he described the man that Witness supposed had taken it, and disposition of money. And therefore the court find the defendant guilty—cost Warrant, 19cts, complaint upon oath 25.7 [25 1/2] Witnesses 87 1/2, Recognizance 25, Mittimus 19, Recognizance or [of] witness 75, Subpoena 18—$268 [$2.68].

Reminiscences of the Trial by Dr. W. D. Purple

The account of the trial by Dr. William D. Purple, as published in the Norwich *Chenango Union*, May 3, 1877, was brought to light through field researches undertaken in Chenango County by Fawn M. Brodie. The same account, reprinted in an unidentified publication, is to be found in a scrapbook in the New York Public Library complied by Charles L. Woodward, "The First Half Century of Mormonism." It also served as the basis of a discussion of Mormonism in James H. Smith, *History of Chenango and Madison Counties*, pp. 153-55.

In a latter work Smith had this to say: "Dr. Purple possesses a remarkably retentive memory, and his mind is a rich store-house of facts and incidents connected with the early settlements in this locality, with which he is probably more conversant than any other individual in the southern part of the county." He also noted that Dr. Purple was admitted to the Chenango County Medical Society on May 10, 1825, having been licensed the preceding October 1, and that he later, in 1838-39, served as president of that society.

Fuller information about Dr. Purple was developed by Mrs. Brodie from a scrapbook found in the public library at Greene, New York. This scrapbook contained medical articles by the doctor, most of them published in the *Transactions* of the New York State Medical Society; two articles clipped from the *Chenango Union* entitled "Reminiscences of the Town of Greene;" the article on Joseph Smith here reprinted; and four or five obituary notices.

These obiturary remarks are important because they go far to establish the credibility of Dr. Purple as a witness. He was born, it appears, in 1802 and died May 18, 1886, at the age of 84. He came to Greene, New York, in 1807, and began to practice medicine in Bainbridge in 1824. In 1830 he moved from Bainbridge to Coventry, and then to Greene, where he practiced medicine until his retirement. He then became postmaster, a position he held for some years. He was a liberal contributor to medical literature, was president of the Chenango County Medical Society, and in 1849 received the degree of Doctor of Medicine from the Regents of the State Medical Society.

One obituary notice said of him: "He was blessed with a most retentive memory, and was thoroughly conversant with the county's history. He was a man of the strictest integrity and uprightness of character." Another remarked: "His articles on current topics contained apt and appropriate matter, often expressed in crisp style. . . . His medical writings were dignified, and contained much originality and sound philosophy, and were so free from technicalities that they were readily comprehended. Many of them are to be found in the 'Transactions of the N. Y. State Medical Society' and the 'Chenango County Medical Society,' and one of his medical articles was translated into French and published abroad. . . . Dr. Purple possessed a remarkably retentive memory, characterized, also, by a surprising facility for the recollection of dates, statistics, and historical occurences, so that he was called sometimes, as veritably he was, a walking encyclopedia. He could tell at once the names of candidates, the year of their nominations, the names, methods, and characteristic, and management of all parties, and the principle history of nearly all political leaders during every year of the past eighty years; would one ascertain the number of miles distance between Utica and Rochester, or Buffalo and Albany, Dr. Purple had it at his tongue's end; also the year and frequently the month when almost any important event had happened in his own country, as well as much that transpired in more remote localities during the period of his lifetime."

In comparing Dr. Purple's reminiscences with the court record, it will be seen that discrepancies appear, some of them no doubt explained by the lapse of half a century. He remembered the trial to have taken place in February 1826; the court record shows the date to have been March 20, 1826. Dr. Purple recalled that Stowell's sons had "caused the arrest of Smith," whereas the court record says the warrant was issued on oath of Peter G. Bridgman, though of course it does not therefore follow that Stowell's sons may not in this manner have "caused the arrest." Dr. Purple's recollection was that Stowell's sons made affidavit or gave their testimony before Joseph Smith was examined; the court record shows that it was the other way around. Dr. Purple remembered the elder Joseph Smith to have followed his son to the witness chair; the court record is silent as to this. In turn, the court record shows the testimony of one McMaster, concerning whom Dr. Purple is silent. The court record and Dr. Pruple's reminiscences agree that the principal witnesses, Joseph Smith, Jun., Josial Stowell, and Jonathan Thompson were examined in that order.

The recollections of the testimony given are fuller than the information that is developed by the laconic court record, and it is not impossible that there had been some enlargement of Dr. Purple's memory with the passing years. But it may also be noted, painful as the idea may be to Mormon sensibilities, that though the fantastic story of the search after a seer stone is not verifiable in other sources, it by no means follows that this story, true or false, was not related to the court. Mormon and non-Mormon accounts alike agree that the youthful Joseph Smith had a remarkable imagination and a well-developed talent as a teller of tales:

JOSEPH SMITH, the Originator of Mormonism

Historical Reminiscences of the Town of Afton

by W. D. Purple

More than fifty years since, at the commencement of his professional career, the writer spent a year in the present village of Afton, in this [Chenango] County. It was then called South Bainbridge, and was in striking contrast with the present village at the same place. It was a mere hamlet, with one store and one tavern. The scenes and incidents of that early day are vividly engraven upon his memory, by reason of having written them when they occurred, and by reason of his public and private rehearsals of them in later years. He will now present them as historical reminiscences of old Chenango, and as a precursor of the advent of that wonder of the age, Mormonism.

In the year 1825 we often saw in that quiet hamlet, Joseph Smith, Jr., the author of the Golden Bible, or the Books of Mormon. He was an inmate of the family of Deacon Isaiah [Josiah] Stowell, who resided some two miles below the village, on the Susquehanna. Mr. Stowell was a man of much force of character, of indomitable will, and well fitted as a pioneer in the unbroken wilderness that this country possessed at the close of the last century. He was one of the Vermont sufferers, who for defective titles, consequent on the forming a new State from a part of Massachusetts, in 1791, received wild lands in Bainbridge. He had been educated in the spirit of orthodox puritanism, and was officially connected with the first Presbyterian church of the town, organized by Rev. Mr. Chapin. He was a very industrious, exemplary man, and by severe labor and frugality had acquired surroundings that excited the envy of many of his less fortunate neighbors. He had at this time grown up sons and daughters to share his prosperity and the honors of his name.

About this time he took upon himself a monamaniacal impression to seek for hidden treasures which he believed were buried in the earth. He hired help and repaired to Northern Pennsylvania, in the vicinity of Lanesboro, to prosecute his search for untold wealth which he believed to be buried there. Whether it was the

"Ninety bars of gold
And dollars many fold"

that Capt. Robert Kidd, the pirate of a preceding century, had despoiled the commerce of the world, we are not able to say, but that he took his help and provisions from home, and camped out on the black hills of that region for weeks at a time, was freely admitted by himself and family.

What success, if any attended these excursions, is unknown, but his hallucination adhered to him like the fabled shirt of Nesus, and had entire control over his mental character. The admonition of his neighbors, the members of his church, and the importunities of his family, had no impression on his wayward spirit.

There had lived a few years previous to this date, in the vicinity of Great Bend, a poor man named Joseph Smith, who with his family had removed to the western part of the State, and lived in squalid poverty near Palmyra, in Ontario County.[14] Mr. Stowell, while at Lanesboro, heard of the fame of one of his sons, named Joseph, who by the aid of a magic stone had become a famous seer of lost or hidden treasures.[15] These stories were fully received into his credulous mind, and kindled into a blaze his cherished hallucination. Visions of untold wealth appeared through this instrumentality, to his longing eyes. He harnessed his team, and filled his wagon with provisions for "man and beast," and started for the residence of the Smith family. In due time he arrived at the humble log-cabin, midway between Canandaigua and Palmyra, and found the sought for treasure in the person of Joseph Smith, Jr., a lad of some eighteen [twenty] years of age. He, with the magic stone, was at once transferred from his humble abode to the more pretentious mansion of Deacon Stowell. Here, in the estimation of the Deacon, he confirmed his conceded powers as a seer, by means of the stone which he placed in his hat, and by excluding the light from all other terrestrial things, could see whatever he wished, even in the depths of the earth. This omniscient attribute he firmly claimed. Deacon Stowell and others as firmly believed it. Mr. Stowell, with his ward and two hired men, who were, or professed to be, believers, spent much time in mining near the State line on the Susquehanna and many other places. I myself have seen the evidences of their nocturnal depredations on the face of Mother Earth, on the Deacon's farm, with what success "this deponent saith not."

In February, 1826, the sons of Mr. Stowell, who lived with their father, were greatly incensed against Smith, as they plainly saw their father squandering his property in the fruitless search for hidden treasures, and saw that the youthful seer had unlimited control over the illusions of their sire. They made up their minds that "patience had ceased to be a virtue," and resolved to rid themselves and their family from this incubus, who, as they believed, was eating up their substance, and depriving them of their anticipated patrimony. They caused the arrest of Smith as a vagrant, without visible means of livelihood. The trial came on in the above mentioned month, before Albert Neeley, Esq.,[16] the father of Bishop [Henry Adams] Neeley, of the State of Maine. I was an intimate friend of the Justice, and was invited to take notes of the trial, which I did.[17] There was a large collection of persons in attendance, and the proceedings attracted much attention.

The affidavits of the sons were read, and Mr. Smith was fully examined by the Court. It elicited little but a history of his life from early boyhood, but this was so unique in character, and so much of a key-note to his subsequent career in the world, I am tempted to give it somewhat *in extenso*. He said when he was a lad, he heard of a neighboring girl some three miles from him, who could look into a glass and see anything however hidden from others, that he was seized with a strong desire to see her and her glass, that after much effort he induced his parents to let him visit her. He did so, and was permitted to look in the glass, which was placed in a hat to exclude the light. He was greatly surprised to see but one thing, which was a small stone, a great way off. It soon became luminous, and dazzled his eyes, and after a short time it became as intense as the mid-day sun. He said that the stone was under the roots of a tree or shrub as large as his arm, situated about a mile up a small stream that puts in on the South side of Lake Erie, not far from the New York and Pennsylvania line. He often had an opportunity to look in the glass, and with the same result. The luminous stone alone attracted his attention. This singular circumstance occupied his mind for some years, when he left his father's house, and with his youthful zeal traveled west in search of this luminous stone.

He took a few shillings in money and some provisions with him. He stopped on the road with a farmer, and worked three days, and replenished his means of support. After traveling some one hundred and fifty miles he found himself at the mouth of the creek. He did not have the glass with him, but he knew its exact location. He borrowed an old ax and hoe, and repaired to the tree. With some labor and exertion he found the stone, carried it to the creek, washed and wiped it dry, sat down on the bank, placed it in his hat, and discovered that time, place, and distance were annihilated; that all intervening obstacles were removed, and that he possessed one of the attributes of Deity, an All-Seeing Eye. He arose with a thankful heart, carried his tools to their owner, turned his feet towards the rising sun, and sought with weary limbs his long deserted home.

On the request of the Court, he exhibited the stone. It was about the size of a small hen's egg, in the shape of a high-instepped shoe. It was composed of layers of different colors passing diagonally through it. It was very hard and smooth, perhaps by being carried in the pocket.

Joseph Smith, Sr., was present, and sworn as a witness. He confirmed at great length all that his son had said in his examination.[18] He delineated his characteristics in his youthful days—his vision of the luminous stone in the glass—his visit to Lake Erie in search of the stone—and his wonderful triumphs as a seer. He described very many instances of his finding hidden and stolen goods. He swore that both he and his son were mortified that this wonderful power which God had so miraculously given him should be used only in search of filthy lucre, or its equivalent in earthly treasures, and with a long-faced, sanctimonious seeming, he said his constant prayer to his Heavenly Father was to manifest His will concerning this marvelous power. He trusted that the son of Righteousness would some day illumine the heart of the boy, and enable him to see His will concerning him. These words have ever had a strong impression on my mind. They seemed to contain a prophetic vision of the future history of that mighty delusion of the present century, Mormonism. The "old man eloquent" with his lank and haggard visage—his form very poorly clad—indicating a wandering vagabond rather than an oracle of future events, has, in view of those events, excited my wonder, if not my admiration.

The next witness called was Deacon Isaiah [Josiah] Stowell. He confirmed all that is said above in relation to himself, and delineated many other circumstances not necessary to accord. He swore that the prisoner possessed all the power he claimed, and declared he could see things fifty feet below the surface of the earth, as plain as the witness could see what was on the Justice's table, and described very many circumstances to confirm his words. Justice Neeley soberly looked at the witness, and in a solemn, dignified voice said, "Deacon Stowell, do I understand you as swearing before God, under the solemn oath you have taken, that you *believe* the prisoner can see by the aid of the stone fifty feet below the surface of the earth, as plainly as you can see what is on my table?" "Do I *believe* it?" says Deacon Stowell, "do I believe it? no, it is not a matter of belief. I positively know it to be true."

Mr. Thompson, an employee of Mr. Stowell, was the next witness. He and another man were employed in digging for treasure, and always attended the Deacon and Smith in their nocturnal labors. He could not assert that anything of value was ever obtained by them. The following scene was described by this witness, and carefully noted: Smith had told the Deacon that very many years before a band of robbers had buried on his flat a box of treasure, and as it was very valuable they had by a sacrifice placed a charm over it to protect it, so that it could not be obtained except by faith, accompanied by certain talismanic influences. So, after arming themselves with fasting and prayer, they sallied forth to the spot designated by Smith. Digging was commenced with fear and trembling, in the presence of this imaginary charm. In a few feet from the surface the box of treasure was struck by the shovel, on which they redoubled their energies, but it gradually receded from their grasp. One of the men placed his hand upon the box, but it gradually sunk from his reach. After some five feet in depth had been attained without success, a council of war against this spirit of darkness was called, and they resolved that the lack of faith, or of some untoward mental emotion, was the cause of their failure.

In this emergency the fruitful mind of Smith was called on to devise a way to obtain the prize. Mr. Stowell went to his flock and selected a fine vigorous lamb, and resolved to sacrifice it to the demon spirit who guarded the coveted treasure. Shortly after the venerable Deacon might be seen on his knees at prayer near the pit, while Smith, with a beacon in one hand to dispel the midnight darkness might be seen making a circuit around the spot, sprinkling the flowing blood from the lamb upon the ground, as a propitiation to the spirit that thwarted them. They then descended the excavation, but the treasure still receded from their grasp, and it was never obtained.

What a picture for the pencil of Hogarth! How difficult to believe it could have been enacted in the nineteenth century of the Christian era! It could have been done only by the hallucination of diseased minds, that drew all their philosophy from the Arabian nights and other kindred literature of that period! But as it was declared under oath, in a Court of Justice, by one of the actors in the scene, and not disputed by his co-laborers it is worthy of recital as evincing the spirit of delusion that characterized those who originated that prince of humbugs, Mormonism.

These scenes occurred some four years before Smith, by the aid of his luminious stone, found [published] the Golden Bible, or the Book of Mormon. The writer may at some subsequent day give your readers a chapter on its discovery, and a synopsis of its contents.[19] It is hardly necessary to say that, as the testimony of Deacon Stowell could not be impeached, the prisoner was discharged,[20] and in a few weeks he left the town.

Greene, April 28, 1877.

A Contemporary Account of the Trial

The following letter is the earliest printed reference to the 1826 trial that has so far come to light. No files of Chenango County newspapers for March and April 1826 are known to exist, and it may be that proceedings before a mere justice's court in any event would not, in a town which itself had no newspaper, have been found worthy of an editor's attention. No more nearly contemporary printed reference to the trial than this now reprinted may ever be found.

The letter is the more interesting for its bearing on the admission made by Oliver Cowdery in 1835 that Joseph Smith had indeed been hauled before a magistrate's court in Chenango County during the period of his association with Josiah Stowell, and before he claimed to have come into possession of the golden plates. Cowdery wrote: "While in that country, some very officious person complained of him [Joseph] as a disorderly person, and brought him before the authorities of the county; but there being no cause for action he was honorably acquitted." It can hardly be argued again that Cowdery had reference to an entirely different affair of which there is no other record. Though the outcome of the trial may be disputed, the fact of its having been held, and the nature of the proceedings, will now doubtless be accepted.

The letter under discussion was published in a Universalist weekly, the *Evangelical Magazine and Gospel Advocate*, April 9, 1831, vol. 2, p. 120. This periodical, which was published at Utica, New York, on February 5, 1831, had printed a caustic account of the Book of Mormon which called forth the present letter. The writer signed it only by his initials, "A. W. B.," but his identity is established in the *Magazine and Advocate* for 1834, which publishes three communications on temperance dated South Bainbridge and signed "A. W. Benton." Further details about him are to be had from Smith's *History of Chenango and Madison Counties*, p. 144, where it is noted, "Abraham Benton, brother of Orange Benton, studied medicine with Dr. Boynton at Bettsburgh and settled in the village on the east side of the river, where he practiced several years nearly fifty years ago. He sold out in 1837 to Elam Bartlett and removed to Illinois." His views on temperance were also recalled.

In Joseph Smith's account of the trials to which he was admittedly subjected in Chenango County in 1830, he makes reference to "a young man named Benton" who "swore out the first warrant against me" (*History of the Church*, 1:97). This may more likely have been Orange than Abraham Benton, as the author of the present was clearly a Universalist, whereas Joseph Smith declares the other Benton to have been of the Presbyterian faith.

For the Evangelical Magazine and Gospel Advocate.

MORMONITES

Messrs. Editors—In the sixth number of your paper I saw a notice of a sect of people called Mormonites; and thinking that a fullller history of their founder, Joseph Smith, jr., might be interesting to community, and particularly to your correspondent in Ohio, where, perhaps, the truth concerning him may be hard to come at, I will take the trouble to make a few remarks on the character of that infamous imposter. For several years preceding the appearance of his book, he was about the country in the character of a glass-looker: pretending, by means of a certain stone, or glass, which he put in a hat, to be able to discover lost goods, hidden treasures, mines of gold and silver, &c. Although he constantly failed in his pretensions, still he had his dupes who put implicit confidence in all his words. In this town, a wealthy farmer, named Josiah Stowell, together with others, spent large sums of money in digging for hidden money, which this Smith pretended he could see, and told them where to dig; but they never found their treasure. At length the public, becoming wearied with the base imposition which he was palming upon the credulity of the ignorant, for the purpose of sponging his living from their earnings, had him arrested as a disorderly person, tried and condemned before a court of Justice. But considering his youth, (he being then a minor,) and thinking he might reform his conduct, he was designedly allowed to escape.[21] This was four or five years ago. From this time he absented himself from this place, returning only privately, and holding clandestine intercourse with his credulous dupes, for two or three years.

It was during this time, and probably by the help of others more skilled in the ways of iniquity than himself, that he formed the blasphemous design of forging a new revelation, which, backed by the terrors of an endless hell, and the testimony of base unprincipled men, he hoped would frighten the ignorant, and open a field of speculation for the vicious,[22] so that he might secure to himself the scandalous honor of being the founder of a new sect, which might rival, perhaps, the Wilkinsonians, or the French Prophets of the 17th century.

During the past Summer he was frequently in this vicinity, and others of baser sort, as Cowdry, Whitmer, etc., holding meetings, and proselyting a few weak and silly women, and still more silly men, whose minds are shrouded in a mist of ignorance which no ray can penetrate, and whose credulity the utmost absurdity cannot equal.

In order to check the progress of delusion, and open the eyes and understandings of those who blindly followed him, and unmask the turpitude and villa[i]ny of those who knowingly abetted him in his infamous designs; he was again arraigned before a bar of Justice, during last Summer, to answer to a charge of misdemeanor. This trial led to an investigation of his character and conduct, which clearly evinced to the unprejudiced, whence the spirit came which dictated his inspirations. During the trial it was shown that the Book of Mormon was brought to light by the same magic power by which he pretended to tell fortunes, discover hidden treasures, &c. Oliver Cowdery, one of the three witnesses to the book, testified under oath, that said Smith found with the plates, from which he translated his book, two transparent stones, resembling glass, set in silver bows. That by looking through these, he was able to read in English, the reformed Egyptian characters, which were engraved on the plates.

So much for the gift and power of God, by which Smith says he translated his book. Two transparent stones, undoubtedly of the same properties, and the gift of the same spirit as the one in which he looked to find his neighbor's goods. It is reported, and probably true, that he commenced his juggling by stealing and hiding property belonging to his neighbors, and when inquiry was made, he would look in his stone, (his gift and power) and tell where it was. Josiah Stowell, a Mormonite, being sworn, testified that he positively knew that said Smith never had lied to, or deceived him, and did not believe he ever tried to deceive any body else. The following questions were then asked him, to which he made the replies annexed.

Did Smith ever tell you there was money hid in a certain glass which he mentioned? Yes. Did he tell you, you could find it by digging? Yes. Did you dig? Yes. Did you find any money? No. Did he not lie to you then, and deceive you? No! the money was there, but we did not get quite to it! How do you know it was there? Smith said it was! Addison Austin was next called upon, who testified, that at the very same time that Stowell was digging for money, he, Austin, was in company with said Smith alone, and asked him to tell him honestly whether he could see this money or not. Smith hesitated some time, but finally replied, "to be candid, between you and me, I cannot, any more than you or any body else; but any way to get a living." Here, then, we have his own confession, that he was a vile, dishonest impostor. As regards the testimony of Josiah Stowell, it needs no comment. He swears positively that Smith did *not* lie to him. So much for a Mormon witness. Paramount to this, in truth and consistency, was the testimony of Joseph Knight, another Mormonite. Newell Knight, son of the former, and also a Mormonite, testified, under oath, that he positively had a devil cast out of himself by the instrumentality of Joseph Smith, jr., and that he saw the devil after it was out, but could not tell how it looked!

Those who have joined them in this place, are, without exception, children who are frightened into the measure, or ignorant adults, whose love for the marvellous is equalled by nothing but their entire devotedness to the will of their leader; with a few who are as destitute of virtue and moral honesty, as they are of truth and consistency. As for his book, it is only the counterpart of his money-digging plan. Fearing the penalty of the law, and wishing still to amuse his followers, he fled for safety to the sanctuary of pretended religion.

A. W. B.
S. Bainbridge, Chen., co., March, 1831.

[Editor's note: The contemporary documentation for the 1826 trial which eluded Dale Morgan—a bill of costs and a writ of mittimus—was unearthed in the early 1970s by Wesley P. Walters and is discussed at some length in Marvin S. Hill, "Joseph Smith and the 1826 Trial: New Evidence and New Difficulties," *Brigham Young University Studies*, Winter 1972.]

APPENDIX B

The Evolution of Claims Concerning the Origin of Joseph Smith's Church

The documents printed in whole or in part below are designed primarily to exhibit the ideas concerning the origins of the Mormon church held by Joseph Smith, his followers, and those who rejected his claims before 1835. These documents are both pro and con in character, but two things in particular they share: their undoubted contemporaneity and their entire lack of information that Joseph Smith had a visitation in 1820 from the Father and the Son.

Just about in this particular region, for some time past, much speculation has existed, concerning a pretended discovery, through superhuman means, of an ancient record, of a religious and divine nature and origin, written in ancient characters, impossible to be interpreted by any to whom the special gift has not been imparted by inspiration. It is generally known and spoken of as the "*Golden Bible*." Most people entertain an idea that the whole matter is the result of a gross imposition, and a grosser superstition. It is pretended that it will be published as soon as the translation is completed. Meanwhile we have been furnished with the following, which is represented to us as intended for the titlepage of the work—we give it as a curiosity: * * *

[Palmyra, New York, *Wayne Sentinel*, 26 June 1829.]

"GOLDEN BIBLE"

The Palmyra Freeman says—The greatest piece of superstition that has come within our knowledge, now occupies the attention of a few individuals of this quarter. It is generally known and spoken of as the "*Golden Bible*." Its proselytes give the following account of it. In the fall of 1827, a person by the name of *Joseph Smith*, of Manchester, Ontario county, reported that he had been visited in a dream by the spirit of the Almighty, and informed that in a certain hill in that town, was deposited the golden Bible, containing an ancient record of a divine nature and origin. After having been thrice thus visited, as he states, he proceeded to the spot, and after penetrating "mother earth" a short distance the Bible was found, together with a huge pair of Spectacles! He had been directed, however, not to let any mortal being examine them, "under no less penalty than instant death." They were therefore, nicely wrapped up and excluded from the "vulgar gaze of poor wicked mortals!" It was said that the *leaves* of the Bible were *plates* of gold, about eight inches thick, on which were engraved characters or Hyeroglyphics. By placing the spectacles in a hat, and looking into it, Smith could (he said so, at least) interpret these characters.

An account of this discovery was soon circulated. The subject was almost invariably as it should have been—with *contempt*. A few, however, believed the "*golden*" story, among whom was *Martin Harris*, an honest and industrious farmer of this town, (Palmyra). So blindly credulous was Harris, that he took some of the characters interpreted by Smith and went in search of some one, besides the interpreter, who was learned enough to *English* them; but all to whom he applied (among the number was a Professor Mitchell of New York,) happened not to be possessed of sufficient knowledge to give satisfaction! Harris returned and set Smith to work at interpreting the Bible. He has at length performed the task, and the work is soon to be put to press in Palmyra. Its language and doctrine are said to be far superior to those of the Book of life!!!

[Rochester, New York, *Advertiser and Telegraph*, 31 Aug. 1829. A summary of the same story appears in the Rochester *Gem*, 5 Sept. 1829.]

A fellow by the name of Joseph Smith, who resides in the upper part of Susquehanna county, has been, for the last two years we are told, employed in dedicating [dictating] as he says, by inspiration, a new bible. He pretended that he had been entrusted by God with a golden bible which had been always hidden from the world. Smith would put his face into a hat in which he had a *white stone*, and pretend to read from it, while his coadjutor transcribed. The book purports to give an account of the "Ten Tribes" and strange as it may seem, there are some who have full faith in his Divine commission. The book it seems is now published. * * *

[*Cincinnati Advertiser and Ohio Phoenix*, 8 June 1830, quoting the Bethany, Pennsylvania, *Wayne County Inquirer*.]

Revelation to Joseph Smith, given in Fayette, New York, June 1830. . . . After that it truly was manifested unto this first elder, that he had received a remission of his sins, he was entangled again in the vanities of the world;

But after truly repenting, God ministered unto him by an holy angel, whose contenance was as lightning, and whose garments were pure and white above all whiteness, and gave unto him commandments which inspired him from on high, and gave unto him power, by the means which were before prepared, that he should translate a book;

Which book contained a record of a fallen people, and also the fulness of the gospel of Jesus Christ to the Gentiles;

And also to the Jews, proving unto them, that the holy scriptures are true;

And also, that God doth inspire men and call them to his holy work, in these last days as well as in days of old, that he might be the same God forever. * * *

[Book of Commandments, Zion, 1833, Chapter 24. Text previously printed in Painesville, Ohio, *Telegraph*, 19 April 1831, and in *Evening and Morning Star*, June 1832 and again in June 1833.]

THE BOOK OF MORMON

Mr. Editor,—I have lately spent between two and three days examining a book of an extraordinary character, bearing the above title, which was lately brought from the state of New York, and is much talked of in some parts of the county of Windham, where it is circulating. I feel inclined to give a short account of it to such of your readers, as may not have opportunity of seeing it. It was printed at Palmyra, contains near six hundred pages, and claims to be divine inspiration, or written by men who had frequent interviews with God & angels. It is stated to have been written in the Egyptian language, on plates of gold, and to have been found in the town of Manchester, and county of Ontario, in a box of stones well cemented together, and buried in the earth, where it must have lain, according to things said in the book ever since A.D. 420. Joseph Smith Jr. found it, and he translated it, not from any knowledge of the language on the plates, but by means of two stones or glasses found with it in the box, which give light, and exhibit objects, when looked into in the dark. Eight persons testify, in a certificate appended to the book, that they have seen the plates, which have the appearance of gold, and are of curious workmanship;— and three more testify, in another certificate, that God showed them the plates, by an angel descending from heaven for the purpose. Thus all either express, or appear to have full confidence in the truth of the book. [There follows a long summary and critical analysis of the contents of the volume.] I am at a loss to determine whether the book originated from speculation only, or from fanaticism, or from both. I am credibly informed, that a church has been formed at the westward, on the plan of this book. If this is true, it may furnish a new denomination in religion.

CLERICUS.

[*Brattleboro' (Vermont) Messenger*, 30 Oct. 1830.]

COMMUNICATION

Mr. Editor.–I have gotten some additional information respecting the Book of Mormon, which I send you for insertion in your paper, if you see fit. It is contained in an extract, which I have just taken from a letter written from a town in the State of New York, where, as I had been previously told, this Jos. Smith had resided some years, and from which he set out, with an attendant, in pursuit of the gold plates, which he found, as they say, about one hundred and fifty miles from the place of starting. The letter is dated Oct. 18th, 1830, and the extract is as follows:

"You have probably heard of the Gold Bible taken from the earth by Joseph, the money-digger. This he has translated from the Egyptian reformed language to English, by a pair of stone spectacles (provided by an angel) and a dark hat before his eyes. The books have been printed, and J. S. [Josiah Stowell?] and Mr. N–s are engaged in peddling the same. The society are increasing. Eighteen have been baptized in a day. H. P. [Hezekiah Peck?] and wife have been baptized, & are very strong in the faith. The girls are under conviction. The leaders pretend to cast out devils and work miracles, heal the sick, &c. We have seen none of their miracles here, except N. N. [Newel Knight] I heard say in meeting, that he had had the devil cast out."

I just add, that I have been almost in contact with these peddlers in different parts of this county, having my information from them only through most credible second hand informers, who state that they said, they know the book, and the manner in which it is said to have been found, was true; or that they did not believe it, but *knew* it. They are said to be respectable men. The wife of one of them, though immersed formerly by an Elder in this county, has been immersed or baptized again into this new system. I only state facts, and leave the judicious and pious to their own reflections.

CLERICUS.

[*Brattleboro' Messenger*, 20 Nov. 1830.]

The Golden Bible.—Some two or three years since, an account was given in the papers, of a book purporting to contain new revelations from Heaven, having been dug out of the ground, in Manchester in Ontario Co. N. Y. The book, it seems, has made its appearance in this vicinity.—It contains about 600 octave pages, which is said to be translated from Egyptian Hieroglyphics, on metal plates, by one Smith, who was enabled to read the characters by instruction from Angels. About two weeks since some persons came along here with the book, one of whom pretends to have seen Angels, and assisted in translating the plates. He proclaims destruction upon the world within a few years,—holds forth that the ordinances of the gospel, have not been regularly administered since the days of the Apostles, till the said Smith and himself commenced the work —and many other marvelous things too numerous to mention. * * * The name of the person here, who pretends to have a divine mission, and to have seen and conversed with Angels, is *Cowdray.* * * *

[*Painesville, Ohio, Telegraph*, 16 Nov. 1830.]

DELUSION.

About a couple of weeks since, three men, calling themselves Oliver Cowdry, David Whitmer and Martin Harris, appeared in our village, laden with a new revelation, which they claim to be a codicil to the New Testament. * * *

The account which they give is substantially as follows:—at a recent period an angel appeared to a poor ignorant man residing in or near Palmyra in Ontario County in the State of New York, directed him to open the earth at a place designated, where he would find the new revelation engraved on plates of metal. In obedience to the celestial messenger, Smith repaired to the spot, and on opening the ground discovered an oblong stone box tightly closed with cement. He opened the sacred depository and found enclosed a bundle of plates resembling gold, carefully united at one edge with three silver wires so that they opened like a book. The plates were about 7 inches long and 6 broad, and the whole pile was about 6 inches deep, each plate about the thickness of tin. They were engraved in a character unintelligible to the learned men of the United States, to many of whom it is said they have been presented. The angel afterwards appeared to the three individuals, and showed them the plates. To Smith was given to translate the character[s] which he was enabled to do by looking through two semi-transparent stones, but as he was ignorant of the art of writing, Cowdry and the others wrote as Smith interpreted. They say that part of the plates escaped from them in a supernatural manner and are to be again revealed when the events of the time shall require them. * * *

[New York *Morning Courier and New-York Enquirer*, 7 Dec. 1830, quoting the Painesville, Ohio, *Geauga Gazette*, ca. 23 Nov. 1830.]

"THE GOLDEN BIBLE."—Yes, reader, strange as it may appear, there is a new Bible just published, entitled the "Book of Mormon," and better known to some as the Golden Bible. * * * We have lately purchased one for the gratification of our curiosity, which was rather excited on learning that its doctrines were taught and believed in this and the adjoining counties.

We have not read it in course, but have perused it sufficiently to be convinced that it is one of the veriest impositions of the day. * * *

This Bible is closed by two certificates commending the work; to the first is attached the name of Oliver Cowdry and two other persons, and to the last are 8 names, among which are those of the father and two brothers of the reputed author.

On reading the name of Oliver Cowdry, in support of the divine authenticity of the work, whatever faith we might have been inspired with on reading the certificate, was banished, for we had known Cowdry some seven or 8 years ago, when he was a dabbler in the art of Printing, and principally occupied in writing and printing pamphlets, with which, as a pedestrian pedlar, he visited the towns and villages of western N. York, and Canada, and the only opinion we have of the origin of this Golden Bible, is that Mr. Cowdry and Mr. Smith the reputed author, have taken the old Bible to keep up a train of circumstances, and by altering names and language, have produced the string of jargon called the "Book of Mormon," with the intention of making money by the sale of their books; and being aware that they would not sell unless an excitement and curiosity could be raised in the public mind, have therefore sent out twleve Apostles to promulgate its doctrines. * * *

[*Ashtabula (Ohio) Journal*, 4 Dec. 1830, quoting the *Cleveland Herald*.]

THE GOLDEN BIBLE.

In the fall of 1827, a man named *Joseph Smith* of Manchester, Ontario county, N. Y. reported that he had three times been visited in a dream, by the spirit of the Almighty, and informed that in a certain hill in that town, was a Golden Bible, containing an ancient record of a divine nature and origin. On going to the spot he found buried the Bible with a huge pair of spectacles: The leaves (he said, tho' he was not permitted to show them) were plates of gold, about 8 inches long, 6 wide, and 1/8th of an inch thick, on which were engraved characters or hieroglyphicks, which with the spectacles he could interpret. Martin Harris an industrious farmer, caught the contagion, took some of the characters to different learned men to translate, but without success. He returned, set Smith to work at translating it, and has had it printed. * * *

[Ravenne *Ohio Star*, 9 Dec. 1830.]

Farmington, Ont. co. Jan. 1, 1831.

Mr. EDITOR–

I observe by the public prints, that this most clumsy of all impositions, known among us as Jo Smith's "Gold Bible," is beginning to excite curiosity abroad, from the novelty of its appearance, and the assurance of its advocates, who in imitation of too many of our religious sects, who have gone before them, very charitably (at least in this region) threaten all who have the hardihood to refuse to subscribe to their rhapsodies, with "dire damnation."

The two papers published in your village, for reasons easily explained,[1] decline at present, throwing any light on this subject. To you, and you alone, do we look for an expose of the principal facts and characters, as connected with this singular business; I say singular, because it was hardly to be expected, that a *mimicry*, like the one in question, should have been gotten up at so late a period, and among a people, *professing* to be enlightened.

It is not from a persecuting spirit, that I solicit an exposure, or my maxim is that "error is never dangerous, where truth is free to combat it," and that liberty of conscience in matters of religion, should be allowed to all. Among the bundle of papers herewith sent to you for inspection, you will find little else, than a dry statement of facts, without much reference to time or order; you will perceive that I have attempted to throw all the light I could upon the "money digging mania," which formerly pervaded this, and many other countries, which eventuated in the discovery of Jo Smith's "Golden Treasure."

For your knowledge of ancient & modern history, by which you will be enabled to relieve the dryness of the subject, by bringing before the public parallel cases, there can be no doubt that much useful information may result from your labors. I shall from time to time, send you such information as I may collect on this piece of legerdemain.

Yours, &c.
PLAIN TRUTH

[Palmyra *Reflector*, 6 Jan. 1831.]

GOLD BIBLE.—We have long been waiting, with considerable anxiety, to see some of our contemporaries attempt to explain the immediate causes, which produced that anomaly in religion and literature, which has most strikingly excited the curiosity of our friends at a distance, generally known under the cognomen of the Book of Mormon, or the Gold Bible.

The few notices heretofore given in the public prints, are quite vague and uncertain, and throw but a faint light on the subjects. While some have evinced a spirit of rancor, without giving the *why* and *wherefores*; others have attached an ominous consequence to this transaction, which may have a tendency to mislead the ignorant.

It is our intention, so far as in us lies, to give, in accordance with the wishes of our friend "Plain Truth," . . . a plain and unvarnished statement of facts, so far as they may come to our knowledge, which may, in our opinion, be considered as having any connection with the origin, rise, and progress of the book in question; so that our readers may not only judge of this, but of *some* other matters for themselves. * * *

[Palmyra *Reflector*, 6 Jan. 1931.]

[Lucy Mack Smith to Solomon Mack and wife, Waterloo, New York, 6 Jan. 1831:]

Dear Brother and Sister:

Although we are at a great distance from each other and have not had the pleasure of seeing each other for many years, yet I feel a great anxiety in your welfare, and especially for the welfare of your souls; and you yourselves must know that it is a thing of greatest importance to be prepared to meet our God in peace, for it is not long before He is to make His appearance on the earth with all the hosts of heaven to take vengeance on the wicked and they that know not God. By searching the prophecies contained in the Old Testament we find it there prophesied that God will set His hand the second time to recover His people the house of Israel. He has now commenced this work; He hath sent forth a revelation in these last days, and this revelation is called the Book of Mormon. * * *

Perhaps you will inquire how this revelation came forth. It has been hid up in the earth fourteen hundred years, and was placed there by Moroni, one of the Nephites; it was engraven upon plates which have the appearance of gold. . . . he hid them up in the earth, having obtained a promise of the Lord that they should come forth in His own due time unto the world; and I feel to thank my God that He hath spared my life to see this day.

Joseph, after repenting of his sins and humbling himself before God, was visited by an holy angel whose countenance was as lightening and whose garments were white above all whiteness, who gave unto him commandments which inspired him from on high; and who gave unto him, by the means of which was before prepared, that he should translate this book. And by reading this our eyes are opened that we can see the situation in which the world now stands; that the eyes of the whole world are blinded; that the churches have all become corrupted, yea every church upon the face of the earth; that the Gospel of Christ is nowhere preached. This is the situation which the world is now in, and you can judge for yourselves if we did not need something more than the wisdom of man to show us the right way.

God, seeing our situation, had compassion upon us, and has sent us this revelation that the stumbling block might be removed, that whomsoever would might enter. He now established His Church upon the earth as it was in the days of the Apostles. * * * I want you to think seriously of these things, for they are the truths of the living God.

Please to accept this from your sister,

LUCY SMITH.

[Ben E. Rich, *Scrap Book of Mormon Literature*, Chicago, 190-, 1:543-45.]

[W. W. Phelps to E. D. Howe, Canandaigua, New York, 15 Jan. 1831:]

DEAR SIR—Yours of the 11th, is before me, but to give you a satisfactory answer, is out of my power. To be sure, I am acquainted with a number of the persons concerned in the publication, called the "*Book of Mormon.*"—Joseph Smith is a person of very limited abilities in common learning—but his knowledge of *divine things*, since the appearance of his book, has astonished many. Mr. Harris, whose name is in the book, is a wealthy farmer, but of small literary acquirements; he is honest, and sincerely declares upon his soul's salvation that the book is true, and was interpreted by Joseph Smith, through a pair of silver spectacles, found with the plates. The places where they dug for the plates, in Manchester, are to be seen. When the plates were said to have been found, a copy of one or two lines of the characters, were taken by Mr. Harris to Utica, Albany and New York; at New York, they were shown to Dr. Mitchell, and he referred to professor Anthon who translated and declared them to be the ancient short-hand Egyptian. So much is true. The family of the Smiths is poor, and generally ignorant in common learning. * * *

Jo Smith, junior, according to the best information we can obtain on this subject, was born in the State of Vermont. His father emigrated to this county (Ontario county, N. Y.) about the year 1815, and located his family in the village of Palmyra. The age of this modern prophet is supposed to be about 24 years. In his person he is tall and slender—*thin favored*—having but little expression of countenance, other than that of dulness; his mental powers appear to be extremely limited, and from the small opportunity he has had at school, he made little or no proficiency, and it is asserted by one of his principle followers, (who also pretends to divine illuminations,) that Jo, even at this day is profoundly ignorant of the meaning of many of the words contained in the Book of Mormon.

Joseph Smith, senior, the father of the personage of whom we are now writing, had by misfortune or otherwise been reduced to extreme poverty before he migrated to Western New-York. His family was large consisting of nine or ten children, among whom Jo junior was the third or fourth in succession. We have never been able to learn that any of the family were ever noted for much else than ignorance and stupidity, to which might be added, so far as it may respect the elder branch, a propensity to superstition and a fondness for every thing *marvelous*.

We have been credibly informed that the mother of the prophet had connected herself with several religious societies before her present illumination; this also was the case with other branches of the family, but how far the father of the prophet, ever advanced in these particulars, we are not precisely informed, it however appears quite certain that the prophet himself never made any serious pretensions to religion until his late pretended revelation.

We are not able to determine whether the elder Smith was ever concerned in moneydigging transactions previous to his emigration from Vermont, or not, but it is a well authenticated fact that soon after his arrival here he evinced a firm belief in the existence of hidden treasures, and that this section of country abounded in them.—He also revived, or in other words propagated the vulgar, yet popular belief that these treasures were held in charge by some *evil* spirit, which was supposed to be either the DEVIL himself, or some one of his most trusty favorites. This opinion however, did not originate by any means with Smith, for we find that the vulgar and ignorant from time immemorial, both in Europe and America, have entertained the same preposterous opinion.

It may not be amiss in this place to mention that the *mania* of money digging soon began rapidly to diffuse itself through many parts of this country; men and women without distinction of age or sex became marvellous wise in the occult sciences, many dreamed, and others saw visions disclosing to them, deep in the bowels of the earth, rich and shining treasures, and to facilitate those *mighty* mining operations, (money was usually if not always sought after in the night time,) divers devices and implements were invented, and although the *spirit* was always able to retain his precious charge, these discomfited as well as deluded beings, would on a succeeding night return to their toil, not in the least doubting that success would eventually attend their labors.

Mineral rods and balls, (as they were called by the imposter who made use of them,) were supposed to be infallible guides to these sources of wealth—"*peep stones*" or pebbles, taken promiscuously from the brook or field, were placed in a hat or other situation excluded from the light, when some *wizard* or *witch* (for these performances were not confined to either sex) applied their eyes, and nearly starting their balls from their sockets, declared they saw all the wonders of nature, including of course, ample stores of silver and gold.

It is more than probable that some of these deluded people, by having their imaginations heated to the highest pitch of excitement, and by straining their eyes until they were suffused with tears, might have, through the medium of some trifling emission of the ray of light, receive imperfect images on the *retina*, when their fancies could create the rest. Be this however as it may, people busied themselves in consulting these blind oracles, while the ground was nightly opened in various places and men who were too lazy or idle to labor for bread in the day time, displayed a zeal and perseverance in this business worthy of a better cause.

[Palmyra *Reflector*, 1 Feb. 1831.]

---

* * * In the commencement, the imposture of the "book of Mormon," had no regular plan or features. At a time when the money digging ardor was somewhat abated, the elder Smith declared that his son Jo had seen the *spirit*, (which he then described as a little old man with a long beard,) and was informed that he (Jo) under *certain* circumstances, eventually should obtain great treasures, and that in due time he (the spirit) would furnish him (Jo) with a book, which would give an account of the Ancient inhabitants (antideluvians,) of this country, and where they had deposited their substance, consisting of costly furniture, &c. at the approach of the great deluge, which had ever since that time remained secure in his (the spirits) charge, in large and spacious *chambers*, in sundry places in this vicinity, and these tidings corresponded precisely with revelations made to, and predictions made by the elder Smith, a number of years before.

The time at length arrived, when young Jo was to receive the book from the hand of the spirit, and he repaired accordingly, alone, and in the night time to the woods in the rear of his father's house (in the town of Manchester about two miles south of this village) and met the spirit as had been appointed. This rogue of a spirit who had baffled all the united efforts of the money diggers, (although they had tried many devices to gain his favor, and at one time sacrificed a barn yard fowl,) intended it would seem to play our prophet a similar trick on this occasion; for no sooner had he delivered the book according to promise, than he made a most desperate attempt, to regain its possession. Our prophet however, like a lad of true metal, stuck to his prize, and attempted to gain his father's dwelling, which it appears, was near at hand. The father being alarmed at the long absence of his son, and probably fearing some trick of the spirit, having known him for many years; sallied forth in quest of the youthful adventurer. He had not however, proceeded far before he fell in with the object of his kind solicitude who appeared to be in the greatest peril. The spirit had become exasperated at the stubborn conduct of the young prophet, in wishing to keep possession of the book, and out of *sheer* spite, raised a whirlwind, which was at that particular juncture, throwing trunks and limbs of trees, about their ears, besides the "elfish sprite" had belabored Jo soundly with blows,—had felled him once to the ground, and bruised him severely in the side. The rescue however, was timely, Jo retained his treasure, and returned to the house with his father, much fatigued and injured. This tale in substance, was told at the time the event was *said* to have happened by both father and son, and is well recollected by many of our citizens. It will be borne in mind that no *divine* interposition had been *dreamed* of at the period.

[Palmyra *Reflector*, 14 Feb. 1831.]

---

* * * It is well known that Jo Smith never pretended to have any communion with angels, until a long period after the *pretended* finding of his book, and that the juggling of himself or father, went no further than the pretended faculty of seeing wonders in a "peep stone," and the occasional interview with the spirit, supposed to have the custody of hidden treasures; and it is also equally well known, that a vagabond fortune-teller by the name of Walters, who then resided in the town of Sodus, and was once commited to the jail of this county for *juggling*, was the constant companion and bosom friend of these money digging imposters.

There remains but little doubt, in the minds of those at all acquainted with these transactions, that Walters, who was sometimes called the conjurer, and was paid three dollars per day for his services by the money diggers in this neighborhood, first suggested to Smith the idea of finding a book. Walters, the better to carry on his own deception with those ignorant & deluded people who employed him, had procured an old copy of Cicero's Orations, in the latin language, out of which he read long and loud to his credulous hearers, uttering at the same time an unintelligible jargon, which he would afterwards pretend to interpret, and explain, as a record of the former inhabitants of America, and a particular account of the numerous situations where they had deposited their treasures previous to their final extirpation.

So far did this impostor carry this diabolical farce, that not long previous to the pretended discovery of the "Book of Mormon," Walters assembled his nightly band of money diggers in the town of Manchester, at a point designated in his magical book, and drawing a circle around the laborers, with the point of an old rusty sword, and using sundry other incantations, for the purpose of propitiating the spirit, absolutely sacrificed a fowl, ("*Rooster*") in the presence of his awe-stricken companions, to the foul spirit, whom ignorance had created, the guardian of hidden wealth; and after *digging* until day-light, his deluded employers retired to their several habitations, fatigued and disappointed.

If the critical reader will examine the "Book of Mormon," he will directly perceive, that in many instances, the style of the Bible, from which it is chiefly copied, has been entirely altered for the worse. In many instances it has been copied *upwards*, without reference to chapter or verse, (taking Jeremiah for an example) and that the old and new Testament, have been promiscuously intermingled, with the simple alteration of names, &c, with some interpolations, which may easily be discovered, by the want of grammatical arrangement. * * *

[Palmyra *Reflector*, 28 Feb. 1831.]

SOMETHING NEW.–THE GOLDEN BIBLE

* * * Some hundreds of the rabble and a few intelligent citizens of the western part of New York and the western [eastern] part of Ohio, have, with the wildest enthusiasm, embraced a feigned revelation purporting to be literally new. From the advocates of this new religion called *Mormonism*, from a letter received from the intelligent Post Master at Palmyra, extracts from Mr. Thomas Campbell's letters and other sources, embracing the subjoined pieces taken from the Telegraph of Painesville, O.: from these different quarters I learn the following particulars. For a long time in the vicinity of Palmyra, there has existed an impression, especially among certain loose classes of society, that treasures of great amount were concealed near the surface of the earth, probably by the Indians, whom they were taught to consider the descendants of the ten lost Israelitish tribes, by the celebrated Jew [M. M. Noah] who a few years since promised to gather Abraham's sons on Grand Island, thus to be made a Paradise. The ignorance and superstition of these fanatics soon conjured up a ghost, who they said was often seen and to whom was committed the care of the precious deposit. This tradition made money diggers of many who had neither intelligence nor industry sufficient to obtain a more reputable livelihood. But they did not succeed and as the money was not dug up, something must be dug up to make money. The plan was laid, doubtless, by some person behind the curtain, who selected suitable tools. One Joseph Smith, a perfect ignoramus, is to be a great prophet of the Lord, the gabled ghost the angel of his presence, a few of the accomplices the apostles or witnesses of the imposition, and, to fill up the measure of their wickedness and the absurdity of their proceedings, the hidden golden treasure, is to be a gold bible and a new revelation. This golden bible consisted of metallic plates six or seven inches square, of the thickness of tin and resembling gold, the surface of which was covered with hieroglyphic characters, unintelligible to Smith, the finder, who could not read English. However, the angel (ghost!) that discovered the plates to him, likewise informed him that he would be inspired to translate the inscriptions without looking at the plates, while an amanuensis would record his infallible reading; all which was accordingly done. But

now the book must be published, the translation of the inscriptions which Smith was authorized to show to no man save a few accomplices, who subscribe a certificate of these pretended facts at the end of the volumes. Truly a wise arrangement! * * *

[Dayton, Ohio, *Evangelical Inquirer*, 7 March 1831.]

We have received the following letter from Palmyra, N. Y. on the subject of Bible impostors. It is signed by ten individuals of the first respectability.

Palmyra, March 12, 1831.

The "gold bible" question excites but little interest in this section of country, its followers being few and generally of the dregs of community, and most unlettered people that can be found anywhere, and besides there is much reason to doubt the sincerity of many of them.

The first idea of a "Book," was doubtless suggested to the Smiths by one Walters, a juggling fortune-teller, who made the ignorant believe that an old book in his possession, in the Latin language, contained an account of the anti-deluvians, &c. and the word was given out that the book Smith has about to find, was a history of hidden treasures.

Smith and his father belonged to a gang of money-diggers, who had followed that business for many years, Jo pretending he could see the gold and silver by the aid of what they called a "*peep stone.*"

The book is chiefly garbled from the Old and New Testaments, the Apocraphy having contributed its share; names and phrases have been altered, and in many instances copied upwards.—A quarto Bible now in this village, was borrowed and nearly worn out and defaced by their dirty handling. Some seven or eight of them spent many months in copying, Cowdery being principal scribe. * * *

The whole gang of these deluded mortals, except a few hypocrites, are profound believers in witchcraft, ghosts, goblins, &c. * * * We have only to add that the facts published in the "Reflector," are true as far as has come to our knowledge.

Yours, &c.

[Painesville, Ohio, *Telegraph*, 22 March 1831.]

There appears to be a great discrepancy, in the stories told by the famous three witnesses to the Gold Bible; and these *pious* reprobates, individually, frequently give different versions of the same transaction. In the first place, it was roundly asserted that the plates on which Mormon wrote his history, (in the *reformed* Egyptian language) were of gold, and hence its name; gentlemen in this vicinity were called on to estimate its value from its weight, (something more than 20 lbs.) Smith and Harris gave out that no mortal save Jo could look upon it and live; and Harris declares, that when he acted as *amanuenses*, and wrote the translation, as Smith dictated, such was his fear of the Divine displeasure, that a screen (sheet) was suspended between the prophet and himself.

Whitmar's description of the Book of Mormon, differs entirely from that given by Harris; both of whom it would seem, have been of late permitted, not only to see and handle it, but to examine its contents. Whitmar relates that he was led by Smith into an open field, on his father's farm near Waterloo, when they found the book lying on the ground; Smith took it up and requested him to examine it, which he did for the space of half an hour or more, when he returned it to Smith, who placed it in its former position, alledging that the book was in the custody of *another*, intimating that some Divine agent would have it in safe keeping.

This *witness* describes the book as being something like 8 inches square; (our informant did not recollect precisely,) the leaves were plates of metal of a *whitish yellow* color, and of the thickness of tin plate; the back was secured with three small rings of the same metal, passing through each leaf in succession;—that the leaves were divided equidistant, between the back & edge, by cutting the plates in two parts, and united again with *solder*, so that the front might be opened, as it were by a hinge, while the back part remained stationary and immoveable, and in this manner remained to him and the other witnesses a *sealed book*, which would not be revealed for ages to come, and that even the prophet himself was not as yet permitted to understand. On opening that portion of the book which was not secured by the *seals*, he discovered inscribed on the aforesaid plates, divers and wonderful *characters*; some of them large and some small, but beyond the wisdom of man to understand without supernatural aid.

Some of the other apostles give somewhat similar accounts, but varying in many particulars, according to their various powers of description.—Harris however gives the lie to a very important part of Whitmar's relation, and declares that the leaves or pages of the book are not cut, and a part of them sealed, but that it opens like any other book, from the edge to the back, the rings operating in the place of common binding.

As these details, under different modifications, (for it must be borne in mind, that these Mormonites have given versions of the same particulars,) are pretty well understood in this vicinity, we shall give our distant readers but small portions at a time. We have on hand a new edition of the prophet's vision, at the time the Gold Bible was revealed to him by the Spirit, and the subsequent transactions, as related by JO's father and his elder brother;—also sundry money digging scenes in whch the Smiths acted conspicuous parts, all of which will be given to the public in due time. * * *

[Palmyra *Reflector*, 19 March 1831.]

For a letter written from South Bainbridge, New York, in March 1831 by A. W. Benton, published in the Utica, New York, *Evangelical Magazine and Gospel Advocate*, April 9, 1831, see Appendix A.

MORMONISM. . . .

CANANDAIGUA, Aug. 15th, 1831.

* * * You have heard of MORMONISM—who has not? * * * The individuals who gave birth to this species of fanaticism are very simple personages, and not known until this thrust them into notice. They are the old and the young Joe Smith's, Harris a farmer, Ringdon [Rigdon] a sort of preacher on general religion from Ohio, together with several other persons equally infatuated, cunning, and hypocritic. The first of these persons, Smith, resided on the borders of Wayne and Ontario counties on the road leading from Canandaigua to Palmyra. Old Joe Smith had been a country pedlar in his younger days, and possessed all the shrewdness, cunning, and small intrigue which are generally and justly attributed to that description of persons. He was a great story teller, full of anecdotes picked up in his peregrinations—and possessed a tongue as smooth as oil and as quick as lightning. He had been quite a speculator in a small way in his younger days, but had been more fortunate in picking up materials for his tongue than stuff for the purse. Of late years he had picked up his living somewhere in the town of Manchester by following a branch of the "American system"—the manufacture of gingerbread and such like domestic wares. In this article he was a considerable speculator, having on hand during a fall price no less than two baskets full, and I believe his son Joe Junr., was at times a partner in the concern. What their dividends were I could not learn, but they used considerable molasses, and were against the duty on that article. Young Joe, who afterwards figured so largely in the Mormon religion, was at that period a careless, indolent, idle, and shiftless fellow. He

hung round the villages and strolled round the taverns without any end or aim—without any positive defect or as little merit in his character. He was a rather stout able bodied fellow, and might have made a good living in such a country as this where any one who is willing to work, can soon get on in the world. He was however, the son of a speculative Yankee pedlar, and was brought up to live by his wits. Harris also one of the fathers of Mormonism was a substantial farmer near Palmyra—full of passages of the scriptures—rather wild and flighty in his talk occasionally—but holding a very respectable character in his neighborhood for sobriety, sense and hard working.

A few years ago the Smith's and others who were influenced by their notions, caught an idea that money was hid in several of the hills which give variety to the country between the Canandaigua Lake and Palmyra on the Erie Canal. Old Smith had in his peddling excursions picked up many stories of men getting rich in New England by digging in certain places and stumbling upon chests of money. The fellow excited the imagination of his few auditors, and make them all anxious to lay hold of the bilk axe and the shovel. As yet no fanatical or religious character had been assumed by the Smith's. They exhibited the simple and ordinary desire of getting rich by some short cut if possible. With this view the Smith's and their associates commenced digging, in the numerous hills which diversify the face of the country in the town of Manchester. The sensible country people paid slight attention to them at first. They knew them to be a thriftless set, more addicted to exerting their wits than their industry, readier at inventing stories and tales than attending church or engaging in any industrious trade. On the side & in the slopes of several of these hills, these excavations are still be to be seen. They would occasionally conceal their purposes, and at other times reveal them by such snatches as might excite curiosity. They dug these holes by day, and at night talked and dreamed over the countless riches they should enjoy, if they could only hit upon an iron chest full of dollars. In excavating the grounds, they began by taking up the green sod in the form of a circle of six feet diameter—then would continue to dig to the depth of ten, twenty, and sometimes thirty feet. At last some persons who joined them spoke of a person in Ohio near Painesville, who had a particular felicity in finding out the spots of ground where money is hid and riches obtained. He related long stories how this person had been along shore in the east—how he dreamt of the very spots where it could be found. "Can we get that man here?" asked the enthusiastic Smith. "Why," said the other, "I guess as how we could by going for him." "How far off?" "I guess some two hundred miles—I would go for him myself but I want a little change to bear my expenses." To work the whole money-digging crew went to get some money to pay the expenses of bringing on a man who could dream out the exact and particular spots where money in iron chests was hid under ground. Old Smith returned to his gingerbread factory—young Smith to his financing faculties, and after some time, by hook or by crook, they contrived to scrape together a little "change" sufficient to fetch on the money dreamer from Ohio.[2]

After the lapse of some weeks the expedition was completed, and the famous Ohio man made his appearance among them. This recruit was the most cunning, intelligent, and odd of the whole. He had been a preacher of almost every religion—a teacher of all sorts of morals.—He was perfectly *au fait* with every species of prejudice, folly or fanaticism, which governs the mass of enthusiasts. In the course of his experiments, he had attended all sorts of camp-meetings, prayer meetings, anxious meetings, and revival meetings. He knew every turn of the human mind in relation to these matters. He had a superior knowledge of human nature, considerable talent, great plausibility, and knew how to work the passions as exactly as a Cape Cod sailor know how to work a whale ship. His name I believe is Heny Rangdon or Ringdon, or some such word. About the time that this person appeared among them, a splendid excavation was begun in a long narrow hill, between Manchester and Palmyra.[3] This hill has since been called by some, the *Golden Bible Hill.* The road from Canandagua to Palmyra, runs along its western base. At the northern extremity the hill is quite abrupt and narrow. It runs to the south for a half mile and then spreads out into a piece of broad table land, covered with beautiful orchards and wheat fields. On the east, the Canandaigua outlet runs past it on its way to the beautiful village of Vienna in Phelps. It is profusely covered to the top with Beach, Maple, Bass, and White-wood—the northern extremity is quite bare of trees. In the face of this hill, the money diggers renewed their work with fresh ardour, Ringdon partly uniting with them in their operations.

About this time a very considerable religious excitement came over New York in the shape of a revival. * * * The singular character of the people of western New-York—their originality, activity, and proneness to excitement furnished admirable materials for enthusiasts in religion or roguery to work upon. * * *

It was during this state of feeling in which the money diggers of Ontario county, by the suggestions of the Ex-Preacher from Ohio, thought of turning their digging concerns into a religious plot, and thereby have a better chance of working upon the credulity and ignorance of their associates and the neighborhood. Money and a good living might be got in this way. It was given out that visions had appeared to Joe Smith—that a set of golden plates on which was engraved the "Book of Mormon," enclosed in an iron chest, was deposited somewhere in the hill I have mentioned. People laughed at the first intimation of the story, but the Smiths and Rangdon persisted in its truth. They began also to talk very seriously, to quote scripture, to read the bible, to be contemplative, and to assume that grave studied character, which so easily imposes on ignorant and superstitious people. Hints were given out that young Joe smith was the chosen one of God to reveal this new mystery to the world; and Joe from being an idle young fellow, lounging about the village, jumped up into a very grave personlike man, who felt he had on his shoulders the salvation of the world, besides a respectable looking sort of blackcoat. Old Joe, the ex-preacher, and several others, were the believers of the new faith, which they admitted was an improvement on christianity, foretold word or words in the bible. They treated their own invention with the utmost religious respect. By the special interposition of God, the golden plates on which was engraved the Book of Mormon, and other works, had been buried for ages in the hill by a wandering tribe of the children of Israel, who had found their way to western New York, before the birth of christianity itself. Joe Smith is discovered to be the second Messiah who was to reveal this word to the world and to reform it anew.

In relation to the finding of the plates and the taking the engraving, a number of ridiculous stories are told. Some unsanctified fellow looked out the other side of the hill. They had to follow it with humility and found it embedded beneath a beautiful grove of maples. Smith's wife, who had a little of the curiosity of her sex, peeped into the large chest in which he kept the the engravings taken from the golden plates, and straightway one half of the new bible vanished, and has not been recovered to this day. Such were the effects of the unbelievers on the sacred treasure. There is no doubt but the ex-parson from Ohio is the author of the book. It is full of strange narratives—in the style of the scriptures, and bearing on its face the marks of some ingenuity, and familiar acquaintance with the Bible. It is probable that Joe Smith is well acquainted with the trick, but Harris the farmer and the recent converts, are true believers. Harris was the first man who gave credit to the story of Smith and the ex-preacher. He was their maiden convert—the Ali of the Ontario Mahomet, who believed without a reason and without a murmur. They attempted to get the Book printed, but could not raise the means till Harris stept forward and raised money on his farm for that purpose. Harris with several manuscripts in his pocket, went to the city of New York, and called upon one of the Professors of Columbia College for the purpose of showing them to him. Harris says that the Professor thought them very curious, but admitted that he could not decypher them. Said he to Harris, "Mr. Harris you had better go to the celebrated Doct. Mitchell and show them to him. He is very learned in these ancient languages, and I have no doubt will be able to give you some satisfaction." "Where does he live," asked Harris. He was told, and off he posted with the engravings from the Golden Plates to submit to Doct. Mitchell. Harris says that the Doctor received him very "purlitely," looked at his engravings—made a learned dissertation on them—compared them with the hieroglyphics discovered [by] Champollion in Egypt—and set them down as the language of a people formerly in existence in the East, but now no more.

The object of his going to the city to get the "Book of Mormon" printed, was not however accomplished. He returned with his manuscript or engravings to Palmyra—tried to raise money by mortgage on his farm from the New York Trust Company—did raise the money, but from what source—whether the Trust Company or not I am uncertain. At last a printer in Palmyra undertook to print the translations of Joe Smith, Harris becoming responsible for the expense. They were called translations, but in fact and in truth they are believed to be the work of the ex-Preacher from Ohio, who stood in the back ground and put forward Joe to father the new bible and the new faith. After the publication of the golden bible, they began to make converts rapidly. The revivals and other religious excitements had thrown up material for the foundation of a new sect, they soon found that they had not dug for money in vain—they began to preach—to pray—to see more visions—to prophesy and perform the most fantastic tricks—there was now no difficulty in getting a living and the gingerbread factory was abandoned. They created considerable talk over all this section of the country. * * *

[*Morning Courier & New-York Enquirer*, 31 Aug., 1 Sept. 1831.]

ENDNOTES

CHAPTER ONE

[1]Pomeroy Tucker, *Origin, Rise, and Progress of Mormonism* (New York, 1867), pp. 12-13; Lucy Mack Smith, *Biographical Sketches of Joseph Smith the Prophet and His Progenitors for Many Generations* (Liverpool, 1853), pp. 70, 92.

[2]So Joseph Smith declared in his journal under date of May 17, 1836, *History of the Church*, 2:443. Orasmus Turner, *History of the Pioneer Settlement of Phelps and Gorham's Purchase* (Rochester, 1851), p. 213, indicates that before his death the eldest son, Alvin, was looked upon within the family as most likely to fulfill the expectation.

[3]Smith, *Biographical Sketches*, p. 66; Lewis D. Stilwell, "Migration from Vermont (1776-1880)," *Proceedings of the Vermont Historical Society* 5 (June 1937): 63-245.

[4]Joseph F. Smith, Jr., "Asahel Smith of Topsfield," *Topsfield Historical Collections*, 8 (1902): 87-101; Mary Audentia Smith Anderson, *Ancestry and Posterity of Joseph Smith and Emma Hale* (Independence, Missouri, 1929), pp. 51-75.

[5]Joseph Smith, *History of the Church*, 4: 191.

[6]Smith, *Biographical Sketches*, pp. 45-69. For the period of the Smith residence in Vermont, see also the fresh information developed by Fawn M. Brodie in her biography of Joseph Smith, *No Man Knows My History* (New York, 1945), pp. 1-9.

[7]Turner, *Phelps and Gorham's Purchase*, p. 213; also compare Lucy Smith's account in *Biographical Sketches*, pp. 56-58, 90.

[8]Smith, *Biographical Sketches*, pp. 56-57.

[9]Tucker, *Origin, Rise, and Progress of Mormonism*, pp. 12, 23; Turner, *Phelps and Gorham's Purchase*, pp. 213-14; E. D. Howe, *Mormonism Unvailed* (Painesville, Ohio, 1834), pp. 232-61; John A. Clark, *Gleanings by the Way* (New York, 1842), p. 225; [La]Fayette Lapham, "An Interview with the Father of Joseph Smith Forty Years Ago," *Historical Magazine* 8 (May 1870): 305-309; Frederick G. Mather, "The Early Days of Mormonism," *Lippincott's Magazine*, 26 (Aug. 1880): 198; Palmyra *Reflector*, Feb. 14, 1831; New York *Morning Courier and New-York Enquirer*, Aug. 31, 1831.

[10]Solomon Mack, *A Narraitve [sic] of the life of Solomon Mack. Containing an Account of the Many Severe Accidents He Met with During a Long Series of Years, Together with the Extraordinary Manner in which He Was Converted to the Christian Faith* (Windsor, 1811?); *Historical Magazine* 8 (Nov. 1870): 318.

[11]Smith, *Biographical Sketches*, pp. 21-23, 30-36, 52-54; Anderson, *Joseph Smith and Emma Hale*, pp. 157-66.

[12]See the advertising columns of the *Palmyra Register* from November 26, 1817. This paper, on file in the New York State Library, is indispensable to any study of Mormon beginnings. The paper had various names: *Palmyra Register*, 1817-21; *Western Farmer*, 1821-22; *Palmyra Herald, and Canal Advertiser*, 1822-23; and *Wayne Sentinel* from 1823.

[13]Willard Bean, *A. B. C. History of Palmyra and the Beginning of "Mormonism"* (Palmyra, 1938), p. 19.

[14]Tucker, *Origin, Rise and Progress of Mormonism*, p. 12.

[15]New York *Morning Courier and New York Enquirer*, Aug. 31, 1831, a dispatch written from Canandaigua under date of Aug. 15, 1831. This account has escaped Mormon historians who have reproached Tucker for originating, long afterwards, the "slander" of the cake and beer shop.

[16]Smith, *Biographical Sketches*, p. 70.

[17]No coherent account of their settlement upon and eventual undertaking to purchase their farm was given by any member of the Smith family, most of what is known about it having to be pieced together from the account by Lucy Smith. In dating for 1818 the removal of the Smiths from Palmyra to the farm in Farmington (later Manchester), however, Pomeroy Tucker has been followed. He says that the Smiths arrived in Palmyra from Vermont in the summer (better, perhaps, the fall) of 1816, and that they lived in the village for two and a half years before moving to the farm. Orasmus Turner writes simply that as early as 1819 the Smiths occupied some new land out the Stafford Road, that here he himself remembered first having seen the family "in the winter of '19, '20, in a rude log house, with but a small spot underbrushed around it." Lucy herself is ambiguous about the move, but implies that they undertook to buy the property within a year of their arrival in Palmyra, and within two years were located on the farm, in "a snug log-house neatly furnished." Joseph has said that his family lived in Palmyra "about four years" before moving to Manchester, but the Smiths were certainly living on the farm at the time of the census of 1820, as is shown by the returns for Ontario county in the National Archives. It seems likely that the log house was built during the summer of 1818 and that the Smiths moved in as soon as it was finished.

It is apparent that they squatted upon the property for several years before contracting to buy it, since Lucy reports that Alvin, during the two years before his death on November 19, 1823, played a major part in finding the funds for the first two payments. How desperately poor the Smiths were at this time is suggested by Ontario County reports. Judgments for $79.09 and $115.61 respectively having been obtained against Joseph Smith by Job J. Brooks, and Abner Woodworth, the sheriff sent to execute the judgements, reported back on November 27, 1822, that Smith had "no goods or chattels lands or tenements whereon to levy." After a second effort, on December 20, 1822, the sheriff reported satisfaction of the Brooks judgement, but made the same report as before on the Woodworth judgement. See entries under "S" in Book of "Executions," Ontario County Clerk's Office, Canandaigua, New York. Tucker speaks of the Smiths as having been at first squatters upon their farm, and what is said by him and other residents of Palmyra, e.g., Thomas L. Cook, *Palmyra and Vicinity* (Palmyra, 1930), pp. 219-20, as to the Smiths' neglect of their property is best explained by their having had no legal interest in it until some years after they located on it. Lucy's recollection that "something like thirty acres of land were got ready for cultivation the first year," and William's remembrance that in all some sixty acres were cleared, would seem to apply to the period after the purchase of the farm was arranged.

[18]The later valuation is given by John Fowler, *Journal of a Tour in the States of New York in the Year 1820* (London, 1831), p. 103, though Fowler thought the farm in question, one of 300 acres, could be bought for ten dollars less. The earlier valuation comes from De Witt Clinton's journal of 1810, both properties being located in the Holland Purchase. Clinton was told by the agent of the Holland Company that the lands were going for from five to eight shillings the acre on ten year contracts, for two years of which the interest was forgiven. See William W. Campbell, ed., *The Life and Writings of De Witt Clinton* (New York, 1849), pp. 117-18.

[19]William Smith, *William Smith on Mormonism* (Lamoni, Iowa, 1883), p. 12; see the extract reprinted in Appendix B.

[20]See the interview with William Smith shortly before his death in November 1893, reprinted in Appendix B. One of the old neighbors of the Smiths, Lorenzo Saunders, who had gone to school with William, recalled that the family once won the county's fifty dollar bounty by producing 7,000 pounds of sugar in a single season (unpublished affidavit dated Reading, Michigan, Sept. 20, 1884, in possession of the Reorganized LDS church).

[21]Tucker, *Origin, Rise, and Progress of Mormonism*, p. 13; Cook, *Palmyra and Vicinity*, pp. 219-20.

[22]See the recitals by Tucker and Turner, and the statements about the Smiths printed in Howe, *Mormonism Unvailed*, pp. 232-61; *Saints' Herald*, June 1, 1881; *Naked Truths about Mormonism*, Jan. 1888; and Thomas Gregg, *The Prophet of Palmyra* (New York, 1890), pp. 34-56.

[23]Smith, *Biographical Sketches*, p. 73.

[24]Palmyra *Reflector*, Feb. 14, 1831; New York *Morning Courier and New-York Enquirer*, Aug. 31, 1831; Clark, *Gleanings by the Way*, p. 225; and the reminiscent accounts by Turner and Tucker.

[25]Orson Pratt, *An Interesting Account of Several Remarkable Visions and of the Late Discovery of Ancient American Records* (Edinburgh, 1840). Although Mormon writers have tended to exaggerate Joseph's ignorance in early life, to make more imperative "the gift and power of God" which alone enabled him to write the Book of Mormon, this summation of his education probably hews to the facts. Joseph got some schooling at Bainbridge, New York, in the winter of 1825-26 which contributed to the attainments here described. A copy of the first edition of the Book of Mormon in the University of Utah library, which was inscribed by Joseph at Harmony, Pennsylvania, in 1830, does not indicate too imperfect a hand. I have not seen an earlier specimen of his handwriting.

[26]Turner, *Phelps and Gorham's Purchase*, p. 214.

[27]The Palmyra *Western Farmer*, Jan. 23, 1822, invites the young people of Palmyra and vicinity to join in this debating society "at the school house near Mr. Billings' on Friday next."

[28]The demonstration, from Mormon and non-Mormon sources alike, that the revival which figures so largely in Joseph Smith's history is of no earlier date, is made in Chapter 3.

[29]Smith, *Biographical Sketches*, p. 84.

[30]Tucker, *Origin, Rise, and Progress of Mormonism*, pp. 17-18.

[31]Campbell, ed., *Life and Writings of De Witt Clinton*, pp. 60, 61.

[32]Smith, "Asahel Smith of Topsfield," p. 92

[33]Mack, *Narrative*, pp. 18-24.

[34]Smith, *Biographical Sketches*, pp. 37, 57-58.

[35]Walter W. Sweet, in *The American Churches* (New York, 1948) and *Revivalism in America* (New York, 1944), has provided short summaries of American religious history, but perhaps the most instructive background work for a study of Mormonism is John M. Mecklin's *The Story of American Dissent* (New York, 1934). In its earlier state Mormonism was a church of the disinherited, yet subsequently in Utah took on something of the character of an establishment, and Mecklin's book exhibits in broad perspective the historical processes involved.

[36]For Nimrod Hughes, see the St. Louis *Louisiana Gazette*, Oct. 3, 1811, May 9, 1812; for McDonald, the Washington, D. C., *Daily National Intelligencer*, Sept. 12, 1823, and the *Wayne Sentinel*, Oct. 8, 1823; for the Shakers, Marguerite Fellows Melcher, *The Shaker Adventure* (Princeton, 1941); for Jemima Wilkinson, Robert P. St. John, "Jemima Wilkinson," *Quarterly Journal of the New York Historical Association* 9 (April 1930): 158-75; for Dylks, R. E. Taneyhill, "The Leatherwood God," *Ohio Valley Historical Miscellanies, No. 3* (Cincinnati, 1871); for Bullard, Z. Thompson, *History of Vermont* (Burlington, 1842), Part 2, pp. 203-204, Bellows Falls *Vermont Intelligencer and Bellows Falls Advertiser*, Nov. 10, 1817, *Wayne Sentinel*, May 26, 1826, and Woodstock *Vermont Chronical*, June 24, 1831.

[37]A little of this background is developed in Whitney R. Cross, "Mormonism in the 'Burned-Over District,'" *New York History* 25 (July 1944): 326-38.

[38]De Witt Clinton, "A Discourse delivered before the New York Historical Society . . . 6th December, 1811," *New-York Historical Society Publications* 2 (1811): 89-90. Also see his journal of 1810, in Campbell, ed., *Life and Writings of De Witt Clinton*, pp. 109, 150, 156-57, 172-73. Many remains in western New York were sketched in 1848 by E. G. Squier. See his *Antiquities of the State of New York* (Buffalo, 1851).

[39]*Palmyra Register*, Jan. 21, 1818, quoting from some remarks by the *North American Review* on discoveries lately described in the *Western Gazetteer*.

[40]William Henry Harrison, "Discourse on the Aborigines of the Ohio Valley," *Ohio Historical and Philosophical Society Transactions* 2 (1839): 11.

[41]In 1810 De Witt Clinton talked with a horticulturist living at Ovid who had dug at six places on his property, without finding anything more than burnt ashes and charcoal. Earlier in the summer he observed near the Little Falls of the Mohawk River "large holes dug, which we are told were made by money-seekers from Stone Arabia." Campbell. ed., *Life and Writings of De Witt Clinton*, pp. 156, 157, 47.

[42]See the affidavit by Peter Ingersoll, Dec. 2, 1833, in Howe, *Mormonism Unvailed*, p. 233. For contemporary accounts of the money-digging craze as it raged in Vermont, see the *Palmyra Herald and Canal Advertiser*, July 24, 1822, and the *Wayne Sentinel*, Feb. 16, 1825. The latter relates how, at Tunbridge, where the Smiths had formerly lived, an old gentleman had been informed in a dream as to the place of the burial of a chest of money in Randolph. With a mineral rod he located it exactly and made an excavation fifteen feet square and seven or eight feet deep, actually coming upon the chest. "One of the company drove an old file through the rotten lid of the chest, and perceiving it to be nearly empty, exclaimed with an oath, 'There's not ten dollars a piece.' No sooner were the words out of his mouth, than the chest moved off through the mud, and has not been seen or heard of since."

[43]*Historical Magazine* 8 (Nov. 1870): 316. This account is perhaps suspect because the source, Judge Daniel Woodward, also says that the senior Joseph had been engaged in counterfeiting activities during his time of residence in Vermont. Brodie, *No Man Knows My History*, p. 7, has shown he was a victim, not an accomplice. See the legal record of this affair, Supreme Court Records, vol. 3, pp. 35, 84-86, 108, in the Windsor County Clerk's Office, Woodstock, Vermont.

[44]*Palmyra Reflector*, Feb. 1, 1831.

[45]See, e.g., Howe, *Mormonism Unvailed*, pp. 232-61; [La] Fayette Lapham, "Interview with the Father of Joseph Smith, the Mormon Prophet, Forty Years Ago," *Historical Magazine* 7 (May 1870): 305-309; and the reminiscences of Dr. W. D. Purple reprinted in Appendix A.

[46]"Journal of Priddy Meeks," *Utah Historical Quarterly* 10 (1942): 179, 180, 200-202. Priddy adds that a neighbor persuaded William by fair promises to go and live with him. He became careless, used bad language, went to the city, after awhile married, "and the last account I had was in the papers: he had a mining lawsuit and got beat." Put in other terms: by the time William grew to manhood the climate had changed and society had no place for a seer in peepstones.

[47]Arturo Castiglioni, *Adventures of the Mind* (New York, 1946), pp. 63-68, 72, 86. This book is to be read with the greater interest if "Joseph Smith" throughout be equated with "magician."

CHAPTER 2

[1]See the accounts of Walters in the *Reflector* for June 12, July 7, 1830, and Feb. 26, 1831, the quotations being from the latter issue. Walters is also mentioned in a letter signed by ten citizens of Palmyra under date of March 12, 1831, in the Painseville, Ohio, *Telegraph*, March 22, 1831. In his debate with E. L. Kelley at Kirtland in 1884, the Campbellite preacher, Clark Braden, remarked that Walters was of British birth and knew something of mesmerism (*The Braden-Kelley Debate* [St. Louis, 1884]). The existence of such a person having been called in question by Mormon writers, it is interesting to note that Pomeroy Tucker, *Origin, Rise, and Progress of Mormonism* (New York, 1867), p. 38, includes among "the pioneer Mormon disciples" one Luman Walters of Pultneyville, New York. The census returns for 1830, in the National Archives, show the presence in Sodus Township of "Luman Walters," aged between thirty and forty, and having a wife and five children. There was no separate return for Pultneyville, then part of the township of Sodus.

[2]See the sworn statement of Mrs. C. R. Smith, a sister of the celebrated Orrin Porter Rockwell, in *Naked Truths about Mormonism*, April 1888: "There was considerable digging for money in our neighborhood by men, women, and children. I never knew of their finding any. I saw a large hole dug on Nathaniel Smith's farm, which was sandy. I saw Joshua Stafford's peep-stone which looked like white marble and had a hole through the center. Sallie Chase, a Methodist, had one and people would go to her to find lost and hidden things." Sally Chase's stone was described by her brother Abel in March 1881 as "dark looking . . . a peculiar stone" (*Saints' Herald*,

June 1, 1881), while Lucy Mack Smith has referred to it as "a green glass" (*Biographical Sketches* [Liverpool, 1853], p. 109).

[3][La]Fayette Lapham, "Interview with the Father of Joseph Smith, the Mormon Prophet, Forty Years Ago," *Historical Magazine* 7 (May 1870): 305-306. Conceivably the seer alluded to was Walters.

[4]Brigham Young described the occasion in his journal under date of Dec. 27, 1841, in *Latter-day Saints' Millennial Star* 26: 118, 119. Therefore Joseph did not give this famous stone to Oliver Cowdery in 1830, as David Whitmer asserted in his *An Address to All Believers in Christ* (Richmond, Missouri, 1887), p. 32. It is possible that the seerstone Cowdery preserved was a whitish stone Joseph made use of later, before and during the writing of the Book of Mormon. This stone was carried off to Utah by Cowdery's brother-in-law, Phineas Young, after the death of the former in 1850 (see the letter of Cowdery's daughter, Maria L. Johnson, to David Whitmer, South West City, Missouri, Jan. 24, 1887, the original of which is preserved in the library of the Reorganized LDS church). Phineas was an elder brother of Brigham Young, and it therefore is quite likely that the church in Salt Lake City today has both of Joseph's stones.

[5]"Journal of Priddy Meeks," *Utah Historical Quarterly* 10 (1942): 179, 180. Hyrum Smith also told Priddy that in ancient times the Nephites (the name given by the Mormons to certain American aborigines) had "had the advantage of their enemies by looking in the seerstone which would reveal whatever they wished to know."

[6]On Pomeroy Tucker's authority, the date is usually given as September 1819, but Willard Chase, clearly the best authority, gives the year as 1822. That date squares well with the court record printed in Appendix A and with what Joseph Smith, Sen., told LaFayette Lapham in 1830. Martin Harris has said that the stone "was dug from the well of Mason Chase, twenty-four feet from the surface," *Tiffany's Monthly* 5 (July 1859): 163-70. Both a Clark and a Mason Chase are shown resident in Manchester by the census returns, the former with many children, the latter with none; Clark seems better to answer the requirements of the sources, and he is named by Pomeroy Tucker. The site of this historic well, which continued in use until filled up in the 1880s, is pointed out by Thomas L. Cook, *Palmyra and Vicinity* (Palmyra, 1930), p. 238.

[7]Affidavit of Willard Chase, Dec. 11, 1833, in E. D. Howe, *Mormonism Unvailed* (Painesville, Ohio, 1834), pp. 241-42, 247.

[8]Tucker, *Origin, Rise, and Progress of Mormonism*, p. 19.

[9]See the reminiscences of Dr. Purple reprinted in Appendix A.

[10]Brigham Young on this evening had exhibited the stone to Stout and other regents of the University of the State of Deseret in Great Salt Lake City as being "the Seer's stone with which The Prophet Joseph discovered the plates of the Book of Mormon." See Stout diary, Feb. 25, 1856. Orasmus Turner, *History of Pioneer Settlement of Phelps and Gorham's Purchase* (Rochester, 1851), p. 216, says the stone was horn blende, which is one of the green, brown, or black forms of the mineral amphibole.

[11]Emma Smith Bidamon to Mrs. Charles Pilgrim, Nauvoo, Illinois, March 27, 1871, original letter in the library of the Reorganized LDS church.

[12]See the court record of 1826 reprinted in Appendix A. Arad Stowell mentioned a second stone "which was white and transparent," and McMaster testified that Joseph claimed he "could discern objects at a distance by holding this white stone to the sun or candle," and "rather declined looking into a Hat at his dark-colored stone as he said that it hurt his eyes." The

white stone reappears prominently in connection with the translation of the Golden Plates.

[13]This was the term Joseph used when, in 1827, he promised his father-in-law, Issac Hale, that he would turn to other pursuits. See Hale's affidavit, March 20, 1834, in Howe, *Mormonism Unvailed*, p. 264.

[14]Theodore Besterman, *Crystal-Gazing: A Study in the History, Distribution, Theory and Practice of Scrying* (London, 1924), and compare Lynn Thorndike, *A History of Magic and Experimental Science During the First Thirteen Centuries of Our Era*, 6 vols. (New York, 1923-41), 6:498-99, 520. A work by Johannes Rivius of Attendorn, published in 1541, says Thorndike, "admitted to a few vestiges of superstition remaining even among the Protestants, some of whom still sought hidden treasure by crystal-gazing or employed incantations and arts of divination." Besterman and Thorndike develop something of the early history of crystal-gazing, but provide no information of any value on its later spread to and development in America.

[15]Arthur J. Ellis, *The Divining Rod: A History of Water Witching*, U.S. Geological Survey Water Supply Paper 416 (Washington, 1938). The faith tenaciously held by the elder Joseph Smith in divining rods has not perished; see *Life Magazine's* story on the American historical novelist, Kenneth Roberts, "Can He Find Water?", Oct. 4, 1948.

[16]Cultural anthropologists have traveled to the ends of the earth to enquire into rain rituals among the Toradya, the power of *bonga* among the Ho, and the making of magicians among the Kaingang, but none have been found, so far as I can learn, willing to travel six blocks by streetcar to begin some investigations into the character and cultural persistence of horoscopy, numerology, palm-reading, crystal-gazing, and kindred practices and beliefs. A fortune-teller in Chicago in 1950, say, strikes me as no less interesting and perishable within a societal complex than a rain-maker in Zuni, and I think the narrow preoccupation of anthropolgists with primitive man should be broadened to include those studies of modern society without which other studies lose much of their meaning.

[17]Palmyra *Reflector*, Feb. 1, 1831. These remarks, made in the third of a series of six articles on the "Gold Bible," appear to have been made not by the editor, as has been inferred, but by a correspondent living in Farmington. See the *Reflector*, Jan. 6, 1831.

[18]As described to Frederick G. Mather, "The Early Days of Mormonism," *Lippincott's Magazine* 26 (Aug. 1880): 199, "When 'peeking' he [Joseph Smith] kneeled and buried his face in his white stovepipe hat, within which was the peek-stone. He declared it to be so much like looking into the water that the 'deflection of flight ' [i.e. deflection of light] sometimes took him out of his course." Martin Harris mentions "the old white hat," and John C. Bennett, *History of the Saints* (Boston, 1842), even prints a letter purporting to have been written by Joseph, signed "Old White Hat." Without specifically describing the hat, Joseph Smith's later father-in-law, Issac Hale, similarly pictures Joseph's methodology with his stone, which was "placed in his hat, and his hat closed over his face."

[19]The emphasis on great caverns not only in the literature of the money-digging but later on in Mormon folklore owed in some part to a "stupendous cavern" discovered near Watertown, New York, in the spring of 1822, which was widely publicized in the contemporary press, e.g., *Nile's Weekly Register* 22 (June 22, 1822): 270, 271, and the *Palmyra Herald, and Canal Advertiser*, June 19, 1822. Other caverns had been described in the press from time to time, but without making quite such an impression.

Willard Chase, in his affidavit of Dec. 11, 1833, pictures Joseph as declaring, at a later date, that he "had discovered on the bank of Black River, in the village of Watertown, Jefferson County, N.Y., a cave, in which he had found a bar of gold, as big as his leg, and about three or four feet long." This allusion clearly derived from the newspaper story of 1822, whether the mind of origin is held to be that of Joseph Smith or Willard Chase. See Howe, *Mormonism Unvailed*, p. 244.

It may be convenient here to point out that various stories published in the newspapers through the early 1820s were by no means of a kind to discourage seekers after treasure. From Vermont to Georgia, pirate treasure and gold and silver mines were universal objects of search. The gold deposits discovered in North Carolina in 1823 were enough to confound the complacence of those who supposed it long since since settled that the United States were barren of this yellow metal. There were reports of a silver mine found in Indianna, another in Westchester County, New York, and even, to give spice to the possibilities, twenty-nine guineas found by a wood-chopper in the trunk of a tree near Utica, all these discoveries duly chronicled in the village paper.

[20]See Howe, *Mormonism Unvailed*, pp. 238-39, 257-58.

[21]Affidavit of Joseph Capron, Nov. 8, 1833, in Howe, *Mormonism Unvailed*, pp. 258-60. This affair of the gold watches was among the better remembered of Joseph's treasure-hunting exploits; it is mentioned by Joshua Stafford and by the Palmyra *Reflector*, July 7, 1830.

[22]Discourse by Brigham Young at Farmington, Utah, June 17, 1877, *Journal of Discourses* (Liverpool, 1878), 19:37-38. Young vouched for Rockwell's veracity: "When he tells a thing he understands, he will tell it just as he knows it; he is a man that does not lie." Joshua Stafford declared in 1833 that "Joseph once showed me a piece of wood which he said he took from a box of money, and the reason he gave for not obtaining the box, was, that it *moved*." Howe, *Mormonism Unvailed*, p. 258.

[23]These are of course the rituals of magic everywhere, the magic circle, and the magic force of blood in sacrifice. The latter reappears in Joseph's church at a later date, in connection with the doctrine of blood atonement.

[24]Stephen S. Harding heard this detail while in Palmyra in the summer of 1829. See his letter of February 1822 to Thomas Gregg, printed in the latter's *The Prophet of Palmyra* (New York, 1890), p. 56.

[25]William Stafford tells the story himself in his affidavit of Dec. 8, 1833, in Howe, *Mormonism Unvailed*, p. 239. The adventure of the black sheep recurs in every reminiscent account of Palmyra. Cook, *Palmyra and Vicinity*, p. 222, on the authority of an old resident, Wallace W. Miner, who had known Stafford well, adds a fresh detail. According to this version, after the sacrifice of the sheep Joseph came to Stafford and offered to make the latter a number of sap-buckets in repayment; this he did to Stafford's satisfaction.

[26]It has remained for a later generation of believers to deny the stories altogether. Joseph himself never denied that he had been a seer in peep-stones before establishing himself as a prophet of God. In the *Latter Day Saint's Messenger and Advocate*, October 1835, speaking through Oliver Cowdery, he admitted to having spent "a few months with some others in excavating the earth," in pursuit of treasure down in the Susquehanna country. Again, in the *Elder's Journal*, July 1838, replying in the third person to the question whether he had ever been a money-digger, Joseph said, "Yes, but it was never a very profitable job to him, as he only got fourteen dollars a

month for it." This may well be taken as a literal statement of so much of the truth as he admitted. Still later, writing in his autobiography of this employment in the Susquehanna country which had paid him the fourteen dollar wage, he concluded somewhat disingenuously, "Hence arose the very prevalent story of my having been a money-digger." At no time did he ever squarely meet the question whether he had used his peepstone in the country roundabout Palmyra for treasure seekers of that neighborhood. As a matter of fact, such early converts to Mormonism as the Rockwell and Beman families had been actively associated with him in the treasure-hunting at Palmyra and Manchester, and others, like Martin Harris, were well informed about it and accepted it naturally as a part of his history.

[27]Brigham H. Roberts, *Comprehensive History of the Church*, 6 vols. (Salt Lake City, 1930), 1:41. Roberts accepted the incontrovertible fact that Joseph had a seerstone, but came only reluctantly to the admission that it was the stone from the Chase well. Compare his *Defense of the Faith and the Saints* (Salt Lake City, 1907), 1:257, and his *Comprehensive History of the Church*, 1:129.

[28]See his testimony in his trial at Bainbridge, New York, in March 1826, reprinted in Appendix A.

[29]The only effort ever made to vindicate the Smiths through interviewing old residents of Palmyra was by William and E. L. Kelley in March 1881. Their inquiries developed little more than that the Smiths had been neither much better nor much worse than their contemporaries. Three of the persons questioned alluded to Joseph's use of a peepstone for money-digging purposes, but detailed inquiries were apparently made only of Abel Chase, brother of Willard, who was too young to be able to say he had seen the stone himself. *Saints' Herald*, June 1, 1881. The accuracy of the Kelleys' report of the interviews was shortly after attacked by some of those who had been interviewed. Their statements are to be found in Charles A. Shook, *The True Origin of Mormon Polygamy* (Mendota, Illinois, 1910), pp. 39-43.

More characteristic of the Mormon reaction to the Palmyra stories has been the vilification of the affiants, "a set of blackguards, liars, horse jockeys and drunkards." See, e.g., Benjamin Winchester, *The Origin of the Spaulding Story* (Philadelphia, 1840).

[30]The stringency of the times is at least suggested by an item in the *Western Farmer*, June 20, 1821, "It appears by a letter written near Cadiz (Ohio) dated April 30, 1821,—that the times there if possible are more embarrasing than here; that wheat will fetch but from 12 1/2 to 25 cents per bushel—Money is not to be had—no means whatever will extort it. Lawsuits are generally stopped as property will not buy money at any rate."

[31]This notice appears in the *Wayne Sentinel* from Sept. 29 through Nov. 3, 1824. It had been supposed on his mother's authority that Alvin died in November 1824, but this card in the *Sentinel*, like his actual gravestone in the Church Street cemetery in Palmyra, demonstrates that the death occured a year earlier. See Willard W. Bean, *A. B. C. History of Palmyra and the Beginnings of "Mormonism"* (Palmyra, 1938).

[32]See Chapter 3.

[33]*Palmyra Reflector*, Feb. 14, 1831.

[34]See his statement in Howe, *Mormonism Unvailed*.

[35]Compare the testimony of Stowell and Joseph himself at Joseph's trial in Bainbridge early in 1826, reprinted in Appendix A. Joseph's mother writes in her *Biographical Sketches*, pp. 91, 92, that Stowell journeyed to Palmyra "with the view of getting Joseph to assist him in digging. . . . He came for

Joseph on account of having heard that he possessed certain keys by which he could discern things invisible to the natural eye." This is the nearest any member of the Smith family ever came to the outright admission that Joseph had a peepstone which he used for the benefit of treasure seekers. Martin Harris, who faced the facts more frankly, mentioned not only the peepstone but the money-digging: "There was a company there in that neighborhood, who were digging for money supposed to have been hidden by the ancients. Of this company were old Mr. Stowell—I think his name was Josiah—also old Mr. Beman, also Samuel Lawrence, George Proper, Joseph Smith, Jr., and his father, and his brother Hiram Smith. They dug for money in Palmyra, Manchester, also in Pennsylvania, and other places. When Joseph found this stone, there was a company digging in Harmony, Pa., and they took Joseph to look in the stone for them" *Tiffany's Monthly* 5 (July 1859): 164. Three of the money-diggers mentioned by Harris—Lawrence, Proper, and the elder Smith—are shown as residents of Manchester by the census returns of 1830, and Alva Brown is located by the same census at Fivonia.

It is assumed that Joseph and his father were given advanced assurances of the fourteen dollar wage, though the only evidence that he was paid such an amount is his statement in *Elders' Journal*, July 1838. There is no reason to think they were seriously concerned about meeting the payments on the farm, and that this was a controlling consideration in their agreement to accompany Stowell back to his home.

[36]Joseph Smith, *History of the Church*, 1:17. Joseph first published this version of his association with Stowell in *Times and Seasons* 3 (May 2, 1842): 772.

[37]*Latter Day Saints' Messenger and Advocate*, Oct. 1835.

[38]See Appendix A and particularly Note 1.

[39]For the full text of this agreement, see Appendix A. The original, the present whereabouts of which is unknown, is declared to have been in Joseph's own hand.

[40]Howe, *Mormonism Unvailed*, pp. 262-63. At the time Hale swore to this statement, March 20, 1834, he had become Joseph Smith's father-in-law. Though published by Howe in 1834, Hale's statement seems to have been published earlier in the Montrose, Pennsylvania, *Susquehanna Register*, and the *New York Baptist Register*. W. R. Hines, whose statement is reprinted in part in Appendix A, Note 8, says that D. P. Hurlbut wrote Hale at his suggestion to obtain the affidavit, and that thereafter he, Hines, publicly defended Hale in Kirtland, Ohio, against Mormon detractors. The embarrassed reaction of the Saints to Hale's story is evidenced by Oliver Cowdery's remarks in the *Evening and Morning Star*, Sept. 1834, and again in *Latter Day Saints', Messenger and Advocate*, Oct. 1835.

[41]In addition to the records reprinted in Appendix A and the contemporary statements printed by Howe, there are many reminiscent accounts of Joseph's experiences as a seer in the country about the Great Bend of the Susquehanna. See, especially, Emily C. Blackman, *History of Susquehanna County* (Philadelphia, 1873), pp. 577-82; Frederick G. Mather, "The Early Days of Mormonism," *Lippincott's Magazine* 26 (Aug. 1880): 198-204; James H. Smith, *History of Chenango and Madison Counties* (Syracruse, 1880), pp. 153-55; and *Naked Truths about Mormonism*, January 1888. Some of these accounts picture Joseph as having been in the region for a year or two prior to 1825, probably a misapprehension arising from the fact that he lived there intermittently from 1825 to 1830.

[42]There are only oblique allusions in the sources to Joseph's sexual maturation, which is interesting and important for its bearing on his later history. He himself mentions the Stowell girls (*History of the Church*, 1:90), while Eliza Winters figures in one of the statements printed in Howe, *Mormonism Unvailed*, p. 268. Under her married name, Eliza Winters Squires, she was one of these who about 1879 gave information to Frederick Mather, concerning the early days of Mormonism in the Susquehanna country. Her life is briefly sketched in Rhamanthus M. Stocker, *Centennial History of Susquehanna County* (Philadelphia, 1887), p. 537.

[43]See the testimony in detail in Appendix A.

[44]In A. W. Benton's language (see Appendix A), "considering his youth, (he being then a minor,) and thinking he might reform his conduct, he [Joseph] was designedly allowed to escape," though condemned. Oliver Cowdery, through whom alone Joseph ever admited to the fact of such a trial, wrote in the *Latter Day Saints' Messenger and Advocate*, Oct. 1835, "some very officious person complained of him (Joseph) as a disorderly person, and brought him before the authorities of the country; but there being no cause for action he was honorably acquitted." Cowdery makes it clear that this occurred during the time of Joseph's association with Stowell, and before he became involved with the Book of Mormon.

From the point of view of Mormon history, it is immaterial what the finding of the court was on the technical charge of being "a disorderly person and an imposter;" what is important is the evidence adduced, and its bearing on the life of Joseph Smith before he announced his claim to be a prophet of God.

CHAPTER 3

[1]The account that follows condenses and paraphrases Joseph's own, as printed in *History of the Church*, 1:2-16. It was first published in *Times and Seasons* 3 (1842): 726-28, 748-49, 753-54, 771.

[2]This history appeared in the form of a series of eight letters published in the *Latter Day Saints' Messenger and Advocate*, Oct. 1834 to Oct. 1835, written by Oliver Cowdery but published directly under Joseph Smith's eye and, as Cowdery advised the Saints at the time, prepared with his actual assistance: "Indeed, there are many items connected with . . . this subject that render his labor indispensable." Brigham H. Roberts, speaking for the Saints in his *Comprehensive History of the Church*, 1:78n, declared that, so far as the facts themselves are concerned, this is "practically the personal narrative of Joseph Smith." The various branches of the church Joseph Smith founded have agreed with Roberts, and the letters have often been reprinted.

[3]In his third letter, which first touched upon the revival that awakened Joseph, Oliver Cowdery placed this event in "the fifteenth year of his life." His fourth letter apologized for this error; this religious excitement began not in the fifteenth but the seventeenth year of Joseph's age: "You will please remember this correction, as it will be necessary for the full understanding of what will follow. . . . This would bring the date down to the year 1823." Cf. *Messenger and Advocate*, Dec. 1834 and Feb. 1835. The account which follows is taken from ibid.

[4]William Smith fully corroborates the Cowdery account in what it says of the decisive role that the Reverend Lane played in the revivals which aroused Joseph Smith on the subject of religion. See the several statements by him reprinted in Appendix B.

[5]Orson Pratt, *An Interesting Account of Several Remarkable Visions and of the Late Discovery of Ancient American Records* (Edinburgh, 1840). The First Vision, it would seem from the internal evidence of Joseph's autobiography, was first put down on paper in the spring of 1838. The conception may have come to him earlier, perhaps as early as the fall of 1835, but the only evidence to support such an assumption is a somewhat ambiguous entry in Joseph's history under date of November 15, 1835, to the effect that he had that day given one Erastus Holmes "a brief relation of my experience while in my juvenile years, say from six years old up to the time that I received my first vision, which was when I was about fourteen years old" (*History of the Church*, 2:312). The documents on which such an entry in the History may have been based are withheld from study, so that it is impossible to determine whether it is a genuine or later interpolation, even conceding that it is a conclusive reference to the Vision of the Father and the Son.

The only other evidence that has been advanced to prove that Joseph's followers knew of the First Vision before 1835 is not persuasive. Edward Stevenson, *Reminiscences of Joseph the Prophet* (Salt Lake City, 1893), p. 4, declares that in 1834, at Pontiac, Michigan, he heard Joseph "testify with great power concerning the vision of the Father and the Son," but apart from the late date of this account, its value is vitiated by the fact that Stevenson's manuscript autobiography, written in 1891, from which the reminiscences were adapted, pictures Joseph on this particular occasion as speaking only of a "vision of an angel."

[Editor's note: Morgan unfortunately did not have access to the earliest accounts of the First Vision, including an 1832 recital in Joseph Smith's own hand, which only began surfacing in the late 1960s. They are most conveniently available in Milton V. Backman, Jr., *Joseph Smith's First Vision* (Salt Lake City, 1971).]

[6]In 1834, Oliver Cowdery became involved in a steamboat argument with a skeptic who would not believe that Christ had been seen upon the earth since his ascension, and though Cowdery published in the *Messenger and Advocate*, Oct. 1834, a lengthy account of his refutation, his argument did not include any reference to a visitation to the Mormon prophet, nor was there any editorial comment calling to the attention of the church membership a circumstance of such striking interest to them.

[7]See the letter as printed in Ben E. Rich, *Scrapbook of Mormon Literature* (Chicago, 190-?), 1:543-45.

[8]See again his various statements reprinted in Appendix B.

[9]Negatively, the Palmyra newspapers as published during the period these visions are asserted to have occured, support the implication of the folklore, since even when printing news of various fanaticisms and delusions, the opportunity was never seized to note the existence of another such at Palmyra. However, that is also true of Joseph's money-digging, supported though it is by so much external evidence. But the folklore is directly backed up by the Palmyra *Reflector*, which declared on February 1, 1831, that it appeared "quite certain that the prophet himself never made any serious pretensions to religion until his late pretended revelation," and again on February 28, 1831, "It is well known that Joe Smith never pre-

tended to have any communion with angels, until a long period after the *pretended* finding of his book."

[10]*Times and Seasons* 3 (1842): 749. Joseph's followers have amended this language to have him say that he "displayed the weaknesses of youth, and the foibles of human nature; which I am sorry to say led me into divers temptations, offensive in the sight of God;" to this they have added, "In making this confession, no one need suppose me guilty of any great or malignant sins. A disposition to commit such was never in my nature" (*History of the Church*, 1:9). Numerous changes of the kind have been made in Joseph's history, analogous to the prudery which has so often retouched the paintings of the old masters.

[11]It so happened that Joseph's paternal great-grandfather was named Jesse; thus scripture was fulfilled in the person of Joseph. Some of the quotations as voiced by the angel differed slightly, as Joseph pointed out, from the King James version; they are, in fact, quoted from the Bible as Joseph revised it during the 1830s.

[12]Three and seven have long been regarded as numbers with mystic significance. See, as a viewpoint contemporary with Joseph, Frederick Henry Quitman, *A Treatise on Magic, or, on the Intercourse between Spirits and Men* (Albany, 1810), pp. 65, 66. Oliver Cowdery, writing in the *Messenger and Advocate*, July 1835, makes an emphatic point of the repetition: "Was he [Joseph] deceived? Far from this; for the vision was renewed twice before morning, unfolding farther and still farther the mysteries of godliness and those things to come."

[13]Joseph's mother, after quoting most of Joseph's account of these events, here tells a divergent story. By her account, the angel had told Joseph the night before to relate to his father what had taken place, and the duty that had been laid upon him. When the angel, on his appearance to Joseph in open daylight, demanded to know why Joseph had not done as he was instructed, the boy answered that he feared his father would not believe him. The angel rejoined, "He will believe every word you say to him," which turned out to be the case.

It is interesting, as almost the only corroboration of Joseph's claim to have had a vision as early as 1823, that Lucy says Alvin was working with Joseph and his father in the field this day; she also pictures Alvin as much enraptured with Joseph's story of the record engraved upon the golden plates. Alvin died in November of this year. See Lucy's *Biographical Sketches* (Liverpool, 1853), pp. 81-84, 89-90.

[14]Oliver Cowdery's remarks in *Evening and Morning Star*, Sept. 1834, make it clear that the history on which he and Joseph collaborated was designed to combat affidavits concerning Joseph's money-digging which had lately been gathered in Susquehanna County, especially from Joseph's in-laws. These had first been printed in the Montrose, Pennsylvania, *Susquehanna Register*, and then more widely circulated by the *New York Baptist Register*.

[15]See Joseph's letter to Oliver Cowdery, in *Messenger and Advocate*, Nov. 1834. Characteristically, when this letter is reprinted as a footnote in *History of the Church*, 1:10, "unchaste" becomes "trifling" conversation.

[16]Here, embedded in the words of Moroni, is the language of Joseph's First Vision, which in fact is simply a dramatization of this pronouncement, undoubtedly suggested by the logical question Oliver Cowdery raised but did not answer in setting down the original version of Joseph's history.

[17]The recurrence of this phrase shows how burr-like the idea was in the Smith family's mind. Nearly two years before the words as here quoted were published in the *Messenger and Advocate*, July 1835, one of the Smith's old neighbors at Palmyra, Joseph Capron, in an affidavit dated Nov. 8, 1833, related some details of a conversation once had with the senior Joseph Smith. The old man, speaking of the Book of Mormon as a speculation rather than a work of religious import, had said, "When it is completed, my family will be placed *on a level* above the generality of mankind." See E. D. Howe, *Mormonism Unvailed* (Painesville, Ohio, 1834), p. 260. See also *Messenger and Advocate*, July and Oct. 1835.

[18]Disagreeing with both of Joseph's accounts concerning the indistinctive character of the years between 1823 and 1827, Lucy Smith tells a remarkable story of Joseph's expectation of bringing home the plates in 1824, and how this was frustrated. The probable basis of fact in her story will be considered in the next chapter, but in any event anything she says upon the subject must be cautiously received, because she says that the family could never bear to hear anything said on the subject of the golden plates after the death of Alvin, which actually occured in 1823, and not, as she says, in 1824. See *Biographical Sketches*, pp. 85-86, 99. See also *Messenger and Advocate*, Oct. 1835.

[19]See Catherine C. Cleveland, *The Great Revival in the West, 1797-1805* (Chicago, 1916), and such contemporary accounts as David Rice, *A Sermon on the Present Revival of Religion* (Lexington, 1804), and Richard McNemar, *The Kentucky Revival* (Cincinnati, 1807).

[20]Rev. Seth Williston to C. Davis, Ontario County, April 29, 1799, *New York Missionary Magazine* 1 (Jan. 1800): 35-38.

[21]This is the language of Reverend Abner Chase, then riding a circuit in Oneida County; see his *Recollections of the Past* (New York, 1846), p. 103. Later, for many years, Chase was presiding elder for the Methodist Episcopal church in Ontario District, most notably, from 1820 to 1824.

[22]See James R. Hotchkin, *A History of the Purchase and Settlement of Western New York, and of the Rise, Progress, and Present State of the Presbyterian Church in that Section* (New York, 1848), pp. 130, 378. A Presbyterian minister in this region from 1801, Hotchkin noted the absence of any extended revivals from the close of the awakening of 1799 to that of 1816-17. He noted, too, that after the second revival there was again a long period of quiescence. The Methodists made the same osbervation. See *Zion's Herald*, April 13, 1825.

[23]Palmyra *Western Farmer*, Jan. 30, 1822, quoting the Lyon's *Republican* of Dec. 7, 1821.

[24]*Western Farmer*, Oct. 17, 1821. Hotchkin, *Purchase and Settlement of Western New York*, p. 378, is specific in remarking on the revivals at Palmyra, dating them for 1817 and 1824, with nothing of moment inbetween.

[25]*Western Farmer*, Jan. 23, March 13, 20, 1822.

[26]George Peck, *Early Methodism Within the Bounds of the Old Genesee Conference from 1788 to 1828* (New York, 1860), pp. 167, 234-38, 313, 447-49, 492-95, provides full details of Lane's life in the ministry. Born in New York state in 1784, Lane was reared in the southern part of the state—in fact, in Windsor Township, scene of some of Joseph Smith's treasure-hunting exploits of 1825-26. He prepared himself for school teaching, but was converted to religion and received into the Methodist Episcopal church in northern Pennsylvania in 1803. Admitted to trial in the Philadelphia confer-

ence in 1805, he became one of the pioneer circuit riders of the Holland Purchase, in 1808 presiding over the first camp-meeting ever held east of the Genesee River. In 1810 he left the itinerancy, becoming a local preacher at Wilkes-Barre, but was re-admitted in 1819, being appointed to the Susquehanna District of the Genesee Conference. That year, as it happened, was also the year the Ontario District was created. After laboring five years in the Susquehanna District, Lane was transferred to the Ontario District at the fifteenth meeting of the Genesee Conference in July 1824. After his single year on that district, he again located at Wilkes-Barre. He returned to the itinerancy in 1834, and two years later was named assistant book agent. In that capacity and as principal book agent he served until he retired, broken in health, in 1852. He died in 1859. In addition to the account by Peck, see F. W. Conable, *History of the Genesee Annual Conference of the Methodist Episcopal Church, from . . . 1810 to the Year 1872* (New York, 1876), pp. 159-232, *passim*.

[27]See Cowdery's full description of Lane and the impression he made upon Joseph at this time.

[28]Peck, *Early Methodism*, pp. 492-95.

[29]See Lane's letter, dated Wilkes-Barre, Jan. 25, 1825, *Methodist Magazine* 8 (April 1825): 158-61, which is his own account of this historic revival.

[30]*Wayne Sentinel*, Sept. 15, 1824.

[31]See Appendix B.

[32]*Methodist Magazine* 8 (April 1825): 160.

[33]Quoted in *Zion's Herald*, Feb. 9, 1825, and in the *Wayne Sentinel*, March 2, 1825.

[34]*Wayne Sentinel*, March 2, 1825.

[35]*Zion's Herald*, May 11, 1825, quoting the *Western Recorder*.

[36]See Appendix B.

[37]See the account elicited from William Smith in 1893, reprinted in Appendix B. The mention of Stockton in this connection is entirely plausible, since Lucy herself makes it clear that the revival took place "after the death of Alvin," and her anxieties over her dead son may have troubled her deeply. The reference to Stockton is another among the innumerable evidences that it is the revival of 1824-25 that figures in Mormon history. The Reverend Stockton was installed as pastor of the Presbyterian church in Palmyra on February 18, 1824, succeeding Reverend Daniel C. Hopkins, who had been the "stated supply" during the two years previous (W. H. McIntosh, *History of Wayne County, New York* [Philadelphia, 1877], p. 147). Hotchkin, p. 378, in his account of the revivals at Palmyra, says that a "copious shower of grace passed over this region in 1824, under the labors of Mr. Stockton, and large numbers were gathered into the church." Stockton continued as Pastor at Palmyra until October 1827.

[38]Smith, *Biographical Sketches*, p. 90.

[39]Orasmus Turner, *History of the Pioneer Settlement of Phelps and Gorham's Purchase* (Rochester, 1851), p. 214; Pomeroy Tucker, *Origin, Rise, and Progress of Mormonism* (New York, 1867), p. 18.

[40]*Messenger and Advocate*, Dec. 1834.

[41]Smith, *Biographical Sketches*, p. 90.

[42]The time could be determined with more assurance if the precise date of Lucy's own conversion could be established, but records of membership for the years before 1832 are not preserved in the West Presbyterian Church of Palmyra. The conversation Lucy remembers may quite possibly have

taken place in the spring of 1825, the basis in fact for Joseph's placement of his First Vision in the springtime.

[43]Note the interesting correspondence in dates between Joseph's employment of his seerstone and his passing interest in religion. Willard Chase says that Joseph had the stone in his possession two years—that is, from 1822 to 1824—before returning it, and that Hyrum came to reborrow the stone "sometime in 1825," after which Chase never saw it again.

[44]*History of the Church*, 1:220n., quoting the manuscript "Far West Record," p. 13.

[45]B. H. Roberts, *Defense of the Faith and the Saints* (Salt Lake City, 1907), 1: 307-308. A quotation by which Roberts supported his point of view remains not without point: "It is no use trying to twist facts to suit theories derived from a past which was destitute of the knowledge we now possess; what we have to do is to adjust our theories to suit the facts."

[46]Elias Smith, *The Life, Conversion, Preaching, Travels and Sufferings of Elias Smith* (Portsmouth, New Hampshire, 1816), p. 58. Elias Smith was born in Lyme, Connecticut, the birthplace of Lucy Mack's father, and migrated to Vermont at about the same time. He was ordained a Baptist minister, but withdrew from that church in 1804 to found his Christian Connection, a church which, like Joseph Smith's, returned literally to the church of Christ. When Joseph began to attract attention in the early 1830s, he was sometimes pictured unflatteringly as Elias Smith's spiritual heir.

[47]John Samuel Thompson, *Christian Guide* (Utica, New York, 1826), pp. 67, 71.

[48]Wild's vision was reprinted from the *Mohawk Herald* by the *Wayne Sentinel*, Oct. 22, 1823, one month to the day from the time when, as Joseph later asserted, the golden plates were first showed to him by the angel Moroni. Wild promised at an early date a pamphlet seting forth his views and visions, and this appeared at Amsterdam in 1824: *A Short Sketch of the Religious Experience, and Spiritual Travels, of Asa Wild, to Which is Added, a Short treatise on the Millennium*.

[49]Charles G. Finney, *Memoirs* (New York, 1876), pp. 15-23. Finney's conversion took place in October 1821. His great career as a revivalist was launched at Antwerp, New York, in the summer of 1824, and his contemporary account of that revival is reprinted in the *Wayne Sentinel*, July 14, 1824.

[50]It is to be remarked that Joseph practically never wrote manually; he always dictated, even his history. Thus he was always in the position of a man vis-a-vis an audience with all the psychological complexities in which such a relationship abounds. Much that Joseph wrote would be inexplicable had he written it in privacy of spirit and by his own hand.

CHAPTER 4

[1]This is the arrangement described by Thomas L. Cook, *Palmyra and Vicinity* (Palmyra, 1930), p. 219, although he pictures Durfee as owner of the property from the beginning. Lucy Mack Smith's confused and pathetic account, *Biographical Sketches* (Liverpool, 1853), pp. 92-98, 129, at any rate agrees that Durfee "became the possessor of the farm," and that the Smiths remained on it thereafter only at Durfee's pleasure. It would seem that

Lucy's pride makes her insist that they missed only the final payment, for it is inconceivable that they could have contracted to buy the farm in no more than five installments, and even more inconceivable that they would have engaged to pay at the rate of a thouand dollars a year, the sum she says they would have needed to save the farm.

[2]Smith, *Biographical Sketches*, p. 40, gives the date of Hyrum's marriage as November 2, 1826, no doubt correct, for a communication to the *Wayne Sentinel* remarks that among three recent weddings in Manchester was that of "Mr. Hiram Smith to Miss Jerusha Barden."

[3]Smith, *Biographical Sketches*, p. 93.

[4]See his statement in E. D. Howe, *Mormonism Unvailed* (Painesville, Ohio, 1834), p. 263.

[5]*History of the Church*, 1:17; see also the statement by W. R. Hines in *Naked Truths about Mormonism*, Jan. 1888, and Emily C. Blackman, *History of Susquehanna County* (Philadelphia, 1873), p. 582. Emma, who was born at Harmony on July 10, 1804, at the time of her marriage was in her twenty-third year, accountable for her own actions before the law. Thus in a legal sense Joseph did not, as has sometimes been said, "steal" his wife.

[6]Smith, *Biographical Sketches*, p. 98. Willard Chase, in his statement in Howe, *Mormonism Unvailed*, pp. 244-45, relates, on the authority of Samuel Lawrence, a remarkable story to the effect that Joseph persuaded Lawrence to take him south with a tale concerning a silver mine found there, and then induced Josiah Stowell to bring him and Emma home with another story of a gold bar he had located in a cave near Watertown. This may possibly have been the case, but the story is unsupported from any other source.

[7]Unpublished affidavit by Lorenzo Saunders, Reading, Michigan, Sept. 20, 1884, in the possession of the Reorganized LDS church.

[8]Affidavit of Issac Hale, March 20, 1834, in Howe, *Mormonism Unvailed*, p. 263.

[9]Howe, *Mormonism Unvailed*, pp. 234, 235. The independent account of this episode, as given by Isaac Hale, agrees substantially with that of Ingersoll. When Joseph and Emma appeared at his home in company with Ingersoll, Hale says, "Smith stated to me, that he had given up what he called 'glass-looking,' and that he expected to work hard for a living, and was willing to do so. He also made arrangements with my son Alva Hale, to go to Palmyra, and move his (Smith's) furniture, &c. to this place. He then returned to Palmyra, and soon after, Alva, agreeable to the arrangement, went up and returned with Smith and his family." Alva is himself on record as having heard Joseph say "that this '*peeping*' was all d——d nonsense," and that Joseph "was deceived himself but did not intend to deceive others;—that he intended to quit the business, (of peeping,) and labor for his livelihood." Howe, *Mormonism Unvailed*, p. 268.

[10]Howe, *Mormonism Unvailed*, p. 235.

[11]This is Martin Harris's version of how the details first got out. *Tiffany's Monthly* 5 (July 1859): 167-68.

[12]Smith, *Biographical Sketches*, pp. 84, 85. As exhibiting the persistent interest of the Smiths during this period in the ancients and their treasures,

see the affidavits of Peter Ingersoll, Roswell Nichols, and William Stafford, in Howe, *Mormonism Unvailed*, pp. 233, 237-38, 257-58.

[13]This was at any rate the content of Joseph's conception as reported in the Palmyra *Reflector*, Feb. 14, 1831.

[14]Willard Chase, for example, says that as early as June 1827 he was given to understand that the record would come to light the following September. Alvin's role is developed in the text.

[15]The evidence that Joseph's peepstone played a key part in the affair of the golden plates is formidable. Orasmus Turner remarks that even after Joseph had begun to spread abroad the story of a visitation from an angel, the other members of the family had a different version. On one occasion they showed a neighbor Joseph's stone, carefully wrapped in cotton and kept in a mysterious box, and told him that "it was by looking at this stone, in a hat, the light excluded, that Joseph discovered the plates. . . . It was the same stone the Smiths had used in money digging, and in some pretended discoveries of stolen property." Turner, *History of the Pioneer Settlement of Phelps and Gorham's Purchase* (Rochester, 1851), p. 216. Martin Harris tells the same story, saying that Joseph told him he found the plates "by looking in the stone found in the well of Mason Chase. The [Smith] family . . . told me the same thing." *Tiffany's Monthly* 5 (July 1859): 169. Willard Chase declares that Joseph made a similar admission to him immediately after coming into possession of the plates; had it not been for the stone from the Chase well, "he would not have obtained the book." Howe, *Mormonism Unvailed*, p. 246. Brigham Young, when exhibiting Joseph's stone in 1856, identified it as "the Seer's stone with which The Prophet Joseph discovered the plates of the Book of Mormon."

[16]Palmyra *Reflector*, Feb. 14, 28, 1831, July 7, 1830; [La]Fayette Lapham, "Interview with the Father of Joseph Smith, the Mormon Prophet, Forty Years Ago," *Historical Magazine* 7 (May 1870): 307-308.

[17]See the letter to James T. Cobb written from Harmony, Pennsylvania, April 23, 1879, by two of Emma's cousins, Hiel and Joseph Lewis. This was Joseph's description of the spirit in talking to their father shortly after the translation of the plates began. William Alexander Linn, *The Story of the Mormons* (New York, 1902), p. 28. The Spaniard may have figured in the story as a result of the digging in the Susquehanna country in 1825. Frederick G. Mather, "The Early days of Mormonism," *Lippincott's Magazine* 26 (Aug. 1880): 200, mentions a "headless Spaniard" said to have guarded the treasure Josiah Stowell sought.

[18]This was Lucy Smith's description as given to Abigail Harris, herself a Quaker, early in 1828. Howe, *Mormonism Unvailed*, p. 253.

[19]Ibid. See also the affidavit by Willard Chase in Howe, *Mormonism Unvailed*, pp. 242-43, where the messenger is identified as "the spirit of the prophet who wrote this book."

[20]The earliest printed reference to this apparition describes it still differently as "the spirit of the Almighty." See the Rochester *Advertiser and Telegraph*, Aug. 31, 1829, quoting the Palmyra *Freeman* of a day or so before.

[21]The account that follows is a blending of three different versions which became current, that of Willard Chase set down in 1833, in Howe, *Mormonism Unvailed*, pp. 242-43; that of John A. Clark, first published in

the *Episcopal Recorder* in 1840 and reprinted two years later in his *Gleanings by the Way* (Philadelphia, 1842), pp. 224-27; and that of LaFayette Lapham, which, though not printed until some forty years later in *Historical Magazine* 7 (May 1870): 307-308, seems to be a reasonably accurate remembrance of a rambling discourse with which the elder Joseph favored Lapham and Jacob Ramsdell. Lapham thought this interview had taken place in 1830, but I am inclined to date it a year earlier. Of the three accounts, the first and third are the most valuable.

[22]These details are from Willard Chase; the Lapham account adds that Joseph was required to carry with him a coverlid and a napkin. The essential injunction laid upon him was that he must not lay down the treasure until he had wrapped it in the napkin.

[23]The power of names is one of the most widespread of magical beliefs. See Arturo Castiglioni, *Adventures of the Mind* (New York, 1946), p. 33. The belief crops up again in Mormon history in some of Joseph Smith's early revelations, and in the mystic names bestowed upon the Saints in the rites of the endowment, by which they are to be summoned at the day of resurrection.

[24]Smith, *Biographical Sketches*, pp. 85-86, tells a story which, allowing for differences in the idiom, is striking in corroboration of the legend as I have reconstructed it from "hostile" sources: In the September before Alvin's death, which Lucy erroneously places in 1824, Joseph made an effort to obtain the plates, but having taken them up, laid them down again for the purpose of covering the box, lest some one chancing to pass that way get whatever treasures remained. When he turned round to take up the record again, "behold it was gone, and where he knew not, neither did he know the means by which it had been taken from him." He kneeled in prayer, whereupon "the angel of the Lord appeared to him, and told him that he had not done as he had been commanded, for in a former revelation he had been commanded not to lay the plates down, or put them for a moment out of his hands, until he got into the house and deposited them in a chest or trunk, having a good lock and key." He had not done this, and so he had been deprived of the record. The angel showed him the plates again, but when he reached forth his hand to take them, "he was hurled back upon the ground with great violence." This story Lucy relates separate and distinct from her son's narrative of having been shown the plates a year earlier.

[25]Ibid., pp. 82-83, 89-90.

[26]See Peter Ingersoll's statement in Howe, *Mormonism Unvailed*, p. 233.

[27]There is a curious lacuna in the various stories which would indicate that one year Joseph forgot all about his September 22 appointment with the spirit. The Lapham account mentions such a lapse, though placing it before rather than after Alvin's death. Willard Chase says that after Joseph informed Samuel Lawrence of the plates, Lawrence waited two years before trying to get the plates, which may be another way of accounting for the same lapse.

There is more than a little reason to believe that the money-diggers of Palmyra and vicinity actively sought the plates with Joseph sometime before 1827, perhaps several years earlier; and the appearance of so confirmed a treasure-seeker as Lawrence in the story may be further evidence of this. David Whitmer, apparently in 1828, talked with some young men who claimed to have dug for such plates in company with Joseph, and they maintained that they "saw the plates in the hill that he took them out of" before Joseph obtained them. See *Kansas City Journal*, June 5, 1881. The story has persisted in Palmyra that before Joseph claimed to have found the plates in the Hill Cumorah, they had been dug after in another hill, see Cook, *Palmyra and Vicinity*, p. 238, in which the hill is pointed out. Also see the confused account in Clark, *Gleanings by the Way*, p. 227.

[28]Affidavit of Joseph Capron, Nov. 8, 1833, in Howe, *Mormonism Unvailed*, p. 260.

[29]Smith, *Biographical Sketches*, p. 99.

[30]*History of the Church*, 1:18.

[31]Smith, *Biographical Sketches*, p. 99; *Tiffany's Monthly* 5 (July 1859): 165.

[32]Smith, *Biographical Sketches*, p. 100. The detail of Joseph's having jounced off with Emma in a borrowed wagon is fully supported, see Howe, *Mormonism Unvailed*, pp. 245-46; *Tiffany's Monthly* 5 (July 1859): 164, 165; *Historical Magazine* 7 (May 1870): 307; and an unpublished statement by Joseph Knight, Jr., dated August 16, 1862, cited in B. H. Roberts, *Comprehensive History of the Church*, 1:84. Martin Harris says the wagon belonged to Stowell.

[33]Smith, *Biographical Sketches*, p. 106.

[34]Howe, *Mormonism Unvailed*, pp. 245-46.

[35]*Tiffany's Monthly* 5 (July 1859): 164, 165. Lucy Smith intimates that the plates were hidden not in a treetop but in a decayed birch log in the woods. *Biographical Sketches*, p. 104.

[36]Smith, *Biographical Sketches*, pp. 101, 106. Joseph himself described this instrument only as "two stones set in silver bows." The most complete description is by Martin Harris: "The two stones set in a bow of silver were about two inches in diameter, perfectly round, and about five-eighths of an inch thick at the centre; but not so thick at the edges where they came into the bow. They were joined by a round bar of silver, about three-eighths of an inch in diameter, and about four inches long, which, with the two stones, would make eight inches. The stones were white, like polished marble, with a few grey streaks." *Tiffany's Monthly* 5 (July 1859): 165-166. Harris seems to have examined these out-size spectacles the following year, in Pennsylvania; Lucy is the only person who claims to have seen them at Palmyra. Pomeroy Tucker, *Origin, Rise, and Progress of Mormonism* (New York, 1867), pp. 32-33, says that the "spectacle pretension . . . is believed to have been purely an afterthought, for it was not heard of outside the family for a considerable period subsequent to the first story [of the finding of the plates]."

[37]Smith, *Biographical Sketches*, p. 101.

[38]Howe, *Mormonism Unvailed*, pp. 245-46. Also see Smith, *Biographical Sketches*, p. 124.

[39]*Tiffany's Monthly* 5 (July 1859): 167.

[40]*History of the Church*, 1: 19.

[41]Interview with Thomas H. Taylor, Manchester, New York, *Saints' Herald*, June 1, 1881.

[42]In his letter to John Wentworth published in *Times and Seasons* 3 (March 1, 1842): 708. On the subject of the persecutions Joseph is not the most reliable of witnesses, but it may be that someone actually did take a shot at him, and that this is the basis in fact for an incident Lucy Smith relates, placed by her however in Joseph's fifteenth year. See her *Biographical Sketches*, p. 72.

[43]Smith, *Biographical Sketches*, p. 102. Chase's own money- digging proclivities are mentioned by Dr. John Stafford, son of William Stafford, see *Saints' Herald*, June 1, 1881.

[44]*Journal of Discourses* 2:180; and see also *Journal of Discourses* 5:55. Young says the conjuror journeyed to and from Palmyra three times in the effort to lay hands on Joseph's plates. It is not unlikely that this is the same person who figured in an episode at Albion in the fall of 1825, while Joseph was in Pennsylvania. With the aid of a mineral stone buried in a hat, a diviner of that locality had spied out a monstrous potash kettle filled with the purest bullion, thought to have been buried prior to the flood. Efforts to obtain it were unavailing because "His Satanic Majesty, or some other invisible agent," kept it under "marching orders." *Wayne Sentinel*, Dec. 27, 1825, quoting the Albion *Orleans Advocate*. Albion lies about fifty miles west of Palmyra by air, upwards of sixty by road or canal.

[45]It is likely that in speaking of the Urim and Thummim Lucy has reference here to Joseph's peepstone, about which her book is extremely reticent. (In her single reference to it she calls it a "key," the same term she applies to the Urim and Thummim.) That this is a sensitive point is indicated by the fact that the editions of her book published in Utah change her language in reference to the peepstone from "key" to "means." Joseph was accustomed to carrying his stone about with him, and he never claimed to be able to see anything in the Urim and Thummim that he could not also see in his stone.

The circumstances of Joseph's going to Macedon to work, and Emma's seeking him there, is mentioned not only by Lucy but by Willard Chase, who places the event about ten days after Joseph claimed to have obtained the plates. Howe, *Mormonism Unvailed*, p. 246.

[46]Smith, *Biographical Sketches*, pp. 102-109. This same story was told to Willard Chase in October 1827 but with Joseph being attacked by two men rather than three. Brigham Young, *Journal of Discourses* 5:55, speaks of Joseph having had to knock down "two or three" men in bringing home the plates. Martin Harris further reduces the number of assailants in saying that Joseph, enroute home, "was met by what appeared to be a man, who demanded the plates, and struck him with a club on his side, which was all black and blue. Joseph knocked the man down, and then ran for home, and was much out of breath. When he arrived at home, he handed the plates in at the window, and they were received from him by his mother." *Tiffany's Monthly* 5 (July 1859): 166.

[47]Palmyra *Reflector*, Feb. 14, 1831; *Historical Magazine* 7 (May 1870): 307. Brigham Young, *Journal of Discourses* 5:55, would have us believe that "millions and millions" of spirits sought to prevent Joseph from getting the

plates. Heber C. Kimball remarked, somewhat ambiguously, "You know that the world has made a great deal of fuss, and told many lies about the devil pitching on to Joseph Smith when he went to get the plates, but they will get to a place where the devils will handle them worse than they did Joseph when he got the plates; if they do not embrace the Gospel it will be so." *Journal of Discourses* 3:230.

[48]Letter to John Wentworth, *Times and Seasons* 3 (March 1, 1842): 707. The only other description of the plates in detail seems to be that by Martin Harris, who says that they were "seven inches wide by eight inches in length, and were of the thickness of plates of tin; and when piled one above the other, they were altogether about four inches thick; and they were put together on the back by three silver rings, so that they would open like a book." *Tiffany's Monthly* 5 (July 1859): 165.

[49]Howe, *Mormonism Unvailed*, pp. 235-36. See also Smith, *Biographical Sketches*, pp. 133-34.

[50]*Tiffany's Monthly* 5 (July 1859): 166-67.

[51]Howe, *Mormonism Unvailed*, p. 246; *Tiffany's Monthly* 5 (July 1859): 166.

[52]Lucy Smith and Martin Harris supply parallel accounts of these events; where they vary I regard Harris as being the better authority, his memory not colored by quite the same obligations.

[53]Smith, *Biographical Sketches*, pp. 107-109. According to Martin Harris, when the plates were taken from the cooper's shop, "they were put into an old Ontario glass-box. Old Mr. Beman sawed off the ends, making the box the right length to put them in, and when they went in he said he heard them jink, but he was not permitted to see them" (*Tiffany's Monthly* 5 [July 1859]: 167). Beman had been one of Joseph's associates in the money-digging, and his daughter Louisa subsequently became one of the prophet's plural wives. He is evidently the "man by the name of Braman" referred to by Lucy. The details of the plates' being kept from this time in a glass box is confirmed by Isaac Hale, who saw the box after the removal to Pennsylvania (Howe, *Mormonism Unvailed*, p. 263).

Lucy would have us believe that not only the plates but a singular breastplate Joseph had obtained with them were thus nailed up. She is the only one who ever claims to have handled this breastplate, and I am inclined to doubt that her memory is substantive. According to her story, one day after he brought the plates home, Joseph called her from work to show her this breastplate, wrapped in a thin muslin handkerchief so thin that she could see the glistening metal. "It was concave on one side and convex on the other, and extended from the neck downwards, as far as the centre of the stomach of a man of extraordinary size. It had four straps of the same material, for the purpose of fastening it to the breast, two of which ran back to go over the shoulders, and the other two were designed to fasten to the hips. They were just the width of two of my fingers, (for I measured them,) and they had holes in the end of them, to be convenient in fastening. The whole plate was worth at least five hundred dollars." Smith, *Biographical Sketches*, p. 107. Fawn M. Brodie, *No Man Knows My History* (New York, 1945), p. 40, has suggested that Joseph may have found a copper breastplate of a kind often found in mounds; had this been the case, however, he would doubtless have made public exhibition of it as he did the Egyptian mummies and papyri he acquired in 1835.

[54]See the statements concerning Harris by his wife Lucy, his cousin Henry, and G. W. Stodard in Howe, *Mormonism Unvailed*, pp. 251-52, 254-57, 260-61; and accounts of him in the *Wayne Sentinel*, May 21, 1831, the Rochester *Daily Democrat*, June, 1841, and Clark, *Gleanings by the Way*, pp. 222-24, 254.

[55]*Tiffany's Monthly* 5 (July 1859): 164.

[56]Smith, *Biographical Sketches*, pp. 111-12. Lucy Smith's account of her visit to the Harris home confirms in general Harris's own story, but she pictures Mrs. Harris as trying to press upon her two hundred dollars or so "to assist in getting the record translated," an offer Lucy Smith declined with dignity. Nothing that is known about Lucy Harris and her views about the proper use of money entitles this to any credence. The story is doubtless explained by the various humiliations Lucy Smith subsequently experienced at the hands of Lucy Harris, and the need that worked upon her memory to put her family in a light befitting their sense of integrity.

[57]*Tiffany's Monthly* 5 (July 1859): 168-70. There is no reason to doubt the substantial accuracy of Harris's account of Joseph's appeal to him for financial aid. Peter Ingersoll, however, says that Joseph came to him seeking to borrow money, his brother-in-law, Alva, to be his security. Ingersoll agreed to let him have the money if he could not obtain it elsewhere. Joseph then went to Palmyra, and, according to the story he told Ingersoll, "I there met that dam fool Martin Harris, and told him that I had a command to ask the first *honest man* I met with, for fifty dollars in money, and he would let me have it. I saw at once . . . that it took his notion, for he promptly gave me the fifty." A variant version owing to Willard Chase is that Joseph met Harris in the street at Palmyra and told him, "I have a commandment from God to ask the first man I meet in the street to give me fifty dollars, to assist me in doing the work of the Lord by translating the Golden Bible." Harris, "being naturally a credulous man," gave him the money. Howe, *Mormonism Unvailed*, pp. 236, 246. In contrast to this is Lucy Smith's story that the first time Harris came over to the farm after the finding of the plates, he stepped immediately up to Joseph, took a bag of silver out of his pocket, and said, "Here, Mr. Smith, is fifty dollars; I give this to you to do the Lord's work with; no, I give it to the Lord for his own work." *Biographical Sketches*, pp. 112-13.

[58]Turner, *Phelps and Gorham's Purchase*, p. 215.

[59]See the affidavit of Abigail Harris in Howe, *Mormonism Unvailed*, p. 253. Lucy's later history at Kirtland and Nauvoo, when she exhibited Joseph's Egyptian mummies and other odds and ends in exactly this way, leaves no room for doubt as to the substantial accuracy of these remarks.

[60]Lucy Mack Smith to Solomon Mack, Waterloo, New York, Jan. 6, 1831, printed in Ben E. Rich, *Scrap Book of Mormon Literature* (Chicago, 190-?), 1:543-45.

CHAPTER 5

[1]See Isaac Hale's statement in E. D. Howe, *Mormonism Unvailed* (Painesville, Ohio), p. 264. With respect to the role Joseph's son was expected to play in the affair of the golden plates, as also some of the curious tales told before Joseph hit upon this explanation of his refusal to show the plates, see Palmyra *Reflector*, March 19, 1831; Howe, *Mormonism Unvailed*, pp. 236, 245, 247, 264, 267-69; Pomeroy Tucker, *Origin, Rise, and Progress of Mormonism* (New York, 1867), pp. 31-32; *Lippincott's Magazine*, 26 (Aug. 1880): 201; John A. Clark, *Gleanings by the Way* (Philadelphia, 1842), p. 226.

[2]Many years later Emma said that Joseph bought her uncle Jesse Hale's place, adjoining her father's farm (*Saints' Herald*, Oct. 1, 1879), but the instrument by which the property was formally conveyed from Isaac Hale to Joseph Smith is still preserved in the Susquehanna County Recorder's Office at Montrose, Pennsylvania. It has been asserted that although Joseph purchased the farm of his father-in-law, he gave it so little attention through the whole period of his residence that it is difficult to conceive what he could have used for money. See also Frederick G. Mather, "The Early Days of Mormonism," *Lippincott's Magazine*, 26 (Aug. 1880): 201; and Emily C. Blackman, *History of Susquehanna County* (Philadelphia, 1873), p. 500.

[3]*History of the Church*, 1:19.

[4]Howe, *Mormonism Unvailed*, pp. 270-71; Clark, *Gleanings by the Way*, p. 234; *Lippincott's Magazine*, 26 (Aug. 1880): 201; and compare Palymra *Reflector*, March 19, 1831.

[5]Exodus 28:30. See Leviticus 8:8; Numbers 27:21; Deuteronomy 33:8; Ezra 2:63; Nehemiah 7:65; and I Samuel 28:6. The words "Urim" and "Thummim" are translated as light (or revelation) and truth, and in the Hebrew may be seen in the Yale University seal.

[6]*History of the Church*, 1:12. This view Joseph incorporated into the Book of Mormon; see Mosiah 8:13, 19; 28:20; Alma 37:21, 24; Ether 3:28. In Mormon usage the Urim and Thummim have been considered not as separate entities but as a whole, hence "Urim and Thummim."

[7]See Harris's description of this "enormous pair of spectacles" to Charles Anthon, Howe, *Mormonism Unvailed*, pp. 270-71; Clark, *Gleanings by the Way*, p. 234. Down through the years, Joseph's followers have speculated that the proportions of the Urim and Thummim indicated that there once existed a species of men and women much larger than any now known.

[8]*Tiffany's Monthly*, 5 (July 1859): 166. With Harris as its apparent source, the *Wayne County Inquirer* of Bethany, Pennsylvania, reported in 1830, "Smith would put his face into a hat in which he had a *white stone*, and pretend to read from it, while his coadjutor transcribed." *Wayne County Inquirer*, quoted in the *Cincinnati Advertiser and Ohio Phoenix*, June 2, 1830. Harris's language in reference to the Urim and Thummim makes it obvious that his thought was shaped by Joseph's seerstone. There could have been no question of placing the awkwardly proportioned Urim and Thummim in a hat. If the stones were detachable from their mounting,

they were only seerstones anyway. In his autobiography, William Smith declared: "The manner in which [the translation] was done was by looking into the Urim and Thummim, which was placed in a hat to exclude the light, (the plates lying near by covered up), and reading off the translation, which appeared in the stone by the power of God." *William Smith on Mormonism* (Lamoni, 1883), p. 11. In this connection, it is significant that when, on December 27, 1841, Joseph Smith exhibited his seerstone to the Twelve, Wilford Woodruff referred to it as being "the Urim and Thummim" (see M. F. Cowley, *Wilford Woodruff* [Salt Lake City, 1909], p. 157).

[9] *History of the Church*, 1:19.

[10] Howe, *Mormonism Unvailed*, p. 266.

[11] Harris told this story to Ezra Booth in the summer of 1831. See Booth's letter of Oct. 2, 1831, in the Ravenna *Ohio Star*, Oct. 20, 1831. Booth did not give the date of the colloquy between Joseph and Harris, but there is little question about it. Compare the language of Joseph's first revelation in July 1828 when God rebukes Joseph, "Behold, you . . . have gone on in the persuasions of men . . . behold, you should not have feared man more than God" (Book of Commandments, Chapter 2).

[12] *Wayne Sentinel*, June 1, 1827. A German scholar working in the Vatican Library declared that he had found evidence that the Mexicans and Egyptians had had intercourse with one another from remotest antiquity, and at the same time he claimed to have found examples of biblical texts written in two different Egyptian dialects, the Sefitic and the Memphitic.

[13] The progress which had been made in deciphering the Egyptian hieroglyphics was summed up in the *Edinburgh Review*, 45 (Dec. 1826 and March 1827): 95-147, 528-39, accompanied by a facsimile giving demotic and hieroglyphic equivalents for the Greek alphabet. These articles were remarked in *Niles' Register*, 33 (Dec. 1, 1827): 218, and it would be unlikely if Joseph's attention was not called to the article in the widely read *Register*.

[14] *Transactions of the American Antiquarian Society*, 1 (Worcester, 1820): 324-25, 340-43.

[15] Concerning Harris's interview with Mitchill, a writer in the New York *Morning Courier and New-York Enquirer*, Sept. 1, 1831, relates: "Harris says that the Doctor received him very 'purlitely,' looked at his engravings—made a learned dissertation on them—compared them with the hieroglyphics discovered by Champollion in Egypt—and set them more as the language of a people formerly in existence in the East, but now no more." Some writers have placed the visit of Harris to Mitchill subsequent to the visit to Anthon, but as Mitchill had by far the greater celebrity and as Anthon himself firmly says that Harris originally come to him with a note of introduction from Mitchill, it must be supposed that the visit to Anthon followed that to Mitchill. The latter died in 1831 and left no account of the incident. In his letter of Jan. 15, 1831, to E. D. Howe, W. W. Phelps remarks that the transcript was taken to Utica, Albany, and New York, and that in the latter city Mitchill referred Harris to Anthon. Howe, *Mormonism Unvailed*, p. 273.

[16] Charles Anthon to E. D. Howe, Feb. 17, 1834, in Howe, *Mormonism Unvailed*, pp. 270-72. Anthon again described the transcript in these terms

in a letter of April 3, 1841, to Rev. T. W. Coit, printed in the *Church Record*, 1841, and reprinted in Clark, *Gleanings by the Way*, pp. 233-38.

[17]The seven-line transcript which has become known as the "Anthon transcript" was preserved by David Whitmer with the secondary manuscript of the Book of Mormon which came to him at Oliver Cowdery's death in 1850, and like that manuscript is now owned by the Reorganized LDS church. The first three lines of the transcript were reproduced in facsimile in *The Prophet*, Dec. 21, 1844, and identified at that time as a representation of the characters taken by Harris to Anthon. A minor puzzle is how and when this three-line transcript was made, for Cowdery had been estranged since 1838.

Accepting the authenticity of the "Anthon transcript," a young Mormon attorney, Ariel L. Crowley, in four articles published in the *Improvement Era*, January to March 1942, and September 1944, attempted to establish by visual demonstration that the characters on the transcript not only derive from demotic Egyptian but that they make "connected thought." Crowley's researches having been received by the Saints as "evidence of the truth of the Book of Mormon," I have referred them to an Egyptian scholar, Carleton T. Hodge. Under date of April 21, 1949, Hodge wrote me:

> I do not believe the transcript to be a copy, even a very rough copy, of a demotic manuscript. If a demotic text was before Joseph Smith at the time the transcript was made, only random characters were copied (and that rather badly), with no continuity and interspersed with signs totally unrelated to demotic. My reasons for this are as follows:
>
> The characters used in demotic are not readily isolated. A "word" or other unit of writing was a fairly closely knit group of signs, with many ligatures. The original hieroglyphs from which demotic writing developed appear in radically different forms according to their position in such a unit. So in order to have a demotic document or even a rough facsimile, a sequence of signs is necessary—a group forming a complete "word." The "Anthon transcript" is almost totally devoid of any sequences which could be so interpreted and has no sequences whatsoever which could form a brief utterance or statement in demotic. The signs which are similar to demotic forms are isolated and hence without any significance. The similarities given in detail in the photographic reproductions [of actual demotic characters compared with characters from the "transcript"] are often forced and just as often parallels could be found in any number of scripts. (Compare David Diringer, *The Alphabet* [New York, 1948], *passim*.) Mr. Crowley himself points out some of the coincidental parallels with completely irrelevant scripts. Any parallels from Assyrian, Sabean, Arabic (*Improvement Era*, Feb. 1942, Figs. 110, 120, 132, etc., March, 1942, *passim*) are not only irrelevant but detrimental to the argument. Egyptian was at no time influenced by any of these scripts (with the possible exception of the so-called "syllabic orthography," which has no bearing on the case). None of the

similarities have any meaning without being in a meaningful sequence.

Gardiner's *Egyptian Grammar*, frequently quoted by Mr. Crowley, has an excellent specimen of demotic with a hieroglyphic transcription. This gives one a good idea of how an actual text looks, and an attempt to connect similar hieroglyphs in the transcription with any particular sign in the demotic will readily show my point about the relation of signs in groups. Mr. Crowley himself admits defeat on the translation of the transcript and on the identification of many signs. Had there been any basis to the contention that this was a demotic document, I am sure his industry would have been rewarded.

The Mormon appeal from this verdict would take the ground that the "Anthon Transcript" is a transcript from "reformed" rather than demotic Egyptian, and therefore not amenable to demotic criticism. This, however, returns the argument to where it was before—a private language interposed between Joseph Smith and the world of scholarship.

[18]See the New York *Morning Courier and New-York Enquirer*, Sept. 1, 1831, and the Rochester *Daily Advertiser and Telegraph*, Aug. 31, 1829. Clark, *Gleanings by the Way*, p. 229, says that shortly after Harris's return from New York he "told me that, the book was written very remarkably, but he could not decide exactly what language they belonged to." On the other hand, W. W. Phelps wrote E. D. Howe from Canandaigua, New York, Jan. 15, 1831, that Anthon had "translated and declared them [the characters] to be the ancient shorthand Egyptian." Howe, *Mormonism Unvailed*, p. 273.

[19]Much was made of these remarks by the early Mormons, but modern scholars within the church acknowledge that Anthon could have had no background, knowledge of Egyptian being what it was, which would have enabled him to pass upon the correctness or otherwise of the "translation" brought him. An alphabet had been worked out by Champollion, but not yet a grammar or a dictionary.

[20]*History of the Church*, 1:20. There is no independent account of this interview which comes from Harris himself, other than a recital preserved by Edward Stevenson in *Millennial Star*, 44 (1882): 79, but one detail of Joseph's own account is supported in Harris's interivew in *Tiffany's Monthly*, 5 (July 1859).

[21]Howe, *Mormonism Unvailed*, pp. 270-71. What appears to be a photographic reproduction of the original of Anthon's letter of 1834 is in the library of the Reorganized LDS church.

[22]Clark, *Gleanings by the Way*, pp. 235-36.

[23]See Isaiah 29:11-12 and, in the Book of Mormon, 2 Nephi 27:15-20. Joseph thought so well of this improvement upon Isaiah that he subsequently incorporated it into his revision of the Bible; see his Holy Scriptures, Isaiah 29:20-22. Since it was Joseph's rule in the Book of Mormon to prophesy only about what had already taken place, this passage is the best possible evidence that some byplay about a sealed book actually occurred in Harris's interview with Anthon.

[24]In both of the letters cited in Note 16 Anthon alludes to this second visit from Harris.

[25]Clark, *Gleanings by the Way*, pp. 229-30.

[26]*History of the Church*, 1:20.

[27]Lucy Mack Smith, *Biographical Sketches* (Liverpool, 1853), pp. 115-16.

[28]Howe, *Mormonism Unvailed*, p. 264.

[29]See her letter to Mrs. Charles Pilgrim, Nauvoo, March 27, 1871, in the Reorganized LDS church library, and compare Ezra Booth's letter in the Ravenna *Ohio Star*: "These treasures [in the earth at Palmyra] were discovered several years since by means of the dark glass, the same with which Smith says he translated the most of the Book of Mormon."

[30]*Saints' Herald*, Oct. 1, 1879.

[31]*Deseret Evening News*, Sept. 5, 1870; and see *Millennial Star*, 44 (1882): 86-7; 48 (1886): 389-91.

[32]Howe, *Mormonism Unvailed*, p. 14.

[33]Ibid., p. 18. Howe also remarks that another account the Mormons gave of the translation was that "it was performed with the big spectacles before mentioned, and which were in fact, the identical *Urim and Thummim* mentioned in Exodus 28-30, and were brought away from Jerusalem by the heroes of the book, handed down from one generation to another, and finally buried up in Ontario county, some fifteen centuries since, to enable Smith to translate the plates *without looking at them*!"

[34]See Note 30.

[35]Interview in *Kansas City Journal*, June 5, 1881; David Whitmer, *An Address to All Believers in Christ* (Richmond, Missouri), p. 12.

[36]The church, faced with the difficulty of accounting for the stories told by Harris and Whitmer, if it is assumed that their information came from Joseph himself, has evaded this awkward question by adopting the position that no one but Joseph was competent to describe the method of translation, and as he, over his own signature, said only that through "the medium of the Urim and Thummim" he translated the record "by the gift and power of God," it is fruitless to pursue the matter further.

[37]B. H. Roberts, *Defense of the Faith and the Saints* (Salt Lake City, 1907), pp. 260, 265, and his *Comprehensive History of the Church*, 1:132-33.

[38]See the preface to the edition of the Book of Mormon published at Kirtland in 1837. The second copy of the Book of Mormon manuscript in the possession of the Reorganized LDS church exhibits in holograph many of the changes made in the text after the first edition. These do not affect the sense. Lamoni Call, *2,000 Changes in the Book of Mormon* (Bountiful, Utah, 1897), examines these in some detail.

CHAPTER 6

[1]*History of the Church*, 1:19-20; Lucy Mack Smith, *Biographical Sketches* (Liverpool, 1853), pp. 117-18.

[2]Smith, *Biographical Sketches*, p. 118; E. D. Howe, *Mormonism Unvailed* (Painesville, Ohio), pp. 267-69; Mary Audentia Smith Anderson, *Ancestry and Posterity of Joseph Smith and Emma Hale* (Independence, Missouri, 1929), on the authority of a family Bible, gives the baby's name as Alva, as does his grave in the old McKune cemetery south of Oakland, Pennsylvania, a few yards from that of Isaac Hale.

[3]Smith, *Biographical Sketches*, p. 121.

[4]Ibid., pp. 122-24.

[5]Book of Commandments, Chapter 2.

[6]*History of the Church*, 1:28.

[7]Smith, *Biographical Sketches*, p. 126. Joseph's autobiography rewrites these events to reflect his later necessities, for he had given his followers to understand that his first revelations were had through the Urim and Thummim. He explains that this instrument had been taken from him because he had wearied the Lord in asking that Harris be permitted to show the "writings" to his family and neighbors; that it was returned long enough for him to have his first revelation; that the plates and the Urim and Thummim were then again taken from him, but returned in a few days; and that he then inquried of the Lord and was granted a second revelation about the lost portion of the Book of Mormon manuscript. *History of the Church*, 1:21, 23. Since demonstrably he had this second revelation in May 1829, it is clear how much credence may be given this recital. [La]fayette Lapham, *Historical Magazine*, 2nd Series, 7 (May 1870): 305-309, says that after the loss of the manuscript "Joseph and Harris returned to Harmony, and found the plates missing—the Lord had taken them also. Then Joseph put on the spectacles, and saw where the Lord had hid them, among the rocks, in the mountains. Though not allowed to get them, he could, by the help of the spectacles, read them where they were, as well as if they were before him. They were directed . . . [to] begin where they left off, and translate until they were directed to stop."

[8]Book of Commandments, Chapter 3.

[9]Isaiah 29:14; I Corinthians 1:8; John 4:35; Revelation 14:15; Matthew 7:7, 8.

[10]Significantly, the words of the Lord quoted by Isaiah, "Therefore, behold, I will proceed to do a marvellous work among this people, even a marvellous work and a wonder," are only one paragraph removed from the figure of a sealed book; the intervening paragraph reads: "Wherefore the Lord said, Forasmuch as this people draw near me with their mouth, and with their lips do honour me, but have removed their heart far from me, and their fear toward me is taught by the precept of men."

[11]Howe, *Mormonism Unvailed*, pp. 264-65.

[12]The bearing of this on Joseph's earlier practice with his seerstone is manifest. But after a church came into being, the language of the revelation became a serious embarrassment, and for the first edition of Doctrine and Covenants (1835) the passage was revised to read: "You have a gift to translate the plates; and this is the first gift that I bestowed upon you; and I have commanded that you should pretend to no other gift until my purpose is fulfilled in this; for I will grant unto you no other gift until it is finished."

Compare Book of Commandments, Chapter 4, cited here in the text, with Doctrine and Covenants (1921 edition), Section 5.

[13]See the letter from Simon Smith to Joseph Smith III, dated Bristol, England, Dec. 29, 1880, in the Reorganized LDS church library, in which he reports an interview with Harris in Utah prior to his death.

[14]They were descendants of John and Mehitable (Rowley) Fuller.

[15]The "Wood Scrape," as it came to be called, is described at length in Barnes Frisbie, *A History of Middletown, Vermont* (Rutland, 1867), pp. 43-64.

[16]*Kansas City Journal*, June 5, 1881.

[17]Smith, *Biographical Sketches*, pp. 128-30.

[18]*Kansas City Journal*, June 5, 1881.

[19]*Latter Day Saints' Messenger and Advocate*, Oct. 1834.

[20]Oliver Cowdery, *Defence in a Rehearsal of My Grounds for Separating Myself from the Latter Day Saints* (Norton, Ohio, 1839). [Editor's note: There is some question among scholars whether this document, which can only be traced to 1906, is legitimate.]

[21]Book of Commandments, Chapter 5.

[22]Joseph had later to disembarrass himself of the language of this revelation (see Book of Commandments, Chapter 7). More ambiguously, the key passage was made to read, "Now this is not all thy gift; for you have another gift, which is the gift of Aaron; behold, it has told you many things; Behold, there is no other power, save the power of God, that can cause this gift of Aaron to be with you. Therefore, doubt not, for it is the gift of God; and you shall hold it in your hands, and do marvelous works; and no power shall be able to take it away out of your hands, for it is the work of God." (Doctrine and Covenants, Section 9.)

[23]Book of Commandments, Chapter 8.

[24]Ibid., Chapter 5.

[25]*Latter Day Saints' Messenger and Advocate*, Oct. 1834.

[26]Curiously, Cowdery wrote four and a half years later that he received baptism from Joseph's hand, "by the direction of the Angel of God, whose voice, as it has since struck me, did most mysteriously resemble the voice of Elder Sidney Rigdon, who, I am sure had no part in the transactions of that day, as the Angel was John the Baptist, which I doubt not and deny not." *A Defence in a Rehearsal of My Grounds for Separating Myself from the Latter Day Saints*. Note Cowdery's tendency to see not only angels but still more supernal personages. He relates, for example, that the Redeemer himself subsequently appeared to him in open vision to inform him that Joseph had "given revelations from his own heart and from a defiled conscience as coming from my mouth and . . . corrupted the covenant and altered words which I had spoken."

Joseph's account of the "restoration of the priesthood" makes much of two priesthoods, Aaronic and Melchizedek, the first of which was conferred at this time by John the Baptist, the second at a later date by Peter, James, and John themselves. This, however, is only another example of his proclivity for rewriting his early history to answer the logic of later events. The concept of two priesthoods evidently dates back no further than March, 1835 (Doctrine and Covenants, Section 107). Neither "Aaronic" nor "Melchizedek" priesthood was mentioned or even implied in any document of prior date. On this point some of the church's historians have been led astray, accepting Doctrine and Covenants, Section 28, as a revelation given on Sept. 4, 1830, whereas the text is a rewritten version of the original that postdates Section 107. Compare the original revelation in Book of Commandments, Chapter 28. It should be added that Smith, *Biographical Sketches*, p. 131, makes no more of this "restoration of the priesthood" on which ultimately the Mormon claim to authority rests than that one morning Joseph and Oliver "sat down to their work, as usual, and the first thing which presented itself through the Urim and Thummim, was a commandment for Joseph and Oliver to repair to the water, and attend to the ordinance of Baptism. They did so." It may be that the incident amounted to no more than this; that Cowdery's broad imagination later supplied the visitation from John the Baptist, and that Joseph seized upon Cowdery's story for its value to his legend.

[27]*History of the Church*, 1:42-44.

[28]Book of Commandments, Chapters 12-14.

[29]Ibid., Chapter 7.

[30]Ibid., Chapter 12.

[31]"Revelation, to Oliver Cowdery, David Whitmer, and Martin Harris, at Fayette, Seneca County, New York, June, 1829, given previous to their viewing the Plates containing the Book of Mormon," printed in the 1835 edition of Doctrine and Covenants as Section 42. If this revelation was extant before 1833, there is no reason why it should not have been included in the Book of Commandments, the only revelation from its period since admitted to the canon, and in view of the wholesale alterations made in the revelations when they were reprinted in Doctrine and Covenants, the historicity of this revelation must remain in question unless and until its 1829 dating can be established from other sources.

[32]Smith, *Biographical Sketches*, p. 138.

[33]See, for example, Howe, *Mormonism Unvailed*, pp. 13, 15.

[34]*Tiffany's Monthly*, 5 (July 1859): 166.

[35]*Millennial Star*, 44 (1882): 37. For a similar statement, see J. M. Sjodahl, *Introduction to the Study of the Book of Mormon*, (Salt Lake City, 1917), p. 59.

[36]A. Metcalf, *Ten Years Before the Mast* (Elk Horn, Idaho, 1888), p. 7. In this interview, Harris said that it was about three days after the other witnesses saw the plates that he was vouchsafed the privilege. He "went into the woods to pray that I might see the plates. While praying I passed into a state of entrancement, and in that state I saw the angel and the plates." Clarke, *Gleanings by the Way*, pp. 256-57: "A gentlemen in Palmyra, bred to the law, a professor of religion, and of undoubted veracity, told me that on one occasion, he appealed to Harris and asked him directly, 'Did you see those plates?' Harris replied, he did. 'Did you see the plates, and the engravings on them with your bodily eyes?' Harris replied, 'Yes, I saw them with my eyes, they were shown unto me by the power of God and not of man.' 'But did you see them with your natural—your bodily eyes, just as you see this pencil-case in my hand? Now say *no* or *yes* to this.' Harris replied, 'Why I did not see them as I do that pencil-case, yet I saw them with the eye of faith; I

saw them just as distinctly as I see any thing around me, though at the time they were covered over with a cloth.' "

[37]Palmyra *Reflector*, March 19, 1831. This is the basis of an account later printed in Howe, *Mormonism Unvailed*, p. 16.

[38]Report of Orson Pratt and Joseph F. Smith, Sept. 17, 1878, in *Millennial Star*, 40. An account to substantially the same effect was published in *Kansas City Journal*, June 5, 1881, and one not dissimilar in the Richmond, Missouri, *Democrat*, Jan. 26, 1888, the day after his death; see *Millennial Star*, 50:139.

[39]David Whitmer to A. Metcalf, April 2, 1887, in the latter's *Ten Years Before the Mast*, pp. 73-74.

[40]Book of Commandments, Chapter 4.

[41]Smith, *Biographical Sketches*, p. 140.

[42]Thomas Ford, *History of Illinois* (Chicago, 1854), pp. 257-58.

[43]Tucker, *Origin, Rise, and Progress of Mormonism*, pp. 50-53.

[44]Smith, *Biographical Sketches*, p. 142.

[45]Ibid., pp. 142-43.

[46]Whitmer, *An Address to All Believers in Christ*, p. 32.

[47]Stephen Harding, later a governor of Utah, somewhat regretfully admitted to this practical joke some years after; see Tucker, *Origin, Rise, and Progress of Mormonism*, pp. 80-81, and Thomas Gregg, *The Prophet of Palmyra* (New York, 1930), pp. 48-49. A contemporary allusion to the escapade is found in the Palmyra *Reflector*, Sept. 23, 1829.

[48]Smith, *Biographical Sketches*, p. 148.

[49]This episode as described by Smith, ibid., pp. 148-51, is one of the few sections of her book which can be checked for accuracy against external sources, and from this criterion it has to be said that all her reminiscences must be received with great caution. In many particulars, her memory was seriously at fault, as becomes at once apparent when recourse is had to the issues of the *Reflector* itself.

[50]Smith, *Biographical Sketches*, pp. 150-51.

[51]Book of Commandments, Chapter 16.

CHAPTER 7

[1]Book of Commandments, Chapter 9; "Preface," Book of Mormon (Palmyra, 1830).

[2]B. H. Roberts, in editing *History of the Church*, 1:23, rejected the date given for this revelation, May 1829, and conjecturally dated it for August or September 1828. In this he followed the vague and rather perilous authority of Joseph's autobiography. It would in fact simplify the problem of dealing with the authorship and text of the Book of Mormon to grant Roberts and Joseph Smith their point. Yet the fact remains that the revelation was dated May 1829 when first printed in the Book of Commandments in 1833, that it appeared in this book as Chapter 9 rather than Chapter 3, and that when reprinted in the various editions of Doctrine and Covenants, published

under Joseph Smith's own eye, the date first given it was retained, even when the revelation itself was internally revised. Convenient as I would find it to date the revelation for 1828, I find it necessary to postulate the correctness of the later date.

[3]The copy of the Book of Mormon manuscript in the possession of the Reorganized LDS church at Independence, Missouri, commonly spoken of as the original, or "one of the original manuscripts," clearly is a secondary copy. I was enabled to study a photostatic reproduction of it in February 1948. The errors it contains are those characteristic of retranscriptions, notable examples of which appear on folios 181 and 426; the numbering of the folios is not interrupted at the critical point, nor the continuity of the transcription; and the testimonies of the three and eight witnesses at the end continue as an integral part of the manuscript. Presumably, therefore, the original manuscript of the Book of Mormon was the copy placed in the cornerstone of the Mansion House in Nauvoo and largely destroyed by the damp. A few pages of this copy were subsequently salvaged, some going to the Reorganized LDS church (subsequently to crumble away), and some to the Utah LDS church, which still preserves them. These pages are withheld from study, even in the form of the photographs which have been made of them, but are understood to comprise some twenty-odd folios from the opening pages of the Book of Mormon, one of which is reproduced in Francis W. Kirkham, *A New Witness for Christ in America* (Independence, 1942), p. 216. The pages thus preserved being a part of the "restored text," they are, unfortunately, not likely to yield much information of value even when made available to scholars.

[Editor's note: Since the early 1970s, the LDS church in Utah has made available to researchers either a photocopy or a microfilm copy of the original manuscript to the Book of Mormon.]

[4]Canandaigua *Ontario Repository*, July 11, 1827. The work referred to, *David Cusick's Sketches of Ancient History of the Six Nations* (Lewistown, New York, 1827), went through several editions. Its content does not suggest that it could have contributed anything to the Book of Mormon beyond the primary idea quoted by the *Repository*.

[5]A formidable literature concerning the Ten Tribes had come into being by this time, and Ethan Smith drew upon much of this for his evidences. Among the better-known works were James Adair, *The History of the American Indians* (London, 1775); Robert Ingram, *Accounts of the Ten Tribes of Israel being in America* (Colchester, England, 1792); Charles Crawford, *An Essay upon the Propagation of the Gospel, in Which There Are Facts to Prove That Many of the Indians in America Are Descended from the Ten Tribes* (Philadelphia, 1799); and Elias Boudinot, *A Star in the West; or a Humble Attempt to Discover the Long Lost Ten Tribes of Israel Preparatory to Their Return to Their Beloved City, Jerusalem* (Trenton, 1816).

[6]Ezra Booth, in his letter of Oct. 24, 1831, in the Ravenna *Ohio Star*, Oct. 27, 1831, most explicitly reports Joseph's views on this point, but see also *History of the Church*, 1.

[7]Since 1870, when Orson Pratt described it to the Saints in a sermon at Salt lake City (*Journal of Discourses* 13:130-31), apologists for the Book of Mormon have periodically referred to a stone decalogue carved in Hebrew

characters, found in a mound at Newark, Ohio, in 1867, as evidence for the authenticity of Joseph Smith's book; this decalogue, however, was a hoax.

See E. O. Randall, "The Mound Builders and the Lost Tribes: The 'Holy Stone of Newark,'" *Ohio Archaeological and Historical Society Publications*, 17 (April 1908). Archaeological research in the Americas has brought to light no single artifact which can be regarded as of Hebrew origin.

[8]These quotations are from the 1825 edition of *View of the Hebrews*, pp. 150, 172-73, 184, 207, 223, 225.

[9]It exhibits the literary kinship of the Book of Mormon and the Procrustean adjustments required in the thinking of believers that such books as Josiah Priest's *American Antiquities* (1833) and Lord Kingsborough's *Antiquities of Mexico* (1830-48) are still cited by apologists for the Book of Mormon, while the disciplined scholarship of modern archaeologists and ethnologists is dismissed as "speculative." The complex states of mind to which the Book of Mormon has given rise could profitably be explored at length; in general, the point of view of earnest church members against the adverse weight of evidence is that not all the evidence is in. However long it takes, Joseph's book will finally be vindicated; the disrepute into which it has fallen is only an incident in the trials by which true believers shall be sifted out from those of little faith.

[10]See Mormon 1:18-19; 2:10; and Helaman 13:19-20, 31, 35-38, for references to aboriginal treasures, read with lively interest by Joseph's early converts.

[11]See 1 Nephi 2:16 and 9:4 for almost the only information we have about the character of that part of Joseph's book which disappeared, and which as rewritten had a more pronounced religious emphasis.

[12]An example may be seen in the *Palmyra Register*, March 8, 1820.

[13]It is curious that at the time Joseph Smith was writing of a visionary Lehi who dwelt in a skin tent in the Valley of Lemuel, his own visionary father was living at Manchester in a drafty house which, together with the land on which it stood, had fallen into the possession of Lemuel Durfee.

[14]The complete texts of the two visions, as derived from the Book of Mormon and Lucy Mack Smith's *Biographical Sketches* (Liverpool, 1853), may be compared in parallel in I. Woodbridge Riley, *The Founder of Mormonism* (New York, 1902), pp. 114-17. The common origin of these visions is evident from the elements common to each. Had the first 116 pages of the original Book of Mormon manuscript not been lost, it might have been possible to identify other "visions of Lehi" with the six additional dreams Lucy Smith describes.

[15]*Millennial Harbinger*, Feb. 7, 1831.

[16]Fawn M. Brodie, *No Man Knows My History* (New York, 1945), p. 67.

[17]See B. H. Roberts, *Defense of the Faith and the Saints* (Salt Lake City, 1907), pp. 335-37, 351, 362-64, in which Roberts could only adduce as new truth the pronouncements (a) "fools mock, but they shall mourn;" (b) "the Lord doth grant unto all nations, of their own nation and tongue, to preach his word;" and (c) "Adam fell that men might be; and men are that they might have joy."

APPENDIX A

[1]The murder of Oliver Harper on May 11, 1824, is celebrated in the annals of Susquehanna county. He was about fifty years old, the owner of a large farm, and was also engaged in lumbering. He had taken a raft of lumber down the Susquehanna River and was returning with about $800 when he was robbed and murdered. Jason Treadwell of Harmony (now Oakland), Pennsylvania, was charged with the crime, arrested, tried in Montrose, September 1-5, 1824, and executed the following January 13, on the only gallows ever erected in Susquehanna County. See Emily C. Blackman, *History of Susquehanna County* (Philadelphia, 1873), pp. 97, 582; Phamanthus M. Stocker, *Centennial History of Susquehanna County* (Philadelphia, 1887), p. 573; and J. B. Wilkinson, *Annals of Binghamton* (Binghamton, New York, 1840), pp. 147-48. A short notice of Harper's murder appears in the Philadelphia *National Gazette*, May 21, 1824. The 1820 census returns, now in the National Archives, show Harper to have lived in Windsor Township, Broome County, New York.

[2]Most of the names appearing in this document are readily verifiable, though the 1820 census returns for Susquehanna County are not available for cross-checking. John Grant is shown by the 1830 census to reside in Colesville Township, Broome County, New York. Isaac Hale, subsequently Joseph Smith's father-in-law, and one of the earliest settlers in Harmony, made affidavit in 1834 regarding his participation in this treasure-hunting and his eventual revulsion against it. David Hale, a son of Isaac, was the tax collector for Harmony in 1820 and later settled in Amboy, Illinois, where he furnished information printed in Emily Blackman's *History of Susquehanna County*, pp. 103-104. William Hale was listed in the 1830 census as residing in Colesville, New York. The two Newtons were possibly sons of Thaddeus Newton, who settled at Bainbridge, New York, about 1790; a son named Charles is reported by James H. Smith, *History of Chenango and Madison Counties* (p. 163), to have died at Oxford, New York, about 1841. One Charles Newton was found in Bainbridge by the 1820 census, and he may be both the son of Thaddeus and the Charles A. of the money-digging agreement. John R. Shephard may have been a son of John Shepherd who was, according to Wilkinson's *Annals of Binghamton* (p. 115), one of those who settled at Tioga Point in 1780. Josiah (or sometimes spelled Isaiah—the last name is also variantly spelled Stowel and Stoal) Stowell appears in Mormon annals as having been responsible for Joseph Smith's "employment" at fourteen dollars a month for money-digging; he is listed by the census in 1820 and 1830 as a resident of Bainbridge. Calvin and Elijah (also spelled Elihu) Stowell were both listed at Bainbridge in the 1820 census, Calvin having been, according to Smith's history of Chenango County (p. 150), the first presiding officer of the "South Presbyterian Society and Meeting-House of the town of Bainbridge" on its organization in 1819. "William Wylie" was located at Bainbridge by the 1820 census.

[3]Peter G. Bridgman is noted in Smith's *History of Chenango and Madison Counties* (p. 152) to have been on February 17, 1829, a trustee of the West Bainbridge Methodist Episcopal Church.

[4]A salt water spring or deposit known to the Indians in the vicinity of the Great Bend of the Susquehanna was often vainly searched for by the white settlers. See J. B. Wilkinson, *Annals of Binghamton*, pp. 103-104. The search for such a spring in the vicinity of Bainbridge was no doubt spurred by the finding of a salt spring in 1824 on a branch of Snake Creek seven miles northeast of Montrose, Pennsylvania. See the account of it in *Zion's Herald*, April 21, 1824.

[5]No person of this name appears in the census returns, but the name itself was obviously a puzzle to the transcriber. In 1820 one Charles Atherton was listed at Bainbridge.

[6]The 1830 census shows Asahel Bacon and Matilda Bacon as heads of households in Windsor Township, Broome County, New York.

[7]At the time of the 1820 census Simpson Stowell lived at Bainbridge, Chenango County, New York. His whereabouts in 1830 I have been unable to establish.

[8]With this testimony compare the statement of W. R. Hines in *Naked Truths About Mormonism*, Jan. 1888: "Jo Smith, who became the Mormon prophet, and his father came from Palmyra or Manchester, N. Y., and dug for salt two summers, near and in sight of my house. [Hines was born at Colesville on February 11, 1803, and lived seven miles above Isaac Hale on the Susquehanna River.] The old settlers used to buy salt from an indian squaw, who often promised to tell the whites where the salt spring was, but she never did. Jo Smith claimed to be a seer. He had a very clear stone about the size and shape of a duck's egg, and claimed that he could see lost or hidden things through it. He said he saw Captin Kidd sailing on the Susquehanna River during a freshet, and that he buried two pots of gold and silver. He claimed he saw writing cut on the rocks in an unknown language telling where Kidd buried it, and he translated it through his peepstone. I have had it many times and could see in it whatever I imagined. Jo claimed it was found in digging a well in Palmyra, N.Y. He said he borrowed it. . . . He had men who did the digging and they and others would take interests. Some would lose faith and others would take their places. They dug one well thirty feet deep and another seventy-five at the foot and south side of the Aquaga Mountain, but found no salt. My nephew now owns the land he dug on. Asa Stowell furnished the means for Jo to dig for silver ore, on Monument Hill. He dug over one year without success. Jo dug next for Kidd's money, on the west bank of the Susquehanna, half a mile from the river, and three miles from his salt wells. . . . He dug for many things and many parties, I never knew him to find anything of value."

[9]Horace Stowell was head of a household at Bainbridge when the 1830 census was made.

[10]Arad Stowell is located at Bainbridge by the census returns of both 1820 and 1830. Smith, *History of Chenango and Madison Counties* (pp. 150-51), shows him to have been a trustee of the "South Presbyterian Society and Meeting-House of the town of Bainbridge" on its organization in 1819, and again a trustee when it was reorganized on February 7, 1825, as the South Bainbridge Presbyterian Church.

[11]David McMaster was a co-trustee with Arad Stowell for the South Bainbridge Presbyterian Church in 1825, and was listed at Bainbridge in the

census of 1830. He thus appears as the McMaster most probably referred to; but in his autobiography, alluding to trials to which he was subjected in Chenango and Broome counties in the summer of 1830, Joseph Smith speaks bitterly of "Cyrus McMaster, a Presbyterian of high standing in his church, [who] was one of the chief instigators of these persecutions" (*History of the Church*, 1:97).

[12]One J. S. Thompson was listed as the head of a household in Bainbridge by the 1830 census, but more probably Jonathan Thompson appears in the census list without name, in the household of Josiah Stowell. In 1830, as in 1826, Thompson testified in Joseph's favor during proceedings against the latter. See *History of the Church*, 1:90.

[13]A number of Yoemans or Yeomans appear in the local annals, among them William, Solomon, and Jeremiah—all listed in 1820 in Windsor Township, Broome County, New York.

[14]Although nothing like a detailed chronology of the movements of the Smith family before 1830 exists, there is no reason to believe that any of the Smiths had been in Chenango prior to 1825.

[15]It is most reasonable to suppose that Stowell had heard about Joseph's pretensions to seership either by letter from or while visiting his son Simpson Stowell, who had removed to Palmyra sometime after 1820. The ingenuous Mormon explanation of why Stowell should have desired to hire Joseph Smith for money-digging is that he had heard some rumor of Smith's being shown the golden plates by the Angel Moroni and consequently thought him suited to seeking out the hidden things of the earth.

[16]James H. Smith's *History of Chenango and Madison Counties* (pp. 168-69) recalls Albert Neely as one of the first owners of a mercantile business in Afton, opening a store about 1820 and going west a few years later. As has been seen in the introduction to the court record, he married Phoebe Pearsall, aunt of Emily Pearsall to whom we are indebted for the court record.

[17]It may be a reasonable presumption that Dr. Purple made these notes in the justice of the peace record itself. That he was equipped for clerical responsibilities is evidenced by the fact that he was, on May 5, 1829, elected first town clerk of Bainbridge Village.

[18]Is it possible that Dr. Purple's recollection is inexact, that these remarks by the elder Joseph Smith were made, not before the court, but in casual conversation to interested listeners before or after the trial?

[19]Evidently this was never done. No clipping of such an article was preserved in the Purple scrapbook, and, at the insistance of Dr. Kirkham, Mrs. Helen L. Fairbanks of the Guernsey Memorial Library, Norwich, New York, searched the files of the *Chenango Union* through 1880 without finding an article of the kind.

[20]To reconcile this statement with the verdict of guilty appearing in the court record itself, see the letter of 1831 reprinted in section 4 of this Appendix.

[21]Here are harmonized the discrepant accounts of the court record and the Purple reminiscences as to the outcome of the trial. Joseph Smith would appear to have been given the equivalent of a suspended sentence. He

was, as asserted, a minor at the the time, not reaching the age of twenty-one until December 23, 1826.

[22]This language was the Universalist idiom of the period in reaction to the hellfire and brimstone teaching of other denominations.

APPENDIX B

[1]Presumably the *Wayne Sentinel* refrained from comment on the Book of Mormon because it had been responsible for printing it, while the Palmyra *Freeman*, being Anti-Masonic in its politics, may have been willing for the anti-Masonic content of the Book of Mormon to influence the public mind in any way it could.

[2]It is interesting to consider whether Sidney Rigdon, who had been in the vicinity of Canandaigua in December 1830 and January 1831 while investigating Joseph Smith and his church, had become locally identified with the conjurer brought to Palmyra from the west in 1827 to find Joseph's golden plates.

[3]This large excavation or cave, though not in the Hill Cumorah proper, became a subject of many legends in and around Palmyra. See Pomeroy Tucker, *Origin, Rise, and Progress of Mormonism* (New York, 1867); *Saints' Herald*, 1 June 1881; and Thomas L. Cook, *Palmyra and Vicinity* (Palmyra, 1930).

The Published Writings of Dale Lowell Morgan

1934

ARTICLES:

"A Student Speaks." *The University Pen,* Autumn 1934. (The *Pen* was a student literary magazine published by the University of Utah.)

1935

ARTICLES:

"Cold." *The University Pen,* Autumn 1935.
"Insight Into Confusion." *The University Pen,* Winter 1935.
"Perspective on Platitude." *The University Pen,* Spring 1935. Reprinted in *The University Pen Centennial,* 1947.

1936

ARTICLES:

"Eve." *The University Pen,* Autumn 1936.
"For the Sun Will be Always Bright." *The University Pen,* Spring 1936.

1937

ARTICLES:

"Business Man." *The University Pen,* Spring 1937.
"On Realism in Literature." *The University Pen,* Winter 1937.

1938

BOOK REVIEWS:

Architects of Ideas, by Ernest R. Trantner. *Salt Lake Tribune,*26 June 1938.
American Years, by Harold Sinclair. *Salt Lake Tribune,* 3 July 1938.
A Political History of the Cherokee Nation, by Morris L. Wardell. *Salt Lake Tribune,* 17 July 1938.
What are We to do?, by John Strachey. *Salt Lake Tribune,* 14 August 1938.
No Star is Lost, by James T. Farrell. *Salt Lake Tribune,* 9 October 1938.

Roads to a New America, by David Cushman Coyle. *Salt Lake Tribune*, 27 November 1938.
The Fifth Column and the First Forty-nine Stories, by Ernest Hemmingway. *Salt Lake Tribune*, 20 November 1938.
The Romance of Human Progress, by Arthur Stanley Riggs. *Salt Lake Tribune*, 18 December 1938.

1939

BOOKS:

Inventory of the County Archives of Utah. Salt Lake City: Utah Historical Records Survey, 1939-41. The essays on Carbon, Daggett, Emery, Tooele, Uintah, Utah, and Weber counties were written by Morgan.

BOOK REVIEWS:

Germany Speaks, a symposium. *Salt Lake Tribune*, 8 January 1939.
Guide to the Philosophy of Morals and Politics, by C. E. M. Joad. *Salt Lake Tribune*, 22 January 1939.
The United States and World Organizations, 1920-1933, by Denna Frank Fleming. *Salt Lake Tribune*, 19 February 1939.
The True History of the Conquest of Mexico, by Captain Bernal Dias Del Castillo. *Salt Lake Tribune*, 26 February 1939.
Betrayal in Central Europe, by G. E. R. Gedye. *Salt Lake Tribune*, 19 March 1939.
Albert Einstein: Maker of Universe, by H. Gordon Garbedian. *Salt Lake Tribune*, 2 April 1939.
Spanish Prisoner, by Peter Elstob. *Salt Lake Tribune*, 23 April 1939.
Mein Kampf, by Adolf Hitler. *Salt Lake Tribune*, 30 April 1939.
Democracy Works, by Arthur Garfield Hays. *Salt Lake Tribune*, 14 May 1939.
America in Midpassage, by Charles A. Beard and Mary E. Beard. *Salt Lake Tribune*, 4 June 1939.
The Bonapartes in America, by C. E. Macartney and Gordon Dorrance. *Salt Lake Tribune*, 2 July 1939.
The Web and the Rock, by Thomas Wolfe. *Salt Lake Tribune*, 9 July 1939.

1940

BOOKS:

Historical Records Survey, Utah. Salt Lake City: Works Projects Administration, 1940.
A History of Ogden. Ogden: Ogden City Commission, 1940.

ARTICLES:

"The State of Deseret." *Utah Historical Quarterly*, April, July, and October 1940.

1941

BOOKS:

Utah: A Guide to the State. American Guide Series. New York: Hastings House, 1941. Written, with others, and edited by Morgan. Reprinted, in whole or in part, in 1945, 1954,1958, and 1983.

ARTICLES:

"Utah: A Viewpoint." *Rocky Mountain Review,* Winter 1941.

1942

BOOKS:

Provo: Pioneer Mormon City. American Guide Series. Portland: Binfords and Mort, 1942. With others.

Tales of Utah, 1941-42. Dale L. Morgan, editor. Salt Lake City: Utah Writers' Project, Works Projects Administration,1942.

ARTICLES:

"Mormon Storytellers." *Rocky Mountain Review,* 1942.

1943

BOOKS:

The Humboldt: Highroad of the West. Rivers of America Series. New York: Farrar and Rinehart, 1943. Reprinted in 1985.

1945

BOOK REVIEWS:

Children of the Covenant, by Richard Scowcroft. *Saturday Review of Literature,* 18 August 1945.

No Man Knows My History, by Fawn M. Brodie. *Saturday Review of Literature,* 24 November 1945.

This is the Place: Utah, by Maurine Whipple. *Saturday Review of Literature,* 10 November 1945.

1946

BOOKS:

"Rain (An Excerpt)" and "Mormon Storytellers." In *Rocky Mountain Reader,* edited by Ray B. West. New York: E. P. Dutton, 1946.

ARTICLES:

"Great Salt Lake." *Think Magazine* (IBM Corporation), 1946.

BOOK REVIEWS:

The Colorado, by Frank Waters. *Saturday Review of Literature*, 28 September 1946.
I Hate Thursday, by Thomas Hornsby Ferril. *Saturday Review of Literature*, 7 December 1946.
Jim Bridger, by Stanley Vestal. *Saturday Review of Literature*, 26 October 1946.
On This Star, by Virginia Sorenson. *Saturday Review of Literature*, 25 May 1946.

1947

BOOKS:

The Great Salt Lake. American Lakes Series. Indianapolis: Bobbs-Merrill Company, 1947. Reprinted in 1973, with an introduction by Ray Allen Billington.
"Introduction." In *The Exploration of the Colorado River in 1869*. Dale L. Morgan, editor. Salt Lake City: Utah State Historical Society, 1947.

ARTICLES:

"Introduction to Powell Documents." *Utah Historical Quarterly*, 1947.

BOOK REVIEWS:

Across the Wide Missouri, by Bernard DeVoto. *Saturday Review of Literature*, 8 November 1947.
Along Sierra Trials, by Joyce and Josef Muench. *Saturday Review of Literature*, 20 September 1947.
Exploring Our National Parks and Monuments, by Devereaux Butcher. *Saturday Review of Literature*, 20 September 1947.
One Hundred Years in Yosemite, by Carl Parcher Russell. *Saturday Review of Literature*, 20 September 1947.
Vermilion, by Idwal Jones. *Saturday Review of Literature*, 17 May 1947.

1948

BOOKS:

"Introduction." In *The Exploration of the Colorado River* and *The High Plateaus of Utah in 1871-72*. 2 vols. Dale L. Morgan, editor. Salt Lake City: Utah State Historical Society, 1948-49.

ARTICLES:

"The Administration of Indian Affairs in Utah, 1851-58." *Pacific Historical Review*, November 1948.

BOOK REVIEWS:

Frederic Remington: Artist of the Old West, by Harold McCracken. *Saturday Review of Literature*, 24 January 1948.
Lewis and Clark: Partners in Discovery, by John Bakeless. *Saturday Review of Literature*, 17 January 1948.

MAPS:

Historical Trails, Map of Utah. Salt Lake City: Utah State Department of Publicity and Industrial Development, 1948. Reprinted ca. 1965.

1949

BOOKS:

Letters by Forty-Niners Written from Great Salt Lake City. Dale L. Morgan, editor. Los Angeles: Dawson's Book Shop, 1949.
"The Mountain States." In *The American Guide*, edited by Henry G. Alsberg. New York: Hastings House, 1949.
"Salt Lake City, City of the Saints." In *Rocky Mountain Cities*, edited by Ray B. West. New York: W. W. Norton, 1949.
Santa Fe and the Far West. Reprinted from *Niles National Register*, 1841. Dale L. Morgan, editor. Los Angeles: Glen Dawson, 1949.

ARTICLES:

"Letters by Forty-Niners." Dale L. Morgan, editor. *Western Humanities Review*, April 1949.
"The Mormon Ferry on the North Platte: The Journal of William A. Empey." Dale L. Morgan, editor. *Annals of Wyoming*, July-October 1949.
"Our History." *The Gospel News*, April 1949.

BOOK REVIEWS:

Beulah Land, by H. L. Davis. *Saturday Review of Literature*, 11 June 1949.
The Big Divide, by David Lavender. *Saturday Review of Literature*, 12 February 1949.
The Bubbling Spring, by Ross Santee. *Saturday Review of Literature*, 3 September 1949.
The Evening and the Morning, by Virginia Sorenson. *Saturday Review of Literature*, 23 April 1949.
Jesse James Was My Neighbor, by Homer Croy. *Saturday Review of Literature*, 25 June 1949.
The Journal of Madison Berryman Moorman 1850-51, edited by Irene D. Poden. *Western Humanities Review*, April 1949.
The Lost Pathfinder, by W. Eugene Hollon. *Saturday Review of Literature*, 17 September 1949.
Sierra-Nevada Lakes, by George and Bliss Hinckle. *Saturday Review of Literature*, 16 April 1949.
Wicked Water, by MacKinlay Kantor. *Saturday Review of Literature*, 12 February 1949.

MONOGRAPHS:

"A Bibliography of the Church of Jesus Christ, Organized at Green Oak, Pennsylvania, July, 1862 [Bickertonites]," *Western Humanities Review*, 1949-50.

1950

BOOK REVIEWS:

Voice in the West, by W. J. Ashton. *Saturday Review of Literature*, 15 July 1950.

MONOGRAPHS:

"A Bibliography of the Church of Jesus Christ of Latter Day Saints [Strangites]," *Western Humanities Review*, 1950-51.

1951

BOOKS:

West From Fort Bridger: The Pioneering of the Immigrant Trails Across Utah, 1846-50, by J. Roderic Korns. Salt Lake City: Utah State Historical Society, 1951. (Morgan completed and edited this book.)

BOOK REVIEWS:

Family Kingdom, by Samuel Taylor. *Saturday Review of Literature*, 12 May 1951.

1952

BOOKS:

Life in America: The West. Grand Rapids: Fideler Company, 1952. Reprinted in 1958, 1960, and 1962.

ARTICLES:

"Introduction and Annotations to: *Three Years in California: William Perkins' Journal of Life at Sonora, 1849-1852*." *Southern California Quarterly*, June 1952.

BOOK REVIEWS:

The Larkin Papers, edited by George P. Hammond. *Utah Historical Quarterly*, October 1952.

Peter Skene Ogden's Snake Country Journals, edited by K. G. Davies. *American Historical Review*, April 1952.

1953

BOOKS:

Jedediah Smith and the Opening of the West. Indianapolis: Bobbs-Merrill Company, 1953. Reprinted in 1964.

ARTICLES:

"Miles Goodyear and the Founding of Ogden." *Utah Historical Quarterly,* July, October 1953.

"Washakie and the Shoshoni: A Selection of Documents from the Records of the Utah Superintendency of Indian Affairs," (Parts 1 to 10). *Annals of Wyoming,* July 1953-April 1958.

BOOK REVIEWS:

Before Lewis and Clark, edited by A. P. Nasatir. *Utah Historical Quarterly,* July 1953.

The Course of Empire, by Bernard DeVoto. *Utah Historical Quarterly,* July 1953.

David Thompson's Journals Relating to Montana and Adjacent Regions, 1808-12, edited by M. Catherine White. *Utah Historical Quarterly,* July 1953.

The Road to Santa Fe, edited by Kate L. Gregg. *Utah Historical Quarterly,* January 1953.

MONOGRAPHS:

"A Bibliography of the Churches of the Dispersion." *Western Humanities Review,* Summer 1953.

Bibliographies of the Lesser Mormon Churches. Salt Lake City: Western Humanities Review, n.d. A compilation of Morgan's complete WHR series.

1954

BOOKS:

Jedediah Smith and His Maps of the American West. With Carl I. Wheat. San Francisco: California Historical Society, 1954.

ARTICLES:

"The Diary of William H. Ashley, March 25 to June 27, 1825." Dale L. Morgan, editor. *Bulletin of the Missouri Historical Society,* October 1954, January and April 1955.

BOOK REVIEWS:

Isn't One Wife Enough? by Kimball Young. *Saturday Review of Literature*, 21 August 1954.

The Larkin Papers, Vol. 4, edited by George P. Hammond. *Utah Historical Quarterly*, Summer 1954.

1955

ARTICLES:

"The Reminiscences of James Holt: A Narrative of the Emmett Company." Dale L. Morgan, editor. *Utah Historical Quarterly*, January, April 1955.

BOOK REVIEWS:

Bent's Fort, by David Lavender. *Saturday Review of Literature*, 29 January 1955.

1956

BOOKS:

Rand McNally's Pioneer Atlas of the American West, . . . 1876. Dale L. Morgan, editor. Chicago: Rand McNally, 1956. Reprinted 1969.

BOOK REVIEWS:

The Fur Hunters of the Far West, by Alexander Ross. *Montana Magazine of Western History*, Summer 1956.

1957

BOOKS:

Mapping the Transmississippi West, 1540-1861, by Carl I. Wheat. 6 vols. San Francisco: Institute of Historical Cartography, 1957-63. Morgan authored approximately one-half of the second volume, 90 percent of the third volume, the chapter on Mormon maps in the fourth volume, and all of the fifth and sixth volumes.

BOOK REVIEWS:

Joseph Reddford Walker and the Arizona Adventure, by Daniel Ellis Connor. *Utah Historical Quarterly*, Summer 1957.

Journal of John R. Bell, edited by Harlin M. Fuller. *Pacific Historical Review*, August 1957.

Massacre: The Tragedy at White River, by Marshall Sprague. *Saturday Review of Literature*, 27 July 1957.

The Mormons, by Thomas F. O'Dea. *Saturday Review of Literature*, 28 December 1957.

This is the West, by Robert West Howard. *Saturday Review of Literature*, 24 August 1957.

1958

BOOKS:

"Letters by Forty-niners." *Among the Mormons*, by William Mulder and A. Russell Mortensen. New York: Alfred Knopf, 1958.

1959

BOOKS:

"The Changing Face of Salt Lake City." In *The Valley of the Great Salt Lake*. Salt Lake City: Utah State Historical Society, 1959. Revised edition, 1963.

The Overland Diary of James A. Pritchard from Kentucky to California in 1849. With a Biography of Captain James A. Pritchard by Hugh Pritchard Williamson. Dale L. Morgan, editor. Denver: Fred A. Rosenstock, 1959.

ARTICLES:

"The Changing Face of Salt Lake City." *Utah Historical Quarterly*, Summer 1959.

"The Ferries of the Forty-Niners." *Annals of Wyoming*, April, October 1959, and April 1960.

BOOK REVIEWS:

Great Basin Kingdom, by Leonard J. Arrington. *Utah Historical Quarterly*, Spring 1959.

1960

BOOKS:

California As I Saw It: Pencillings by the Way of Its Gold and Gold Diggers, and Incidnets of Travel by Land and Water. Dale L. Morgan, Editor. Los Gatos, California: Talisman Press, 1960.

BOOK REVIEWS:

Army Exploration in the American West, by William H. Goetzmann. *California Historical Society Quarterly*, March 1960.

Bill Sublette, Mountain Man, by John E. Sunder. *Pacific Northwest Quarterly*, April 1960.

Robert Newell's Memoranda: Travels in the Territory of Mississippi, by Dorothy O. Johansen. *Oregon Historical Quarterly*, March 1960.

1961

BOOKS:

Kansas in Maps. Topeka: Kansas State Historical Society, 1961.
"The Significance and Value of the Overland Journal." In *Probing the American West: Papers of the Conference on the History of Western America.* Santa Fe: Museum of New Mexico Press, 1961.
Trappers and Mountain Men, by the editors of *American Heritage,* in consultation with Dale L. Morgan. New York: American Heritage: 1961.

BOOK REVIEWS:

The Diary of James J. Strang, edited by Mark A. Strang. *Michigan History,* September 1961.
The Fur Trade, by Paul Chrisler Phillips. *New York Times Book Review,* 13 August 1961.
The Gila Trail, by Benjamin Butler Harris. *Arizona and the West,* August 1961.

1962

BOOKS:

"Introduction." In *California Manuscripts: Being a Collection of Important, Unpublished & Unknown Original Historical Sources.* New York: Edward Eberstadt & Sons, 1962.
Mexico: Ancient and Modern; An Exhibition Celebrating the Acquisition of the Silvestre Terrazas Collection. Berkeley: Friends of the Bancroft Library, 1962. Dale L. Morgan, editor.

ARTICLES:

"The Significance and Value of the Overland Journal." *El Palacio,* Summer 1962.

1963

BOOKS:

A Guide to the Manuscript Collections of the Bancroft Library. Volume 1. Dale L. Morgan, editor, with George P. Hammond. Berkeley: University of California Press, 1963.
"Introduction." In *Travelers' Guide Across the Plains Upon the Overland Route to California,* by P. L. Platt and N. Slater. San Francisco: John Howell, 1963.
"Mountain Men of the American West." In *The Book of the American West.* New York: Julian Messner, 1963.
Overland in 1846: Diaries and Letter of the California-Oregon Trail. 2 vols. Dale L. Morgan, editor. Georgetown, California: Talisman Press, 1963.

ARTICLES:

"Contemporary Biography: George P. Hammond." *The Pacific Historian,* August 1963.

"Introduction to *Upon the Overland Route to California,* by P. L. Pratt (reprint)." *Journal of the West,* July 1963.

BOOK REVIEWS:

John Doyle Lee, by Juanita Brooks. *Southern California Quarterly,* December 1963.

Josiah Belden, 1841 California Overland Pioneer, edited by Doyce B. Nunis. *California Historical Society Quarterly,* December 1963.

Peter Skene Ogden's Snake Country Journal, 1826-27, edited by K. G. Davies. *Pacific Northwest Quarterly,* July 1963.

1964

BOOKS:

"Introduction." In *Geographical Memoir Upon Upper California,* by John C. Fremont. Dale L. Morgan, editor, with Allan Nevins. Sacramento: Book Club of California, 1964.

"Introduction." In *Three Years in California: William Perkins' Journal of Life at Sonora, 1849-52.* Dale L. Morgan, editor, with James R. Scobie. Berkeley: University of California Press, 1964.

The West of William H. Ashley: The International Struggle for the Fur Trade of the Missouri, the Rocky Mountains, and the Columbia, with Explorations Beyond the Continental Divide, Recorded in the Diaries and Letters of William H. Ashley and his Contemporaries, 1822-1838. Denver: Fred A. Rosenstock, Old West Publishing Company, 1964.

ARTICLES:

"Early Maps." *Nevada Highways and Parks,* centennial issue, 1964. Morgan also edited this issue.

BOOK REVIEWS:

The Field Notes of Captain William Clark, 1803-1805, edited by Ernest Staples Osgood. *Minnesota History,* Winter 1964.

1965

BOOKS:

Dakota War Whoop: Indian Massacres and War in Minnesota, by Harriett E. Bishop McConkey. Dale L. Morgan, editor. Chicago: R. R. Donnelley & Sons Co., 1965.

GPH: An Informal Record of George P. Hammond and His Era in the Bancroft Library. Berkeley: Friends of the Bancroft Library, 1965.

Old Greenwood: The Story of Caleb Greenwood, Trapper, Pathfinder, and Early Pioneer. With Charles Kelly. Revised edition. Georgetown, California: Talisman Press, 1965.

ARTICLES:

"The Fur Trade and Its Historians." *The American West*, Spring 1965.
"A Western Diary: A Review-Essay." *The American West*, Spring 1965.

BOOK REVIEWS:

The Beaver Men: Shepherds of Empire, by Mari Sandoz. *The American West*, Winter 1965.
The Gathering of Zion, by Wallace Stegner. *Saturday Review of Literature*, 16 January 1965.

1966

BOOKS:

Captain Charles M. Weber: Pioneer of the San Joaquin and Founder of Stockton, California. Dale L. Morgan, editor, with George P. Hammond. Berkeley: Friends of the Bancroft Library, 1966.
Honolulu: Sketches of Life in the Hawaiian Islands from 1828 to 1861, by Laura Fish Judd. Dale L. Morgan, editor. Chicago: R. R. Donnelley & Sons Co., 1966.

ARTICLES:

"The [Carl I.] Wheat Legacy." *Bancroftiana*, November 1966.
"The Fur Trade and Its Historians." *Minnesota History*, Winter 1966.

BOOK REVIEWS:

Mountain Men and the Fur Trade of the Far West, Volume 1 and 2, edited by LeRoy R. Hafen. *Utah Historical Quarterly*, Spring 1966.

1967

BOOKS:

North American Fur Trade Conference, St. Paul, 1965. Selected papers of the 1965 North American Fur Trade Conference. With others. St. Paul: Minnesota Historical Society, 1967.
The Rocky Mountain Journals of William Marshall Anderson: The West in 1834. Dale L. Morgan, editor, with Eleanor Towles Harris. San Marino: Huntington Library, 1967.
Three Years in the Klondike, by Jeremiah Lynch. Dale L. Morgan, editor. Chicago: R. R. Donnelley & Sons, Co., 1967.

ARTICLES:

"Brigham Young." In *Encyclopedia Britannica*. New York: Encyclopedia Britannica, Inc., 1967.
"Jedediah Smith Today." *Pacific Historian*, Spring 1967.
"Tribute to Susanna Bryant Dakin." *Bancroftiana*, May 1967.

BOOK REVIEWS:

Mountain Men and The Fur Trade of the Far West, Volume 3, edited by LeRoy R. Hafen. *Utah Historical Quarterly*, Summer 1967.
Quest for Empire, by Klaus J. Hansen. *Utah Historical Quarterly*, Fall 1967.

1968

ARTICLES:

"The Archivist, the Librarian, and the Historian." *Library Journal*, 15 December 1968.
"Kit Carson's Early Uncertain Chronology." *Montana Western History*, Summer 1968.
"Let's Have Good Luck." *The Pacific Historian*, Winter 1968.
"The Mormon Way-Bill." *Bancroftiana*, May 1968.
"New Light on Ashley and Jedediah Smith." *The Pacific Historian*, Winter 1968.
"Utah Before the Mormons." *Utah Historical Quarterly*, Winter 1968.
"The [Carl I.] Wheat Collection." *Bancroftiana*, May 1968.

BOOK REVIEWS:

America's Western Frontier, by John A. Hawgood. *Minnesota History*, Spring 1968.
Australians and the Gold Rush, by Jay Monaghan. *Arizona and the West*, Spring 1968.
The California Gold Discovery, by Rodman W. Paul. *Pacific Historical Review*, May 1968.
Exploration and Empire, by William H. Goetzmann. *Journal of American History*, June 1968.
Father Kino in Arizona, by Fay Jackson Smith. *Journal of American History*, June 1968.
The Recollections of Philander Prescott, by Donald Dean Parker. *Journal of Illinois State Historical Society*, Summer 1968.
Wilderness Kingdom, by Joseph P. Donnelly. *Oregon Historical Quarterly*, March 1968.

1969

ARTICLES:

"Literature in the History of the Church: The Importance of Involvement." *Dialogue: A Journal of Mormon Thought*, Autumn 1969.

1970

BOOKS:

In Pursuit of the Golden Dream: Reminiscences of San Francisco and the Northern and Southern Mines, 1849-57, by Howard Calhoun Gardiner. Dale L. Morgan, editor. Stoughton, Massachusetts: Western Hemisphere, Inc., 1970.

"Western Travels and Travelers in the Bancroft Library." In *Travelers on the Western Frontier*, edited by John F. McDermott. Urbana: University of Illinois Press, 1970.

BOOK REVIEWS:

An Artist on the Overland Trail, by James F. Wilkins. *Western Historical Quarterly*, January 1970.

The California Gold Rush Diary of a German Sailor, by W. Turrentine Jackson. *Pacific Historical Review*, February 1970.

The Lion of the Lord, by Stanely P. Hirschon. *Utah Historical Quarterly*, Fall 1970.

Posthumous Publications

BOOKS:

Dale Morgan's Introduction to A Mormon Bibliography, 1830-1930. Salt Lake City: University of Utah Press, 1978.

A Mormon Bibliography, 1830-1930. Chad J. Flake, editor. Salt Lake City: University of Utah Press, 1978. Introduction by Dale Morgan, who also acted as co-editor before his death.

Dale Morgan on Early Mormonism: Correspondence and a New History. Edited, with a biographical introduction by John Phillip Walker, and a preface by William Mulder. Salt Lake City: Signature Books, 1986.

ARTICLES:

"A Bibliography of the Published Writings of Juanita Brooks." *Dialogue: A Journal of Mormon Thought*, Spring 1974.

BOOK REVIEWS:

The Mountain Men and the Fur Trade of the Far West, Vol. 4, edited by Leroy C. Hafen. *Utah Historical Quarterly*, Fall 1971.

JOHN PHILLIP WALKER lives in Salt Lake City, where he is vice-president of marketing for Magic Chemical Company. He also owns a management consulting business.

WILLIAM MULDER is Professor of English at the University of Utah. His publications include *Homeward to Zion: The Mormon Migration From Scandinavia* and *Among the Mormons: Historic Accounts by Contemporary Observers*.